To the Weiserman,
with deep thanks
for all you do
for the Jewish community)
VI + me!

Lawrence J. Aronson
8/21/0

New Essays in American Jewish History

Commemorating the Sixtieth Anniversary of the Founding of the American Jewish Archives

Published by
The American Jewish Archives
of
Hebrew Union College–Jewish Institute of Religion
Cincinnati, Ohio

Library of Congress Cataloging-in-Publication Data

New essays in American Jewish history : commemorating the sixtieth anniversary of the founding of the American Jewish Archives.
     p. cm.
   Includes index.
   ISBN 978-1-60280-148-6
   1. Jews--United States--History. 2. Marcus, Jacob Rader, 1896-1995.
   E184.35.N49 2010
   973'.04924--dc22

2010019808

Distributed by
KTAV Publishing House, Inc.
930 Newark Avenue
Jersey City, NJ 07306
bernie@ktav.com
www.ktav.com
(201) 963-9524
Fax (201) 963-0102

Sponsors of the American Jewish Archives
Sixtieth Anniversary Volume

Jean and William Soman

Congregation Emanu-El of the City of New York

and the

Dolores and Walter Neustadt
American Jewish Archives Journal Endowment Fund

Contents

Preface

The festschrift is a unique genre for scholars. Methodologically serious, it is also purposefully celebratory in spirit. Like a first-class music festival, a distant cultural and etymological cousin, it combines both new and representative work and seeks to create a communal scholarly statement that is simultaneously joyous and important to the advancement of a given field of study.

Even the casual reader of this volume, *New Essays in American Jewish History* (*NEAJH*), will quickly recognize all of these features in this impressive collection of new and original scholarly studies of the American Jewish experience. *NEAJH* has a sweeping range of historical themes, is chronologically comprehensive, and contains the seasoned work of a highly diverse group of scholars. For students of the American Jewish experience, *NEAJH* is a historical marker that records the continued vitality and increasing sophistication of their field of study. Indeed, the scholarship in this volume is something to celebrate and worthy of continued support, particularly in difficult economic times.

An exemplary festschrift, *NEAJH* is both celebratory in spirit and a serious scholarly statement. Its principal goal is to *commemorate* the confluence of three important events. First, it celebrates the sixtieth anniversary of the founding of the American Jewish Archives (AJA) on the Cincinnati campus of the Hebrew Union College (HUC) in 1947. *The American Jewish Archives Journal* was first published in 1948— only one year after the late Dr. Jacob R. Marcus (1896–1995) founded the AJA. Finally, it is a tribute to the current, indefatigable executive director of the AJA, Professor Gary P. Zola. Since its jubilee, Dr. Zola has not only continued the work of Dr. Marcus but has expanded the scope of the AJA's activities in many remarkable ways. Indeed, it is a time to celebrate, and this volume is a highly meaningful way to laud the work of the institution and its amiable and energetic director.

xi

The title of this volume was purposefully crafted to link it to the first festschrift generated by the AJA, *Essays in American Jewish History* (1958). Published in honor of the tenth anniversary of the AJA's founding, that volume is a rich collection of twenty-four individual contributions that mostly focused on nineteenth-century themes. In 1976, the AJA sponsored the publication of *A Bicentennial Festschrift for Jacob Rader Marcus*, who was then celebrating his own eightieth birthday. Edited by one of Marcus's principal students, Dr. Bertram Wallace Korn, senior rabbi of Reform Congregation Keneseth Israel (Elkins Park, Pennsylvania), the *Bicentennial Festschrift* contains thirty-four articles with a broader range of topics and a more diverse group of scholarly contributors than its predecessor.

Similar in size to the AJA's first festschrift, this volume includes a still wider range of themes and methodologies than its older siblings. It also fully affirms what Dr. Korn concluded in his preface to the 1958 volume: that "the time will come . . .when other minds will guide the Archives, but always it will continue to be an extension of the mind, the personality, and the insight of its founder," Jacob Rader Marcus. In many ways, this book confirms the accuracy of Korn's prediction.

Jacob R. Marcus was born in 1896 in Connellsville, Pennsylvania, and spent much of his childhood in Wheeling, West Virginia. At the age of fifteen, he moved to Cincinnati to study for the rabbinate. Following military service in the U.S. Army during World War I, Marcus was ordained by HUC in 1920 and was appointed to the school's faculty. In 1922, he left for Germany and earned a doctorate in history from the University of Berlin in 1925, after which he returned to HUC. An active scholar of the European Jewish experience, Marcus deepened the festschrift tradition among Jewish scholars in the United States when he, along with Albert T. Bilgray, published an *Index to Jewish Festschriften* (1937), which included four thousand entries to articles in more than fifty-three festschriften.

Marcus, whose early scholarship primarily focused on Europe and particularly on Germany, was deeply affected by the Holocaust. In his opinion, the Nazis' destruction of the thousand-year-old Jewish center in Europe resulted in the shift of Jewish cultural hegemony to America in the postwar era. Accordingly, Marcus refocused his teaching and scholarly efforts and, to that end, founded the AJA in 1947. He quickly assembled a first-class staff, worked tirelessly to build the archive's core collection, and remained its director until his death at the age of ninety-nine in 1995. However, what did not change during the course of Marcus's long and distinguished career was his deep, almost redemptive belief in scientific critical scholarship and his love of the Jewish people and the lofty ideals of progressive Judaism.

"No scientific society," Dr. Korn wrote in 1958, "no scholarly library, no college, ever moved from a prospectus on paper to fulfillment in reality without the affectionate and whole-hearted devotion of one man." Indeed, Marcus was "whole-souled" in his devotion to building the AJA. He traveled around the country in search of minutes books, collections of documents, and other scholarly sources. If he could not obtain originals, he made copies to bring back to Cincinnati. He gathered professional scholars to his cause and trained several generations of new scholars at HUC. He recruited a professional staff to process the ever-increasing holdings of the AJA; created his own scholarly journal; published dozens of monographs, books, and anthologies; and lectured widely on American Jewish history. In turn, he was recognized as the "doyen" of his field, often simply referred to as "The Doctor." He urged scientific caution in research and boldly and repeatedly reminded other scholars, in his unique playful way, that "I know where all the bodies are buried."

In 1977, Marcus established a fellowship program at the AJA. Thirty-three years later, the program has been responsible for bringing more than 350 scholars from twenty different countries to the AJA to do original research and to participate in ongoing formal and informal scholarly conversations about their work in American Jewish history. The diversity of scholars reflected in this festscrift is due, in part, to the success of the fellowship program over the past three decades in catching rising academic stars and maintaining lasting relationships with seasoned scholars.

Marcus also cultivated and nurtured personal ties with hundreds of Reform rabbis, many of whom were his own students at HUC. (In 1950, HUC merged with the Jewish Institute of Religion and is now the Hebrew Union College–Jewish Institute of Religion [HUC-JIR.]) Offering all of their synagogue libraries free subscriptions to the *American Jewish Archives* (now *The American Jewish Archives*

Journal), he delighted in annually *schnorring* his rabbinic colleagues and asking them to support the AJA on an ongoing basis. Marcus served as president of the Central Conference of American Rabbis (CCAR) in 1949–1950 and subsequently was named honorary president of the conference for life, a unique distinction. He referred to all members of the CCAR, both male and female, as "his boys." Marcus was also particularly proud of an honorary doctorate bestowed by the Jewish Theological Seminary, the fountainhead of the Conservative movement in American Judaism.

On July 1, 1998, Marcus was formally succeeded as executive director of the American Jewish Archives by his last doctoral student, Gary P. Zola, an ordained rabbi and former national dean of admissions at HUC-JIR. Already an accomplished scholar in American Jewish history when he took the helm at the archives, Zola quickly built on foundations Marcus created, both preserving his predecessor's dedication to original critical scholarship and moving the AJA into new academic and cultural realms. Like Marcus, Zola combines genuine human warmth with a passion for his work and a firm commitment to cultivating first-class original scholarship through the collections of the American Jewish Archives.

During his first few years, Zola worked to expand and upgrade the AJA's physical plant. At the heart of this expansion was the erection of a four-story, state-of-the-art archival repository that holds the AJA's rich collection. In 2005, the Edwin A. Malloy Education Building was dedicated, complete with electronic classrooms, distance learning centers, and public exhibition galleries. Zola helped to pioneer the application of digitization in American Jewish research, launching an online archive of the papers of Isaac M. Wise, with more than thirty-three hundred searchable items, and has worked diligently to secure and preserve rare audio and video recordings as part of the American Jewish record. At present, the AJA houses approximately ten million documents in its 10,000 linear foot collection.

In addition to his full-length critical study, *Isaac Harby of Charleston, 1788–1828: Jewish Reformer and Intellectual* (1994), Zola has been prolific in his own scholarly output. In 1996, he edited *Women Rabbis: Exploration and Celebration,* which was followed by a festschrift titled *A Place of Our Own: The Rise of Reform Camping* in honor of the fiftieth anniversary of the founding of the Olin-Sang Ruby Union Institute in Oconomowoc, Wisconsin. Among his many scholarly articles are contributions to the study of American Reform Judaism, southern Jewish History, and Canadian Jewish History.

Always forward-looking, Zola organized an academic advisory and editorial board to use as his sounding board in managing and developing the American Jewish Archives. Along with Zola, Professor Jonathan D. Sarna of Brandeis University serves as the board's co-chair, and all three editors of this volume are members of that board. Again building on Marcus's lead, Zola created the B'nai Yaakov Council, a rabbinic group dedicated to supporting the AJA, which meets formally at every national CCAR conference. Dr. Zola also formalized Dr. Marcus's vast network of lay support into The Ezra Consortium, and, together with Professor Sara Lee of HUC-JIR (Los Angeles), created an educational advisory council that ties together leading Jewish educators with scholars of the American Jewish experience to advance further the study and appreciation of American Jewish history at every level on the educational continuum.

As with Marcus, Zola's passion for the study of the American Jewish experience and his dedication to the AJA has carried him far beyond his Cincinnati home. Zola played a leading national role in framing the year-long 2004 observance of the 350th anniversary of Jewish settlement in North America, served on the academic advisory council of the United States Congress's Abraham Lincoln Bicentennial Commission, and has even appeared on ABC's *Nightline*. Ultimately, it is not just his national presence and his scholarship that have earned Zola the mantle of leadership at the AJA but also his warmth and generosity, which attract scholars to the Marcus Center, including all the editors of and contributors to this volume.

It is important to note that the contributors to this volume are not only from the United States but also from Israel and Germany. Moreover, the scholars who prepared studies for this book teach at institutions both Jewish and secular, private and public. The number of women contributing to this volume triples the role women scholars played in the pages of the *Bicentennial Festschrift*. Articles by Natalie

Zemon Davis, Cornelia Wilhelm, Dianne Ashton, Hasia Diner, Shuly Rubin Schwartz, and Pamela S. Nadell greatly add to the general and feminist historiographies that inform this collection of studies.

While far from a comprehensive study of the American Jewish experience, the essays in this volume represent the full breadth of scholarship in the field of American Jewish history today. The volume spans the different movements in Judaism and includes studies of the southern and western Jewish experience in America and in Caribbean communities, in addition to historical aspects of Jewish life in the enduring American "Pale of Settlement," the seaboard communities stretching from Boston to Washington, DC. It also includes two studies on Jews and slavery and offers a legal scholar's perspective on the history of the Jewish community of colonial New Amsterdam. It includes both Jonathan D. Sarna's study of the grand theme of American Judaism and William Toll's sophisticated microstudy of Jewish life at the University of Oregon. Students of American Reform Judaism will be particularly delighted to see the first full study of the publication of the old *Union Prayer Book*. Jews and science, the history of biblical scholarship in America, Holocaust studies, American Jewish historiography, Zionism, cinema studies—all are represented in this festschrift, all reflect contemporary currents in the field of American Jewish history, and together they form a microcosm of what scholarly visitors to the AJA are currently investigating.

Finally, a special word of thanks is due to the team that edited and produced this very special festschrift. My coeditors, Professors Jonathan D. Sarna and Pamela S. Nadell, worked diligently to secure contributions to this volume. Kevin Proffitt, the senior archivist for research and collections at the American Jewish Archives, not only offered his usual extraordinary level of support to all research needed for this project but contributed an article of his own to this collection. Behind the scenes, Dr. Dana Herman, managing editor of *The American Jewish Archives Journal* and academic associate, attended to every detail in the creation of the final manuscript for this book and saw it through its publication with extraordinary skill and remarkable patience. The editors of this volume are particularly grateful to David Ellenson, president of HUC-JIR, Michael Marmur, academic vice-president of HUC-JIR, and Alfred Gottschalk *z"l*, former president and chancellor of HUC-JIR and the rabbi who ordained Dr. Zola in 1982, for their unstinting support of this project. For his part, Professor Zola modestly "sat this one out" and waited to see what his colleagues would produce. All of us can only hope he is pleased with our final product.

New Essays in American Jewish History was published to mark the sixtieth anniversary of the AJA and its distinguished journal, as well as a decade of Gary P. Zola's tenure as the AJA's executive director. "We who are engaged in American Jewish historical and sociological studies are busy enough with our own commitments without having to interrupt ourselves midstream to contribute to a miscellany," Bertram W. Korn protested in his "Preface" to the AJA's *Bicentennial Festschrift*. But, he continued, "when we are invited to associate ourselves with a project" to honor the archives and its esteemed leader, "we have considered it to be our honor and privilege to participate in this *Festschrift*." Indeed, what was true in 1976 is just as true in 2010.

Lance J. Sussman

After Sixty Years: An Appreciation

The rich collection of scholarly essays contained in this sixtieth anniversary commemorative volume displays the enduring vitality and foresight of Jacob Rader Marcus, and celebrates the tenth anniversary of Gary P. Zola as Executive Director of the AJA and Editor of *The American Jewish Archives Journal*. *Talmid muvhak* of Jacob Rader Marcus, Gary Zola has followed in the footsteps of his teacher, building upon and extending the structures Professor Marcus created. The American Jewish Archives has moved into renovated and expanded new quarters under his leadership, and Dr. Zola has made the AJA and its unparalleled resources available to the world of scholars and interested laypeople alike. *The American Jewish Archives Journal* itself has maintained its tradition of scholarly excellence under his editorship, and has addressed an ever-expanding range of topics and subjects related to the American Jewish experience. This volume is ample testimony to that assessment, and reflects the high esteem in which Gary Zola is held by his academic peers. Following in the tradition of the 1958 publication, *Essays in American Jewish History*—which marked the tenth anniversary of the founding of the AJA—it is a pleasure and an honor to salute the achievements of the executive director on this occasion, and to wish the AJA and its journal many more years of continued success under his leadership.

As President of HUC-JIR, I cannot avoid noting that this sixtieth anniversary of *The American Jewish Archives Journal* parallels the sixtieth anniversary year of the State of Israel. Both were born in the crucible that was Jewish life after the Shoah, and this moment of joy—as we celebrate sixty years of the publication of *The American Jewish Archives Journal*, and of the AJA itself, as well as the decade of leadership Dr. Zola has contributed—invites reflection upon the

1

philosophy that guides and animates HUC-JIR as well as the role that the AJA plays at the College-Institute as this institution seeks to fulfill its mission of service to the Jewish and academic worlds.

Simply put, Hebrew Union College–Jewish Institute of Religion affirms the spiritual-religious assertion that the late Brandeis University Professor Simon Rawidowicz put forth in his famed work, *Babylon and Jerusalem*. In that book, Professor Rawidowicz employed the two ancient sites contained in the title of his book as emblematic of the reality and indivisibility that marks Jewish existence—whether in the Diaspora or the Land of Israel. He unquestionably considered Israel as a center of Jewish life, but, at the same time, affirmed the Diaspora as a center of Jewish life as well. By affirming as a core Jewish belief the integral connectedness that binds Jews and Jewish settlements everywhere, Professor Rawidowicz affirmed the moral obligations that bind Jews worldwide to one another and proclaimed a broad notion of Jewish peoplehood that included both the Land of Israel and the Diaspora. He refused to accept the notion of Zion as *the* spiritual center of Jewish life and instead employed the notion of an ellipsis—a figure with neither center nor beginning or end—to conceptualize the unending ties that bind Jews in Israel and the Diaspora together as one.

It is within this larger context that the story of the American Jewish Archives must be placed and its importance emphasized, for the philosophy that informed Jacob Rader Marcus in conceptualizing the American Jewish Archives surely parallels and echoes the stance that Rawidowicz articulated in his *Babylon and Jerusalem*. After the slaughter of more than 6,000,000 Jews during World War II and the wholesale destruction of Jewish settlements and cultural institutions by the Nazis during the 1940s, Dr. Marcus—despite his training as a European Jewish historian—came to the conclusion that the United States was now going to occupy a central role in the unfolding narrative of Jewish history. As his 1933 essay, "Zionism and the American Jew," indicates, Marcus had a keen appreciation of the Zionist Movement and the role that Israel could play as a land of refuge and as *a* spiritual center for Jews worldwide.[1] However, Professor Marcus would not cede primacy to Israel and insisted that the United States was no less a center of Jewish life than Zion. Hence, his dream of building the American Jewish Archives testified to his belief that the

American experience was now as central to Jewish life and history as Israel.

Informed by this philosophy and aware that no first-rate archives containing the records of the American Jewish community then existed, Dr. Marcus was led by this ideological stance to conclude immediately after World War II that the American Jewish story could not be properly told without such a repository—that the leadership of the American Jewish community would fail in fulfilling the role that it was now being called upon to play in the stream of Jewish history and life without the intellectual foundation such a scholarly resource would provide. Determined to address this need and rectify this lack, and with the active assistance of his HUC classmate and friend President Nelson Glueck, Marcus established the American Jewish Archives on the campus of HUC in Cincinnati in 1947. He believed that the AJA would allow for the gathering and housing of documents that would enable American Jewish history to be written, and, as the past six decades have demonstrated, the growth of the AJA has confirmed the wisdom of his belief. The American Jewish Archives has now unquestionably become the premiere research center in the world for materials related to the American Jewish experience.

At the same time that he established the AJA, Dr. Marcus also had the breadth of vision to realize that the narratives and descriptions that the scholars and students of American Jewish history would compose would require an appropriate journal for their dissemination. He therefore published the first volume of *American Jewish Archives* in 1948 as a vehicle for the display of that scholarship, and for sixty years this journal has embodied the highest standards of academic integrity and excellence in the field. In so doing, *The American Jewish Archives Journal* has garnered worldwide fame in academic and lay circles alike and has fulfilled the highest vision of its founder.

During these anniversary years of the State of Israel, the AJA, and its distinguished journal, we have great reason to rejoice in these two arenas of Jewish life and culture and to be proud that HUC-JIR has vibrant campuses and programs in both Jerusalem and North America where our students imbibe the philosophy of Jewish peoplehood which Professor Marcus advanced and which our College-Institute still champions. May the American Jewish Archives and its journal, under the guidance of Gary Zola, continue to devote itself to this vision and may it continue to contribute—as I am certain it will—to the ongoing strength and quality of Jewish life in the United States, Israel, and the world.

David Ellenson
November 21, 2008–23 Cheshvan 5768

Jacob Rader Marcus and the Archive He Built

Kevin Proffitt

Introduction

Concurrent with the founding of the American Jewish Archives (AJA), Jacob Rader Marcus also founded *The American Jewish Archives Journal* (known until 1998 as *American Jewish Archives*). From its genesis, Marcus envisioned archives and scholarship as a joint project at the AJA, each supporting and enhancing the other. Marcus's inspiration in founding the AJA was his awareness of lacunae in the gathering and preservation of primary source materials on American Jewish life. His motivation was to create an institution, located in the Midwest, that was "devoted to the preservation of American Jewish historical records and their study," particularly for "those students and researchers living between the Rockies and the Cumberland plateau."[1]

This essay will discuss Marcus's creation of the AJA and its joint ventures of scholarship and publication as intertwined, and will consider these subjects within a larger context of archival thought and practice. The creation of the AJA is a fascinating case study. It encompasses two emerging disciplines in the historical community in the mid-twentieth century: the creation of a scholarly discipline for the study of American Jewish history and the emergence of an American archival profession. Jacob Rader Marcus was a leader in laying a foundation for both scholarship and archives in American Jewish history. Through the combination of his scholarly training, his rabbinic background, his leadership vision, and his personal devotion to Judaism, Marcus led the way in making important contributions which established organized efforts in both movements.

Marcus was a historian, not an archivist. His focus in creating the AJA was from a historian's perspective of scholarship rather than from the archivist's view of professional theory and practice. Ordained as a rabbi at Hebrew Union College, trained in Europe for his Ph.D., and a professor of rabbinic students at Hebrew Union College, Marcus was immersed in Jewish culture and learning, and had no connection to the U.S. archival profession and its theories, which were beginning to emerge concurrent with the establishment of the National Archives in 1935. Yet, as we shall see, in founding the AJA, Marcus followed—and often anticipated—the accepted archival forms and conventions of his time.[2]

Marcus's motivation in founding the American Jewish Archives was to enhance and advance what he called the "scientific" inquiry of American Jewry. Originally a historian of European and German Jewry, Marcus began in the late 1930s to work in American Jewish history. Marcus was one of a small number of historians (among them Columbia University historian Salo Baron and Harvard scholar Oscar Handlin)[3] who worked to establish the study of American Jewish history as an academic discipline. In the early 1940s, he hosted the first known graduate level seminar in American Jewish history at Hebrew Union College. His teaching load in the subject increased steadily as American Jewish history became a required course of study for rabbinic students at HUC.

In this context, we are able to see, not coincidentally, that Marcus's interest in fostering the growth of American Jewish history as an academic discipline paralleled the expansion of his own teaching and writing in American Jewish history. He quickly learned, however, that few of what he called the "basic tools" necessary for research in American Jewry—archives, manuscripts, and primary sources, together with reference volumes and other secondary sources—were available to support his, or others' work. Commenting in 1951 on the lack of sources available to students of American Jewry, Marcus wrote, "it is no more difficult to write American Jewish history than it is to make bricks without clay….The basic tools are still missing."

With the founding of the AJA, it became Marcus's mission to provide these tools.[4]

The Historian-Interpreter

In founding the AJA, Marcus patterned his new project broadly along the lines of what is now known as the historical manuscripts tradition. The historical manuscripts tradition dates to the late eighteenth century and the founding of the Massachusetts Historical Society, which itself was modeled after the Societies of Antiquaries in London. The historical manuscripts tradition sprang from mostly private (as opposed to public, or government) repositories and historical societies that focused "on the collection, preservation and dissemination (generally through editing and publication) of artificial collections of historical materials by historical societies and libraries."[5]

The archival profession as it is known and practiced today was in its infancy in the 1940s. Modern archival thought and practice—which was based on the European principle of provenance, *respect des fonds*—would not gain a clear foothold in the U.S. until nearly 1960. Until that time, the historical manuscripts tradition was a predominant model. Rooted in the mindset and philosophy of the historian, its methodologies were based in principles of librarianship. It was overseen by historian-interpreters who had a desire to preserve documents and study history, but were not trained as archivists or librarians. The historical manuscripts tradition emphasized the collection of documents of "remote vintage" over those of recent origin. It cataloged and described documents more as discrete items (i.e., through the use of calendars or catalogs) rather than in bulk as was emphasized in public archival theory. The historical manuscript tradition also boasted a strong legacy of publishing—which was a key component of Marcus's vision and must have been an obvious point of attraction as he examined the existing landscape for models to emulate. Many if not most of this first generation of historical societies had programs in place to publish speeches, articles and documents, usually based upon holdings in their possession.[6]

In following the historical manuscripts tradition, Marcus not only copied the prevailing archival model of the time; he also, no doubt, reflected his own training, interests, and background. In many ways, Marcus was the prototypical "historian-interpreter." Though he knew little about the details of librarianship or archival practice, Marcus had a vision of preserving American Jewish history and providing information to his patrons with a maximum amount of service and a minimum of bureaucracy or cost. In establishing the AJA, Marcus was attempting to create a venue where research and scholarship could be pursued on demand by a broad community of users (including himself).

Coming from the historical manuscripts tradition, Marcus was concerned with implementing his broad mission of scholarship and research as a means to further Jewish culture, not with the development of archival theory and practice. The leaders of the public archives movement were attempting to form a profession of records keepers. In terms of publications, Marcus was interested in pursuing and promoting humanities-based scholarship on the American Jewish experience. The public archives advocates pursued social sciences-based research that focused on the processes of their work in order to create an intellectual framework for what they did and who they were. What Marcus and the emerging archival profession shared, however, was the common goal of wanting to better document American life and culture while—perhaps most importantly—gaining legitimacy for their work through their publications and research.[7]

Marcus often showed his iconoclastic side, however, and aligned with the public archival theorists against the traditionalists. For example, he eschewed the "antiquarianism" of most historical societies in their policy of collecting only original documents, and believed that the informational value of a reproduction was equal to the intrinsic value of an original document—not to mention more accessible. In his introductory essay about the AJA, Marcus foreshadowed in broad form the 1980s archival concept of documentation strategies in his vision to collect collaboratively records of American Jewry from coast to coast. He created networks of individuals and organizations to assist in collecting and in documenting specific regions and topics of interest. He became not just a collector of documents, but in many ways a creator of records as well. He documented social and cultural movements (such as the 1960s civil rights movement) not just after the fact, but as they occurred. He often invited individuals to write about their thoughts and their involvement in contemporary events to keep as a record for future researchers. He regularly polled different parts of the American Jewish community for their views and reactions to various happenings that he then stored at the AJA. In sum, he used oral history to great effect.[8]

In matters of arrangement and description, Marcus led the way again. Rather than relying on his or his staff's memory to provide information about holdings to patrons as was then a common practice, particularly at Jewish libraries and archives (which information would then be lost when the staff member no longer worked there), Marcus had his staff prepare and publish a cataloging manual. This was a very important—and groundbreaking—reform because it promoted professionalism in methodology, increased access through greater transparency, and ensured consistent description and access to material at the AJA over time. Although meant as an internal document, Marcus later allowed this manual to be circulated as a model for other institutions (such as synagogues) that were collecting records or creating archives. Another of Marcus's important reforms in archival description was his implementation of pragmatic processing guidelines (due to the limited staffing and budget of his bare-boned archive) that some fifty years later are now being discussed in modern archival practice and thought.[9]

Marcus also differed with the historical manuscripts tradition in that he took a populist approach in his vision for the AJA. Though emphasizing scholarly research and study, Marcus did not want the AJA to be a repository where materials were collected and then kept isolated in a storeroom only for safekeeping—or only for the use of the intellectual or cultural elite. Atypical of most historical societies of that time, which were open only to dues-paying members and limited their services to a select few, Marcus insisted that the AJA's holdings be available to the public and accessed on demand. He also insisted that the AJA be free of what he felt were unnecessary rules and regulations (i.e. excessive visitor registration, etc.), the sort of which he had been subjected to in visits to many of Europe's finest archives and made sure to offer regular and convenient hours of operation during which time researchers would have as much access to material as they desired. The atmosphere for patrons at the AJA was relaxed, fees were nominal, service was emphasized, and researchers were made to feel like guests rather than unwelcome intruders.[10]

In collecting, Marcus emphasized local history—and the preservation of local records—at a time when most Jewish communities were little concerned with preserving their own past. Most importantly, Marcus was at the forefront in going beyond the "great man" theory of history in documenting the diversity of the American Jewish community in gender, belief, observance, class, culture and profession.[11]

Establishing a Jewish Archive

In following the larger rubric of the historical manuscripts tradition as he created the AJA (and its journal), it seems clear Marcus was following the example of the American Jewish Historical Society. Founded in 1892, the AJHS is the oldest ethnic historical society in the United States. It was founded during the mass immigration of east European Jews to the U.S., when an emerging and then uncertain identity for American Jews was evolving. Not only at this time were thousands of Jewish immigrants struggling to accommodate to their new social, political and cultural environments; the members of the Jewish community were adapting internally to each other and to their place in the larger society as well. As Elisabeth Kaplan has written in a beautifully nuanced essay on archives and the construction of identity, the problem facing this emerging American Jewish community "was that no ideology had been developed to justify or account for [their] state of affairs." As a result, the founders of the AJHS attempted to create an organization that would—through many means, including publications—help advance what historian Michael A. Meyer has called "the appearance of a new historical consciousness [that would] play a crucial role in the formation of modern Jewish identity."[12]

It is no coincidence Marcus would use the AJHS as a model for the AJA. Until 1947, the AJHS was the singular institution in the United States for preserving and documenting American Jewish history. In its mission, reputation and services, the AJHS was not only a valued resource but—maybe most importantly—a symbol of Jewish identity and culture to the American Jewish community of that time, particularly to Jewish historians such as Marcus. The Society's journal, begun in 1893 as *Publications of the American Jewish Historical Society* (now titled *American Jewish History)*, was the voice of record for scholarship on American Jewish life. And it is doubtful anyone at that time was more familiar with the AJHS and its publications than Marcus. Through his work and contacts at Hebrew Union College, as well as through his research and scholarship, Marcus knew many of AJHS's founders and benefactors. He used the Society's collections for his own research and was a contributor to the Society's annual conferences and journal. His first publication to appear in *PAJHS* was an article in the September 1948 issue on Civil War veteran, Major Louis A. Gratz.[13] A few years after the AJA was founded, from 1956–1959, Marcus served as president of the AJHS and was later named its honorary president.

Considering the AJHS's tradition and Marcus's many points of involvement therein, it makes sense that the AJHS would loom large in his plan to create a related organization. In his introduction to the AJA, Marcus went to great lengths to praise the AJHS, calling its work "pioneering," and adding that no scholar "can afford to neglect" their publications. He also made clear that the AJA was not being created as a challenge or replacement to AJHS. Rather, Marcus implied that the AJA was the progeny of the AJHS, and described his Cincinnati-based archive as "but one phase of the inevitable [westward] geographic expansion of American Jewish culture."[14]

Scholarship and Publications

Though clearly an admirer and supporter of the AJHS, Marcus was (if politely so) ambivalent about the quality of their publications. This assessment was not based on any personal agenda or criticism of those who worked at AJHS, but was rooted in a disagreement in principle stemming from the Society's origin and mission. As Kaplan notes, the AJHS was founded by a group of mostly successful German Jews who traced their American heritage to the mid-eighteenth century. Through their establishment of the AJHS, Kaplan argues, this group sought a way to "relieve internal strife" in the American Jewish community as they tried to "construct a single viable Jewish identity." In other words, the founders of the AJHS attempted to establish internal and external legitimacy for American Jewry by establishing historical context and justification for regarding Jews as equal partners in the fabric and context of American history.[15]

Publicly, the extent of Marcus's criticism of *PAJHS* was mild—he only went so far as to say that their work was "uneven." However, one need not read between the lines to see that part of Marcus's rationale in creating his own journal was his desire to improve the level of scholarship in the field. Writing in 1960, Marcus said the American Jewish Archives (and, by connection, the AJA's journal) "was the response to a need—a need for accurate, objective, scientific research in an area that had previously known little more than apologetics." Marcus's goal was to create a "bulletin" that would "inform the interested public and co-workers in the field of American Jewish history," and "further a knowledge of the American Jew."[16]

For Marcus, the non-negotiable requirement for scholarship was that it must rely on what he called the "scientific" method. How Marcus defined "scientific"—and more importantly, how he practiced it—may have been fluid at times and is a topic to be researched and discussed in greater detail.[17] But there is no doubt Marcus had an unwavering belief that scholarship should be a discovery process that was impartial and accurate, based on documentary research, and as much as possible unaffected by speculation, advocacy, or partisanship. In Marcus's view, scholarship was not a tool to be used to validate anyone's status or belief. He wanted his journal to present reasoned, documented research that would encourage thought and provoke discussion, but never provoke any questioning of its motives or methods. Being "scientific" also meant that no topic or subject was out of bounds. Beyond insisting on a high level of scholarship, Marcus did not want his journal to avoid or censor controversial topics or authors. He wanted to be open to controversial topics such as Zionism, anti-semitism, left-wing politics and the like. He also wanted to publish work that could be read both by scholars and lay persons. In his oft-quoted introduction to the American Jewish Archives, published in the inaugural issue of his journal, Marcus wrote these lines: "We seek to ascertain the facts as they actually are: and we desire to promote the study of those materials which will further a knowledge of the American Jew."[18]

This was Marcus's approach to scholarship, and it contained no apologetics or filiopietism. This is not to say Marcus disdained analysis or interpretation or avoided controversy or occasional hyperbole. But he viewed his job as presenting the facts—across a broad spectrum—with the intent of revealing events "as they actually are." In saying this, Marcus undoubtedly understood, as Kaplan notes, that "there was simply no way to weave together all of the varied strands of culture and background that [American Jews] brought as individuals, in order to create one American Jewish identity."[19]

As mentioned earlier, Marcus envisioned the dual functions of archives and scholarship as intertwined. His progressive thought and work in collecting material on American Jewish life fulfilled and reflected his vision of effective publishing. His new publication (which he called his "journal" or in shorthand, the *AJAr*—to distinguish it from the AJA and the archival arm of his operation) became the public arm of the AJA. And, as he did in developing the AJA's collection, Marcus was innovative and progressive in the work of his journal, seeking new opportunities to reach a broad audience and inviting participation from inside and outside the Jewish and scholarly communities.

Marcus wanted the AJA to be proactive in creating publications—designed for both scholars and laypersons—that would educate and enlighten the public about American Jewish history and, by extension, about Judaism in general. Looking at the AJA from this angle it can be argued that the AJA's publication programs, particularly *The American Jewish Archives Journal*, were the vehicle through which Marcus felt he made his most important contribution to Jewish life: the creation of a venue where intellectual learning and discourse in American Jewish history would be pursued through rigorous and unbiased scholarly pursuit.

Following his populist bent concerning access to the AJA's collections, Marcus insisted the AJA's publications were not just for a scholarly audience. Decades before the internet made outreach *de rigueur* for archives, Marcus was very active in reaching out to a broad community of patrons and users, and in finding creative ways to do so. For example, Marcus created a series of educational tools for laypersons and school children—such as posters, filmstrips, and curriculum drafts—that were based on documents at the AJA. He printed and distributed these primarily to synagogues and religious schools. He also published many of his own talks in pamphlet form, using them as tools for laypersons who were interested in learning about American Jewish history, but not on a scholarly level. He published instructional booklets on preserving synagogue records and on how to write the history of local Jewish communities, and also published the AJA's manuscript catalog (with regular updates)—at a time when few other institutions were doing so—and placed these in libraries across the U.S. and Europe.[20]

In its early days, the AJA's journal was thin and printed on glossy paper, similar to a magazine. Each issue contained usually one "meat and potatoes" historical study, which was often written by one of Marcus's students as part of their studies in his classes, or by colleagues in the Reform rabbinate. Marcus often sought to fill what he thought were areas of void in the literature by soliciting authors to write on specific subjects. Book reviews and lists of new acquisitions to the collection of the AJA were staples of each volume. In the first ten years nearly every issue contained a documentary analysis or excerpt from a historic document: a diary, a letter, or a memoir. Highlights of the first ten years include two issues devoted to the American Jewish Tercentenary; an issue devoted to Jewish history in the American West; and what Marcus called "an imposing monograph" on social justice and the American Reform rabbinate.[21]

As mentioned earlier, Marcus did not shy away from controversy with his new publication. The most interesting exchange in the journal's early years stemmed from Ellis Rivkin's review essay of Morris Schappes's, *A Documentary History of the Jews in the United States, 1654–1875.*[22] Writing in the June 1952 issue of the journal, Rivkin—then an Associate Professor of History at the Hebrew Union College–Jewish Institute of Religion (HUC-JIR) in Cincinnati—considered Schappes's work in light of Schappes's alleged connection with the Communist party. Rivkin wrote that Schappes's book was "an exact reproduction of official Communist policy as it was at the time Mr. Schappes was compiling his work." In the next issue (January 1953), Marcus published a lengthy rejoinder by Schappes (longer than Rivkin's original essay), where Schappes passionately defended himself and his work, saying Rivkin had "set up a straw-man and has had a hollow and petty triumph knocking down his creation."[23] The matter did not end until the next issue (June 1953) when Louis Harap, then the editor of the journal *Jewish Life*, wrote a letter to the editor to defend his magazine against charges leveled by Rivkin that *Jewish Life* was the official organ of the American Communist Party.[24]

Considering the political and social tenor of the early 1950s—the rise of McCarthyism, the Cold War, and the Rosenberg case (and the specter of antisemitism that encompassed all of it)—the mere mention of Communism was a hot-button, no-win, issue no one would have blamed Marcus for avoiding. Yet, there is no record of Marcus making any attempt to temper or censor Rivkin's approach. Instead, Marcus seemed more concerned with propriety than with any larger social or political repercussions. "I am inclined to publish [Schappes's response]," Marcus wrote to Rivkin, "after I have deleted what I consider to be personal attacks....If you [want to make] a counter-rebuttal...make it very brief. I have no desire to carry on controversies and counter-controversies." In a later letter to Rivkin, Marcus wrote: "Schappes' [rejoinder] left me cold. It reads dialectical."[25]

As the years passed, Marcus ceded much of the work of preparing and editing the journal to others—particularly to his associate directors Stanley Chyet and Abraham Peck—so he could concentrate on his own scholarship. As a result, the tone and content of the journal began to shift, reflecting changes in modern scholarship as well as the new editors' varying interests. The size of the journal expanded, the layout was modernized, and the number of essays per issue increased to three or more.

Chyet was a rabbi and graduate of HUC-JIR.[26] Though he was a professor of history at HUC-JIR, Chyet's interests went beyond history and increasingly centered on literature and poetry. During his tenure at the AJA (1960–1976), the journal continued with basic historical studies and documentary analyses, including several anniversary issues (such as centennial anniversaries of the Civil War, the Union of American Hebrew Congregations, and HUC-JIR). However, under Chyet's influence, the intellectual content of the journal noticeably expanded. Articles on the arts, Hebrew and Yiddish literature, and poetry appeared with more frequency, together with articles reflective of contemporary life and scholarship—such as analyses of Black anti-semitism and Jews and the New Left.[27]

Peck joined the AJA in 1977.[28] Born in a German DP camp, and raised in the United States as the child of Holocaust survivors, Peck, who was also not a rabbi, contributed a new perspective—from outside the HUC orbit—which further diversified the scope of the journal. Peck often used themes as the basis for entire issues: Sephardim in America, Latin American Jewry, history of the American rabbinate, etc. Under Peck's direction, the journal included articles that were based more on secondary literature and analysis than was common in earlier years of the journal. Guest editors for special issues became common as well, and authors were increasingly more often doctoral students and post-doctoral scholars from the U.S. and abroad, who worked professionally in the field. In this way, the journal became more intertwined with the broader intellectual discourse of the academy and expanded its content beyond the fact-based narratives of events and persons that represented much of its early content.[29]

In its current manifestation, under the editorship of Gary P. Zola, the journal is an amalgam of old and new. In *The American Jewish Archives Journal*—which has returned to regular publishing—modern historical scholarship and analysis coexist with traditional research and study in a publication which reflects, and continues to be a tribute to, its earliest days.

Conclusion

Though successful beyond any expectation, Marcus's project was not perfect. In collecting, Marcus's eagerness to gather materials led to complaints of "poaching" from other repositories from which Marcus (and his surrogates) obtained copies which were then placed in the AJA. Marcus's eagerness to collect the widest possible range of material (often sight-unseen) sometimes led to a lack of appraisal and the result that a lot of chaff was brought in with the archival wheat—cluttering the collection and leading to vagueness and confusion about the true scope of the AJA's collecting policy. With his journal, Marcus struggled to find a consistent voice. The quality of the articles was mixed, and his vision of appealing to both scholarly and popular audiences led sometimes to a lack of focus. In scholarly circles the *AJAJ* trailed in importance to the *PAJHS*. Marcus's journal had a different audience (largely centered in the American Reform rabbinate) and did not have the same circulation or number of readers as the Society's journal.[30]

As those who knew him can attest, Jacob Marcus was far from modest in his self-assessment. Yet, he managed this without presumption or self-congratulation. He was disdainful of self-reflection, both personally and professionally. That is why—despite many pleas from colleagues and friends—he never wrote an autobiography or published a memoir.[31] It is not surprising, then, that in an essay noting the publication of the first twenty-five volumes of the journal, Marcus was matter-of-fact (neither pensive nor shy) in pointing out the many ways the vision he had outlined in 1947 had come to pass. He noted the increasing "hegemony" of the American Jewish community as the most influential and powerful in the history of the world, and thereby affirmed, without saying so directly, his validation for creating the AJA. He cited the rise of "scientific" scholarship in American Jewish history that "has begun to produce works of quality," and reported—as he had predicted in 1947—on the creation of regional Jewish archives across the country that were now collecting records and "publishing their own magazines."

Marcus also made other predictions that have proven prescient. "A new generation of college and university students is turning, albeit slowly," Marcus wrote, "to the study of American Jewry as an interesting and significant segment of the national past; the phenomenon reflects an interest in ethnic studies undoubtedly heightened by the devotion of [ethnic groups] to their own history." Predicting an increasing growth of study in American Jewish historiography in the American academy, Marcus concluded by restating (most assuredly quite deliberately) what was both affirmation and justification for his creation of the AJA and its journal: "If this prediction (of increasing interest in American Jewish history) is a correct one, then there is every reason to expect that this emergent cultural pluralism will produce notable works which cannot fail to throw light on the general history of the American people."[32] As Marcus often noted to those who were closest to him when they asked for advice or an opinion, there was "no question" that he was correct.

"The task of the Archives is as endless as history itself," Marcus wrote. The task Marcus sought was to create a venue where interested persons could gather to examine and discuss the divergent and varying identities that comprise American Jewry throughout its history. As Jonathan Sarna writes: "To study the history of American Judaism is…to be reminded anew of the theme of human potential." The AJA and its journal were created not to validate or affirm American Jewry but to document it. As Kaplan notes, "the reification of ethnic identity does not foster tolerance or acceptance." Attempting to do so, Kaplan notes (and as Marcus realized decades earlier), gives archivists and historians "the potential for destroying the very diversity that [their] efforts hope to sustain." Rather, Marcus's vision for the AJA was to preserve the diversity and complexity of the Jewish experience in American society for present and future generations so that—both as individuals and as a community—we can, in Sarna's words, "make a difference [and know] that the future is [ours] to create." This is why the work of the AJA, in collecting and publishing, remains—as its founder stated—to look "forward as well as backward in its service to a scientific study and compilation of the records of American Jewish history."[33]

"A Land That Needs People for Its Increase:" How the Jews Won the Right to Remain in New Netherland

Paul Finkelman

Despite the relatively few Jews in the New Netherland colony in the seventeenth century, an examination of their experience is critical for understanding subsequent Jewish history and the history of religious freedom in the colonies and eventually the United States.[1] Put simply, this initial Jewish experience set down patterns for both Jewish and non-Jewish actions that paved the way for the flowering of American Jewry in the next three centuries. Equally important, the handful of Jews in seventeenth century Manhattan helped shape a culture of religious diversity that became an important prologue not only for their future co-religionists, but for all Americans. A full history of the Jewish experience in the New Netherland colony remains to be written.[2] The aim of this article is more modest. My goal is to explain the complexity of the arrival of the first Jews and what they faced when they came to New Amsterdam. In exploring the history of these first Jews this article departs from the traditional account.

The Traditional Account

The traditional account of the first Jews in America can be quickly summarized. In 1654, twenty-three Portuguese Jews arrived from Brazil aboard a French ship, the *St. Charles*. They were not, however, welcome in New Amsterdam. Petrus Stuyvesant, the highest ranking official in the colony (his title was director-general), did not want these Jews to stay. According to the traditional account, Stuyvesant, a classic antisemite, was prepared to throw the Jews out as quickly as he could. Within two weeks after their arrival Stuyvesant wrote officials of the Dutch West India Company (Westindische Compagnie) in Amsterdam, asking permission to expel the Jews. As one historian recently put it: "Jews experienced anti-Semitism from the moment they set foot in North America."[3] According to the usual rendition of the story, Jewish investors in the West India Company (WIC) then interceded on behalf of their co-religionists, Stuyvesant was thwarted, and the Jews were allowed to remain. As the traditional story goes, the Directors of the WIC told Stuyvesant that he had to respect the rights of the Jews in part because of "the large amount of capital which they [the Jews] still have invested in the shares of this Company."[4]

This traditional tale resonates well with American Jews. The moral of the story is that Jews help each other, with commercially successful Jews helping their less fortunate brethren in the face of omnipresent antisemitism. It is a comfortable story that reinforced Jewish notions of elite charity to immigrants through the Hebrew Immigrant Aid Society (HIAS) from the 1870s to World War I, and Zionist notions of American Jewish support for Israel in the rest of the twentieth century.

This story, however much it is ingrained in American Jewish culture, does not ring completely true. The "first" Jews—those that Stuyvesant tried to expel—turn out not to have actually been the "first" Jews to come to New Amsterdam, and Stuyvesant's antisemitism may not have been what motivated him to attempt to expel the twenty-three Portuguese Jews. His descriptions of the Jews were crudely antisemitic, but his actual actions were not particularly oppressive and pale in comparison to his rough treatment of Lutherans and his truly brutal treatment of Quakers. The arrival of the "first Jews" also undermines the theme of Jewish solidarity, as it turns out that the "first

Jews" in New Amsterdam refused even to lend money to the refugees from Recife. Finally, we now know that the ship they arrived on was the *St. Catrina*, not the *Charles*, and that it was Dutch, not French.[5]

The emphasis on Jewish influence in the WIC is also problematic. Jewish participation in the Company was negligible. In 1623, when the WIC began, just eighteen Jewish residents of Amsterdam invested a total of about 36,000 florins—about 1.27 percent of the initial capitalization of 3,000,000 florins. None of these investors—or any other future Jewish stockholders—would ever become directors of the WIC. In 1656, nearly three years *after* the first Jews arrived in New Netherland, only seven Jews in Amsterdam were main stockholders (*hoofdparticipanten*) in the WIC, making up about 4 percent of the Company's main stockholders (7 Jewish stockholders in the company out of 169). However, it is not clear that even this number of Jewish stockholders existed in 1653–1654, when the Portuguese Merchants wrote the directors of the WIC, because Jewish investment in the WIC increased "mostly after the loss of Dutch Brazil" in the late 1650s and beyond.[6] It is hard to imagine that the Jewish investment had much influence on the Company. On the other hand, even as a small number of main participants, the Jewish investors had some access to the management of the Company, and thus at least may have been able to make the case to the WIC directors that the Portuguese Jews should be allowed to stay. To the extent that some Jews had access to the WIC directors and lobbied on behalf of the Jews in New Amsterdam, the traditional account remains valid. But it is not the whole story or even the most important story.

The intervention of the Jews in Amsterdam is also not exactly what the traditional story implies. In January 1655, the WIC received a petition, not from the few Jewish investors in the WIC, but from a larger group of Dutch Jews, who referred to themselves as "the merchants of the Portuguese Nation residing in this city [Amsterdam]." This petition only indirectly referred to the twenty-three Jewish refugees in New Amsterdam by noting many Jews had "lost their possessions" with the fall of the Dutch colony in Brazil, "arrived from there in great poverty," and "have been dispersed here and there." These "merchants of the Portuguese Nation" asked not merely for permission for those Jews "dispersed here and there" to stay in New Amsterdam, but that "the Jewish nation be permitted, together with other inhabitants, to travel, live and traffic there, and with them enjoy liberty on condition of contributing like others."[7] This petition was in effect on behalf of all Jews in Holland.

The petition of the Jewish merchants and the existence of a few Jewish investors in the WIC were not the only factors influencing the Company's attitude toward Jews. For a number of years, the WIC had been doing business with Jewish merchants in its other colonies, and thus the leaders of the WIC were not much concerned about the presence of Jews in New Amsterdam. In 1624 the WIC had seized the Portuguese colony at Bahia and in 1630 soldiers and sailors working for the Company seized Pernambuco, with its main city of Recife. Jews in Amsterdam had helped finance this attack on the Portuguese and Jewish soldiers had been involved in the military operations that led to Dutch rule. Some Portuguese Jews from Amsterdam probably served as interpreters for the invading Dutch forces, since they spoke both the local language as well as Dutch. In deciding to move into these Brazilian ports, the WIC had counted on support from the Jews and "New Christians" living there. The WIC directors correctly knew that in Brazil the Jews (and "New Christians" who might want to return to their original faith) would help them seize and control the colony, and correctly anticipated they would also help make it profitable. Once the colony was in Dutch hands, the WIC guaranteed them freedom of religion in the privacy of their homes, and ordered that no Dutch official should "molest them or subject them to inquiries in matters of conscience."[8] Some of these Jews of course would later come to New Amsterdam.

After the conquest of Bahia and Pernambuco, the Jews played an important role in the development of Dutch Brazil. By the mid-1640s, there were between 850 and 1,000 Jews in all of Dutch Brazil and they constituted about half of the European population of Recife.[9] Their many contributions to the success of the WIC in Brazil led to the Jews gaining tremendous liberty in the colony. In 1646 the States-General of the United Netherlands praised members of the "Jewish Nation, living in faraway lands" for their service to the WIC "particularly for the conservation and maintenance of the conquests in Brazil." Thus the States-General ordered the Dutch authorities in Brazil to "take care, and make such provisions where necessary, that the aforesaid Jewish Nation in said Brazil . . . shall be protected and sheltered in the same way as the other inhabitants of the United Netherlands themselves." In 1651, while the Company still held Recife, the Directors informed Stuyvesant that it had entered into a contract with "a Jew, *Jan de Illau* . . . who intends to bring a considerable number" of his co-religionists "to settle and cultivate" the Dutch colony at Curaçao. The Company directors actually believed that Illau "and his associates" were also planning "to trade from there to the *West Indies* and the [Spanish] *Main*," but the Company was still "willing to make the experiment," and thus ordered Stuyvesant to help "accommodate" Illau.[10] In 1654, when the Portuguese recaptured Recife, a number of Jews died defending Dutch rule. The remaining Jews in the colony, who had been stalwart supporters of the Dutch administration, were forced to seek refuge elsewhere. This was how the twenty-three Jews ended up in New Amsterdam.[11] By this time the WIC understood that Jews had made important contributions to its mission and the growth of its colonies. Jews were good settlers for the WIC. The Directors of WIC understood, as had Johan Mauritis, the Dutch governor-general in Brazil, that the Jews "had always been 'reliable political allies.'"[12] The States-General had understood this as well, and thus reminded the WIC in Brazil "to take care, and make such provisions where necessary, that the aforesaid Jewish Nation in said Brazil . . . shall be protected and sheltered in the same way as the other inhabitants of the United Netherlands themselves." As Jonathan Sarna has observed, "the Jews of Dutch Brazil enjoyed rights unmatched by any other seventeenth-century Jewish community in the world."[13]

Clearly, by the time the first Jews came to New Amsterdam the WIC had no qualms about having Jewish investors, Jewish business associates, or Jewish colonists, and the Dutch government was on record supporting Jewish immigration to its overseas outposts. This understanding of the Jewish experience in Holland and in the Dutch new world colonies before 1654 places the arrival of the Jews in New Netherland in perspective and sheds light on the development of religious liberty in America. The place to begin is with the arrival of Jews in New Amsterdam.

The Arrival

In the spring of 1655, authorities in New Amsterdam reported that during the previous summer (1654), "Some Jews came from Holland" as merchants.[14] In late August of 1654, Jacob Barsimson[15] arrived in New Amsterdam on the *Peereboom* from Amsterdam. He is considered the first Jewish immigrant into what would become the United States. It is possible that Asser Levy and Solomon Pietersen were also on this ship,[16] but they may also have come earlier. We know Barsimson was on the ship because there is a record of the fare he paid, seventy-two Florins, which also indicated that he did not come empty-handed. He may have been sent there by the Jews in Holland to investigate the possibility of encouraging further Jewish emigration to the New Netherland colony.[17] The arrival of Barsimson, Levy, Pieterson, and, perhaps other Jews before the Portuguese Jews later that year is not just a matter of antiquarian interest—a search for the "first" Jew in what became the United States. Rather, the reaction to the arrival of Barsimson and other Jews is important because it sheds light on Stuyvesant's response to the subsequent arrival of the Portuguese Jews.

Significantly, neither the civil officials in New Amsterdam nor the Dutch religious leaders seem to have been bothered by the trickling-in of Dutch Jews in the summer of 1654. Their arrivals are matter-of-factly reported without any editorial comment or very much detail. From the records it is impossible to know how many Jews came before the twenty-three arrived from Recife, or even who they were. There are a number of complex reasons for this. Because these Jews were coming directly from Holland they were not foreigners, even though from the perspective of Dutch Calvinists they followed a foreign faith. Indeed, Barsimson came at the behest of the Dutch West India Company, with a passport or some other papers "as one of a party of emigrants from Holland sent" by the Company.[18] It would have been politically inexpedient, or worse, for Stuyvesant to have challenged his right to be there.

Even if he did not want Dutch Jews in his community, Stuyvesant must have known that Jews in Holland had relative religious freedom at this time. In 1572 and 1579, the Dutch Republic had established freedom of religious practice and in 1585, the Dutch States General had invited Jewish merchants in Antwerp to move to Amsterdam, where they were promised religious freedom. In the 1590s, the Amsterdam city council granted citizenship to a few Sephardic merchants, even though citizenship was in theory only available to members of the Dutch Reformed Church. As one scholar recently noted, "It is likely that once these Portuguese immigrants settled in Amsterdam and shared their valuable trade connections with the Dutch merchants the authorities closed their eyes to the fact that they had really let in Jews."[19] At the time of the settlement of New Amsterdam, Jews in Holland had, at least by the standards of the period, enormous religious freedom even though they lacked political and legal equality. By the beginning of the seventeenth century Jews in Holland had established synagogues, burial grounds, schools, and rabbinical leadership. Amsterdam's eight hundred or so Jewish residents had three synagogues before the English Pilgrims migrated to Plymouth in 1620. In 1642 the Prince of Orange made an official state visit to the newly consecrated Portuguese Synagogue.[20] After the Peace of Münster (1648), Dutch authorities insisted (although with little success) that Dutch Jews should have the same rights as other Dutch citizens when doing business in Spain. They were allowed to be naturalized citizens, although they could not inherit citizenship, and, unlike almost everywhere else in Europe, they were allowed to attend universities. Barred from many professions, such as the law, they were mostly merchants, physicians (a profession that was open to them), or involved in printing and book selling.[21] By 1630, Amsterdam would become "the chief centre of Hebrew printing for the entire Jewish world." In general, Dutch Jews would "play a larger role . . . in commerce, finance, colonial trade, intellectual life, and publishing . . . than was possible before the 1790s in any other European country."[22] A few invested in the WIC. As Jacob Marcus observed, "As far as the Jew was concerned, in no place was the new age of tolerance better documented than Holland."[23] Thus, it would have been inappropriate—almost anti-Dutch—for the authorities in New Amsterdam to complain about the arrival of Barsimson and any other Dutch Jews in 1654.

The situation for Jews in New Amsterdam and for Stuyvesant changed dramatically in early September 1654, with the arrival of the twenty-three Jewish refugees from Recife. We do not know whether they went directly to New Amsterdam or came by a circuitous route that may have included an unplanned and unwanted stop in the Spanish Caribbean, [24] but by the time they arrived they were virtually penniless and were soon being sued for non-payment of their passage. On 7 September 1654, the New Amsterdam Court ordered the Jewish refugees to pay the ship captain for their passage, and allowed him to hold all their furniture and other belongings as security until payment. The spokesman for this group of "23 souls, big and little," was Solomon Pietersen, described in the record as "a Jew." Pietersen does not, however, appear to be one of the twenty-three. Rather, he was one of the "first" Jews who came to New Amsterdam in the summer of 1654, before the arrival of the Recife refugees. Two days later, the Court held a special meeting at which it ordered that David Israel and Moses Ambrosius be jailed until the remaining balance was paid to the captain of the *St. Catrina*. The case was still being disputed in early October, with the Jewish defendants now claiming that they should not have to pay any more because their furniture and other goods had been sold, when in fact they were supposed to be held as security with the specific condition that they not be sold.[25]

Once these debts were finally settled, the Jews had little to survive on. The Jewish refugees from Recife immediately became dependant on the charity of the colonial government, the Dutch Reformed Church, and individual Dutch settlers. Initially Dominie Johannes Megapolensis, the Dutch cleric in the colony, "directed them to the Jewish merchants," who had arrived that summer. Megapolensis thought "it would have been proper, that they should have been supported by their own people." But, according to Megapolensis's account, the Dutch Jews in the colony "would not even lend them a few stivers," and thus he later reported, "they have been at our charge, so that we have had to spend several hundred guilders for their support." He noted that the Jews from Recife "came several times to my house, weeping and bemoaning their misery."[26]

It is not clear from Megapolensis's account if the "we" and "our" in this letter refers to the New Amsterdam government or the Dutch Reformed Church or both. It is also not clear if Megapolensis personally gave them alms when they came "weeping" to his house or only gave them money from the church's coffers.[27] What is clear, however, is that Megapolensis thought the Jews an unnecessary burden on the community and he was reluctant to see them settle in the colony.

Compounding Megapolensis's complaints over the cost of supporting these Jews was his correct assumption that the refugees were planning to remain and develop a community. The twenty-three consisted of four families, including children who would presumably begin to make families of their own in the not-too-distant future. That the Jews wanted to stay in New Amsterdam made sense. They were homeless, stateless people. They had no place to return to, no nation to protect them. As long as they could stay in New Amsterdam they indicated they would.[28]

The Rev. Megapolensis was not alone in this evaluation of the Jews. Within two weeks of their arrival, Director-General Petrus Stuyvesant wrote to the directors of the WIC, asking permission to expel the Jews. Stuyvesant did not immediately write such a letter because he was apparently waiting to see what the Jewish refugees actually wanted. If they were only planning to stay for a short time, he was willing to offer them sanctuary, just as Rev. Megapolensis begrudgingly gave them food and other charity. But, when Stuyvesant found that "they would nearly all like to remain here," he felt it best to take steps to be rid of the Portuguese Jews. So, he sought permission from officials of the Dutch West India Company "to require them in a friendly way to depart."[29] Stuyvesant offered three reasons for his position.

First, Stuyvesant suggested that the Jews were "very repugnant to the inferior magistrates" of the colony. The source of this repugnancy is not entirely clear, although most likely their Jewishness and the fact that they were not Dutch was enough to make them "repugnant" to the leadership of the colony. Their poverty no doubt reinforced this view. However, even while worrying about their poverty, Stuyvesant claimed he feared their "customary usury and deceitful trading with the Christians."[30] This fairly standard antisemitic canard was especially absurd in light of the actual circumstances of these immigrants. The newly arrived Portuguese Jews could hardly have been involved in money lending or trading. On the contrary, they were money borrowers, having almost nothing of their own.

These comments, in the context of the previous Jewish immigration, also illustrate the apparent ambivalence of the New Netherland authorities towards Jews. Neither Stuyvesant nor anyone else in the community seems to have been bothered when the Dutch Jewish businessmen—who might very well have become involved in trading or money lending—arrived earlier that summer. Their arrival did not lead to any antisemitic outbursts. Neither Stuyvesant nor Rev. Megapolensis were apparently concerned about Barsimson's business plans. Why then were the authorities in New Amsterdam concerned about the arrival of a few more Jews in September? The two other reasons Stuyvesant gave for wanting to expel these new Jews suggest the answer.

Stuyvesant noted that the church authorities feared that "owing to their present indigence they [the Portuguese Jews] might become a charge in the coming winter."[31] This seems to have been a major concern of both the religious and secular leaders of the colony. In this matter Stuyvesant's desire to force the Portuguese Jews to leave reflected the accepted seventeenth century solution to the immigration of poor people—expulsion. This was done in England and the New England colonies. Well into the nineteenth century, American courts would hear cases of one town or county suing another for the maintenance of indigents. Simply stated, Director-General Stuyvesant did not feel his colony should be held responsible for the maintenance of poor people from another country. It is likely he would have reacted the same way to indigent immigrants—whatever their religion—from anyplace in the world other than, perhaps, Holland.

Stuyvesant's third reason for wanting to get rid of the new Jews appears, at first glance, to be a classic example of antisemitism. On careful examination, however, Stuyvesant's position emerges as more complex. Stuyvesant concluded this portion of his letter to the authorities in Amsterdam, "praying also most seriously in this connection, for ourselves as also for the general community of your worships, that the deceitful race—such hateful enemies and blasphemers of the name of Christ—not be allowed further to infect and trouble this new colony, to the dissatisfaction of your worships' most affectionate subjects."[32]

The phrases "deceitful race" and "hateful enemies" of Christ reflect the anti-Jewish attitudes of some Calvinists. However, dislike of Jews *per se* does not seem to be Stuyvesant's main concern. Rather, he is worried that the Jews will "infect and trouble" the colony. This suggests that Stuyvesant is mostly concerned with the increasingly polyglot nature of the community. He objects to the Portuguese Jews, not merely because they are Jews, but because they are neither Calvinists nor Dutch, and are thus doubly foreign. This analysis is supported by an understanding of how most Europeans viewed ethnic and religious diversity and an examination of how Stuyvesant treated other non-Dutch or non-Calvinist immigrants.

The Problem of Religious Toleration in the Seventeenth Century

At the beginning of the seventeenth century, virtually all political leaders accepted the idea that religious diversity was dangerous to the stability of any government. Most Europeans believed that in any kingdom the ruler and the subjects should have the same religion. This was based on the assumption that religious difference could create conflict within the country that might lead to civil war and anarchy. This was certainly true during the brutal wars of the sixteenth century. Thus, the Peace of Augsburg in 1555 ended years of religious wars in the Holy Roman Empire by establishing throughout most of the Empire the concept of *cuius regio, eius religio* (whose the region, his the religion). This rule allowed local rulers to decide the religion of their subjects. In 1648, European leaders reaffirmed this principle in the Treaty of Westphalia, which ended the Thirty Years' War.

The one great exception to this general rule was The Netherlands.[33] In the last part of the sixteenth century, The Netherlands began to emerge as the most tolerant nation in Europe. By the 1620s, Amsterdam's Jews, while officially second-class citizens "enjoyed virtual freedom of religion in all essential respects" and as noted above, some Jews were granted citizenship. Roman Catholics were even more despised than Jews in Holland, but nevertheless, despite the best efforts of the Dutch Reformed Church, "Roman Catholicism flourished in Amsterdam." By the 1630s, "in practice the Roman Catholics had total religious freedom in Amsterdam" although "they could build no churches with towers in the public streets."[34]

This tolerance partially migrated to the New World along with the Dutch flag. From the beginning, officials of the WIC realized the virtue of both a religious establishment and religious tolerance. In 1638 the Company declared that religion in New Netherland should "be taught and practiced" according the same "confession and formalities of union" which were "publicly accepted" in Holland. This meant that the Dutch Reformed Church was the established church of the colony. However, the WIC leaders also declared that this directive should be implemented "without . . . it being inferred from this that any person shall hereby in any wise be constrained or aggrieved in his conscience."[35] This endorsement of religious toleration was promulgated by Company officials in Amsterdam, but, with a few exceptions, the leadership in New Amsterdam resisted their superiors in Amsterdam. The history of the New Netherland Colony shows one of constant conflict between the tolerance of the Heeren XIX,[36] who made up the governing body of the WIC in Amsterdam, and the intolerance of the local political and religious leadership in New Amsterdam, especially under Petrus Stuyvesant.

The local religious and secular leaders in New Netherland believed that religious toleration was dangerous to the stability of any government. These Dutch Calvinists "interpreted a harmonious state to mean one in which the magistracy and church worked together to preserve doctrine and therefore civil unity. Conversely, they held that doctrinal diversity must necessarily lead to civil anarchy and disintegration of the state."[37] Such ideas were of course common throughout Europe and its colonies at this time. But, in contrast to these views, the Dutch government, the Heeren XIX, and the other leaders of the WIC in Amsterdam were on the cutting edge of appreciating the value of toleration.[38]

But the older ideas—that "doctrinal diversity must necessarily lead to civil anarchy and disintegration of the state"[39]—resonated with the leaders of New Netherland. Theirs was a weak and underdeveloped colony, precariously sandwiched between French settlements to the north, powerful Indian tribes to the west, Swedish settlements to the west and south, and strong English colonies to the east and south. "Because the colony was intended to be an efficient, disciplined trading center in a strange and unaccommodating wilderness, its leaders thought it essential to enforce existing social controls in a rigorous manner."[40] The rulers of New Netherland naturally established the Dutch Reformed Church.

Initially, the colonial officials were able to sustain religious homogeneity, but this goal could not be maintained. Refugees, including the religiously oppressed, were more likely to move to the New World than were prosperous and contented Dutch citizens. The tolerance of The Netherlands also undermined the intolerance of New Netherland. Despite persecution by the local authorities, religious dissenters moved to the colony in the 1640s and 1650s. The Heeren XIX usually allowed the dissenters to remain with some religious freedom, often overruling the colony's director-general on these matters. Once they were allowed to live in the colony, they quickly sought other privileges, including citizenship and the right of public religious observance. When denied the latter right, they either appealed to authorities in Holland or sometimes practiced in defiance of the law.

Religious minorities reached the colony in the 1640s, but not until the 1650s did their presence lead to political difficulties. In the 1640s, the WIC director in New Netherland, Willem Kieft, allowed various New England dissidents to settle in the colony, offering them not only religious freedom, but also "the liberty to appoint their own magistrates" subject to the approval of the Dutch leadership. Among those settling in New Netherland was the radical separatist Anne Hutchinson, who was chased from Massachusetts and ultimately moved to Long Island in 1642. These refugees from New England orthodoxy tended to live by themselves in small villages and communities. They did not threaten Dutch hegemony or Dutch Reformed orthodoxy, while at the same time, they added much to the colony.[41] Moreover, most were Calvinists, like the Dutch, although some, like Hutchinson, were extremist in their views and practices. Thus, as early as 1640, officials in New Netherland accommodated a small number of non-Dutch fellow Calvinists because they would help populate the large and mostly empty colony. While not members of the Dutch Reformed Church, these English settlers were theologically similar to the Dutch and at the same time posed no threat to the colony's established orthodoxy. The arrival of Lutherans, Quakers, and Jews was more problematic.

Petrus Stuyvesant and the Non-Dutch Immigrants

Petrus Stuyvesant, the Director-General of the colony after 1646, was a professional soldier who had lost a limb fighting the Spanish. The peg-legged Director-General was "fiercely patriotic, fearless in battle, capable of towering rages, and an autocratic leader with a reputation for discipline and work."[42] The WIC sent him to the New World to bring order and stability to a teetering colony run by a company that was going bankrupt. He was replacing Willem Kieft, who had nearly destroyed the colony in an unnecessary and costly Indian war. Stuyvesant "arrived in New Netherland at the colony's darkest hour, and he must have fancied himself something of a savior because from the moment he stepped ashore he became a whirlwind of activity, issuing proclamations, closing down brothels and taverns, and setting a new tone of optimism." The residents of the colony never loved him or even liked him, rather they "respected" and "feared" the military man who, for all his faults of arrogance, narrow mindedness, and authoritarianism, was "the most capable man the Company had ever sent" to govern New Netherland.[43] He would also serve longer than any other colonial governor of either Dutch New Netherland or English New York. His autocratic nature probably saved the colony from total chaos in the late 1640s and into the 1650s, but in the end his authoritarianism also undermined Dutch rule, so that the English takeover of the colony in 1664 would be accomplished without firing a shot. The English offered fair terms, and the burghers of New Amsterdam were quick to surrender their colony and their director-general.

While a towering figure in early American history and in the history of New York, Petrus Stuyvesant looms even larger in the history of American Jews. He was the first official to encounter the Jews, and the first to espouse an antisemitic response to them. He is, in a sense, an American Haman: He tried to do harm to the Jews and was stopped before he could complete his work.

However, Stuyvesant's response to the Jews must be put in a larger perspective. The WIC had sent Stuyvesant to run the colony and to rescue it from mismanagement and chaos. Stuyvesant was the son of a clergyman and as an adult became an elder in the Dutch

Reformed Church. He "believed strongly in the Old World axiom that the combined forces of church and state were the best promoters of morality and social harmony."[44] Basically, he was opposed to the arrival of anyone who was not Dutch. Furthermore, he preferred that any Dutch who came to New Netherland be members of the Dutch Reformed Church. His attempt to prevent the Recife Jews from remaining in New Netherland must be seen in part as the actions of a political functionary, trying to implement what he deeply believed were the policies best suited for the colony. His actions were colored by his strong devotion to the Dutch Reformed Church, his xenophobia, and his antisemitism. But Stuyvesant's antisemitism, while transparent and hateful, was in the end not particularly vicious, especially when compared to his response to other religious outsiders. He allowed the Jews to land in New Amsterdam, unlike the Quakers, and while trying to get rid of the Jews he did not physically abuse them. Unlike the Lutherans, Quakers, and even some Puritans, he never jailed any Jews. His preferred method was "to require them in a friendly way to depart,"[45] which was far more gentle than throwing them in jail until he could put them on the next ship leaving his colony, which is how he later treated some Lutherans and Quakers. In the spring of 1655, he was preparing to place the Jews on ships to send them to Holland, but was still waiting for authorization to do so before acting. He did not even seek authorization to do this to some Lutherans and Quakers and jailed them while waiting to expel them.

Stuyvesant's response to the Recife Jews contrasts sharply with his response to the arrival of Quakers three years later. The director-general tried to prevent Quakers from even landing in the colony and when they secretly came ashore, he jailed them under horrible conditions. The response of others in the Dutch colony to the presence of Jews, especially the response of Dutch Reform cleric Dominie Johannes Megapolensis, also reveals a nasty antisemitism which was directly tied to the public policy of the colony. Yet, even as Rev. Megapolensis wrote antisemitic tirades to his superiors in Holland, he also provided the Jews with charity through the winter of 1654–1655. The contradictions between the words of Stuyvesant and Megapolensis and their actions underscore the complexity of the history of the first

Jews in New Netherland. The history of Stuyvesant's responses to other non-Dutch settlers—Puritans, Lutherans, and Quakers—illustrates the complexity of this story.

The Lutherans in the New Netherland

The experience of the Lutherans in New Netherland helps put the history of Jews in the colony in perspective. In 1648 the Dutch began to encroach on the Swedish settlements in what is today Delaware. This would lead to a Dutch victory in 1655 that extended the Dutch colony as far south as present-day Wilmington, Delaware. By 1649, Lutherans from Holland (where they had substantial religious freedom) were drifting into the colony and privately practicing their faith.[46] In 1653, the year before the Jews arrived, the Dutch Lutherans in the colony asked for the right to import a minister and build a church. The Church leaders in New Netherland vehemently opposed this, noting that a Lutheran minister and church "would tend to the injury of our [Dutch Reformed] church, the diminution of hearers of the Word of God, and increase of dissensions." They feared it would "pave the way for other sects, so that in time our place [the New Netherland colony] would become the receptacle of all sorts of heretics and fanatics." The leaders of the Church in the colony happily noted that Stuyvesant agreed with them that allowing a Lutheran minister and church would be "contrary to the first article of his commission" which required that he not allow "any other than the Reformed doctrine." The ministers reported that Stuyvesant was "zealous for the Reformed Religion" and "would rather relinquish his office than grant permission" for the Lutherans to have a minister or a church.[47] The Directors of the WIC agreed with this position, resolving in February 1654 that no Lutheran ministers would be allowed.[48] Stuyvesant's war on the Lutherans did not end here, however. In 1655, he summarily expelled two Lutheran ministers from the recently captured colony at New Sweden (Delaware), although one was allowed to stay on humanitarian grounds, at least for the short term.[49] The subsequent Treaty with Sweden ceding the territory to the Dutch allowed the remaining Swedes to keep this minister and openly practice their faith. But, what Stuyvesant had to allow in the old Swedish colony did not affect his rule in the rest of New Netherland.

In 1656, the Lutherans once again demanded a minister, arguing that in Holland they were allowed to openly practice their faith. Stuyvesant responded by publishing a placard, which was the equivalent of an executive order or ordinance, against the Lutherans, and then jailing some of them.[50] The Directors of the WIC reprimanded the director-general for both acts. The WIC would not allow the Lutherans to have a church or a minister, but would also not tolerate their persecution. He was ordered to "let them have free religious exercises in their houses."[51] Lutherans in Holland then directly petitioned the directors of the WIC for the right to have public worship and a minister, and in October, the Lutherans in New Netherland petitioned Stuyvesant for the same right, claiming that the directors of the WIC in Holland had allowed this. The authorities in New Amsterdam denied the request, reiterating that the Lutherans were only allowed private worship, and sent the petition to the Heeren XIX in Holland. The Lutherans in New Amsterdam argued that if their co-religionists in what had been New Sweden could have a minister, so should they. But in March 1657, the Directors in Holland reaffirmed that the Lutherans could not have a church or a minister.[52] Significantly, at least three Lutherans were Directors of the WIC at this time, but they were unable to win the right to public worship for their co-religionists.

The Lutherans were not satisfied, however, with worshipping at home without a preacher. They directly petitioned the States-General, Holland's legislature, for relief, but at the same time smuggled a minister, Rev. Johannes Ernestus Gutwasser (also called Goetwater in some of the letters), from Holland into the New Netherland colony.[53] The Dutch Reformed clergy emphatically opposed this. In July, Rev. Johannes Megapolensis and Rev. Samuel Drisius petitioned the New Amsterdam government to prevent the Lutherans from having a minister and having full religious freedom. They warned, if this happened "the Papist, Mennonites, and others, would soon make similar claims. Thus we would soon become a Babel of confusion, instead of remaining a united and peaceful people. Indeed it would prove a plan of Satan to smother this infant, rising congregation, almost in its birth, or at least to obstruct the march of its truth in its progress."[54] The "rising congregation" was of course the Dutch Reformed Church in New Netherland. Significantly, while worrying about "a Babel of confusion," the Dutch Reformed Ministers did not mention any threats from the city's growing Jewish community. The real threats to them came from other Christians, especially Lutherans, Mennonites, Quakers, and Catholics.

New Amsterdam's officials responded quickly to the petition of the Dutch ministers concerning the Lutheran minister, Rev. Gutwasser. The Mayor and Aldermen ordered Rev. Gutwasser to appear before them, to respond to the charges that he was secretly a Lutheran minister. He did not deny this. In fact, he "frankly answered, he had been sent on behalf of their [the Lutheran's] Consistory, to occupy the position of a preacher here, as far as it would be allowed." He also claimed that the Heeren XIX were sending a "letter of permit" to allow him to preach in New Netherland. The local officials explained these events to the WIC and expressed grave doubts that "the Hon. Directors would tolerate in this place any other doctrine, than the true Reformed Religion." The city officials ordered Rev. Gutwasser "not to hold public or private exercise" in New Amsterdam until they heard back from the Directors in Holland.[55]

In October, Stuyvesant resolved the crisis by ordering Rev. Gutwasser to immediately leave the colony. The Lutherans protested and petitioned, as did Gutwasser himself, but to no avail. Having missed the opportunity to leave on his own, he was arrested and summarily forced to sail back to Europe, or at least that is what was reported to the Directors of the WIC. In May 1658, the Directors of the WIC confirmed that Stuyvesant was correct in expelling Gutwasser: "That you have sent back here the Lutheran preacher is not contrary to, but rather in accordance with our good intentions." Significantly, in contrast to his treatment of Jews, Stuyvesant did this without prior authorization for the WIC Directors in Amsterdam. While the Directors approved what Stuyvesant did, they thought he "might have proceeded less vigorously." The Directors suggested that next time something like this happened, the director-general should "use the least offensive, and most tolerant means" of removing an unwanted clergyman, "so that people of other persuasions may not be deterred" from attending the Dutch Reformed Church, "but in time [might] be induced to listen and finally gained over."[56]

Meanwhile, Gutwasser had not in fact left the colony, but had "concealed himself with a Lutheran farmer." In the summer of 1658, he was discovered. The Dutch Reformed ministers reported this information to Stuyvesant, pointing out that the "perverseness" of the Lutherans had "led them to make false representations" to the government. The New Netherland government then took steps to finally remove Pastor Gutwasser, but the Lutherans appealed to Stuyvesant claiming that their pastor was too ill to travel. The government granted him time to recover.[57] Meanwhile, Rev. Gutwasser continued to evade expulsion and to preach. Finally, in the spring of 1659, Stuyvesant had Gutwasser arrested and placed on a ship, which took him back to Holland. In September, the Dutch clerics reported that there was "now again quietness among the people" because the Lutherans were attending the Dutch Reformed Church. However Revs. Megapolensis and Drisius worried that the Lutherans were still planning to try to bring a minister over. But for the moment, "imminent injury to this infant church" had "been averted" by the "vigilance and discretion of the Dutch ministers and the director-general." In Holland the authorities of the Dutch Reformed Church reported that "the minister Gutwasser, has been put in jail and was sent to the Fatherland [Holland] with the first ships." The Assembly of the Church in Amsterdam "rejoiced in this."[58]

The crisis over Rev. Gutwasser was over, and from the perspective of Stuyvesant and the Dutch Reformed Church this was cause for rejoicing. But the Lutherans did not go away. In 1660, Lutherans at Fort Orange (Albany) began to collect money to bring over a preacher. No Lutheran minister seems to have been brought over at this time, but the fear continued to rattle the Dutch clergy in the colony. Finally, in 1666, the new governor of what was by then the New York colony would grant Lutherans religious freedom and the right to have their own ministers.[59]

While Megapolensis and Drisius were battling the Lutherans and Pastor Gutwasser, they sent a very long letter to the religious authorities in Amsterdam, explaining the situation in New Amsterdam. They complained about the Lutheran pastor, and explained how they had petitioned the local government demanding his expulsion. They also complained about the Swedes in Delaware and the fact that the "Swedish Governor made a condition in his capitulation, they might retain one Lutheran preacher," which in fact they had. The Dutch Clergy declared that this preacher was "a man of impious and scandalous habits, a wild, drunken, unmannerly clown, more inclined to look into the wine can than into the Bible." He would, they proclaimed, "prefer drinking brandy two hours to preaching one" and he often "wants to fight whomever he meets." The ministers also complained about Englishmen on Long Island, Mennonites who "reject the baptism of infants" and a "cobbler from Rhode Island" who had come to preach "saying he had a commission from Christ." They worried about "Independents" and Presbyterians in some towns and Puritans in others. In a postscript they noted the arrival, in early August, of Quakers. The ministers at first thought the Quakers had all gone on to Rhode Island, "for that is the receptacle of all sorts of riff-raff people, and is nothing else than the sewer [*latrina*] of New England." But then they discovered that a few Quakers had secretly landed in New Netherland. Fortunately, the ministers reported these Quakers had been jailed and so they hoped "God will baffle the designs of the devil" and save the colony from "these machinations of Satan." Significantly, once again the leaders of the church in New Netherland took no notice of the Jews while complaining about religious diversity.[60]

Indeed, by this time the Jews were no longer very much on the minds of the authorities in New Amsterdam. The Lutheran problem and the secret arrival of Rev. Gutwasser had perplexed and bedeviled Stuyvesant and the ministers. However, the Quakers would create an even greater challenge.

The Quakers in New Netherland

In the seventeenth century, Quakers were notorious for their opposition to most forms of political authority. With little exaggeration, one historian has argued that "As Bolsheviks were feared after the Russian Revolution of the twentieth century, so the very thought of Quakers frightened people of the seventeenth."[61]

The Society of Friends was founded by George Fox in 1652. The religion grew out of Puritanism and is an extreme example of "the relentless movement of the Puritan-Reformed impulse away from the hierarchical, sacramental, and objective Christianity of the Middle Ages towards various radical extremes in which intensely individualistic and spiritual motifs become predominant." Quaker teaching "undermined the establishment by minimizing the liturgical and teaching function of an ordained ministry, abandoning the idea of objective sacraments, and inspiring conduct which was attributed to the promptings of an inner voice. Most ominous of all to the authorities was the phenomenal missionary zeal which flowed from the Quaker conviction of the universality of the Holy Spirit's work."[62] The Friends became known as the "Quakers" because of their shaking or "quaking" while praying and giving sermons.

The description of the arrival of a shipload of Quakers in New Amsterdam provided by Revs. Megapolensis and Drisius illustrates the consternation the Quakers could cause government officials. In early August 1657, a ship "having no flag" came into the harbor. This ship "fired no salute before the fort, as is usual with ships on their arrival." People in the colony "could not decide whether she was Dutch, French, or English." And, when a government official boarded the ship, those on board "tendered him no honor or respect." When the ship's master came before Stuyvesant "he rendered him no respect, but stood still with his hat firm on his head, as if a goat." The ship was allowed to remain in the harbor for only one night.[63]

The Dutch ministers believed that after it was sent away the ship went to Rhode Island— "the receptacle of all sorts of riff-raff people." Since "all the cranks of New England" had moved there, the Dutch assumed these Quakers would do the same. However, before the ship left, two Quaker women somehow managed to disembark and hide on Long Island, and "as soon as the ship had fairly departed, these began to quake and go into a frenzy, and cry out loudly in the middle of the street, that men should repent, for the day of the judgment was at hand." The two women were soon jailed. Other Quakers coming to New Netherland were expelled, jailed, and tortured.[64]

This was the beginning of the longest and most brutal religious suppression in the colony's history. Over the next six years, a number of Quakers were jailed, expelled, fined, placed at hard labor, and tortured for preaching in the colony. Non-Quakers were also jailed and fined for aiding or harboring Quakers.[65] The story provides a significant contrast to the treatment of the Recife Jews, who were not only allowed to disembark, but given charity when they landed.

This persecution proved futile. Each new persecution seemed to strengthen the Quakers, especially in the English-speaking settlements on Long Island. The persecutions also stimulated some colonists to argue for religious toleration as a duty of Christian love. In the "Flushing Remonstrance" of 1658, thirty-one settlers, including the sheriff, called on Stuyvesant to rescind his orders levying heavy fines on anyone who harbored a known Quaker. The petitioners, who were mostly English, declared that "wee desire therefore in this case not to judge least wee be judged, neither to Condem, least wee bee Condemed, but rather let every man stand and fall on his own." They felt bound by God's law "to doe good unto all men," and thus, by Stuyvesant's decree, they were trapped between the law of God and that of man. Rather than persecute the Quakers, they would allow them freedom, on the theory that "if God justify who can Condem, and if God Condem there is none can justifye."[66] Stuyvesant not only rejected the petition, but arrested the leading petitioners for sedition.

Ultimately, officials in Holland ended the persecutions. The directors of the WIC told Stuyvesant that they too wished no Quakers had moved into the colony. But once in the colony, the directors asserted "we doubt very much, whether we can proceed against them rigorously without diminishing the population and stopping immigration, which must be favored at a so tender stage of the country's existence."[67] In other words, the colony could not grow and prosper, and the profits of the investors with it, without tolerance.[68] The directors told the director-general to "shut your eyes" to the Quakers, and "not force people's consciences, but allow every one to have his own belief, as long as he behaves quietly and legally, gives no offence to his neighbors, and does not oppose the government." The directors pointed out that this had been the practice in old Amsterdam "and consequently" the city had "often had a considerable influx of people." New Amsterdam too "would be benefitted by" this practice.[69]

The Arrival of the Jews and the Struggle to Stay

It is useful to revisit the history of the Jews in New Netherland in the context of the treatment of Quakers and Lutherans by both

Stuyvesant and the religious leaders of the colony. When a handful of Jews arrived in 1654, Dominie Megapolensis, the clerical leader of the Dutch Reformed Church in the colony, sided with Stuyvesant in an attempt to expel them. Megapolensis clearly disliked Jews, who, he believed, had "no other God than the unrighteous Mammon, and no other aim than to get possession of Christian property." He thought Jews were "godless rascals" and hoped authorities in Holland would order their expulsion. Significantly, however, after all of his antisemitic ranting, Megapolensis in the end did not make his case for expelling the Jews on antisemitic or on theological grounds. Rather, he defended his position by arguing that if the Jews settled in the community it would be one more step on the road to ethnic and religious chaos. He noted "we have here Papists, Mennonites and Lutherans among the Dutch; also many Puritans or Independents, and many Atheists and various other servants of Baal among the English under this government, who conceal themselves under the name of Christians; it would create a still further confusion, if the obstinate and immovable Jews came to settle here."[70] This outburst is fascinating, because it is aimed as much at non-Jews as it is at Jews. As already noted, Megapolensis was vigorous in his opposition to Lutherans and Quakers. Similarly, as noted earlier, Stuyvesant opposed allowing the Jews to stay for a variety of economic and political reasons that were reinforced by his antisemitism.

In the end, Stuyvesant and the Dutch Reformed clerics were fundamentally unsuccessful in their attempts to control the growth of the Jewish population. Indeed, conditions outside the colony were particularly good for the Jewish immigrants coming to New Netherland. At the very time that Stuyvesant wanted to stop Jewish immigration, the Dutch government had a growing interest in the toleration of Jews. For example, in 1655–1656, the Dutch Ambassador to Great Britain kept his superiors in Amsterdam informed about the status of changes in England that would allow toleration of Jews.[71]

Thus, although the Recife Jews arrived in September 1654 to a cold welcome, they were allowed to disembark from their ship and initially given some alms. Only when Stuyvesant realized these Jews planned to remain did he take steps to expel them. On 22 September 1654, Stuyvesant wrote the directors of the Company, asking to be allowed to send the Recife Jews away. The substance of this letter is in part II of this article.[72]

In January, the Directors of the WIC received a long and detailed argument, in the form of a petition from a group of Jews in Amsterdam, who referred to themselves as "the merchants of the Portuguese Nation residing in this city [Amsterdam]." They complained that it had "come to their knowledge" that the Directors had "raise[d] obstacles to the giving of permits or passports to the Portuguese Jews to travel and to go to reside in New Netherland, which if persisted in will result to the great disadvantage of the Jewish nation." They also noted it could "be of no advantage to the general company but rather damaging." They reminded the Directors that many of the Portuguese Jews had "lost their possessions at Pernambuco," been oppressed by the Inquisition, and "have at all times been faithful and have striven to guard and maintain" the Dutch colonies in Brazil "risking for that purpose their possessions and their blood." The petitioners noted that the English and French colonies in the New World were at this time welcoming the Portuguese Jews, and thus the Portuguese Jewish petitioners were perplexed as to why the Amsterdam Jews could not go to all the Dutch colonies. They also noted that some members of their community had been living in that city for "about sixty years" and many in their community were "born here and confirmed burghers." Thus they wondered why, as burghers of the city of Amsterdam, they were not allowed to move to the Dutch settlement.[73]

This was an impressive petition, as it touched on a series of strong arguments for allowing Jewish immigration to New Netherland. Politics, economics, foreign policy, loyalty, and fairness all favored Jewish immigration. So too did the reality that the New Netherland colony "needs people for its increase." Significantly, this petition said very little about the Jews from Recife. The Portuguese Jewish community was seeking permission not just for the twenty-three refugees from Brazil, but for any of the Jews in Holland who might want to move to New Netherland. The Jewish merchants ended by asking the Directors of the WIC to issue a resolution declaring that "the Jewish nation be permitted, together with other inhabitants, to travel, live and traffic there, and with them enjoy liberty on condition of contributing like others."[74]

In effect, the petition of the Portuguese Jews was also an offer to the WIC to help the Company make New Netherland a success. It was a powerful argument. In April the company responded to Stuyvesant. The directors were clearly underwhelmed by Stuyvesant's letter of 22 September,[75] and may have wondered what possessed the director-general to expend so much energy and time on the arrival of a handful of Jews. Politely, but firmly, they informed him:

> We would have liked to agree to your wishes and request that the new territories should not be further invaded by people of the Jewish race, for we forsee from such immigration the same difficulties which you fear, but after having further weighed and considered the matter, we observe that it would be unreasonable and unfair, especially because of the considerable loss, sustained by the Jews in the taking of Brazil and also because of the large amount of capital, which they have invested in shares of this Company. After many consultations we have decided and resolved upon a certain petition made by said Portuguese Jews, that they shall have permission to sail to and trade in New Netherland and to live and remain there, provided the poor among them shall not become a burden to the Company or the community, but be supported by their own nation. You will govern yourself accordingly.[76]

As they had with the arrival of the Lutherans, and as they would when Quakers came to the colony, the directors of the Company acknowledged Stuyvesant's fears that a polyglot community would be difficult. But, this was all they were willing to concede to their director-general. In rejecting his request to be authorized to remove the Jews, the Directors reminded Stuyvesant of the important Jewish contributions the settlements of the WIC in Brazil, pointing out that it would be "unreasonable and unfair, especially because of the considerable loss, sustained by the Jews" in Brazil for the company to now suddenly turn its back on the Jewish refugees from Recife. Morality dictated that the Jews be allowed to stay. So too did good policy, because the Jews had been good citizens and good colonists for the Company.

The other reason the WIC Directors gave Stuyvesant was that the Jews had a "large amount of capital" invested in the Company.[77] But, as already noted, only a very few Jews in Amsterdam were actual investors in the Company, and they had not invested much. The "large amount of capital" argument may have been a convenient answer to Stuyvesant, who surely understood that economic influence mattered in this for-profit company. But surely the relatively small amount of Jewish investment in the Company could not have been decisive. On the other hand, Jews in Amsterdam, in addition to those who had invested in the Company, had also contacted the WIC on behalf of their co-religionists in New Amsterdam. That local influence, combined with the mere fact that there were Jewish stockholders, surely had some influence on the Directors of the WIC. Significantly, in this letter the Directors told Stuyvesant they were acting "upon a certain petition made by said Portuguese Jews." This was not a reference to the Jews already in New Netherland, but to the Jews in Holland, the "merchants of the Portuguese Nation residing in this city [Amsterdam]." This petition of Jews in old Amsterdam, concerning their own business interests helped determine the fate of the handful of Jews in New Amsterdam.

Finally, the Directors of the Company must have been influenced by the very practical matter that the WIC needed settlers in the colony. The Jews were there, and they were willing to stay there. They had been good settlers in Recife and the rest of Dutch Brazil. It would have been foolish to expel them from another WIC colony without a very compelling reason. Added to this general tolerance for Jews in Amsterdam was the growing Dutch national interest in attracting Jews to Holland. The WIC was also probably influenced by the fact that these Jews had been loyal residents of the WIC colony in Recife. From Stuyvesant's perspective they may have been foreigners, but from the perspective of the WIC, they were very much a known commodity. All of these reasons combined to frustrate Stuyvesant's goals. The Jews would stay and he would "govern" himself "accordingly." As the petition of the Jewish merchants noted, this was "a land that needs people for its increase."[78]

A year later the company further strengthened its position on religious diversity. Stuyvesant had been complaining about the continuing presence of Jews, worrying that they would soon want their own house of worship. As with the controversy over the Lutheran minister, here the Directors of the Company could accede to one of the director-general's demands, but they did so in such a way that could not have made Stuyvesant very happy. In March 1656, the company reaffirmed the "permission given to the *Jews*" to "enjoy" "civil and political rights" but not full religious freedom. The Directors in Amsterdam wrote:

> The permission given to the *Jews*, to go to *New-Netherland* and enjoy there the same privileges, as they have here, has been granted only as far as civil and political rights are concerned, without giving the said *Jews* a claim to the privilege of exercising their religion in a synagogue or at a gathering; as long therefore, as you receive no request for granting them this liberty of religious exercise, your considerations and anxiety about this matter, are premature and when later something shall be said about it, you can do no better, than to refer them to us and await the necessary order.[79]

Thus, the Jews would remain. By this time, as noted above, both the civil and religious authorities were focusing on the dangers, as they saw them, from Lutherans and then Quakers. The Jews were clearly no longer a major annoyance.

Jews and the Struggle for Equality

It is hardly remarkable or surprising that the Jews in New Amsterdam faced antisemitism from the authorities. The Dutch Reformed clerics were deeply hostile to anyone who was not of their faith. Stuyvesant was not a tolerant man, and as a professional soldier he was probably not much given to reflection or philosophical musings. Indeed, his hot temper seems to have been one of his most famous traits. That he spouted antisemitic canards at the Jews, or made equally bigoted statements about Catholics, Lutherans, Quakers, Mennonites, and others seems to be exactly what we should have expected from him.

What is remarkable, however, is how the Jews in New Amsterdam were able to gain significant concessions from the Stuyvesant regime. These would not come all at once. Throughout the rest of the Dutch period, which would end in 1664, the Jews would have to petition the government, and then appeal to Amsterdam, for the right to own property, live where they wanted, have their own burial ground, have full access to business and trading opportunities, and even serve in the town guard like other burghers.[80] The Jews of New Amsterdam persisted in asserting their rights and participating in the community. They did not shy away from commerce and public life, but became actors in both phases of the community, and, in the process, put themselves into a position where they could claim the status of burghers.

As the Jews fought for and won concessions, they created an atmosphere where religious toleration worked. By the end of the Dutch period, persons of almost any religious faith were able to live in the colony. Catholics, Jews, Lutherans, and Quakers, among others, were allowed to hold their "superstitious" religious services—as the Dutch authorities called them—in private homes. The reason for this was not the desire to protect religion from government interference that motivated Roger Williams of Rhode Island.[81] This toleration was also not a function of Christian charity, love, or fear of God, although some in the colony thought it should be. Nor was toleration the result of an enlightenment philosophy that denied any role for the government in the saving of souls.

Toleration in New Netherland had almost no theory or philosophy behind it. It evolved out of the need to populate a frontier and encourage trade and commerce. Put simply, the Dutch West India Company placed worldly success above theology. For Petrus Stuyvesant, "religion was an important instrument of social control," and the failure to exercise such control was "an invitation to an anarchy of contesting beliefs."[82] However, his superiors in Amsterdam understood that too much control of religion might lead to tyranny and would certainly discourage settlement. Lutherans, Jews, Quakers, Catholics and others were allowed to settle and trade in the colony because they could make the colony grow and prosper. To put it another way, they had no need for a theoretical or philosophical defense of tolerance because they had the practical argument that the practice of tolerance had real economic benefits. This was the message the Dutch officials conveyed to Stuyvesant whenever he wanted to suppress religious minorities. Stuyvesant and other overly devout colonial officials were simply told to "shut your eyes" to persons of other religions, and let everyone in the colony go about their business. Indeed, business, not religion, was the purpose of the colony. Toleration stimulated growth and trade. And as the Merchants of the Portuguese nation had reminded the Directors of the WIC, "Yonder land is extensive and spacious. The more of loyal people that go to live there, the better it is. . . ." That was reason enough to allow persons of any faith to discreetly practice their religion and openly ply their trades.[83]

In 1664, an English fleet seized New Amsterdam and, with it, the entire Dutch empire on the mainland of North America. New Netherland was renamed New York, after the colony's new proprietor, James, Duke of York. The English of the 1660s differed somewhat from the rest of Europe in their support for the old concept of *cuius regio, eius religio*—"whose the region, his the religion." Some dissenting Protestants in England had religious liberty; Catholics faced discrimination, but not persecution; and Jews had been trickling into the country since the 1640s. The very fact that England had taken over a Dutch colony meant that a certain amount of religious toleration was necessary, because the overwhelming majority of the residents of the colony were not members of the Church of England.

In fact, the colony that James claimed was probably the most polyglot in the New World. A religious census at the time would have found members of the Dutch Reformed Church; Lutherans from Holland, Germany, and Sweden; French Calvinists; Presbyterians from the British Isles; Puritans; Separatists; Baptists and Quakers from England, Germany and elsewhere; a variety of other Protestant sects; and small numbers of Jews and Catholics. The only conspicuous absence was anyone who claimed membership in the Church of England.

Most of the residents of this new English colony were members of the Dutch Reformed Church. No official in the "Duke's Colony" ever contemplated expelling them or forcing them to accept the Church of England. This would have been impossible and impractical.

Instead, the Duke and his deputies adopted an unusually tolerant policy on religious matters. The Articles of Capitulation, which the Dutch were compelled to sign, provided that the "Dutch here shall enjoy the liberty of their consciences in Divine Worship and church discipline."[84] What the Duke gave to the Dutch he also had to give to the Protestant dissenters living on Long Island. Initially, all towns in the colony were allowed to establish whatever church they wished. Minority faiths were granted the right to conduct meetings openly. In 1666, Lutherans gained the right, long denied under the Dutch, to build their own churches. In 1674, the Duke of York ordered his new governor, Edmund Andros, to "permitt all persons of what Religion soever, quietly to inhabitt wthin ye precincts of yor jurisdiccon, wthout giveing ym any disturbance or disquiet whatsoever, for or by reasons of their differring opinions in matter of Religion."[85] In 1683, the New York Assembly partially codified this tolerance in the colony's Charter of Liberties and Privileges, which declared:

> Noe person or persons which professe ffaith in God by Jesus Christ Shall at any time be any wayes molested punished disquieted or called in Question for any Difference in opinion or Matter of Religious Concernemnt . . . But that all and Every such person or persons may . . . at all times freely have and fully enjoy his or their Judgments or Consciencyes in matters of Religion throughout all the province.[86]

This charter did not separate church and state, but explicitly provided for government support for all Christian churches. John W. Pratt, in his study of religion in New York, asserts that the Charter of Liberties "amounted to a full grant of religious freedom to Christians."[87] Yet, even this understates the reality in New York, because in 1682, the colony's Jews were allowed to have their own house of worship, even though they clearly did not "professe faith in God by Jesus Christ." While not given access to tax monies to support their teachers and clergymen, the Jews nevertheless had complete freedom of public worship, something the Dutch had denied them.[88]

Even without statutes and explicit protections of religion, no one seems to have been turned away from the colony for their religious beliefs. New York was already a commercial entrepôt and something of a melting pot. In 1678, Governor Andros reported to his superiors in London that he could find "Noe account" of "childrens births or christenings" because ministers had kept few records. Further complicating his attempts to take a complete census, Andros noted: "There are Religions of all sorts, one Church of England, severall Presbiterians and Independents, Quakers and Anabaptists, of serverall sects, some Jews. . . ."[89] A decade later, Andros's successor, Governor Thomas Dongan reported: "Here bee not many of the Church of England; [a] few Roman Catholicks; abundance of Quakers preachers men and women especially; Singing Quakers, Ranting Quakers; Sabbatarians; Antisabbatarians; Some Anabaptists; some Independents; some Jews; in short of all opinions there are some, and the most part none at all."[90]

At one level, the fears of Stuyvesant and the Dutch clerics had been realized. The colony they helped govern was no longer homogenous. It was a polyglot of religions and sects and ethnicities. But, it was on its way to becoming the most economically successful city in the New World.

The Jews played a crucial role in the development of this economic and cultural polyglot, not just as businessmen and entrepreneurs, but as pioneers who helped successfully force the issue of toleration on the local government. In this sense, the story of the first Jews suggests a different moral for modern Americans than the traditional narrative. The Jews succeeded in the New World in part because of help from the Old, but also because in the New World they persistently demanded the right to be part of the polity, to build houses, participate in the economy, and stand guard at night like other burghers.[91] They also succeeded because the directors of the WIC understood the value of hard-working immigrants who would help an empty colony grow. Finally, their success was directly tied to the success of other minority groups. For these mid-seventeenth century Jews heterogeneity—what an early generation of historians called pluralism and what modern scholars call cultural diversity—was a blessing. The more diversity New Netherland had, the more the Jews could prosper and the more the colony could prosper. Stuyvesant opposed Jews and Lutherans and Quakers and just about everyone else who was not Dutch who might come to his colony because he feared instability and chaos.

He never understood that diversity could also lead to stability. Fortunately, Stuyvesant was defeated by Jews, Lutherans, and other immigrants who persisted in helping the colony prosper in spite of its narrow-minded director general. Equally important, wiser leaders in Amsterdam, who understood that in diversity there was strength, overruled Stuyvesant.

Architecture of Autonomy: The Blessing and Peace Synagogue of Suriname

Aviva Ben-Ur and Rachel Frankel

The Jewish Community of Suriname

On 12 October 1785 the oldest synagogue building in the Americas, located in the Dutch colony of Suriname, celebrated its hundredth anniversary. The colony's Governor Wichers, its Councils of Police, notable citizens from the capital city of Paramaribo, and some 1,600 others attended the festivities. One thousand Chinese lanterns illuminated the tabletops; guests feasted on hundreds of delicacies and were plied with beverages; speeches were delivered; Dutch and Hebrew prayers were recited; and poems were declaimed to the accompaniment of a lively orchestra. To mark the event Surinamese cantor David Baruh Louzada composed a Hebrew poem praising the congregation as a surrogate Jerusalem Temple. The concluding celebration, a splendid ball at midnight, lasted until dawn.[1] This lavish celebration recognized a pioneering institution of colonial Suriname. But even more, the centenary provided Jews an occasion for a nostalgic pilgrimage to a disintegrating religious and political center whose architecture both symbolized unparalleled autonomy and, perhaps, suggested messianic sentiment.[2]

51

The synagogue had been consecrated in 1685 as Beraha VeSalom, Hebrew for "Blessing and Peace." Its founders were Jews of Iberian origin, most of whom identified themselves as members of the "Portuguese Jewish nation," who had arrived, beginning in the 1650s, from various parts of Europe, northern Africa, and other regions of the Americas.[3] These Portuguese Jews descended from refugees of the Iberian Inquisitions and Spanish Expulsion, and many had been *conversos* (forced converts to Christianity) before openly returning to the Jewish faith. Under tolerant English (1650–1667) and Dutch (1667–1975) colonial rule they established an agrarian settlement in the midst of the Surinamese jungle, some fifty miles south of the capital city. Situated along the Suriname River, this settlement developed into an autonomous village known as Jodensavanne—Dutch for "Jews' Savannah." By the mid-eighteenth century, Jodensavanne was surrounded by dozens of satellite Jewish plantations sprawling north- and southward and dominating the stretch of the river. These plots, mostly devoted to the cultivation and processing of sugar and worked by African slaves, at the time collectively formed the largest Jewish agricultural community in the world[4] and the only Jewish settlement in the Americas granted virtual self rule. From the 1660s, the decade of Jodensavanne's establishment, the few hundred recently settled Portuguese Jews of this enclave held privileges which granted them rights, exemptions and immunities both as an ethnic minority and as burghers. These privileges were arguably the most liberal Jews had ever received in the Christian world.[5]

Architectural Inspiration: Jerusalem and Amsterdam

It would be natural for the founders of Jodensavanne, the capital of an autonomous Jewish community, to be inspired by visions of ancient Jerusalem. The First Temple, built in that city by King Solomon in the tenth century B.C.E., attracted special interest among both Jews and Christians, particularly during and after the Renaissance, since many believed that God dictated architectural instructions directly to the Israelite king. This Temple was destroyed by the Babylonians in 586 B.C.E. and was rebuilt by 516/515 B.C.E. as the "Second Temple," only to be demolished again by the Romans in 70 C.E.[6] According to the Hebrew Bible, only the First Temple had God as its direct architect,[7] and Rabbinic tradition stipulates that, upon the arrival of the Messiah, Jews will be responsible for rebuilding the ancient structure. Gathering details on the physical appearance of the Temple was thus an act of messianic anticipation. One scholar fascinated with this theme was Jacob Judah Leon (1602–1675), a Dutch Sephardic teacher so entrenched in recreating the first Jerusalem sanctuary that he earned the nickname "Templo." His detailed, illustrated description of Solomon's Temple, first published in 1642 and subsequently reprinted and translated several times, became accessible to a wide audience, both lay and scholarly. Drawing on the erudite work of Spanish Jesuit predecessors and combining their ideas with his own, Templo conceived a "more sober, less baroque" and pronouncedly Dutch vision of the Temple. The model he displayed in his home attracted visitors from far and wide and directly informed the construction of Amsterdam's Sephardic *esnoga* (synagogue), inaugurated in 1675.[8] (fig.1)

Figure 1

The *esnoga*, the Portuguese synagogue of Amsterdam, consecrated in 1675. Southwest view. The auxiliary buildings in the foreground surround the sanctuary building. Photograph by Rachel Frankel, 1996.

Renowned for its majesty, that *esnoga* became an influential model for Portuguese Jewish sanctuaries both in Europe and the New World. While the "mother synagogue" served as inspiration, each community added idiosyncrasies to its own religious architecture. London's Bevis Marks building (1701) bears typical English detailing and embellishments, Curaçao's Mikvé Israel (1730) features double-curved gables and a mahogany interior, painted white in 1876 in order to reflect more light, and Paramaribo's Sephardic synagogue, Sedek VeSalom (1737), is painted white and features a slate roof.[9] Jodensavanne, situated in altogether different surroundings, produced perhaps the most dramatic architectural variations.

In both Suriname and in the Dutch Republic, congregations used outsiders to design and build their synagogues. In Amsterdam, where Jews were banned from guilds, the congregation's leaders selected Elias Bouman (b. 1636), a Dutch gentile, as their architect. Another non-Jew, Gillis van der Veen, was its master carpenter.[10] In Jodensavanne, as in Suriname in general, skilled personnel were scarce, so Jews likewise depended on others, presumably gentile Africans,[11] to build their synagogue. The architect of Beraha VeSalom remains unknown, but may have been Jewish, as were the designers of an Iberian-Jewish settlement in Recife, Brazil earlier in the seventeenth century.[12] In Amsterdam, master architect Bouman had to contend with municipal regulations, including the prohibition of direct access from the public road to sanctuaries other than Reformed churches.[13] Jodensavanne's anonymous designer was apparently unimpeded by such restrictions.

Other fundamental differences further distinguished the settlement at Jodensavanne from Amsterdam's Jewish community. Amsterdam's Jews lived in an urban and cosmopolitan environment surrounded and dominated by gentiles. Their Surinamese co-religionists, by contrast, lived in an isolated, autonomous colonial agricultural settlement where, in 1684, 105 Jewish men outnumbered Jewish women by a ratio of almost two to one, and enslaved Africans constituted 84 percent of the total Jodensavanne population.[14] A small minority of enslaved American Indians, as well as many others who maintained their freedom, also populated the settlement.[15] Moreover, in Amsterdam, the monumental Great Synagogue of the self-described High German Jews (Jews of primarily Central European origin) preceded and stood opposite the Portuguese *esnoga*.[16] If Jews of Germanic descent resided in Jodensavanne at all, they were few in number, lived there by virtue of marital bonds, and were banned from property ownership.[17] Although other Europeans and religious minorities lived in rural Suriname at the time of the construction of Beraha VeSalom (including the pietistic sect of Labadists, whose utopian settlement existed further up along the Suriname River), the various European groups lived geographically and socially apart from one another.[18]

Prior to Beraha VeSalom's consecration in 1685, no known synagogue of major architectural stature existed in the Portuguese Jewish communities of West Africa or in the New World. New Christian merchants and religious leaders, who had returned to their ancestral Jewish faith and later relocated to Joal, Senegal, established their synagogue around the year 1612. Located within a compound of private homes, this edifice seems to have been purposely tucked away from view and was probably a provisional structure.[19] Crypto-Jews in Portuguese Brazil, in addition to many confessing Jews (later under Dutch rule), worshipped in private homes.[20] Brazil's first congregation, Kahal Kadosh Tsur Israel in Recife, met in a rented house until its building was erected in 1640/1641. The composition of this first Jewish house of worship in the Americas was undistinguished, described as "some large, multi-level houses...facing Jews' Street, which served as their synagogue, and which is of stone and lime, with two stores on the main floor; which these Jews also built."[21] Around 1637 the Mahamad of Tsur Israel granted Iberian-origin Jews permission to found Brazil's second congregation—Kahal Kadosh Magen Abraham—and to build it on the Ilha de Antônio Vaz (Mauritsstad, across the river from Recife). The island's residents wished to avoid profaning the Sabbath and holidays, as reaching Tsur Israel would have entailed a boat ride before 1644, when a bridge was built. Given the status of Tsur Israel as Recife's "mother synagogue,"[22] and the elders' protectiveness of its standing as the leading congregation in the colony, it is questionable whether the building in Mauritsstad could have been architecturally noteworthy. Later, members of Magen Abraham tried to secede from the parent congregation—rebelliousness which may hint at earlier discord. But it seems doubtful that Tsur Israel would have granted permission for the building of a second synagogue had they known of any grandiose architectural plans. Finally, what Bruno Feitler calls "informal synagogues" existed in Paraíba, in Penedo along the São Fransisco River, in Olinda, and in various other locations in Brazil. It is likely that all were private houses; in fact, some are explicitly referred to as such in archival records.[23]

Nor, apparently, did the Beraha VeSalom synagogue have imitable precedents in the Caribbean or North America. Before 1656, Curaçao's congregation, established in 1651, worshipped in a small wooden house, probably located in the fields where the early colonists labored. The congregation acquired a piece of land around 1687, and in 1692 inaugurated the first of three successive stone synagogue buildings—unremarkable edifices if we are to judge by their frequent demolition and replacement.[24] In 1658 David Cohen Nassy founded a Jewish settlement in Nova Zeelandia (in present-day Guyana), but sources do not describe its physical appearance.[25] On 12 September 1659 Nassy received permission to establish a parallel colony in Dutch-ruled Cayenne,[26] in present-day French Guiana. Colonial authorities granted Cayenne's Jewish settlers freedom of conscience, including the right to establish a synagogue and school "in the same manner as is allowed in the city of Amsterdam, in accordance with the doctrines of their elders."[27] From admonitions to remain "so far from the [already established] colony on Cajana that they will not interfere with the inhabitants of that [colony]," we may surmise that the Jews of Cayenne lived in their own village.[28] Traveling to Cayenne in 1660–1661, Captain Languillet, in the employment of the Dutch, found there about fifteen to twenty Jewish families, all of them planters.[29] But these two Jewish communities were not long-lived: Cayenne fell to the French in 1664, and the Nova Zeelandian settlements of Pomeroon and Essequibo to the English in 1665. Material analysis is of no help in determining architectural emulation. The synagogues and cemeteries of the early Jewish settlements of contemporary Guyana and French Guiana have left not a trace.[30]

Continuing further northward, New York's first synagogue building, complete with a woman's balcony, would not be erected until 1728,[31] and Montreal's Congregation Shearith Israel was only founded in 1768.[32] The designers of Jodensavanne, far removed from European Christian restrictions and Germanic Jewish populations, and with possibly no architectural examples from which to draw inspiration, were poised to shape a new Jewish environment, at once distinctively messianic, Iberian, Dutch, and African.

Messianism and Design Intent

Beraha VeSalom was constructed on high ground, 30 to 36 feet above the river, to which it was adjacent. It sat in the middle of a spacious rectilinear plaza, measuring 450 feet long by 300 feet wide. Four cross streets defined the plaza's edges. At the corners of the crossroads were several houses, described in 1788 as "large and commodious," most of "a mediocre architecture," though some were "passably attractive."[33] Lithographs of Pierre Jacques Benoit, the Belgian painter who visited Suriname during the years 1829–1830, and G. W. C. Voorduin, a marine officer stationed in the colony in the 1850s, confirm the synagogue's hilltop location and its status as the tallest building of Jodensavanne's center. The site choice is not surprising. According to the Talmud, a synagogue should be located at the highest point of a town and should stand taller than other local houses.[34] Furthermore, the proximity of the synagogue to water greatly facilitated the ritual bath and other purification observances demanding naturally flowing water. Many ancient synagogues in both Palestine and the Diaspora were situated near bodies of water, likewise attesting to a concern with ritual purity.[35]

Considering the expanse of available land, the congregation's building was modest in size (a paradox addressed later in this article). The ruins of the synagogue measure 94 feet along its east-west axis and 43 feet across its north-south width (4,042 square feet or 375 square meters).[36] By contrast, Amsterdam's *esnoga* (consecrated in 1675) dominated nearly an entire block and stretched 125 feet by 95 feet (11,875 square feet or 1,008 square meters; 36 by 28 meters).[37] Even if we consider that additional adjoining land was bestowed upon the Jodensavanne community in 1691 (six years after the synagogue's consecration), when communal leader Samuel Nassy and Governor Joan van Scherpenhuysen respectively contributed an additional 25 and 100 acres,[38] Beraha VeSalom was still relatively small, taking up only three percent of the plaza space (135,000 square feet or 12,542 square meters).

If the rainforest synagogue was not notable for its dimensions, its structure compensated. "Everything there is so properly built," community leader David Cohen Nassy marveled in 1788, "and the synagogue has such an indescribable majesty, that although its size is quite ordinary, it elicits the admiration of those who see it for the first time."[39] Originally assembled with brick (in early modern Dutch: *gebakken steenen*, or "baked stones") and topped with a flat tile gabled roof, the house of worship stretched 33 feet high, and inside featured a "properly constructed vault" supported by "large wooden columns."[40] Again comparing Jodensavanne to the Dutch metropolis, the exterior of the Amsterdam synagogue expressed classical symmetrical architecture,[41] whereas Beraha VeSalom's façade resembled Dutch vernacular structures and exhibited asymmetry on its north and south sides. Beraha VeSalom's squared-off gables on the end brick walls also evoked a typical Dutch-style profile. In the Dutch Republic these features would have served two purposes: to create an architectural detail for chimneys, and, concurrently, to provide a practical way to finish off masonry, as pointed top-ends do not typically or practically exist in masonry construction. In tropical Suriname there would have been no need for a chimney to provide heat to the building. Furthermore, it is unlikely that the synagogue contained a hearth for ritual baking, since the colony's kitchens were typically open-air and set apart from edifices in order to avoid the spread of conflagration. These distinctively Dutch characteristics may have been part of the vision of a commissioned (non-Jewish) architect in Amsterdam. Or perhaps the typically Dutch style of the synagogue building expressed Surinamese Jewry's patriotism for the United Provinces—the republic that gave them, and their brethren in Amsterdam, such ample religious privileges. Squared-off gables are also visible in some of Paramaribo's more elegant buildings and Jodensavanne's finer homes, as Benoit depicted them in the 1830s.[42] The chimney in itself may have also served to distinguish the building from humble dwellings that lacked this status symbol.[43]

Spatially, Beraha VeSalom also differed from its Amsterdam precedent. The latter synagogue plan, like the imagined layout of Solomon's Temple, is a complex of buildings, at the center of which is the sanctuary building. An asymmetrical courtyard surrounds the sanctuary building on three sides. Auxiliary buildings, such as the religious school, the library, and the *mikvah* (ritual bath), surround the courtyard and form the perimeter of the complex. Although there are several entrances through the wall of auxiliary buildings leading to the courtyard, and then several more entrances leading from the courtyard into the sanctuary building at the center, the western entrance dominates the plan. This perimeter buffer of buildings enclosed and protected the inner sanctuary, concealing it from view. Furthermore, as mentioned earlier, the design complied with restrictions stipulating that only Dutch Protestant Reform churches could have direct access from a public road to a sanctuary.[44] (fig.1)

In contrast, Jodensavanne's synagogue, which stood at the center of a plaza, included the sanctuary and auxiliary spaces all assembled in one building. Instead of being surrounded by a buffer of buildings, the plaza was enclosed only by a wooden fence with four identical gate entrances located at the center point of each of the four sides. Three of the four gates led directly to the three entrances to the synagogue. Of these three entrances (on the north, west, and south sides), the west gate led to a façade in which most likely there were three doors. The center door opened to what probably served as a foyer. This foyer was flanked by two auxiliary spaces, and led to an interior room that served as the meeting place of the Jewish court of justice. The other two doors, as suggested in the schematic floor plan (fig. 3), opened directly into stairwells leading to the women's balcony. The north and south gates brought the visitor to the entrances leading directly into the sanctuary. In contrast to Amsterdam's inner sanctuary building, Beraha VeSalom was built in open view, unfettered by perimeter constructions.[45]

The consolidation at Beraha VeSalom of various rooms within one building with their own separate functions may simply reflect the economical use of materials (shared walls, foundation, and roof). On the other hand, commissioned synagogue architects were concerned not only with municipal regulations and functional requirements of worship, but also with creating symbolism through their design.[46] The configuration of Suriname's synagogue thus lends itself to symbolic interpretation: it evokes the freedom and optimism perhaps felt by these uniquely privileged New World Jews, anticipating, with open arms and architecture, the Messianic Age.

Like the early sixteenth-century Spanish founders of the City of Kings (Lima, Peru), whose utopian and Christian urban center plan "reflected a sense of order and a desire for permanence,"[47] the site plan for Jodensavanne also seems to communicate messianic elements. Unlike any other synagogue in the Sephardic diaspora, Beraha VeSalom was entered through an open plaza—unencumbered and exposed. This imposing layout compensated for the modest size of the synagogue, as if the city planners were focusing less on projected population size and more on emphasizing the precedent of autonomy and environment. This layout invited approach to the synagogue courtyard from all sides: north, south, east, and west. Despite the threat of slave revolts and attacks from maroons (fugitive slaves and their descendants), American Indians, or invading European powers, the town was laid out as if in a perfect world.[48] Four roads, positioned in parallel and perpendicular pairs beside the riverfront, came together in idealized geometry to form the synagogue plaza. In an environment where the river was the essential medium of transport, it seems odd that in Jodensavanne—which, like other settlements parallel to the Suriname River, was surrounded by thick vegetation and rainforest—two of the four roads ran parallel to the river. What purpose would these roads have served? The construction of these parallel thoroughfares suggests that Jodensavanne's planners envisioned this site as a fledgling town, informed by the relatively new discipline of town planning as conceived by the Dutch.[49]

Moreover, the quadri-directional layout brings to mind one of the three passages in the Hebrew Bible where "ideal (i.e., not extant) town planning is described."[50] In the first, Numbers 2:1–31, the Lord directed each tribe "to encamp by its own standard, three tribes each on the north, south, east and west sides of a square in the center of which was the tent of meeting." Jodensavanne's quadrilateral town plan was remarkably similar to that of colonial New Haven (1638), and to the imaginary utopian state described in Johann Valentin Andreae's *Christianopolis* (1619). If the architects of the riverside village did not have these models in mind, perhaps they, like Andreae and the Connecticut visionaries seeking to model their ideal or fledgling settlements on Christian utopianism, drew inspiration directly from biblical directives for creating a "new Jerusalem."[51]

The geometrically idealized village square also brings to mind the Jewish anticipation of the messianic age, as expressed in the thrice-daily recitation of the *amidah* prayer:

Sound on the great Shofar the summons for our freedom; set up the banner to gather our exiles, and bring us together from the four corners of the earth soon to our own land. Blessed are You, Lord who will gather in the dispersed of Your people Israel.[52]

The town plan of Jodensavanne, an unprecedented diasporic village where Jewish rule was dominant and self-determining, symbolically, spatially, and architecturally suggests the ideal of an age of peace and an end to war and oppression, as evoked in Isaiah 43: 5–7:

Fear not, for I am with you; I will bring your folk from the East, Will gather you out of the West. I will say to the North, "Give back!" And to the South, "Do not withhold! Bring My sons from afar, And my daughters from the end of the earth—All who are linked to My name, Whom I have created, Formed and made for My glory.[53]

Despite the sanctioning of slavery in the Hebrew Bible, there is much irony in the apparent design intent. The vast majority of Jodensavanne's inhabitants were held in lifelong bondage with scant chances of manumission.[54] Perhaps at no time in the village's history were sanctity and brutality more shockingly juxtaposed than when transgressing slaves, secured immobile along the synagogue's fence, were punished with the *spaansche bok*, a system of flogging that tore all the flesh from the back.[55] For most residents of Jodensavanne, the village probably symbolized not redemption, but hell.

The Place and Role of Women and Eurafrican Jews

An analysis of the synagogue's interior may also speak to the role of gender in the ritual lives of free and enslaved residents of Jodensavanne. Jewish houses of worship have historically not been the realm of women, and many medieval congregations preferred that their female members worship at home. Still, most synagogues reserved special sections or even separate buildings for females,[56] in conformity with the operative rabbinic law calling for the physical separation of men and women in religious public spheres. In many Jewish houses of worship in Europe women had been seated separately from men since the thirteenth and fourteenth centuries, sometimes to the side of the main sanctuary and other times in an elevated balcony above the men.[57] Not until the end of the sixteenth century, when the attendance of women in synagogue became commonplace, did the women's section acquire full architectural importance. Italy's major synagogues, as well as Isaac Jacobowicz's synagogue in Cracow, Poland, were forerunners of well-planned accommodations for female worshippers.[58] In Amsterdam's Portuguese synagogue, women wishing to attend services sat separately in an elevated gallery reserved for them and situated directly above the main sanctuary of the men.[59]

Beraha VeSalom also maintained a spatial gender division, but its women's gallery was different from its counterpart in Amsterdam (fig. 2). In Jodensavanne's main sanctuary, traditionally reserved for men, a large ark of beautiful cedar wood, which held the scrolls of the Law, stood along the east wall. Opposite this cedar ark, on a kind of raised platform or second story towards the back of the main sanctuary, was the section for the women, perched above the synagogue's auxiliary spaces. These auxiliary spaces were enclosed rooms separate and inaccessible from the sanctuary (fig. 3).

The most sacred area of the synagogue is the space assigned to the Torah, which, considered in its most encompassing sense, is the Lord's will and deed.[60] Vestments in which the Torah is stored and the spaces it traverses on its way to being publicly read become sacred.[61] The Torah is kept in the *heikhal* (ark)[62] and read from the *teivah* (reader's platform), upon which the cantor (or other designated leader) conducts the services. Typical of Spanish-Portuguese synagogues as far back as those of sixteenth-century Ferrara, Leghorn, and Venice

Figure 2
Interior view, facing east, of the *esnoga*. The *teivah* (reader's platform) is in the foreground; the *heikhal* (ark) is in the background. Photograph by Rachel Frankel, with permission of the Amsterdam Portuguese congregation.

(which are thought to have influenced that of Amsterdam) is a bifocal layout with the *heikhal* and *teivah* at opposite ends of the sanctuary. The *heikhal* is always on the side of the sanctuary facing Jerusalem. In the western world, this is the eastern wall. The *teivah* stands opposite it, at the western end of the sanctuary.[63]

Also typical of Iberian diasporic synagogues is their seating con-figuration: half the congregation sits on the north side of the sanctuary and the other half on the south side. Between the split congregation is, in some places, an ample void; in others there is simply a direct path linking the *heikhal* and the *teivah*, which stand at opposite ends of the path. This configuration allows each half of the congregation to face both the *heikhal* and the *teivah*. Similar to a soccer stadium, this split-congregation, bifocal layout activates the Torah ritual as the scroll is paraded from one end of the sanctuary to another, from the *heikhal* to the *teivah*, before and after it is read. This processional allows the worshipper to participate as much as possible in the ceremony without actually being a "player"—that is, an active religious official or hon-oree. In addition, this stadium-like layout, exemplified in Amsterdam,

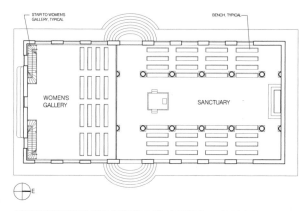

RECONSTRUCTED UPPER FLOOR PLAN OF BERAHA VESALOM BASED ON 1997 FIELD SURVEY
BY RACHEL FRANKEL AND CARIBBEAN VOLUNTEER EXPEDITIONS

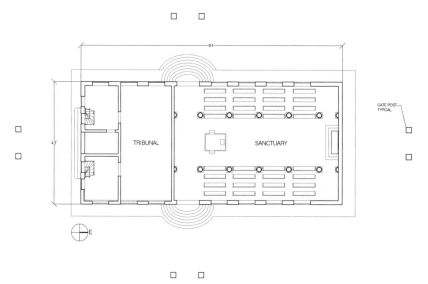

RECONSTRUCTED LOWER FLOOR PLAN OF BERAHA VESALOM BASED ON 1997 FIELD SURVEY
BY RACHEL FRANKEL AND CARIBBEAN VOLUNTEER EXPEDITIONS

Figure 3
Reconstructed plans of the Beraha VeSalom synagogue. Drawings based on 1997 field survey by Rachel Frankel and Caribbean Volunteer Expeditions.

enables worshippers in both the main sanctuary and the women's gallery above to focus their attention on both the ark and the reader's pulpit without impediments. Whether the Torah is moving or being read, from the viewer's perspective it is always in the foreground (never in the background), and invites those seated to shift their gaze left or right. This floor plan configuration has been exemplified in Amsterdam's synagogue and many other Sephardic congregations, such as those of Leghorn and Venice, ever since the style took shape in the sixteenth and seventeenth centuries[64] (fig. 2).

The extant remains and historical descriptions of Jodensavanne's main sanctuary confirm that it duplicates this north-south, split-congregation, bifocal layout with the seating facing both the ark and reader's platform. However, at Beraha VeSalom, the women's seating did not parallel the men's as it did in Amsterdam and in other Sephardic synagogues. At Jodensavanne women faced the ark and the east wall with the whole of the men's sanctuary in the foreground. The women in their gallery viewed the sanctuary much like a conventional balcony audience does a stage. Thus, the women's gallery was set back from the men's sanctuary, rather than being elevated directly above it along the east-west axes of the building. In comparison to Amsterdam's synagogue, the women's gallery in Beraha VeSalom was visually and spatially restricted. Furthermore, it was elevated, and thus removed from the arena of worship. Thus, the seating arrangement prevented women from dynamically participating in the procession of the Torah. When the holy scroll was taken out from the ark to be read at the *teivah* and proudly paraded around the aisles of the main sanctuary, from the women's perspective the Torah moved from background to foreground. From the men's aisles, both the Torah and its varying locations throughout the religious service were always in the foreground. Left to their own devices, the designers of Beraha VeSalom apparently did not value the rich and inclusive religious experience afforded their sisters in the Portuguese synagogues of Europe, characterized by typical bipolar floor plans.[65]

Ironically, spatial restriction in the women's gallery may have enhanced the role of female worshippers. Copper crowns found in the women's section suggest the presence of Torah scrolls there at least by the mid-nineteenth century.[66] Did the gallery double as a storage area, or do these relics indicate actual use? An epitaph in the community's first known burial ground, the Cassipora Creek Cemetery, refers to a female cantor ("*hazan*"), who died in 1715. Unless this was a carving error, Rachel Mendez Meza's tombstone may indicate that women did indeed serve as religious leaders.[67] Given the traditional Jewish prohibition against females assuming public religious roles in a mixed gender setting, this cantor likely paralleled the Askhenazic *firzogerin* (foresayer) of Central and Eastern Europe. As early as the thirteenth century in the Rhineland, female lead singers or prayer leaders provided simultaneous auxiliary services in women's synagogues, separate rooms—or even houses, connected to the main sanctuary by a gallery—adjacent to the main (male) synagogue.[68] In Jodensavanne, this room was designated as the "women's synagogue" or "apartment,"[69] and was most likely the balcony above the main sanctuary, which was referred to as the men's synagogue.[70] While archival and architectural evidence demonstrates that there was no separate female synagogue, the locution describing space designated for females ("women's synagogue" or "apartment") supports the possibility that independent worship was conducted in the women's prayer quarters as parallel to the services of men in the main sanctuary.

Furthermore, women were, on certain occasions, endowed with a special religious status. According to her epitaph, [Deborah] Rebecca, wife of Benjamin Henriquez da Costa, died after childbirth in 1771 while "a Bride of Genesis" (*Noiva de Beresit*).[71] This honorary ritual role was sometimes assigned to a bride on the eve of her nuptials. But since Rebecca was both married and pregnant, it is more likely that in this case "Bride of Genesis" referred to the honor of being called up to read the first chapter of the Pentateuch in synagogue on the holiday of Simhat Torah. While such a title was usually conferred when a woman's husband received the honor of "Bridegroom of Genesis," the *Noiva de Beresit* may suggest that there were parallel religious services in the woman's section of Beraha VeSalom. That this honor required some kind of active participation is suggested in the epitaph of Esther Hanna, wife of Joseph Gabay Faro, who passed away just before she was to "undertake the charge of a Bride of Genesis" in 1725.[72] Similarly, in Curaçao in 1783, Sara Hanna, wife of Joseph Hisquiau Hoheb, died during her so-called "nuptials." The epitaph refers to her husband's "marriage" and to Sara Hanna's departure for synagogue that day, decked out like a bride.[73]

The women's section of Beraha VeSalom could have held at least eighty women, about twenty more Jewish females than resided in Jodensavanne in 1684.[74] Each row could have included four five-person benches and there could have been at least four rows of benches, with leftover room in the rear of the gallery, where views to the sanctuary would have been more or less obscured. However, when the females in the women's apartment worshipped autonomously, an unobstructed view of the female prayer leader, presumably stationed at the east end of the gallery, would have been possible even from the rear of the gallery. The men's section had a capacity for at least 160 individuals, roughly 55 more Jewish males than the settlement had in 1684. Amsterdam's *esnoga*, in comparison, had a seating capacity for 1,200 men and for over 400 women. Naturally, in 1685 Jodensavanne's Jews would have built a structure that could support an expanding population. The proportion of seats to Jewish residents suggests that the anticipated growth of the congregation in its founding year was modest. In this respect, Jodensavanne's synagogue was similar to early colonial Jewish sanctuaries elsewhere in the Caribbean and in New York.[75] Beraha VeSalom's design may have been inspired by Solomon's Temple, but its vision was a decidedly modest one—more on the scale of the diasporic lesser sanctuary (*mikdash me'at*) promised by God in Ezekiel 11:16.[76]

This paradox—the modest architectural use of a huge expanse of land, reflected in both the synagogue's dimensions and its seating capacity—suggests that if Jodensavanne was conceived of as an ideal town, its messianism was localized. In the eyes of some Portuguese Jewish settlers, elements of redemption had already materialized in the small village—as hinted in the very name of its sanctuary, Blessing and Peace. The true redemption, though, the true ingathering of Jewish exiles from the four corners of the world, could only be carried out in Jerusalem.[77]

The self-confident messianic intent of Jodensavanne's Jewish founders is emphasized when "Blessing and Peace" is contrasted with the names of North American congregations founded by Iberian-origin Jews (e.g. Philadelphia's Mikveh Israel [Hope of Israel] and Montreal's and New York's Shearith Israel [Remnant of Israel]), which suggest *anticipatory*, as opposed to *actualized*, redemption. A commentary on the *Zohar* (Book of Splendor), which many contemporary scholars attribute to a Jewish mystic (kabbalist) of thirteenth-century Castile,[78] suggests the messianic anticipation of Suriname's first Jewish settlers. This mystical commentary on the Pentateuch indicates that Eden is to be found in the place of "the secrets of life, blessing, and peace [*beraha vesalom*]."[79] Jodensavanne, a village where Jews were permitted to live autonomously and according to the strictures revealed to them by God, was thus akin to Eden—the paradise Adam and Eve enjoyed before their expulsion. Jews' Savannah was intended to be the site of *actualized* redemption. Here, in this secluded place, the messiah had symbolically already arrived.

Just as they apparently did not expect their population to expand significantly, the founders of Jodensavanne's community likely did not anticipate the growth of an entire class of Jews that would become a thorn in the side of the ruling elite. In 1684, one year prior to the construction of Beraha VeSalom, Jodensavanne was home to at least 1,158 people, with Africans outnumbering Jews at least six to one.[80] The conjunction of Jewish male polygamy, predicated on rape or consensual relations,[81] and the skewed proportion of Jews to Africans, gave rise to a marginal group that disrupted the order of a once neatly bifurcated society. Spawned by Iberian-origin men and African women, these "in-between" Jews—henceforth Eurafrican Jews—were granted membership in the congregation but were sidelined to its margins. The synagogue was an important space where racial status was contested. There, like women, Eurafrican Jews were restricted to designated spaces within the sanctuary. In the case of the latter, however, there was no opportunity within that space for separate but parallel religious ceremonies. Instead, male Jews of African descent were obliged to passively observe the ceremony from the bench of *abelim* (mourners).[82] These Eurafrican males were classified as congregants (in Portuguese, *congregantes*), as opposed to first-class members, *jehidim* (singular: *jahid*), who were generally of "undiluted" European Jewish descent. Through the years, some Eurafrican Jews succeeded in attaining a *jahid* status, despite their partial non-Jewish, African ancestry. But by the mid-eighteenth century, Jodensavanne's communal leaders had discovered "the danger and impropriety there is of admitting Mulattos as *jehidim*, and placing them in this community, in which some have intervened in cases of leadership of the synagogue."[83] Similarly, in Amsterdam, male converts to Judaism were never appointed to official posts in the Jewish community, rabbinic law stipulating that a convert may not be given a post with coercive communal authority.[84] Moreover, Amsterdam's Mahamad decreed in 1644 that "circumcised Negro Jews" were not to be called to the Torah or given any honorary commandments to perform in the synagogue.[85]

Females of African (and Native American) descent were, by the mid-eighteenth century, officially unwelcome in the Beraha VeSalom synagogue. In the communal ordinances of 1754, these females (*"Negras, Mulatas ou Indias"*) appear as threats to the "decency of the sacred place," and are prohibited from attending, with or without children. A reference to the responsibility of their masters to remove them suggests that this prohibition applied only to the enslaved and that free women of African (or Native) descent were too few in number to justify specific legislation.[86]

For Suriname's free Eurafrican Jews striving for equal status in ritual life and worship, the only option seemed to be secession. Beginning in the late 1780s a handful of Eurafrican Jewish males began an ultimately unsuccessful protest against their exclusion from certain funerary honors.[87] By the early 1790s they were demanding full congregational membership: *jahid*, rather than *congregante* status which barred them from full participation in prayer rites and confined males to the mourner's bench. By this point, females such as Roza Mendes Meza (a.k.a. Roza Judia) and Mariana Pinto had joined the struggle, presumably not only out of solidarity with their male contemporaries, but also because *congregante* status applied in similar ways to their sex.[88] The ongoing controversy concerning the social status of Eurafrican Jews would not be legally resolved until 1841, when all ritual distinctions between *congregantes* and *jehidim* were (at least officially) annulled.[89]

These intensifying campaigns, as Robert Cohen has noted, are indicative of the breakdown of internal communal control in Jodensavanne and the village's replacement by Paramaribo as Suriname's dominant Jewish center during the second half of the eighteenth century.[90] By the last quarter of the eighteenth century, the Jewish agricultural community along the Suriname River entered a period of decline. Soil depletion hampered the growth of crops and sugar prices had dropped. Many planters found themselves in default on their loans and absentee ownership further deteriorated the viability of plantations. Slave rebellions and maroon raids on the plantations were a continual threat. But these social revolts also reflected a pan-Caribbean phenomenon whereby Eurafricans came to form the majority of the free population. Their demands and very existence challenged accepted definitions of whiteness and stretched the boundaries of full communal membership.

"Houses of Prayer" in Paramaribo

In the early eighteenth century some of Jodensavanne's Jews had already moved to Paramaribo, where they constructed new prayer houses and cemeteries and established themselves primarily as merchants. These new religious edifices were both of wooden construction. The first, completed in 1716, replaced an earlier building that was converted into a house for the sexton of the Spanish-Portuguese congregation. A new congregational building, Neveh Salom (Oasis of Peace), was completed in 1723, completely rebuilt between 1835 and 1842, and rededicated in 1837 (fig. 4 and fig. 5). Neveh Salom was sold in 1735 to the High German Jewish community, with the stipulation that it maintain its Portuguese rite, and Iberian-origin Jews built a new prayer house, Sedek VeSalom (Justice and Peace), that same year. That structure was significantly altered when its roof was raised to provide gallery space for the women in 1813[91] (fig. 6 and fig. 7).

Despite the grandeur of these buildings, Portuguese Jews considered Sedek VeSalom merely a "house of prayer," not a "synagogue," hearkening back to a 1678 communal ordinance that attempted to eternalize Beraha VeSalom as the colony's only synagogue.[92] In proclaiming the rainforest congregation as irreplaceable and inimitable, Jodensavanne's leaders attempted to exert long-distance control and ensure their own political clout and religious authority.[93] But over the course of the eighteenth century the 1678 precept was increasingly ignored, and both congregations, Sedek VeSalom and Neveh Salom, effectively assumed the functions of a synagogue.

Figure 4
The house of prayer Neveh Salom, built in Paramaribo in 1723 and rebuilt from 1834
to 1842.
The south and west façades of the building. The sanctuary is entered from doors on
the south façade (under the pediment and columns), the north (not shown), and the
center door on the western façade. Each of the two doors flanking the center door on
the western façade opens onto a respective staircase, which leads to the second story
women's gallery. Photograph by Rachel Frankel, 1997.

At the end of the eighteenth century, a third prayer house, this
one for Jews of Eurafrican descent, appeared in Paramaribo. This
was probably the first successful effort by *congregantes* to organize
communally since the founding of the Eurafrican Jewish brotherhood
Darkhei Jesarim (The Ways of the Righteous) in 1759.[94] The common on which the prayer house stood was known as the *sivaplein*
("siva square"), after the Hebrew word for "society."[95] Its existence
was short-lived—by 1794 the building was advertised for sale and
by around 1800 it was demolished[96]—and nothing is known of its architecture. However, the earlier two prayer houses in Paramaribo exist to this day and manage, against great odds, to survive.[97] Although
these two buildings share some architectural features with the one at
Jodensavanne and with other Portuguese synagogues in the Caribbean, they lack Jodensavanne's singular elements. Absent are the messianic design elements in the synagogue complex plan, the Dutch-style

Figure 5
The house of prayer Neveh Salom, interior view looking east. At left, a portion of the women's gallery is shown where it wraps along the north side of the sanctuary. The *teivah* (reader's platform) is in the foreground; the *heikhal* (ark) is in the background. The minimal fenestration on the east wall and the sand-covered floor are similar to the *esnoga* of Amsterdam, and probably to Beraha VeSalom. Photograph by Rachel Frankel, 1997.

Figure 6
The house of prayer Sedek VeSalom, built in Paramaribo in 1735 and at a later date renovated to include a women's gallery. The original interior was recently removed from the building and sent to the Israel Museum in Jerusalem. North and east façades of the building. Photograph by Rachel Frankel, 1998.

Figure 7
Interior of Sedek VeSalom, looking east from the women's gallery. The *teivah* (reader's platform) is in the foreground below; the *heikhal* (ark) is in the background. Photograph by Rachel Frankel, 1998.

Figure 8
Ruins of the Beraha VeSalom synagogue. Photograph by Rachel Frankel, 1995.

building profile, the interior auxiliary spaces, the setback and perpendicularly aligned women's gallery, and most conspicuously, the brick construction. Beraha VeSalom was most distinguished in its building materials. The use of brick in the seventeenth- and eighteenth-century Caribbean was not only a status symbol, but also evidence of reluctance to creolize.[98] Materials such as wood and thatch, which grew in the wild, indicate some degree of adaptation to local usage, while the technology for producing "baked stones" was a European importation.[99] Finally, the materials of Paramaribo's prayer houses either reflect limited expectations for the urban community's longevity or its inability (or unwillingness) to invest in more expensive architecture. Brick, as stone, can endure indefinitely; but the wooden *gebedshuizen* of Paramaribo, subject to fire and rot, were ephemeral. Only Beraha VeSalom, it seems, was built to last.

The Demise of Jodensavanne

As Paramaribo's Jews established their new communities, Jodensavanne continued its downward spiral. At the time of the hundred-year anniversary celebration in 1785, Beraha VeSalom was already a relic of the past, visited and cherished largely as a historic monument by Jodensavanne's former inhabitants and their descendants. By 1787 meetings of the Sephardic communal government (Mahamad) were no longer held at Jodensavanne, but in Paramaribo. The devastating fire of 1832 destroyed most of the village's edifices, but spared the synagogue. By 1833 the only residents of Jodensavanne were synagogue officials, the "trusted slaves" of wealthy Jews living in Paramaribo and abroad, and "some elderly people too much connected to the ground of their forefathers" to abandon "the lonely existence of this village."[100]

Detailed descriptions from this long period of decline help to explain the mystique of Jodensavanne. An account from 1788 depicts a sumptuous synagogue interior. The *heikhal* was "of a beautiful architecture, and ornamented with very well executed sculptures which reflect much honor (considering the infancy of the colony when it was built) upon the one who fashioned it."[101] Among the sanctuary's ornaments were "crowns of silver with which the Scrolls of the Law are decorated, and other necessary furnishings of the same metal, large

candlesticks of yellow copper with several branches, and chandeliers of several kinds, which cost the individuals who donated them
a considerable sum."[102] As late as 1827, an inventory listed ten Torah
scrolls, some topped with ornamental silver pomegranates, as well as
silver and gold crowns, silver pointers (an embellished implement that
eases the reading of the text), and sacramental cups.[103] A visitor in
1833 described the synagogue as "the principal jewel of this currently
very impoverished village," though it was by that time bereft of ornaments, save "copper crowns which are lit at the evening service with
wax candles."[104]

Suriname's Jewish community was reluctant to allow Jodensavanne to die. In 1838 the Hozer Holim[105] (Aid to the Sick) brotherhood in Paramaribo conceived of a plan to resuscitate the decrepit
village. Praising its "beautiful location where one can admire nature in
its full glory," the health of the air, its formerly large population, considerable buildings, splendid synagogue, extensive wood trade, and
military presence, brotherhood leaders bemoaned the present state of
Jodensavanne, "almost abandoned and approaching its complete decay."[106] Only a fundraising campaign would enable its remaining inhabitants to generate an economic revival. The brotherhood proposed
two objectives. First, they would erect buildings in Jodensavanne as
new residences for the poor whose own houses had become uninhabit-
able. These buildings would also entice artisans and other productive
migrants to establish themselves in Jodensavanne. Second, they would
provide new residents with monetary advances so that they could purchase items necessary for their work.[107]

The brotherhood's campaign may have been at least partially successful, as a synagogue inventory of 1848 lists ten functional Torah
scrolls, some enrobed in silken textiles. For their embellishment were
a few pairs of silver pomegranates, some with dangling bells, and
multi-pronged copper crowns engraved with the names of donors. The
interior was illuminated with dozens of large and small copper and
silver chandeliers, a few bearing engraved names, and silver memorial
lamps. Wooden calendars for ritually counting the Omer (the 49 days
between the second day of Passover and the first day of Pentecost) and
two copper charity boxes adorned the walls. Reliquia, also suggesting
the active use of the congregation, included a silver cup, a spice box

to observe the departure of the Sabbath and holidays, a copper cande-labrum for Hanukkah (described as a "Maccabean lamp"), and silver pointers to guide the Torah reader.[108]

But nostalgia alone could not rejuvenate a village past economic viability. In 1865, worshippers visited the synagogue for the last time. Then, in 1873, its roof collapsed, and no subsequent repairs were made. Over time, visitors dismantled the masonry, pilfering bricks for their own use (fig. 8). But abandonment and vandalism have not mitigated the long-enduring enchantment of this autonomous Jewish settlement. Today it is identified by the ruins of its synagogue and cemetery and is widely regarded as a "national" or "Jewish shrine."[109]

Conclusion

A creative contemplation of the architecture of the Beraha VeSa-lom synagogue, informed by archival research and historical context, suggests that messianic sentiment may have animated some of Joden-savanne's founding settlers and anonymous architect. But this inter-pretation is admittedly speculative. More importantly, the foregoing discussion speaks to the underestimated role of messianism among early modern Sephardic pioneers. Messianism was one of the many religious currents informing early Sephardic communities in Bra-zil and the Caribbean and is only now receiving serious attention.[110] During the mid-seventeenth century many Europeans considered the Americas to be the end of the earth, and messianists—Christians and Jews alike—often regarded the dispersal of Jews all over the world as a prerequisite for the coming of the Messiah.[111]

Both Isaac Aboab (1605–1693), who served in the Dutch colony of Pernambuco in the 1640s and 1650s as the first New World rabbi, and João de Yllan (1609–1696), Curaçao's first Jewish settler, were later secret followers of Sabbatai Zevi.[112] Another devotee was Moises Pereyra, who was born in Madrid in 1635[113] and became a denizen of Barbados in 1671. Pereyra had set out on a journey to the Land of Israel in 1666, following in the footsteps of his likeminded father, the wealthy merchant Abraham Pereyra.[114] Recent archival research demonstrates that by at least 1650 de Yllan maintained commercial ties with David Nassy, the mastermind of a number of Jewish colonies in the Caribbean, including Suriname.[115] With the debacle of Sabbatai

Zevi behind them, Nassy and his contemporaries may have viewed their self-ruling agrarian community in Suriname as a diasporic fulfillment of the messianic promise. Millennialism coexisted with the ruthless pragmatism characteristic of most early modern pioneers.[116] In the Jewish context, this meant that a diasporic "Eden" would not be built without slavery.

David Nassy's "Furlough" and the Slave Mattheus

Natalie Zemon Davis

In February 1792, David Nassy, secretary and associate treasurer to the *Mahamad* of the Portuguese Jewish Nation of Suriname, penned a letter of lament and supplication to the *"Dignissimos Senhores"* of that august body and to its *Adjuntos*, the council members of the Nation.[1]

He signed his letter David Nassy rather than David de Isaac Cohen Nassy, the name he was given at his birth in 1747 to Sarah Abigail Bueno de Mesquita and Isaac de Joseph Cohen Nassy, a descendant of early settlers of the colony. Before this, though, David had written his full name often enough, as, through the decades, he carried out the obligations of his many roles in the community: he followed his father for a term as sworn notary (*jurator*) of the Portuguese Jewish Nation; served as *gabay*, secretary, and one of the regents (*parnasim*) for the *Mahamad*; translated texts from Portuguese and Spanish into Dutch for the Suriname Court of Policy; ordered inventories to be made of his plantation and possessions; purchased medicines for his pharmacy, and contributed manuscripts in French and Dutch to the more general intellectual culture of the colony. Then, in January 1790, he went before the current jurator of the Nation and formally shortened his name to David Nassy: he claimed it was for the sake of simplicity—too many men had similar long names—but he also wanted to appear more modern.[2]

The tone of Nassy's supplication to the *Mahamad* and *Adjuntos* was plaintive, but this did not mean that he could not look back from 1792 on a life of accomplishment and some fulfilled hopes—for himself, for the "benefit of the Nation and the glory of the Jewish name," and for the literary life of Suriname, where, despite limitations, he and his fellow Jews enjoyed "a kind of Political Patrimony."[3]

Nassy married his cousin Esther Abigail de Samuel Cohen Nassy in 1763, and four years later Esther gave birth to their daughter Sarah. Nassy's purchase of the Tulpenberg coffee plantation on the Suriname River in 1770 had ended, partly through mismanagement, in financial disaster by 1773. (A fate suffered by other Suriname planters who had relied naively on easy credit arrangements offered from Amsterdam). But, thanks to bequests from his father Isaac, who died in 1774, and property brought to the marriage by his wife, David Nassy still owned land on creeks off the Suriname River, houses at Jodensavanne on the Suriname River and in the town of Paramaribo, and slaves. In 1777, he set up a partnership with Solomon Gomes Soares, "doctor and apothecary" at Jodensavanne: they would practice pharmacy together and Gomes Soares would instruct him in the art of healing. The partnership fared so well that by 1782, Nassy and his wife hired an agent in Paramaribo to acquire medicines for them. That same year, Esther's jewelry case included diamond rings and gold bracelets.[4]

In the 1780s, Nassy was also able to celebrate the Portuguese Jewish Nation. The year 1785 was the hundredth anniversary of Beraha VeSalom (Blessing and Peace), the synagogue at Jodensavanne. By that time, a wooden synagogue had been built at Paramaribo for the Portuguese Jews (the synagogue for the Jews of the German Nation was nearby), but Beraha VeSalom was a splendid brick construction and the oldest religious building in the colony. David Nassy was impresario and director for the Anniversary Jubilee held in October 1785. Tableaux on themes of persecution, tolerance, and charity were presented to the Governor, the councilors of the Suriname courts, the militia officers and the Jewish dignitaries; songs were sung, Hebrew prayers recited, and poems declaimed. Then, Christians and Jews banqueted and danced the night away.[5]

At about this same time, Nassy began to agitate for the reform of the *Ascamoth*—the ordinances of the Jews of the Portuguese Nation— that had been last issued in 1754. His plea reflects the language and ideas of the European Enlightenment: "it is necessary to purge our ecclesiastical institutions of their errors, to uproot our old habits, and cut away our prejudices, the source of all our divisions." Nassy won his case, and, with support from the Suriname government, submitted a revised *Ascamoth* that was approved in 1789. In fact, the new ordinances strengthened the hand of the *parnasim* against restive members of the congregation and the possible criticism of the rabbi, "who [was] not to preach about anything but morals in general."[6]

In these same decades, David Nassy's role also expanded in the wider cultural life of Suriname. The Portuguese Jews had been pioneers in the acquisition of books in European languages from Amsterdam, and Nassy's own collection, inventoried in 1782, was perhaps the largest. His shelves contained approximately 450 volumes in French, Spanish, Portuguese, Dutch, Latin, and Hebrew—a collection that included classics of the Enlightenment, European poetry, romance, and history, and medical and pharmacological texts. Collectors, both Jewish and Christian, later established a public library, which, according to Nassy's perhaps exaggerated boast about his fellow settlers, "was filled with books on every subject, and yielded to no other library in all of America."[7]

In 1774, the first printing press was set up in Suriname, and learned societies emerged alongside it. Nassy, unsurprisingly, took part in these societies; he read a paper on medicinal plants to the new Natural History Society, and another, on the meanings of the words *roman* (novel) and romance, to the new Society of Friends of Letters.[8]

The Portuguese Jews founded their own literary society as well, the *Docendo Docemur* ("we are taught by teaching"), and devoted many of their meetings, in 1786, to a French translation of Christian Wilhelm von Dohm's recent plea for Jewish emancipation, *Über die bürgerliche Verbesserung der Juden*. Out of their discussions of this work came Nassy's decision to write a book about the history, economy, government and cultural life of Suriname, which would give full and hitherto unacknowledged credit to the role of its Jews. A few years later the two-volume *Essai historique sur la Colonie de Surinam* (*Historical Essay on Suriname*) appeared. The work's title page named the Regents of the Portuguese Jewish Nation as author, and gave its place and date of printing as Paramaribo, 1788. In fact, David Nassy was the author, (who wrote in his preferred literary language of French), and the book had been printed by the busy

Amsterdam publisher Hendrik Gartman, who did not get the pages back to Suriname until the spring boats of 1789.[9]

Looking merely at this public record, we would be hard-pressed to understand the melancholy mood of David Nassy's 1792 supplication to the *Mahamad* and *Adjuntos*. But there is more to the story. In November 1789, Nassy's wife, Esther Abigail, died, leaving him with their only child, Sarah, who remained unmarried in 1792 at the age of twenty-four—an age when three-quarters of Portuguese Jewish women had already found a husbands and borne children.[10] Sarah was mentally astute, as shown by commercial transactions, signed in a fine, clear hand, in which she was involved even as a teenager. But she seems to have faced some other difficulty. In detailing his unhappy lot to the *Mahamad* and *Adjuntos*, Nassy did not explicitly mention the death of his wife, but he did speak of the "well-known infirmity . . . of this poor daughter, to whom nature has assigned me all the care."[11]

The main burden of Nassy's complaint to the *Mahamad* and *Adjuntos* concerned calumnies against him, uttered by "a vile conspiracy" (*"hua vila Cabala"*), which were making it difficult for him to continue his many services to the Nation and were endangering his livelihood in Suriname. What was behind these intrigues? Possibly some men from established Portuguese Jewish families objected to Nassy's restructuring of the *Ascamoth*. In any case, that *Ascamoth,* and Nassy as its framer, were the targets of strong criticism by the newer mulatto Jews, whose status as lesser members of the congregation of Portuguese Jews—mere *congregaten*, with special seating arrangements, rather than full *jehidim*—Nassy had maintained in the 1789 *Ascamoth*. But attacks from the *congregaten* may not have worried Nassy much: in 1791 he was writing against their claims to full ritual and ceremonial status, and he was fully backed in this by the *parnasim*.[12]

Instead, the "calumnies" and "conspiracy" that troubled Nassy were those provoked by his *Essai historique*. Fending off these criticisms, he reminded the *Mahamad* and *Adjuntos* how he had "courageously written a defense of our Nation" and made public "facts unknown to our own people and forgotten in the old papers of [our] Archives, [which] do honor to the Portuguese Jews of Suriname."[13] (Nassy might have added how much the book contributed to the general history of Suriname, including its economy and population, but he was here trying to persuade the *parnasim* and other worthies.) Possibly some members of the Nation itself had been put out by the way the *Essai* favored certain families—the Nassys, the Pintos, the de La Parras—and paid less attention to others. But it is sure that the directors of the Societeit van Surinam, which owned the colony, made objections from Amsterdam, and questions were raised in Paramaribo by its current governor, Wichers, even though Nassy had written of his fiscal and cultural policies with praise. Meanwhile, a faction among the Christian planters who had long been unhappy about the Jews' political role in the colony would have found much to disagree with in the *Essai*. Indeed, Nassy was later to write of his book that while English and French journalists had spoken of it "to advantage," the *Essai* had been "disparaged" ("*décrié*") in the colony.[14]

Faced with this "conspiracy," Nassy told the *Mahamad* and *Adjuntos* he had no other choice but, with "tearful sentiments . . . shortly to leave my native land. . . to abandon my responsibility and care for the interests of the Nation and deprive myself of the company and affection of my worthy friends and protectors." Reviewing the many services he had performed for the community over the years, Nassy requested that the *Mahamad* and *Adjuntos* grant him a three-year leave of absence, or "furlough" (he used the Dutch word *Verlof*), reminding them that his salary as secretary to the community had been raised in 1789, and that in addition his salary covered his extra work as translator. It would be difficult to maintain himself and his "poor and helpless daughter" ("*pobre e desvalida filha*") in foreign lands; the climate would be different, his health was fragile. Thus, he requested some funding for the three years of his leave, although the bulk of his salary would of course be going to his replacement as secretary. For the latter post, he nominated Abraham Bueno de Mesquita, current *jurator* of the community. Nassy described him as his friend and relative (Nassy's mother was a Mesquita), and indeed, as a friend to most of the *parnasim*—a man of "zeal and integrity in his service to the Nation."[15]

But Nassy had another request. Since 1774, he had had on rental and "under his authority" a young slave named Mattheus and his sister Sebele. Mattheus and Sebele were part of the estate of the late David

Baruch Louzado, bequeathed to and administered by the Portuguese Jewish Nation. Mattheus had learned the art of carpentry, Nassy's request went on, but, through some misfortune, around 1788 swollen spots began to appear on his body. Doubts were raised about whether his disease was contagious—Nassy himself believed that Mattheus had a skin condition particular to Africans and *not* leprosy—but the *Mahamad* and *Adjuntos* decided he could not be put up for public sale in 1790, when some other slaves from the Louzada estate were auctioned off. In fact, a government ordinance prohibited public sale in such circumstances.

Nassy asked that he be allowed to purchase Mattheus. The young man had shown such loyalty and goodness caring for the sick in Nassy's house that Nassy believed he would be a great help to him as well in his "sad days . . . in foreign lands." Since Nassy could never sell Mattheus publicly and was therefore taking a risk in purchasing him, he thought it fitting for the *Mahamad* and *Adjuntos* to sell him Mattheus at a reasonable price.[16]

How would Mattheus have regarded all this? We can track him down and perhaps provide some answers to this question through the *Mahamad*'s accounts of the Louzada estate. Mattheus was born about 1770 to Diana, slave of David Baruch Louzada, and an unknown black father, and lived with his mother, his older sister, Siberi, and another slave family in Louzada's household. Louzada did not own a plantation, so Mattheus's earliest memories would have been of the hills and fields of Jodensavanne. At Louzada's death in 1774, the *Mahamad* rented Diana, Mattheus and Siberi not directly to David Nassy, but to his mother Sarah Abigail for ninety-one guilders a year. Because his father, Isaac Nassy, had just died, and David Nassy's plantation had gone bankrupt and been sold the year before, David was thus an inappropriate lessor; he and his widowed mother probably set up household together in those years of financial trouble.[17]

Mattheus spent his boyhood in Jodensavanne, where David Nassy's daughter Sarah, three years older than he, was growing up as well. The language used most frequently between slaves and their owners at that time was presumably Dju-tongo, the Portuguese-based creole spoken among slaves on the Jewish plantations of Suriname. Although Nassy himself considered creole tongues mere "jargon," he probably taught Portuguese only to those few mulatto slaves in his household whom he "instructed in the Jewish religion." In the 1770s, Mattheus would have known Nassy's mulatto slaves Moses, Ishmael and Isaac, all of whom were circumcised after their birth and destined for manumission.[18]

In the 1780s, when Nassy's relations with his creditors had eased up, he was able to establish his household once again on Green Street in Paramaribo. There Mattheus received his training as a carpenter and was rented out by Nassy (as were other slave carpenters) for building tasks in town. Mattheus became familiar with the town's markets and varied population, including its free blacks and persons of color. Much outnumbered by the slaves in Paramaribo, free blacks and people of color plied trades of all kinds, peddled goods, and mounted balls attended by men and women dressed in fine silk and chintz. Sometimes they as well would own a slave or two, whom, at their deaths, they would manumit or bequeath to a relative. Mattheus would also have taken note of the Paramaribo prayer house of Darhe Jesarim (Way of Righteousness), the brotherhood of the free Jewish persons of color, whose status as an independent institution was soon to be of great concern to David Nassy and the *Mahamad*. Mattheus would have seen the slaves who accompanied their owners as they went about activities in town and who were dressed to do honor to their masters and mistresses. He himself, perhaps, carried an umbrella over the heads of David and Esther Nassy on their way to the Paramaribo synagogue of the Portuguese Nation and waited for them outside until the service was over.[19]

This period was also a time of loss for Mattheus. In 1783, the *Mahamad* announced in the *Surinaamse Courant* the sale of some slaves from the Louzada estate, and we can deduce that Mattheus's mother was likely to have been among them, as David Nassy's rental payments to the *Mahamad* for 1788 mention only Mattheus and his sister, now called Sebele (Sebele may be a version of Siberi, but perhaps Diana had another daughter).[20]

It was also in this year that the swollen spots cropped up on Mattheus's body. Physicians and close observers of slave life in Suriname in the eighteenth century have described two serious illnesses of the skin especially affecting persons of African origin:

yaws, and an incurable illness known in the Suriname Creole as "boisi" or "boassi," which was compared variously to leprosy and elephantiasis.[21] Nassy's denial to the *Mahamad* that Mattheus was afflicted with "boassi" (in his request to purchase him) would lead us to believe that Mattheus's lesions evidently *suggested* the disease, and we can imagine Mattheus's anxious conversations with his fellow slaves about remedies and rituals for healing. Nassy also must have done his best, and he may even have used herbal baths learned from African healers in his attempts to cure Mattheus, for, despite his contempt for their "frightful ceremonies," Nassy admired the healers' knowledge of local medicinal plants.[22] In any case, despite Mattheus's skin condition, he was very much alive and ready for travel four years later.

The *Mahamad* and the *Adjuntos* granted both of David Nassy's requests, though Mesquita's replacement salary and Nassy's leave benefit may have been less than requested. Interestingly enough, Mattheus is recorded in the accounts as sold to Sarah Nassy rather than to David, similar to how he had been, previously, leased to her grandmother. In the next months, father and daughter were busy with preparations for what they now specified as a trip to North America: they settled with creditors and gave power of attorney to Mordechai de La Parra to represent them in their absence.[23] And they arranged for passage on a spring boat from Paramaribo to Philadelphia.

Why Philadelphia? News from North America was printed regularly in the *Surinaamse Courant*: Nassy could read there of the successful revolution of the English colonies against their mother country and of the debates about the new constitution in Philadelphia's Independence Hall. News also came to Suriname through travelers and letters. The Moravian missionaries in Suriname, for example, had frequent exchanges with their Brethren in Pennsylvania, and Jews had connections as well. In 1784, Eliazer Cohen, a schoolmaster in Philadelphia, set up two German Jews in Suriname to be his agents for the estate of his father Eliazer David Cohen, who had lived and died in Suriname. By the early 1790s, Eliazer Abraham Cohen—possibly the schoolmaster himself—was cantor and then rabbi at the German Jewish synagogue in Paramaribo.[24] In Philadelphia, Nassy could expect a political and intellectual atmosphere suited to his Enlightenment curiosity and his constant interest in projects for betterment, a Jewish community in which he and his daughter could make a start, and a medical establishment that would perhaps welcome him.

Nassy must have, in some ways, prepared Mattheus for the trip. By now, since Mattheus had served not only as a carpenter but also as a close personal servant in the household, Nassy may well have taught him Portuguese or, perhaps, French, Nassy's preferred second language. In any case, both master and slave had a language challenge ahead of them, for neither knew English beyond those words embedded in the Suriname creole. Possibly Mattheus got news through the slave and free-black networks in Paramaribo of the flourishing movement in Philadelphia for the abolition of slavery, but David Nassy would have been loath to broach the subject with his slave even if he had had information about it. No friend of abolition, Nassy went no further in his views than the most enlightened of the Suriname planters and preachers: slavery was an acceptable institution but must be conducted with humanity and beneficence, without (as Nassy wrote in the 1789 *Essai*) the "rage that [some] Whites conceive against the Blacks," and without "the cruel tortures they make them suffer."[25]

On 21 April 1792, David Nassy, his daughter Sarah Nassy, "and her slaves Mattheus and Amina," left Paramaribo on the American ship *Active* for Philadelphia. Amina was a little girl of about ten, a mulatto, and evidently important to Sarah.[26]

David Nassy's first stops that we can trace in Philadelphia were the Mikveh Israel synagogue and the court for manumission. Built in 1782, the Mikveh Israel synagogue drew Jewish families of varied geographical origin, but its ritual followed the Sephardic liturgical practice familiar to Nassy. By the Jewish New Year of 5553 (September 1792), he had paid his synagogue dues for the entire past year of 5552, even though he had arrived in Philadelphia only in the spring.[27]

Among the worshippers at Mikveh Israel Nassy soon met the merchant and entrepreneur Solomon Marache. This was an appealing connection for Nassy because, among other reasons, the two men could chat in Dutch: Marache had been born in Curaçao and lived there until, as a teenager in 1749, he was taken to New York by his widowed mother to learn his trade. Marache had since flourished in Philadelphia and become an important figure in the congregation Mikveh Israel already in the years before the synagogue was built. After 1787, when he took a widowed non-Jewish woman as his second wife, Marache no longer served as treasurer to the congregation, but continued to attend services. As Nassy himself described it: "The Maraches . . . and [men of] several other families [are] lawfully married to Christian women who go to their own churches, the men going to their synagogues, and who, when together, frequent the best society."[28]

Through his second wife, Solomon Marache was in fact in contact with people who believed in the abolition of slavery. Since the 1780s, a number of worshippers at Mikveh Israel had been manumitting their slaves, especially encouraged to do so by two of their brethren, Solomon Bush and Solomon Marache. Bush, a member of the Pennsylvania Abolition Society in 1789, was the only Jew to be associated with the organization in its early days. He married a Quaker woman in 1791, and, when he died in 1795, Bush at his own earlier request was buried in the Friends cemetery, where he would lie among those who had founded the Society. Solomon Marache's second wife—born Mary Smith—had a Quaker mother and cousins, and her brothers and maternal cousin George Aston, who was both an officer of the society and especially close to Mary, were members of the Abolition Society.[29]

On 9 August 1792, Solomon Marache accompanied David Nassy together with his daughter Sarah, Mattheus and Amina to the court chambers of Philadelphia. There David Nassy "late of Surinam now of the City of Philadelphia, Doctor of Physick" manumitted and set free "his Negroe man Matheus aged about twenty two Years." Nassy went on to "reserve his servitude," that is, to indenture Mattheus for seven years. At this time he also changed Amina's name to Mina—"my Mulatto Girl named Mina aged about ten years"—and after freeing her reserved her servitude as well, to himself or to those he would assign, for eighteen years.[30] In this ungenerous manumission, Nassy was following Pennsylvania's Gradual Emancipation Act of 1780, which provided that any personal slave brought into Pennsylvania by a new resident must be freed at the end of six months, but within that period of six months, the master could indenture a slave until the age of twenty-eight (the case of Mina) or for seven years if the slave was not a minor (the case of Mattheus).[31]

Solomon Marache must have tried to persuade David Nassy to become more open to the importance of abolition. Also, Nassy is known to have had conversations with other Philadelphia opponents of slavery, such as the celebrated physician Benjamin Rush, a major figure in the Pennsylvania Abolition Society, to whom Nassy presented a copy of his *Essai historique* in June 1793. But Nassy's three years in Philadelphia seem to have moved his thoughts little on this score. Writing in February 1795 about "the means of improving the colony of Suriname" and referring undoubtedly to recent events in Saint Domingue, he commented that:

> for Blacks who have not come to a certain level of civilization, the ideas of liberty and equality throw them into a state of drunkenness (*"espèce d'ivresse"*), which does not pass until they have destroyed everything . . . Until freedom has been preceded by enlightenment . . . it will be the most disastrous present one can give to Blacks.

Nassy recalled manumitted slaves in Suriname who, he claimed, "had of their own volition returned to the discipline of their former masters to be fed, clothed, and cared for in their maladies."[32] Nassy may also have been justifying here the seven years of service he was in the midst of requiring from Mattheus.

Much went on in the medical, pharmaceutical, intellectual, and political life of David Nassy during his "furlough" in Philadelphia which we cannot consider here. Nor can we here speculate on the discoveries made during those years by Sarah Nassy and her mulatto servant Mina, and the interesting possibility that Sarah took Mina with her to the women's section of Mikveh Israel.

But, we do wish to imagine some of the experiences of the indentured servant Mattheus. Philadelphia was a hub of black— especially free black—life in the new United States. In contrast to Paramaribo, the free black population of Philadelphia (somewhat more than 1800 when Mattheus arrived there) outnumbered the slave population more than six to one. If David Nassy arranged for Mattheus to work as a carpenter in Philadelphia, he would have come into direct contact with this world. Surely he was aware of the Free

African Society, a benevolent association founded in 1787 by two remarkable ex-slaves, Absalom Jones and Richard Allen (Jones went on to establish the African Episcopal Church, where the first sermon was delivered in July 1794, while Allen set up a place of worship for black Methodists the same year). Rather than accepting a pattern of life in which manumitted slaves went on to acquire slaves of their own, as in Suriname, Jones and Allen entreated "the people of color . . . favored with freedom...to consider the obligations we lay under to help forward the cause of freedom, we who know how bitter the cup is of which the slave hath to drink, O how ought we to feel for those who yet remain in bondage?"[33] Part of a Jewish household, Mattheus would probably not have attended such services, but he surely heard word of the pleas of Jones and Allen.

Mattheus may well have been involved, however, in the assistance provided by Philadelphia blacks during the devastating yellow fever epidemic of August through November 1793. Benjamin Rush believed—mistakenly as it turned out, but perhaps conveniently— that blacks were immune to the illness; thus they were called upon, or volunteered themselves, to care for the sick and bury the dead. Nassy, whose wise and moderate methods of treatment managed to keep most of his patients alive, did not subscribe to Rush's view. He speculated, rather, that "foreigners," that is, those not native to Philadelphia, were less susceptible to the epidemic because their "temperaments" and "constitution" were linked to the climate and air of the places in which they had grown up; those whose constitution was linked to the climate and air of Philadelphia were more likely to be infected.[34] Thus, Mattheus would have served at Nassy's right hand, or in attendance to others, during the epidemic not as a black man, but as a "foreigner" like the master to whom he was indentured.

Finally, Mattheus met with adventures and conversations of a less risky sort as well. Nassy had early made contact with Peter Legaux, a Frenchman from Lorraine, who was trying to establish viticulture in Pennsylvania. Legaux gave a copy of Nassy's *Essai historique* to the American Philosophical Society in the autumn of 1792, and not long after presented Nassy himself; but, of more import to Mattheus, Legaux introduced Nassy to the French aviationist Jean Pierre Blanchard, who had come to Philadelphia for North America's first aerial voyage. On 9 January 1793, when Blanchard prepared to rise in his hydrogen-filled gas balloon, Pierre Legaux and David Nassy were holding the restraining ropes. President George Washington had shaken Blanchard's hand before he boarded his basket, but the servant Mattheus was surely nearby, watching the balloon rise and drift away on its successful fifteen mile flight.[35]

Legaux had spent some years in Saint Domingue before coming to Philadelphia in 1785, but Nassy also had connections with émigrés who had witnessed and fled the later great revolts on that island. Solomon Moline came to Philadelphia with his family and slaves not long after the first Saint-Domingue slave uprising in 1791; Nassy would have seen him at Mikveh Israel, where Moline was close to Benjamin Nones, a leading figure in the congregation. Indeed, Nones accompanied Moline to court when he manumitted his slaves without requiring further servitude.[36] Later, in August 1793, as the end of slavery in Saint Domingue seemed assured, the physician Jean Devèze arrived with his family and slaves from Cap de François with tales of a recent bloody battle, of continuing uprisings, destruction, and slaughter. In Philadelphia, Devèze immediately plunged into the treatment of those stricken by the epidemic, and, with a medical approach very similar to that of Nassy, they became friends. Reports from Moline and Devèze must have been among the sources fuelling Nassy's image of the "state of drunkenness," into which he believed blacks were thrown when they had not yet been "enlightened" by instruction.[37]

For Mattheus, however, conversations with the slaves that Moline and Devèze had brought with them—soon to become ex-slaves by Pennsylvania law—would have had a different tenor.[38] They would have found a way to communicate—either in French if they knew it—or in a pidgin constructed from their differing creole languages. From such exchange Mattheus could hear of a hoped-for republic, where blacks and people of color would be free citizens administering their own polity, in contrast with the societies of free Maroons he knew of in Suriname, living in tribal clans with respected kings, and with the free black communities in Philadelphia, enterprising and aspiring, but still subaltern in a society dominated by white folks.[39]

In the spring of 1795, the three years of David Nassy's furlough were up, and he sat down to write a letter in English to the merchant house of Brown, Benson and Ives in Providence, Rhode Island asking for passage on one of their boats to Suriname. His "family of four" would make their way by land to Providence, he wrote, making clear that Mina and Mattheus were still part of the picture.[40] We may wonder why Mattheus did not run away rather than return with his master to Suriname. His previous illness and residual skin condition, which surely made Mattheus dependent on the physician Nassy—or at least less able to initiate new permanent relations in a foreign land—may have been a factor. Also, in Suriname, Mattheus had his sister Sebele and other kin. Furthermore, Nassy's 1792 letter to the *Mahamad* and *Adjuntos* suggested his paternalistic attachment to the young man.

The "family" left sometime after 19 June 1795, the date when Nassy bade farewell to the American Philosophical Society. On the way back, Nassy decided to have the four of them disembark at the Danish island of Saint Thomas, where he visited its growing Jewish community and had himself examined by a learned Danish royal physician who was there on a brief visit. By January 1796 he was back in Paramaribo, recounting his adventures to the *Mahamad* of the Portuguese Jewish Nation; a few months later he was signing documents once again as Secretary to the community.[41]

If his furlough in Philadelphia had not changed Nassy's mind about the legitimacy of slavery, it had deepened his commitment to educational reform. By the fall of 1796 he had published a new proposal for a college in Suriname and was far advanced in raising money for it: the school would be dedicated to letters and sciences, liberal arts and crafts and trades suitable for "American lands in the tropics." It would be for boys only, but for boys both rich and poor (funding would be provided for the latter), and for Jews and Christians both. The pupils would, of course, be free in status (the only slaves listed in his prospectus are those rented for kitchen, washing, and maintenance duty), but there is no mention in Nassy's prospectus of a color bar. I think we can see here the influence of what he had observed in Philadelphia: the intensive social and cultural exchange between Jews and Christians and the energetic efforts of free people of African descent to achieve the "enlightenment" that he thought essential to the "social man" and "civilization."[42]

As for Mattheus, his contracted service to Nassy was to last until the spring of 1799. We may wonder whether Nassy taught him to read and write Portuguese and/or Dutch in those years, if he had not already done so. There is no sign of him, however, among the *congregaten* of the Portuguese Jewish Nation in the late 1790s or the early years of the nineteenth century, although he may well have remained associated with the blacks and people of color that he had known in the Jewish households in which he had grown up. In 1799, now twenty-nine years of age, Mattheus was free to put up his own wooden sign as a carpenter, with a surname added on. Because manumitted slaves in Suriname took the last name of their former master or mistress preceded by "de" or "van, Mattheus's surname would almost certainly have been de Nassy or van Nassy."[43] We can imagine Mattheus in one of the small Paramaribo shops, recounting to his neighbors stories of Blanchard's balloon, the frightening epidemic, and the Free African Society. And we can find it likely that when he needed help in his carpentry, he hired a young lad for wages rather than acquiring a slave. From Philadelphia, he could have carried with him, if not the words, then the spirit of Absalom Jones and Richard Allen: "to consider the obligations we l[ie] under to help forward the cause of freedom, we who know how bitter the cup is of which the slave hath to drink."[44]

The Democratization of American Judaism

Jonathan D. Sarna

In an influential volume titled *The Democratization of American Christianity*, Nathan Hatch proclaimed that the "American Revolution and the beliefs flowing from it created a cultural ferment over the meaning of freedom." Common people, he showed, became significant actors on the American religious scene in the Revolution's wake. Turmoil swirled "around the crucial issues of authority, organization and leadership." The tension between traditional religious values and new American values, he concluded, provoked "a period of religious ferment, chaos, and originality unmatched in American history."[1]

Hatch confined his evidence to the world of American Christianity, including early Mormonism. Was the story the same with respect to America's small community of Jews? We might have supposed that Jews would have been wary of religious ferment. The small size of the American Jewish community (estimates range from one thousand to twenty-five hundred[2]); the fact that Jews were scattered over six communities (Savannah, Charleston, Richmond, Philadelphia, New York, and Newport); and Jews' centuries-old emphasis on tradition and deference would presumably have made Jews wary of "chaos and originality." They had lived through the Protestant Great Awakening without its transforming, in any discernible way, Jewish religious life.[3] The impact of the Revolution, we might have conjectured, would likewise have been muted.

And yet, the more we learn, the clearer it becomes that the Revolution's impact on the American Jewish community was anything but muted. Instead, in response to the political, social, and spiritual revolution wrought by independence and the beliefs flowing from it, Judaism in America was challenged and radically transformed. The values of the American Revolution—liberty, freedom, and especially democracy—profoundly affected the Jewish community. In the first quarter of the nineteenth century, before masses of central and eastern European Jews arrived, a new American Judaism took shape. In this early period, as so often later, American Judaism and American Protestantism experienced similar influences and developed in parallel ways. More often than we realize, the individuals who brought about change in both faiths marched to the sounds of similar drumbeats.[4]

As a rule, in talking about early American Judaism, scholars look first to New York, for that is where the bulk of the Jews lived and the bulk of the surviving documents remain. But I begin here in the unlikely Jewish community of Richmond, Virginia, which took shape in the very midst of the American Revolution. Jacob I. Cohen and Isaiah Isaacs, the city's earliest known Jewish residents, arrived about 1781 from Charleston, South Carolina.[5] Both men had fought, in 1779, under Captain Richard Lushington as part of the Charleston Regiment of Militia ("Free Citizens"), known at the time as the "Jew Company," although only a minority of its members were actually Jewish. Cohen fought in the Battle of Beaufort under General William Moultrie and, according to Lushington, "in every respect conducted himself as a good soldier and a man of courage."[6] Isaacs may well have been in Richmond previously,[7] but now the two veterans established the commercial firm of Cohen & Isaacs, locally known as "The Jews' Store." Subsequently, it expanded to include a tavern inn, known as the "The Bird in the Hand," as well as assorted other properties.[8]

A year after the original store's founding, in 1782, Cohen traveled to Philadelphia on a prolonged buying trip, and in May of that year he applied to join Philadelphia's Mikveh Israel synagogue. Having established himself in business, he may also have been looking around for a wife: He was, after all, thirty-eight years old and still single. Within three months he had fallen in love with a recently widowed woman of his own age, Esther Mordecai, whose husband had left her impoverished and with three children. Since Esther Mordecai had applied to the congregation for nine pounds to pay her rent, the community had reason to be especially gladdened by this turn of events; the match likely seemed providential.[9]

But then a problem arose, for Esther Mordecai was a convert to Judaism. Her original name was Elizabeth Whitlock, and she had converted as a teenager to marry her much older first husband, Moses Mordecai. Who converted her and where she was converted remains uncertain,[10] but few at the time seem to have doubted the legitimacy of her conversion. The real problem was that the marriage of a kohen, a Jew of priestly descent, to a convert is explicitly prohibited by *halakhah* (Jewish law); a kohen may only marry the daughter of a Jew.[11] In much of the Jewish world, this obstacle would almost certainly have doomed the match, no matter how extenuating the circumstances.[12]

What is therefore remarkable, and extremely revealing, is that Cohen proved defiant. Although informed of the law, he spurned it. Why, he must have wondered, should he be denied the right to marry a convert to Judaism just because his ancestors had been descendants of Aaron, the high priest? The dictates of the synagogue and of Jewish law ran counter to his newfound sense of democracy and freedom.

Nor was he alone. According to the laconic minutes of the congregation, "great while was spent in debating" the marriage—a sure sign of communal restiveness. In the end, Congregation Mikveh Israel prohibited its *hazzan* (minister) from conducting the marriage or even from mentioning the couple's name within the synagogue's portals. Interestingly, stricter punishments, which some proposed, were voted down.[13]

The response on the part of Cohen and his friends was a public act of defiance. The congregation's leading member, Haym Salomon, along with the Revolutionary War hero Mordecai Sheftall of Savannah and the well-respected old-time Philadelphian, Israel Jacobs, privately conducted and witnessed the wedding ceremony.[14] The *ketubbah* (wedding document) survives, and the copy in the American Jewish Archives makes clear that the officiants acted in conscious awareness of what they were doing. Esther Mordecai is described in the Aramaic *ketubbah* as an *armalta giyorret*—"a widow and convert"—and her husband is listed as *Yaakov Ben Reb Yehoshua Hacohen,* Jacob, the son of Joshua the priest.[15] The three highly respected signators on the document, having been apprised of Jewish law, thus knowingly placed personal liberty above its dictates. In performing this wedding in the face of the synagogue's objections, they served notice that times had changed and that the congregation's power to regulate Jewish life was waning.

This conclusion is reinforced by a second document that survives, this one from 1785 and written in Western Yiddish (Judeo-German).[16] The document is a fascinating letter written by the leaders of Congregation Mikveh Israel of Philadelphia to Rabbi Saul Halevi Loewenstamm (1717–1790),[17] Ashkenazic chief rabbi of Amsterdam, seeking his advice and support in a battle against one of their most learned (and contentious) lay members, Mordecai M. Mordecai (1727–1809), a native of Telz, Lithuania.[18] Mordecai—no relation to Esther Mordecai who married Jacob I. Cohen—was akin to one of the "common people" whom Hatch highlights as emergent religious actors in this period. A distiller and unsuccessful businessman, he, like so many of his Protestant counterparts, did not feel bound by people of privilege and status, such as the *hazzan* and the members of the synagogue's governing body (*adjunta*). Himself the son of a rabbi, he felt that he understood Jewish law better than they did, and he therefore took the law into his own hands, much as some Protestants of that time insisted that, based on their own independent reading, they could interpret the Bible.[19]

"Reb Mordecai," according to our document, took the law into his own hands on two separate occasions. First, in an apparent attempt to reconcile members of his extended family, he performed an unauthorized Jewish marriage ceremony on a previously intermarried couple: his niece, Judith Hart, and her unconverted husband, Lt. James Pettigrew. On another occasion, the document charges, he openly flouted synagogue authority by performing the traditional last rites on Benjamin Clava, an identifying but intermarried Jew whom the synagogue, as a warning to others, had ordered buried "without ritual ablution, without shrouds and without funeral rites." Since on both occasions Mordecai vigorously defended his actions, insisting that he knew Jewish law better than those who judged him, the congregation sought "the illuminating light" of the Dutch rabbi's opinion.[20]

The real question here plainly had less to do with Jewish law than with Jewish religious authority in a democratic age. Mordecai, echoing the spirit of the American revolutionary tradition, and like many Protestant rebels of his day, challenged his religious superiors and claimed the right to interpret God's law as he personally understood it. Nor was he alone. According to the document, "In this country . . . everyone does as he pleases. . . .Yet, the <u>Kahal</u> (community) has no authority to restrain or punish anyone, except for the nominal penalty of denying them synagogue honors, or of withholding from them sacred rites. However, these vicious people completely disregard such measures and continue to attend our synagogue, because under the laws of the country it is impossible to enjoin them from so doing."[21] In other words, the problem, from the perspective of Mikveh Israel, was that Jews in post-Revolutionary America were making their own rules concerning how to live Jewishly, and there was little that the synagogue could do about it.

Returning to Richmond, where Jacob I. Cohen had also returned, we see more evidence of "democratization." In 1789, the city's first synagogue, Beth Shalome, adopted a constitution. The very term "constitution" is noteworthy. In the colonial era, Jews called such documents by traditional Hebrew terms, *haskamoth* or *ascamoth,* meaning agreements or covenants, and they followed a traditional Sephardic formula.[22] Now, two years after the American Constitution was ratified, we see the English term, "constitution," employed. The Beth Shalome document echoes its American counterpart.[23] "We the subscribers of the Israelite religion, resident in this place," it begins. And it continues with three striking clauses, never to my knowledge previously found in a synagogue constitution, and all of them highly revealing:

"Every free man residing in this city for the term of three months, of the age of 21 years, and who congregates with us, shall be a yahid [first-class member] of the kehilla and entitled to every right and privilege of the same." (Article 1)

The key word here is "every." In the colonial era, *yehidim* were the equivalent of what Protestants called "communicants." They were men of status who materially supported the congregation, and they were different from women, the poor, and visitors, who occupied seats but had no authority. In New York's Shearith Israel, according to the congregation's 1761 constitution, the waiting time to become a *yahid* was set at "at least one Year," and the cost was twenty shillings—a respectable sum.[24] Now in Richmond, *every* free man, rich and poor alike, could become a *yahid* after only three months. Although women and slaves were still excluded, democratization was evident nevertheless. Just as the franchise nationwide was broadening, so too was the franchise within the world of the American synagogue.[25]

"The parnas and assistants shall not be connected in family or in partnership in trade, in order to preserve an equal and an independent representation." (Article 2)

With these words, Beth Shalome's constitution outlawed the traditional practice of having only wealthy families run the synagogue. In colonial New York, interconnected merchant families had dominated congregational life for more than fifty years, and such was the case in much of early modern Europe.[26] Post-Revolutionary Richmond Jews, however, rebelled against such undemocratic practices. The phrase "an equal and an independent representation" is particularly revealing. These were good Virginia values in 1789, but by no means traditional Jewish ones.

"No rules or regulations shall be considered as binding on the congregation until it is read 2 Shabbath or holidays separately in the synagogue. Should any member object to the same, it must be by a letter to the parnas within 24 hours after the last publication, who shall be obliged to call a meeting of all the members in toto. . . . A majority present at such meeting, which must be 2/3 of the members in town, shall deterim [determine] the same and the [de]teremination shall be binding on the objecting member and all the rest." [Article 3]

This provision of the Richmond synagogue constitution promoted the goal of communal consensus by offering dissenters unprecedented opportunity to have their views heard. Even a single dissenter could bring about a meeting of "all the members in toto" to render a binding decision. The practice never became normative in American synagogue life; it was totally impractical. The intent, nevertheless, is fascinating, for a key source of dissatisfaction within colonial-era synagogues was the stifling of dissenting voices. Following the Revolution, at least for a brief period, synagogue dissenters in Richmond received a guarantee that their views would be heard and voted upon.[27]

Young people likewise found their voices heard in the immediate post-Revolutionary years. Whereas before, at least in New York, leaders had tended to be older men, the leadership at Shearith Israel now became progressively younger. From 1783–1801, the age of the *parnasim* (presidents) of that congregation averaged about fifty-eight. From 1801–1824, the average age dropped to forty![28] So dramatic a change cannot fully be explained based on the data at hand, but the generational shift certainly adds credence to the sense that a rising post-Revolutionary generation was demanding to be heard. Moreover, in Judaism, as in Protestantism, religious leadership was becoming divorced from social position, in keeping with the ideology of a democratic age.

The same trend reveals itself in 1805, with the dramatic change in the way that congregants were seated in the Shearith Israel synagogue. Throughout the colonial period, the synagogue seated its members much as Protestant churches did. An anonymous colonial-era poem summed up the system:

> In the goodly house of worship
> Where in order due and fit,
> As by public vote directed
> Classed and ranked the people sit.[29]

In Shearith Israel and, so far as we know, every other synagogue, the congregation carefully allocated a "proper" seat to each person based on his or her status, and each seat was then assessed a membership tax. Members of the wealthy Gomez family regularly enjoyed the most prestigious seats and paid the highest assessments. Others paid less and sat much farther away from the holy ark. The system generated a great deal of bad feeling, usually on the part of those dissatisfied for one reason or another with the seats assigned to them, but it produced a steady stream of revenue and accurately reflected the social stratification of Jewish society. The synagogue seating chart, in the colonial era, provided an annual map of society's inequalities.[30]

Unsurprisingly, this system offended Jews of the post-Revolutionary era. As early as 1786 a special *banca* (bench) reserved for the aristocratic women of the Gomez family was removed. Elite families such as the Gomezes no longer could impose their will on everybody else.[31] In 1805, in a much more radical move, the congregation abandoned its whole system of assigned seats and assessments and committed itself to a system of what churches call pew rent. Under this procedure, the trustees assigned different values to different seats (as in a theater), and then leased them on a first-come, first-served basis. Practically speaking, this hardly changed the social stratification of the synagogue, since wealthy people rented better seats than poor people did. In the eyes of contemporaries, however, the change represented a dramatic triumph for democracy in American Judaism, for under the new system members enjoyed much more freedom of choice.[32]

The next twenty years, from 1805–1825, witnessed a great deal more ferment in American Jewish religious life, much of which I have described elsewhere.[33] First, women gained new visibility, thanks to the adoption of the open-style women's gallery in New York (1818) and Philadelphia (1825). No longer did they have to sit, as they had earlier, hidden by a "breast-work as high as their chins." The number of seats available to women likewise increased—to 44 percent of the seats in New York, and 46 percent in Philadelphia—suggesting that women were regularly expected to attend religious services, much as their Protestant counterparts did. The presence of so many women within the synagogue's portals often proved a source of contention, especially when disputes arose concerning who should sit where.[34]

In Charleston, so-called "vagrant Jews"—the counterparts to Hatch's "common people"—literally brawled with synagogue leaders in 1812 over issues of authority that pit the congregation's minister against its governing board. A one-sided version of what took place is preserved in a letter from the future Jewish leader Mordecai M. Noah, then twenty-seven years old and living in Charleston, to his uncle Naphtali Phillips in New York:

In my last I enclosed to you a bill of fare relative to a singing match established by Mr. [Emanuel Nunes] Carvalho[.] [W]ithin this last week the Congregation has been in a state of warfare sanctioned & approved by that gentleman unheard of in the annals of religion—It appears he had taught the children to sing the concluding psalms of the Sabbath Morning Service in a very handsome manner which in a measure did away [with] the discordance which attends every Synagogue [.] [F]or a whim or caper he discontinued this ceremony & forbid the children to sing[.] The private adjunta conceiving it to be his duty to continue a system which was generally approved of respectfully requested him to allow the children to continue which he refused to do and on application for some other branch of his duty he treated the adjunta with disrespect & they suspended him for five days which suspension terminated on Saturday at 10 oclock when he performed the prayers[.] --Saturday evening being a meeting of the adjunta in general body he collected a rabble composed of all the vagrant Jews & had a petition signed by them to give him redress[.] [T]his petition was handed the Parnass who could not act upon it being in express violation to the constitution[.] Mr. Carvalho in person aided and abetted the confusion & riot which took place[.] [I]n a short time the whole meeting parnass & all were battling with clubs & bruising boxing &c during which his reverence & brother & friend [Abraham?] Lipman came off with a few thumps[.] [T]his outrageous & disgraceful [*sic*] produced by the interference & cooperation of Mr Carvalho terminated without any serious injury[.] The result has completely destroyed the small remnant of respectability & character yet left for Mr C[.] [H]is duty was not to take the law in his own hands but to submit with respect to the conduct & resolve of the private adjunta who are composed of the most respected & indeed the most enlightened part of the Congregation[.] [35]

Fascinatingly, Noah describes Carvalho in terms similar to those that synagogue leaders of Philadelphia used against Mordecai Mordecai.

In both cases, the offenders were charged with the same kinds of offenses: taking the law into their own hands, spurning authority, and making common cause with congregational malcontents. Moreover, there proved to be little, in both cases, that synagogue authorities could do about the situation. However much the "enlightened" part of the congregation sought to have dissenters "submit" to the *parnas* and the *adjunta*, the new world of American religion conspired against these efforts and favored the forces of change.

The synagogue's reduced power was amply illustrated just a year later in New York City, when its authority to regulate kosher meat was challenged. Formerly in New York, as the historian of Jewish ritual slaughtering details, "all Jewish slaughtering was done by one man, the elected shohet [ritual slaughterer] of the Shearith Israel Congregation. The meat was distributed through a number of Christian meat dealers who had entered into contracts with the Congregation." In 1813, the shohet, Jacob Abrahams, failed to win reelection and instead set himself up as an independent ritual slaughterer, slaughtering meat "without warrant of the Congregation and for butchers with whom the Congregation had no contract." Horrified, the synagogue's leaders petitioned the New York Common Council to have their sole authority over kosher meat restored. The Common Council obligingly agreed, approving an ordinance that "no Butcher, or other person, shall hereafter expose for sale in the public Markets any Meat sealed as Jews Meat, who shall not be engaged for that purpose by the Trustees of the congregation Shearith Israel." But in an era that exalted freedom and democracy, an ordinance that granted monopoly power to synagogue trustees provoked immediate opposition. Eight dissident congregants who supported Abrahams protested the ordinance as "an encroachment on our religious rites [*sic*] and a restriction of those general privileges to which we are entitled." They asked that it be "immediately abolished" and privately complained that it was an "infringement on the rights of the people." The Common Council, unwilling to enter into what it now understood to be an internal Jewish dispute, quickly backed down. It expunged its original ordinance and washed its hands of the whole matter. Once again, synagogue dissidents emerged victorious, while the traditional authorities of the congregation lost both power and face.[36]

Back in Charleston, the leadership of the synagogue experienced a similar loss of face when it attempted to crack down on the move to establish private Jewish cemeteries. Historically, control over the cemetery served as a potent source of power for synagogues and organized Jewish communities. Dissidents, transgressors, and defaulters knew that unless they submitted to authority they risked being shamed at their death. The intermarried Benjamin Clava, we have seen, was ordered buried "without ritual ablution, without shrouds and without funeral rites." In extreme cases, individuals might be denied a Jewish burial altogether. Seeking to preserve this venerable authority, which was perhaps the strongest deterrent in the congregation's disciplinary arsenal,[37] Beth Elohim reacted strongly when several notable families purchased their own "places of interment." It proclaimed in its 1820 constitution that "there shall be one Congregational Burial Ground only, . . ." although in the interests of peace it conceded "that this law shall not extend to any family place of interment already established." The proclamation, however, made no noticeable impact. In a free country, Beth Elohim proved no more able to control where Jews would choose to be buried than Shearith Israel was able to control whose kosher meat they would choose to eat.[38]

Whether all of this adds up to what Hatch calls "democratization" may be open to dispute. The word "democratization" itself—which means "the process of becoming democratic"—was actually unknown in early America, and it only appears in print in the second half of the nineteenth century.[39] But if the word was unknown, the process, if anything, was accelerating. Synagogues, much like the Protestant churches that Hatch described, experienced burgeoning religious ferment, challenges from below to established communal authority, and appeals to American values ("freedom," "rights of the people") in order to legitimate expressions of religious dissent. Over time, the hierarchic, deferential, and tradition-based world of colonial Judaism gave way to a new Jewish world: one where Jewish law and the authority of synagogue leaders could be openly challenged; where *every* man was a "yahid" (first-class member); and where power no longer lay exclusively in the hands of wealthy "elders." Most of all, this new Jewish world was characterized by freedom: the freedom to choose seats within the synagogue, the freedom to buy kosher meat outside the synagogue, and the freedom to bury dear ones in a private cemetery if that is what one chose to do.

After years of stirring, this new Jewish world emerged into the fullness of life in the mid-1820s. The hallowed "synagogue-community" model of American Judaism, which assumed that each community would be organized around a single synagogue that governed all aspects of Jewish life, collapsed at that time. In its place came a more free-wheeling marketplace model of American Judaism, the "community of synagogues."[40]

Two nearly simultaneous "revolts" between 1824 and 1826 occasioned this transformation: the secession from Shearith Israel that led to the establishment of Congregation B'nai Jeshurun in New York, and the secession from Beth Elohim that led to the creation of the Reformed Society of Israelites in Charleston. Both of these well-known episodes sought to bring a greater measure of freedom and democracy into Jewish religious life, legitimating religious change on the basis of American political values.

The developments in Charleston have been amply described elsewhere.[41] Young people, dissatisfied with the "apathy and neglect which have been manifested towards our holy religion" and fearful that Judaism would not survive unless it changed, sought far-reaching changes in their synagogue, advocating, among other things, an abbreviated worship service, vernacular prayers, a weekly sermon, and an end to traditional free will offerings during the Torah service. When their 1824 petition for change was coldly denied, they seceded from Beth Elohim and formed what was officially known as "The Reformed Society of Israelites for Promoting True Principles of Judaism According to its Purity and Spirit."[42]

This development is often recalled as the beginning of Reform Judaism in the United States, which in many ways it was. But in addition to ritual reform, the new congregation also provided for a good deal more democracy. For example, a key article of the Reformed Society's constitution declared, "Any Israelite whatsoever, who makes a donation or leaves a legacy of not less than fifty dollars for the benefit of this Society, shall receive every mark of respect, have the right of burial, and be entitled to every religious attention to which members are entitled." This article, a silent critique of Beth Elohim, aimed to move away from the plutocracy and authoritarianism characteristic of that synagogue and to link the Reformed Society with the nationwide movement for democracy and equal rights. The "birthright of ourselves . . . is equal liberty," Reformed Society of Israelites leader Isaac Harby reiterated on the society's first anniversary. He and his fellow reformers argued, in effect, that a new democratic country needed a more democratic Judaism.[43]

The same argument characterized the Jewish secessionists of New York.[44] In 1825, young members of Shearith Israel petitioned not for reform, but simply for an early worship service "on the Sabbath morning during the summer months." When their petition was refused (for violating the "rules and customs of our ancestors"), the young people formed an independent society "to promote the study of our Holy Law and . . . to extend a knowledge of its divine precepts, ceremonies, and worship among our brethren generally, and the enquiring youth in particular." The goal, in this case, was a worship service run much less formally than at Shearith Israel, without a permanent leader, and with no "distinctions made among the member rich and poor." The movement reflected all of the themes familiar to us from the history of Protestantism in this era: revivalism, challenge to authority, a new form of organization, anti-elitism, and radical democratization. Within a short time, the young people created B'nai Jeshurun, a new and competing synagogue to Shearith Israel.

Revealingly, the new congregation justified itself in the preamble to its constitution by appealing to American democratic values. "The wise and republican laws of this country are based upon universal toleration giving to every citizen and sojourner the right to worship according to the dictate of his conscience,"[45] it explained. In New York as in Charleston, ritual change and democratization marched hand in hand.

Later, congregations elsewhere in the country echoed — practically word for word—the stirring value-laden language that the secessionists at B'nai Jeshurun employed.[46] In addition to mutual influence, this demonstrates the power of rhetoric in a democratic age. The emphasis on toleration, on equality, on conscience, and above all on the "wise and republican laws of this country" bespoke the new values that entered the world of American Judaism in the years following the American Revolution. Following "a period of religious ferment, chaos, and originality unmatched in American history,"[47] a new and more democratic American Judaism had emerged.

Jonas Phillips Levy: A Jewish Naval Captain in the Early Republic

William Pencak

At the age of sixteen, Jonas Phillips Levy (1807–1883) followed in the footsteps of his older brother Uriah Phillips Levy (1792–1862)—the first Jew to command a fleet in the United States navy—by running away to sea. Jonas took little interest in Jewish affairs until 1854 when he became the leading member of the then infant Washington Hebrew Congregation, the first in the nation's capital, and served as the point man for the American Jewish community as it lobbied the State Department to protest injustices against Jews abroad. But why did Jonas Levy so suddenly associate himself with the Jewish community, and, furthermore, why did he completely omit these achievements from the fascinating autobiography that detailed his life of adventure on the high seas—a life which included the restoration of a Peruvian president to power and the facilitation of the United States' conquest of Vera Cruz during the Mexican War? Why, also, did he have little or nothing to do with the Jewish community after 1860?

Jonas was a rebel, and rebellion seemed to run in his family. Jonas Phillips, the maternal grandfather whose name he bore, supported the Revolution and led the Jewish community as President of Philadelphia's only synagogue, Mikveh Israel. He petitioned the United States Constitutional Convention of 1787 not to discriminate against the Jews in the new frame of government, given their valuable contributions to the cause. (The delegates did not condone explicit

109

discrimination, but left the question of political rights to the states, which meant the Jews had to win the right to vote and hold public office on this level.)[1]

Jonas's father Michael, too, was something of an outsider, if not a rebel: he was one of the few prominent Jewish Federalists in Philadelphia during Thomas Jefferson's presidency, and abandoned his father-in-law's synagogue to join Rodeph Shalom, the German congregation founded in the city in 1802.[2] Did the fact the brothers ran away from their Federalist father's home have something to do with the fact that they idolized Thomas Jefferson, a man they never met? Uriah, in fact, donated a statue of Jefferson to the United States government—the first of many statues which now adorn the nation's capital—and, in 1836, purchased a decaying Monticello which he would maintain for the rest of his life. One of Jonas's sons, Jefferson Monroe, eventually inherited Monticello from his uncle (after Jonas tried without success to sell the property and iron out his brother's tangled estate) and went on to become a Congressman from New York.[3]

The Levy brothers also endured a childhood in which the high social status of their families clashed with harsh reality. The problem was too many children: Jonas Phillips had twenty-one, and Michael Levy fourteen. Few fortunes in the new republic could be spread significantly among so many heirs.[4]

A daguerrotype of Jonas survives. His piercing expression exudes the grim determination with which he strove for success, but his plaid jacket depicts the maverick who resisted authority and did not hesitate to use force and deceit to achieve his ends. Although he never achieved the fame of either his brother or his son, he was an important figure who lived a fascinating life and made his mark on history although his grandest scheme—to build an Atlantic-Pacific route across Mexico and run the entire United States mail service between California and the east— came to naught. In the 1850s Jonas's personal ambitions and the goals of the American Jewish community coincided. Like his better-known brother Uriah, whose famous 1857 defense of American Jews before a naval review board was primarily a means to restore his command on the grounds he was a victim of antisemitism, Jonas's concurrent emergence as a champion of Jewish rights was undoubtedly

Daguerrotype of Jonas P. Levy, courtesy of the American Jewish Historical Society, New York City and Newton Centre, Massachusetts.

self-interested. But that his efforts also merit a prominent place in the history of American Jews who stood up for their community cannot be denied. His is a story that deserves to be known.

Fortunately, we can learn much of that story thanks to Jonas himself. At the age of seventy he left his children a colorful autobiography of twenty-seven pages, typed (certainly at his dictation) on legal-size paper, and describing how he "traversed the thousands of miles over the Briny Ocean, so full of pleasure and danger to those who faced the music of old Boreas, and Neptune's Home."[5] In some respects Jonas's was the typical story of poor-boy makes-good after many trials and tribulations. But its poignancy resides in his inability ever to forgive or forget a loss, or to find peace or what he considered real success despite the considerable wealth and comfortable family life he was finally able to enjoy.

Much like Benjamin Franklin in his autobiography, Jonas did not hide his "errata"—as Franklin called his parade of youthful mistakes. But, unlike Franklin, he did not apologize for them: he was out to avenge injustice and looked for opportunities to do so from the very first. Hating school, he set a trap for his teacher which overturned an inkstand on her "beautiful ash colored silk dress," then ran away from

Portrait of Jonas P. Levy, courtesy of the Washington Hebrew Congregation.

Philadelphia where, as a teenager, he learned how to build and paint houses. Looking for better opportunities, Jonas walked to Lancaster, where he was equally dissatisfied working in his brother Louis's china shop. Jonas's next stop was Columbia, Pennsylvania, and from there Baltimore (where his brother Joseph lived), before he returned to Philadelphia from whence, in the middle of the winter of 1823, he walked to New York, where his widowed mother lived with his uncle. So eager was he to get away that he wore only one pair of stockings until he was rescued, clothed properly, and fed by a kindly country couple, whose sympathy he won with the lie that his clothes had been stolen. By the age of sixteen, Jonas had already rejected school, "the great city of brotherly love," and a life with two of his brothers (1–3). It turned out Jonas's mother did not want him either, as she was a poor dependant of her brother: she gave him "a good box on the ears" and told him to return to Philadelphia. This is the only glimpse of her personality we get from either brother; is it any wonder they ran away from home? At the same time, however, Jonas went on at length—for nearly a full page—about the warm welcome he received from his cousins: "what a pretty curly haired boy I was and how tall I was, and the blond ringlets took the eyes of my fair cousins" (4). (A portrait of Jonas survives at the Washington Hebrew Congregation as a young man: his hair was indeed light and curly.) Clearly Jonas had never experienced this kind of affection before, or it would not have figured so prominently in his memory over a half-century later. Nonetheless he was compelled to leave this scene of domestic bliss immediately— the very next day—as his mother did not want him to be a burden to her brother. But, instead of returning to Philadelphia, Jonas went to sea, inspired by a fabulous dream of foreign lands which came to him the one night he spent under his uncle's roof: "mountains of fruit and lakes of honey and molasses and all the other nice things together with parrots, monkeys, poodle dogs and dogs without any hair on them and beds of roses with castles in the air" (4). It is not the sea itself that attracted him, but the exotic places he hoped to visit, and the things and adventures he hoped to have. Lying again, this time asserting to a sea captain that he had no family, Jonas took voyage for New Orleans, discovering, instead of the paradise he had envisioned, "the finest kind of cockroaches" and a bed "equal to lying on a hard plank with no soft spot on it." But he was philosophical: "I stood the sea voyage well." He cooked for the crew, and, in New Orleans, discovered that his brother Morton was the pilot of a Mississippi River boat. Morton turned out to be the family member to whom Jonas repeatedly returned and who shared his tragedies and successes (5–6).

Yet, before he began his own tale in earnest, Jonas paused to tell the story of yet another brother, Benjamin, commander of the ship "Paragon." Ben had been apprenticed to the Philadelphia merchant and philanthropist Stephen Girard, whose charity did not extend to Ben, for Girard did not promote him to captain despite "the various occasions he had saved his ship and cargo for him," which "was more than his high sense of duty to himself could stand" (3). Ben's story foretold Jonas's own future. Respectable society (and no one was more respectable than Girard) offered nothing for a man of his talents, who was frequently done in by duplicitous associates and unsympathetic governments. The sea was a siren, promising riches but yielding tribulation. When Ben took command of his own ship in 1824, he was stabbed through the heart by the vessel's Spanish cook, much as Jonas was to be confronted by mutinous crews and pirates, and as he was, figuratively, to be stabbed through the heart by potential in-laws and business associates—treacherous events which undid his dreams of wealth and fame in Mexico. Jonas related how the United States sent a ship, the "Hornet," to Havana to demand Ben's murderer's execution, which the authorities carried out within sight of the ship after the captain threatened to attack the city. By writing his autobiography, Jonas similarly sought posthumous satisfaction, similar to that which Ben had received. But, while he did not lose his life, and attained what most people would consider substantial success through his extensive trading with Latin America, Jonas nonetheless dwelled on the injustices and losses he suffered (1–2).

Repeated encounters with danger and potential disaster fill Jonas's narrative. After a career on the inland waterways of the United States (5–7), he had his first major brush with authority on a voyage to Liverpool out of New York. The drunken captain fell asleep and nearly blew up the ship while smoking his pipe, as his stateroom was located above two kegs of powder. Jonas assumed command of the ship, but only received his wages from the ungrateful captain when he threatened to report him to Lloyd's of London, which had insured the ship (8). After returning to Philadelphia, pirates seized Jonas's ships on a subsequent voyage to the Caribbean, but he saved the day by hiding the gold and allowing the pirates to get away only with the crew's provisions. Next, he again wound up in New Orleans, from there made his way to New York via Savannah, and then sailed to France, joining the crew from LeHavre that had sailed to America with Lafayette on board on 4 July 1824.

It is hard to imagine that Jonas did everything mentioned in the last paragraph during his first half-year at sea; surely after over half a century he was conflating several years' early experiences. Yet, despite Jonas's probable inaccuracies, he soon met Lafayette again, while the general was undertaking his year-long travels through the United States, and received a finger ring from him (8–9). Next in Jonas's adventures came an expedition to capture seals in the South Atlantic which led to battles with the Indians of Patagonia—the famed "Patagonian giants"— (whom, he attested, frequently attained seven feet in height), and subsequent voyages to the South Seas and China (10–13). All this in his early twenties! Although he was neither rich nor famous, Jonas demonstrated his superior intelligence by evading catastrophe on at least two occasions and obtained the recognition of the great Lafayette.

Still in his early twenties, Jonas became involved at the highest level of Latin American affairs, and was occupied by this involvement on and off for a quarter of a century. In this he represented an expanding United States whose final boundaries were yet to be determined, and whose navy (and as his case shows, merchant marine as well) intervened regularly in South America to rescue sailors or punish ports and nations interfering with American business. Joining various crews on the Pacific Coast of South America, Jonas hired his ship out to President de Orbegoso of Peru, and was so important in keeping him in power that at the age of twenty-seven he received the freedom (or citizenship) of Peru from the national congress (13–14). Trading sealskins, sugar, rice, and hides for gold and silver, he returned to New York in 1835 a wealthy man. Indeed, Jonas's fortune was based on supplying the gold and silver-rich Latin American markets with items they required for food and clothing, as his subsequent ventures into Mexico and the West Indies demonstrate. Unable to find a carriage upon his return to New York, Jonas went on foot to visit his mother and relatives for the first time in twelve years—"a nice walk for a Spanish man from Peru dressed in that gaudy style."(14) Jonas had lost his identity: he was neither Jew nor North American, but a man of the world, flaunting his individuality and identifying with the South American voyages that gave him his wealth and defined his character.

To be sure, Jonas took nearly a page to recount the delights of returning to his mother, whom he found asleep. He "laid [his] head on her dear and beloved breast, where [he] first nourished of life" (15).

But given how his mother had treated him in the past, and the fact that he took his time returning, Jonas's reverie strikes a false note. His description suggests that he was likely wishing his mother *had* been nurturing, and had provided the comfortable family setting he actually never enjoyed. But he was now addicted to the sea, to adventure, and the pursuit of wealth. Soon he was off to Monticello to visit his brother Uriah—whom he had not seen for thirteen years—and he certainly spent more time describing this attractive estate than he spent recounting his visit with his mother. Here at Monticello was the status to which Jonas aspired: his brother had made a fortune in New York real estate and purchased one of the two most famous houses in the nation, and had seen the world and risen in the navy as well (16–17). Uriah was a cantankerous fellow, whose personal disposition combined with his verbal and physical responses to the antisemitism of some of his fellow officers led him to be court-martialed six times, still a record in the navy. Jonas shared with (and possibly acquired from) his brother a propensity for relentlessly taking legal action and pursuing both legislative and bureaucratic channels at the highest levels of government to secure his own interests.[6]

In less than a year Jonas was off again, wealthy enough to outfit his own ship and load it with trade goods bound for the Pacific via Cape Horn. Unfortunately, though, disaster struck: the ship was wrecked off the coast of Brazil, Jonas's crew deserted, and a second crew, which he picked up in Rio de Janeiro, mutinied—an uprising he was only able to quell, with the aid of his officers, by killing one of the leaders. When he heard the men were planning a second revolt, Jonas lined them up, shot a man who bolted, imprisoned the ringleaders, and dumped the crew in Valparaiso, Chile (17–18). Jonas, clearly, did not tolerate opposition. Undaunted, he headed up the coast to Peru, where he saved President de Orbegoso a second time by bombarding a fortress held by the rebel General Talavera [*sic*] from the sea while staging a simultaneous land assault—an effort which led to his appointment as an admiral in the Peruvian navy.[7] He then went to Panama before paying a call on his sister Fanny Lopez and her husband in Kingston, Jamaica, and, while there, also enjoyed "a very pleasant visit" to the parents of his future sister-in-law, Virginia, who married Uriah Levy in 1850 when he was fifty-eight and she was fifteen (18–19).

Painting by James Guy Evans of Captain J. Levy's Ship USS Transport American 1847 off Vera Cruz, courtesy of Arnold and Deanne Kaplan Collection of American Judaica.

In 1837, aged thirty, Jonas returned home a successful man. But his quest for community and affection still eluded him. He nearly married a Miss R. H—ks [*sic*] upon his return to New York, but her family spirited her away that she might be "secretly married to her cousin in the West Indies"—apparently an arranged marriage of the sort Sephardic Jews sometimes practiced in early America. Jonas described this turn of events as "a disgrace to her family and heart-rending to me for many years before I got over it." Given the dashes he placed in her name, Jonas clearly wanted his readers to know that he understood it would be improper to name the family (since the autobiography was never published, he was not worried about libel.) But by including the "ks", Jonas made sure everyone who read it would know he meant the Hendricks family—the nation's largest copper manufacturers before the Civil War—whose plot adjoins the Levys' at the highest point of the Shearith Israel Cemetery in Cypress Hills, Brooklyn, New York. One wonders what made Jonas an undesirable match. It was clearly not a lack of wealth, for later that year, when his store in New York burned down, Jonas incurred losses of $15,000. After the failure of his attempt to marry, Jonas returned to Monticello and New York from whence he transported his sister Elisa, who had herself married a Hendricks, and her children to New Orleans (19–21). Apparently the Hendrickses had no objection to the Levys, but rather to Jonas personally.

Jonas remained in New Orleans, and set himself up in business with his brother Morton. After a bout of yellow fever, which his brother was able to cure with calomel, castor oil, and mustard plasters, Jonas became Morton's business partner, and for the next several years Morton gave him the family he never had.

After an unfortunate trip, in 1842, to St. Thomas in the West Indies, which was a total loss for Jonas and Morton financially, the brothers commenced a prolonged and frustrating series of adventures which began in Mexico. The Levys were promised the right to land their goods and equipment duty free at Laguna in the Yucatan, where they planned to build a sugar mill and brickyard. They also hoped to sell wine, cotton goods, steel, and pepper.[8] But Jonas and Morton could not have picked a worse location. At that time the Yucatan was in rebellion against Mexico—with some help from the then independent nation of Texas—while the Mayan Indians were in turn in rebellion against the Yucatan's creole elite. This was no place to start a business, as the Yucatan's leader would soon offer his "country" to France, Britain, and the United States—anyone who agreed to protect it from Mexico.[9] Once again, Jonas met with deceit, as he and Morton, who brought his wife and six children along, were fleeced out of $15,000 by local officials through "forced loans and contributions" (21). Jonas nevertheless returned to New York for more materials and goods, while in the meantime his brother's family became destitute: Morton's youngest child died, and was then disinterred by the local Roman Catholics after it had been buried not even *in*, but adjacent to, the local cemetery. This is the only incident of antisemitism, or mention of religion in any manner, that Jonas included in his entire autobiography (21–23).

When war broke out with Mexico in 1846, the Mexican government denied Jonas and Morton their rights under a treaty of 1839 which gave them twelve months to close their business and leave. Instead, like all Americans, they were ordered to depart in twenty-four hours. The Levys were put ashore in New Orleans, after having to fork over $300 to a ship's captain bound for Havana. There, through friends, Jonas made his way to Washington where he filed a claim for his losses, and then to New York, where, on behalf of a purchasing agent, he took command of the "American"—a ship of seven hundred tons— to transport supplies and forty-four landing (surf) boats for General Winfield Scott's invasion of Vera Cruz (23).

At this point Jonas became something of a hero, and dwells at length on his wartime experiences in his autobiography. He proved indispensable to the invading army, anchoring his ship safely in a gale. But, instead of praising Jonas for his skill, the fleet's commander, who had run his own ship aground, told him he had risked the whole expedition—as he carried many of its landing boats—by bringing his ship up in a storm. Jonas's temper flared: "when Commander Conner knew the Gulf of Mexico, its reef and shoals as well as Captain Jonas P. Levy did, he would not have run his ship ashore, as the commander did" (23). Jonas then unloaded the surfboats and allowed Scott's forces to disembark, without help from the petulant Conner. As a reward for his services, General Worth, with the approval of Scott, appointed Jonas harbormaster of Vera Cruz on 1 April 1847—a post he held for only two weeks following which he returned to New Orleans, and made two further trips to bring troops from Kentucky, Illinois, and Louisiana, whom he described as "very unruly," and Massachusetts, whom he termed "almost mutinous" (23).

To read his account, Jonas's masterful handling of his vessel was the only bright spot of the landing (24–25). He commemorated the episode by commissioning a dramatic painting of his ship by James Guy Evans (c. 1810–after 1860)—the foremost painter of ships in New Orleans at the time, whose works were distinguished by written descriptions of the ship and perhaps an event connected with it at the bottom. Jonas ran into a gale when he left Vera Cruz on 15 April, and the painting shows the ship triumphantly surmounting the storm. It is interesting to speculate why Jonas would have chosen that gale, rather than his equally spectacular landing of the "American," as the theme of the painting. Commissioning this work was an expensive and important decision for Jonas: at the time even wealthy people only ordered paintings for exceptional reasons (their wedding, before leaving on a voyage, or to commemorate a lifetime of achievement). Significantly, Jonas had his crew individually painted on the side of the ship, and thus shares the credit for their preservation as well.[10]

As the war ended, Jonas finally found domestic happiness. Perhaps his success emboldened him quickly to court and then, on 22 November 1848, marry Fanny Mitchell, whom he had met when he visited New York that February and March and had therefore known only for a month. The Reverend Ansel Leo married them (26). Leo was the second rabbi of B'nai Jeshurun (he was paid $1000 a year as opposed to the first rabbi Morris Raphall's $2000), founded in 1821 as New York City's first German synagogue, and second synagogue of any type. Jonas's father-in-law Abraham Mitchell (as the Mitchell grave marker adjoining the Levy plot in the Shearith Israel cemetery notes in an almost totally faded inscription) was both a "founding member" of the synagogue and for "many years its parnass," or president.[11]

Mitchell was also a liquor merchant with offices in both New York and Philadelphia, and, like his son-in-law, not above some skullduggery to advance his interests. In 1842 Mitchell had gone bankrupt, and appointed two of his brothers-in-law, Louis Allen of Philadelphia and Jonas Hart of New York, along with Hart's son Henry, as his preferred creditors to distribute his assets, which he was legally allowed to do provided they proved honest and competent. However, given Allen's out-of-state residence, and the fact that Jonas was blind and Henry illiterate, it was clear to the New York Chancery Court that Mitchell had selected these men "to keep the control of the property in his own hands." The judges found for his creditors in their lawsuit.[12]

Jonas valued his wife's company to the extent that he risked her life by bringing her to Vera Cruz, where he opened a store after the war. On the way, they survived a cholera epidemic in New Orleans, and then a yellow fever outbreak in Vera Cruz. They had five children: Isabella (1849); Jefferson Monroe Levy (1852); Louis Napoleon (1854); Mitchell Abraham Cass (1856); and finally, Amelia (1858).

Mitchell and Amelia were named after their maternal grandparents, with Abraham Mitchell's first and last names inverted, suggesting that Jonas may have considered them more of a mother and father to him than he ever considered his own parents. Lewis Cass was not only Jonas's friend, but was also the 1848 Democratic presidential candidate, Michigan Senator, and later, Secretary of State under James Buchanan. He was a man on whom Jonas would rely heavily for political favors and who was also present at his namesake's birth. Jonas and Fanny's other children's names—Isabella was the Queen of Spain who also was fascinated by the Indies—reflected Jonas's heroes and aspirations to greatness (26–27).

Having a family seemed to give Jonas the stability he needed to embark on even grander schemes. A notable example was his plan to have stagecoaches traverse the narrowest part of Mexico connecting the Atlantic and Pacific Oceans, thereby cutting the time and danger required to reach the gold fields of California. In addition, new steamships Jonas hoped to build would sail from New York to Havana or New Orleans, and then to Vera Cruz, where their goods would be unloaded and taken across Mexico via rail and roads to Huatulco on the Pacific, where more steamers would be available. Jonas predicted he could ensure that mail and passengers would reach San Francisco from New York in twenty days: "no shorter or quicker route can be had on the continent of America, nor opened at less expense." After receiving approval from the Mexican government in 1850, he proposed to the United States Congress that he be allowed to carry all the mail from coast to coast for $575,000 a year, an enormous sum of money at the time. (In 1855, Jonas's brother Uriah was probably the wealthiest Jew in New York with an estimated wealth of about half a million dollars.) The Mexican government promised Jonas (and presumably his heirs or company) a contract for fifty years, renewable for another forty-nine, in return for 10 percent of the profits and exemption from import duties for all goods Jonas handled. Had Congress approved, Jonas's route might have supplanted Commodore Cornelius Vanderbilt's Central America corridor as the quickest and safest path to the gold fields. But, he was turned down.[13]

Another major effort Jonas undertook was lobbying Congress to obtain approximately $55,000 in compensation for his losses in

Mexico before and during the war, out of a total of $3.25 million Mexico had promised to pay United States businessmen under the terms of the peace Treaty of Guadalupe Hidalgo, signed in 1848. This seems to be the principal reason Jonas moved to Washington, DC and remained there for seven years, from the spring of 1854 to 1 April 1861 (the only period of his life when he was actively involved in Jewish affairs). In 1854 Congress allowed that he had a claim, its amount to be determined subject to the auditing of his accounts, but Jonas misinterpreted this approval to mean he was legally entitled to all he was asking for. Jonas's calculation of his losses would have made Herman Melville's "Confidence Man" blush. Deprived of his brickyard and other commercial ventures by the Mexican government when war was declared in 1846, he simply estimated his earnings at $10,000 per year and put in for five years' worth of profit! Apparently, too, the State Department lost his evidence, and the testimonials he did present scarcely seemed credible: documents from a Mexican general and the court of the state of Tabasco attesting to the value of his property.[14]

Jonas's principal bone to pick was with Elisha Whittlesey, Comptroller of the Treasury, who audited his accounts in 1855. Whittlesey ruled that Jonas was trying to hold the government responsible for profits that were exceedingly unlikely to occur in so unstable an economic climate as Mexico: "the prospective gain or loss, however, in managing his work of business is a matter of such perfect uncertainty . . . that my opinion is decidedly opposed to allowing any sense in this or any other similar claim as a loss . . . for many circumstances may have occurred which would have ruined his whole establishment." Unwilling to give up, Jonas published a pamphlet criticizing Whittlesey for his "multifarious suppressions of the truth, its imaginary additions to the truth, its perversion of the testimony, its scarcely plausible inferences, its unwarranted and malignant aspersion upon private character, never before assailed, even by the tongue of calumnious malice or unscrupulous and causeless vindictiveness." Enraged that no jury heard his claim, Jonas went on to conflate the Declaration of Independence and the Constitution, insisting Whittlesey's action was "unconstitutional and not according to public law, justice, and equity, <u>nor shall a citizen of the United States be deprived of life, liberty, or property without due process of law.</u>"[15]

Whether to aid his friend Jonas, because he really thought there was a case, or because he hoped his political clout would get the claim approved, on 1 February 1856 Louisiana Senator Judah P. Benjamin, that body's only Jewish member, presented one of the many memorials to Congress that Jonas would draw up over the next quarter-century. On 20 February Senator Albert Gallatin Brown of Mississippi—who would be present along with Lewis Cass at Jonas's son's birth later that year—presented the further claim that the government owed Jonas bounty land for his military service (although he was a civilian contractor hired by the military) and two guns he had personally supplied, at which time he also introduced General Winfield Scott's "warm" commendation of his "gallant" service.[16] In the pro-Southern administration of Democrat Franklin Pierce, these Senators carried great influence (ironically, Pierce had defeated the Whig candidate, General Scott, in the presidential election of 1852). But Congress, presented with numerous claims of varying validity concerning Mexican losses, followed its usual procedure of referring both claims back to be determined by the courts and the auditors. For the rest of his life Jonas would periodically return to Washington, to argue his case without success (27). He presented his final memorial, with over eighty pieces of supporting evidence, in 1882, the year before he died.[17]

It is possible to view Jonas's involvement with the Washington Hebrew Congregation, of which Jonas became the most energetic member and first president when it was formally organized in December 1855, as an expression of both his attempt to claim his place in history—as was the trans-Mexican route—and of his desire to find a community and a place for his family to attend worship.[18] Jonas obtained the congregation's charter from Congress. As it was customary for synagogues to be incorporated by *state* legislatures (which enabled them to own property, collect money, sue or be sued, etc.), Washington's Jews enjoyed the only federal charter in the nation. Jonas's friend Senator Cass introduced the measure, and Jonas was rewarded for his efforts by election as the president of the congregation. He copied the charter with his own hand and gave it to the congregation.[19]

At the same time, Jonas also became the American Jewish community's major defender in the capital. In March 1854, shortly before he moved to Washington, Jonas had joined with other New York Jews to protest a treaty the Pierce administration had signed with Switzerland. Only seven of twenty-four cantons allowed Jews full citizenship: the rest either imposed disabilities or (in seven cases) did not even allow them to settle there. Whereas Daniel Webster, Secretary of State during the previous administration of the Whig party's Millard Fillmore, had assured America's Jews that "this government will not ratify a treaty with the Swiss confederacy which makes any discrimination against citizens of the United States of Jewish persuasion," the actual treaty the Democrats under Pierce agreed to had an important qualifier: "where such admission and treatment shall not conflict with the constitutional or local provisions, as well federal as cantonal, of the contracting parties."[20]

Foiled by Pierce, in October 1857 leading Jews met in Washington with his successor, Democrat James Buchanan, and again put their case. Buchanan promised to remove the discriminatory provision, but failed to follow through. At this juncture Jonas became the point man for the American Jewish community: not only was he the leader of Washington's Jewish congregation, but he also was a personal friend of Secretary of State Lewis Cass, after whom, as noted above, he named one of his sons. Hoping to convince Cass that Jews were both a major lobby and a source of significant commercial prosperity for both nations if Switzerland would change its policies, and that thousands of Jews would probably settle in Switzerland if given equal rights, Jonas stated that there were about 400,000 Jews in the United States "on average" equal in worth to "the wealthiest Christian citizens." These latter two assertions were gross overstatements: there were probably about 150,000 to 200,000 Jews in the nation most of whom had recently arrived from Germany and were anything but wealthy. Jonas was clearly thinking of—and extrapolating from—Sephardic Jews he knew from B'nai Jeshurun and Shearith Israel rather than those he represented in Washington.[21]

But Cass explained that the United States government could not compel the cantons to grant the Jews citizenship. The Swiss had, in fact, argued that the situation was similar to states rights in the United States, a position the Buchanan administration supported when it came to the critical slavery issue. Jonas pleaded in vain that "the public," presumably the American Jewish public, "were much dissatisfied with this delay."[22] Despite the fact that many American Jews, especially prominent New York Jews, were firm supporters of the Democratic Party and the Buchanan administration—Uriah Levy had successfully called on leading Democrats to back up his ability to command a ship when he was reinstated as a captain in 1857—neither Buchanan nor Cass pushed the issue. They had more important things on their minds: the fiasco of "Bleeding Kansas," the Dred Scott decision, and their efforts to acquire Cuba to placate the slave states.[23]

Jonas, upon its formation in 1859, became the Washington delegate on the Board of Delegates of American Israelites, the first effort made by American Jews to form a lobby that spoke for the nation's entire Jewish community. On its behalf he also communicated with French Jews who, at the same time, were trying to create a worldwide Jewish alliance and also to convince Switzerland to repeal its discriminatory legislation. But although Jonas received letters from Theodore Fay, the American consul in Switzerland, stating that the Jews were making progress and receiving more and more favorable hearings, the treaty remained in place and it was not until 1874 that Jews received equal rights.[24]

Jonas took up other Jewish causes while in Washington. In 1859 he tried to persuade Mayor James G. Barrett to allow Jews to work on Sundays, only to receive the reply that "that day has become consecrated over the civilized world for more than eighteen hundred years, and the best interests of morality and of humanity require that it should be kept 'holy' according to sacred injunction."[25] The same year Jonas asked Isaac Leeser, leader of the nation's Orthodox Jewish community and editor of the *Occident*, its primary organ, to find a way for a Jewish rabbi to take his turn with clergy of other denominations opening sessions of Congress with prayer.[26] When Indiana's Schuyler Colfax, Chairman of the House Committee on the District of Columbia, responded that they were unaware of any Jewish rabbi in Washington, DC, Jonas agreed that his congregation's *hazzan*—the wealthy merchant Solomon Landsburg—did not speak English well enough to handle the job. Because Colfax promised that Congress would request a rabbi to lead their prayers the following year, Jonas pleaded with Leeser to ask for nationwide contributions so the congregation could afford to hire a bilingual rabbi. Leeser responded that it would help if the Jews of Washington would first build a synagogue—to show their commitment and give the Jewish community in the capital a visible presence. Jonas himself encouraged the Jewish community in a speech urging his congregation to "yield more to your religion than you do."[27]

When Congress convened in 1860 Jonas tried again, this time approaching the Board of Delegates, and appealed to synagogues throughout the nation to contribute $10 or $20 a year toward raising the $2000 needed to pay a rabbi fluent in English and German (necessary for most of the congregation's members). He told the Board that this would be "a credit to our holy religion" and the means of attracting "particularly those [congregations] who have not joined the delegation." An added benefit, Jonas continued, would be that the fund-raising drive for the rabbi might be "the means of uniting the present dissidents with you," since the Board represented only Orthodox congregations and Leeser and other leaders were divided over whether the Board should become an authoritative body for American Jews, much as existed in European countries. Jonas was trying to use the *Occident*, the Board, and the American Jewish community to build a synagogue for his small congregation.[28] In 1863, thanks to about $12,000 in donations, Jonas's dream materialized, and a permanent synagogue opened in Washington— although he was by then living in Wilmington, North Carolina.[29]

In February 1860 Colfax did ask Jonas for a rabbi, but, as none was available in Washington, Jonas attempted to find one elsewhere. David Einhorn in Baltimore proved unacceptable because of his accent (his strong anti-slavery stance may have also been a reason), so Jonas put out the call to a number of northern rabbis. Morris Raphall of New York was the first to accept the invitation, and was the first Jew ever to open a day's session of Congress with a prayer, two days later.[30] Jonas informed Sir Moses Montefiore, the leader of the British Jewish community, of the event. Montefiore responded with joy and took the liberty of conveying this news to the British public: "[I]t gave me extreme satisfaction to learn from your letter that the cause of religious toleration has made such progress that it leaves scarcely anything to be asked for, and has led to a triumphant recognition of our faith in the hall of so illustrious an assembly as the Congress." At this time, Britain's Jews were trying to gain the right for Jews to sit in Parliament.[31]

While his personal and community causes were pending, Jonas supported himself in Washington, as one of his advertisements proclaimed, as "an importer and dealer in wines, liquor, sugars, and fine groceries."[32] He became involved in at least two other projects in the capital that fell through. In 1856, Congress tabled his suggestion that the government appoint schoolmasters to provide an education for boys who wanted to join the navy so they could receive appointments as midshipmen. This sounds like an idea his brother Uriah—who had taken special care to educate midshipmen in seamanship on his voyages—may have suggested. The same year, Jonas's plan to incorporate a company called Benzole to supply gas to light the city streets also went nowhere.[33]

But Jonas's final request to the Board of Delegates may suggest what he had in mind all along: by trying to solidify his ties with both the Jewish administration and the Democratic party he hoped to advance his commercial interests in Mexico. In March 1860, Jonas solicited the Board of Delegates and asked them to endorse his appointment as the United States consul in Acapulco, Mexico, which would have been the closest major city to Huatulco, his projected Pacific port for the mail service, adding that he would also accept "any other foreign post of honor."[34] Hoping the Board would be proud to have a Jew in this position and also that they would take this opportunity to reward him for his efforts on their behalf, Jonas was disappointed. The Board's reply, although negative, was the essence of tact and revealed genuine appreciation and friendship. They began by noting their "warm feelings…out of regard of the interest you at all times so warmly evince in matters appertaining to the welfare and progress of the community." However, they went on, "our official existence debars us from the satisfaction we should derive from serving you. Mingling in politics is forbidden to the Board by its constitution. Even so meritorious a case as yours might compromise its very existence." Nevertheless, they wished him luck in obtaining support through other channels, hoped that he would obtain the position, and thereby "gladden those [hearts] of [his] numerous friends and well wishers."[35]

Politics was indeed an issue. Given Jonas's close contacts with the Buchanan administration, and his friendship with Cass, Judah P. Benjamin, and Albert Gallatin Brown of Mississippi, Jonas was identified with the administration and its pro-Southern policies. In fact, in 1860 the *New York Times* spread the rumor that Jonas was planning a campaign to run with Benjamin for President on the Democratic ticket. Although false, the statement would not have been printed if Jonas's Southern connections did not lend it some plausibility. New York Jews did organize a political club—the German Hebrew Democrats—to support Democratic candidates that year, which was much to Leeser's consternation as he feared that such partisanship would compromise the Jews' reputation in the severely divided nation. These New York Jews were typical of the city's commercial elite, in that they made much of their money trading southern cotton for English manufactures. New York City was adamantly pro-Southern. It was the scene of the nation's bloodiest anti-draft riots in 1863, and Mayor Fernando Wood actually tried to have the city secede and become a Confederate state.[36]

Jonas continued to work for the Board of Delegates even after they refused to endorse him for the consulate. In December 1860 he wrote to Cass's successor, Jeremiah Black, urging him to join with Great Britain in protesting the mistreatment of Jews by the Turks at Damascus, hoping Black could find the time, "concerned as he [was] with the difficult state of preserving the union." Black instructed the United States consul at Constantinople to protest, but clearly was too preoccupied with the disintegrating republic to do anything more.[37]

After failing to obtain his Mexican claim, despite the friendships he had carefully cultivated within the Buchanan administration, Jonas moved to Baltimore in early April 1861. He had no intention of helping to suppress "the revolution with the South," as he called it (27). After all, his dearest relative—his brother Morton—had been a businessman in New Orleans until his death in the previous year, and Morton's family still lived in the city.[38] Jonas briefly commanded the Baltimore City Marine Guard, until Union troops arrived at Fort McHenry, before he set off again for Mexico to continue his business. The Union blockade, though, prevented him from proceeding past Wilmington, North Carolina, which, fortunately for him, remained unconquered and undamaged until late February 1865. In Wilmington he bought a farm, and also set up a shop during the war. His accounts with the Union troops who briefly occupied the city reveal that he sold them pens, pencils, stationery, oil, locks, and leather totaling $453.05. Once again, Jonas thought the government was cheating him. He protested that he was forced to sell his goods at New York prices although goods in the South were far cheaper. Nevertheless, the fact that Jonas left the Union and somehow managed to be stranded in the South raised eyebrows. In 1874, in fact, New Jersey's Senator Frelinghuysen objected to Jonas's Mexican claim on the grounds he had supported the South in the Civil War, which Jonas denied although he admitted "he was absent in the South at that time." In any event, the Mexican government had allocated the money to the United States and he had incurred his damages well before the war.[39]

Just as Mexico was Jonas's main venture in the 1840s and Jewish affairs were his interest in the 1850s, in the years after the Civil War he turned his energies toward acquiring Monticello for his family, wishing to manage it himself—or at least to make as much of a profit from it as he could. His brother Uriah had died in 1862, and his estate was a mess. Six of the eight executors were unwilling to fulfill their duties, which left the task to Jonas and his and Uriah's mutual nephew Asahel Levy, whom Uriah had treated as the son he never had. The estate was not the only controversial item in the will. For starters, Uriah had also hoped to become the first Jew in human history to build a statue to himself, and had insisted that this statue be at least life-sized and cost at least $6000. Just two years before Uriah's intention, the nation's Jews had debated at length—and had even called upon Europe's leading rabbis for help—over whether New Orleans Jews could build a statue to honor philanthropist Judah Touro. In the end, the decision was that they could not, as the statue would indeed constitute a graven image. Although Uriah's statue was never built, his impressive naval monument is next to Jonas's tomb.[40]

Uriah had divided his New York real estate principally between his twenty-seven-year-old wife Virginia (sale value $66,048.26)— who was his sister's daughter and whom he married in 1850 when she was 15 and he was 58! —and his nephew Asahel (sale value $239,194.20).[41] He then willed that Monticello should become a school where the orphaned boys of naval officers would be taught agriculture, with the state of Virginia being given right of first refusal (followed by the state of New York and Congregation Shearith Israel) to take it over. Uriah may have been hoping that the boys would follow in his own footsteps, and turn from the sea to agriculture, as he had perforce done, dabbling in manual labor as a gentleman farmer at Monticello during the years he was deprived of a command at sea—that is, for over thirty years during most of the early 1820s to the late 1850s. But agriculture was only Uriah Levy's hobby; he was also at this time becoming the richest Jew in New York City thanks to his real estate investments, according to Moses Beach's account of the wealthiest people in the city, and furthermore, officers generally had sufficient funds that their sons would not have to descend to manual labor.[42]

When the state of Virginia did not move to take over Monticello, Jonas and his lawyer on the scene, former Virginia Judge William Robertson, petitioned the courts in 1868 on behalf of Uriah's heirs— forty-nine brothers, sisters, nieces, nephews and other relatives—to obtain the estate. But standing in their way now were two Virginias: the state, which took a sudden interest in the property, and Uriah's widow, who had remarried William Rée in 1865 and needed money. Virginia's new husband had been "arrested for various crime," and the couple was bankrupt, having managed to go through, in less than three years, all the money Uriah had left Virginia in his will. Jonas tried to annul her claim (which, like her New York dower, would equal approximately a fifth of the estate) on the grounds that an uncle and niece could not be legally married in the state of Virginia, but his attempt fell through as the Old Dominion recognized marriages performed in other states, such as New York. Jonas thus had to include the Reés among the family heirs, but, of course, his earlier efforts to exclude them ended all friendly discourse.[43] Jonas also fell out with and sued Asahel Levy, who had cut down and sold two hundred acres of Monticello's timber and pocketed the profits. To make matters even more complicated, various heirs had sold off their shares, and others refused to join Jonas's consortium.[44]

Jonas was making plans to sell Monticello as early as 1868, although its title was still uncertain until 1873 when the family finally won its suit. All the while, he had as much trouble with the hands-on management of Monticello itself as he did with its legal entanglements. He repeatedly nagged George Carr, appointed by the court to oversee the grounds in the interim, complaining that the actual groundskeeper, one Wheeler, had permitted the place to become "dilapidated" by allowing "ruthless visitors to carry off pieces of the house for consideration of money to himself." Even though there is no record that he visited Monticello, he claimed that "Every day of my life, my attention is called to the ruin he has made of it," Jonas wrote Robertson, making it his mission "to save it from destruction." But Wheeler was still on the job when Jonas sold out to his son in 1876. Carr, too, tried to resign in 1873, although Judge Robertson persuaded him to stay on and Jonas allowed him to do so.[45]

Jonas's interest in Monticello seems to have been pecuniary rather than patriotic. When advertisements were placed for Monticello and some potential buyers expressed interest, Jonas told Carr that he would not sell for less than $200 per acre, and insisted that 91 acres his brother had acquired, in addition to Jefferson's original 218, be included as well, thereby making the total acreage about 300 and thus raising his asking price to about $60,000. (In contrast to Jonas's hopes, the final price Jefferson Monroe Levy paid was $10,500). In a burst of sentimentality Jonas refused to sell, "as our ever-lamented mother," whom he saw only twice in his life after the age of sixteen, "is buried on that sacred mountain." (In fact, her grave is the only remaining sign the Levys ever owned the place.) Finally, in 1873 he called off the sale, having "very particular motives why the property should not be sold."[46]

These motives Jonas expressed in a memorial, which he persuaded Pennsylvania Congressman Robert Milton Speer to present to the national legislature. He hoped the federal government would buy the property on "fair and suitable terms" as a memorial to Jefferson for the patriotic if inaccurate reason that the property "where that valuable instrument the Declaration of the Independence [*sic*] of the

United States was written and that sacred spot where the ashes and the bronze statue of Jefferson [would be housed] . . . should be held by the government." Jonas planned to bring the bronze statue to Monticello, and, about the same time, petitioned Congress for the return of the Jefferson statue which his brother had donated in 1834 on the grounds that Congress had not formally accepted it and that it remained on the White House lawn rather than on display, as Uriah intended, inside the Capitol. The Committee on Public Buildings and Grounds responded that while "coldly greeted by some of the representatives," the statue "was at one time or another accepted by each house of Congress."[47]

Neither of Jonas's schemes worked out. The only buyer for Monticello turned out to be Jonas's own son, Jefferson Monroe Levy, who lovingly restored it over the years. The statue Uriah had presented to the government remained in Washington, but at least Jonas's petition persuaded Congress to move it into the Rotunda of the Capitol, where it remains today. And while Jonas was hoping not only to honor Jefferson but to enrich himself, what he requested of Congress has ultimately become the happy fate of Jefferson's home: "Monticello can never be purchased from the heirs for any purpose other than for some Institution to be dedicated to the memory of its founder."[48]

Aside from the Monticello dealings, Jonas's post-war activities suggest that despite his complaints of financial losses he still had plenty of money. He moved four times in New York City, always to upper-class addresses, and had three consecutive offices on Wall and Fulton Streets and Broadway where he bought and sold real estate and served as "Sole Agent of the Ward Burton Breech-Loading Rifle and Carbine."[49] A farm he owned in Bedford, Westchester County, did not attract him; he lived there for only five months in 1870 (27).

Jonas concluded his autobiography by noting that his son Mitchell Cass opened a printing office in 1876 on Franklin Street—the very street where he had left his mother over fifty years before. He had at last obtained a place, through his son, on a street named for the Founding Father whose rise from rags to riches (as a printer, no less) most resembled his own. Finally, he had his own and his wife's portraits painted in January 1877, noting they were executed by Ramon D. Eldriaga, "a Spanish artist from Rome." That he hired a prestigious artist to take his likeness at the age of three score and ten may have been a final effort to place a seal of accomplishment on his life (27).[50]

Jonas's sons were actually his true accomplishments. Although a successful printer, Mitchell was the least noteworthy. Jefferson Monroe Levy graduated from New York law school, and made a fortune in the New York real estate market in his early twenties. In 1876 he purchased his parents' shares of Monticello, and, by 1883, became its sole proprietor and, later, a Congressman from New York. Louis Napoleon Levy, another successful attorney, was President of Shearith Israel from 1893 until his death in 1921. They are both buried near their parents' tomb, although Congressman Levy's plain, flat stone is conspicuously modest next to those of his parents and his uncle Uriah.[51]

Jonas left these last words in his autobiography for his children: "Up to present date nothing of note occurred except heavy snow storm and cold weather" —a fitting ending to a life filled with much adventure but little peace and happiness (27). To the last, Jonas seemed to be a restless, dissatisfied man: he could not stay in the same place even when he could afford it, and was unquiet even in the peaceful Westchester town where Chief Justice John Jay's descendants escaped from the hubbub of the city (the Jays lived there from 1798 until 1953). Throughout his life he continued to build the "castles in the air" he dreamed of the night before he went to sea. Monticello was about as close to a castle in the air as America offered, and the New York real estate market, in which he invested late in life, undoubtedly provided at least a pale reflection of the excitement of his early maritime adventures. In fact, Jonas's participation in the Washington Hebrew Congregation could be regarded as a similar effort to make his mark, and indeed, his work with the Board of Delegates and his success in obtaining a rabbi to speak for Congress led to the growth of the congregation and helped in the erection of its synagogue. But in his autobiography, Jonas always dwelled on his substantial financial losses—never on the fact that he always seemed to land on his feet or have a substantial sum in reserve. But Jonas did find, from the 1840s on, two families, Morton's and his own, on which he could rely for companionship and support. It is fitting that the final personal recorded reference to Jonas Levy appeared in the records of Shearith

Israel and confirmed his family ties: on 15 January 1879, at 108 E. 40 Street—the house he had bought in 1869—his daughter Isabella married Marcus, son of Joseph and Libby (née Rothschild) Rittenberg of Sumter, South Carolina (27).[52]

What does Jonas Levy's story tell us about American Jewry in the nineteenth century? Similar to Jews before him in the colonial and revolutionary periods, Jonas was among those Jews who were at the forefront of American commerce and expansion, as were his brothers Uriah the naval captain, and Louis the entrepreneur in New Orleans, the West Indies, and Mexico. Other Levys could be found as well in the West Indies, Maryland, and Pennsylvania—they were a typical Jewish merchant clan that did not hesitate to disperse their family in order to pursue the main chance. Jonas's pursuit of wealth and status, and his use of powerful personal connections to further his career, brought out the antisemitism of some of his contemporaries—for example, the Mexican Catholics and the (then) Republican *The New York Times*—but at the same time attested to his acceptance by some of the leading figures in America and the world: Senators Benjamin, Cass, and Brown, Peruvian President de Orbegoso, General Winfield Scott, and leading members of the Jewish community in France, Britain, and the United States.

Like many American Jews of his era, it was difficult for Jonas to maintain an ongoing interest in practicing his religion. Before he moved to Washington his sole connections with the Jewish religious community of New York seem to have been through his wedding in 1848 and his brief service in 1853 and 1854 as one of thirty-nine initial directors for the school opened by his father-in-law's congregation B'nai Jeshurun, the first Hebrew school in New York City.[53] After he settled in New York after the Civil War, he did not take any recorded interest in either B'nai Jeshurun or Shearith Israel, where his daughter was married and which his brother Uriah and his widow Virginia supported.[54]

But when Jonas Levy got his dander up, even if he did have a personal agenda, he stood up as strongly for the rights of Jews throughout the world as he did for his own personal interests. Isaac Leeser acknowledged that no one helped the Washington Hebrew Congregation acquire a rabbi, a synagogue, and national attention and support more than Jonas Levy.[55] Despite his absorption with his maritime and international enterprises, Jonas should be remembered among those who significantly furthered the cause of American Jewry. In the mid-nineteenth century he helped his community move beyond formal political and civil rights toward the full acceptance of Jews as socially equal citizens of the United States who played an important role on both the national and international stage.

Beyond the Parochial Image of Southern Jewry: Studies in National and International Leadership and Interactive Mechanisms

Mark K. Bauman

It is most fitting to celebrate the sixtieth anniversary of the American Jewish Archives, *The American Jewish Archives Journal*, and the tenth anniversary of Gary P. Zola's directorate.[1] Like his mentor, Jacob Rader Marcus, Zola frequently uses individual lives to explicate social and religious history. This article follows that lead in order to challenge assumptions apparent in the historiography of the last thirty-five years concerning southern Jewish distinctiveness, and to introduce alternative ways to view southern and American Jewish history.

The Debate in Historiography

The prevailing paradigm concerning the relatively small number of Jews who settled in the South has been that they found greater acceptance in that region than they found elsewhere. Furthermore the Jews of the South adapted the mores and lifestyle of the area in order to cement that acceptance, and, as they became more deeply rooted in the region, their southern identity and orientation subsumed their Jewish background. Southern Jews fought duels, owned slaves, and participated in the slave trade, fervently supported the Confederacy, and celebrated the Lost Cause after the Civil War. Reform congregations were disproportionately represented in the South, and adherence to Classical Reform was both more widespread and sustained than it was elsewhere. Thus, according to the southern distinctiveness school, by the late nineteenth century southern Jews had diverged dramatically from the national Jewish norm, and lived in isolation from Jews and Jewish experiences in the North. In essence, forces toward acculturation and assimilation are said to have fostered this divergence from the experiences of northern Jews, and, because of this, Jews in the South can best be described as provincial cousins of their northern brethren, with whom they were often at odds over issues as divergent as theology, Zionism, and the African American struggle for civil rights. As Melvin I. Urofsky maintains, Jews in the south were impacted by the region far more than they impacted it.[2]

People are, of course, influenced by where they live. The Jews in the South were no exception to this, and many of the contentions of this southern distinctiveness school of historiography are correct. Yet, other historians began to question key contentions of the school during the early 1990s. Lee Shai Weissbach began his pioneering work on Jews in small towns with studies in Kentucky, which revealed little difference between these towns and similar communities in the rest of the country. I followed with a controversial monograph in which I argued that regional distinctiveness has been exaggerated. Expanding on Weissbach, I stressed that the impact of local environments—small towns, port cities, commercial versus industrial centers, and the size of Jewish communities—far exceeded regional influence. When comparing communities with like characteristics, similarities far outweigh differences.[3]

The debate has raged unabated, although, frequently— as I originally argued— it seems to be based more on emphasis than on deep seated differences.[4] Nonetheless, I would contend that practitioners of the distinctiveness school assert many points without sufficient evidence or logic to support their claims. For example, were Jews accepted in the South more than they were elsewhere? Historians of western Jewry make the same claim for the West, and both sets of historians use extensive office-holding as evidence of acceptance although no actual comparative study has appeared showing that this criterion provides any conclusive information.[5] Also, racism against African Americans in the South shielded Jews from antisemitism, but prejudice against Hispanics and Asians could have had the same effect in the West. If the South was such a genial environment for Jews, why do practitioners of the distinctiveness school describe Jews as almost constantly responding to antisemitism? And, if Jews were so bent on conformity, why were their behavioral responses to antisemitism so often geared to the maintenance of Jewish distinctiveness? If the price of acceptance was conformity to southern mores and the blurring if not obliteration of Jewish culture, does this not imply the existence of antisemitism? Jews in the South, as opposed to the general society, opposed prohibition, prayer, and the reading of *The Merchant of Venice* in the public schools, and supported the passage of the Nineteenth Amendment granting women the right to vote. Although a mini-debate rages, Jews also tended to treat African Americans more humanely and reacted differently to the civil rights movement than did virtually any other group of European descent in the region. Still, fears of violence, of loss of business, and of the loss of the precarious acceptance of their community affected Jews in the South.

Consequently, those supportive of blacks civil rights tended to espouse different means to reach these goals than did Jewish integrationists elsewhere. Nonetheless, a very high percentage of white Christians openly and fervently supported segregation and massive resistance. This was clearly not the case among southern Jews. The one or two rabbis (notably Benjamin Schultz) who defended segregation were largely ostracized by other rabbis in the South. In contrast, Schultz would have fit in and been accepted among Southern Baptists, Methodists, and Presbyterians. Jews simply did not conform so neatly to the portrait drawn by distinctiveness school historians.

This article expands the revisionist critique of distinctiveness school assumptions. It argues that, contrary to the latter, Jews in the South did not live in isolation from national and international Jewish events. Rather, many actively participated in and substantially contributed to national and international affairs. Anything but provincials, they migrated from place to place and were strongly linked by ties of family, business, religious institutions, and ethnic identity. A discussion of the backgrounds, actions, and beliefs of two such individuals also brings to light the types of new findings that can be discerned when one searches beyond New York/Philadelphia leadership.[6]

The individuals discussed in this paper are not necessarily typical or representative, although numerous others played similar roles. Nonetheless, the institutions these people nurtured, the communications and interactive mechanisms they employed, and their explication of multiple Jewish identities all reflect broad patterns that transcend individual biographies.

Rosanna Dyer Osterman (1809–1865) of Baltimore and Galveston[7]

The John Dyer family emigrated from the Germanic states to Baltimore in 1812. According to local historians, the Dyers' Baltimore butcher shop became the first meat- packing house in the United States. The major organizer and first president of Baltimore Hebrew Congregation, John Dyer and his family were integrally involved in and comfortable with this traditional congregation. They did not choose to join Har Sinai Verein— the first long-term congregation in America begun as a Reform body— when Rabbi Abraham Rice's insistence on tradition and attacks on ritual laxity resulted in a split. Instead, Dyer's son Leon facilitated the building of the Lloyd Street synagogue of Baltimore Hebrew Congregation, and served seven years as its president—years which included the 1842 Har Sinai Verein schism. (Ironically, Leon Dyer later planted the seeds of Reform in California, when he settled in San Francisco and helped found Congregation Emanu El, the first synagogue on the west coast.) Leon Dyer worked for his father in the family business, but also pursued impressive military and political careers. As acting mayor of Baltimore, for example, he quelled bread riots. He also served as a major on General Winfield Scott's staff in Florida during the Seminole Wars and as his quartermaster-general in the Mexican War, which position he also held for the state of Louisiana. Leon Dyer later operated a meat-packing house in New Orleans as a branch of his father's Baltimore firm, and volunteered, as well, to serve as a major in Texas's struggle for independence. Leon

Dyer crowned his many achievements with an appointment as special envoy to Germany from President Martin Van Buren.

Another of John Dyer's sons, Isadore, fostered Reform in Galveston, Texas, where he had resided since 1840. In 1856, on Yom Kippur, Galveston's small Jewish community met for their first of many religious services in a room designated for the purpose in Isadore Dyer's home. A merchant who retired in 1861, he presided over the Union Marine and Life Insurance Company during the post-bellum period, joined the boards of the National Bank of Texas and the Galveston Wharf Company, and served as a grandmaster of the Odd Fellows in addition to winning election to the county commission.[8]

The case of the Dyer family illustrates how the internal migration of people transported ideas and institutions throughout the country. Jews deeply involved in congregational and general Jewish communal affairs in east coast cities, including Baltimore and Charleston, moved ever westward seeking economic opportunity. As was typical of so many other immigrant and migrant groups, they sought to transplant cultural patterns and institutions rather than break from their roots.[9] Thus, they built congregations and other institutions important for religious continuity in virtually every town and city in which they settled. Yet, such reconstruction did not necessarily mean replication. The Dyers, stalwarts of traditionalism in Baltimore, mixed orthodoxy with reform as necessity dictated and choice allowed when they ventured to new sites of Jewish settlement.

The experiences and actions of John Dyer's daughter Rosanna reinforce and expand the themes apparent in her brothers' lives. Born in Bayreuth, Bavaria, she immigrated with her parents as a young child and, in 1835, married Joseph Osterman (1796–1862), a native of Amsterdam, Holland, and a charter member of Baltimore Hebrew Congregation. Multiple factors motivated the Osterman's move to Galveston in the Republic of Texas in 1838. Physicians suggested the change for reasons of Rosanna's health, but Joseph's jewelry and diamond-cutting business had, also, recently failed. Leon Dyer, stationed in Texas with the military, acted as catalyst. He recommended the small village for its commercial possibilities and also supplied his brother in-law with funding for merchandise. Joseph soon arrived, and set up a tent on the Galveston wharf where he began to sell his wares.

Rosanna joined him shortly thereafter, and the couple, who purchased land in the city at the initial public offering, achieved phenomenal success. From their retail store stocked with goods from Europe, the Caribbean, and elsewhere in America, Joseph and Rosanna sent out mule pack trains loaded with merchandise and traded extensively with Native Americans. Joseph Osterman Dyer explains that his uncle was among the first to offer credit to farmers based on future crops, and also to export cotton to Holland, from whence he imported wine. Joseph Osterman started a banking business by offering interest on deposits of money and valuables and, in addition, financed post roads and underwrote the first ferry to Virginia Point.

When Joseph died in 1862 Rosanna took over the reins of the business. Her position as the head of the company acted as a culminating point of the activities she had pursued throughout her married life. She, too, had acted as a city booster. Concerned with city beautification, she had brought palm, olive, rubber, banana, and almond trees, in addition to coffee, tea, and oleander from Jamaica on the schooner her husband used to import rum and sugar. She developed meat biscuits— important as a food for western travelers— and also, possibly, condensed milk which she allegedly created while experimenting as a cook. Gail Borden, Jr., a friend who, as a customs official, had met Joseph at the wharf, developed the recipes commercially with partial funding from the Ostermans. Rosanna used Peruvian bark, imported from South America by Joseph, to nurse yellow fever sufferers during the epidemic of 1853. During the Civil War she opened her house as a hospital for soldiers from both sides who were wounded in the Battle of Galveston. Although she had freed her slaves (several of whom remained in her employ) prior to the war, she, nonetheless, used her contact with the wounded Union soldiers to spy for the Confederacy. The information she transmitted as a courier to Confederate forces in Houston led to the temporary re-taking of the city on New Years day, 1863.[10]

Along with her civic and altruistic endeavors, Rosanna Dyer Osterman became deeply involved in Jewish affairs. When brother Isadore's six year old son died in 1852, she confronted Galveston's Jews with the need for a cemetery. The Jewish community thereupon successfully petitioned the city government to allocate a section of the municipal cemetery for that purpose, which was purchased with funds supplied by Isadore. During Federal occupation during the war, business declined and most Jews fled the city. As commerce thrived at the war's end, Rosanna, who had remained in Galveston, welcomed and assisted newly arriving Jews who hailed originally from Germany, Alsace, Russia, and Poland.[11]

At her death by drowning after the explosion of the Mississippi steamboat J. W. Carter in 1866, Rosanna Dyer Osterman, whose only child had died at age five, left a quarter of a million dollars to secular and Jewish charities. She recognized, as did other women, that, although she could not vote, hold office, or participate as an equal in Jewish communal activities, money could drive men to follow a female's will. In this case, similar to her practice during her life, she placed provisions in her will forcing people to create and build Jewish institutions as conditions to receive the bequests. She allocated $5,000 to Galveston and $2,500 to Houston to build synagogues, $1,000 each to incorporate Hebrew benevolent societies, and $1,000 each to establish school funds for poor Jewish children. Both synagogues, constructed of brick, had to have been one third completed and approved by her executors before the money, with interest, would be allocated. Eighteen months after her death, from the impetus that she had given Jewish Galvestonians formally organized B'nai Israel as their synagogue and almost immediately purchased a plot for a sanctuary. Rosanna's stipulation that money would be allocated only to the first benevolent society "organized and incorporated" in Galveston squared off the community's men against its women, and the men quickly established a benevolent society within only three months of her death.[12]

Other bequests went to the Jewish Foster Home of Philadelphia, to the "Hebrew Talmud Yelodim School" in Cincinnati as well as to similar schools in New York and Philadelphia, to Jewish hospitals in Cincinnati, New Orleans, and New York, and to men's and women's Hebrew benevolent societies in New Orleans. Money granted to the Ladies Hebrew Benevolent Society of Philadelphia listed Rebecca Gratz specifically as secretary, an indication of the national communications network employed by women. The Osterman Building ultimately became the Widow's and Orphan's Home, and fifty shares of Galveston City Wharf stock was contributed to "the support of indigent Israelites, if any there be; if not, to any other denominations, residing in Galveston." Galveston's secular charities received numerous other donations.

Osterman's identity as a Jew included ethnic as well as religious aspects, and her knowledge of activities extended beyond the United States. She gave $1,000 to the "'North American Relief Society' for indigent Jews of Jerusalem, Palestine, of the city and state of New York, Sir Moses Montefiore of London, their agent."

The Jewish cemeteries in Galveston and New Orleans, both of which received allocations, were close to her heart because family members were interred in each, and she requested that she be buried in the family plot in the "Portuguese cemetery if not in violation of our holy religion." In Galveston, the money was to be used to extend the current plot—something she preferred to the purchase of a second cemetery. Although it is impossible to determine why she stipulated the latter, her desire to be buried in the New Orleans cemetery according to traditional practices speaks to her beliefs. She had been forced to compromise in the borderlands environment that was Jewish Galveston. Accepting membership and participation in a Reform congregation in life, in death she sought orthodoxy.

Osterman's will shares remarkable similarities to that of America's first great Jewish philanthropist, Judah Touro, who preceded her in death by fourteen years.[13] Although Touro's bequest doubled that of Osterman and was allocated to more Jewish institutions, both gave to the Hebrew Foreign Mission Society of New Orleans, and, using the same wording, to the same Jewish schools in Philadelphia, New York, and Cincinnati. Their bequests to the Ladies Hebrew Benevolent Society of Philadelphia and to the indigent Jews in Jerusalem also contained identical wording.[14] Whether this was accidental or a conscious copying on Osterman's part is impossible to determine with certainty.[15] Yet her knowledge of Touro's will is highly likely. She had family contacts through her brother Abraham with New Orleans, and New Orleans served as a trade and transportation hub which she often visited. Both the Dyer/Osterman family and Touro associated with Nefutzoth Yehudah (Disbursed of Judah), the Portuguese congregation begun by Gershom Kursheedt, and both Rosanna Dyer Osterman and Judah Touro were buried in its cemetery. Touro died in 1854 and Osterman's will was composed prior to her husband's death in 1862.

What takes this conjecture beyond curiosity is the mixture between tradition and actual practice in the lives of these two prominent Jews. Judah Touro, the son of the Reverend Isaac Touro who had ministered to the colonial Newport, Rhode Island congregation, did not participate in organized Judaism as an adult before coming under the influence of traditionalist Gershom Kursheedt. This association exerted a dramatic impact on Judah Touro's benefactions and regular synagogue attendance. Rosanna Dyer Osterman, raised in a traditional household and a backbone of early Galveston Jewry, lived in a Reform environment as an adult, nurtured a mixture of Reform and traditional institutions in her will, and sought burial according to *halakhah*, or Jewish law. Theirs was an American Judaism in which individuals were influenced by their environment, and chose degrees of observance as they saw fit. Boundaries which could characterize religious affiliation, like those of region, remained blurred.

Lessons Learned

Rosanna Dyer Osterman exemplifies those Jewish women who became active in business, politics, and Jewish institution-building during the nineteenth century. As previously indicated the distinctiveness school of historiography describes Jews who, having sunk deep roots in the South, became provincial and isolated in relation to Jews elsewhere.[16] Rosanna Dyer Osterman's family history and actions challenge these notions. Joseph Osterman migrated from Holland to Baltimore; she and her family from the Germanic states to Baltimore. He conducted business with his native land and the Caribbean as well as in various locations within the United States. Joseph and Rosanna Dyer Osterman, like her siblings, moved from place to place within America with the ebb and flow of economic opportunity. Her awareness and association with Jews and Jewish institutions throughout America and in Palestine are obvious from her bequests. The Dyer/Osterman family thus illustrates an internal Jewish migration from key cities along the east coast across the country, and the impact of that migration on the spread of Jewish congregations and benevolent societies, and on reform, traditional modes of practice, and philanthropy. The family and business connections, the Jewish institutional ties, and the expressions of ethnic identity integral to the stories of Rosanna

Dyer Osterman and, as we will see, Leo N. Levi— the individuals highlighted in this article— served as critical mechanisms that unified Jews and Jewish communities and transcended state, region, and even country. Jews and Jewish communities moved and functioned along a transnational borderland that spanned the Atlantic and included the Caribbean. All of these are patterns common to American Jewish history before and after the nineteenth century.

The Dyer/Osterman saga also speaks to the role of Jews in the westward march of America. Jews facilitated this expansion by introducing merchandise from world markets, acting as agents for sales elsewhere in America and overseas, creating new products, moving from business to banking and then to the financing of infrastructure, and, finally, offering culture and assistance to their host communities.

The Dyer/Osterman story is more typical than unique. Harby,[17] Labatt,[18] and Hyams[19] family members went from Charleston, South Carolina to Louisiana, Texas, and California joining or forming congregations as they traveled. These names stand out more than others because these families had led Charleston's Reformed Society of Israelites. Albeit traditionalists in Baltimore, Dyers married Reform-minded Labatts and Labbatts married Hyams. All cooperated in congregational and benevolent activities as well as civic affairs. The cross-country movement of these people and the Jewish organizations they nurtured linked American Jewry through informal networks that functioned before, and later beside, national Jewish communal structures. It also acted effectively against regional identity, provincialism, and isolation.

Leo Napoleon Levi (1858–1904) of Galveston and New York

Much has been written concerning Leo Napoleon Levi,[20] so here I will only briefly summarize his life and instead concentrate on specific issues not fully explored previously. His father, Abraham, began peddling at age thirteen in his native Alsace before immigrating to New Orleans in 1846. Within two years Abraham worked his way up from laborer to butcher, to peddler, to an employee for a Mississippi merchant. He investigated prospects for a store in the newly incorporated Victoria, Texas, for the merchant, and, upon its establishment, worked there selling a variety of items. Abraham married into the merchant's family, and the partnership eventually became southwest Texas' largest emporium. When a fire destroyed the business during the Civil War, Abraham chose to spend the remaining war years in France. After the war, he unsuccessfully launched a business in Mexico before returning to Victoria, where he moved from the grocery business into banking. His enterprise grew into the largest chartered bank in the state and his wholesale grocery became the largest firm in Victoria. He also acquired 25,000 acres of land and extensive cattle interests. Abraham Levi presided over Victoria's B'nai B'rith Israel synagogue for over two decades and actively participated in civic affairs.

Thus, Leo Levi was born into an affluent family with a strong tradition of religious and civic activism. His older brother was trained to head the business empire, which freed him to practice law. At sixteen he matriculated at the University of Virginia, where he won awards as the author of a university magazine article, as a debater, and as the top student. Leo Levi received his law degree four years later. From Charlottesville, Levi moved to Galveston for a position, and eventual partnership, in a law firm. He also ran advertisements soliciting loan applications for the Texas Land and Loan Company.[21] In addition to his civic and professional activities, Levi was deeply involved in Jewish concerns. He presided over Congregation B'nai Israel (1887–1889), the synagogue instigated by Rosanna Dyer Osterman's bequest, where he brought Rabbi Henry Cohen to the pulpit. The two worked cooperatively on many projects. For example, besides immigrant relocation efforts, Levi influenced the creation of the American Jewish Historical Society of which Cohen became an active member and frequent contributor.[22] Joining the local B'nai B'rith lodge, Levi rose to the presidency of District Lodge No. 7, and finally to the presidency of the I.O.B.B (1900–1904). After election at the Chicago convention he moved to New York to better fulfill the responsibilities of the position.

As president of the international fraternal order Levi became deeply involved in protesting the Kishinev massacre of 1903. He collaborated with Simon Wolf, whose firm was on retainer by the Order and who served as his vice-president, lobbying with Secretary of State John Hay, President Theodore Roosevelt and other administration officials, writing and organizing the protest petition to Russian Tsar Nicholas II ultimately sent by the State Department (the Tsar refused to receive it), and aiding immigrants from Rumania and Russia.[23] (Future Zionist leader Louis Lipsky served as Levi's secretary.) Under Levi, B'nai B'rith lodges assisted the Rumanian Relief Committee (RRC; 1900), over which he served as first chairperson, placing immigrants where employment opportunities existed outside of the Northeast. In conjunction with the Baron de Hirsch Fund, Levi participated in the transformation of the RRC into the Immigrant Removal Office (1901) designed to disperse Jewish immigrants.[24] The I.O.B.B. was seemingly well-positioned to place immigrants through local lodges, although in practice the program achieved only marginal success. Levi, along with Cyrus L. Sulzberger and David M. Bressler, originally manager of the RRC and in 1903 of I.R.O, toured communities informing them about the philosophy behind the movement and fostering cooperation and enthusiasm. Levy believed in a Jewish peoplehood transcending differences and, unlike many other leaders, foresaw the intermingling of American Jews of central and eastern European origin.[25]

Thus far we have learned about a father who followed the almost mythical path of Jewish immigrant success and set the stage for an American generation of business people and professionals. Commitment to Jewish causes expanded from generation to generation, but other themes also loom large. One of these is mobility— social, economic, and also geographic. The father moved to and from France, Mexico, and Texas. The son uprooted himself from Texas to New York where he easily fit in with a national (read: New York and Philadelphia) Jewish elite which included Cyrus Sulzberger and Jacob Schiff. Moving from the outline of Leo N. Levi's career to an analysis of his ideas in critical areas will provide insight into the ways a Texan and southerner by birth transcended sectionalism.

As diplomatic as Levi tried to be, he never evaded controversy. This trait can be seen in his challenges to the Reform rabbinate as well as to contemporary Reform practices. His activities reflected contemporary interaction between laypeople and rabbis, as well as his sanguine perception of the latter and his relatively moderate view concerning Reform.

Levi used several communications mechanisms to drive home his messages. These included speeches to Jewish organizations such as the Union of American Hebrew Congregations (UAHC) and the

Central Conference of American Rabbis (CCAR) in addition to the I.O.B.B. His speeches, along with other writings, were often published in the Jewish press, especially *Menorah* and *The American Israelite.* His publications in the latter and presentations at conferences of the Reform organizations that Isaac M. Wise headed imply a longstanding relationship between the two. The Jewish media of the era served as personal organs of their editors, who were frequently rabbis. From the study of Leo N. Levi it becomes clear that the Jewish press also served as a tool for laymen to air their grievances and offer their positions on issues. This could involve confronting and exerting influence on rabbis.

Levi's second letter to *The American Israelite* (4 January 1878, 5–6), written at age twenty-one and launching his debate with parts of the Reform movement, concerned the spiritual side of Galveston's Jewish community. Levi indicated that Jews gave money to, but rarely attended synagogue, and that the rabbi was amply compensated but had few duties. The synagogue, a beautiful edifice, like the rabbi's salary, was designed to show off the stature of the community rather than commitment to Jewish practices.

In July 1887 the *Menorah* published "A Layman's Open Letter to the Rabbis," addressed to "Reverend Sirs," in which Levi blamed Reform Judaism and the rabbis for the chaotic state of Judaism. Levi avers that he had been taught that Judaism was a religion based on specific doctrines, practices, and ceremonies, but that specific ceremonies and practices reflected adaptation to time and circumstance and were thus open to interpretation and change. Yet, each of the three hundred rabbis in America seemed to have an equal number of opinions defining what was essential, or peripheral, to Judaism. Compounding the problem, rabbis did not seem to believe what they taught. Many of these hypocrites were "rabbis for revenue only" and preached whatever they thought the congregants wanted to hear including denunciations of Judaism. Lectures on contemporary issues had replaced sermons advocating doctrine. Levi might define Jews as a racial group, but many rabbis rejected that notion in favor of a religious identity. Levi asked whether Reform would preserve Judaism by eliminating "trivial forms and ceremonies," or did it amount to "a revolution which if allowed to ripen will separate the Jews in America from Judaism and make them easy prey for other denominations?" Levi demanded a clear definition of Judaism that he hoped to obtain through responses to a list of thirty questions which he provided.[26]

Levi's article generated comments from Jewish periodicals throughout the country, as well as letters to the editor in that press from numerous rabbis. Levi responded with disdain to the rabbis. He took as his venue the UAHC council meeting in New Orleans in December 1894, where he delivered an address titled: "Judaism in America from the Standpoint of a Layman." Levy had been invited to give the presentation by Julius Freiberg, president of the executive board and a resident of Cincinnati since his emigration from Germany in 1847. Freiberg had participated in the call to establish the UAHC, gave the welcome address at the conference that created it, and presided over the UAHC from 1889 to 1903. He also acted as vice president of the board of governors of Hebrew Union College from its inception in 1875 until his death in 1905. Although not a member of Isaac M. Wise's congregation, the two men worked together closely through these and other organizations in which Freiberg held high office.[27]

In the introduction to his address, Levi refers to a rabbinic conference that was soon to take place, and in doing so was clearly attempting to influence the deliberations of the conferring rabbis. Whereas rabbis routinely criticized congregants for lack of piety and adherence to ritual observance with the latter lacking "an opportunity to say one word by way of rejoinder," Levy would "venture for once to 'talk back.'"[28]

Reverend Dr. L. Kleeberg of New Haven had defined the essence of Judaism as an ethical system that, Levy contended, made it indistinguishable from Christianity or Islam. Jacob Voorsanger of San Francisco similarly noted that one could be a good Jew by living "a pure and virtuous life"—a definition which, for Levi, would not distinguish Jews from followers of Buddha and Confucius. Chicago's Bernhard Felsenthal provided what Levi called a "nebulous answer" in which a Jew was defined as anyone who claimed the designation. M. Stanfield of Memphis simply avoided Levi's question by arguing that the responses "would involve the publication of fifteen octavo volumes." Levi identified only Isaac M. Wise's response as satisfactory, although not "sufficiently comprehensive." Wise used Bible quotations as his

sources in defining Judaism as a religion based upon covenants between the Jewish people and God.[29]

Levi then quoted a variety of sources on the nature of religion to
conclude that, beyond faith, Judaism required the embracing of specific doctrines and rituals in one's life, which distinguished Judaism
from universal ethical beliefs and behaviors. Thus Judaism would retain its distinctiveness vis-à-vis other religions. Levi demanded a catechism of beliefs understandable to adults and children which would
include explanations why the beliefs should be upheld. Such a catechism would provide laypeople with a clear definition of the essentials
of Judaism—"what is necessary to *believe,* and what is necessary to
do to bring myself *within the defined limits of Judaism"* (emphasis in
original)—based on the Torah and illustrating the differences between
it and other religions. It would not be based solely on reason but, instead, must rely on "divine law." Once again Levy urged the rabbis to
take a moderate approach: one of reform without revolution. To him,
a critical strength of Judaism had been the ability of Jews to "ris[e]
superior to the errors of their time, and preserving in their purity the
laws, doctrines and practices of their ancient faith."[30]

Levi had not finished with "the so-called reform rabbis." He informed the conferees:

> Jewish laymen should persist in their demand that the Rab-
> bis shall define Judaism, *and shall stand by it or leave
> it.*"(emphasis in original) The ideal rabbi…will be a man im-
> bued with a perfect faith in God's law as written in Torah; he
> will study it with a broad and liberal mind, seeking always
> to comprehend the will of the Creator…devoting himself to
> teaching and practicing the ancient religion, not as a mere
> matter of form, but as a vital and forceful agency to accom-
> plish the true development of man's highest nature. To him
> eloquence will consist in deeds, not words; to him entertain-
> ment will only be an incident to instruction; to him theology
> only an aid to piety; to him ceremonies will be divinely or-
> dered means to a divinely ordered end; to him the human in-
> tellect will be infinitely small compared with the infinite mind
> of God…[31]

It will be recalled that in 1888 Levi hand-picked Henry Cohen, a moderate reformer and a man of deeds—who stuttered— as the rabbi for his Galveston congregation. Cohen required of his confirmands responses to forty-five questions, the first of which asked: "What is the fundamental principle of our religion?" Levi's advocacy of a Jewish catechism was, then, actuated at B'nai Israel. Cohen was extolled for "living his religion, by providing young and old with a model of the righteous life," characteristics demanded by Levi of the ideal rabbi.[32]

When on 4 December 1894 a motion was made to thank Levi for his address and publish it in the UAHC proceedings, a parliamentary storm struck.[33] When the motion was divided in two and considered as separate motions of thanks and publication, both passed and a motion to reconsider the publication vote was defeated. A final motion to publish with the stipulation that such an action should not be viewed as an endorsement was delayed one day. A "Protest Against the Address," signed by the officers of the CCAR—Wise as president, David Philipson as corresponding secretary, and Charles S. Levi as recording secretary—was drawn up and submitted to the UAHC at the same time the last motion was voted upon. Both the stipulation and the protest won adoption.

In their protest the CCAR officers lambasted Levi's "strictures made upon the rabbis and their work.... [as] not founded on fact." The rabbis called Levi's analysis of the Reform movement and his conclusions "erroneous" and "hastily arrived at..." Furthermore, they asserted, the answers to his questions could be found in *Judaism at the World's Parliament of Religions* published by UAHC.[34]

The real elephant in the room, so to speak, was the Pittsburgh Platform, promulgated by a group of radical Reform rabbis in 1885. Levi's July 1887 article in *Menorah* and his 1894 address to the UAHC council meeting in New Orleans can be viewed as responses to that document. In May 1884 Levi had delivered an extemporaneous address in which he supplied answers to the questions he later submitted to the rabbis. Calls for its publication led to a series of articles titled, "The Jews of Today" published in the same year in *The American Israelite* and reprinted separately in 1887, after the Pittsburgh conference. Levi defined Judaism clearly as a distinct religion but also as what his contemporaries called a race or what is defined today as a people or ethnic group.[35] In this and on other issues he directly challenged the positions those rabbis took at the Pittsburgh conference and thereby joined in the "storm of indignation" against ideas that he believed would lead to the demise of Jews as a distinct entity.

Lessons Learned

The discord between Levi and the rabbis is striking. Contrary to their protest, he based his conclusions on substantial study and analysis. The real differences arose over ways of viewing Jews and of practicing Judaism, and the power relationship between rabbi and layperson. Much of the intellectual history of American Judaism emphasizes the thoughts and actions of rabbis. The study of Levi suggests the need to include the roles of laypeople in the development American Jewish thought and ideology. Did Levi receive the same scorn from laypeople? To the contrary—within five years he won election to the presidency of B'nai B'rith, a fraternal order that offered an alternate source of Jewish identity from the synagogues. As president, Levi again demonstrated his position as a national and ultimately international figure. Had he not died prematurely there is no telling what he might have accomplished.

Studies of people like Levi challenge the image of regional parochialism and illustrate the existence and importance of a Jewish leadership structure joined with, and transcending, the New York/Philadelphia nexus.

Overview

The stories of Osterman, Levi, and their families span a century. Each represented important positions under-reported in the historiography of the region and country. Osterman was a traditionalist who nurtured Judaism in an acculturated, Reform environment. Levi, a Reform Jew, believed that Classical Reform was too radical. Additional studies of leadership beyond New York are likely, similarly, to disclose patterns of religious expression seemingly out of the norm.

Although unusual in their involvement and impact, these individuals were far from unique. Equally important, "average" Jews listened to speeches, read newspaper articles, participated in local, state, regional, national, and international organizational networks through memberships, donations, publications, and attending meetings and conferences, and otherwise remained aware of forces and events outside of their towns and cities. Jews defined Judaism not only as a religion but also as a source of ethnic identity or peoplehood—another unifying force. The resultant cosmopolitan perspective transcends paradigms of local and regional historiography. The movement of Jews across the country, their family ties, and the nature of Jewish business ventures and contacts, reinforce these religious and institutional factors.

However much it changed over time, however difficult it is to define, and however varied its impact was on divergent subgroups, regional identity did exist.[36] Furthermore, some families did remain rooted in one location across generations. Nonetheless, the examples of the Dyer/Ostermans, Leo N. Levi, and others illustrate the variety of experiences of Jews in the South and add nuance to an oversimplified picture. These Jews were neither isolated nor provincial. They remained aware of national and international events of significance to Jews and actively participated in them. The new dynamic picture that emerges is one of migration of people and institutions and of an integrated national leadership and communications network. It is a framework unifying American Jewish history without ignoring or denying divisions. The themes in this essay thus illustrate a national, rather than a New York-based, model of American Jewish history.

An Ambivalent Relationship: Isaac M. Wise and the Independent Order of B'nai B'rith

Cornelia Wilhelm

Isaac M. Wise is well-known as the energetic and charismatic organizational leader of the American Reform Movement and the founding president of Hebrew Union College—America's first rabbinical seminary—in Cincinnati. Little is known, however, of his struggles with the first *secular* national organization of Jewish life in America, the Independent Order of B'nai B'rith. This Jewish fraternal order predated Wise's concept of union by thirty years and, for the first time, introduced an important organizational *alternative* to the synagogue which offered both Jewish cohesion and access to a new civil Jewish identity outside the congregation.

The Independent Order of B'nai B'rith was founded in 1843 in New York's Lower East Side. It was the project of a group of Jewish laymen who tried to "uplift and educate" immigrants at a time when the stream of German Jewish immigration to the United States was swelling. This increase in the German Jewish population challenged religious and ethnic cohesion and made immigrant Jews' civil integration more difficult as well.[1] Therefore, the Independent Order of B'nai

B'rith, a "secular but not secularist"[2] organization, sought to maintain Jewish community by redefining Jewish identity in both civil and religious contexts, and thus to explore new forms of community and cohesion outside the synagogue. The creation of B'nai B'rith was one approach toward the formation of a modern Judaism fit for the civil arena which would meet both the special challenge which America's religious liberty imposed on a modern Judaism and the obligation to preserve a common Jewish identity and group consciousness. To achieve these goals, the B'nai B'rith used the fraternal model of the Independent Order of Odd Fellows—which fostered group cohesion as well as a universalistic mission—as an organizational template. While remaining a secular organization, the B'nai B'rith made use of a religious framework that defined its members as Jews *and* as a priestly people. Like other modern Jewish organizations in Germany outside the *Einheitsgemeinde* or European-style *kehillah*—such as the *Gesellschaft der Freunde*—the Order used the peculiar characteristics of fraternal organization consciously to create a venue for Jewish identity formation and civil integration. Most importantly, organizing Jewish identity on a secular platform enabled American Jews to become visible on a national level and to identify as *American* Jews, and at the same time allowed for individual *religious* belief and full liberty of conscience.[3]

Isaac M. Wise, like many prominent Reform Jews,[4] had been an active Mason. He also sought respectability and inter-religious contact through membership in numerous lodges such as the Odd Fellows, the Druids and the Harugari. He wholeheartedly supported these groups' non-denominational and practical religiosity, charitable projects, and cosmopolitan attitude. Although one would suppose, accordingly, that Wise's relationship to the largest *Jewish* fraternal order, the Independent Order of B'nai B'rith, would have been an even closer and particularly cordial one, this was not, in fact, the case. Wise, who had emigrated with his family from Bohemia in 1846, had joined B'nai B'rith Zion Lodge No. 2 in New York City during his first rabbinate in Albany, probably in 1849.[5] He continued his membership in the order after moving to Cincinnati in 1854, where he accepted a new pulpit in congregation Bene Yeshurun, which was at the time America's second largest congregation.

Cincinnati was at this time the center of B'nai B'rith's huge Western District Grand Lodge No. 2, which included a region stretching from Chicago to New Orleans and from Louisville to the Rocky Mountains. District Grand Lodge No. 2 was much larger territorially than the Eastern Grand Lodges Nos.1 and 3, which were based in New York City and Philadelphia in the densely populated regions of the Eastern seaboard. Wise ascended to the presidency of District No. 2 in 1857, and consequently gained membership in the Council of Skenim, a council composed of past presidents which was the highest authority in the Order. This office made him the most powerful man of the Order in the "West," where now, in the second half of the 19th century, membership and influence was rapidly growing due to westward migration. However, although Wise was such a central figure in B'nai B'rith, he frequently and bitingly criticized the Order in his autobiography, *Reminiscences*, and in his newspaper, the *American Israelite*. In the *American Israelite*, Wise derogatively referred to B'nai B'rith members as "lodgers," claimed that the Order had "destroyed everything [he] ever aimed at" and complained bitterly that he could "…not think of a single public act of injustice of which [he had] been the victim that was not inspired by B'nai B'rith brethren and members."[6] Wise also sought to downplay the influence of the Order as America's first national platform for Jewish union by belittling it as "only a benevolent society," and a "group of agnostics."

Wise's prominent function within B'nai B'rith and the fact that B'nai B'rith's identity was closely intertwined with the idea of a modern Judaism contributed to the confusion about Wise's ambivalence, and even hostility, toward the Order and its high officials. At first glance, the Order and Wise seem to have sought to accomplish almost identical goals: the redefinition and modernization of Jewish identity within an American framework. Upon closer examination, though, the relationship between B'nai B'rith and Wise reflects a more complex picture which gives us new insight into the nature of both. Although Reform Jewish thought was deeply ingrained in both, Wise and B'nai B'rith represented two alternative models of Jewish "union" for modern American Jews. An investigation of these differing models will explain Wise's increasing hostility towards the "civil Judaism" represented by the Order.

As early as 1849, right after Wise initially joined the Order, conflict arose around these two diverging visions of American Judaism.
Because of the chaotic religious and communal situation of Jews and
Judaism in New York's quickly growing and continuously changing
immigrant community and its growing lack of standards and institutions, Isaac M. Wise and Isaac Leeser were moved, in 1849, to attempt
to realize their first concept of a Jewish "union"—a synod and a network of congregations based on common belief and the coordination
of Jewish religious matters, education and rabbinical training. In his
Reminiscences, Wise claimed that, since his arrival in America, his
thought had been dominated by the *vision* to maintain Jewish religious
identity by shaping a Jewish religious movement—similar to *American* Christian denominations[7]—which would entail the establishment
of a "church" or religious authority like a synod. For the sake of such
an ecclesiastical organization which would represent a cohesive and
respectable "American Judaism" based on a majority of congregations, Wise was willing to compromise ideologically with modern
Orthodoxy—represented by Isaac Leeser—and sacrifice some of his
own Reform principles in order to maintain union among Jewish congregations. He considered such a "union" the first step toward creating
a network of communal institutions such as a seminary for rabbinical
training, a library, hospitals and orphan-asylums—all of which were
desperately needed by American Jewish congregations but could not
be provided by them individually.

However, as several sources reveal,[8] Leeser's and Wise's concept
for union met with immediate opposition from recent German Jewish
immigrants who were identified as refugees of the revolution—supporters of the liberal movement and radical rationalists called *Lichtfreunde*, or friends of light. This group vehemently refused Wise's and
Leeser's plans for the German Jewish community of New York City,
and rejected any central "coordination" of religious matters and the
establishment of religious hierarchies.[9]

Although we know little about the *Lichtfreunde* of New York
City—who were only known under this name for about six months—
the *Israel's Herold* explains that the group's most active adherents
were Isidor Busch and Rabbi Max Lilienthal. The *Lichtfreunde*'s history, goals, background, and name indicate a connection, or at least

identification, with a larger German movement that emerged among all religious denominations during the pre-revolutionary era (like-minded German Christian groups were frequently found in America and are well documented).[10] In this movement, active laymen and women sought to overcome religious authority and the limits of liberty of conscience as posed by the connection of church and state by establishing new democratic forms of religious community as well as by encouraging the rationalization of religion within independent congregations. In their quest for "independence" from religious authority, the *Lichtfreunde* rejected hierarchical structures of established "churches," and demanded instead strictly egalitarian democratic organization within the congregations. These congregations were governed only by laymen (and women), democratically elected their preachers, addressed each other as "brothers" and "sisters," and tried to live according to the laws of "brotherly love." Jews were part of this confessionally overarching movement, and ultra-modern Jewish groups such as the *Frankfurt Reformfreunde* explicitly sought contact with this larger movement.[11]

In America, as in the old world, Jews continued to be part of this movement. Groups of people from similar backgrounds sprang up among the refugees of the revolution in Philadelphia and in Chicago, where they used the Hebrew name *Ohabe Or* instead of *Lichtfreunde* or "friends of light," and constituted several early proto-Reform congregations whose members were also an integral part of the non-Jewish German immigrant community.[12] Religious liberty—the separation of church and state and the rooting of the American congregation organizationally in "associations"—very much accommodated *Lichtfreunde* ideals of a democratic religiosity and liberty of conscience. Therefore, it is no surprise that these groups opposed Wise and Leeser's attempt to establish a Jewish synod in the U.S. from the very first moment on. The beginning of Wise's ambivalence towards B'nai B'rith, on the other hand, likely occurred when the *Lichtfreunde* did not survive as a separate organization and, after six months of existence, decided to merge with the New York based Independent Order of B'nai B'rith. In B'nai B'rith they found a strong overlap of ideals, which induced the merger of the two groups.[13] The fact that they shared much common ground ideologically is reflected in the immediate appointment of Isidor Busch to the presidency of the Order. It also suggests that within B'nai B'rith the *Lichtfreunde* found a larger nationwide platform for Jewish identity without any confinement of their liberty of conscience. The Order offered a cohesive network of "lodges"—independent Jewish grassroots groups apart from a synod, established religious authority or "church"—which were intended to define the guidelines of a "civil" American Judaism. Another important motivation for the merger with the Order might have been its national presence, which, unlike local groups, could accommodate the immigrants' mobility.[14]

By the mid-1850s the B'nai B'rith had spread throughout the United States and had brought together American Jews from New York, Chicago, New Orleans, San Francisco, and places between. While diversity among American Jewish congregations grew, the grassroots model of the lodge motivated its members to joint communal action but left the individual room for his own interpretation of religiosity. This was important since ethnic and religious factionalism in American Judaism grew side by side with immigration. The lodge could function as a proto-congregation or simply as a source of community, and provided access to Jewish identity in the public sphere along with the utmost liberty of conscience for the individual member in religious matters. Also, the lodge, by its very nature, motivated the individual to engage in society and in projects of community-building. The so-called "ritual"—the degree system of the Order through which an individual ascended to full membership as he submitted to the values of the Order—challenged the member to cultivate his character and live up to an ethical and civil role model as a Jew, inside and outside the lodge. The ritual demanded that Jews act according to the laws of "brotherly love." Parallel to the Reform Movement's principle of the "fatherhood of God and the brotherhood of men," this demand called upon modern Jews to seek their place in society within the *human* family and to reject any Jewish particularism.

Although Wise downplayed or consciously camouflaged his first defeat by the Independent Order of B'nai B'rith in his own autobiographical record, the *Lichtfreunde*'s merger with B'nai B'rith commenced a longstanding rivalry between Wise and the Order which only increased once Wise moved to Cincinnati. Here in the American West, in a place where charismatic leadership outweighed adherence to theological principle, Wise's pulpit at Bene Yeshurun added strong lay support to his leadership role. Under the influence of religious structures in the West, increasing immigration and a growing diversity among American Jewish congregations, Wise found it ever more necessary to promote Jewish cohesion under a broad Reform umbrella and to establish facilities and find venues for the shaping of an American Judaism. He had managed to introduce reforms in his congregation and also successfully founded two Jewish newspapers, the *American Israelite*, in English, and *Die Deborah*, in German.

Because of his special leadership role in American Judaism, Wise managed to call for another rabbinical meeting—a conference that was to embrace a majority of American Jews. The purposes of this gathering were to reach an agreement on union, to establish a regular synod, to develop a common prayer book and liturgy called *Minhag America*, and to found a rabbinical college which would secure Jewish education in America.[15] In his eyes, the founding of a rabbinical seminary was key to the establishment of an *American* Judaism, and would both provide a new generation of university-trained English-speaking rabbis and prevent a culture of immigrant-rabbis which would foster ethnic and theological disagreement. Although not all of the originally interested nine rabbis actually attended the rabbinical gathering in October 1855—which became known as the Cleveland Conference—the most important leaders, who felt they could reach common ground, did attend. At first, the meeting in Cleveland seemed promising. But the conference, and the attempt to establish a congregational union and synod, failed again. It had found its harshest opponent in David Einhorn, a German radical Reform rabbi who had arrived in the US right before the conference started, and who was, theologically and intellectually, the most prominent of the German immigrant rabbis of the time.

Einhorn was convinced of the importance of the realization of an ideologically uncompromising religious Reform in America, where such a departure from religious authority and tradition was possible for the first time in history. In his eyes, America gave Judaism a unique chance actively to shape itself upon a modern model. Because Einhorn was seriously concerned about the future of Reform Judaism he was driven to strict opposition to Wise and Leeser, the two rabbis who favored union over the ideological maintenance of Reform principle. Although he had only recently immigrated and taken the position of rabbi at Baltimore's Har Sinai congregation, Einhorn's vehement attacks against the Cleveland Conference, as well as the absence of orthodox rabbis such as Abraham Rice and Morris Raphall, made the enterprise a failure.[16] Also, although Einhorn had never become a B'nai B'rith member, his arrival lent support to a group of his old-world friends who had key functions within B'nai B'rith, namely, the circle of radical reform leadership which governed the Council of Skenim, the central authority of the Order. This circle included rabbis Maurice Mayer, Bernhard Felsenthal, Emanuel Friedlein and Henry Jones.[17] Having been a victim of both religious and secular authorities in Germany, which restricted and undermined both his liberal thought and his professional career as a rabbi, Einhorn stressed the importance of congregational independence from an established ecclesiastic authority.

When the Cleveland conference failed B'nai B'rith was automatically strengthened as the national platform for American Jews. This lack of a religious platform left the establishment of communal institutions largely to local communities and to B'nai B'rith as the only national Jewish network available. The Order continued to serve as the prime source for organization, consensus and "communal" cooperation, and in fact, after Wise and Leeser's first attempt for a synod and rabbinical college had failed, B'nai B'rith prospered enormously. The Order was so successful that it had not only founded lodges across the country, including chapters in New Orleans, San Francisco and Chicago, but, by 1854, had also sought to direct its energies toward a suitable and prestigious project that would represent "the higher aims of the order."[18] This *formulation* naturally triggered a debate about what these "higher aims" would actually be. The preamble to the B'nai B'rith constitution expressed the purpose of the organization, but left room for vast interpretation, stating that the Order's task was educational and benevolent engagement, but also that the Order was dedicated to "foster the teachings of Judaism."[19]

Isaac M. Wise, who was already running his Zion College in Cincinnati, felt intrigued to see in B'nai B'rith a potential ally for the financing of what he considered most important for the development of an American Judaism:[20] a rabbinical college in Cincinnati which would give a future generation of American, English-speaking rabbis a standardized and up-to-date university training. Wise imagined such a college to be an important point of departure from European influences on American Judaism,[21] which he felt would be harmful to establishing a modern and uniquely *American* Judaism. Therefore, in 1857, when Wise was President of the quickly growing Second District, and thus a member of the B'nai B'rith Council of Skenim, he felt the time had come to win over B'nai B'rith support for an educational institution for Judaism which he could initiate during the national General Convention in Philadelphia. Wise argued that this project would be in the Order's interest, since it was committed to education, *Bildung* and the fostering of the teachings of Judaism.[22]

The success and presence of B'nai B'rith as the sole national Jewish organization may have both frightened as well as appealed to Wise. On the one hand, the well-accepted and financially well-endowed Order seemed to be a possible ally in the emergence of a modern American Jewish community. On the other hand, Wise feared the secular Order's continued interest in religious matters, i.e. "Judaism," and was concerned with the possibility that this organization would turn into a platform which might compete with his idea of a congregational union. Wise rejected the idea that Jewish cohesion could be maintained through a civil, secular organization which left religious matters entirely to individual congregations and which would neither define the congregation as the center of American Judaism nor develop a communal network around the synagogue.[23]

The Council of Skenim, the central authority of the Order, was strongly influenced by a group of radical reform thinkers—laymen and rabbis alike—who shared a German background and were well-acquainted with or strongly inspired by David Einhorn. When these thinkers were discussing Wise's suggestion of a B'nai B'rith-sponsored rabbinical college, they rejected his idea as "not in the best interests of the order." They feared that supporting a Reform college would bring religious conflict into the Order and create an opportunity for Wise to utilize B'nai B'rith and coordinate it with his larger concept of religious "union,"—thus causing their organization to lose its independent status. These thinkers strongly stressed the view that a civil platform was necessary for a modern Judaism, since it guaranteed the utmost liberty of each congregation in religious terms while enabling American Jews to develop an American Jewish identity outside the synagogue in the American civil arena. To counter Wise efficiently and to limit his power in the "West," the Skenim added to the emerging conflict by declaring New York City the permanent seat of the Constitution Grand Lodge, which weakened Cincinnati,[24] and they modified B'nai B'rith's organizational structure, mission and ritual to accord with their strong universalist vision.

The new ritual, introduced by B'nai B'rith in 1858, reflected a strong *Jewish* universalism and abolished the wearing of regalia and of aprons (as was enthusiastically practised by laymen in the Western lodges), in order to stress the importance of social equality to American lodges. The innovated ritual also reduced the initial six degrees to three, and reflected the strong influence of Einhorn's theological outlook with its emphasis on universalistic mission. Although Einhorn had never been a member of B'nai B'rith, his influence on the new ritual has been stressed by historians[25] and may be rooted in his close relations with Merzbacher, Ellinger and Friedlein, who were childhood friends from Germany and regularly met in Einhorn's home to discuss issues related to the Order.[26]

From this point on, the Order increasingly split into two camps, referred to as "East" and "West." The first stood for radical Reform, and the latter embraced a more moderate Reform which would adapt to American religious and social structures and be willing to compromise beyond theological consistency. Although the two camps originated in East and West on the compass, if we think of the original conflict between Isaac M. Wise and the Council of Skenim the regional division did not hold for long: over the course of the dispute the "West" soon found support from lodges in Philadelphia—the northern part of District No.3 which was under the presidency of Isaac Leeser and a more conservative lay leadership. Likewise, allies of "the Eastern" radicals soon established themselves in Chicago and northern parts of the Second District of the Order, which were clearly part of the Western states but vehemently opposed what was agreed to in Cincinnati, the center of District No.2. Since the members of the Order continued to use the terms "East" and "West" to distinguish between those two camps, I shall do likewise, but it is important to remember that the terms refer to *ideological* differences between radicals ("East") and moderates ("West") rather than to precise *geographical* differences.

Unlike Wise, who was more pragmatic, radical Reform ideologues made a conscious distinction between American fraternal orders and the B'nai B'rith with its special *Jewish* mission. The changes in ritual aroused great resentment among some of the rank and file lay-membership, for whom the Order fulfilled different needs than it did for its intellectual leadership. This was particularly true for the so-called "Western" districts, where the Jewish lodge, to a much larger degree, satisfied communal needs and was a platform for the demonstration of an equal civil and civic presence while serving the material needs of immigrants as well. Here, religious principle and theological consistency in the process of modernizing Judaism were less important than civic cooperation and practical support. Therefore, in "the West," the majority of laymen sought an adaptation to the organizational forms of Christian institutions. They sought to be outwardly similar to their Protestant brothers, rather than adhere to theological principles rooted in the intellectual debates of Central Europe. Interestingly, this was also reflected in the discussion over women's membership in the Order, an issue debated since 1846. While those who rejected the universalistic ritual were willing to discuss an "*auxiliary* degree" for the wives of members, as instituted in some non-Jewish orders, the radical Reform wing supported an *independent* women's order, the United Order of True Sisters, and officially acknowledged them in 1874 as an "equivalent" and partner organization to the B'nai B'rith.[27]

Wise, too, thought in these terms with regard to the religious development of an American Judaism, and wished to secure Jewish cohesion and organization similar to that of an American denomination. Challenged by his old enemies, he claimed that the Eastern radical Reform faction would seek to dominate B'nai B'rith, and feared the Order would, under its current leadership, become too powerful an organization in American Israel. Seeking to gain the popular support of the lay-membership in the West, Wise refused to adopt the ritual and the new constitution in his district and demanded the abolishment of the Skenim, whom he claimed to be an "undemocratic life aristocracy."[28]

On top of this, using his popular lay support Wise tried to go further and did not hesitate to launch open conflict by appearing with a group of confidants, rather than the elected delegates, at the next meeting of the Council of Skenim in 1858. A letter from lodge official Baruch Rothschild to Maurice Mayer tells us that during the meeting Wise burst out: "Why shall I be for the Order? I cannot be for it, for in this Order I have my greatest opponents, who have defeated all I aimed at!"[29] Shaking with fury, Wise demanded a public statement from the B'nai B'rith declaring that "the Order had nothing to do with religion and Judaism and was only a benevolent institution,"[30] and expressed his fear that the B'nai B'rith would actively become involved in the shaping of an American Judaism.

During the General Convention in 1859 Wise forced the Order to make an official statement about "The Order's role as *Jewish* agent" that precisely explained the relationship of the B'nai B'rith to religious matters inside or outside the organization and which would state:

> ...that the Convention declares most emphatically that it is not the duty nor the object of the Order B'ne B'rith to interfere with, nor to influence the religious opinion of any man inside or outside the Order. And while it is the true and avowed object of the Order to elevate the moral and social condition of all its members, and thus make them good Israelites, questions of purely religious character should not be brought forward in any lodge of the Order, as they would tend to produce serious trouble and disastrous effects.[31]

To calm Wise and prevent an escalation of internal conflict, the Order accepted Wise's suggestion. Wise therefore felt empowered, in 1860, to reintroduce his college plan within his district only. Having connected his plan with the decision concerning the newly introduced universalistic ritual, Wise felt quite sure that his project would be supported by the moderate "Western" laymen of the Order, namely Districts nos. 2 and 3. Wise was, at this time, still maintaining his alliance with Isaac Leeser, who was serving as president of the B'nai B'rith Grand Lodge No. 3, headquartered in Philadelphia. Both rabbis managed to gain a victory over the universalistic District No. 1 during the convention of 1863, and as a consequence of their agitation against the council of elders as a "life aristocracy,"[32] the Constitution Grand Lodge was forced to abolish the Council of Skenim and replace it with a democratically elected "Constitution Grand Lodge" to function as a central body for all districts. They also reintroduced the wearing of regalia into the Order. These changes brought the divided Order to the brink of extinction, and only major changes in the constitution, which introduced complete independence of the individual district grand lodges and allowed them to operate largely according to their own regional needs,[33] kept the B'nai B'rith from dissolution. Under these new conditions Wise felt secure enough once again to submit his college plans to the Second District of the B'nai B'rith as a project that would represent "the higher goals of the order." But, to his great surprise, his own district supported the establishment of an Orphan Asylum in Cleveland rather than the theological seminary.[34] It is hard to judge if this was the result of disinterest on the part of the Western laymen in theological education, or if they feared Wise's dominance.

At the same time, the establishment of Bernhard Felsenthal's Chicago Sinai Congregation created a hub of radical Reform opposition right in Wise's own district,[35] and Felsenthal's presence and activity in Chicago's Ramah Lodge increased the pressure on Wise. Felsenthal, a scholar and community leader, outspokenly rejected an explicitly *Jewish* university as a project modelled on concepts of traditional religious seclusion which copied the particularist and "sectarian" institutions of the Old World. He attacked ritual and secrecy in the Order as "un-Jewish" and contrary to the goals of a modern universalistic Judaism which sought to define a new role in civil society, rather than to maintain the old particularism.[36]

By this time, Felsenthal and the radical reform circle around Ramah Lodge in Chicago had become an "outpost of the Eastern opposition to Wise" in his own Western District. The group not only criticized Wise for a lack of theological principle, but also fought his increasing attempts to coordinate the District in order to realize his own goals. The Chicago group noticed that Wise was willing to give the lay element an important voice over issues they considered crucial for the future image of Judaism in America.[37] Felsenthal condemned what he saw as Wise siding with the laymen to build a majority in the conflict that would support his own plans. To draw public attention to these tactics Felsenthal alerted the Jewish public to the importance of preserving consistency with reform principles such as universalism and the abolishment of any form of secrecy.[38] Felsenthal argued that the B'nai B'rith was created to serve as an "open society," rather than a secret order which would preserve some kind of particularism. After all, he concluded, a modern Judaism had nothing to hide from the world.[39] At the same time, Wise openly argued in the *Israelite* in favor of a much more pragmatic approach—he announced that no matter what conflicts may arise around the Order, the B'nai B'rith offered a unique practical possibility for a successful Jewish union which should be taken advantage of, without excessive discussion about principle:

> The objections against this order are its secrets…This is a mistake, however. In the first place, the age is far from being enlightened…the generality of mankind clings tenaciously to social and religious prejudices, so much so, indeed, that the most absurd doctrines win the most admirers, and pure reason counts its votaries by individuals only, while absurdity can reckon upon communities…it is a mistake that enlightened men should have no mistakes. The means of union, if legitimate must be efficient; it is perfectly indifferent whether they are secret or public. All attempts to cement a union of American Israelites on the basis of voluntary adherence failed decidedly; the Cleveland conference and the New York Board of delegates proved abortive; this order has succeeded in uniting 5,000 Israelites, and it will unite 5,000 more in less than ten years. If you can do it by public means, do it. The order does it by means which prove efficient. If one contemplates the disunion of congregations in one and the same city he must admit that this order performs wonders.[40]

This conflict escalated when the laymen of the Second and Third Districts caused Felsenthal's worst fears to come true—they attempted to define principal issues about the nature of the Order that were based upon the theological definition of what made a person a Jew (and thus allowed an individual to be a member of the order).[41] In 1867 the Second District voted that intermarried candidates should be prohibited from membership, and considered denying benefits to their families as well. In 1868 they also sought to restrict membership in the Order to "male Jews" only.[42] This created an uproar. For radical Reform, which was so strictly tied to theological consistency, it was untenable for laymen to make decisions about religious issues such as definitions of Jewishness in the framework of a secular organization such as B'nai B'rith. B'nai B'rith was "civil" by definition. It was not intended to erect new religious boundaries, but to level existing ones in order to promote a common religion of humanity and to enhance the idea of human brotherhood. From the point of view of radical Reform, laymen were not to judge issues which fell into the realm of Jewish law and which rightly should be decided by a *Sanhedrin*. Therefore, Felsenthal argued, the Order could only require that its applicants for membership submit to the ideal of joining the "mission of Israel," and vehemently rejected making membership accessible only to one confession.[43] This episode proved that the attempt to utilize the B'nai B'rith in the discussion about a Jewish union had developed dynamics beyond anyone's control. The original concept of the Order—as well as hopes to create a modern Judaism with the privilege of absolute liberty of conscience—was now itself on shaky ground.

Other developments further shook the Order. In 1867 radical reformers in Districts nos. 2 and 3 in Baltimore and Chicago expressed their desire to break off from their mother districts to become independent as Districts no. 5 (Baltimore) and 6 (Chicago).[44] Baruch Rothschild, one of the founders of the Order, explains in his correspondence that the decision to organize two new districts was consciously sought by radical Reform leaders because these new organizational units seemingly added independence to the District Grand Lodges, and also—and more importantly—because they secured the majority of the "East" in the Constitution Grand Lodge, which was the new national platform of the Order and successor of the "Skenim." In the same spirit, the decision was reached to limit the sessions of the CGL General Meetings to take place only every five years. The aim of this decision was to stop continual disruption and conflict and to add some stability to the Order's leadership. Also, it was suggested that an Executive Committee decide the Order's everyday business, while individual districts were allowed to build their own profile.

At the forefront of the 1869 Philadelphia Conference—a rabbinical meeting launched by the radical Reform supporters David Einhorn and Samuel Adler to establish a platform which would separate Reform from Orthodoxy in the United States—was the fact that the Order was facing almost total collapse. Benjamin Peixotto of the Second District, and president of the Order, used his power to order the new ritual to be "invalid," and at the same time reintroduced the wearing of aprons. Peixotto's decisions were interpreted as "autocratic," and triggered the worst fears of his opponents—who did not only fear that these decisions were made in order to please his regional membership, but believed that they were also an intentional favor to his friend Wise. These suspicions proved true when Peixotto soon after also reintroduced the idea of a B'nai B'rith funded rabbinical college—now called "B'nai B'rith University"—to make the project sound more appealing. The college was labelled as *Jewish*, yet represented the idea of a secular university which would also offer theological studies for a future American rabbinate. After the convention, which gave the Grand Lodges the possibility to pursue their own goals, silence dominated the Order, whose districts turned inward. While this was generally perceived as a chance for healing, it was obvious to everyone that these conflicts would reassert themselves at the next General Convention in 1874.

In preparation for that convention Julius Bien and Bernhard Felsenthal made a bold move and discussed a new democratic structure and the abolishment of secrecy within the entire Order. They envisioned the B'nai B'rith as a future platform for a loose alliance of Jews, and thus formulated for the first time an alternative model to Wise's conception of religious union.

Their plans, however, were undermined when leading laymen of the West, only a few months before the B'nai B'rith convention, initiated a union of Reform congregations and thus finally materialized Wise's plans for congregational union. Unlike his earlier plans, the newly founded UAHC did not seek theological authority through a "synod." The Union instead expressed the desire of the laymen to institute a congregational platform for Judaism which would enhance practical cooperation in communal matters such as the establishment of Jewish schools, a theological seminary and other communal institutions. For Wise, the Union was a limited success because one of his main goals, the founding of an American rabbinical seminary, still lacked finances. However, in 1870 Henry Adler, a wealthy layman from Lawrenceburg, Indiana, donated $10,000 toward Wise's college project, under the condition that the project be realized by 1875. This conditional "donation" put Wise under new pressure to raise more funds to secure the survival of the seminary, and he tried one last time, in the months preceding the 1874 convention, to win over the B'nai B'rith as an ally in this endeavor.

In his *Israelite*, Wise continued to insist that it was now time for the B'nai B'rith to *prove* its *service to Judaism* and the *Jewish religion*. He stressed that the Order was still merely a "benevolent organization," and tried to clearly define the options the Order had with respect to its future relationship with the UAHC—aiming to convince the Order that it had to submit to the UAHC if it wanted to maintain its claim to be an agent of the *Jewish* community.[45]

Chicago, the new seat of the Sixth District Grand Lodge and the center of rebellion against Wise, had been purposely chosen by radical Reform supporters as a provocation to Wise. For the first time, the General Convention was held publicly in the city's Music Hall, and Moritz Ellinger, the editor of the *Jewish Times*, served as secretary of the Convention and organized its schedules and meetings. The relationship between the B'nai B'rith and the UAHC was one of the most important issues to be discussed at the convention, but was not put on the agenda as such. Instead, Wise's College project and the suggestion for establishing a "Home for the Helpless" were placed on the agenda. Significantly, the latter was combined with the proposition "that the BB would give the Union every moral and practical support," as Wise suggested. Both issues were discussed, without the public, in a separate meeting at Wabash St. Temple, and the Committee that decided these questions—as Wise claimed later—*intentionally* appointed one of Wise's worst enemies, Moritz Ellinger, as its head. This committee predictably succeeded completely to defeat Wise's proposition to tie the B'nai B'rith to the Union. Likewise, several other issues were decided in favor of the radical reform leadership. Among them were the acknowledgement of the United Order of True Sisters as an official partner organization for women, and a ritual with even less decorum. Oaths which were regarded as "un-Jewish" were also eliminated from the ritual.[46]

Only a week after the Convention the *Israelite* and *Die Deborah* reacted bitterly: "So we know now and forever that the B'nai B'rith Order has nothing to do with Judaism as a religion, and will not meddle with it."[47] This attitude determined Wise's sentiment towards the B'nai B'rith forever after. He withdrew from all activities within the Order, and the *Israelite* used the emergence of the Ethical Culture Movement to hint at the B'nai B'rith's supposedly "agnostic" nature. The paper saw the B'nai B'rith in danger of following this movement as it moved away from its connection with the centre of Jewish religious identity—the congregations.

Nonetheless, after many disappointments with the Order and the successful organization of a national Union of Congregations which was even joined by the "Eastern" congregations of his former opponents, Wise was still conscious that the communal component which the B'nai B'rith added to Jewish life in America, and its potential to activate laymen, was crucial for an American Judaism. While the rabbinate and the Reform Movement's intellectual leadership were increasingly dominated by rationalism and critical thought and could not provide much of a sense of community, Wise sensed that the Order would be a powerful tool to actively shape Jewish identity and would provide those who could not easily connect to the new intellectual style in the synagogue with a modern sense of Jewishness. Shortly before his death in 1898 Wise wrote to his long-time friend Simon Wolf, who had helped him coordinate the Board of Delegates with the Union, expressing his hope for a closer union between the two organizations, and mentioning with regret that he himself never succeeded in this endeavor.[48]

Ironically, shortly after Wise's death, and after Julius Bien had been replaced as President of the B'nai B'rith, a new generation of B'nai B'rith presidents—especially Leo N. Levi—sought a closer cooperation between the Order and the Reform Movement. This discourse was actively picked up by the Social Gospel activist Emil G. Hirsch, which infused the B'nai B'rith with new life.[49] Although the

Order never gave up its independence from the Reform or any other congregational movements, its leaders began to realize that the B'nai B'rith needed the discourse with American Judaism's religious and intellectual leadership to carry out its mission: to pioneer new areas of societal engagement and to synchronize and re-negotiate Jewishness with universalism in order to contribute to social progress, create a modern Judaism, and fulfill the mission of the Reform idea.

The Odyssey of a Liturgist: Isaac S. Moses as Architect of the Union Prayer Book

Eric L. Friedland

The Context

It was only shortly after the historic liberal *Rabbinerversammlungen* (Rabbinical Conferences) in Braunschweig (1844), Frankfurt am Main (1845) and Breslau (1846) that Jews yearning for freedom began emigrating in large numbers from German-speaking countries in Central Europe to America. Challenged by the need to adapt to a new post-ghetto era, those conferences had deliberated on what changes could be made in liturgy, theology and law which would, if at all possible, not exceed the perimeters of the millennial Jewish tradition. Among the multitudes leaving the Old World were those imbued with the idea of Reform, including young learned rabbis (some of whom had fought in the Revolutions of 1848)[1] who were singularly equipped to implement the new religious perspective. While not nearly as bound to tradition as their European counterparts, the non-Orthodox prayerbooks edited in America during that first generation of arrivals from the 1840s and 1850s were in the main marked by a relative fidelity to the old forms.[2] While new prayerbooks were being composed for individual premier congregations, notably on the eastern seaboard, the wish was sounded early on that a single *minhag* (rite) be molded to unify all of American Jewry.[3] The next decade saw incremental editorial changes, generally in the direction of greater brevity and textual political correctness,[4] while in the 1870s (when Isaac S. Moses, the subject of our essay, reached America) bolder, more substantive alterations found their place in the various Progressive rites and, in several instances, paved the way for radical transformations of the classical Jewish liturgy. One of the more far-reaching changes during this next phase was experimentation with Sunday morning services[5] in many Reform synagogues—an innovation which pushed the liturgical envelope in daring ways. By the end of the century the process of Americanization for the offspring of the newcomers from *Mitteleuropa* had reached the point where the time was ripe to forge a *siddur* to meet their needs and their sensibilities. The one liturgist who was practiced in this process, responsive to the pull and tug between tradition and modernity, and ready for the task of the hour was Isaac S. Moses (1847–1926).

A Thumbnail Biographical Sketch[6]

A native of the Prussian province of Posen (now Poznan, in Poland) and son of a poor rabbi and teacher, Isaac S. Moses did well in his Jewish and secular studies, but discontinued them in order to immigrate to America, where he arrived in the early 1870s. Moses started out as a religious teacher in St. Louis, and then served as a rabbi in Quincy, Illinois, Milwaukee (for nine years), Nashville, and Chicago (for twelve years) before being invited to New York City to assume the pulpit of a prominent metropolitan synagogue. It was during his tenure in Milwaukee that Moses began the liturgical activity that was to occupy him for at least three decades. Between the early 1890s and 1916 he was intimately involved with the gestation, birth, and growing pains of the first combined Reform prayerbook for American Jewry, *The Union Prayer Book for Jewish Worship.*[7]

A Preliminary Bibliographical Listing[8]

What follows below is a preliminary bibliographical list of Isaac S. Moses's liturgical efforts, which he began not very long after his arrival in America. These will be itemized chronologically and, where possible, include the name of the primary congregation for which each was originally intended:

1) *Tefillah le-Mosheh: Order of Prayers and Responsive Readings for Jewish Worship* (Milwaukee, WI: self-published, 1884); hereafter *Tefillah le-Mosheh 1884*—Congregation Emanu-El.

2) *Order of Prayers and Responsive Readings for Jewish Worship: Tefillat Yisrael* (Milwaukee WI: self-published, 1887); hereafter *Tefillat Yisrael 1887*—Congregation Emanu-El.

3) *Tefillot Yisrael: The Jewish Prayer Book: Order of Worship for Sabbaths and Holidays*, "Printed as Manuscript for the Ritual Committee appointed by the Rabbinical Conference held in Baltimore, MD, July, 1891" [composed by Moses alone] (Chicago, 1891); hereafter *Ms. 1891*—originally undertaken for Temple Israel in Chicago.

4) *Jewish Prayer Book: Tefillot Yisrael*, edited by Ritual Committee (of the Central Conference of American Rabbis) and printed as manuscript (Chicago, 1892) [for Sabbaths, Festivals and Weekdays]; hereafter *Ms. 1892*.

5) *Tefillot Yisrael: Union Prayer Book*, adapted by the CCAR and published by the Ritual Committee (Chicago, 1892); hereafter *UPB 1892*—for sale to the general public.

6) *Union Payer Book: Tefillot Yisrael*, vol. 2, edited with the Ritual Committee (of the CCAR) printed as manuscript (Chicago, 1893) [for the High Holy Days]; hereafter *Ms. 1893*.

7) *The Sabbath School Hymnal: A Collection of Songs, Services and Responses for Jewish Sabbath Schools and Homes*, 2nd rev. ed. (Chicago: Bloch, 1894); hereafter *Sabbath School Hymnal 1894*.

8) *Hymns and Anthems for Jewish Worship* (New York: Bloch, 1904); hereafter *Hymns and Anthems 1904*—Temple Ahawath Chesed-Shaar Hashamayim.

9) *The Sabbath-School Hymnal: A Collection of Songs, Services and Responsive Readings for the School, Synagogue and Home*, 6th rev. and enlarged ed. (New York: Bloch, 1904); hereafter *Sabbath-School Hymnal 1904*—Temple Ahawath Chesed-Shaar Hashamayim.

10) *Divine Service for the Congregation Ahawath Chesed Shaar Hashamayim*, arranged by Adolph Huebsch [as revised by Moses] (New York, 1916); hereafter *Huebsch 1916*—Temple Ahawath Chesed-Shaar Hashamayim.

Premier American Influences: Leo Merzbacher and David Einhorn

There were notable American as well as European influences on Isaac S. Moses's liturgical efforts, all of them still current in his own day. The American influence least noticed was perhaps the most important—certainly, at least, in terms of his preferred version of Hebrew text, organization and layout. Indeed, this was the prayerbook that may be said to have heightened his esthetic sense in terms of how the book should look and feel, how the prayers and their rubrics should be arranged, and what sort of typography would be the most appealing. This pivotal prayerbook was the neatly-wrought, exceptionally compact *The Order of Prayer for Divine Service: Seder Tefillah* (New York: J. Muhlhausen, 1855) which the Bavarian-born Rabbi Leo Merzbacher (1810–1856) prepared for Congregation Emanu-El in New York, where he served during the last decade of his all-too-brief life (the second [New York: Thalmesser, Cahn & Benedicks, 1860] and third [New York: Thalmesser, 1864] editions were revised by Merzbacher's successor at Temple Emanu-El, Samuel Adler [1809–1891]).[9] Another rite whose theological persuasiveness and power increased over time was the epoch-making German-Hebrew *'Olat Tamid: Gebetbuch fuer israelitische Reform-Gemeinden* (Baltimore: E.W. Schneidereith, 1858) by the liturgical virtuoso—and Merzbacher's fellow-Bavarian—David Einhorn (1809–1879). In the preface to his *Tefillah le-Mosheh 1884*, Moses himself identifies yet other nineteenth-century *siddurim* that helped shape his own efforts. These were in actuality secondary or peripheral, and they include Benjamin Szold and Marcus Jastrow's *Avodat Yisrael: Israelitish Prayer Book for the Public Services of the Year* (Philadelphia: self-published, 1873), and Max Landsberg's all-but-monolingual *Ritual for Jewish Worship* (Rochester, NY: Charles Mann, 1884).

As for the European rites that transfused Moses's prayerbooks, the key ones that deserve to be given prominence are the nonconformist and intensely spiritual manual of prayers for the *Reformgemeinde* in Berlin: the *Gebetbuch der Genossenschaft fuer Reform in Judenthum* (Berlin, 1848), and its many subsequent editions, which were re-titled *Gebetbuch fuer juedische Reformgemeinden*. Over time this prayerbook came to show more of the influence of the congregation's highly original rabbi and preacher, Samuel Holdheim (1806–1860).[10] Not much later a more conservative prayerbook which caught Moses's imagination and aroused his esthetic consciousness was the single-handed effort by the poetic and musical Leopold Stein (1810–1882),[11] *Seder ha-Avodah: Gebetbuch fuer israelitische Gemeinden*, specifically its second, 1882 edition, published in Mannheim. To these we will return below.

Reform temples founded in the United States during the second half of the nineteenth century that bore the name Emanu-El, such as the ones in San Francisco and Milwaukee, adopted the rite initially designed for the standard-bearer New York congregation and emulated its pattern of worship. Thus, when Moses arrived to assume the rabbinical leadership of the Milwaukee congregation in 1879, he inherited Merzbacher's *Order of Prayer*, as revised by the learned Samuel Adler. The polished framework of that slender book became the fixed foundation of all Moses's liturgical labors. The sole exception was the High Holy Day volume of Adolph Huebsch's right-of-center Reform *Gebete fuer den oeffentlichen Gottesdienst: Seder Tefillah* (New York: Rubens & Freund, 1872) in use at Temple Ahawath Chesed,[12] in New York City, which rite Moses reworked and partially retranslated as late as 1916.

Making Do With Merzbacher's *Order of Prayer*

What, then, were those features in the Merzbacher/Adler service-book that Moses appropriated in his own revisions of the Prayerbook? The opening parts of the Morning Service, which were never subject to strict *halakhic* regulation and vary considerably among the traditional rites, were a good place for him to start. In the name of brevity and focus, Moses accepted Adler's dismantlement of the structure of both the *Birkhot ha-Shachar* (Preliminary Benedictions) and the *Pesuqey de-Zimrah* (Introductory Hymns and Psalms)[13] and the substitution in their place of a single psalm, the jubilant Ps. 100 (Adler, 30–31).[14] However, for the Evening Service, Merzbacher chose, as a kind of introductory anthem—and in a somewhat individualist fashion—a different psalm for each different occasion: Ps. 121("I will lift up mine eyes unto the hills") for Purim, Ps. 124 ("If it had not been the LORD who was on our side") for Hanukkah, Ps. 129 ("Often have they attacked me from my youth") for Tish'ah be-Av, Ps. 122 ("I was glad when they said to me") for all the Three Festivals, Ps. 81 ("Sing aloud to God our strength") for Rosh Hashanah, and Ps. 130 ("Out of the depths I cry to you, O LORD") for Yom Kippur (Merzbacher, 4–11).[15] When we examine which psalms Moses chose as preambles, after *Mah Tovu*, for his prayer manuals, we will notice that there was a good bit of fluctuation from one prayerbook to the next in Moses's choice of prefatory psalm, and will also see that the psalms were more often than not sung as choral anthems, sometimes in place of *Mah Tovu*.

To give us some idea of which "new" selections were made, let us see what we find in *Ms. 1891*, the first draft to be submitted by Moses to the Central Conference of American Rabbis. For Sabbath Evening the usual Pss. 95, 92 and 93 are offered as choices, along with *Mah Tovu*, as the opening anthem, while for '*Arvit* of the Three Festivals the options are Ps. 122, 113, 115:14-18 and 116:12-18—the last three of course being from the Hallel. As for Sabbath Morning the alternatives are *Mah Tovu*, Pss. 100 ("Make joyful noise to the LORD"), 150 ("Halleujah, praise the LORD in His sanctuary") and 124 ("If it had not been the LORD who was on our side"), while for the Festivals they are Pss.100, 125 ("Those who trust in the LORD are like Mount Zion"), 124 and 29 (*Ms. 1891*, 13–16, 33–36, 45–48, 95–98). In the subsequent drafts, up to *UPB 1892,* such a varied array of psalms no longer exists quite in the same way, doubtless to Moses's regret. The Hebrew texts of the *Qeriat Shema' u-Virkhoteha* (the Shema and its [encompassing] Benedictions) in all of the foregoing revisions are virtually identical with, or at any rate, very close to, Adler's modifications, both subtle and significant, of Merzbacher's liturgical infrastructure and phraseology (Adler, 10–15, 30–34). Their remarkable durability is attested by their relative persistence throughout all the editions of the *Union Prayer Book* and, to a considerable degree, the rites following—at the very least in the prayers' lean proportions and in their rewording according to Reform principle.[16] As an example, one might cite the benediction immediately preceding the *Shema'*, *Ahavah Rabbah*, where the line "O bring us in peace from the four corners of the earth, and make us go upright to our land" is removed,[17] as are the preferential "from all peoples and tongues," from the penultimate phrase *u-vanu vacharta mi-kol 'am ve-lashon* (without, however, negating the doctrine of the Chosen People; Adler, 32–33).[18]

The Torah Service in virtually all of Moses's rites is Merzbacher's (Merzbacher, 82–85), which in turn is derived, by and large, from the principally Sephardic-based Hamburg Temple *Gebetbuch*.[19] From this premier Reform rite Merzbacher took up the psalmodic verses *Se'u She'arim*,[20] the Elevation of the Scroll (to the accompaniment of *ve-zot ha-torah*) *prior* to the reading, and dispensed with the prophetic lesson (*haftarah*). Here is where Merzbacher and, later on, Moses did things differently from the Hamburg Temple prototype. As soon as the Reader took the Torah scroll out of the ark, he elevated it while reciting (or perhaps even chanting) *ve-zot ha-torah*, whereupon the congregation responded with the *Shema*, followed by the Reader's "O magnify the Lord with me" (*gaddelu l-adonai itti*) as he brought it to the reading-desk (*holekhin la-bimah*, as the rubric puts it). Then the congregation sang *lekha adonay*. As the Torah was read, there were naturally the requisite blessings before and after, but no salutatory *bar'khu et adonay hamevorakh* with its usual response (these already having been recited at the start of the statutory portion of the service). Merzbacher's procedure, as mediated through Moses and with gradual modifications, was the universal norm in American Reform until the arrival of the *Gates of Prayer: The New Union Prayer Book* in 1975.

Like Merzbacher, Moses initially placed his Festival Hallel *after* the Return of the Scroll to the Ark, serving as a holiday substitute, as it were, for *Ashrei*, customarily said at this point in the service (*Tefillah le-Mosheh 1884*, 25; *Tefillat Yisrael 1887*, 46ff.). The placement of Pss. 113–118 here no doubt acted as a smart celebratory surrogate for the suspended Additional Service with its many warm *yomtov* associations. Moses did not drop this eccentric practice until *Ms. 1891* when he moved it back to its habitual position between the end of the Festival Morning *'Amidah* and the Torah Service.

The opening paragraph of the classical *'Aleynu* has always been a matter of concern in European and American Reform because of its perceived chauvinism and ethnocentricity.[21] Merzbacher (24–25) took a bold initiative with regard to this quandary in two ways. First, he blue-penciled the objectionable lines "has not made us like the nations of other lands…nor is our lot like unto all their multitude" and exchanged them for the more cosmic *shehu noteh shamayim* until *hu eloheynu, eyn 'od* from after the crowning "We bend the knee...." The previously invidious *'Aleynu* lead-in now reads, in Merzbacher's (but not Adler's) literal rendition:[22]

It is peculiarly our duty to praise the Lord of all; to ascribe greatness to him who founded the world in the beginning; he who stretched out the heavens, and laid the foundations of the earth; the residence of whose glory is in the heavens above; and the divine majesty of whose power is in the highest heavens. He is our God, and there is no other!

Cong. Thus we bend the knee and prostrate ourselves before the Supreme King of kings, the holy and blessed one!

Here the prayer picks up again with "In truth He is our King" through the end of "We therefore hope in You, O Lord our God."[23] Incidentally, this was the identical *'Aleynu* that Isaac M. Wise embraced in his *Minhag Amerika.*[24] Moses even seized upon the new name Merzbacher had given the ancient prayer: Adoration.[25]

Further proof of Merzbacher's verbal inventiveness is the more inclusive nomenclature he came up with for the Mourners' Kaddish. The traditional terminology is *Qaddish Yatom, Orphan's* Kaddish. To accommodate the bereft parent, the grieving spouse and sorrowful others as well, Merzbacher coined the more comprehensive phrase *Qaddish da-Avelim* (the *Mourners'* Kaddish; Merzbacher, 26–27). Moses even utilized the novel expression—in Hebrew characters, unvocalized!—as its heading in his Anglicizing *Tefillah le-Mosheh 1884* (27).[26]

The all-pervasive reality of death throughout the nineteenth century—before vaccines and modern medical technology—is mirrored in all the prayer manuals of the time. *The Order of Prayer* and all of Moses's recreations devote considerable space to death and mourning. For a special trilingual 1871 edition for the House of Mourning, essentially a modified Evening Service, Adler thought up a new *'Amidah* comprised of a restyled *Havinenu* (a single-paragraph digest of the twelve Intermediate Benedictions with a novel and Hebraically well-crafted *'Anenu*, ending in "Blessed are You, O Eternal, who comforts the mourners"). The following prayer, in English and in German, is really an *'Aleynu* retooled for mourners, with the climactic *va-anach-nu kore'im* now reading: "Before thee, therefore, we bow and bend the knee, and with humility, resignation and unfailing trust submit to thy holy decrees." In place of *ve-hayah adonai le-melekh—u-shemo echad*, Adler turned out an innovative *chatimah*: "Blessed art thou, O Lord, our God, in all thy dispensations; honor and glory to thy holy name for ever and ever. Amen."[27] Moses commandeered this format in various ways in every one of his rites for the House of Mourners (1884. 37–39; 1887, 124; *Ms. 1892*, 201–203; *UPB 1892*, 201–202). With continuing adjustments, it made its way into the Evening Service at the House of Mourning in the first and revised editions of the *Union Prayer Book I* (1895, 250–253; 1918, 306–309).

Those nineteenth century Progressive prayerbooks which contained a Burial Service would invariably encompass a *Tsidduq ha-Din* (biblical verses justifying the divine decree). *The Order of Prayer* (296–297) is no exception, except, remarkably enough, it offers nothing else in addition, such as the predictable Ps. 91 ("You who live in the shelter of the Most High") and/or the Ashkenazic *El Male Racha-mim* or—by way of the Hamburg Temple *Gebetbuch*—the Sephardic *Hashkavah* (usually in either German or English), which Einhorn or Huebsch took in before ending with the Mourners' Kaddish. Moses does attach, in Hebrew and in translation, the last confession of sins and faith (*Vidduy Shekhiv Meira'*), which might be viewed as a sign of pastoral concern for his parishioners.[28] In this regard Moses was without a doubt prompted by *'Olat Tamid*.

David Einhorn's Influence: A Case Study

The influence of David Einhorn's *'Olat Tamid*[29] on all of Isaac S. Moses's liturgical work is considerable, notably in theology and interpretive translation. For purposes of illustration, we will make use of one example alone—the handling of the Shofar Service (specifically the tripartite *Malkhuyot-Zikhronot-Shofarot* sequence which traditionally forms the nucleus of the *Musaf* Service for Rosh Hashanah). Since there is no Additional Service in *'Olat Tamid*, the triadic chain is broken up and expediently spread over the Morning Service, with simply a single series of shofar[30] blasts (*teqi'ah, teru'ah, teqi'ah*) at the very end. Thus, the *Zikhronot* section (taking up all of four pages [179–182] in Einhorn's inspired German paraphrase), minus a *chatimah* (the benedictory seal: "Blessed are You, O Eternal...),[31] is placed, at variance with established usage, *before* the Hebrew Intermediate Benediction (the accustomed locus of the *Malkhuyot* section) of the Morning *'Amidah*. The climactic *Shofarot* (with its grand German adaptation of *Attah Nigleyta*) is positioned where the *Teqi'ot di-Meyushav* are authorized in the traditional *Machzor*, that is, prior the Return of the Scroll to the Ark. All of the foregoing is, of course, technical and quite involved and, in the final analysis—it must be said—quite impressive and indeed brilliant.

What then did Moses do with this unprecedented rearrangement of *Malkhuyot-Zikhronot-Shofarot*[32] by Einhorn? In the virtually-all-English *Tefillah le-Mosheh 1884* (29–31, 34) the triadic disposition remains entirely Einhorn's, but some of the language is taken from Landsberg's *Ritual* adaptation (Landsberg, 18–23). The key difference is that for *Shofarot* the text is based very loosely on Adler's in the 1860 and 1864 editions of the *Order of Prayer* (124–127). The re-Hebraized *Tefillat Yisrael 1887* has, within the Morning *'Amidah* for Rosh Hashanah—this time *following Malkhuyot*—the traditional *Zikhronot* on the Hebrew side (93, 95, including the customary *chatimah*, [*zokher ha-berit*])—with an excerpt from the medieval poem *U-Netanneh Toqef* inserted in the middle!—and Einhorn's recreation thereof on the opposite page. *After* the Return of the Torah to the Ark, where the *Musaf* would have been, the climactic *Shofarot* (104–105) is again Adler's (the Hebrew text essentially identical with Adler's, the English a slight revision of *Tefillah le-Mosheh 1884*), with the notes *teqi'ah, shevarim, teru'ah, teqi'ah* blown on the shofar. The choir then sings either Ps. 89:16 or 98:6 and Ps. 150. When we turn to *Ms. 1893*, however, we discover that Einhorn is joined by Isaac M. Wise. As in *'Olat Tamid*, an affecting interpretive *Zikhronot* appears before a Hebrew *qaddeshenu be-mitsvotekha—melekh 'al kol ha-aretz, meqaddesh yisra'el (ha-shabbat) ve-yom ha-zikkaron* (technically, the *Malkhuyot section*), while, after the scroll has been replaced in the ark and the sermon has been delivered, the choir sings vigorously the whole of Ps. 98 ("O sing to the LORD a new song"). The rabbi then repeats the ensuing remodeled Adler's confident *Shofarot*, as further refined from that found in *Tefillah le-Mosheh 1884* and *Tefillat Yisrael 1887*:

O Lord and Father, Thou didst reveal Thyself unto Thy people; Thy glory shone forth unto our ancestors, when Thou didst teach them Thy law of truth and love. Reveal Thyself unto us also, O Heavenly Father. May the cornet's sounds remind us that Thou alone art the Creator and Sustainer of the universe, our King, Law-giver and Judge; and that to Thee alone are due worship, honor and adoration. Cause, O Lord, our God, the trumpet of freedom to be sounded over the earth; and may all who still sigh under the burden of oppression hear the sound of deliverance; may the banner of Israel, Thy people, be exalted wherever Thou hast sent them to proclaim and to sanctify Thy name. Praise be to Thee, Eternal, who graciously acceptest the adoration of Israel. Amen.

Now here is where Wise's influence comes in. For dramatic effect, four (as opposed to Einhorn's one) series of shofar blasts are sounded, introduced with *adonay melekh, adonay malakh, adonay yimlokh le-'olam va'ed* and interspersed with I Chron. 16:15 and Ps. 98:6 and drawn to a close with Ps. 86:16, much like in *Minhag Amerika* (vol. 2 [1866], 162).

Paradoxically enough, in working on the more traditional *Huebsch 1916* Moses was able to be more faithful to his radical Einhorn legacy. While he places *Zikhronot* after *Malkhuyot* in Huebsch's Morning *'Amidah*[33] (85–89, thereby reverting to the accustomed sequence), *Attah Zokher* is none other than Einhorn's elevated five-page rendering in Emil G. Hirsch's English. After the Torah is put back in the ark, we are presented with a hymn composed by Huebsch (in Moses's rendition) "Hark! The Shofar's sounds awake thee," *Attah Nigleyta* in Einhorn's imposing style and Hirsch's unabridged version, the *berakhot* before sounding the shofar (as Huebsch would have had it), the minimalist four notes *teqi'ah, shevarim, teru'ah, teqi'ah*, Ps. 86:16, and, finally, the ebullient *Ha-Yom Te'ammetsenu* (110–115).

In all these various modernized handlings of the tripartite Shofar Service taken over from the *Musaf* of Rosh Hashanah we can see, all at the same time, Moses's keen sense of the pastorally feasible, the artistically tasteful, and the theologically compelling. Meanwhile, Einhorn's sway is never far off.

Berakhot Or No?

Another idiosyncrasy of much of early American Reform is the virtually wholesale abandonment of benedictions for everyday use, whether of the "commanding" variety (*asher qiddeshanu be-mits-votav*) or those before, during or after partaking of or enjoying any of God's creations (e.g., while beholding a rainbow or putting on a new item of clothing). All that is left of the benedictory scaffolding are the *Stammgebete*: the aforesaid *Shema* and its surrounding Benedictions and the *'Amidah*. Among the more traditionalist Reformers, for example, Szold and Jastrow provided *berakhot* for the donning of *tefillin*, taking of the *lulav* or hearkening to the call of the *shofar*, as they are all seen as prescribed in the Torah (*mi-de-orayeta*, in talmudic parlance).[34] As for those usages ordained by the Rabbis (*mi-de-rab-banan*), such as kindling the Sabbath light or reading the Megillah, no "prescriptive" benedictions are offered in any shape or form. This was a distinction these proto-Conservatives were careful to maintain,[35] and was one Isaac Mayer Wise upheld as well.[36] Although no radical in other respects, Leo Merzbacher was hardly of the conviction that God was the kind of deity who would command, let alone worry about, ritual observances. As a result, there was not a single benediction with the formula "who has sanctified us by Your commandments and commanded us to" for pentateuchal *mitzvot* or rabbinic "ordinances" to be found in either volume of Merzbacher's prayerbook;[37] for the most part this too was true of Moses's future liturgical works.[38] Nonetheless, in *Huebsch 1916* for the High Holy Days, Moses kept unaltered his predecessor's *berakhot* mandating the blowing of the *shofar* (114), solely out of deference to the congregation's love and loyalty to the Huebsch/Kohut *minhag*.[39]

Following suit, the *Union Prayer Book* also did not have any *be-rakhot* until the revised edition of 1918, where the one and only "commanding" benediction—for the lighting of the Hanukkah candles—is recited amid ceremonial pomp and circumstance at a Friday night service during Hanukkah (53). Interestingly, in the section "Private

Devotion" of the selfsame edition it is suggested, by striking contrast, that the "wife" of "the head of the household" say, in the vernacular, "May our home be consecrated, O God, by Thy light. May it shine upon us all in blessing as the light of love and truth, the light of peace and goodwill. Amen" (345).[40]

European Influences: Abraham Geiger, The *Reformgemeinde* And Leopold Stein

Moses periodically turned to European liturgy-writers for inspiration. While Abraham Geiger[41] was unquestionably a groundbreaking *Wissenschaftler* and foremost Reform theologian, he was nowhere near as audacious as Moses in the liturgical reforms he was responsible for in his *Devar Yom be-Yomo: Israelitisches Gebetbuch fuer den oeffentlichen Gottesdienst im ganzen Jahre* (Breslau: Julius Hainauer, 1854 and Berlin: Louis Gerschel, 1870). Because of restrictions entailed by the overriding *Gemeinde* structure of the Jewish communities he shepherded, he settled on a relatively conservative, or gradualist, approach in the *siddurim* he edited. Fortunately, his innovative side eloquently manifested itself in the deeply spiritual and personalized German paraphrases—or should one say transfigurations?—of the standard Hebrew text. This approach was to serve Moses well in his later English compositions.

The *Reformgemeinde*'s Rite As Formative For Moses

One of the most far-reaching and interior prayerbooks to come out of Europe was the avant-garde and all-purpose *Gebetbuch* of the Berlin *Reformgemeinde* (1848),[42] which over time came to reflect more and more the influence of Samuel Holdheim, the congregation's rabbi from 1847 until his death in 1860. Less than a handful of its devotional outpourings were translated by Moses for the prayerbooks he edited. It is entirely possible that he first became acquainted with those prayers that had been borrowed by Einhorn for his *'Olat Tamid*. A good illustration of this is the transmutation of the time-honored post-*'Amidah* meditation, *Elohay Netsor Leshoni*. The *Reformgemeinde*'s acrimony-free and soulful—and exquisite—reconstruction (echoed in *'Olat Tamid*) reads in German (63):

Gemeinde in stiller Andacht

*Mein Gott, bewahre meine Zunge vor Boesem, meine
Lippen vor Trug. Verleih' mir Sanftmuth gegen die, die
mir uebel wollen; pflanze Demuth in meine Seele und Gott-
vertrauen in mein Herz. Sei mein Hort, wenn ich in Schmerz
verstumme, mein Trost, wenn meine Seele gebeugt ist. Lass
mich wandeln in Deiner Wahrheit; leite mich, denn Du bist
mein Gott und meine Hilfe, auf Dich hoffe ich alltaeglich.
Nimm in Wohlgefallen auf die Worte meines Mundes, die Regung meines Herzens komme vor Dich, Gott, mein Schoepfer
und Erloeser! Amen.*

Vorbeter

*Nimm in Wohlgefallen auf die Worte meines Mundes,
die Regung meines Herzens komme vor Dich, Gott, mein
Schoepfer und Erloeser! Der Du den ewigen Frieden erhaeltst
In den Himmelshoehen, erhalte auch den Frieden uns und
Allen, die Deinen Namen anrufen. Amen.*[43]

Moses (*UPB 1892*, 16) rendered it in no less graceful and agreeable
manner:

The Congregation in Silent Devotion

O God, keep my tongue from evil, and my lips from ut-
tering deceit, and grant that I may be meek and kind to those
who bear ill-will against me. Implant humility in my heart
and strengthen my faith in Thee. Be my support when grief
oppresses me and my comfort in affliction. Let Thy truth il-
lumine my path and guide me; for Thou art my God and my
aid; in Thee I trust every day. May the words of my lips and
the meditation of my heart be acceptable in Thy sight, O God,
my Strength and my Deliverer. Thou who preservest peace
in the heavenly spheres, grant it to me and to all who invoke
Thy name.

Minister

May the words of my lips…..

The Union Prayer Book (vol. 1, newly revised, 1940, 24) eventually smoothed out the wrinkles here into:

Silent Prayer
(or such other prayer as the heart may prompt)
O God, keep my tongue from evil and my lips from speaking guile. Be my support when grief silences my voice, and my comfort when woe bends my spirit. Implant humility in my soul, and strengthen my heart with perfect faith in Thee. Help me to be strong in temptation and to be patient and forgiving when others wrong me. Guide me by the light of Thy counsel, that I may ever find strength in Thee, my Rock and my Redeemer. Amen.
Choir
May the words of my mouth and the meditation of my heart be acceptable unto Thee, O Lord, my Rock and my Redeemer. Amen.

Not to be overlooked is the moving personal prayer for peace, also taken from the *Reformgemeinde*'s prayerbook (1848, 50). Moses first put part of it to use as a parting benediction in *Ms. 1892* (60):

Lord, Thy peace be with us, the peace that spreadeth out like the heavens, like a tent to dwell in. May there be peace within us; peace in our houses, that works and words of love be in them. Let us hear what God will speak; for Thou wilt speak peace unto Thy people.[44]

A fuller version appears in *Ms. 1893* (28) (to which, compare *Huebsch 1916*, 96) as a post-*'Amidah* meditation:

O Lord, may Thy peace be vouchsafed to me. Let it enter my soul that I may live in peace with myself and be content with what is allotted to me. Let my heart be in perfect peace with Thee, my God.

Let peace ever abide in my house, that works of love may be seen therein; only words of love be heard in it, and that no discord may ever separate those whom Thou hast created for each other.

Oh, grant peace unto all who seek Thee, O Lord of peace. Accept graciously the words of my mouth and the meditation of my heart, O God, my Strength and my Redeemer. Amen.

Leopold Stein's Influence

The first edition (1860) of Leopold Stein's *Seder ha-'Avodah: Gebetbuch fuer israelitische Gemeinden*, designed to serve the recently renovated *Hauptsynagoge* in Frankfurt am Main, was basically a traditional *siddur* with many Reform touches; the second edition (Mannheim: J. Schneider, 1882), now independent, is a Reform rite with a strong attachment to the tradition. In both editions, taking up over forty pages, is the entire Psalter in German verse intended to be treated either musically, with cantor and/or choir (and, at times, congregation too) as chorales and anthems, or simply as responsive readings. This was a practice that Moses made his own in the majority of his prayerbook revisions. The Psalms, for the most part grouped according to theme (as he understood it), would be placed in an appendix. That these ancient sacred songs were always close to his heart, for both their emotional candor and their literary quality come through in a spontaneous remark he made at a session of the CCAR: "I am in favor of going to the Bible for our songs—put the entire book of Psalms in [a hymnal]. Let the congregation get familiar with the Psalms by singing and chanting them."[45]

"O Day of God"

Set to the perdurable strains of *Kol Nidrey, O Tag des Herrn*[45] ("O Day of God") is Stein's revampment of the legal formula as a rallying call to reconciliation and pardon that found its way into many a Liberal and Reform prayerbook. The earliest English translation I have been able to uncover is the fairly literal, if labored, one by Marcus Jastrow for the Atonement Eve Service in his 1873 revision of Benjamin Szold's Proto-Conservative *'Avodat Yisrael* (246–247). In due course another equally wooden but anonymous rendition appears in perhaps the most nonconformist, truly pioneering of nineteenth-century American Reform prayerbooks, *The Service Manual* (Philadelphia: Edward Stein & Co., 1892) by Joseph Krauskopf (1858–1923), before the sermon on Yom Kippur Eve towards the end of service (297–298). The effortless and natural translation that wound up in the *Union Prayer Book II,* and that was avidly promoted by Isaac S. Moses, was carried out by a colleague of his in Quincy, Illinois—a Unitarian minister and native of Boston who was a recognized authority on hymnody and fecund maker of the same, Frederick Lucian Hosmer (1840–1929).[47] Here are some verses from Hosmer's close yet sweet-sounding rendition of Leopold Stein's second stanza:

> Brothers, come! Here be renewed
> Bonds of love and brotherhood!
> Hearts of the morn shall see
> From all hatred free –
> Speed the reconciling!
> Hark, who weeps?
> They weep for thy friendship vanished –
> The bond renew!
> Hark, who grieves?
> The brother thy hate has banished –
> The wrong undo!
> God loveth all who live,
> As He forgives, forgive,
> Loyal be, and true.

Stein's Passover Melodies In American Guise

Nineteenth-century American Jewry did not enjoy such a plethora of non-Orthodox Passover *haggadot* as we do today. Moses stepped into the breach by singlehandedly translating into English Leopold Stein's singularly user-friendly, predominantly-German *Haggadah* (*Hagada, oder Erzaehlung vom Auszuge aus Aegypten* [Frankfurt am Main: J.S. Adler, 1841]). Stein was preeminently gifted in that he succeeded in putting into the vernacular countless Hebrew melodies, such as familiar Sabbath Eve *zemirot* and many of the songs customarily sung at the Passover Seder. For his part, Moses sought to achieve the same, but to a much more limited degree.[46] It has doubtless been taken for granted that the standard English counterpart of the universally singable Passover hymn *Addir Hu* is "God of Might, God of Right" by the adept Reform hymnographer and rabbi, Gustav Gottheil (1827–1903).[47] Another hymn, set to the same exuberant melody, was sung for a good while in Reform and Conservative synagogues across the land, "Praise the Lord! One accord."[48] Here we will reproduce in English three stanzas of Moses's reasonably accurate translation of Stein's zestful, upbeat seven-stanza *Lobt den Herrn/Nah und fern*:[49]

Praise the Lord! One accord
Sound through all creation!
Laud and sing! Honor bring
Him without cessation!
And His fame loud proclaim
Every land and nation!

* * * *

Lo, the spring joy doth bring:
Winter's frosts are ended;
Gladness reigns, life remains
With sweet pleasures blended.
We can bear what His care
And His love intended.

Father, we pray of Thee:
Let Thy grace be o'er us!
Let Thy light in the night
Show Thy path before us!
Our Thy love from above,
And the strength which bore us.[50]

Moses's Esthetic

Although conversant in the theological developments in Judaism[51]—and much else outside its purview—Isaac S. Moses was something of an esthete. He preferred the artistic over the intellectual, and made sure his prayerbooks were not only easy to hold but pleasant to the eye. Typography and layout were matters of continual concern to him, as was the delicate balance between the spoken text and the chorally (and congregationally) sung pieces during worship. His love of music without fail shone through in the hymns he wrote, translated and incorporated in his hymn-books. In the preface to *Tefillah le-Mosheh 1884* Moses reveals his captivation with the Psalms and his determination to give them greater exposure.[52] In his sermons he often dilated on the grandeur of nature in all things great and small, delighted in the sensuous as much as in the spiritual, and exulted in the beauties of form, symmetry and sound. He scarcely ever hid his conviction that access to and knowledge of the Divine may be gained through the esthetic, no less than the interhuman[53] and the ethical.

In this connection, the end of his sermon to the twenty-eighth convention of the Central Conference of American Rabbis in 1916 at Buffalo captured the artistic, deeply religious soul of a man who, through his distinctive fusion of talents, evolved into a successful liturgist: "We must move the hindrances that divide us from divine communion. One of our medieval poets sang, in that fine poem, *Ha-Aderet veha-Emunah*[54]: 'Beauty and power come from the Ever-living One, Communion and sweetness come from the Ever-living One.' Beauty, loveliness and permanence—these are divine elements."

A New Understanding of the Cantor's Role

It should then not come as a surprise that Moses's last rabbinical post, in New York in 1901, opened him up to a new appreciation of the cantor's role in the synagogue. We discover from the preface to *The Sabbath-School Hymnal* 1904 (4)[55] that *Hazzan* Theo Guinsburg helped Moses greatly to re-judaize the hymnal by applying familiar Jewish melodies associated with traditional Hebrew texts to new English verse. He was undoubtedly instrumental in exposing Moses to something of the range of the cantorial tradition. Moses came to see the cantor as a *sheliach tsibbur* or "*Vorbeter*, a leader in prayer, ministering to the spiritual needs of the congregation." In an address titled "The Cantor as a Religious Functionary," delivered by Moses before the Society of American Cantors on 22 March 1904, he had this to say:

Ever since I came to this pulpit [of Ahawath Chesed-Shaar Hashamayim] I have experienced the blessed effect of a truly religious, a genuinely Jewish service. While the cantor recites or chants the prayers I am, as it were, under the spell of a holy influence; thoughts flash out, emotions well forth, memories rise, fears are allayed and doubts are stilled, courage and hope are winged, the soul is stirred and chastened, uplifted and calmed—by the noble, dignified, melodious voice of the cantor.[56]

A Summation

From Moses's work one can infer quite a bit about his strategy in prayerbook-making.[57] First and foremost, he was practical and pastoral. He was manifestly not a liturgical scholar of the rank of a Zunz; nor did he possess the originality of Fraenkel and Bresselau—the two men behind the creation of the Hamburg Temple *Gebetbuch*—or the solid Hebrew learning of a Merzbacher or a Szold, or the soaring intellect of an Einhorn. In the preface to each of his first two prayerbooks he claimed "the merit of this book is the lack of originality." All the same, his easy bilingualism,[58] his deep encounters with earlier high-calibered American and German Reform prayerbooks, his readiness to do the spadework in each new liturgical undertaking,[59] his energetic resourcefulness and, his hands-on experience with widely divergent rites, not to mention his canny esthetic sense, all served him in good stead.

But the road was not easy. Moses made considerable financial sacrifices and, along the way, encountered frustration, disappointment, and hurt. Because two of his congregations, Temple Emanu-El[60] in Milwaukee and Kehilath Anshe Maarav (KAM)[61] in Chicago, were already using the Merzbacher/Adler rite, *The Order of Prayer*, it was that *siddur* he primarily worked with, emulated and tweaked in all his years as a liturgist. There were causes for some dissatisfaction for Moses—and perhaps for either or both of his congregations as well. Theologically, it did not go far enough. Reform consisted chiefly of what was weeded out of the Classical Prayerbook or an occasional alteration in the Hebrew text. David Einhorn's cutting-edge Jewish worldview, as embodied, for example, in his liturgical tour de force *'Olat*

Tamid, filled that void admirably.[62] Because one of Moses's ongoing passions was to provide a prayer manual accessible to the younger, Americanized generation, he issued his *Tefillah le-Mosheh 1884*—an all-English edition but for a handful of individual Hebrew sentences. The models in this case were, as noted earlier, the highly innovative prayerbook of the *Reformgemeinde* and Max Landberg's *Ritual*. When that experiment failed, Moses used the experience as a chance to try something else. *Tefillat Yisrael 1887* has the bulk of Merzbacher's Hebrew text restored, along with most of the psalms for *Qabbalat Shabbat* and a sampling of the *Pesuqey de-Zimrah*, in English.[63] Yet, when the opportunity arose to change his focus from solely the congregational sphere to one embracing an entire movement—imaginably with some fear and trembling—Moses rose to the challenge and collaborated with colleagues of varying positions, temperaments and tastes to put forward a uniform prayerbook for all American Reform Jewry. No doubt this is why he was able to accomplish what Isaac Mayer Wise, with his *Minhag Amerika*, could not.[64] To be sure, although Moses made a number of accommodations as he prepared his final project, fundamentally he was able to avoid having "too many cooks spoil the broth" or having to surrender his vision of what a union prayerbook should be. The final product, in essence, shape, form, and *élan*, is all Isaac S. Moses's triumph.

Modern Maccabees: Remaking Hanukkah in Nineteenth Century America

Dianne Ashton

Most Jews in nineteenth-century America, in common with the majority of America's Jewish population throughout its history, shared a desire to fit in with American society. Except for a small minority of fervently orthodox Jews who sought to maintain an insular Jewish culture, in each era of American history Jews embraced elements of the broader culture in order to demonstrate that they, too, were genuinely American. In this respect they were much like other religious "outsiders."[1] Twentieth century observers of American Jewish life often point to the case of Hanukkah as a paradigmatic illustration of this pattern, explaining that the "magnification" of Hanukkah grew from American Jews' desire to celebrate their own December holiday during the "national festival" of Christmas.[2] The domestic customs of Christmas, such as decorated evergreens and gift-giving, became widespread among Christian Americans who sought moral frames for the nation's developing culture of consumption as early as the mid-nineteenth century.[3] Jews, likewise, in order to lend a religious cover to their own participation in the general consumer festival each December, turned to Hanukkah.

But there is more than this to the story of Hanukkah's transformation from a minor festival to an elaborate celebration. In the nineteenth century—before it became an occasion best noted for the eagerness with which Jewish children awaited it—serious-minded Jews had already transformed Hanukkah's meaning. These thinkers redefined Hanukkah to express their own religious understanding of the holiday, and in doing so redrew the past to serve the present. Other Jews fought against the new picture of Hanukkah developed by these thinkers, but in this battle of interpretation American principles and cultural forms entered nearly every conception of Hanukkah expressed by American Jews. A synthesis of Jewish and American culture not only supported Jews' claim to a rightful place as American patriots, it also asserted Judaism's relevance to modern Western culture.[4]

American Judaism took shape in the early nineteenth century with new prayer books, new hymns, and new forms of congregational governance that featured written constitutions.[5] These innovations elicited wide-ranging disagreements and discussions: about Judaism's religious core versus its specific practice; about God's commandments versus human invention, and about the demands of modernity. In the midst of the competition over control of the future of Jewish religious life in the United States, Hanukkah became contested cultural ground as Jews expressed an array of opinions that both redefined the holiday and shaped a new place for it within Jewish life. As American society invented new holidays like Thanksgiving (1863), Memorial Day (1868), Arbor Day (1885), Labor Day (1886), and Mothers' Day (1914) in order to inculcate values and behaviors that seemed to be slipping away in an industrializing, diversifying, and urbanizing society, American Jews took a new look at their own religious holiday calendar.[6] Hanukkah seemed especially suited to illuminate a view of Jewish faith and heritage relevant in the post-Civil War American context.

In an 1885 open letter to America's Jews, Reform Rabbi Emanuel Schreiber of Denver, Colorado, hoped to clarify the heated competition between Jewish religious reformers and traditionalists by framing their debates in the stark terms suggested by the upcoming Hanukkah holiday. "Reform Judaism " he said, was "the modern Maccabee" that "stepped in with a religion of the heart keeping Jews away from proselytizers" and unbelief, and rescuing Judaism from what he believed would have been its certain death in America.[7] Because Christians seemed to define the American way of life, the trend to modify Jewish customs to allow Jews to live and worship in a manner more like their Christian neighbors was a major factor in the Jewish com-· munity's process of assimilation. In the 1870s this new approach to Judaism enjoyed widespread popularity and seemed to hold the future in its hand. Reformers established both an organization uniting American Jewish congregations and a seminary to train rabbis—at that time the only such institutions in the country. More than one third of the country's Jewish congregations formally identified themselves with the new trend, and, by 1879, out of two hundred seventy eight Jewish congregations nationwide one hundred and five affiliated with the Union of American Hebrew Congregations (UAHC).[8] Yet many congregations who did not affiliate with the UAHC also experimented with reforms. Reformers sanctioned abandonment of the Jewish dietary laws, streamlined the liturgy and translated it into the vernacular, added edifying sermons, adorned synagogue worship with instrumental music from the great composers of Europe, such as Bach, Mendelssohn, and Handel, and encouraged family-style seating. Many American Jews found these changes appealing, although controversy consistently surrounded them and actual synagogue practices varied widely. Reformers touted their approach to Judaism as the best way to keep American Jews within the Jewish fold, and, convinced that Talmud-driven Jewish practice could never survive in the modern world, they wrote essays and sermons advancing their cause. Published in various Jewish newspapers and magazines geared to ordinary American Jews, these essays gave advice to modern Jews navigating between American and Jewish customs. Looking back upon Reform's achievements during the past century, Rabbi Schreiber defended Reform's changes, and went so far as to compare its champions to the ancient Maccabees.

On the opposite side of the religious divide from Schreiber, tradition-minded Rabbi Sabato Morais also turned to the heroes of Hanukkah's story, in his case to illustrate the virtues of a more traditional view. Unlike Schreiber, Morais urged Jews to remember the "illustrious... brave men who ventured their lives to transmit to us unity of religion." He insisted that the Maccabees hoped to *preserve* Judaism—not transform it.[9] Speaking in 1850, one year before his arrival in Philadelphia from London, Morais found in the Maccabees a symbol of Jewish devotion that might inspire contemporary Jews to rededicate themselves to their ancient faith. A native of the Italian port city of Livorno, Morais felt that he understood the Jews of London and Philadelphia, themselves port cities where Jews participated in a cosmopolitan world. He believed that these cosmopolitan Jews should better their Jewish and larger communities through religious "self cultivation" which led "away from the self . . . towards political and social activity." The religious self-cultivation he had in mind required education, and Morais taught Jewish culture as well as religion.[10] He developed Philadelphia's Hebrew Literary Society into a lively organization that soon became part of the national Young Men's Hebrew Association.[11] In 1887, Morais began serving as the first president of the Jewish Theological Seminary, a rabbinical school in New York City that instructed its pupils in a more tradition-oriented Judaism than that promulgated at Reform's rabbinical school, Cincinnati's Hebrew Union College.[12]

Tradition-minded American rabbis like Morais believed America's freedoms offered Jews an opportunity to embrace their religion even more fully than they had been able to under the more homogeneous but oppressive conditions of the past. Hanukkah could provide a vehicle for modern Jews to rededicate themselves to their faith. To the Jews scattered around the country and divided over religious practices, these rabbis talked of Maccabees joining together to advance and defend their religion and people. Samuel Isaacs, a traditionalist living in New York, fumed over this attitude, and felt that going to these lengths was both unnecessary and "self-abasing." "Here in these shores of freedom," he wrote, "where we have every right guaranteed us by the constitution, where we have every reason to thank God for His goodness to us, and where we have every cause to manifest by our acts that we are Israelites, observing the commandments delegated to us - how humiliating is the idea that [Judaism's] most sacred ordinances are totally disregarded."[13]

Thus, American rabbis as different in their approach to Judaism as were Schreiber and Morais utilized the image of the Maccabees to encourage American Jews to enliven their religious lives, believing as they did that the future of Jewish life in America rested upon their ability to motivate ordinary Jews.[14] Talk of ancient Maccabees fighting an oppressive imperial power in order to practice their own religion dotted the rhetoric of rabbis who hoped to modify Judaism to fit the modern age, as well as that of rabbis who hoped to generate a flowering of traditional Jewish religious observance. Reformers sometimes claimed that they themselves were Maccabees, and often told the ancient story in contemporary language. Traditionalists more often spoke of the grandeur of the Maccabean past and the duty of modern Jews to honor it. Both sides also blended America's rhetoric of liberty and revolution into the story of the Maccabean revolt. In doing so, they contributed to a larger trend that dominated American Jewish life as American Jews wove their own story into the fabric of American culture.[15] These nineteenth-century Hanukkah debates were an important factor in the reinterpretation of the holiday, which resulted in a new significance for the heretofore minor festival.

Hanukkah and Jews' Encounter with the Modern Age

Whether reformers like Schreiber or traditionalists like Morais, many nineteenth century rabbis studied the process of Jewish integration into Western culture in North America and Western Europe. On the face of it, the nineteenth century seemed to be good for the Jews of the West. Late eighteenth-century political revolutions in France and the United States had proclaimed the dawn of a new age, and promoted liberty in England and Germany. In Europe, the Napoleonic conquests tore down ghetto walls and invited Jews into the general citizenry. In the United States, federal law granted Jews equal status with Christians and state laws followed suit over the course of the century. The era's industrial growth seemed to further define the modern era as an age of progress. Some leading American Protestants concluded that providence was advancing material conditions to bring about the kingdom of God.[16] The leading American minister, Henry Ward Beecher, confidently told an 1876 audience that "The Revolutionary generation built a great nation, but we are building a greater one."[17]

But in both Western Europe and North America, Christianity shaped cultural values and public festivals, subtly spreading Christian articles of belief across the population, while, at the same time, Enlightenment rationalism suggested to educated individuals that religion ought not to interfere too much in any civilization. In Europe and the United States, this meant restricting religion's legal reach and its governmental supports. Religion's inability to obtain support from public coffers or to call upon public officials to enforce religious rules, caused the clergy of many denominations to worry about their own weakening influence. Complicating matters, "[F]aith in individual autonomy . . . (was) a central tenet of the modern world view."[18] The modern world encouraged individual Jews to solve their religious confusions for themselves, if only with the guidance of a religious leader of their own choosing.

These trends concerned nineteenth century American rabbis, many of whom hailed from Western Europe, where the great centers of Jewish religious learning and authority remained. Living in nineteenth-century Jewish America, on the other hand, meant to struggle along on the distant periphery of the Jewish world. At the time of the Revolution, the Jews of the United States numbered no more than 2500 individuals scattered in five communities along the eastern seaboard and comprised less than .1 % of the general population. (As a result, between 1776 and 1840, marriages with Christians reached 28.7% of all known Jewish marriages.) Immigration from central Europe, though, greatly expanded the American Jewish population to 250,000 by 1880. Adventurous young Jews made their way in a new country that offered them citizenship without segregation and unparalleled economic opportunities. Yet, with immigrants' attention focused upon learning a new language, new customs, and new places, Jewish religious obligations sometimes fell by the wayside. Many immigrant men who began as peddlers traveled to small towns across the countryside to serve rural gentile customers.[19] The peddlers arrived in these outlying towns as bachelors, but would frequently marry local gentile women. Many of these couples raised their children as Christians.[20] Lacking the support of kin and community that Jewish immigrants had left behind, and devoid of any authoritative body to teach or enforce religious practices, American Jewish life rested upon myriad individual decisions about how—or whether—to participate in religion. American rabbis wondered how Judaism would survive.

Some rabbis compared the contemporary American Jewish dilemma to that faced by Jews in ancient Judea, who embraced Hellenic culture yet disagreed about the degree to which they could do so and still retain Jewish identity.[21] These rabbis often focused on a moment that seemed to resolve the confusion: the rededication of the Jerusalem Temple in 165 B.C.E., when Jewish ritual standards replaced the remnants of Greek worship established there by Syrian king, Antiochus IV. To some, this ancient experience seemed to prefigure the contemporary situation, and to provide hope for its resolution. The Jerusalem Temple might be gone, but the image of those Jews who fought for some sort of religious standard inspired nineteenth century rabbis to look at Hanukkah with new eyes.

By bringing the Maccabees into the debate over how Judaism might survive in the modern world, all sides revealed the emotions that animated them. The polemic polarized differences that actually fell along a continuum of approaches to Jewish life. Baltimore rabbi Benjamin Szold, for example, compiled a well-received prayer book for his congregation that "closely followed traditional lines," yet included German translations. (Szold's prayer book replaced the more radical prayer book compiled by Reform leader Isaac M. Wise, used by the congregation before Szold's arrival in 1859.) Under Szold's leadership, the congregation gained a reputation for strict observance of the Sabbath. He characterized himself as opposing "radicalism," not change.[22] Szold's colleague, Philadelphia's Rabbi Marcus Jastrow, held both rabbinic ordination and a doctorate from the University of Halle—an education sufficiently secular that it might have convinced him to join the ranks of those seeking Judaism's reform. Instead, after coming to Philadelphia in 1866, Jastrow taught Bible and Jewish history at Maimonides College, the brainchild of one of the first American Jewish leaders to oppose reform, Isaac Leeser. Jastrow, although unable to prevent liberalization, slowed the pace of his Philadelphia congregation's ultimate embrace of Reform. Traditionalist Isaac Leeser, older than Jastrow, Szold, Morais, and Schreiber, deemed the trend toward religious laxity that washed over Western Europe—and influenced America—in the wake of the French revolution a "calamity." "Instead of illustrating the old methods of worship and making them lovely to the multitude," Leeser said, reformers introduced "changes and modifications unknown…unauthorized…(and) unlawful."[23] Like most American Jews at mid-century, Leeser came from central Europe. He arrived in the United States from Westphalia in 1824, and five years later Philadelphia's oldest congregation, *Mikveh Israel*, hired him to serve as its religious leader. Although Leeser had no training as a rabbi, his religious education far exceeded that of his congregants. He left his stamp on the Jacksonian era through his monthly periodical on Jewish affairs, his English translation of the Hebrew Bible, his volumes of sermons, and the various institutions for Jewish education that he helped to establish.

Traditionalists themselves did not always agree upon every matter regarding Judaism. Some traditionalists stepped out of Talmudic norms in their own lives, yet wished the synagogue service to remain unchanged.[24] Leeser, a bachelor who rented rooms at the home of a gentile widow, caused some members of his congregation to suspect that this arrangement would prevent him from adhering to Judaism's dietary laws, despite his traditional values.[25] Also, Leeser and some other traditionalists, such as Morris Raphall, hoped their own congregations would adopt the decorum they noticed in Protestant churches without otherwise changing the Jewish worship service.[26] However, despite their disagreements, when the traditionalists compared themselves to ancient Maccabees who defeated an alien oppressor and restored correct Jewish worship to the Jerusalem Temple, they erased their differences and instead conveyed an image of united support for historic Judaism.

Nineteenth century rabbis' disputes lent Hanukkah new significance. No account of the Maccabean revolt appears in the Hebrew Bible, and the holiday's rites, which are minimal, categorize Hanukkah as only a minor festival. Sages who compiled the Talmud mentioned Hanukkah mostly as part of a larger discussion about Shabbat, and explained the Maccabean victory as evidence of God's continuing protection of the Jews. Written several centuries after Judea's fall in 70 C.E., their interest in the historical details of the revolt lay in matters pertaining to religious life, the Temple and the Torah. They had little interest in the political gains the Hasmoneans achieved for Judea, a country that no longer existed by the time they wrote.[27]

The rabbis touted an entirely different way of dealing with domination by foreign powers than the armed revolt conducted against Antiochus IV led by the Hasmoneans. Rabbinics scholar Daniel Boyarin explains that the "earliest Jewish texts" of the Roman era "present a culture of men who are resisting, renouncing, and disowning" the Roman ideal of manliness identified through the assertion of male physical power and status. "None of the rabbis were pacifists," Boyarin tells us, but they asserted an attitude that is probably best expressed in the phrase, "Where there is life, there is hope," or "Where there is life, there is Torah."[28] Rather than being quick to take up arms against an oppressor, the rabbis advocated lying low, being obscure, and if necessary, resorting to appeasement and bribery. In other words, they advocated a tactical relationship to the larger power that allowed for survival, rather than outright rebellion using the "manly" arts of violent resistance. The rabbis went so far as to give an entirely different account of bravery than one found in two of the books of the Maccabees which concern an elderly teacher named Eleazar. In these earlier accounts, Eleazar died a courageous death, tortured by Antiochus's forces for refusing to pretend to eat forbidden food—an act that would set a bad example to other Jews. Flayed alive, he nonetheless kept his reason and kept his eyes raised to heaven.[29]

Boyarin sees the rabbis' story of Eleazar as "almost a parody" of the one found in Maccabees. In their story, which includes three miracles, Rabbi Eleazar survives by fooling the Romans who confront him.[30] The values of this story are that "(a)ny sort of deception is legitimate, as long as it gets you off the hook with the oppressor, because his rule is absolutely illegitimate. The purpose of the rabbis' version is to "bring out the opposition between the Torah and modes of violence per se."[31] This approach to dealing with a larger power is common to diasporic peoples in many parts of the world.

Historians suggest a second explanation for the rabbinic reluctance to laud Maccabean militarism. Throughout much of their exilic history, Jews looked to the highest governing authorities to protect them from violence at the hands of local mobs or local authorities. Yosef Hayim Yerushalmi described the situation as one in which "the practice of the Jewish religion and the vital substructure of Jewish civilization all depended on as much stability and continuity in the rule of law as possible, and on the establishment of a mutuality of interest with those ruling powers most capable of providing it. Jews, in other words, sought direct vertical alliances.[32] Even when rulers failed to protect them, this "royal alliance," as historian Salo Baron termed it, endured as a cultural myth among Jews.[33] This perspective, seen in their own tactical approach to Jewish survival, may have influenced rabbinic writers to dampen Jews' regard for the Maccabean revolt against Antiochus IV.

The Talmudic rabbis also designed Hanukkah celebrations to focus upon God's power. In the daily prayers these rabbis compiled— still used in the twenty-first century—Jews at Hanukkah thank God for delivering "the strong into the hands of the weak." In synagogues, Psalms 113–118, which praise God, continue to be recited, and God is specially thanked for miracles in the *Amida* (Standing) prayer. The same prayer expressing gratitude for miracles is added to the grace after meals during Hanukkah,[34] and on the Sabbath that falls during Hanukkah, a special reading from the prophet Zekharia includes the phrase, "not by might, nor by power, but by my spirit, saith the Lord." Together, these readings seem to completely deny Maccabean military effectiveness and to praise only God's power.

The blessing to be recited when lighting the Hanukkah lamp can be found in other tractates of the Talmud. Anthropologist Catherine Bell tells us that rituals usually convey their meanings in multiple and redundant ways, and this certainly applies to the ritual associated with Hanukkah.[35] Hanukkah's ritual commemorates a second miracle that *explains* the Maccabees' miraculous victory. According to the Talmud, the lighting of the menorah on Hanukkah commemorates a miracle, which occurred as Jews cleaned out remnants of Greek sacrifices and general desecration after they defeated Antiochus's army. As they cleaned, the Jews found that only a small amount of the oil prepared by their own priests remained, yet they needed that ritually prepared oil to complete their rededication of the Temple and light the flame required to burn constantly to indicate God's presence. The small amount of oil, burning for a week until more could be prepared, was regarded by the rabbis of the Talmud as a miracle through which God conveyed to the ancient Jews that their victory also had been his work.

Hanukkah's ritual primarily recalls the miracle of the oil, not the Maccabean victory. According to the Talmud, on each evening of Hanukkah Jews light small candles or oil lamps, and recite a blessing praising God for miracles performed at this season in ancient days. Each evening of the holiday an additional candle is placed in the lamp. Increasing in number from right to left; they are lit from left to right by means of an additional ninth candle. Except for the time when the lamps are lit, Jews need not refrain from everyday work during Hanukkah. The Talmud also instructs Jews to place the lighted menorah in public view to advertise the miracle, and for women to join in lighting the lamp. Women took it upon themselves to observe Hanukkah more stringently than men, the Talmud says, because the ancient Greeks forced sexual immorality upon them.[36] The miracle, as the Talmud calls the Maccabean uprising, also rescued these women. In the sixteenth century Joseph Caro compiled a guide to rabbinic law, which, with an addition by Moses Isserles, quickly became the standard for Jewish observance. Called the *Shulchan Arukh* (Set Table), its rules regarding the placement and lighting of the Hanukkah candelabra reasserted the holiday's central meaning as commemorating the miracle of the oil.[37] It is also customary for Jews to eat foods fried in oil on Hanukkah, as another reminder of the miracle of the Temple oil. The focus upon Hanukkah miracles expressed in the Talmud and the *Shulchan Arukh* harmonized with the belief in miracles common among Jews' gentile neighbors.[38]

The Maccabees also earned scant mention in the American Jewish press before the debate over reforms flared at mid-century.[39] Hanukkah seldom appears in the letters or diaries of nineteenth century American Jews, and even New York journalist Robert Lyon's tellingly named newspaper, *The Asmonean,* seldom noted the Maccabees. Published between 1849 and 1858, before the religious debate turned rancorous, British born Lyon thought the best route to solving the religious differences dividing American Jews would be the establishment of a centralized religious authority, such as a *beth din* (religious court) that "would standardize religious law and practice."[40] Leeser's own magazine, *The Occident and American Jewish Advocate*, mentioned the Maccabees only five times in nearly a decade. Two of those occasions were simple reprints of self-congratulatory speeches given at the anniversary dinners of charitable societies, and another noted that the Jews of China owned two books of the Maccabees. In addition, a Hanukkah sermon by Rabbi Max Lilienthal urged Jewish parents to provide Jewish educations for their children. However, Leeser printed one item in 1845 that signaled the coming trend: a "manifesto" by

German rabbis fighting reformers abroad. "At the time of the Maccabees," it said, "Israel . . . valiantly fortified their hearts with courage . . . and saved their holy faith."[41] Rabbis in America were soon using this image, although not always to the same end.

Reformers and the Heart of Hanukkah

Reformers in the United States felt that a simplified style of Judaism could keep American Jews loyal to the faith. Their emphasis on the synagogue, and a reshaping and streamlining of worship, they believed, would help Judaism to fit the American environment where Christians expected religion to focus upon a church.[42] Reforming rabbis like Schreiber, immigrants themselves, felt that they understood the needs of their fellow Jews. Schreiber, originally from Moravia, studied for his Ph.D. in Berlin and served several congregations in the U.S., including Denver, Colorado's Congregation Emanuel, formed in 1873.[43] When Schreiber claimed that reformers offered Jews a "religion of the heart," he may have had in mind liberal Judaism's loosening of the bonds of dietary laws and daily worship services that he felt "fail[ed] to impress the modern Jew with a spirit of priestly holiness."[44] Reform rabbis fully articulated these positions ten months later—after Schreiber urged American Jews to view reformers as Maccabees for the modern age—in their statement of principles known as the Pittsburgh Platform.

Nineteenth century American Jewish Reform leaders refocused Jews' attention away from the miracle of the oil and toward the Maccabees and their struggle with Hellenism. Reformers compared the changes they had made in Jewish law to the ancient Maccabean decree allowing Jews to militarily defend themselves on the Sabbath, contrary to the older religious law forbidding it. Isaac M. Wise, the most influential reformer in nineteenth-century America, told American Jews that reformers had "regenerated and rejuvenated" Hanukkah as part of their goal to rejuvenate Judaism itself. Reform Judaism participated, through its throwing off of tradition, in the drive toward a universal religion touted by Unitarians and other liberal Protestants in the United States in the latter nineteenth century. But, by insisting upon Judaism's ultimate destiny to become the universal "religion of humanity," Wise also refuted the claims made by conservative Christians that Christianity would reign supreme.[45] Wise believed that Judaism's "theology" did not depend upon a belief in miracles like the one historically linked to Hanukkah, and he even eliminated the mention of miracles from his prayer book, *Minhag America*, in 1857.[46] That same year, focusing on the Maccabees as heroes, he ranked their importance to history with that of Oliver Cromwell, and praised the Maccabees' "indestructible tenacity, strength, power of mind and force of character." Had "Israel yielded . . . (to Syria)," Wise wrote, "the entire history of mankind would have taken another turn . . . (there would have been) no Jesus of Nazareth and no Mohammet of Mecca . . . none can say how modern civilization would look now."[47] For that reason, he agreed with the German reforming rabbis who unanimously had decided to put forward a less miracle-focused and "more suitable and solemn celebration of Chanukah."[48]

Worship in Reform synagogues included hymns in the vernacular. Among the first American Jewish hymns expressing a Reform perspective was the 1842 work for Hanukkah written by Charleston, South Carolina poet Penina Moïse. Moïse, regarded by Charleston as its poet laureate for her widely praised volume of poetry, was a member of the Reformed Society of Israelites—a group of congregants who urged reforms to the traditional worship in their local synagogue, Beth Elohim. Moïse and her group acknowledged that many members of their congregation did not understand Hebrew, and desired that English should be included in the synagogue to provide meaning to the service. The Reformed Society of Israelites broke away from their synagogue in 1824, but the original congregation ultimately accommodated their requests when, sixteen years later in 1840, a new hymnal, most of it written by Moïse, who also ran her congregations' Sunday school, was added to the by that time liberalized congregation's worship.[49]

Like some others in her congregation, Moïse considered herself a Sephardi Jew, and traced her ancestry to Iberia and the Mediterranean area. Sephardi Jews customarily sang Psalm 30 at Hanukkah, which is noted in the Tanakh as a song "for the dedication of the house." (The word Hanukkah means "dedication.") Its four stanzas begin, "I extol you, O Lord, for you have lifted me up, and not let my enemies rejoice over me." The hymn goes on to thank God for being merciful and promises to praise God forever.[50] Other Beth Elohim congregants claimed Ashkenazi descent from central or eastern Europe, where at Hanukkah Jews often sang *Maoz Tsur*, a six-stanza song that recounted various episodes in which God rescued Jews from calamities.

Taking advantage of the opportunity to write hymns that would express the sentiments of the Charleston group, Moïse wrote a song that voiced a new approach to the holiday by blending Jewish and American religious viewpoints and modified a customary Hanukkah perspective. First, unlike both Psalm 30 and *Maoz Tsur*, her song was intended specifically for Hanukkah, suggesting that her congregation felt the need to sing something special for the holiday. Although she borrowed her Protestant neighbors' terminology and titled her work "Hanucca Hymn," its opening line affirms her belief in Judaism's God. "Great arbiter of human fate! Whose glory ne'er decays, To Thee alone we dedicate, the song and soul of praise"—words which counter the evangelical assertion that Jesus is the deity to whom prayers ought now to be offered. The rest of the hymn supports her opening assertion by briefly recounting the Hanukkah story wherein God provided the "power . . . Which . . . to triumph led." Second, Moïse's hymn mines the Hanukkah story for ways to describe an *individual's* spiritual crisis. When Antiochus installed Greek worship in the ancient Temple in Jerusalem he deprived Jews of the place where they formally sought forgiveness for their sins. Moïse's hymn imagines the personal anguish of an ancient Jew whose sacred Temple had been desecrated, asserting "in bitterness of soul they wept." After describing the Temple restored and reporting that "priests of God his role resumed," she concludes by using the defiled temple as a metaphor for a contemporary "blemished heart" needing cleansing. "Oh! Thus shall mercy's hand delight, To cleanse the blemished heart; Rekindle virtue's waning light, And peace and truth impart." The hymn speaks of virtue, whose guiding light may be waning, and addresses the inner turmoil that results from such a spiritual crisis. It asks not for an end to exile, as does *Maoz Tsur*, but for a comforting personal salvation that soothes religious anguish. Although Moïse, like most rabbis and religious Jews before her, believed that God guided the Maccabean victory, her hymn turned the familiar story in a different direction: it elaborated the personal anguish of ancient Jews whose sacred temple had been desecrated, and assured modern readers that just as God ultimately purified the temple, He could also lead nineteenth century Jews to their own pure spiritual lives. Her poem gave Hanukkah a place in the emerging style of American religious culture—a culture dominated by the language of individualism and personal conscience and derived from both Protestantism and the Enlightenment. Interestingly, though, neither Talmud nor the *Shulchan Aruch* identifies Hanukkah as a special occasion to ask for the forgiveness of sins. Why is Moïse focusing upon sin?

The answer to this question lies in the fact that Moïse's hymn shares a particular religious discourse that reigned in her area of the country. Born in 1797, Moïse lived in a South dominated by a Protestantism that emphasized the anguish suffered by individuals unsure of Jesus's mercy. A half-century before her birth, evangelicals, who had spilled into the South from the Mid-Atlantic region, began transforming the established Anglican order. Presbyterians, Baptists, and Methodists challenged the religious status quo by reaching out to women, workers, and slaves. After the American Revolution dismantled legal and tax support for Anglicanism—now called Episcopalianism—these evangelicals expanded their influence. By the time Moïse wrote, Southern women evangelicals were helping their families, friends, and neighbors to find salvation in Jesus.[51] The procedure they used would always be the same: to convince the neighbor that the unhappiness and fears in their lives were due to sin, which, unforgiven, would provoke God's vengeance. The evangelists would then offer release from these fears through salvation through Jesus. Moïse's Hanukkah hymn suggests that she was familiar with these arguments, and the psychological and religious needs they addressed. She offered American Jews a way to express their own personal religious confusions or difficulties, but used Jewish images and provided a well-formed Jewish plea for God's reassurance at a particular time in the Jewish religious calendar. Moïse's hymn provided an individual voice for prayer and an expression of the inner need for God, and tied these elements, through imagery, to the Hanukkah story. Finally, by not mentioning exile, Moïse suggests that Jews are satisfied with life in America—an opinion we also find evidence of in letters written by American Jews since the mid 1700s.[52] The hymn proved so popular that it was reprinted many times, (most recently in 1959), in songbooks used by both Reform and Conservative Jews. Moïse's personalized Hanukkah hymn suited the personalized religious style of American Jews.

Schreiber may have had Moïse's hymn in mind when he penned his open letter forty-three years later. He may also have been thinking of another way reformers were attempting to create a "religion of the heart" for modern Jews, namely, by changing their attitude toward Jewish history. While reformers emphasized Judaism's faith and pro-phetic ethics as divine gifts whose significance never dimmed, they also encouraged Jews to understand that throughout history Judaism had undergone many changes. This was a perspective which, naturally, helped reformers to legitimize the changes *they* advocated.[53] Abraham Geiger, a leading voice for Reform in Frankfurt am Main, and an in-fluential voice among reformers in nineteenth century America, wrote: "Wherever a new culture springs up, where the mind develops itself untrammeled, where a fresh nationality or a fresh spiritual develop-ment is manifested, there Judaism quickly joins the movement and its professors soon adopt the new culture, digest it, and regard the country which offers them the highest boon, mental and spiritual liberty, as their home." Geiger argued that even Hellenism initially provided that boon, but the "Syrio-Grecian" ruler, Antiochus IV, crushed Judea. The Maccabean revolt occurred because "the heart of the people could not endure oppression."[54] Geiger and other reformers looked to the Mac-cabees' strength of heart to provide a model for their own initiative in taking new steps to adapt Judaism to the modern world. In both Talmud and *Shulchan Arukh*, fighters and martyrs alike were referred to simply as Jews—willing to die for their faith and whose devotion convinced God to rescue them.[55] Now, instead, reformers sought to cultivate among Jews an appreciation of religious courage in the lan-guage of military heroism, thereby suggesting to them that Jews could themselves control their religion's future.[56]

To illustrate this viewpoint, Isaac M. Wise, America's leading re-former and the founder of Hebrew Union College in Cincinnati, wrote, in 1860, a romantic fiction based upon the Maccabean revolt, which he serialized over thirty-nine weeks in his national Jewish magazine, *The Israelite*.[57] In his story Wise recast the Maccabean revolt in popular language to appeal to ordinary American Jews. (*The Israelite* reached more Jews in more towns than any other Jewish publication.)[58] Years later, referring to his earlier writing, Wise claimed to have written his several works of historical fiction simply to fill the space allotted for them in his magazine—sending them immediately to the press without any editing or revision. By that account, he wrote them quickly and without a second thought.[59] Yet, such easily written pieces suggest that they could likely have expressed Wise's genuine views. Wise had worked tirelessly on a scholarly history of the Jewish people that found few readers,[60] but his serialized historical romances, which popularized an approach to the Jewish past emphasizing human agency rather than miracles and divine intervention, made, with more success, the same point he had struggled to convey in his scholarly work. Likewise, when Wise compiled his own prayer book, *Minhag America*, in 1857, he rewrote the Hanukkah blessings to omit the mention of miracles.[61] Actually, in Wise's hands, the story of the Maccabees fit right in with other popular fiction of the Victorian era. Victorians expected to find religious virtues, patriotism, and strong gender distinctions in their literary romances, and Wise delivered. On the eve of the Civil War, Wise also borrowed language from contemporary political debates about liberty's defense.

Wise was not the first to tell the Maccabean story in the language of liberty and revolution. By 1860, portions of Georg Frederic Handel's oratorio *Judas Maccabeus* had been performed many times in the United States, probably beginning with a 1796 Philadelphia performance of the march alone.[62] One of the most prolific composers in revolutionary era Europe, Handel's oratorios on religious themes provided non-liturgical, popular religious entertainments. Born in 1685 in Halle, and educated in the Lutheran Pietistic tradition noted for its humanistic views and sympathy for Jews, by the time Handel relocated to England he seemed to have identified "the Jewish cause with the humanitarian strivings of an era dedicated to social progress."[63] Jews in England enjoyed far greater freedoms than he had seen among Jews living on the Continent, and Handel himself knew Jews and often worked with them in his adopted country. When commissioned to write an oratorio to honor the Duke of Cumberland, who had quashed a Jacobite uprising in Scotland, Handel looked to ancient Jewish history and composed *Judas Maccabeus*, which was first performed in 1747.

Pertinently, two years before the completion of *Judas Maccabeus* London's Jewish brokers and merchants had helped England avert national disaster during an economic panic. Moreover, Jewish merchants had put their ships—fully outfitted—at the government's disposal, and many Jewish men signed up for the national militia. With *Judas Maccabeus*, Handel and his librettist, Rev. Thomas Morrell, recalled Jews' service to England and provided the country's stage with a rare image of a heroic Jew, rather than a villain. British Jews flocked to the oratorio's six performances in its opening year, and frequented its thirty performances during Handel's lifetime.[64] Performances of *Judas Maccabeus* frequently included the aria, "See, the Conquering Hero Comes," originally written by Handel for his oratorio, *Joshua*.[65] When Judas sings that his father had died urging his sons to choose "liberty or death!" the oratorio merged the ancient Maccabean military battle to retake the Jerusalem Temple with the eighteenth century's revolutionary values.[66] Handel's works quickly traveled to North America, and by 1818 Bostonians performed his oratorio, *Messiah*, every year, either at Christmas or Easter.[67] By 1873 Bostonians enjoyed full performances of *Judas Maccabeus*, as well.[68] A decade later, a Bostonian admitted that "Now . . . Cincinnati (is) striving for that supremacy which Boston has long been fully entitled to through her Handel and Haydn Society... (and) New York (is) . . . to be credited with the establishment of the American Opera."[69] When nineteenth century American Jews sought performances of *Judas Maccabeus* at Hanukkah, they participated in the nation's musical tastes, but in a manner that suited their Jewish sensibilities. Its productions taught them that the Maccabees fought for the same revolutionary values extolled in nineteenth century American culture.

In writing historical Jewish fiction, Wise also participated in a movement popular among modernizing Jews on both sides of the Atlantic. In both Europe and the United States Jewish writers penned fiction and poetry in the vernacular, which helped to shape a modern Jewish culture. A Hanukkah poem written in 1848 in German for a Jewish audience praised the Maccabees and their "courageous fight for freedom."[70] In central Europe, some Jewish readers considered Jewish historical fiction important for its capacity to depict "the ethical grandeur of the Jewish past."[71] Wise drew upon Handel's oratorio,

American cultural values, and Europe's trend in Jewish historical fiction when writing his fictional Hanukkah narrative. His male Jewish characters exemplified contemporary American masculine values, as they fought for liberty, justice, truth, and manliness itself. One figure explains, "death is not the greatest evil ... [it is]...sacrific[ing] truth, justice and liberty." Wise told his readers to "kindle your Chanukah lights and forget not your God and country."[72]

Wise also knew that women made up much of the readership of American magazines and fiction, and his romance about the Maccabean revolt provided novel female characters who motivated soldiers and helped to secure victories. Wise encouraged his readers to imagine that ancient Jewish women, like their men, also embodied the attributes esteemed by Victorian Americans. Wise's female character, Miriam, mother to Judah and his brothers, embodied a Victorian maternal and spousal ideal. At her husband's deathbed, Miriam describes her faith in his eternal life, and hears angels singing as God receives him and grants him "eternal bliss." Also in Wise's story, and in this differing from the account in the ancient first Book of the Maccabees where Judah's father takes this role, Miriam instructs her sons to continue the revolt. "I dedicate my five sons to thy service, O God of Israel," she says after her husband's death. For many American Jews, who recalled tradition-minded parents and older family members remaining in Europe, a character like Miriam, an elderly mother who guided her grown sons' religious commitments, would have carried emotional power.

Wise also added the character of lovely young Iphegine, named for his own daughter born that same year. In his fiction she provided the love interest for a younger Maccabee brother, Jonathan. Iphegine's spy missions among the invaders, her dangerous encounters, and her repeated rescues by Jonathan enhance the story's drama. Her women friends discuss their trials under foreign rule, as their husbands, lovers, brothers, and fathers leave to fight and risk death at the hands of their enemies. Iphegine expressed the conundrum of many American Jews, who had adopted much of general American culture and who practiced little Judaism, yet who nonetheless considered themselves loyal Jews. She explained that although she acts like a gentile, she believes in Judaism. "I worship no Gods besides the God of Israel," she begins. "I love beauty and chastity, therefore I am a devotee of . . . Venus. . . . But I worship only the God of heaven and earth." (The hero, by the way—Jonathan—rebuked her for worshiping Venus and urged Iphegine to dedicate herself more completely to Jewish traditions.)[73] Wise expected some of his readers to see themselves in Iphegine, a young person attracted to the style and form of non-Jewish culture. Interestingly, Wise's use of his own daughter's name may suggest personal messages of his hopes for her, embedded in his popular text. Wise's story was another example of a text which asserted that American values matched Jewish values, and that Jewish men and women who remained loyal to Judaism could embody them both. Thus armed with new hymns, dedicated rabbis, comfortable modifications to Judaism and an instructive popular press, American Jewish reformers set about saving Judaism for contemporary Jews, thinking of themselves as modern Maccabees.

American Traditionalists and the Maccabees

Tradition-minded leaders, on the other hand, sought to inspire American Jews with a Maccabean model of self-sacrifice and religious devotion. In 1879, for example, a group of young American-born Jewish men influenced by Morais determined to advance Judaism among ordinary Jews with an exciting Hanukkah spectacle featuring a Maccabean pageant. Both reformers and traditionalists claimed to be Maccabees for the modern era, heroes saving Judaism from extinction in a larger, attractive American culture dominated by foreign beliefs and ideals.

Traditionalists shared an aversion to the sweeping nature of the changes made by reformers. They believed that the Talmudic method, by which rabbis long had adapted biblical law to changing historical circumstances, was the best way for Jews to adapt their religious lives to the modern world.[74] *Halakhah*, derived from this method, set forth many of the rites that reformers denounced, and explained Jewish religious life as a matter of laws which Jews needed to follow because they had been commanded to do so by God. Tradition-minded Jews argued that Hanukkah's story justified their trust in God and their loyalty to Jewish traditions. They turned to Hanukkah's story to refute reformers, pointing out that the Maccabees insisted on maintaining some of the very Jewish "prohibitions" which reformers cancelled, for example, the dietary laws. Rather than keeping Jews loyal, traditionalists said, reformers provided a route *out* of Judaism, and so encouraged its demise.

Philadelphia traditionalist Isaac Leeser believed that the commands and customs of Judaism had been set in place by God, and that they promoted a sense of personal piety and devotion to God that stirred the heart to more than just sentimentality.[75] Leeser believed that most Jews accepted tradition's authority and only needed better resources, such as religious schools, kosher foods, and supportive, committed congregations, to assist them in fulfilling their religious duties. He publicized special Hanukkah events and rituals conducted by Jewish congregations around the country to expedite this aim, praised a Cleveland congregation's Hanukkah dedication of its new synagogue, and noted that benevolent societies in both Cleveland and Baltimore hosted annual Hanukkah banquets. Leeser scoffed at a reform-minded leader in San Francisco who told his congregation that Hanukkah's meaning was simply to keep "the light of religion in our hearts," and that Jews need not light the Hanukkah lamps. That synagogue's lamps remained dark—prompting Leeser to ask his readers: "Is this . . . progress?" He insisted that many San Franciscans lit Hanukkah lamps in their homes and contended that the dark synagogue prompted some members to leave and found another congregation under more traditional principles. Provoking discord was one more way that Leeser felt San Franciscan reformers acted like modern-day Hellenists who embraced principles opposed to Judaism, and not like Maccabees.[76]

From Leeser's perspective, reformers "deformed" Judaism to accommodate an uninformed laity, rather than educating the common Jewish person to appreciate Judaism's purpose and meaning.[77] Other traditionalists felt similarly.[78] Tradition-minded New Yorker Samuel Isaacs, who edited *The Jewish Messenger*, insisted that the Maccabees should be studied by "our children to kindle the spark of (Jewish) patriotism latent in the hearts of their parents."[79] Traditionalists encouraged Jews to proudly fulfill their traditional religious duties along with their obligations as citizens of the larger nation.[80]

Philadelphia traditionalist Sabato Morais and New York's tradition-minded English-born rabbi Henry Pereira Mendes inspired a small cadre of young YMHA laymen in their cities. That diverse group would include, as it matured, a Semitics scholar, a judge, a physician and poet, a librarian, businessmen and inventors.[81] In October 1879 New York members Max Cohen, Philip Cowen, and Mendes met with the Philadelphia members, Solomon Solis-Cohen, Mayer Sulzberger, Joseph and Samuel Fels, Cyrus Adler, and Cyrus Sulzberger, to pledge themselves to "perpetuate and elevate" Judaism. Calling themselves *Keyam Dishmaya*, or loosely, "upholding the dictates of Heaven" in Aramaic, they spearheaded new lay educational and defense organizations that laid the foundation for twentieth century Jewish intellectual life. These included the American Jewish Historical Society, the American Jewish Publication Society, Gratz College, and the Jewish Chatauqua Society.[82] *Keyam Deshmaya* also supported the writing of a *Jewish Encyclopedia* and a new English translation of the Hebrew Bible, but their first step was a new national Jewish magazine, the *American Hebrew*, launched in 1879 to "stir up our brethren to pride in our time-honored faith."[83] In their view, previous generations had felt the "crushing impositions and restrictions of a bigoted Europe," and their own parents' generation was burdened by the "all-absorbing cares of bread-and-butter labor." But perhaps thinking of both the Maccabees and the American revolutionists, they described themselves as "combative,"—and like the "youth of every manly nation that has a soul and a history"[84]—and uniquely suited to "awaken" their coreligionists to greater devotion.

The young YMHA men were also the driving force behind a new kind of Hanukkah entertainment: the spectacle. The already popular American fetes that celebrated the American nation influenced their efforts. Only three years earlier, hundreds of public historical orations delivered in thirty-eight states commemorated the centennial of American independence. These orations commonly blended religion with nationalism—some even comparing the country's destiny to that of ancient Israel—and offered their listeners "timeless, universal moral principles" to guide the present. Offering history lessons as "holy heirlooms," orators spoke to crowds from stages elaborately decorated with arches and greenery, and flanked by women costumed to depict various virtues. These events encouraged even more spectacular pageantry to appear in many locations around the country.[85] The YMHA men hoped to rejuvenate commitment to Jewish life among American Jewish men in the same way that American Centennial activities aimed to rejuvenate national patriotism. Hanukkah, the holiday of dedication, seemed an ideal occasion to display manly Jewish devotion by performing elaborately costumed scenes from Judaism's ancient drama.

In December 1879 New York YMHA members and their friends staged a massive Hanukkah pageant at New York's Academy of Music, which they called "The Grand Revival of the National Holiday of Chanucka." Their title drew upon the popular Christian religious revivals of the same period, but instead of the religious exhortations and hymns that characterized Protestant revivals, evidence suggests that the YMHA staged scenes from *Judas Maccabeus*, accompanied by an orchestra and a professional military band. Several hundred costumed men and women comprised its six tableaux vivants depicting episodes from Hanukkah's history in a manner designed to inspire the participants and the audience to take up Hanukkah celebrations with new zest. Advertising promised "historically correct" costumes "especially designed to illustrate the Maccabean period."[86] Depicting the Maccabees dressed in battle armor triumphantly reclaiming the Temple in Jerusalem, cleansing it of Greek gods and sacrificial objects, and re-dedicating it to the God of the Jews by lighting the sacred candles, the spectacle asserted that Jewish religious life was a manly and exciting endeavor. This approach refuted the Victorian trend of female-led piety that seemed to contribute to religious apathy among American men and, as a consequence, increase the popularity of ritual-rich fraternal associations.[87] The following year Jews in Baltimore and Philadelphia staged similar events, and New Yorkers repeated their pageant.[88]

Americans throughout the country who read *Frank Leslie's Illustrated Newspaper* on 3 January 1880 learned about the grand event. Its tableaux, set up by an arranger of children's festivals, (which was common for such events) offered visually rich, costumed and posed presentations without any actual acting, and children from the Hebrew Orphan Asylum sang choruses.[89] Two young sisters led off the "grand procession," followed by over a hundred "young ladies with cymbals, incense-bearers, slaves carrying precious vessels and jewels," and Judah Maccabee carrying a banner with Hebrew words meaning "Who

Is Like To Thee, oh God?" Excerpted from the biblical book of Exodus, the phrase even used the first letters of each word to spell MAKABI. Judah preceded his "brothers, Jewish soldiers, trumpeters, banner bearers, Syrian captives, and young women with harps," and, according to Leslie's *Newspaper*, "After the parade, forty Jewish maidens with cymbals danced. They were divided into four parts: one division wore blue, another red, another white and gold, and the fourth silver and white. In the stately dance these colors blended or separated like a kaleidoscope. At a stroke from a pair of cymbals behind the scenes, the lights . . . changed from gold to green, or to blue, or to red, while the dancers grouped themselves into motionless statues. Suddenly the curtain at the rear of the stage lifted and a very brilliant light streamed out" to reveal the Temple's interior. "On one side was the *Minorah*, [*sic*] in the center the altar of sacrifice, and on the other side the altar of incense. High priests and Levites, in Biblical dress, were performing their official duties. Judah and his brothers were in the attitude of worship." The reviewer judged it a "grand work of realistic art." It was nearly midnight when the curtain fell and social dancing began.[90]

The sixth tableau earned a particular place in Leslie's *Newspaper*. Its full-page illustration shows the women—who have completed their dances—on their knees, bowing down, on the floor below a stage. On the stage, men dressed as priests and as warriors are lighting a human-size menorah in a mock-up of the Jerusalem Temple. This is a clearly organized scene: male heroes and priests above, the divine light of the temple shining upon them, other warriors standing below, and women kneeling before them all. Such pageantry portrayed the Jewish past with grandeur, while at the same time including a Victorian sense of social order and piety. It conveyed the message that Judaism deserved admiration and respect from its audience.

In deeming the Hanukkah tableaux art, Leslie articulated a view shared by most Americans at mid-century. For two decades after his magazine's start in 1855, Leslie felt confident that he and his readers shared a "common moral map" based both upon piety and upon a gendered and racially divided social order. By the 1880s, suffragists, immigrant radicals, trade unionists, working women and freedmen, among others, comprised a new, fractured public with which Leslie did not communicate. His style became associated with elite society, for whom a hierarchical social order held increasing appeal as threats to its power arose.[91] The Hanukkah revival's tableaux perfectly suited Leslie's search for moralistic narrative art.

For older Jews viewing the event, the "Grand Chanucka Revival" countered a common perception that Jewish young people felt alienated from religious life—a perception that was not completely incorrect. Many young Jews preferred YMHA activities to synagogue worship. Some young people voiced distaste for the dry sermons that had become the centerpiece of many Reform Sabbath services. Others accused affluent congregations of indifference to social ills, and many women resented their exclusion from formal temple or synagogue membership.[92] Yet hundreds of Jewish young adults donned costumes for the Hanukkah revival, a uniquely exciting, one-time event. Perhaps even more surprising, by embodying Handel's *Judas Maccabeus*, young, nineteenth century American Jewish activists suggested to their audience that they should be seen as modern Maccabees.

Hanukkah's story of military revolt also countered the stereotype of the effeminate male Jew that sometimes appeared in the American and the German press. Folklore about Jews, brought to America with European immigrants, depicted Jewish men fighting only with their wits, like women.[93] As the Civil War increased American regard for male bravery, physical power, and aggression, Hanukkah's militarism became more meaningful to American Jews.[94] Longfellow's dramatic poem, *Judas Maccabeus*, published only eight years earlier, provided a similarly heroic image of Jews, despite its focus upon Antiochus's rise and fall.[95] The men of *Keyam Dishmaya* also saw the Maccabees as models for their own courageous devotion to Judaism in the face of what many American newspapers called "universal" Christmas celebrations.[96]

The pageant's parading Maccabean fighters also mirrored a staple of post Civil War American culture. Nearly two and a half million men had served in the war, and veterans were climbing the country's social and political ladders. Processions of such leaders, opened, for example, Philadelphia's Centennial City.[97] Memorial Day, sometimes called Decoration Day, also took shape at this time as a national holiday in towns large and small as veterans paraded, cheered on by women and children. Speeches and anthems lauding veterans' courage, leadership, and self-sacrifice enhanced each parade's emotional impact.[98] A few months before the Hanukkah revival, New York's Academy of Music hosted that city's Memorial Day exercises. The Chanucka Revival's parade of warriors displayed Jewish male power and its importance to Judaism in a similar style. Its parading heroes offered Jews a picture of themselves that refuted the more common images of Jews on America's stages—those of greedy Shylock, the villainous Nathan the Jew, the perfidious Isaac, father of Rebecca in *Ivanhoe*, or the laughable Jewish junk or old clothes dealer.[99]

Like many Memorial Day events, the Hanukkah pageant framed soldiers with costumed women who represented cultural ideals, such as the mourning widow or mother who served as the feminine ideal at Memorial Day. But, in place of sentimental Victorian ideals, the revival's young organizers created images of robust youth from Judaism's ancient past. Women became dancing maidens like those who danced before David's army on its successful return to Jerusalem more than eight hundred years before the Maccabean victory. Their dances stamped the Jewish past with beauty, and suggested to Jewish men that if they too became courageous Jews, maidens might dance for them. Images of dancing women contrasted with those of parading warriors to create distinct gender ideals that mirrored both Jewish and American culture.

When Baltimore's YMHA mounted a similar event the following year, women found more important roles on stage. One young woman read an "explanatory address" specially written by twenty-year old Henrietta Szold. A second young woman read the poem, "Hannah and Her Seven Sons," written by New York philanthropist Minnie Desau Louis, based upon the ancient mother who saw her children tortured to death for refusing to eat forbidden food.[100] Women's roles in these holiday pageants were to provide female models of piety within a manly Hanukkah. Just as the marching Maccabees offered a more appealing image of Jewish men, the pageant's dancing maidens and poets offered more genteel images of Jewish women than commonly were seen upon the popular stage, where the frequently performed play, *Leah the Forsaken*, depicted a wild and uncivilized Jewish woman.[101]

The *Keyam Dishmaya* men believed a bold Hanukkah event could capture the imagination of ordinary Jews, and especially energize Jewish youth. As Max Cohen put it, "Israel must be whatever its children make it."[102] The previous year, New Yorkers had attended a Hanukkah concert featuring *Judas Maccabeus*,[103] but Cohen and his colleagues hoped that when flesh-and-blood young Jews depicted its themes they could inspire other American Jews to have pride in their ancestry and loyalty to their traditions. Poet Solomon Solis-Cohen, a *Keyam Dishmaya* member, believed Hanukkah to be so important that he composed a poem describing a Hanukkah menorah's candles catching the flame from the burning bush during Moses's encounter with God on Mt. Sinai. Solis-Cohen's poem suggested Hanukkah ought to be considered among Judaism's founding events.[104] Organizers judged the Grand Hanukkah Revival a success. As Max Cohen said: "Every worker in the cause of a revived Judaism must have felt the inspiration exhaled from the enthusiastic interest evinced by such a mass of Israel's people."[105]

Five separate Hanukkah articles in one December 1888 issue of the *American Hebrew* argued that manly Jews must preserve the Maccabean spirit with self-defense and religious devotion. For example, many Jewish men felt compelled to labor on Saturday—the Jewish Sabbath—because of American laws that banned work on Sunday. These men did not want to, or perhaps felt they were not able to, sacrifice income by opening their shops only five days per week. Yet, the young members of *Keyam Dishmaya*, few of whom yet supported families, had little sympathy for Jewish men who "succumb[ed]" to the "so-called force of circumstances." "Pitiful" they called such men.[106] They hoped their efforts to revive Hanukkah would be the first step in revivifying Sabbath observance.

Keyam Dishmaya aimed for a more religiously inspirational effect than that achieved by the popular Purim Balls of the same era. Led by lawyer, judge, and co-editor of the *Jewish Messenger*, Myer S. Isaacs, the Purim Ball Association of New York arranged fancy-dress balls each year during the holiday to raise funds for Jewish charities. Most of these charities were in New York, but sometimes also included institutions as distant as the Touro Infirmary and Hebrew Benevolent Society in New Orleans and the Vicksburg Hebrew Relief Society in Mississippi. People of all faiths could be invited to the balls. Respectable establishments such as the Metropolitan Opera House, Madison

Square Garden, the Academy of Music, and Carnegie Music Hall housed the events, and themes chosen for the balls often reflected trends in American society. For the March 1866 ball, attended by an exceptionally large number of Christians, organizers decorated the room in red, white and blue and staged a procession depicting the history of Jewish persecution ending in the triumph of "Religious Liberty over Prejudice." Accomplished and wealthy young men founded and led the Purim Ball Association, which achieved its period of greatest activity in the 1870s and 1880s.[107] The ball reflected their interests in philanthropy, their desire to create a social event grounded in the Jewish religious calendar, and the popular American elite practice of providing entertainment to raise funds for charities. In contrast, the Grand Chanucka Revival aimed to affect Jews' religious observances by instilling pride in their religious heritage and affirming God's continuing protection.

Conclusion

Hanukkah emerged as a newly meaningful holiday for nineteenth century American Jews because it provided images and lessons useful to clergy on all sides of a heated debate about how Judaism should adapt to America. By linking the image of the Maccabees with modernity, American Jews inserted the particularities of their own religious tradition into the secular universalism espoused by modernist philosophers whose Enlightenment ideals informed the founding documents of the United States.[108] At the same time, rabbis and Hanukkah advocates among ordinary Jews created an image of Jewish military bravery and success comparable to the nation's own patriotic rhetoric, taking another opportunity to assert their own "fit" with American society.[109] Moreover, Hanukkah's story was given contemporary importance by drawing parallels between ancient Maccabees and America's own military heroes. In their magazines, reformers and traditionalists alike drew upon the Hanukkah story to support their positions. The Hanukkah story's unlikely victory of a small band of zealots over a great power seemed to parallel the American revolution, and helped American Jewish readers find American values in Judaism as they sought to synthesize their religion with American culture.[110] For the Jewish clergy, Hanukkah became a flashpoint in the struggle between reformers and traditionalists over how best to promote Judaism among an American Jewish population who seemed disturbingly lax in their religious observance. Traditionalists and reformers alike claimed the mantle of modern Maccabee and set out to save Judaism from an appealing but foreign religious culture corroding religious practice in American Jews' households and congregations.

Young Jewish laymen in an American society that valued both militarism and piety also found that Hanukkah "spoke" to them. One Jewish soldier's memoir of his Civil War experience described the "descendants of the . . . Hebrew patriarchs who . . . under the Maccabees, triumphed over the Syrian despot . . . [as being] quite satisfied to fight with [their] Christian comrades for one cause, one country, and the UNION."[111] The *Keyam Dishmaya* men determined to embody its message of dedication and to invite their coreligionist to join them by organizing the same sort of value-laden yet pleasurable entertainment that had become the hallmark of Victorian America's drive to standardize American civilization.[112] In what has been called their "period of most intense creativity and wrestling over issues of group continuity" American Jews turned to the Maccabees to help them explain and envision their best hopes for American Jewish life.[113]

Our *Moreh nevukhei ha-Zeman: Alfred Gottschalk, z"l*

The unexpected death of Rabbi Dr. Alfred Gottschalk on 12 September 2009 was a deep personal loss for everyone associated with the American Jewish Archives, an institution he loved and supported throughout his nearly sixty-year association with the Hebrew Union College–Jewish Institute of Religion (HUC-JIR). His passing also adds significance to this, his final scholarly contribution to the field of modern Jewish studies.

Born in Oberwesel, Germany in 1930, "Fred" Gottschalk resettled in the United States in 1939, graduated from Brooklyn College, and then went to Cincinnati, where he received his rabbinic ordination from HUC-JIR in 1957. The president of HUC-JIR, Nelson Glueck, took note of young Gottschalk and selected him from the ordination class to serve as dean of the fledgling Los Angeles campus. In Los Angeles, Gottschalk completed his doctorate at the University of Southern California (USC) in 1965 and simultaneously spearheaded an ambitious expansion and relocation of the Los Angeles campus to a site adjacent to USC. Upon Glueck's death in 1971, Gottschalk was elected to serve as HUC-JIR's sixth president and, subsequently, the school's chancellor. As president of HUC-JIR for more than a quarter century, Gottschalk guided the college in new directions. By ordaining Sally Priesand in 1972, Gottschalk helped to pave the way for the entrance of women into the mainstream of the American Reform rabbinate and cantorate. In 1992, he underscored the importance of gender equality in Reform Judaism by ordaining the first woman rabbi in Israel.

Since the early 1960s, much of Gottschalk's scholarly work had focused on the thought of Ahad Ha'am (1856–1927)— its roots, its construction and expression and, most of all, its enduring influence. In the article below, he shares, for the final time, important insights into the "Spirit" of Jewish history as understood by Ahad Ha'am and his intellectual predecessor, Nachman Krochmal (1785–1840). Not only does Gottschalk reconnect Ahad Ha'am to Krochmal with respect to the role of the foundational idea of "Spirit" in Jewish history, but in so doing he makes a larger statement about shifts in Jewish philosophy and culture during the long nineteenth century. Understanding those nuanced changes today, when questions of the interrelationship of the spiritual and the secular in the Jewish experience face renewed scrutiny, particularly in American Jewish circles, is of inestimable historical, philosophical, and cultural value.

"The Spirit of Jewish History:" From Nachman Krochmal to Ahad Ha-Am

Alfred Gottschalk *z"l*

This auspicious occasion marking the sixtieth anniversary of the American Jewish Archives' (AJA) founding needs to be relished and celebrated. Its founding genius, Jacob Rader Marcus, envisaged a formidable institution whose primary purpose was to document the American Jewish experience, its history, ethos and rich demographic contours. The AJA's journal has brilliantly presented its contents in a meticulous scholarly style true to its basic commitments to *Wissenschaft*.

We also take cognizance of the ten year anniversary of the devoted term of office of Dr. Gary P. Zola, who has brought brilliance and passion to his role as executive director of the AJA. Under his leadership the AJA has grown to new prominence in the world of Jewish scholarship and particularly in the broad field of American Jewish history.

It was my privilege as president of Hebrew Union College–Jewish Institute of Religion to have the Board of Governors name the AJA as The Jacob Rader Marcus Center and to place Dr. Zola as its director. His commitment to the Center and to the Hebrew Union College–Jewish Institute of Religion (HUC-JIR), which he served previously in another capacity, more than justifies this high honor of special recognition.

* * * *

It is in the tradition of commemorative festschriften to focus on a central theme. Our present theme is the phenomenon of Jewish history in its rich diversity. *Ruah Hayahadut*, the "spirit" of Jewish life and history, has been a central theme for Jewish thinkers of the modern period. This essay will concentrate on two major figures, Nachman Krochmal (1785–1840) and Ahad Ha-Am (1856–1927). These thinkers lived in different periods and were affected by diverse intellectual trends. Nevertheless, the influence of Krochmal on Ahad Ha-Am is not only interesting in itself, but is also representative of broader spiritual developments in modern Jewish thought.

Nachman Krochmal

Nachman Krochmal, active in the first half of the nineteenth century, was a distinguished thinker from the Galician branch of the Haskalah movement. He was part of an intellectual movement whose goal was not only to adjust Judaism to the modern world, but also "to analyze Judaism, to discover its substance and demonstrate its eternity with the help of the tools forged by Western civilization and European philosophy...."[1] Although known in his day, it was only after Krochmal's death that his major work *Moreh nevukhei ha-Zeman* (*Guide for the Perplexed of [Our] Time*) was prepared for publication by Leopold Zunz.[2] The title of Krochmal's work, probably selected by Zunz,[3] harkens back to the title of Maimonides's philosophic work, *Moreh nevukhim* (*Guide for the Perplexed*).

In dealing with the text of Krochmal's work, a number of technical problems become evident. What is available to us of Krochmal's philosophy was published, as previously noted, posthumously. Because of serious illness in the years immediately preceding his death, Krochmal was unable to finish most of his work or to edit his lecture notes, essays and letters. The result leaves the reader in doubt, at times, as to whether he is getting the complete thought of the author. Solomon Schechter summarized the problem as follows: "... Krochmal's work...is full of misprints and the text is sometimes confused with the notes."[4]

Krochmal's *Guide* contains some seventeen chapters of diverse material—philosophical and historical—written for the most part, the above problems notwithstanding, according to the exacting standards of the method which came to characterize the *Wissenschaft des Judentums*. Krochmal's aim was to so present his material that it would naturally lead to *emunah zerufah* (a purified faith). According to a statement attributed to Zunz, Krochmal was inspired in his philosophic speculation because of his study of Hegel, just as Maimonides had undertaken his *Moreh nevukhim* as a result of his confrontation with Aristotle.[5] The precise influence of Hegel on Krochmal's thought has been the source of much disputation, due in no small part to Krochmal himself who, for example, discussing Hegel in his sixteenth chapter of the *Moreh nevukhei ha-Zeman*, often blends his own thought with Hegel's and makes it impossible to isolate the intertwined threads of both philosophies.[6] Although Simon Rawidowicz denies pervasive Hegelian influences on Krochmal,[7] Julius Guttmann holds that Krochmal's "doctrine of the nature and essence of religion and its relation to philosophy was completely taken over from Hegel."[8] Krochmal's indebtedness to German idealism is generally admitted, although in Krochmal's work proper only Hegel is alluded to.[9] Another influence on Krochmal was that of the German philosopher Johann Gottfried Herder (1744–1803). Like him, Krochmal built an analogy between the nation and a biological organism: both undergo birth, efflorescence, decay and death. Herder had written that "history is nothing but the uninterrupted progress of natural development."[10] Drawing his example from nature and applying it to human history, Herder stated:

Now nature has given the whole earth to mankind, her children; and has allowed everything that place, time and power would permit to spring up thereon. Every thing that can exist, exists; every thing that is possible to be produced, will be produced; if not today, tomorrow."[11]

So it was also with regard to human history. Herder enunciated what he called his "first grand principle": "Whatever can take place among mankind, within the sphere of given circumstances of time, place and nation, actually does take place."[12] Nations bud, and "the cultivation of a people is the flower of its existence; its display is pleasing indeed, but transitory."[13] How long a state lasts depends not on "the point of its highest cultivation, but on a wise or fortunate equilibrium of its active living powers."[14] However, everything in history, as in all terrestrial phenomena, is transient. The cause of this transience lies both in the essence and environment of specific historical instantiations, and in the "general laws to which our nature is subject."[15] Therefore, just as individuals die, so do nations. "Nations flourish and decay; but in a faded nation no new flower, not to say a more beautiful one, ever blooms."[16] In history we bequeath at our death all that we have created, for good or ill, to that which succeeds us. "The sun sets, that night may succeed, and mankind rejoice at the beams of a new morn."[17]

Herder's *Ideen zur Philosophie der Geschichte der Menschheit* (1784–1791), from which the quotations above are excerpts, had already been published before Krochmal was born. That Herder's concept of history in terms of its cyclical configuration had made an impact upon Krochmal seems evident from *Moreh nevukhei ha-Zeman* itself, and is confirmed by researchers of Krochmal who have tried to understand his work in reference to his *Zeitgeist*.[18]

What was specific in Krochmal's approach and justifies his claim to eminence in modern Jewish thought was his "unification of historical inquiry with the philosophical interpretation of that historical process...."[19] In the first six chapters of Krochmal's work he dealt with religion in general. He delineated the characteristics of three types of religious persuasions which are fallacious and harmful: *Schwärmerei* (fantasy), *Aberglaube* (superstition), and *Werkheiligkeit* (ceremonialism).[20] In his view, religious fantasies such as "angels" beget cynicism, which leads to a denial of all spirit; superstition produces skepticism and the denial of God and revelation, and ceremonialism produces disembodied theory, devoid of all significant action.[21] Krochmal, who translated general philosophic thought into Jewish categories, engaged in an epistemological excursus which stated that it is the very nature of the spirit of reason to develop the raw conceptualizations derived from sense data into *Begriffe* (concepts), which in turn undergo a further transformation into *Ideen* (ideas),[22]—which are part of reason and hence eternal.

The process of conceptualization depicted above is precisely what the rabbis of the Talmud used in their interpretation of the Bible.

Through the application of reason and the hermeneutical principles they developed, the Talmudists explained the eternal principles of the Bible, emancipating them from their original environment and context. By stripping the teachings of the Bible from their environmental conditioning, the rabbis were able to extend the fundamental truth of the biblical faith to their own day. This happened not only with regard to the legal aspects contained within the Bible but even more basically for its religious assertions.[23] Proceeding from this point, Krochmal reasoned that it was the significant import of the Bible, the Talmud, and all Jewish religious teachings, however expressed, to address themselves to the Spirit (*ruah*), who is God. Even idolatrous faith (*avodah zarah*) was worship of the Spirit believed to be manifest in objects. "Know, that every religious belief is grounded in Spirit (*beruhani*)"[24]—which in Krochmal's use corresponded to the Absolute Spirit of Hegel.[25] The Absolute Spirit was the source of all truth, all causes, and the source of all existence. Krochmal uses the sentence in Isaiah, "I am the first and the last and beside Me there is no other Elohim,"[26] to prove this point. As Julius Guttmann observed:

Only as faith in the absolute spirit can religion express that which is fully embedded in its essence. The adoration of God corresponds to this conception of God. Such adoration depends on man's recognition that only by reason of his spiritual essence can he grasp the love of God and thus assure himself of everlasting life.... Theoretically, religion was spiritual perception, and in its highest reach it was the grasp of the absolute spirit; practically, it was the striving towards unification with this spirit so as to become identical with it.[27]

For Krochmal, biblical religion was the highest form of religion because of its faith in the Absolute Spirit.[28] While philosophy, for Krochmal, also taught "that the spirit was the essence of all being," the manner in which philosophy and religion presented this truth constituted their essential difference in approach. "Philosophy explains the spirit as a concept, and religion in the form of a representation, to which Krochmal occasionally added the dimension of feeling."[29] Like Hegel, Krochmal believed that it was not possible to separate truth from the particular guise in which it was represented. "...It was impossible, therefore, that this identity of religious and philosophic truth should be an absolute one."[30] Krochmal argued that conceptualization of religion, which included the knowledge of God and led to the spirit becoming known to itself,[31] was *emunah zerufah*, or "purified faith." As far as Judaism was concerned, the proper perception of the unfolding of its spirit could only be carried on for the sake of self-knowledge, or, as Shalom Spiegel put it, in order "that 'the perplexities of the time' might be surmounted, and that 'we should make ourselves wise for the future.'"[32]

In order to explain the phenomenon of Judaism in relation to the Spirit from which all emanates—Absolute Spirit—Krochmal undertakes an examination of Jewish history. "For Krochmal, the ideal order of the spirit ... is not merely an eternity beyond time; the ideal order of the spirit is an order in time, is historical."[33] The idea of order presupposes the recognition of the teleological principle as operative not only in nature but in the history of man as well. As Mordecai Kaplan explained:

> To Krochmal, all organisms point to an aspect of reality which cannot be accounted for merely in terms of mechanical necessity, insofar as they display a certain degree of freedom from environmental influence on each of its parts, and each part on the organism as a whole. That constitutes the organicity of living beings, which is a manifestation of purpose. Purpose, according to Krochmal, functions on a far larger scale in the life of a people; it reveals itself in that people's culture or civilization, which is tantamount to its consciousness.[34]

People, Krochmal believed, being different from other orders of life, have sociability as one of their characteristic traits. Human beings banding together into social groups makes the development of certain higher qualities such as love, compassion, honor, and "the fear of the Lord," possible—and raises human concern above the mere need to subsist in the struggle for survival. These traits are then transmitted either by individuals—such as Abraham or Melchizedek—or by specially developed groups, to other social units.[35] The cause underpinning the development of these qualities and higher traits within the history of humanity in general, and within specific nations in particular, is the progressive realization of the Absolute Spirit.[36] The *ruah* ("spirit") of each nation is its innermost soul and genius and the determining factor of its individual characteristics.

Krochmal differentiated between the universal and the particular spirit, which expresses itself in the diverse aspects of a nation's life and gives it its character. While at times it appears difficult to single out the specific national manifestations of the Spirit, it can be done when nations, as complete historical entities, are set next to one another. While the physical aspects of a nation are subject by analogy to birth, growth and decay, its spirit never perishes. Should a nation disappear from the face of the earth—which was common among the smaller nations—its spirit transfers to its successor or its neighbor in time or space. If it was a mighty nation with a formidable national spirit, its spirit is absorbed by civilization at large and becomes "the inheritance of mankind and its collective spirit."[37] In the Torah and the Former Prophets there are examples of national spirits which are called the "gods of the nations" (*elohei ha-uma*). These gods were spirits which united a people internally, but only partook of the Absolute Spirit in a relative and fragmentary way. This was not the case with Israel, which, in terms of its basic striving, sought only the recognition of the one God. In support of his view Krochmal quoted Jeremiah: "The portion of Jacob is not like them for he is the former of all things; and Israel is the rod of his inheritance; the Lord of Hosts is his name."[38] That is to say, He is the Absolute Spirit (*ha-ruhani ha-muhlat*) and beside him there is none else, [he is] the source of all spiritual being ... the all-encompassing...the *en sof* (who is without end).[39]

Israel enjoys a unique role because its spirit as a nation unites with the Absolute Spirit, which has ordained it to become a "kingdom of priests, teachers to mankind of the great biblical faith which is absolute."[40] Since the Absolute Spirit reveals itself directly only to the Jewish nation (*uma*), its spirit is immortal. Unlike in other nations, where the Absolute Spirit reveals itself only as a temporary phenomenon and departs when the people have faded from history, Spirit remains forever with the Jewish people throughout the crests and troughs of history's fortune.[41]

Krochmal goes on to chart the course of Jewish history and asserts
that the history of Israel, similar to the histories of other nations, underwent the processes of birth, of growth into a nation, of a period of
maturity, strength and accomplishment, and afterwards of decay and
death. In Krochmal's discussion of the third phase, he again stresses
the analogy of the nation to a biological organism, for which death is
an inevitable consequence of the life process.[42] Israel, insofar as it par-
takes of the natural order, is also subject to this cycle. There is, however, a fundamental difference between Israel and all the other nations
since Absolute Spirit is inextricably embedded within it. At the point
of national extinction, the Spirit propels Israel into a new cycle. "And
when we fell, we rose again and restored, for the Lord our God had
not forsaken us."[43] It was Israel's destiny to go through three historical cycles, each of which was characterized by three different phases:

First Cycle
   Phase one: From Abraham to the death of Moses.[44]
   Phase two: From the entrance into the land of Canaan until the
   demise of Solomon.[45]
   Phase three: From the death of Solomon to the slaying of
   Gedaliah.[46]
Second Cycle
   Phase one: From the destruction of the first Temple to the con-
   quest of Persia by Greece.[47]
   Phase two: From the conquest of Asia by the Greeks until the
   fall of the Hasmonean dynasty.[48]
   Phase three: From the death of Queen Alexandra to the fall of
   Betar, ca. 135 C.E.[49]
Third Cycle
   (Krochmal was very sketchy with regard to the third cycle,
   quickly delineating the phases with sparse comment)
   Phase one: From Antonius, ca. 138 C.E. and the period of
   forced conversions, to the Geonic period.
   Phase two: From the zenith of early Moslem power, ca. 740,
   to the Golden Age of Spain.
   Phase three: From the death of Nahmanides until after the ex-

pulsions of the fifteenth century and the pogroms in the seventeenth century.[50]

Krochmal was certain that this pattern of historic development would continue and that future historians would be left ample opportunity for further interpretation.[51]

Krochmal's depiction of the last cycle of Jewish history is so abbreviated that questions may well arise as to how important he thought this cycle was. It is our opinion that the sketchiness of this cycle has no relevance to Krochmal's estimation of its importance, since he was interested in depicting a method of history. His lack of projection of a fourth or fifth cycle also cannot be taken to mean that he believed in a cessation of the cyclical process. "The cycles of Jewish history continue, because in each new cycle the Absolute Spirit is perceived and comprehended in more penetrating terms."[52] The Absolute Spirit, while it abides temporarily in all peoples, remains continuously embedded in the Jewish people. The spirit of the Jewish people is universal and eternal, as is the Absolute Spirit itself.[53] Within the cycles of Jewish history, progress within the self-realization of the idea is evident. Jacob Taubes held that Krochmal, like Hegel, believed that in his own time the consciousness of the Spirit had become self-consciousness; "…that the Spirit has come into its own and has become manifest."[54] He based this conclusion on a phrase in Krochmal's work in which he alluded to his own time as *aharit ha-yamim* (the end of days).[55] Taubes found here "unmistakably eschatological undertones" and concluded that Krochmal, as Hegel, believed that in his own time "history has come to an end in order that a philosophy of history may be possible."[56] It is very unlikely, though, taking the totality of Krochmal's thought into consideration, that this is what he meant. It is more likely that Krochmal implied, as Taubes himself observes, that history had come to the end of an epoch, the last phase of a cycle.[57] It was only natural to conclude from the method of exposition characteristic of Krochmal that a new cycle was in formation, the details of which he could not possibly know. That there would be a revival of the Jewish spirit which would lead Judaism to new crests of spiritual accomplishment was implicit in the cyclical process of the development of Jewish history which Krochmal had so cogently constructed.

There were those among the Jewish intellectual aristocracy of Poland and Russia who were schooled in the esoteric biblical exegetical method of *remez* (hint). *Remez* was a hermeneutical device whereby one attempted to explain a verse of the Bible which was on the surface unclear, by looking for a "hint" which would point to another portion of Scripture in which would resolve and bring into focus the meaning of the first text. Krochmal, analogously, had more than hinted that a fourth and even a fifth cycle of Jewish history was in the offing. It was, however, left to the architects of the East European Zionist movement to link the hint in Krochmal to the emergence of the first phase of the Zionist movement, which sought the reason for its existence as much in the history of the past as in the need to alleviate the burning problems of the present. Nahum Sokolow, the historian of early Zionism (*Hibbat Zion*), evaluates Krochmal in the following terms:

> The great value of Krochmal's system is exactly this—that it brings the reader to a dilemma in which he must finally choose one of the two courses. Either he must stand and fall by the theory of one cycle in the life of the Jewish nation, and then he must give up as hopeless the idea of a national Revival; or he must accept the truth regarding the vitality of the nation, a living nation, with all its spirituality, and believe in a Revival.[58]

Ahad Ha-Am[59]

In its formative phase the Zionist movement had two dominant ideological tendencies. One, which emanated from Western Europe, reflected for the most part the need to cope with and be an antidote to the growing problem of antisemitism.[60] The contours of Zionism created in Western Europe, and particularly in Germany, were political in nature. Although its theoreticians also outlined ideas for Jewish survival in a hostile environment, that program was devoid—at least in the estimate of Ahad Ha-Am, foremost among the Zionists who believed in the need for a revival of the Jewish spirit —of the inner strength that would enable Judaism to survive in the modern world.[61]

Ahad Ha-Am was a prestigious figure in the other ideological camp of the earlier Zionist movement, which emerged mainly from eastern Europe. Although relatively open-minded with regard to the practical steps it considered, the representatives of this group saw the plight of Jews and of Judaism as intertwined and insisted that the national character of Judaism was in a fundamental sense "the historic reality of the Jewish people."[62]

Ahad Ha-Am elaborated the main ideas of what came to be known as Spiritual Zionism. The essence of Spiritual Zionism was to participate in a cultural renaissance of the Jewish people and to usher in a new era which would find, at least in the beginning, the elect of the Jewish people— those within whom the "national spirit" was strong—re-established in their historical homeland.[63] Through them, *Eretz Israel* would become the Spiritual Center of the Jewish people— the hub of the wheel of the world whose spokes would extend to the four corners of the Diaspora.[64]

In a stinging rebuke to Herzl (the head of the Zionist movement and the outstanding spokesman of the political approach) written on the occasion of the Third Zionist Congress (Basel, 1899), Ahad Ha-Am referred to what the Congress regarded as the great problems of Jewish life of the day. Apparently unvoiced until this time among political Zionists was the awareness, long present with Ahad Ha-Am, of the fallen state of the spiritual condition of the Jewish people:

> Thus we hear how our spirituality (to use Krochmal's term) decreases from year to year; how our young people are becoming more and more estranged from the spirit of our people; how Torah is forgotten and the Jewish heart is emptying itself out....And yet the people is not heartsick over all this and does not feel the great sin that it has sinned against itself and against all of mankind by raising up a generation of Jews such as this, who do not themselves nor do others know their nature, the reason for their existence, or why they suffer.[65]

Clearly, at this time Ahad Ha-Am felt that there should be an appropriate mandate to the Congress and its leaders, who at long last had seen what the status of contemporary Jewry was, and who had also been awakened to the need to work for the preservation of Judaism. Ahad Ha-Am believed that the "leader of the Zionists" would understand what "Hebrew culture is and what benefit there is in it for the Zionist purpose."[66]

A careful examination of the ideas of Ahad Ha-Am points toward the influence of Nachman Krochmal. Ahad Ha-Am wrote in his *Memoirs* that he "immersed himself night and day" in Jewish philosophical literature "from Maimonides to Krochmal."[67] His acknowledgement of Krochmal as being the author of the *only* distinguished book in Modern Hebrew literature was, for Ahad Ha-Am, a most unusual encomium:

> Those who have read the book feel at once that there is no nexus between the *Moreh nevukhei ha-Zeman* and the rest of the *Haskalah* literature of its period. Its content, structure and style is reminiscent of the older literature, characterized by profound thought and precise, unembellished language. It is not reading for youngsters, but learning for mature adults. Even those who do not agree with the contents of the book do not mock it, for it is a work which does honor to the reader.[68]

It was Krochmal and his system, which emanated from German idealism and particularly from the ideas of Hegel, together with Jewish theological notions elaborated in modern philosophic style, which created the ideological framework from which Ahad Ha-Am developed the key concepts expressed in his philosophy of Spiritual Zionism.[69] It is our contention that Ahad Ha-Am's notions of *ruah* (spirit) and *ruhaniut* (spirituality), as they manifest themselves in such concepts as *tehiyat ha-ruah* (the revival of the spirit), *ha-ruah ha-leumi* (the national spirit), *ha-leumiut ha-ruhanit* (spiritual nationalism), *ha-zedek ha-muhlat* (absolute justice), as well as in his interpretation of Jewish history, are strongly related to Krochmal's theory about the existence of the Jewish people and his philosophy of history in general.

Nevertheless, there was also a major ideological chasm between Ahad Ha-Am and Krochmal, and a difference in the line of thought each related to in modern Jewish philosophy. Krochmal's use of *ruah* and its manifestations was theological, while Ahad Ha-Am's was secular. Krochmal was one of the founders of a stance in the modern *Haskalah* whose adepts, despite the differences among them, worked out of a framework of religious Judaism. For them, God and the Commandments, whether the emphasis was legalistic, ritualistic or ethical, were the basic realities of Jewish existence. For Ahad Ha-Am, on the other hand, religious Judaism was the creation of the Jewish "national spirit," and the workings of that national spirit—not the idea of God—were for Ahad Ha-Am central for the understanding of Jewish history.[70] Ahad Ha-Am stressed that the ethical nature of Judaism was conceived in secular and national terms, and that the religious characteristics of the Jewish people were an outgrowth of this originally secular ethic.[71] For him it was the *ethical* in "ethical monotheism" that needed to be underscored. The religious manifestation of the ethical dimension of Judaism was clearly of secondary importance and conditioned with regard to time and place.

Given such essential differences, where exactly *were* the points of contact between Ahad Ha-Am and Krochmal? Apparently, the matter caused Ahad Ha-Am much reflection. Ahad Ha-Am's avoidance of Krochmal's central concept, *ha-ruhani ha-muhlat* (the Absolute Spirit), was not accidental. His non-use of Krochmal's key term for his conceptual system is undoubtedly related to his own agnosticism. It might appear that Ahad Ha-Am borrowed Krochmal's intellectual framework, and filled it with his own thoughts about the essential spiritual qualities of Judaism, which, in his view, needed both renewal and an opportunity to burst forth again in a natural and congenial environment—in Palestine, the historic fountainhead of the Jewish "national spirit."[72]

Nevertheless, it seems clear that the influence of Krochmal on Ahad Ha-Am ran deeper than this, and not only because Ahad Ha-Am's messianic goals were, although of a secular nature, infused with a religious feeling in which Jewish tradition, as the sancta of a nation, had a major weight. An important point of contact between Ahad Ha-Am and Krochmal was the very idea of a renewal of the Jewish spirit which would allow the manifest purpose of the Jewish people to be realized in history.[73] It seems that Ahad Ha-Am had understood the full import of Krochmal's depiction of the third cycle of Jewish history, which Ahad Ha-Am extended also to include the events of his own time.

One main difference between the two men was in the external intellectual influences upon them. Yehezkel Kaufmann states that in Ahad Ha-Am's day "the time had already passed for the sufficing of popular religion or even for such ideas as Krochmal's 'ha-ruhani ha-muhlat,' or the 'mission of Israel' idea of the savants of the West."[74] Jacob B. Agus puts it more forcefully when he observes that "in contrast to the generation of Krochmal, the contemporaries of Ahad Ha-Am no longer believed implicitly in God. The eternity of the Jewish people could not, therefore, be postulated on the basis of attachment to the Absolute Idea."[75] Joseph Heller, in his exposition of Ahad Ha-Am's thought, points out that from the outset he was influenced by two concurrent ideological streams: positivism and idealism. Heller maintains, correctly I believe, that both influences remained characteristic of Ahad Ha-Am's system throughout his work.[76]

Opposing this viewpoint is Me'ir Turtel, who holds that Ahad Ha-Am gave up idealism in his later writings for Lamarck's notion of vitalism and a mechanistic view of the universe.[77] Yehezkel Kaufmann's thesis, on the other hand, is that there is a logical flaw in Ahad Ha-Am's system because he is inconsistent in using a positivist vocabulary side by side with such notions as "absolute morality" and the "spirit of Judaism." It is Kaufmann's contention that the biological-positivist view preceded the later idealist view, and explains that at first Ahad Ha-Am was concerned with the question of Jewish survival, and therefore gave precedence in his thought to "the will to live." But, Kaufmann reasons, when Ahad Ha-Am realized that his position was devoid of what, for him, was an essential component, namely, the specific survival of Judaism, he resorted to idealistic philosophy, and identified the prophetic absolute ethic with the "spirit of Judaism."[78] Ezra Spicehandler, while agreeing with Heller that "this chronological distinction simply does not fit the facts," has developed a hypothesis of his own in which he reasons that the contradiction inherent in the combination of positivism and idealism, as they appear in Ahad Ha-Am's thought, was characteristic of late French positivism and had its roots in the philosophy of Auguste Comte. Spicehandler observes that Comte's "…preoccupation with 'humanity' and his development of the 'religion of humanity' (priesthood and all!) indicate that even the father of positivism was compelled to abandon the early utilitarian avoidance of ultimates. In place of the presupposition of random ends he is forced into a voluntaristic view of society."[79] Spicehandler concluded that Ahad Ha-Am's "….'deviation' might be explained as either the development of his late positivistic orientation or as a result of his being directly influence by the late French positivists whom he frequently quotes, including Durkheim himself.[80]

The problems in the position of Ahad Ha-Am referred to by Turtel, Kaufmann, Spicehandler and others reflect the extent to which he was influenced by diverse nineteenth century thinkers. Ahad Ha-Am was affected by the positivism of Auguste Comte and Emile Durkheim, as well as by the adaptation of their *Weltanschauung* by Charles Darwin and Herbert Spencer. The latter was apparently especially important: Spencer conceived the universe as a succession of cycles—"alternate eras of evolution and dissolution"[81]— and made the evolution of societies as social organisms explainable as the result of the same process that was operative in the physical universe.[82] Nevertheless, many of the difficulties in Ahad Ha-Am's thought can be explained when one relates his views to the philosophical influence of Krochmal.

At stated above, Krochmal had made the analogy of the nation to a biological organism—a view which showed the influence of Herder. Krochmal, however, departed from Herder in a most fundamental sense: he did not accept Herder's verdict of the inevitability of the death of the Jewish people, which would follow from the general life-cycle that Herder had established for all nations. While there are other significant differences between the two thinkers, the immortality which Krochmal ascribes to the spirit of the Jewish people, because it is at one with the Absolute Spirit, is of foremost importance.[83] This aspect of Krochmal's thought particularly appealed to Ahad Ha-Am, although he had a different approach for the idea of Jewish immortality: Ahad Ha-Am secularized the idea and transformed it into a Jewish "national spirit" (*ha-ruah ha-leumi*).

…For it is surely an error among those who think that the national spirit is an abstract idea denoting the sum of all the spiritual principles that reveal themselves in each generation in the life of the people and when its manifestation ceases in the life of the people its instance also ceases. The national spirit is really a collective notion only in the manner in which it came into being, as a result of the collective life of a group of people closely connected with one another for generations under given conditions. However, after it has once come into being and has rooted itself in men's hearts because of a long history, then it becomes a personal psychological notion, whose truth is inherent in the individual himself and is not at all dependent on that which is external to him.[84]

Although Ahad Ha-Am mentions that he read and enjoyed Herder's works,[85] it was in all likelihood Herder as transmitted through Krochmal's *Moreh nevukhei ha-Zeman* that Ahad Ha-Am confronted in his formative years. Ahad Ha-Am, like Krochmal, believed that nations were analogous to biological organisms; that the Jewish people had defied the third phase that all organisms undergo, namely death; that there were three cycles to Jewish history;[86] and that Jewish history had a teleological principle—(*ha-zedek ha-muhlat*) "absolute justice"—inherent within it.[87]

Ahad Ha-Am's thought was in agreement with Herder's in the same measure that Krochmal's was, but where Krochmal's thought differs from Herder's only in content Ahad Ha-Am's differs in structure as well. Yet, Ahad Ha-Am differs also from Krochmal, not only in his secularization of the spirit of the Jewish people by making of it a psychological phenomenon, but also in his reason as to why the Jewish nation escaped the extinction of all other national organisms. The content of the three cycles of Jewish history is grouped strictly around the national facets of Jewish historical experience.[88] While this is also the case regarding Krochmal, the position is accentuated in Ahad Ha-Am. The teleological principle in Krochmal is unambiguously the Absolute Spirit, who is the God of Israel. With Ahad Ha-Am, on the other hand, the thrust of Jewish history ultimately leads to the full realization of the idea of "absolute justice" (*ha-zedek ha-muhlat*).[89] It is from within the context of Jewish history and the Bible that Ahad Ha-Am draws the data to flesh out the structural skeleton that he absorbed from Krochmal.

* * * *

In the century that separated the births of Krochmal and Ahad Ha-Am, new philosophic currents were astir in the world. Darwinism, positivism and nationalism were on the ascendancy and it was as natural for Ahad Ha-Am to turn to these new intellectual trends to seek a solution for the "plight of Judaism" as it was for Krochmal to turn to the German idealism in vogue in his own day. As Ahad Ha-Am himself had noted, there are "survivals" of the old in every new system, and he preserved aspects of German idealism conceptually, as well as in his philosophical vocabulary, from the very outset of his writings. Krochmal had bequeathed an arsenal of such ideas to him, which Krochmal had already adapted to the temper of Judaism by equating the concepts of German idealism to the traditional vocabulary of Jewish theology. Ahad Ha-Am took over Krochmal's powerful philosophy of Jewish survival and applied it to the needs of his own day. He saw, as Krochmal had seen, that the formative epoch of the Jewish "national spirit" was mirrored in the Bible and in the history of the Hebrew people. It is to that period that he turned to formulate anew a doctrine of Jewish survival. Ahad Ha-Am believed that *Hibbat Zion* (another designation for "Spiritual Zionism") was not a just a part of Judaism or an addition to it, but that it was a concept which contained within it the totality of Judaism.[90]

In his own formulation of the evolution of Judaism Ahad Ha-Am saw fit to replace Herder's biological categories with those of Herbert Spencer, and the Absolute Spirit which animated and sustained the Jewish historical experience gave way to the Darwinist notion of the "drive for self-preservation" in individuals and social units. Nationalism, in its several manifestations, became identified with Jewish culture and the religious heritage, which were both conceived as by-products of the Jewish "national spirit." As he interwove these various ideologies with the Bible and Jewish history, Ahad Ha-Am hoped that he, like Maimonides and Krochmal before him, might serve as the *moreh nevukhim*, "the guide for the perplexed," of his own time.

Creating Cultural Space: Jews and Judaism at a Public University in the 1920s

William Toll

The Campus Context in the 1920s

As the affluence of the 1920s enabled growing numbers of young American Jews to attend college, they encountered different dilemmas at different kinds of schools. Most scholarly interest in Jewish college attendance in the 1920s has focused on the policy of selective admissions implemented by elite private institutions in the northeastern region of the United States, especially in major cities. These restrictive policies have been linked to a national mood of xenophobia in reaction to American involvement in World War I and to the tide of east European immigrants that arrived in the United States just before and after the war.[1] As Congress imposed a numerical limit on immigration, which was further refined by differential quotas based on national origins, Columbia, Harvard, Yale and other colleges altered their admissions protocols to protect an image of America based on Anglo-Protestant dominance. They hoped to accomplish this by controlling the most immediate threat to their own image, the presence of a growing number of students of Russian Jewish parentage. Columbia, situated in the port of entry for European immigrants, was the first university to feel the pressure of Jewish enrollment. By 1921 its administrators had established new criteria for admission that quickly cut Jewish enrollment from over forty percent to about twenty percent. Harvard and Yale, which had smaller proportions of Jews—drawn largely from the much smaller Russian Jewish enclaves in Boston and New Haven—had similar fears. They also enacted new admissions criteria to lower Jewish enrollment.[2]

In a related counter-development, however, the curriculum at these schools began to reflect the more cosmopolitan views of their own professional scholars. Jewish philanthropy had enabled Harvard, Columbia, as well as the University of Pennsylvania to pioneer in the study of the Ancient Near East.[3] Jewish students who gained admission to these schools might find a small number of professors and courses providing some academic validation for the ancient sources of their tradition.[4] They might also find a chapter of the Jewish literary club, The Menorah Society, where, in the company of a small group of supportive faculty, interested students might create a Jewish cultural enclave.[5] From the summer of 1915 through 1917, Horace Kallen, a founder of the first Menorah Society at Harvard, and later a professor of philosophy at the University of Wisconsin, traveled through the Midwest and even as far as Berkeley, California, to energize Jewish faculty and students, primarily at state universities, who belonged to Menorah Society chapters.[6] By late 1917, Henry Hurwitz, the Society's principal founder and director, reported that chapters existed on fifty-five campuses in the United States and Canada.[7]

This pattern of restricted acceptance accompanied by the potential for scholarly validation affected a large number of Jewish students in the 1920s and 1930s because Harvard, Yale and Columbia, despite their elite status, were among the largest universities in the country. In 1919, for example, Columbia enrolled almost 7,000 students and was surpassed only by the Universities of Michigan and of California at Berkeley. Harvard and the University of Pennsylvania enrolled about 4,000 students, considerably less than the Universities of Illinois and Nebraska and the Ohio State University, but only slightly less than the University of Wisconsin. (See table 1) The rejection by Harvard, Yale and Columbia of several thousand Jewish young men during the 1920s—a decade when more and more young men and women saw higher education as a prerequisite for white collar and professional employment—represented discrimination against a significant portion of the most academically ambitious Jews. Nevertheless, at some prestigious private schools like the University of Chicago, the University of Pennsylvania and New York University, Jewish enrollment increased with apparently few overt complaints.[8]

Table 1: Enrollment at Selected American Colleges and Universities, 1919*

Name	Total enrollment		Jewish enrollment	
	Male enroll	Female enroll	Male enroll	Female enroll
Columbia U	3,749	3,194	1,226	249
Fordham	1,077	170	286	4
NYU	4,269	1,267	2,113	419
CCNY	1,961	0	1,544	0
Hunter College	0	1,295	0	502
Tufts College	1,452	183	291	19
Harvard	3,843	0	385	0
U of Penn	3,471	601	545	51
Temple U	987	867	207	59
Johns Hopkins	1,496	487	283	39
U of Pittsburgh	2,621	1,006	372	71
West. Reserve	1,147	691	205	64
U of Chicago	2,507	1,599	571	190
Northwestern U	1,738	1,456	184	37
U of Michigan	6,006	1,245	269	28
U of Illinois	4.465	1,742	245	19
Ohio State U	3,699	1,489	201	33
U of Wisconsin	2,441	1,873	91	52
U of California	3,831	3,455	175	93
U of So. Calif.	2,346	1,290	49	12
Reed College	187	151	9	1
U of Oregon	767	833	15	0

*Source: *American Jewish Yearbook, 1920–1921* (Philadelphia: JPS, 1920), 387–389

But most Jewish undergraduates in the 1920s faced a very different experience. As many scholars have noted, undergraduate enrollment expanded substantially after World War I, rising from about

600,000 in 1919–1920, to over one million in 1929–1930, and—despite the Depression —to over 1.3 million in 1939–1940.[9] Jews who might be denied admission at one school could find a place at a less prestigious—and cheaper—alternative nearby.[10] New schools of business, engineering, and education sprang up on hundreds of campuses, new dormitories and student centers were built, and fraternities and inter-collegiate athletics became a virtual mania. Institutions drawing their students from different social classes, of course, faced different campus situations. The public commuter colleges of CCNY and Hunter had growing Jewish majorities, but unlike Columbia or Harvard, their faculty and curriculum made little effort to accommodate the cultural background of their students.[11]

Large and highly regarded state universities in California, Michigan, and Illinois, as well as smaller state universities everywhere, readily admitted growing numbers of Jews. Here, however, Jews faced the anxiety of being a self-conscious minority, often in an overwhelmingly Protestant college town with virtually no Jewish subjects in the curriculum. In 1924 the Jewish men's fraternal order, B'nai B'rith, acknowledged the cultural isolation of the growing numbers of Jewish students attending state universities by creating Hillel Houses, first at Illinois in 1925, then quickly at Michigan, Ohio State, and Wisconsin, and in 1927 a fifth house at the University of California at Berkeley.[12] Young Reform rabbis were hired to create religious and cultural centers, whose activities were intended to provide informal Jewish study and to train future Jewish communal leaders.

At smaller state universities that lacked B'nai B'rith largesse, Jewish students were largely on their own without social or curricular support. The University of Oregon in Eugene affords a useful window through which to observe the dilemmas attendant on the arrival of a small but growing number of Jewish students at a small, public university in a small, overwhelmingly Protestant town. Here the president, Prince Lucien Campbell, a Harvard graduate (1886) with a classical education and a late nineteenth century liberal spirit, wished to welcome Jewish students and some instruction in Judaism to his growing school. But he—and his Jewish students—encountered many dilemmas. As a public university, Oregon could not in its admissions procedures discriminate on the basis of religion or race. Even before

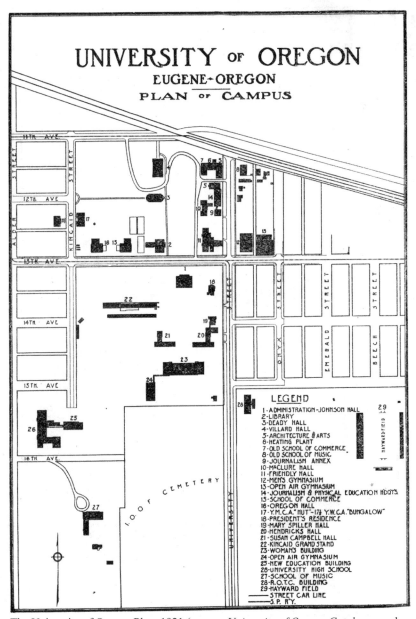

The University of Oregon Plan, 1921 (source: *University of Oregon Catalogue*, vol. 8, 1921–1922, Summer Session Announcements 1921, p. 2)

American entry into World War I, Campbell tried to persuade Portland's Jewish community of perhaps ten thousand to send its sons and daughters to his school. But for a variety of reasons, perhaps its lack of prestige or its location in a small town, few sons and daughters of Portland's Jewish families enrolled there.[13]

If the University of Oregon's charter disallowed it from discriminating against people, it required—like those of most western public universities—that it distance itself from their religions.[14] The prospect of soliciting Jewish philanthropic support for a program in Semitics enticed faculties at five private institutions—Harvard, Yale, Columbia, the University of Pennsylvania, and Johns Hopkins—and at the public University of California. In the more cosmopolitan world of Berkeley, Rabbi Jacob Voorsanger had taught Semitics, with his courses funded by Jewish philanthropy, from 1894 until his death in 1908. In the early 1920s his successor, Rabbi Martin Meyer, and two colleagues with earned doctorates were teaching courses in Semitic languages and ancient cultures.[15] At the time scholars in America believed that the graduate study of Semitics would resolve intellectual conundrums by revealing the origins of Western Civilization's foundation myths, and would elevate the status of their institutions to that of the great European universities.[16] Though the University of Oregon in the 1920s was beginning to support graduate research, including archaeological studies of Native Americans, President Campbell could not imagine funding a graduate program in Semitics. Instead, he struggled with the dilemmas of a more limited civic mandate, that of providing ethical guidance free of sectarian bias for undergraduates—including a small Jewish contingent—who would be the state's future leaders.[17] Because the results of his labors were meager, when Jewish students began to arrive in larger numbers in the mid-1920s, they found themselves socially isolated and culturally marginal. Their effort to create a Jewish physical and cultural presence illustrates how the first generation of Jewish students seeking an educational pathway to social and economic mobility faced a variety of dilemmas in addition to quotas.

Judaism on a Public/Protestant Campus: Searching for a Heuristic Religion

Efforts to attract Jewish students to the University of Oregon were directly related to the effort by President Campbell to bring some form of Jewish cultural presence to his campus. Conscious of his role as president of a public university, he tried to balance a set of often contradictory responsibilities. As the mentor of young men and women, he wished to expose them to the moral guidance he had received in his earliest higher education in the late 1870s and early 1880s at his father's Christian college in Monmouth, Oregon. But as presiding officer of a state institution, he could not allow denominational interests to intrude on public space. In addition, as a classically trained scholar, he believed in exposing his students to diverse cultural experiences, while offering them the freedom to choose their own specific courses, as he himself had done during his more mature college training at Harvard. An informal census of almost one thousand University of Oregon students in 1919 showed that of those declaring membership in a specific denomination, the largest groups were Presbyterians (158) and Methodists (136), with Campbell's own denomination, the Disciples of Christ, standing third (105), and Episcopalians (80) fourth.[18] Though only three Jewish students were counted, at the commencement in 1921, one of them, Abraham E. Rosenberg, received the Failing Prize for the best original oration by a senior.[19]

Many of the University's faculty taught at local Sunday schools— a practice which Campbell greatly encouraged—and as early as 1916 the faculty appointed a Students' Religious, Moral and Social Service committee to advise students on these apparently integrally related matters.[20] A few years later Campbell assured one Detroit businessman, anxious over the scourge of atheism on college campuses, that eighty per cent of Oregon students, when polled, indicated a church preference.[21] To reinforce this moral atmosphere, Campbell hoped that the various churches would assign clergymen to campus ministries and would erect buildings where an array of educational and cultural events could be held. During the 1920s he encouraged Father Edwin V. O'Hara to teach classes on Catholicism for university students at an off-campus venue, and encouraged fund-raising for a Newman Hall.[22]

Campbell and his staff hoped that one of the larger Protestant denominations would assign a pastor to work full-time with students, because, as enrollment grew rapidly, local clergymen could devote little time to the work. They responded supportively when local clergymen proposed to offer classes on religious subjects for students at venues near campus. In 1921 The Presbyterian Church assigned to the campus a young minister, Bruce J. Giffen, who offered courses to students and recruited them for missionary work. By the mid-1920s, he and his wife moved into a Koinonia Center, a new building on the west edge of campus and across the street from the space that had been set aside for the university's new library. Two blocks to the north a Methodist Wesley center was erected across the street from the inter-denominational YMCA, which occupied a building on the campus grounds. The Episcopal church of Portland also owned ground on the east side of campus and planned to develop it, though to what purpose was not entirely clear.[23]

Discussion about the creation of an inter-denominational school of religion, organized by the Presbyterians, was broached in the early 1920s, but defining its relationship to a public university remained highly problematic. In 1923 the secretary of the campus YMCA proposed to form a United Board of Religious Education, consisting of faculty, students and local clergy. Denominations willing to select and fund their own minister-instructors would consult with it, and the new "clerical faculty" would minister to students and organize classes "on various phases of the Christian faith." Students would not initially receive university credit for the classes, "but if they are of a high caliber they will win credit standing, as they have at other universities within a few years." Dean Colin Dyment informed President Campbell, "it is probably in the interest of the University…that the school of religion should be a joint one, since it is somewhat contrary to the general spirit of higher education that several denominations should be competing with one another in religious effort, and each perhaps hammering at our door for our recognition."[24]

These plans never reached fruition, perhaps because they would have violated faculty legislation, but also because the denominations would not commit funds. Consequently, Karl Onthank, president Campbell's private secretary, informed the director of the YMCA in

Portland that the campus YMCA would continue as the focus of outreach to students. "We hope to unite with the YMCA the combined strength of the churches in the religious work on campus rather than to permit them to neglect campus work as has been the case in the past or to build up separate denominational establishments, inevitably competitive in character, on the edge of campus."[25]

Eugene's tiny Jewish community, which consisted of a few merchants and their families, remained unorganized, and could render little assistance to the small number of Jewish students and none to the cultural aspirations of President Campbell. Eugene's most prominent Jewish merchant for over forty years had been S. H. Friendly, who had welcomed student accounts at his store and served on the university's Board of Regents from 1895 until his death in 1915. Shortly after his death, the University's first dormitory was named in his honor. But as a local person, Friendly's relationship to the University seems to have been unique.[26]

Campbell, of course, was acutely aware of the support that prominent Jewish merchants in Portland gave to increasing the legislature's appropriations for the university in a state whose rural members often saw little use for his institution.[27] As President of the University during an era of expanding state interest in urban social problems, Campbell was invited to join state boards to deal with a range of issues from sex education, to the prevention of tuberculosis, the promotion of social work, and mental health.[28] At meetings in Portland he became familiar with merchants such as Adolph Wolfe, Charles F. Berg, and Julius Meier, and clubwomen such as Mrs. S. M. Blumauer and Mrs. Isaac Swett, who also served on these boards. He also came to know Portland's most prominent philanthropist, Ben Selling, who as president of the state senate had strongly supported appropriations for the University, and who had personally endowed a statewide scholarship fund for college students. Selling, however, remained suspicious of the University's social atmosphere, which he felt exuded hostility to Jews and Judaism— which he had sensed over several decades in many small towns.[29]

Campbell and his staff remained sensitive to Selling's views and moved in a variety of ways to alter his opinion. Most important, Campbell, as early as 1915, cultivated a relationship with Rabbi Jonah Wise of Temple Beth Israel, to which Portland's prominent merchants such as Selling, Adolph Wolfe, Julius Meier, and others belonged. Through Wise, Campbell hoped to expose Oregon's students to a Reform Judaism, which prominent Portland ministers like the Unitarian Thomas Lamb Eliot could attest to be a progressive moral philosophy. Campbell also knew that very few Jewish families in Portland sent their children to the University of Oregon. Elite families sent their sons to Ivy League schools, while the children of Portland's Jewish middle class then attended the University of Washington[30] in rapidly growing Seattle, or the new non-denominational Reed College in southeast Portland.[31]

To create contacts, in December, 1915, Campbell invited Wise to lecture at his University. Though Wise was unable to come at the time, Campbell accepted an invitation to speak at Temple Beth Israel, "to present the University's interest to the members of your congregation, many of whom have been warm friends of the University in its past tribulations over appropriations."[32] Over the next several years Wise was invited to the unveiling of a statue on campus sponsored by Joseph Teal, a prominent Portland Jewish lawyer, and to a football game in Corvallis between the University of Oregon and Oregon Agricultural College, although he was unable to attend either event. During that time, Campbell's secretary tried to bring Rabbi Stephen Wise, Rabbi Martin Meyer of San Francisco's Temple Emanu-El, and Lillian Wald to campus, hoping to take advantage of popular speaking tours which could bring such prominent American Jews to Portland. But in every case the tours were cancelled and the speakers never appeared.[33]

Finally, in 1920, an opportunity arose for Campbell to bring a more sustained cultural presence for Judaism to campus as part of his more general effort to promote the moral instruction of the student body. As a disciple of the liberal spirit of President Charles Eliot of Harvard, Campbell believed that ecumenical instruction might counter Christian teachings that had demonized Jews. He reflected the views of his fellow Harvard alumnus and Eliot disciple, Horace Kallen, who wrote in *The Nation* in 1923, "If you can end this teaching that the Jews are the enemies of God and mankind you will strike anti-Semitism to its foundations."[34] To that end, Campbell hoped that Wise might initiate a course of lectures.

Photo of Jonah Bondi Wise, 1930 (Courtesy The Jacob Rader
Marcus Center of the American Jewish Archives)

Wise and two highly qualified Jewish colleagues, Ralph P. Boas, a
literary scholar,[35] and Samuel H. Kohs, a recent Stanford Ph.D. in Psychology then teaching at Reed College and serving as a psychologist
at Portland's juvenile court, proposed to offer a twelve week course.
Expenses for travel and supplies would be borne by the Portland B'nai
B'rith Lodge through its new lecture bureau. Rabbi Wise would begin the course with material on Biblical and synagogue history, Boas
would discuss Jewish contributions to art, science and literature, and
Kohs would discuss social, political and economic issues that Jews
have "confronted" through their history. Students could enroll for one
unit of credit, and others could also attend.[36] The course, however,

was never offered on campus, and the convoluted and frustrating attempt to do so exemplified all of the dilemmas that Jews and Judaism encountered when they ventured into an American small town.

After Wise suggested in mid-September, 1920, a convenient day and time for holding the course, which might start as early as 30 September, delays began. Over the summer, perhaps at the instigation of faculty, Campbell's secretary, Karl Onthank, wrote to the presidents of a dozen public universities including Cornell, Michigan Agricultural College, the Universities of Wisconsin, Michigan, California, Illinois and Kansas to determine how they treated courses with religious content that were supported by religious organizations. Those courses proposed to be offered at the University of Oregon included Jewish History, Christian Apologetics, History of the Christian Religion, and Biblical Literature. The courses were "to be conducted on the same basis and at the same standard as regular university work," and it was proposed that students receive some university credit for completing them.[37] In the meantime, the faculty, though including many Sunday school teachers, began to consider whether they would permit credit being given for courses that were "of a religious nature," and that they did not teach. While Father O'Hara began teaching a course on Christian Ethics in the fall of 1920, and Reverend Giffen proposed to give his course in the winter, Rabbi Wise's course was delayed.

He and the other interested clergymen were invited to a meeting with President Campbell and a representative of the faculty to discuss whether a state university might accredit "courses of an essentially religious nature."[38] Rabbi Wise apparently attended this meeting, and in December, 1920, the faculty appointed a committee to report on the matter. Campbell assured Wise that the course on Jewish History and Literature would be "welcomed on campus," but that "the matter of credits" was becoming more controversial.[39] At a faculty meeting on 3 March 1921, the committee recommended—and the faculty approved—a resolution that sympathized with the need that religious organizations had to educate their young people, but recognized the principle that "the university does not give credit for course work it does not offer or which it does not consider a proper part of the curriculum of a state-supported university."[40] Plans by Wise and Kohs to come from Portland to offer their course were placed in abeyance.

By 1921 Wise had initiated an annual campus visit to meet with Jewish students, and Campbell asked him if he might be able to speak to a campus assembly in early 1922. Campbell also suggested a different approach for offering the Jewish History course. Instead of trying to schedule a time for offering the course on campus in Eugene, he suggested it be offered through the University Extension Service in Portland. Dozens of courses were offered through this agency by non-faculty people, including Psychology courses by Samuel Kohs and courses in Modern Hebrew taught by Bert Treiger, the principal of the non-denominational Portland Hebrew School.[41] In mid-January 1922 a course similar to the one that had been planned by Wise and Kohs was finally offered in Portland rather than on campus in Eugene. The *Scribe* announced a series of lectures by Wise alone and sponsored by the University's Extension Service to be delivered at the public library on Monday evenings. The titles of the lectures suggest a chronological account of the contacts from Biblical through Medieval times between Jews, as a national entity, with the Romans, Christian Europe and Islam.[42] The director of the extension services reported favorably on it to Campbell, who advised him "to keep your eye on this course in Portland so as to be able to judge in regard to its suitability for campus purposes."[43]

Over the next four years Rabbi Wise met with students and spoke on the University campus on several occasions.[44] In March 1925, he gave two talks on successive days on "Judaism" and on "Some Creative Forces and Their Evidence" as part of a series delivered by various speakers on topics like the Psychology of Religion and the Philosophy of Religion. Campbell's secretary, Karl Onthank, wrote to Mrs. Campbell that "both addresses were very good and pleased the students greatly."[45]

Within five months, however, Campbell succumbed to a debilitating illness, and shortly thereafter Rabbi Wise left Portland to take a pulpit in New York City. While their relationship seems to have been cordial, it had failed to enable Wise's course or any other with a Jewish content (with or without credit) to be offered on campus. In 1930 a new rabbi at Beth Israel, the erudite Henry Berkowitz, lectured on Judaism at Reed College as part of a series of talks by clergymen from a variety of denominations. An editorial in the Portland *Scribe* hailed the lecture series as part of a new "trend" on campuses to study religions historically and comparatively, rather than with didactic intent.[46] A decade earlier, however, neither Campbell nor his faculty had quite separated the didactic from the heuristic study of religion, and had missed an opportunity that the Jewish religious talent in Portland afforded Reed College. Respect for Beth Israel's Reform rabbis apparently persisted at the University of Oregon, however, because in June, 1930, Rabbi Berkowitz delivered the Baccalaureate Address at the graduation ceremony.[47]

In the early 1930s, after acquiring private funds to cover the expenses, the university did manage discreetly to initiate a very modest undergraduate program in "Religion," which included Judaism. Like the earlier unsuccessful efforts of President Campbell, this program had no relationship to graduate programs in Semitics, such as the one then supported in part with public funding at Berkeley.[48] Nor did it foreshadow undergraduate programs in Judaic Studies that would be initiated around the country in the 1960s and 1970s.[49] Instead, in 1933 the faculty created a committee on Religious and Spiritual Activities to supervise a sequence of three courses intended as a comparative survey that would complement recently introduced courses in the Philosophy Department on the Ethics and Philosophy of Religion, and in the Sociology Department on the Sociological Aspects of Religion. The year sequence was to cover (1) the Origins of Religion among primitive peoples, (2) the Great Religions of the Orient—Hinduism, Buddhism and Confucianism, and (3) the Great Religions of Palestine and Arabia—Judaism, Christianity and Islam.[50] In 1934 the program in Religion became a "non-major service department in the College of Social Science," but with no permanently assigned faculty. The catalogue assured students that while "instruction is planned in accordance with the same standards of authoritative scholarship recognized in other departments of the institution," the courses were intended to explain the broader processes of religious thought so that students after graduation might provide leadership in the religious and spiritual life of their communities.[51]

To further emphasize the undergraduate focus and inspirational intent of the new courses, the University initially hired as instructor the director of Oregon State University's Department of Religion,

Portrait of Prince Lucien Campbell (Courtesy University
of Oregon Photo Archive Collection, UA REF 3)

Ernest W. Warrington. Hardly a scholar, Warrington had received an
M.A. from Princeton in 1907, and had come to Oregon State in 1921
to be the secretary of the Student YMCA, a position he held until
1926 when he became director of their Department of Religion. Warrington never relinquished that position, and apparently taught at the
University of Oregon for only one year.[52] In subsequent years the catalogue entries describing the courses remained unchanged, though no
instructor was indicated and Warrington was not included in the list of
University of Oregon faculty.

Fulfilling the original intent of Prince Lucien Campbell, the new
courses added to an undergraduate curriculum that for decades had in-

cluded History and Philosophy surveys of Greece and Rome, and that had recently added a new professor to teach courses that included a survey of China and Japan. As the University's faculty and administrators moved gradually at their public institution to cleanse the study of religions—including Judaism—of sectarian bias, the heuristic rather than the scholarly intent of the project remained squarely in the foreground. The courses, however, contextualized Judaism as an ancient antecedent of its "successor" religions, Christianity and Islam. Given the historical context within which Judaism was presented as well as the choice of instructors, the courses would have no relationship to the growing graduate programs in Semitics at a few elite private universities, nor would they address contemporary philosophical or theological disputes within Judaism. The latter, however, would be the very issues about which the University's new Jewish students would come to have substantial knowledge.

Jewish Students in a Protestant Town: Dilemmas of Community

As the numbers of Jewish students on campus grew by the mid-1920s, they were largely left to their own devices to create a Jewish life. By the fall of 1927, the *Scribe* noted that the University had twenty-five Jewish students, which was believed to be the largest number ever enrolled.[53] As several scholars have noted, universities in the 1920s were just beginning to provide eating and sleeping facilities for their students, so students had to arrange for their own accommodations, based largely in fraternities.[54] The University of Oregon's Friendly Hall, then the only dormitory for men, could accommodate only eighty-five male students. All others, the University's catalogue noted, would have to find room and board either in the "invitational" living places (meaning the fraternities), or from a list of boarding houses made available through the YMCA.[55] Jews here, as elsewhere, were rarely admitted to fraternities, and there were very few Jewish families in town. Consequently, Jewish students had to arrange for their basic accommodations, and, as at many state universities, they did so by forming their own fraternities.[56] But to gain additional social support in Eugene, the new Jewish students took the rather unusual step of creating a collective relationship with local families. This dual work to create a Jewish presence on and off campus seemed to occupy their attention.

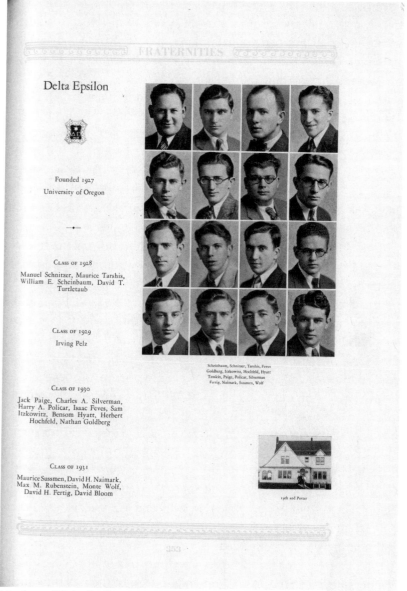

Members of Delta Epsilon Fraternity, 1928 (source: *The Oregana* [University of Oregon Yearbook], p. 353)

In December 1927 the Portland *Scribe* noted that, of the twenty-five Jewish students enrolled at the University of Oregon, nineteen young men, all but one from Portland, had started an independent fraternity, Delta Epsilon. With the assistance of the dean of men and of Portland Jewish philanthropists, they rented a house, and within a year, as membership increased, they moved to a larger building at 1860 Potter Street, which they continued to occupy through the 1930s. Rabbi Benjamin Goldstein, of the Hillel House at the University of California, who was visiting in Portland to address the B'nai B'rith, may also have stopped in Eugene to encourage the young men.[57] Rabbi Goldstein believed that a Hillel house should be the focus of Jewish student life by providing an array of social, cultural and religious events, including the organization of meetings and discussions with non-Jewish groups on campus. Through its student committees it would provide young people with the responsibility for organizing group life, and preparing themselves to become leaders when they returned to their communities.[58]

Eugene, of course, lacked a critical mass of students to warrant support of a Hillel House, and did not even have a Menorah Society to discuss social or scholarly issues and to bring speakers to campus. But the students did what they could to organize a social life for themselves. Under the leadership of William Scheinbaum, who had graduated from Reed College and then enrolled in the University's law school, the fraternity seems to have become the center for Jewish cultural as well as social activities. Scheinbaum, for example, with a freshman colleague, David Fertig, formed a team to debate with a team from the University of Washington's Menorah Society.[59] When he graduated from the law school in 1929 and left to study at Cornell, Scheinbaum was succeeded as fraternity president by Jack Paige, who had also transferred from Reed.

To exercise broader social responsibility and to utilize the Jewish training they had received in Portland, several of the fraternity members created a close relationship with local Jewish families, some of whom may have provided them with room and board prior to founding the fraternity. Local families had organized a Eugene Social Club, through which they hoped to initiate some religious worship and a rudimentary religious education for their children. The *Scribe* reported that as part of a general effort to awaken interest in Judaism among local families, Scheinbaum, a 1924 alumnus of the Portland Hebrew School, had opened a Sunday school, which he continued to direct for the next two academic years.[60] In March 1928 the Jewish ladies of Eugene presented a Holy Ark to the Social Club to enable proper Sabbath services, and gave a medal to Scheinbaum for his efforts with their children. Rabbi Herbert Parzen, newly hired by Conservative synagogue Ahavai Shalom, came from Portland in April as a guest of the fraternity to dedicate the ark.[61]

In the fall of 1928, Eugene's Jews for the first time had Rosh Hashanah and Yom Kippur services, led by a layman from Portland. As the members of Delta Epsilon returned for fall classes and inducted seven new boys from Portland, the *Scribe* believed that the work of the Jewish Social Club of Eugene could resume. When the Club elected officers, the president and vice-president were adults from Eugene, but the secretary was Manuel Schnitzer, a fraternity member from Portland.[62] At a meeting to mark the first anniversary of the Social Club, Rabbi Meyer Rubin of the Conservative synagogue Neveh Tzedek, who was also staying at the fraternity house, delivered the main address.[63]

While the University's administrators still solicited lectures from Portland's Reform rabbi, they seem never to have approached those Conservative rabbis who were now coming to campus at the invitation of the Jewish students. The university administrators believed that an ethically refined Judaism could legitimately be invited onto campus to add to an ecumenical and liberalized religious atmosphere. They never seem to have imagined that the philosophical differences within Judaism might be as substantial as those between their own Protestant denominations, and that rabbis other than Reform might have religious views to which their Jewish students adhered and to which their gentile students should be exposed. The University, along with others in the Pacific Northwest, gave high school foreign language credit for the Hebrew studied at the Portland Hebrew School.[64] But this did not lead the administrators or the faculty to explore the possibility that the Hebrew School and the Reform rabbinate might represent different philosophies of Judaism.

The University's Jewish students, however, had been acquiring an ethnically based and intellectually vibrant Jewish education in the Conservative synagogues to which their families belonged, and at the Portland Hebrew School.[65] The principal, Bert Treiger, had graduate training at Columbia and the Jewish Theological Seminary, and had dedicated his career to making Hebrew teaching the key ingredient for rejuvenating Jewish culture in Portland.[66] His instruction was based on the *Ivrit Bi-Ivrit* method, which used command of simple Modern Hebrew by young students to acquire more sophisticated language through a graded curriculum. Five days each week after attendance at public school, his pupils studied Bible, Jewish History and current affairs. The school had its own Hebrew newspaper and essay contests, and students completing the course were subject to public examination at graduation ceremonies.[67] By 1928 one graduate was then supervising a new Sunday school opened in East Portland, three others were teaching Sunday school at Rabbi Parzen's Ahavai Shalom, and Scheinbaum was applying his knowledge in Eugene.[68] Treiger himself, recognizing the movement of many Jewish families to East Portland, opened a branch of the school in this district, and committed himself to teaching there until permanent instructors could be found.[69]

Hebrew language training came with an intensive commitment to social and cultural institutions, and with acute political awareness. Treiger, Rabbi Parzen and Rabbi Rubin were ardent Zionists, relentless promoters of instruction in Hebrew for adults as well as children, wrote on Zionism for the *Scribe*, and sponsored Zionist lecturers at their synagogues.[70] Inspired by this religious leadership, prominent east European businessmen in 1928 started the Jewish Education Association of Portland to raise funds and to bring some coordination to the various efforts to promote Hebrew education in the city. Principal Treiger was its secretary,[71] and by January 1929 this work was augmented by Rabbis Parzen and Rubin, who started an Institute of Jewish Studies. The rabbis offered courses to adults in Advanced Hebrew and Jewish History, Biblical Literature, and Current Jewish Problems.[72] Only such religious and cultural instruction in such an intense atmosphere could have given the University of Oregon's Jewish students the knowledge and enthusiasm to act as a catalyst for the Jewish families they encountered in Eugene. And only such instruction would have enabled them and their friends to sustain a Jewish life in such a Protestant town.

Although initially formed as a local fraternity, as membership in Delta Epsilon grew with pledge classes of between six and eight a year, and as financing stabilized, its members chose to affiliate with the national fraternity, Sigma Alpha Mu.[73] Started in 1909 at CCNY, Sigma Alpha Mu was intended to provide a sense of community for upwardly mobile east European young men who were commuting daily to campus. As a measure of the ability and interest of east European Jews on the Pacific coast to send their sons to college, in the years just prior to the affiliation decision by the fraternity in Eugene Sigma Alpha Mu chapters had been initiated at UCLA, the University of Washington and at the University of California.[74] Despite the deepening Depression, the network seems to have sustained itself. While membership in the fraternity at the University Oregon dwindled to about a dozen in 1934, by 1939 it had rejuvenated to number twenty-four.[75]

An informal assessment of the family background of the members of Oregon's Sigma Alpha Mu chapter through the early 1930s verifies that virtually all were from families of east European origins with a pattern of social mobility that was projecting them toward communal leadership.[76] They were at the same time moving culturally from orthodoxy to the Conservative Movement. These were the young men whom Rabbi Parzen and Rabbi Rubin would have nurtured in their synagogues, and the rabbis would have been well-known to the students prior to their arrival in Eugene. Indeed, a member of the class of 1930 was Sam Itzkowitz, son of Jacob Itzkowitz, the assistant rabbi at Orthodox Sha'arei Torah.

Of the fifty-one fraternity members and two other male Jewish students who could be identified between 1928 and 1936, thirty-nine, as well as their parents, could be located in Portland city directories of the early 1930s. Virtually all either still lived in or near South Portland or in several adjacent districts of East Portland to which south Portlanders were rapidly moving.[77] Many, like South Portlanders Alex Tamkin, Sam Itzkowitz, Milton Zell and Benson Hyatt of the class of 1930, had spent part of their childhood within a few blocks of a fraternity brother. Their classmate and fraternity brother, Harry Policar, was of Sephardic origins, but his inclusion in their social circle suggests how the two Jewish groups mingled in South Portland. Samuel and Morris Rotenberg and Lester Goldschmidt of the classes of 1933 and 1935 also came from families still residing in South Portland. Louis Mesher and Harold Schectman of the class of 1934 still lived within a few houses of each other on East 14th Street, and Isaac and Louis Feves and Charles Silverman lived within a block of each other on the 700 blocks of east Taylor and east Main Streets.

These were the sons of upwardly mobile artisans, who had transferred their European village skills to Portland, and had built successful businesses in the expanding commercial city. Among the thirty-nine fathers, ten men operated small business, while eight were tailors, a few of whose stores also included dry cleaning. One father was a shoemaker, one a cabinetmaker, and one owned a bakery; four were in the junk business and one was an auctioneer. Six others were salesmen, one manufactured bags, another mattresses. After World War II several of the families—the Schnitzers, Zells, Directors, Meshers—would create very large businesses and become quite prominent.

The education and the college experience their sons received surely assisted them in carving out careers despite the Depression, which they faced when they left school. But the well-meaning though ill-informed administrators of the public university that welcomed them could offer very little social or cultural support. Jewish elites in the northeast in the 1920s might expend their energy battling quotas, but the majority of Jewish college students were struggling to sustain a Jewish presence on public campuses far from Jewish communities. This battle required inner resources and coordinated efforts, for which, at least in Eugene, the young men had to rely on prior education and on-going contacts with home.

Table #2: Delta Epsilon/SAM Fraternity, University of Oregon, Occupation of Fathers, 1930-31*

Occupation	Number	Per cent
store	10	25.5
tailor	8	20.4
Salesman/manufct agent	6	15.3
junk	4	10.3
manufacturer	4	10.3
shoemaker	1	2.6
manager	1	2.6
Rabbi	1	2.6
laborer	2	5.2
Other	2	5.2
Total	39	100.0

*Students identified in *Oregana*, 1928–1933, and *Scribe*; families traced in Portland city directories

APPENDIX: MEMBERS & FAMILY DATA,
DELTA EPSILON/ SAM, U OF OREGON, 1927–1933

Name –class year	Father	Occupation	Portland Addr 1930/31
Sol Beadner-33			
David Bloom –31	Max	expressman	1063 E 23rd
Stanley Bromberg –36	Jacob	salesman	3017 NE 14th av
Sylvan Campfe –32	Sam	fitter	3016 NE 12th
Jerome Clement – 35			
Cecil Cohen –33	Isidore	tailor & cleaner	402 Ivy
Sol Director-32	Sam	auction mrkt	404 College
Isaac Donin –34	Lewis	tailor	585 5th
Zanly C Edelson –35	Charles	mattress mfc	820 Thompson
David H Fertig –31	Charles	mfc agent (clth)	307 Grant
Isaac Feves –30	Myer	shoemaker	737 E Main
Louis Feves –32	Myer	shoemaker	737 E Main
Leo Freeman-33	Sam	grocer	3625 NE Multnomah
Milton Gilbert –33	John	Mont Ward manager	580 E 11th N
Nathan Goldberg –30	William	Bag mfc co	664 E 25th
David A Goldberg –35			
Lester Goldschmidt–35	Sidney	real estate slsmn	471 W Park
Edward Harris –35			
Earl Hart –34	Samuel	tailor	415 11th #110
Herbert Hochfield –30	Marcus	sport gds	450 E 17th N
Benson Hyatt –30	James	laborer	607 2nd
Sam Itzkowitz-30	Jacob	rabbi, Shaarei Torah	608 4th
Max Kaffeseider	Joseph	restaurnt	2324 NE 14th St
Max Kessler-33	Morris	sew mach operator	2032 SW Broadway
Henry Levoff –32	Benj	junk	587 2nd
Harold Lewis –34			
Jack Litchgarn –32	Abe (d) Dora		
Reuben Lockitch –32	David	tailor	353 Grant St.
Calmin Margulies –31	Sam	salesman	781 Multnomah St
Louis Mesher –34	Morris	plumbing supply	629 E 14th N
David Naimark –31	Moses	bag mfc	267 Grant
Jack Paige –30	Benj	tailor	715 1st
Irving Pelz –29	Joseph	musician	855 Hancock
Harry Policar –30	Isaac	salesman	551 Broadway, S
Morris H Rotenberg–35	Hyman	bakery	471 1/2 w Park
Samuel Rotenberg –33	Hyman	bakery	471 1/2 Park St
Max M Rubinstein –31 (EUG)			
Bertram Schatz –35	Harry	tailor	314 Jackson
Harold Schectman–34	Max	tailor	636 e 14th N
William E Scheinbaum –28			
Manuel Schnitzer –28	Harry	junk	467 10th
Manuel Schnitzer –32	Sam	junk	403 Front
Charles A Silverman –30	Morris	salesman	755 E Taylor
Maurice Sussman –31	Osias	shoe store	211 Pennoyer
Alex Tamkin- 30 (not frat)	Morris	cabinet maker	475 1/2 Broadway, S
Morris Tarshis –28	Wm	jobber	233 1/2 Grant
Al Tuch –33 (Hollywood)			
Harry Tuch –33 (Hollywood)			
David Turtletaub –28	Abe	jobber	1054 Schuyler
Monte Wolf –31	Harry	junk co	328 Jackson
Milton Zell-30 (not frat)	Mrs Taube	jewelers	393 College

Robert King Merton, his Science, and the Promise of the Enlightenment[1]

Samuel Haber

In order to better appreciate the work and career of Robert King Merton, the twentieth century American founder of the sociology of science, it is helpful to examine some of the ideas of the eighteenth century Enlightenment. One of the purposes of this essay is to consider how much Merton's social thought, career, and even personal life owed to the doctrines and promises of that great intellectual movement. Of course, the Enlightenment was a complex historic event joining often conflicting ideas and expectations. Nonetheless, for the purpose of this essay one might focus upon a strain within Enlightenment thought particularly pervasive in America.[2] It embraced three linked notions: that there was order in the universe, that this order could be understood by reason (a universal faculty), and that such understanding would help make humankind better and happier. These ideas stretched far back into Western history, but what gave them a special and exciting coherence and cogency in the eighteenth century was the new Newtonian system of physics and astronomy. It marked the culmination of the great scientific discoveries of the previous century, and Newton became one of the heroes of the era. It is not surprising to find that his portrait hung in Jefferson's study, and that Alexander Pope was prompted to declare that "Nature and Nature's laws lay hid in night / God said, *Let Newton be!* and all was light!"[3]

In addition to portraiture and poetry, the good news was spread by books, pamphlets, lectures, and even devices that, to present day observers, might seem like scientific toys. Yet these gadgets inspired awe and reflected intellectual audacity. They were mechanical models of the solar system called orreries, after a spectacular version built under the patronage of Charles Boyle, fourth Earl of Orrery. Orreries of varying sizes and sophistication were built in England, France, and the North American colonies. These seemed to be physical embodiments of the optimistic perspective in the Enlightenment that linked order, reason and human betterment. David Rittenhouse, the builder of America's most elaborate orreries, claimed that they fostered belief in the "Divine Architect," discouraged bigotry and superstition, and encouraged universal benevolence. After the four hundred members of the Pennsylvania Assembly came to visit one of his works, they, in gratitude, awarded Rittenhouse an unprecedented three hundred and fifty pounds, and hired him to build another for public use. The inscription, most likely suggested by the Reverend William Smith, provost of the College of Philadelphia, read in elegant Latin: "Hic! Intima panduntur victi penetralia Caeli!" which translates "Here, heaven [or the sky] having been conquered, its innermost recesses are thrown open." This quote has a Faustian undertone, but of that, more later.[4]

The Latinity of that phrase highlights an important issue: the reach of the Enlightenment. In England, France and the German states, Enlightenment thought was an upper class persuasion. It took hold among the various middle classes, but the lowest ranges of society were rarely touched by its doctrines. As one moved east and south in Europe, the influence of its major ideas often faded. North America received the Enlightenment largely from England and France, but it took a special place in the culture of the United States. The Revolution against Britain was fought on its terms and the Declaration of Independence and the Constitution, our nation's most hallowed and perdurable documents, embody many of the Enlightenment's most popular themes.[5]

For the Jews, the Enlightenment held special meanings, promises and threats. It granted new intellectual and economic opportunities to individual Jews, yet it brought widespread upheaval to their communities. Like the Enlightenment itself, these changes varied significantly in place, time, and penetration. Jewish life in Europe had been largely sequestered and was only slightly affected by the great cultural transformations of the Renaissance, Reformations, and the Scientific Revolution. However, the Enlightenment, for reasons of State and for reasons of sentiment, broke down ghetto walls and abolished some of the laws that established and maintained Jewish civic disabilities. At the same time, rabbinic power within Jewish communities was significantly diminished. In some places, Jews were granted many of the rights of citizenship. Washington's famous letter to the Hebrew Congregation at Newport, gave "to mankind an example" that toleration was not a grant of one class of people to another, but "an inherent natural right." It pledged that the United States would give "to bigotry no sanction, to persecution no assistance." For Jews, this was the Enlightenment at its best. While in various places Jews were granted many of the rights of citizens, they rarely found social acceptance. Nonetheless, some hastened to seek the opportunities of a broader public life. Mrs. Abigail Franks of New York, writing to her son in London in 1739, disconsolately admitted that Jewish faith was clogged with superstition and that she heartily wished that "a Calvin or Luther would rise amongst Us" to sweep away "the idle Ceremonies & works of Supperoregations [*sic*]." For a considerable number of Jews, their traditional way of life seemed shamefully backward.[6]

* * * *

When Meyer R. Schkolnick was nineteen years old he legally changed his name to Robert King Merton.[7] The year was 1929, and for someone like the young impoverished Schkolnick, chances could not seem too promising. Since the end of World War I, anti-foreign feeling had been growing in America. By the mid-twenties even the respectable middle-class journal, *The Saturday Evening Post,* featured recurrent articles expressing disapproval of foreigners and immigrants. The immigrant exclusion acts of the 1920s gave legal force to such sentiments.[8]

More particularly, East European Jews like the Schkolnicks were disparaged, and usually barred from various employments, "good" neighborhoods, clubs, resorts, and country clubs. The most prestigious colleges and universities limited the admission of Jews to fixed quotas.

At the University of Chicago, one of the most liberal of schools, Jews were excluded from general social dances, and a leading Jewish fraternity accepted only those Jews who did not look too "Jewish." More significant for Merton, who had decided to become a sociologist, was the impact of antisemitism on job opportunities in the discipline. William F. Ogburn, a leading sociologist of the era, writing about a job candidate in 1930, explained that "he has a very keen mind. He is Jewish however." Reed Bain, an editor of *The American Sociological Review*, in a 1935 letter to a member of the sociology department at the University of Chicago, stipulated that he wanted to hire "a bright young non-Jewish, non-Negro male." Even more dismal was the letter of 1939 by Professor E. B. Wilson, a colleague of Talcott Parsons, suggesting that in light of the difficulty that Harvard was having in placing students like Paul Samuelson (later Nobel Prize winner in economics), they should not admit Jewish graduate students nor hire Jewish faculty. This is the academic milieu Merton had entered.[9]

As Robert King Merton, he seems not to have directly suffered from it. For those who were not particularly attached to their Jewish origins and whose physiognomy and speech did not fit the prevailing stereotypes of Jews, this form of individualistic "auto-emancipation"—becoming a Robert King Merton—was not unheard of. Changing one's name was a complex event and people changed their names for various reasons. Often it was when they felt that they had crossed a significant threshold, and crossing the boundary between outsider and insider (if only in their minds) led some of them to take up new names.[10]

Merton had been born in the slums of South Philadelphia to East European immigrant parents. His father, Harry David Schkolnick, was an unprosperous tradesman who shifted the family residence almost as rapidly as he changed his occupation. Ida, young Schkolnick's mother, was a vigorous, handsome woman who adjusted more readily to American ways. Her son described her outlook as "philosophical anarchism"—a form of cosmopolitanism that attracted a following among the first waves of Eastern European Jewish immigration. Ida was also an ardent Americanizer. Although official records listed Meyer's birth date as 5 July 1910, Ida claimed that it was 4 July and insisted on celebrating it on that patriotic date. Her son ultimately came to accept his mother's claim. When he decided to legally change his name, his mother enthusiastically approved and his father seemed to be indifferent.[11]

Even when quite young, Schkolnick had demonstrated remarkable intellectual talents. He won a scholarship to Temple University, where he was adopted as a protégé by leading faculty members and gained entry to Harvard's Graduate School with a fellowship in the Sociology Department. The name change seemed to have worked like magic.[12] The Harvard Sociology Department was a difficult and discordant place when Merton arrived in 1931. It had just been established and the differences among its faculty as to the discipline's purpose, scope and methods were becoming increasingly sharp. Pitirim A. Sorokin, the chairman, saw himself as a thinker on a grand scale whose chief task was to create a scholarly *Weltanschauung*—a social philosophy of civilization. At that time, his philosophy was one of cultural pessimism, owing something to Spengler, and supported, apparently, by extensive statistical materials. Challenging that approach was Talcott Parsons, who was then closer to reform traditions of American Sociology although sophisticated by extensive study of the leading European sociologists.[13]

At first, Merton seemed to be working primarily with Sorokin; however he quickly shifted his intellectual allegiance to Parsons. When the time came for Merton to write his dissertation, the rivalry in the department created difficulties for him. Sorokin was a man whom one did not want to estrange unnecessarily. Merton adroitly chose someone outside the department but acceptable to all. George Sarton, in fact, was in no department and drew a salary from none. He held an anomalous position as a scholar in residence at Harvard, with access to the Widener Library, but drew his income from the Carnegie Institution of Washington. Yet, even more exotic was the fact that he was a Comtean. This did not mean that Sarton accepted all of Auguste Comte's extravagant teachings, but he did uphold Comte's dictum that the progress of humankind was inextricably and inevitably linked to the progress of "positive knowledge." The epitome of this "positive knowledge" was science. For young Merton this seemed naïve, too simple a variant of Enlightenment thinking. For, if social progress was simply a matter of intellectual and scientific progress, how could one explain the factors that promoted and constrained science itself? Nonetheless, whatever their differences, Sarton wholeheartedly encouraged and supported Merton's work.[14]

Merton wrote his dissertation on the growth of science in seventeenth century England. This work became the source of what later was called "The Merton Thesis." It underscored the importance of Protestantism for the development of science. This was a transference, in a modified form, of Max Weber's *Protestant Ethic and the Spirit of Capitalism* (which Parsons had recently translated) to the realm of science. However, if the dissertation drew from Weber and Parsons, it also drew from Marx. Merton later recalled that he was "a dedicated socialist" in the early years of the Great Depression. This is surely not surprising. Many young people who came of age in that era readily concluded that the existing economic system could not work. A Marxist perspective, taken with various levels of attachment and different kinds of qualifications, seemed to make sense to many intellectuals. In his dissertation, Merton argued that while some of the impetus for the growth of science in seventeenth century England arose from Protestant belief, the direction that science and technology took was in great measure influenced by economic developments. This argument could be accepted by any "sophisticated" Marxist, and part of the dissertation was published in the Marxist journal *Science and Society*.[15]

Merton received his doctorate in 1936 and served as instructor and tutor in the Harvard sociology department for the next three years. He then took up his first permanent position at Tulane, where he rose rapidly to the rank of full professor and became chairman of the department. This was a very productive period in his career. Merton published an unusually large number of articles and reviews, many of which are still quoted and can still be found in anthologies and collections today. These articles are on diverse subjects and give little indication of the direction that Merton's mature work would take. Yet four of these articles suggest something of his frame of mind at this time.[16]

The first is an ostensibly methodological critique of a paper by the eminent sociologist George Lundberg. Lundberg had used an early form of public opinion poll to measure prejudice against Blacks. Merton's criticism was harsh. He found the categories that Lundberg had used too loose and his statistical methods inadequate. Therefore, Lundberg's conclusions had to be set aside in the name of a more rigorous and scientific sociology. Lundberg had concluded that Jews were less prejudiced against Blacks than were Protestants and Catholics. But Merton showed that Lundberg's assertion that Jews were different than anyone else in this regard was scientifically unwarranted. This was a delicate issue. At a time when racial theorists claimed that Jews had special characteristics, usually in order to derogate those considered racial outsiders, many Jews were wary of any theory that singled out Jews. This was particularly true of Jews who themselves wanted to be like everyone else.[17]

Another of Merton's early papers with an unusual resonance was his study of intermarriage and social structure. This was perhaps the least rigorous and least "scientific" paper that Merton ever published. Merton himself had intermarried. He had met his wife in college—a lovely young woman of Quaker background from a small New Jersey agricultural community who had trained as a social worker. She was definitely a social asset in Merton's early career. Yet, Merton chose to write about Black/White intermarriage. On this subject, the data was notoriously skimpy and haphazardly collected. Such marriages were illegal in many States. Merton's conclusion was that most of these marriages were between White women of higher social status than their Black husbands. He excluded concubinage, in which White men had taken Black women as sexual partners, although surely social structure was an important element there. What is surprising is that Merton turned his back upon the intermarriage that was legal and for which statistics were plentiful and reliable: between Jews and Gentiles.[18]

When Merton came to deal directly with racial theorists, his critique was sharp and unremitting, yet seemingly in the interest of disinterested science. In 1939, Professor Earnest A. Hooton, the Harvard physical anthropologist, published the results of his twelve years of research on the American criminal. His work was based upon biological and racial categories. Merton and his friend M. F. Ashley Montagu spent twenty-four pages of the *American Anthropologist* tearing Hooton's work to shreds, perhaps justifiably. The statistical sloppiness, the overlapping categories, the inadequate sampling, the *obiter dicta*, the underlying assumptions were all reviewed in detail. It seems odd that a major scholarly periodical gave so much space to what apparently was such an unworthy book. One also wonders whether this blast would have had a different impact if the authors had signed their birth names, Meyer Schkolnick and Israel Ehrenberg rather than their professional names, Robert King Merton and M. F. Ashley Montagu. Most likely, they believed that they could be both objective and partisan, because science apparently was on their side.[19]

"Social Structure and Anomie," which focuses on the problem of deviance, is certainly one of the most famous of Merton's early papers. One of Merton's students has claimed that it is the most cited article in American sociology. Its argument is relatively simple. Merton asserts that the possibility of achieving American society's goals, primarily financial success, varies greatly according to one's place in the social structure. This leads to estrangement from society's norms by those who fail. The outcome is deviance. This was the sociological disproof of the Horatio Alger legend. What was the fate of all those Ragged Dicks who lacked the luck and pluck to stop the runaway horse pulling the carriage with the beautiful daughter of the kindly millionaire in it? Such an argument, in line with parallel contentions in the other social sciences, suggested the lightening of personal responsibility. It also provided twentieth century support for the eighteenth century virtue of toleration.[20]

Merton also mentioned a special type of deviant: those who did not fail, but rather chose not to make financial success their upper-most goal. Among these, no doubt, was the group that most excited Merton's admiration throughout his career: those who accepted the discipline of science. He wrote two early papers on science which presaged his later work in the sociology of science. The first of these papers, "Science and the Social Order," published in 1938, took as its starting point the mistreatment of scientists in Nazi Germany. Merton tried to strike an objective tone; "Much of what is said here can prob-ably be applied to the cases of other countries," he wrote. Merton then discussed the dismissal of scientists from universities and scientific in-stitutes. Surely Merton knew that the overwhelming majority of these were Jews, and that they were singled out for punishment because of their Jewishness and not because of their science. Yet it is striking that in this long article the word Jew was mentioned only twice, and nev-er in reference to actual Jews; Merton quotes an ardent Nazi calling

Heisenberg a "White Jew" for not rejecting Einstein's relativity, and then, in a footnote, quotes a Nazi periodical castigating other German scientists for not divorcing themselves from the "Jewish physics" of Einstein. For Merton, the entire question is abstracted into an issue of "institutional dynamics." The political institutions of Nazi Germany were encroaching upon the autonomy and "ethos" of the scientific institutions. Germany was just an extreme case of a widespread anti-science movement for which there was much evidence elsewhere. Merton cautiously disavowed any "program of action." Yet he observed that "as long as the locus of social power resides in any one institution other than science and as long as scientists themselves are uncertain of their primary loyalty, their position becomes tenuous."[21]

Four years later, in 1942, Merton took up the issues of the autonomy of science and the scientific ethos once more. By this time, America had entered the war against the Axis Powers, and the abstractness as well as the seeming "evenhandedness" of Merton's tone had diminished. In this paper, entitled "A Note on Science and Democracy," Merton argued that while it was true that science had advanced in very diverse settings, nevertheless democracy seemed to be more conducive to scientific development than totalitarianism, where power was centralized in political institutions for political purposes. This centralization impinged upon scientific autonomy and the "scientific ethos," making science less productive. Previously Merton had discussed "the scientific ethos" in a scattered and off-hand way. In this essay, he focused sharply upon it and expanded its meaning. Most significantly, Merton argued that the ethos derived not only from general culture, but also from the institutional requirements of the workings of science itself.[22] This echoed the notions of those Enlightenment thinkers who extolled the benefits of science—but with a difference. While Jefferson thought that science would make the people aware of their natural rights, and Rittenhouse believed that science would somehow spread the spirit of benevolence far and wide, for Merton the benefits of science were of a more specialized sort. If there was less fraud among scientists than among car salesmen, it was not because scientists were naturally more virtuous than salesmen, but rather because the claims of the scientist were quickly checked by his peers, while the salesman was confronted by a relatively ignorant customer. Nevertheless, if science could make the scientist better within his work, the technology that his work made possible could make the layman happier with a longer life-span and a higher standard of living.[23]

Merton grouped the "ethos of science" under four headings: Universalism, Disinterestedness, Organized Skepticism, and surprisingly, Communism! These categories leak into each other and some of Merton's explications take unusual turns, yet all these norms, in his depiction, seem laudatory. He sometimes used the terms "ethos" and "norms" interchangeably, but he usually made clear that he was not discussing the attributes of particular scientists, but rather a code of behavior necessary to an institution whose overall purpose was the advancement of "certified" knowledge. "Universalism" was a common theme in the Enlightenment, and there as well it owed something to science. When David Rittenhouse lectured before the American Philosophical Society in 1775, dedicating his speech to the Second Continental Congress, he lovingly described the great scientific revolution of the previous century as the work of men of many nations. Yet the task of advancing Universalism was often seen as the destiny of a particular nation. Washington thought that America would instruct the world in the meaning of toleration, and Jefferson thought similarly about the virtues of self-government. For Merton, Universalism meant the avoidance of parochialism and ethnocentrism, which were its enemies. "Race, nationality, religion, class and personal qualities" were irrelevant to truth claims. In addition, Universalism endorsed Napoleon's maxim, "Careers open to talent!" Even a Meyer Schkolnick might apply. There would no longer be insiders and outsiders, only the talented and the less talented.[24]

"Disinterestedness," in Merton's view, indicates the absence of selfish bias in professional judgments and claims. Again, such avoidance was not because scientists lack prejudice and are not self-seeking, but because, in the interest of institutional stability, various policing devices are set up to check such influences. Merton's third norm, "Organized Skepticism," seems to have a more direct effect upon society at large. The Enlightenment had made the ancient philosophical doctrine of skepticism come alive in the eighteenth century and thereafter, and its most controversial impact was upon traditional religion. Religion was no longer a significant issue, Merton thought. Instead, traditional economic and political structures would now feel skepticism's influence, which might come through particular findings or the diffusion of skeptical attitudes toward current economic or political "dogmas."[25]

The last element in Merton's scientific ethos, "Communism," was the most audacious and perhaps whimsical. However, it served a serious purpose as it helped make science seem as deviant as possible in a capitalist society. Although he described himself as having once been "a dedicated socialist," at this point Merton was clearly not a Marxist. He had rejected Marx's central concept: class. It was too simple, too amorphous, too imprecise. He would endeavor to develop a notion of social structure that was closer to social reality. In this last element of the scientific ethos, he used the word communism as an analogy, comparing ownership in the fund of worldly goods with "ownership" in the fund of knowledge. But the analogy is incongruous at too many points. Most obviously, the fund of knowledge is not diminished by use, while the fund of goods usually is. Nonetheless, Merton continued to defend the analogy even late in his career. "From each according to his abilities, to each according to his needs," he quoted Marx, who was quoting the revolutionary Enlightenment ideologue Gracchus Babeuf.[26]

For Merton, the world of the Enlightenment, which had taken so much of its vitality from the world of science, had, in the darker days of the twentieth century, retreated back into the world of science. Merton wanted to be part of that world.[27] The autonomy of science, for him, was not simply an epistemological argument; it was a personal and moral need. Moreover, if he could transform sociology into a science, he might win a similar autonomy for that discipline. The sociology of science was a likely field in which to accomplish this aim, for science itself had a sociology—although it could produce autonomous "certified" knowledge, it was still in part shaped by its surroundings. Discovering how all this worked was Merton's overall project during his long career at Columbia University. After he had finished his dissertation at Harvard and took his first regular job at Tulane, he was quickly snapped up by Columbia. Merton became a brilliant lecturer, a productive scholar, and was ultimately appointed to the highest professorial rank that Columbia offered, that of University Professor.[28]

Merton's career at Columbia helped shape his outlook and style. Unlike Harvard, Columbia had a very diverse graduate student enrollment, drawing some of its scholars from the lower reaches of society. Many of these students supported their studies with part-time work as cabbies, hotel workers, and temporary teachers. There were also many Jewish students. New York had the largest population of Jews of any city in the world, and, after World War II, when restrictive Jewish quotas were gradually eliminated at Columbia, Jewish students rushed to its gates. All this made for an exciting, strenuous, and somewhat contentious graduate student body. Moreover, the secular Jewish intellectual life of New York was dominated by many varieties of socialism, and Merton's textbooks often seemed to be addressing students with socialist backgrounds. In each edition, Merton presented a long discussion of the points of agreement of functional analysis (his scientifically styled sociology) with dialectical materialism, in order to demonstrate that, like the physical sciences, functional analysis could be ideologically neutral. Merton's sociology may have had the latent function of providing a way station for young socialists on their way to a broader and more acceptable American social vision.[29]

However, the manifest purpose of Merton's program was to give the findings of sociology something like the validity and effectiveness that were generally accorded to the discoveries of science. The growing popularity of the sociology of knowledge, which interpreted knowledge as a social construction, threatened to undermine the cogency of sociology itself. However, the physical sciences, at this point, appeared impervious to the acids of this kind of relativism, and to the extent that sociology could be made scientific it might develop a similar autonomy and invulnerability. The most likely methodology for bringing sociology closer to the physical sciences, Merton believed, was functional and structural analysis. However, behind functional analysis, as it was commonly employed, stood the metaphor of the organism. Implicit in that metaphor is an assumption of social harmony. Merton wished to free his functional analysis from direct dependence on any such metaphor by sublimating it through abstraction. His functional analysis became an orientation that focused upon the complex interrelation of events, "the practice of interpreting data by establishing their consequences for larger structures in which they are implicated"[30]

While most forms of functionalism were accused of containing an inherent conservative proclivity, Merton insisted that his functional analysis would avoid any tacit bias in favor of the status quo. It would emphasize social dysfunctions as well as functions, functional substitutes and equivalents as well as functional needs; most important, it would not overlook "the important role of sheer power in society."[31] It was not clear how this would be accomplished; an organic analogy, even if sublimated, cannot address the concentration of power, since power is distributed throughout an organism. Social dysfunction could not clearly encompass the concept and the practice of social exploitation.[32]

If Merton's functional analysis was an enhanced version of Parsons's, his structural analysis was a discriminating and enriched revision of Marx's class analysis. Although class, Merton had long argued, was too loose a category to be useful in illuminating the workings of society, it need not be totally rejected. It could be resolved, amplified, and made pluralist by such notions as status, group and role. Nonetheless, as Merton himself explained, he owed to Marx the general notion that social position in large part influenced social vision and behavior; and upon that principle most structural analysis rested.[33]

At this stage in the development of sociological theory, Merton urged, practitioners should avoid any attempts to create grand theories or total systems. It would be more effective to develop small sets of empirically verified theorems, "theories of the middle range." Using functional and structural analysis, this kind of theory and its verifying research might be consolidated and codified to yield broad and reliable theoretic gains. Merton also urged only a restricted use of the great founding social theorists of the discipline. Their works might be sifted for suggestions that could be empirically tested, but one must not be distracted by their imposing imaginative visions, which eluded adequate evidence and proof. What was needed, he believed, was not a new social philosophy, but a new social science. A social philosophy was inescapably a subjective, personal vision, whereas a social science, he hoped, would be a cumulative, progressive, collective, social vision. At the head of all three editions of his textbook, Merton placed the epigraph, "A science which hesitates to forget its founders is lost." Although, Talcott Parsons, Merton's former teacher, was at that time trying to construct a grand theory, this led to no estrangement. Both optimistically felt that their scholarly works would meet sometime in the future.[34]

But what was the basis of Merton's optimism? How could the disparate sociological studies of "the middle range," even if they all employed functional structural analysis, be consolidated into a grand theory? Something of the sort had been done by Newton at the end of the seventeenth century, but Newton had believed that there was order in the universe and that it could be understood by reason. Did Merton implicitly share that vision? The notion of an ordered universe would make Merton's preachments on the importance of empiricism (in fact, it was Dewey's hypothetical-inductive method) seem plausible. If there was such order, then extrapolating from the part to the whole might be feasible and somewhat reliable. Yet, in practice it did not always work out. Two of Merton's closest students, ardent Mertonians, applied his structural/functional analysis to the same subject and came away with widely differing and diverging conclusions. Perhaps, as William James suggested, the universe is a complex congeries and concatenation of thises and thats. Even Dewey's hypothetical-inductive method (which Merton recommended) would yield, in large part, lucky hits and unlucky misses.[35]

* * * *

At Columbia, Merton turned from his study of the interaction of science and society (which had been the focus of his dissertation) and from the explicit discussion of the ethos of science (the subject of some of his early programmatic articles) to an investigation into the inner structure of the institution of science in America. Just about the time when Merton's work was taking this new direction, the relation of American science to its setting was changing drastically. Previously, the major patrons of scientific work had been private foundations working through the science departments of the universities. During the war such support was largely overshadowed by federal funding for the development of weapons. The great success of the Manhattan Project and the development of radar persuaded a wide public that government support for science was truly advantageous. Vannevar Bush, who had directed government-funded research during the war, proposed a National Science Foundation to continue such work in peacetime. By the mid-1960s the federal government was pouring fifteen billion dollars a year into scientific research. The number of professional scientists rapidly increased. A common witticism of the day pointed out that there were more scientists alive at that moment than had lived in all ages past. Moreover, the part that these scientists played in American life had become markedly more significant than ever before. Merton had picked up the banner of the sociology of science in the early 1930s, and much later he suddenly found himself at the head of a parade. Yet, it was not his parade. His impetus and direction were largely his own.[36]

To understand that impetus and direction one must return to his dissertation. The dissertation was a study of the social and intellectual context of the growth of science in seventeenth century England. It had been influenced by a provocative paper by a Jewish mathematician and physicist, Boris Hessen, who at the time was among the top-ranking Soviet academicians. Hessen had presented his paper to the International Congress of the History of Science and Technology in London in 1931. Entitled "The Social and Economic roots of Newton's *Principia*," it caused quite a stir at the Congress. Hessen had come to London with an invisible gun to his head. In the early 1930s it was not only the Nazi zealots who were attacking Einstein's work. Marxist fundamentalists in Russia were denouncing it as anti-materialist and contradictory to the teachings of Marxism. Back in Russia, Hessen was in a tight spot because he ardently defended the cognitive autonomy of Einstein's work. He went to London, and with a paper lavishly decorated with quotes from Marx and Engels, argued the importance of Newton's social setting for the writing of *Principia*. Yet, when read closely, it becomes apparent that Hessen also believed in the cognitive autonomy of what Newton had done. When Hessen returned home, he was thrown into jail, where he died some time later. Fortunately for Western scholars, the issue was not a matter of life and death. Many innocently applauded Hessen's paper, and found the argument—that social context influences the direction of science—fresh and exciting. That the findings of science had their own cognitive integrity, they simply took for granted.[37]

As did Merton—for a while. But, in the early 1940s, Merton came up against Karl Mannheim's sociology of knowledge and found it perplexing. Like so many other notions that seemed so persuasive in the 1930s and early 1940s, the sociology of knowledge owed much to Marx. "It is not the consciousness of men that determines their existence, but, on the contrary, it is their social existence that determines their consciousness," Marx announced.[38] Did that make all thought relativistic? If so, Marx's assertion would apply to relativism itself. Mannheim found a way out by granting to the "free-floating intelligentsia" the ability to strip off class blinders. But Merton looked to the scientists who, through their ethos and institutional structures, enabled themselves to find verified reliable truths.[39]

At Columbia, Merton amassed admirable erudition both on the history of science and on the practices of a wide range of present-day sciences. Not all that he found was to his liking and some information did not fit easily with his earlier notions. Yet his intellectual style aimed at openness, incorporating somehow what at first seemed discordant. When he found eminent scientists, from Newton to James Watson, intensely competitive and anxious about priority of discovery, he ascribed this apparent self-promotion to the esteem that scientists placed upon creativity and innovation. When he found a great discrepancy of rewards provided within the scientific establishment, he explained this seeming inequity as a means of distributing limited funds according to scientific talent, which promoted the efficient advancement of knowledge. The system of peer review within departments, academic journals, and most important, the National Science Foundation that Vannevar Bush had established to distribute Federal funds among scientists, was the instrument for matching funds to talent. Peer review, he believed, meant that autonomous scientific standards would govern the scientific establishment. This was what most concerned him, for he believed that "scientists embody some of the prime values of world civilization."[40]

That was Merton at his most self-assured—the disposition which was linked to his untroubled confidence in science. When that confidence came under attack, Merton shifted to a more defensive stance. This shift became apparent during the revolt at Columbia, when students tried to close down the University.[41] That was perplexing to Merton. The University was dedicated to the advancement of knowledge, and its science departments to a special "certified" knowledge. But the students and some sympathetic faculty were asserting that knowledge was a mask for power and scientific knowledge for the most oppressive and deadly power. For Merton, science and technology meant enabling men through the "means of production" to create higher living standards, a longer life span and more leisure for the mass of the people. For the students and their sympathizers, science and technology meant empowering men through the "means of destruction" to perpetrate Hiroshima, the Holocaust, and, now, Robert McNamara's direction of the Vietnam war, with his scientific "systems analysis" and his strategy of overwhelming American fire power.[42]

More troubling for Merton was the attack upon his work by his colleagues within the sociology profession. These attacks were usually from younger colleagues who assailed him from various angles. There were the neo-Marxists who complained that Merton's work was dominated by notions of equilibrium that ignored development and historical change. They also claimed that Merton ignored the importance of conflict as a moving force within society and within the sociology of science.[43] Other sociologists provided more particular critiques. One scholar who studied scientists at work found little trace of the "scientific ethos" and suggested that it was an ideology that scientists used to ward off interference from their patrons. Some attacked the notion that peer review effectively warded off favoritism, and others claimed that Merton's notion of science was outmoded. It is surprising how bitter some of these criticisms could be. If one can find a unifying sense in these very diverse critiques, perhaps it is anger at what the critics believed was Merton's sense of complacency in the face of the inauspicious world that confronted them. It was especially sad to see that at Merton's memorial one of his most prominent students, who was given the task of discussing Merton's contribution to the sociology of science, simply shrugged off the assignment and provided two small-minded and self-promoting criticisms of his former teacher's work. Perhaps the highpoint of hostile criticism had appeared six years earlier in an extended negative review of Merton's work which had ended with the blast "Sic transit gloria mundi."[44]

It would be a foolish mistake to link Merton's declining prestige with his increasing openness about his Jewish origins. That new openness must owe much to many factors. However, in itself it is deeply interesting. A lengthy *New Yorker* profile published in January 1961, when Merton was at the height of his fame, gives no hint that he was in any sense Jewish. In fact, the article describes him as "the Hollywood stereotype of a minister." Yet a little more than a decade later, his friend, Werner J. Cahnman, persuaded Merton to permit the *Encyclopaedia Judaica* to insert a short biographical notice of him. In the 1970's Merton struck up a warm friendship with two Israeli scholars working in the sociology of science, who shared his view on the cognitive autonomy of scientific knowledge. In 1980 he went to Israel to accept an honorary Ph.D. at the Hebrew University and to dance a *hora*. In 1994 Merton's autobiographical talk, *A Life of Learning*, given before the American Council of Learned Societies was published. In it he explained that he had originally been named Meyer Schkolnick, and was the son of Russian Jews, Ida and Harry David Schkolnick; he also recounted the joys of growing up in the slums of South Philadelphia. The following year Merton's given name and parentage was reported for the first time in his *Who's Who in America* entry.[45]

Merton kept writing and publishing almost into the twenty-first century, all the while insisting that science had a cognitive autonomy and therefore should have institutional autonomy. Much more important, however, than its place in society, was the fact that this cognitive autonomy was the essence and foundation of Merton's universalism— just as "reason" had served the Enlightenment's universalism. Even after he had publicly owned his Jewish origins, Merton gave no evidence of feeling less wary of the intellectual dangers of group attachments.[46] Yet, the prevailing winds of doctrine, and more broadly, the climate of opinion and sentiment, were shifting in another direction. There was a widespread growing skepticism, though clearly not an "organized skepticism" about science itself. (Can a profound skepticism ever be organized?) This skepticism was built on the writings of such diverse thinkers as Kuhn (incommensurability), Quine (indeterminacy), Derrida (deconstruction), Rorty (solidarity over objectivity) and Gödel (incompleteness). Taken together these thinkers seem to undermine the Enlightenment credo upon which Merton's science rested.[47] To the extent that there is order in the universe, it could only be understood in a partial way, and that understanding would surely not make people better and happier.

When Harry Met Max

Leonard Greenspoon

In the fall of 1931, Harry M. Orlinsky, then twenty-three-years old, began his graduate studies at Dropsie College in Philadelphia. The main reason for his having chosen Dropsie was "in order to specialize in biblical studies under [Max L.] Margolis." After little more than a month of classes, Margolis "was stricken and I [Orlinsky] never saw him again."[1] Margolis was unable to return to Dropsie, and died on 2 April 1932, at the age of sixty-five.[2]

Max L. Margolis (1866–1932) and Harry M. Orlinsky (1908–1992) were two preeminent twentieth century Jewish scholars of the Hebrew Bible and related fields. In a very real sense, they spanned the century, with Margolis publishing his first articles in the last decade of the nineteenth century and Orlinsky's last work appearing in the final decade of the twentieth.

Although the amount of time Orlinsky spent with Margolis was limited, it would be a mistake to assume that the senior scholar's influence on Orlinsky was likely minimal as well. Quite the contrary. Margolis was a formative and formidable influence on the nature of Orlinsky's academic career. Based on hitherto unpublished letters to and from Orlinsky,[3] this influence can be traced primarily to two areas of Orlinsky's multifaceted, decades-long scholarly activities: Septuagint studies and Bible translation. These letters also provide additional insight into how we should evaluate Margolis's contributions.

When, stricken by illness, Margolis left the classroom for what would prove to be the last time, in December 1931, he had every expectation that he would soon return. As he looked forward to further projects, he could justifiably take pride in decades filled with singular achievements. He was undoubtedly best known to the general public as co-author, with Alexander Marx, of *A History of the Jewish People* (1927), which went through numerous reprintings and was widely used in educational settings. Surely, many would also recognize his name as editor-in-chief of the Jewish Publication Society's (JPS) English-language version of the Bible that appeared in 1917 (*The Holy Scriptures, according to the Masoretic Text*); it is not difficult to imagine its presence in the early to mid-twentieth century libraries of Jewish families, from Orthodox to Reform, throughout North America.[4]

As truly significant as these and other publications were, it is undoubtedly the case that Margolis viewed his research and writing on the Septuagint (the Greek translation of the Old Testament) version of the Book of Joshua, which occupied most of his energies for over thirty years, as his crowning achievement—and one that, as his expression "my damn Joshua" gives voice to, he regarded with a mixture of frustration and affection as a member of the family.[5] Margolis did not live long enough to complete his publications on the Greek Joshua, although we might speculate that even if he had achieved the proverbial lifetime of 120 years, he would have found still more to do.

Where was Harry Orlinsky in the early 1930s? We are fortunate to have Orlinsky's words on this period, extending from a contemporary note he wrote in the 1930s to a reminiscence from the 1980s. We start with the latter. In November 1980, the Society of Biblical Literature (SBL) celebrated its centennial with a banquet in Dallas. Orlinsky was scheduled to speak at what had turned out to be a particularly tense moment (arising from friction among some of the members of the SBL leadership) in the proceedings. For a moment, he considered retreating from the podium, but, as he wrote in a letter, dated 30 November 1980 to G. P. Richardson, Principal of University College, University of Toronto: "George [McRae] got up and introduced me; and there I stood before a howling-wailing mike, an innocent sufferer with no deceit in my mouth. But unlike the central character of Isaiah 53, who opened not his mouth, I had to open mine!"[6] I was among the hundreds in attendance who breathed a good deal more easily as Orlinsky regaled us with his tales of collegiate "pool-shooting" at University College, the scheduling of which (so he repeatedly averred) led him to take courses with Theophile Meek, a renowned biblical scholar who decisively influenced Orlinsky's academic interests in a similar direction. Beyond that, as Orlinsky elaborates in his letter to Principal Richardson:

After completing four years at Parkdale Collegiate Institute, I opted for the fifth year at P.C.I.—like so many other poor Jewish students whose parents had come from Eastern Europe— instead of for the first year at U.C. [University College], because of the saving in tuition. I did well enough in my Senior Matriculation examinations to merit admission to the second year at U.C., in General Arts. Because of the rare combination of Snooker and Meek, I repeated the second year, in Honour Orientals (that was before "Near East" was discovered); and by the time I received the B.A. degree in Honour Orientals, I had had three years of Arabic, two of Assyrian, three of Advanced Hebrew and Aramaic, etc. (Nowadays one receives the Ph.D. degree for less.)[7]

Orlinsky was considerably more formal, but no less convinced of his fine academic training in Toronto, when he wrote the following to Cyrus Adler, President of Dropsie College, nearly fifty years earlier on 30 March 1931. Orlinsky's hand-written letter was in response to Adler's typed "invitation" to Orlinsky to come to Philadelphia, "in order to have a personal interview with Professor Max L. Margolis, the head of the Biblical Department," prior to deciding whether Orlinsky should be admitted for study with a fellowship at Dropsie (as Adler observed, "There are a number of candidates and we find it difficult sometimes to decide upon the basis of documents alone")[8]:

Gentlemen,
    With reference to your desire to have me personally interviewed by your Professor Max L. Margolis, the head of the Biblical Department, I must regretfully advise you that at present I am short of funds and therefore unable to appear personally.
    In addition to the documents already sent to you, I might add that I am shortly completing a thesis for my Bachelor of

Arts degree on "Movements in Jewish Ranks," from the fall of Jerusalem to the present day. I shall have it completed within three weeks, and I shall be glad to mail it to you, should you desire to use it as a reference to my application for a Fellowship. I shall also send you a graduation photograph of myself [in this way, Orlinsky anticipated by half a century Facebook and its competitors!]. Trusting that this will be satisfactory to you, I remain
Yours sincerely,
Harry M. Orlinsky[9]

As it turned out, the documents themselves were satisfactory, and Orlinsky was admitted. The time that Orlinsky and Margolis spent together was brief, but, as we noted above, the brevity of their acquaintance should not mask or obscure the profound influence Margolis had on Orlinsky. Although evidence for this belongs largely to the "genre" of letter—or, more grandly, epistle—these letters differ considerably in tone, style, and content.

Sometimes the debt to Margolis is explicit; at other times, we must, as it were, read between the lines. The latter is the case with a letter sent from Cyrus Adler, editor of the *Jewish Quarterly Review* (JQR), to Orlinsky, dated 16 June 1938; by then, Orlinsky was on the faculty of Baltimore Hebrew College (later, University). Evaluating a submission by Orlinsky on "the Greek and Hebrew Texts of 2 Kings 20:4," Adler complains:

It is not so much a question of typing as the manuscript is in pretty good shape, but just from a cursory examination of it, it seems to me that you have gone into unnecessary detail with regard to a single text. If I undertook to publish articles of this length, all told I think nearly twenty-two pages, including the notes, on each passage in the Bible, that you or anybody else submitted, I could fill the Quarterly with such articles.[10]

It was a hallmark, as it were, of Margolis's pedagogy, as of his publishing, that he would devote an extended and extensive amount of time or space to the detailed, in-depth analysis of a single verse, a single phrase, or even a single word. Orlinsky had the opportunity to observe Margolis teaching a seminar. He described it to me in this way:

> I distinctly remember how Margolis conducted a class. It took at least two full sessions (four hours) to cover one verse. After about twenty hours, we didn't get past about verse 5 in Job 32. Margolis would talk about different versions, variant readings, how variant readings came into being....I was fascinated by this approach and was able to absorb because Margolis didn't go too fast....I learned more methodologically from five verses in Elihu than I could have any other way.[11]

In this sense, then, Orlinsky's proposed study for *JQR* was a tribute to his teacher. Adler's words of exasperation addressed to Orlinsky echoed similar messages, probably many of them, that he had penned in previous decades to Margolis.

At the same time, Orlinsky early demonstrated his own independent streak of scholarship. This also can be observed in the same letter from Adler: "Likewise too, I am not always clear as to what you mean. If you mean by textus receptus, the masoretic text, why not say so?"[12] Throughout his career, Orlinsky cautioned against the common usage of terminology that would privilege any Hebrew transmission as THE masoretic text. So far as we know, Margolis expressed no such reservations. An example of Orlinsky's views on this issue, stated with the candor that is characteristic of his letters, can be found in a note fairly late in his career, dated 1 April 1979, addressed to Samuel Noah Kramer:

> Everyone talks about "the masoretic text." Every editor of every edition of the Hebrew Bible asserts that he is producing "the masoretic text." So I come along...and argue that there ain't never was (nor can there ever be) any such thing as "the masoretic text." Anyone who edits a Hebrew text of the Bible with masoretic notes is editing "a masoretic text." No list of masoretic notes agrees with another....Not infrequently the list of masoretic notes attached to a Hebrew text

actually derived from another Hebrew text....If the status quo people would at least argue the theories and methodology and facts, we'd all get somewhere; but they simply ignore my arguments, and continue to repeat what they heard from their teacher [something of which Orlinsky was not "guilty"].[13]

Orlinsky was as direct in his laudation as he was in his criticism. What follows are two examples of Orlinsky's direct epistolary praise for Margolis (to these can be added his many similar published statements). The first, dated 8 June 1940, is from one of his many letters to James Montgomery of the University of Pennsylvania, whom Orlinsky appears to have revered as the second most formative teacher of his graduate days. Coming upon Margolis's *Notes* to the 1917 JPS translation of the Bible, Orlinsky writes: "[This work] has authority and reliability, the product of Margolis's independent and considered judgment, like everything else of his. At any rate, this is how I was impressed by the book in general and by Job in particular."[14]

Early in his career, Orlinsky struck up a professional and personal friendship with W. F. Albright of Johns Hopkins University, who is universally recognized as the most influential North American biblical scholar of the mid-twentieth century. In a letter dated 21 May 1951, and written from New York where Orlinsky had moved when he began service on the faculty of the Jewish Institute of Religion, he describes the care with which he led other students and colleagues of Margolis's in the preparation of a volume in Margolis's honor:[15]

I have had to interrupt my work to get out a chapter on Margolis' contributions to LXX study for the Margolis Memorial Volume. We hope to have the volume out before 1951 goes into history. There will be a biographical sketch (Gordis), M.'s contributions to Bible and Talmud (Zimmerman), to the history and philosophy of Judaism (Joshua Bloch), to Semitic Grammar (Speiser), a complete bibliography (Reider), and an Index to passages, words, etc, discussed by Margolis. We are limited to about 10 pages [each], so that the book does not go beyond about 120 pages and $1,000.00 [financial exigencies played their role then, as now!].[16]

Particularly poignant are letters from Max Margolis's widow to Orlinksy. From them, we derive the distinct impression that Orlinsky was seen, not only by the scholarly community but also by the Margolis family, as the heir to Margolis's work on the Septuagint (LXX). The fact that Orlinsky was selected to write about Margolis's "contributions to LXX study for the Margolis Memorial Volume" (as noted in the previous paragraph) is also indicative of this. Something of the tenor or tone of this relationship can be gleaned from portions of three letters. The first was sent by Mrs. Margolis to Orlinsky in July 1941:

> I cannot tell you how touched I was at receiving a reprint of your article, "On the Present State of Proto-Septuagint Studies" [which featured Margolis's work]. As I read it, it took me back not just the ten or twelve years when Dr. Margolis was really writing the Joshua[17] but all the way back thirty-five years to when I used to read the Greek foot notes in an edition of the Hexapla which he used in Munich because the letters were too small for him to read….It is truly tragic that a great scholar's years of labor can be so quickly forgotten, and I am always grateful when some of the younger men who were influenced by my husband publicly acknowledge their indebtedness.[18]

The Archives does not contain Orlinsky's immediate response to Mrs. Margolis's letter. However, there is a letter from him to her, dated 17 February 1942, that picks up this thread: "So far there is at least the satisfaction that my article on the Septuagint, dedicated to the memory of Prof. Margolis, has more than ever brought his works and method, as well as their correctness and importance, to the attention of scholarship."[19] A decade later, when Mrs. Margolis was honored by the Jewish Community of Philadelphia, Orlinsky and his wife spoke of Mrs. Margolis in these especially appropriate words: "The home of the first Hebrew Bible printed in the western hemisphere, and of the first English translations of the Hebrew Bible for the Jewish people, Philadelphia is the home also of the First Lady."[20]

In the letter cited above, the Orlinskys speak of Philadelphia as "the home...of the first English translations of the Hebrew Bible." In the first instance, this is a reference to the translation prepared by Isaac Leeser.[21] Philadelphia was (and continues to be) the home of JPS, which sponsored and published the two main English-language versions of the Hebrew Bible during the twentieth century. The main academic and intellectual force behind the first was Max L. Margolis; the force behind the second, Harry M. Orlinsky. This is no coincidence. Even when Orlinsky differed considerably from his teacher's method of translating, there is no doubt that he felt deeply indebted to, and inextricably linked with, Margolis.

Moving chronologically, we find that Orlinsky was involved in Bible translation even before the onset of the new JPS volume. In fact, in 1945, he was selected to be among the editors charged with the preparation of the Revised Standard Version (RSV), and was the first Jewish scholar to serve on such a committee. Although he does not note that fact in the following letter to James Montgomery, dated 20 July 1945, his service on the RSV committee, and later on the NRSV committee of editors is, to this day, unique:[22]

> As you may have heard, I was appointed to the Committee which is revising the American Standard Bible. In years past, such a distinguished trio as the late [James] Moffat, [C. C.] Torrey, and yourself, graced the Committee. Among the newcomers are Albright, [James] Muilenberg, and perhaps [Herbert] May and [J. Philip] Hyatt; [H. S.] Gehman just didn't feel that he had the time to give up for it, and so too Ernest Wright. I spent four very profitable days up at Yale the first week in June...working on [Millar] Burrows' first (and excellent) draft of Proverbs 1–9.[23]

The RSV Committee was no stranger to intrigue (we would expect nothing more—or less—in an academic setting). So, Albright wrote to Orlinsky on 6 August 1945:

> I do wish that you would accept the assignment in Job!! Since [William A.] Irwin has agreed, there is no reason not to ac-

cept. You know better than I that Irwin will go into a sulk if we start changing what he offers, but that exactly the reverse is likely to be true if he can criticize somebody else's translation. You will facilitate the work of the committee immensely if you do accept this assignment—and I cannot see any reason for not taking it.[24]

In a letter dated three days later, Orlinsky agrees: "You probably are right in advising me to accept Job for the Committee; accordingly I am writing to Dean Weigle that I am accepting the job."[25]

As early as 1951 (that is, a year prior to the publication of the RSV Old Testament), serious thought was being given by JPS to the promulgation of a new English-language version of the Hebrew Bible—and to Orlinsky's role in this project. Thus, Orlinsky writes on 4 April 1951 to Luther A. Weigle (Yale Divinity School Dean), who headed the RSV Committee:

I have been approached by the Jewish Publication Society with regards to the possibility of revising their translation of the Hebrew Bible. It is my opinion that their present English translation should be used as the "Basic Text" in the manner that we have been operating in our Revision; and that emendations of the Masoretic text be held to a minimum. (This matter is still only in the "talking" stage, and is confidential.)[26]

This letter is especially interesting because, in subsequent years, Orlinsky radically changed his view of what was needed for a new Jewish version, moving as he did from a revision of the 1917 version to the adoption of an entirely different mode of translation; that is, dynamic or functional equivalence.[27]

Orlinsky's "change of heart" and his efforts to move the JPS in this new direction were gradual. This can be seen from the following letter, dated 21 March 1955 (that is, four years later) to Weigle from JPS's Solomon Grayzel:

We have undertaken to make the revision, despite the fact that many of us are rather timid about it and have misgivings about the urgency of the task....It is understood that such a revision of our translation will concern itself mainly with two areas: the modernization of some of the English and the taking into consideration of the scholarly and archaeological findings since 1917, when our translation was first issued.... We thought it best to entrust the task to one scholar rather than a group. We have chosen Harry Orlinsky for obvious reasons. He will have the advice of a small group....It is our hope that Dr. Orlinsky will complete his task in five years.[28]

As is so often the case, the best made plans, even (or perhaps, especially) for Bible versions, are typically expanded and extended far beyond the scope initially envisioned.

By 1962 the magnitude of the disparity between original conception and ongoing reality must have been clear to everyone.[29] Here is how Orlinsky himself described some of the key features of the new version, in a draft of a letter to the editor of *The Jewish Chronicle*, dated 23 October 1962 (Orlinsky made many of the same points in his voluminous writing on this topic, but I find it particularly revealing to read, and reproduce, some of his thoughts that were not necessarily intended for public consumption):

What the Press Release on the new translation of the Torah meant to convey was (1) that our translation is not to be understood as constituting a revision of any prior or existing translation of the Bible, and (2) that our Committee of translators quite deliberately, to begin with, ignored the interpretation of the Hebrew text as found in the Septuagint, Targum, Syriac, Talmud, Vulgate, Saadia, Rashi, Ibn Ezra, David Kimhi...the 1917 JPS Bible, etc.... We considered ourselves obligated to no prior interpretation of Scripture.... Let me be more specific. The original attempt at a new draft for the new version was made directly from the Hebrew text, chapter by chapter.... Only then, after the Hebrew text had first had its say, began the laborious and detailed search through the older and newer translations and commentaries, to determine what could be incorporated from them into the new version.[30]

Such a task, or rather series of tasks, could not be undertaken by (or to use Grayzel's wording, "entrusted to") a single scholar, even one of Orlinsky's industry, erudition, and insight. Rather, as noted in many pubic statements by JPS and in Orlinsky's published works, a committee was established for the Torah (and later also for the Nevi'im and the Ketuvim). Again, I find it useful to cite some of Orlinsky's less well-known sentiments, in this case on the value of the committee structure. These appear in a letter from Orlinsky to Grayzel (addressed as Sol), dated 6 September 1963:

> In re the minutes of our August 8th meeting, on the volume of Notes [to accompany the appearance of the Torah translation]:[31] these should state flatly and at the very outset that the Bible Translation Committee is the sole and final authority in all matters pertaining to the volume. No one single person can decide what is or what is not to go into the volume, or precisely how a note or comment is to be worded; the final decision rests with the Committee as a whole. By the same token, no indication may be made in the volume as to which member or group of members favored or opposed any given note or comment. So far as the reader of the Notes is concerned, this volume is no less a Committee product than the translation of the Torah.[32]

By the early 1980s Orlinsky was again involved in a new and major undertaking with respect to Bible translation. In this case, it was the New Revised Standard Version (NRSV). As noted above, Orlinsky was the only Jewish scholar on the NRSV committee, as he had been for the RSV. In a letter, dated 27 June 1980, he wrote to Eugene Ulrich of the University of Notre Dame about his NRSV assignment:

> I had spent several months on preparing the draft of Leviticus for the new edition of the RSV [that is, the NRSV]; it was a considerable chore, but worth doing. Our RSV committee adopted a considerable proportion of the draft; and I believe that it will prove superior not only to the 1952 RSV and the 1962

NJV [New Jewish Version] (which I had drafted) but to any
that are now available.[33]

Orlinsky's continued involvement in Bible translation naturally
led to his becoming embroiled in some of the major controversies surrounding these versions. Here, for example, is a letter, dated 8 December 1980, to Bruce Metzger of Princeton Theological Seminary, head
of the NRSV Committee, in response to Metzger's report of a vote "to
request that steps be taken to assure that additional scholars with feminist perspectives become regular members of the RSVB Committee":

> I'm unhappy with the last sentence in paragraph 2 of the let-
> ter: "...with feminist perspectives." My reaction is: to hell
> with such perspectives! Either we are competent philologians,
> textual critics, stylists (in English), etc., with balanced judg-
> ment and relatively even temperament, or we are unaccept-
> able as a member of a team of translators. Such "perspectives"
> as "feminist" are, to my mind, extraneous—and even begin to
> smack of a form of prior censorship.
> You know well that I led the fight in our revision of the Book
> of Psalms to eliminate "(Happy) is the man" in Psalm 1 to
> "(Blessed) are those"—not because of any "feminist perspec-
> tive" but because the correct understanding of the Hebrew text
> demanded it....More recently, in my considerable revision of
> Leviticus, I have proposed the elimination of male-oriented
> language ("man" for ish, or adam, or nefesh) in a number of
> instances—all on the ground of Biblical Hebrew usage.
> I wonder whether the feminist "patriots" aren't going a bit
> overboard, and are encroaching on philological-textual ter-
> ritory not only beyond their comprehension but where even
> knowing male angels would fear to tread.[34]

In another letter to Bruce Metzger almost three years later, Orlinsky returns to this topic. He first establishes that "manslayer" is the
proper rendering for a term that appears in the Hebrew at Joshua 20:3
and elsewhere. In response to those who would support some termino-

logical distinction when a woman was involved as either perpetrator or victim, Orlinsky writes:

There is something basic involved in the "inclusive" approach to these chapters, as to the Bible generally, and that is the lack of respect (and feeling) for the Hebrew text....We all know that the Hebrew writers had ways and means of indicating inclusiveness....And in the Ex. and Josh. chapters involved, I am most doubtful that female manslayers were covered by these cities of refuge in the manner that male manslayers were. Inclusiveness here may indeed constitute a rewriting of the law!

....I'd also propose that unless the "inclusive Sub-committee" was only a one-shot project, that it not be asked to continue; we should put our faith in the overall prudence of each sub-section of the O.T. (and N.T.) Committee.[35]

Like Margolis, Orlinsky continued to conduct research, write, and publish until illness rendered these activities impossible. The last of Orlinsky's major works was devoted to translation of the Bible. Thus, on 5 July 1990, he wrote to Chaim Potok:

I do not remember sending you a copy of the Table of Contents of a book that Dr. Robert G. Bratcher...and I have written for the SBL's Centennial Publications Series, A History of Bible Translation and the North American Contribution.... The role of Jewish scholars and translators, culminating in the New Jewish Version, comes through prominently.[36]

This last comment by Orlinsky raises a question that I had earlier explored with respect to Margolis,[37] namely, in what sense did Orlinsky see himself and his scholarship as distinctively Jewish? A question of this magnitude for a scholar of Orlinsky's magnitude requires more than a few paragraphs. Here again, drawing from epistolary material in the Archives, I wish to point to three specific references that, I think, would otherwise be virtually unknown.

In the first instance, in a letter to Albright dated 11 July 1945, Orlinsky speaks up against the imposition of the quota system with regards to the admission of Jewish students:

> I have been told by various people that the Princeton person now in charge of admissions to The Johns Hopkins is quite openly applying the quota system so far as Jewish students are concerned. I have learned of a number of specific instances where inferior Gentile boys from City College were admitted, while superior Jewish boys, so far as their records at City College are concerned, were rejected. One of the rejected boys later applied to Marshall and Franklin [*sic*] and got a four-year scholarship on his City College record. Another boy was told openly and bluntly by the person in charge of admissions that only a certain percentage of Jewish students would be admitted. My first reaction to this information was: No quota system was applied to the Jewish boys when their Country needed (and needs) them to fight the common enemy, and this is still my reaction. It seems that I have heard about this from too many independent sources to be a baseless rumor.[38]

In the second case, it is fellow scholars about whom Orlinsky is concerned. The relevant letter, dated 15 November 1951, was addressed to Karl Elliger at the University of Tübingen in Germany:

> I have seen the letter which you sent out on September 25th, 1951 as a member of the Editorial Board of the "Internationale Zeitschriftenschau für Bibelwissenschaft und Grenzgebiete." I think that your project is a very worthy one and should interest all professors of Bible.
> In your letter you state specifically that the Editorial Board of the projected journal will consist of Protestant and Catholic scholars. I am very much surprised that for the work of this scholarly journal you excluded Jewish scholars.[39]

The third letter, which I am sure is representative of many that he wrote along the same lines, seeks to correct misunderstandings of

Judaism on the part of Christians, especially as they arose from the publication of the RSV Old Testament in 1952. This particular letter, addressed to Luther A. Weigle, is dated 18 January 1953:

> It would be wrong to assert [as was done by a letter writer] that "for many centuries the Jewish people have taught their daughters that in fulfillment of this very prophecy (Isaiah 7:14) they must keep themselves chaste and pure in order that one day they might be The Virgin referred to in the prophecy." Neither I nor any of the many competent Jews to whom I have spoken about the matter know of any such teachings in Jewish life....The Jewish concept of the Messiah has nothing to do with Isaiah 7:14.
>
> I should ask your questioner to ask his so-called Jewish authorities to submit in writing what he says they told him. Either these Jewish friends find it impossible to say "I don't know" when they are asked something about Jewish life and thought about which they are ignorant, or else they are pulling his leg.[40]

Everyone who knew Orlinsky, or knew someone who knew him, was familiar with Orlinsky's direct manner of speaking and his love of humor. These are traits that he also brought out in his many friends and correspondents. Thus, there is no better way to end an article on Harry M. Orlinsky and Max L. Margolis than this letter, dated 3 December 1982, written to Orlinsky by Maurice Jacobs, whose Philadelphia print shop was for decades the source of beautifully produced Jewish books. Jacobs writes in his own hand:

> Dear Harry:--
> You are going to be honored by your friends at the Copley Plaza. I was there when Jake Marcus [Jacob Rader Marcus] was honored, but now I am an old man....
> You were the one Jew called on to help the goyim on their new translation. You stand out like a sore thumb to those who try to knock you—too much baseball, they say, and not

enough Bible. A good combination, EXCEPT the ball players get the money.

J.P.S. has been giving you credit for the new translation and how <u>you</u> deserved it....

I am for Harry Orlinsky, Max Margolis' <u>greatest</u> product.[41]

Indeed he was, I may add, indeed he was.

Rethinking the History of Nonobservance as an American Orthodox Jewish Lifestyle

Jeffrey S. Gurock

In 1965, sociologist Charles S. Liebman characterized the religious lifestyles of most Jews who identified with Orthodox Judaism both then and during the prior century of American Jewish history as "uncommitted" to its teachings and strictures. For Liebman, those who "nominally affiliated" with that traditional faith were largely "residual" immigrant types who "conformed superficially to Orthodoxy." Their loyalties stemmed primarily from "cultural and social inertia rather than out of religious choice." That meant, for example, that if these American newcomers attended a synagogue, it had to be an Orthodox one, most likely a *shtibl* (store-front congregation) named after the shtetl, city, or province of their European origin. They knew of no other denominational alternatives. But when they attended services, they were more interested in conversing with their fellow Jews from their old hometown than in communing with God.

Liebman looked at two fundamental rubrics of personal piety—keeping Sabbath as a day of rest and women's observance of the laws of family purity—and found that these Jews frequently strayed from *halakhah* (Jewish law) in both of those areas. They were often absent from shul on the Sabbath, because they were out working to provide for their families. This was in gross contravention of *halakhah*, as work is the most fundamental biblical prohibition during the Sabbath. Lieb-man also suggested that there was a significant lack of interest among most residual Orthodox women in observing the laws of family purity. For Liebman, it was noteworthy as a marker of decline in religious motivation that there was "at least anecdotal evidence that *mikvaot* (pl. collection of water for immersion) were scarce and inaccessible out-side New York City, and sometimes within it." Liebman did not reflect on a third indicator: whether these masses of Jews—who he said "at one time probably constituted the majority of all Jews in the United States"—neglected the kosher laws, another cardinal Orthodox teach-ing. Perhaps here a positive proclivity persisted out of the immigrants' lack of knowledge of alternative American culinary options.

This tradition of lack of commitment, said Liebman, continued into subsequent generations among those whom he called the "nonob-servant Orthodox" Jews. Though by the time of his study, the "residual Orthodox represent[ed] a dying generation," their spiritual—and ac-tual—descendents still made up the majority of those who frequented American Orthodox synagogues. These Jews typically "affiliated with Orthodox synagogues but [had] no commitment to the *halakhah* or even to the rituals which the residual Orthodox practice." Some of these "marginal" associates were, in fact, "almost indifferent about synagogue affiliation but, having been raised in an Orthodox environ-ment, find nostalgic satisfaction in attendance at familiar Rosh Ha-Shanah and Yom Kippur services." But though they only attended shul three times a year, these seasonal Orthodox loyalists, Liebman divined, might still perceive the Orthodoxy that they did not follow as "more religious" than Conservatism or Reform. Predicting Ortho-doxy's future, Liebman asserted that in time this cohort was destined to decline. Its disappearance would be due not so much to the nonob-servant soon passing from the scene, but rather because its "children are far more likely to be drawn into the network of intensive and supe-rior Talmud Torahs and all-day schools than were the children of the older residual Orthodox."

These well-educated youngsters, Liebman suggested, would align themselves with the "committed" Orthodox, that staunch minority of devout Jews who throughout American history did "strive to conduct their lives within the framework of the halakhah." Some of these strong adherents—Liebman used "traditional Sabbath observance" as an admittedly "crude measurement" of their fidelity to the faith— were designated as "modern Orthodox." These were the devotees who "seek to demonstrate the viability of the *halakhah* for contemporary life; on the other hand, they emphasize what they have in common with all other Jews rather than what separates them." Their counterparts among the profoundly committed, the "sectarian" Orthodox, lived separatist lives, tried to shelter their people from the lures of the secular outside world, and stayed clear of "communal participation with other Jewish groups."[1]

The understanding that American Orthodoxy's rank and file commonly did not observe cardinal *mitzvot* has long informed my vision of the behavior of that movement's affiliates and loyalists. Indeed, a decade ago, in speaking of the religious lifestyles of the men and women who sat in—or often absented themselves from—Orthodox congregational pews for most of the twentieth century, I argued that "nonobservance of the Sabbath, a very useful metaphor for irreligiosity"—the same benchmark Liebman used—"was already evident within the community that attended, with ever decreasing frequency, the immigrant synagogues of the downtown district." In a parallel piece, I further submitted that "during the first half of the twentieth century. . . most . . . Orthodox synagogue-goers, drawn from among the masses of Eastern European Jews and their children. . . were not especially punctilious in their adherence to the demands and requirements of Jewish law as prescribed in the Shulhan Arukh [Code of Jewish Law]." In all instances, when I characterized these miscreants, I was sure to make clear that they harbored no doctrinal difficulties with what the tradition taught. "Their problem was not so much with Orthodoxy's dogmas but rather with their inability to integrate the traditions with their new ambitions and lifestyle." And, I pointed out that in most cases these men and women evidenced no great desire to affiliate with another Jewish denominational alternative. Interestingly, others who have written about nonobservance, particularly as it applied to that phenomenon in modern Europe, tended to conflate heretical attitudes and affinities for oppositional movements with simple personal noncompliance, with the *halakhah* even as they examined how Orthodox establishments there dealt with these challenges and challengers. For me, the prototypical American Orthodox Jew was rather historically the man or woman who felt very comfortable in the most traditional of synagogue precincts, cared little for—if they knew anything about—Conservative, Reform, or Reconstructionist doctrines, but did not observe the *halakhah* outside of the most sacred of spaces.[2]

Recently, however, in writing a comprehensive history of Orthodox Jews in America over more than three and half centuries that exposes the diversity of behavior among those who chose to identify within that movement, I came to realize that neither Liebman nor I took into our accounts wide degrees of commitment—or nuances of "uncommitment," for that matter—within what we defined statically as so-called "observant" vs. "nonobservant" lifestyles.[3]

To begin with, in judging Orthodox practice, we focused solely on ritual performance. Our myopia led us to ignore the inescapable reality that throughout American Jewish history there have been those who ostensibly have dedicated themselves to devout observance of the Torah's teachings through strictly upholding day-to-day ritual requirements. But in actuality, they have been egregious violators of the *halakhah* by committing acts of unethical and even illegal turpitude. As such, they have denigrated Orthodox Judaism's most fundamental teachings. It is axiomatic that the faith sees itself as both a divinely ordained system of laws and customs and as a community rooted in an exacting set of moral principles. Though only a distinct minority within each generation, these moral transgressors have included, for example, those who have substituted unkosher for kosher meat to maximize their profits; those rabbis in name only, who, during Prohibition, sold bootleg kosher wines in violation of the intent of the Volstead Act; and those male offenders who, in our more contemporary times, have refused to grant their estranged wives a *get* (writ of religious divorce) to torture and extort monies from them. While such Orthodox Jews have been nonobservant to a fault of this different set of essential religious scruples, conversely, many of those who have not kept the Sabbath or observed the kosher laws may have been most scrupulous when it came to upholding Judaism's code of moral rectitude.[4]

But putting aside the cases of Orthodoxy's social sinners, to properly understand the religious lifestyles of ritual transgressors requires rethinking and recalibrating their acts not against *halakhic* absolutes but rather as Jews who, in a voluntaristic American context, chose to affirm certain traditions and to disdain others. For example, what are we to make of the Orthodox conformity and affiliation of a Jew whom I profiled in my newest work that presented in the midtwentieth century the following complicated religious values? On the one hand, he and his wife were the quintessential committed Orthodox Jews of their time. They maintained a strictly Sabbath-observant home—no electric lights turned on or off on the holy day. They kept an unquestionably kosher kitchen and dined out only in properly supervised kosher eateries. He attended synagogue daily, considered the rabbi's study group his favorite pastime, was uncommonly charitable to Jewish causes, and scraped and scrimped with his wife to put their child through an Orthodox day school. However, occasionally, during his busy season or when the Jewish calendar linked together two days of a holiday—as when the first and last days of Passover occur on Thursday and Friday before the onset of the Sabbath, which, in total, call for a seventy-two-hour cessation from mundane activities—he disappeared from his local synagogue's life. He went to work early in the morning of the holy day to support his family. He may have mitigated his deviance somewhat when he stopped off at an Orthodox synagogue near his workplace and sat among similarly conflicted Jews who wanted to say their holiday or Sabbath prayers—prayers that spoke explicitly about the biblical prohibition against labor on those days.

To simply call this man "nonobservant," as just another miscreant, a violator of the *halakhah* because of his noteworthy lapse, fails to take into account how he chose to affirm, within a free and uncontrolled environment, so many Orthodox teachings. It also ignores how, through his pious religious acts, he stood above most of his contemporaries who observed far fewer of the precepts, even as he harbored an intense desire to be counted among those who practiced Jewish law more punctiliously.[5]

Comparably difficult judgment calls that defy facile categorization need to be made to properly contextualize the religious values of Orthodox Jews who were far less devout than this iconic Sabbath-working Jew. Throughout American Jewish history, there have been seasonal and occasional observers of Jewish tradition whose levels of piety have not been acknowledged. As we will see presently, very few Jews in this country evinced "*no* commitment to the halakhah." Indeed, positive affinities can be found even among Jews who have been held up as emblematic of the long-term sorry state of observance in America.

Such negativism toward the practices of her fellow Jews permeates a letter that the devout central European Jewish immigrant Rachel Samuels wrote in the early 1790s to her pious parents in Hamburg. She was stuck—as she described herself—in Petersburg, Virginia, a "place [lacking] in *Yehudishkeit* [Jewishness]." Linguistically, she would not have used the term "Orthodoxy," since that designation would not enter the Jewish lexicon until the nineteenth century, when religiously liberal critics of traditional theology and practice used that term to denigrate their opponents as fossilized and unresponsive to modern times.[6]

In any event, she pilloried the "ten or twelve Jews" in town as "not worthy of being called Jews." They do not know, she complained, "what the Sabbath and holidays are. On the Sabbath all the Jewish shops are open as they do during the whole week." When they came together, "on Rosh ha-Shanah and on Yom Kippur the people worshipped" without a Torah scroll and "not one of them [the men]" save her husband and an "old man of sixty from Holland" wore "a *tallit* [prayer shawl] or the *arba kanfot* [fringe garment undershirt]." Moreover, the meat that they consumed was unkosher because the "*shohet* [ritual slaughterer] . . . goes to market and buys *terefah* [non-kosher] meat and then brings it home." For her, the transcendent problem was that in the United States, "anyone can do as he wants." Had Samuels had her religious druthers and lived in a very different type of Jewish community, punishments would have been rained down on miscreants. But, "there is no rabbi in all of America to excommunicate anyone." The only answer for the Samuels family was to flee from an aggregation of transgressors and to set off for Charleston, South Carolina, where there is a "blessed community of three hundred Jews."

But in her dissatisfaction, Samuels failed to notice or to countenance the *halakhic* values that her neighbors affirmed. Clearly there was interest in town for kosher food; otherwise there would be no customer base for a *shohet*. That the slaughterer may have exploited this desire surely evidences his own personal, moral turpitude; it does not speak ill of the religious commitment of his fellow Jews to *kashrut*. Similarly, her depiction of High Holiday services, where congregants prayed without essential ritual objects, overlooks the fact that these Jews esteemed these central days in their faith's calendar enough to *worship* in their synagogue. Of course, they conducted an "Orthodox" service even if they probably read the portion of the Law from a printed book. As noted previously, in the late eighteenth century there were no Jewish denominational alternatives. Arguably, in that locale, the only Jews who were fully uncommitted were those who absented from the minyan on those holiest of days and cared not at all about what they ate.[7]

A half century after Samuels lamented Judaism's fate in Virginia, I.J.Benjamin, an Orthodox Jew from Moldavia who traveled throughout the frontiers of the expanding United States, harbored comparable disappointment about his coreligionists' behaviors. He saw many as tossing "religious duties and observances overboard as burdensome ballast," as if they were aboard a boat about to be shipwrecked even as they calmly crossed the Ohio, Mississippi, Missouri, or Colorado rivers in the American wilderness of the late 1850s and 1860s. To be sure, there were those on the frontier who were totally uncommitted. However, Benjamin's travelogues also reveal—even if he did not consciously recognize this alternative narrative—that the Jews out west who supposedly were divorced from the *halakhah* made all sorts of efforts to uphold semblances of devout religious observances. To begin with, "no matter how indifferent and cold our fellow Jews are towards their religion" this critic observed, "nevertheless they are never so estranged from all religious feeling that it is a matter of total indifference to them where they bury their dead." Beyond that fundamental act of nonreciprocal loving kindness, for most Jews, "New Year's and the Day of Atonement [had] still some meaning for them." Their emotional ties were rooted, Benjamin recognized, in "all the dear, slumbering memories of the past [that] awoke and wished to live again." In places not unlike Petersburg, where "during the rest of the year, no one thinks about performing Jewish ceremonies," the "cemetery is practically all that discloses the presence of Jews"—"public services are held" on the High Holidays. Dietary laws, particularly Passover food traditions, also retained much importance, even while these Jews erred when it came to "related laws and precepts." The unknowing might bake the unleavened bread "of the flour usually offered for sale in the market, no attention being paid to the regulation for grinding flour"; in these cases, a level of commitment to the strictures of the *halakhah* was evident, even if ignorance of what the tradition prescribed undermined the precise fulfillment of the *mitzvah*. Others who ate matzah that they purchased "at great expense, but along with it ate the usual food" were either likewise oblivious to what the *halakhah* prescribed, or they were just not as concerned as other Jews.[8]

Indeed, degrees of commitment to Orthodox traditions seems to have been common practice among these pioneers; and their practice, while often conducted with some abridgments, never conveyed disdain for the *halakhah*, Take, for example, this almost legendary saga of two young men who were peddlers in northern Westchester County, New York, during the early 1840s. These men made extraordinary efforts to keep up with, even if they did not exactly follow, prescribed practice. Determined as they were to "hurry . . . to the city on a holiday to be there for the service," they started out at four o'clock on the morning of the festival in the upstate and hustled seven miles to Sing Sing to catch a steamboat down the Hudson. But they missed their connection by a few minutes and had "no alternative [but] to walk" toward the city to meet up with a streetcar that would deliver them downtown. Unfortunately, while they "tramped and tramped" toward the station, they arrived after nine o'clock that evening, "when the last car had left." Evidently and significantly, they would have boarded that late train after sundown in violation of a holiday precept rather than spend the holiday in Harlem, which "was then a suburb" of Manhattan. "Impelled," as they were, "by the religious fervor and devotion instilled under the parental roof"—or at least a degree of such piety—the young men traveled by foot "the remainder of the distance, which in all made fifty-six miles, and in consequence, of over-exertion were compelled to take to their beds for three days."[9]

Then there were those who were deeply grieved about their inability to lead devout Jewish lives amid so many environmental difficulties and tried to make the best of religiously trying situations. Their stories are arguably part of the longest-standing narrative of committed Orthodox Jews at work who did not always live up to the requirements of the *halakhah*. For example, from 1842 to 1843, Bavarian immigrant Abraham Kohn articulated the utter despair of a peddler in constant transit who was unable to live as he would have wanted. In his classic statement penned while trekking through "the icy cold winter of New England," he confided to his diary, both about himself and "thousands" of other guilt-ridden "young strong men [who] forget their Creator . . .[who] pray neither on working day nor on the Sabbath . . . hav[ing] given up their religion for the pack which is on their backs." His sentiments are reminiscent of the iconic mid-twentieth-century Orthodox Sabbath worker whom I profiled above. Ashamed that "one must profane the Sabbath, observing Sunday instead," Kohn hoped that God "knowest my thoughts . . . knowest my grief when on the Sabbath eve, I must retire to my lodging and on Saturday morning carry my pack on my back, profaning the holy day, God's gift to His people." So distressed, he prayed in "the open field," which was his "temple," that a forgiving "Father in heaven comforts me and lends me strength and courage and endurance for my sufferings."[10]

Perhaps Kohn derived some additional consolation beyond what God might offer him when he came across other peddlers who bemoaned similar religious fates. Once, for example, he met up with a fellow immigrant named Marx, an acquaintance from Kohn's home region in Bavaria, who "in pursuit of [his] daily bread" was "compelled to profane [the] Holy Sabbath." Marx reportedly lamented to Kohn that he was able to "observe the Sabbath less than ten times" in three years in the new country. Knowledge of what Marx suffered through only caused Kohn to wonder whether "this is the cherished liberty of America."[11]

Ultimately, Kohn, Marx, and many other Jews who were isolated just did their best to keep the commandments whenever and wherever they could. These peddlers certainly were not unconcerned about the call of the *halakhah*, even if they could not answer it in regular or timely manners. At points where the smallest groups of merchants found themselves together, they tried to spend the Sabbath as a community at rest. The person who knew the most about Jewish law might serve as their religious leader. In one small town in Mississippi, the first Jewish institution established was a peddlers' cemetery, as once again Jews performed this fundamental *mitzvah*.[12]

These Jews' desire to observe Jewish traditions, as conditions allowed, became even more apparent when the successful ones set up their stores in small towns. Constant calls were sent back east, seemingly from everywhere across the country, for personal and communal religious needs. Starting with the most basic, they sought the services of a *mohel* (circumciser) for their infant sons. However, they had to be patient and flexible about the "rabbi's" date of arrival. The family's desire to follow the *halakhah* on this most basic rite was there, and arguably most Jews valued it, but given the difficulties of transportation, many boys from outpost families did not formally enter the covenant on their eighth day.[13]

Jewish newcomers like these to America also sided with Orthodoxy when there finally were enough of them in a locale to organize a synagogue, even if their choices were preordained by what religious life had been like for them back in the old country. While these immigrants' decisions to move to America coincided with an era of tumultuous changes in Jewish religious life in central Europe, with Reform and Historical School Judaism challenging Orthodox allegiances, the maelstrom of new ideas and practices in the old country did not influence most Jews who chose American futures. Coming as they did from Bavarian or Bohemian villages and hamlets or from within the Polish provinces under Prussian control, their major concerns back home had been finding ways of eking out subsistence living, not the rarified social and political goals of emancipation. Thus, liberal Judaism was not the talk of their towns as it was in cities such as Berlin, Hamburg, Frankfurt, or Breslau, where aspiring, upwardly mobile Jews gravitated toward religious transformations as a means of promoting equality in their country. Accordingly, when formerly poor, peddler community builders gathered to pray in this country, their forms of prayer resembled, in all essential ways, the Orthodox synagogues of their European villages. They really had no prior exposure to new ideas and practices. In time, as they Americanized, they might—and certainly many did—find the modern Jewish expressions intriguing and ultimately compelling, leading them to leave the Orthodox fold.[14]

During the subsequent period of east European migration, the rabbis who accompanied the masses on board, in steerage, and into the downtown hubs echoed Samuels's and Benjamin's disparagement of the commitment to Orthodox practice of many Jews whom they would attempt to influence. Using powerful and evocative metaphorical language, they decried the disloyal actions of immigrants who emerged from their steerage quarters to throw their *tefilin* (phylacteries) overboard as they crossed the Atlantic Ocean. To properly engender this story—though rabbis of that time would not have spoken in these terms—they also could have lamented those females who disposed of their candlesticks in the sea symbolic of rejection of a positive commandment that the tradition imposes upon women. In any event, for these critics, the voyage was a turning point—the beginning of the end of fidelity to Judaism and the dramatic head start on the road to disaffection. "Like Jonah of old who boarded a boat to Tarshish," prior to his legendary encounter with that big fish, fleeing "from before the face of the Lord," so were these travelers depicted as making a statement, in the midst of their passage to America, that they now wished to put the religious commitments of their ancestral past behind them.[15]

When, for example, Lithuanian rabbi Moshe Shimon Sivitz settled in Pittsburgh, he preached about and decried the behavior of those who "fled from God while still on the boat that first stopped praying and then committed their talis and tefillin to the deep." Tragically, for him, modern Jewish migrants could have emulated the most ancient of Jewish travelers, their forefather Abraham, who "left his home and birth place, but who, instead of distancing himself from God's call, accepted the yoke of the Commandments even more completely." But such was neither the mindset nor the destiny of the Russian Jews coming to America.[16]

There certainly were those in steerage who threw their *tefilin* overboard. But at most only one half of the Jewish population could have acted that way. At that point, women did not have that ritual item in their possessions. There also were many Jewish men—secularists and radicals of varying stripes—who did not even bring *tefilin* aboard. By the time they decided to leave Russia—either because they had given up hope that change was coming or because the tsars' police was chasing them—many of the men who had once dreamed either of freedom and acceptance or who conspired for revolutionary change had long since dispensed with the morning commandment of donning phylacteries. Women of these political and social dispositions did not have to put the *mitzvah* of *tefilin* behind them, since the *halakhah* had never required them to allocate time for prayer daily. But if they had become Sabbath desecrators, most likely it had been a long time since they had lit Friday night candles. As secularists, these men and women also would not have been careful about what they ate, even if kosher foods were available on board.[17]

The most profoundly radical among these migrants found ways to express their dissent from religious Judaism in the most obnoxious of ways. Among the most noticed outright rejectionists were Jewish anarchists who, beginning in the late 1880s, organized and participated in Yom Kippur balls where the solemn religious Kol Nidre service was parodied through song, dance, and drink. Though these antagonistic atheists had their say, most immigrant Jews did not maintain such radical antireligious values.[18]

Nor were the majority of Jews who left for America resolute assimilationists who consciously committed to separating themselves from their fellow Jews as completely and as quickly as possible. The religious values of most immigrants of this period, rather, can be better symbolized—using the rabbi's metaphor—as Jews who carried their *tefilin* on the long trek to America but over the course of time utilized them with ever-decreasing frequency. They certainly did not angrily commit these sacred objects to the deep. These were the Jews whom Liebman would later call "residual" affiliates who, if and when they attended a shul, prayed in an Orthodox one of the transplanted variety because they knew, from their Russian, Polish, Hungarian, or Romanian experiences, no other religious alternatives. More important, as we properly nuance their religious behaviors, many were the men and women who remained deeply attached to Orthodox traditions even as the force of circumstances often precluded their completely fulfilling all religious commitments.

The lures of America surely transformed many newcomers into what one devout critic would call the "*Poshe Yisrael*" (sinners of Israel).[19] On the cultural level, the Jews' desire to look and act like other Americans caused them to change their appearances and dress, sometimes in violation of the *halakhic* codes. In this regard, the metaphor for the abandonment of tradition was the image of men shaving their beards as soon as they settled in the immigrant Jewish quarter. Another version of this act of disaffection with the past has the men emerging from steerage clean shaven as their boat passed Lady Liberty in New York harbor. Meanwhile, it was said that their wives, upon their first encounters with America, immodestly took off their head coverings forever. An alternate reading of this transformation has wives joining their husbands on deck, anxious to toss their scarves or kerchiefs overboard as symbolic of their new life in America. Where, however, these depictions proved to be inaccurate was in their categorical assertion that the clean-shaven men and the kerchief-less women abandoned their commitment to Judaism. Rather, in so many ways and through so many practices, these Jews affirmed tenets of the faith.[20]

Jews without beards may still have occasionally used their *tefilin,* and they constantly identified with other Jewish traditions in myriad ways. Married women could have appeared in public sans scarves but may have confirmed their continued affinity for the faith every week when they lit Sabbath candles in the kosher homes that they monitored scrupulously. Anecdotal evidence—accounts that are very different, by the way, from Liebman's—also suggests that a goodly percentage of immigrant women regularly utilized *mikvaot,* at least upon arrival. As always, the very private nature of this family law precludes uncovering hard numbers on patterns of observance. But this much is known: In 1884, *The New York Tribune* reported that some fifteen downtown synagogues maintained *mikvaot.* In 1905, a Jewish social worker observed that the "religious rites and customs [of *mikveh*] are carefully observed by the older generation who are pious." In time, many of them would come to perform this commandment in ways that the *halakhah* did not prescribe. Perhaps, however, those who immersed in their private baths at the appropriate moment in their menstrual cycle may have perceived themselves as not only physically clean but ritually pure as well. Nonetheless, the point is that while this latter group of women erred in their understanding of Orthodox religious prescriptions, they were not uncommitted to the *halakhah*'s calls.[21]

The greatest challenge to traditional observance was, however, as it had always been in America—the immigrants' drive to succeed economically. An early twentieth century immigrant poet set this scene, both metaphorically and dramatically, when he wrote of the masses of Jewish workers "trampl[ing] with their weekday boots the train of [the Sabbath Queen's] bridal gown" as they shuffled of to their jobs. (Radical Jews, to extend the imagery, would have intentionally kicked mud in the Sabbath Queen's face. But they were not the downtown community's rank and file.)[22]

Indeed, many Jews who were compelled to work on the Sabbath demonstrated an otherwise deep devotion to keeping that day holy. In thousands of immigrant homes, the Sabbath Queen still ruled as the family gathered around the table for a traditional Friday night meal at sundown or when the father could get off from his job.[23] Many men said Sabbath prayers at a minyan conducted very early in the morning before the long day of labor began. They did so in a neighborhood synagogue before the fortunate ones who did not have to work arrived for their more leisurely devotions some hours later. Heartfelt rituals also were performed in the workplaces themselves. None of these Jews came close to renouncing their Judaism. This pattern of religious behavior, as we have seen, would long endure within twentieth-century American Orthodoxy.[24]

Then there were those within the broad continuum of commitment who hallowed the start of the quiet Sabbath evening with prayers and perhaps with religious song before leaving their sacred home precincts for the decidedly secular environs of the local Yiddish theatres. While they prioritized Jewish popular culture over strict religious observance, some of these ticket-holders may have paid their entrance fees before the Sabbath to avoid a gross violation of the holy day and perhaps squirmed in their orchestra or balcony seats. In response, the conflicted projected their ambivalence upon the thespians who, in their view, were *really* violating the Sabbath. As Hutchins Hapgood, a Christian muckraker who lived among the downtown poor, reported:

> The Orthodox Jews who go to the theatre on Friday night, the beginning of the Sabbath are commonly somewhat ashamed of themselves and try to quiet their consciences by a vociferous condemnation of the actors on the stage. The actor, who through the exigencies of his role, is compelled to appear on

Friday night with a cigar in his mouth is frequently greeted with hisses and strenuous cries of "Shame, shame, smoke on the Sabbath! from the proletarian hypocrites in the gallery.[25]

At the same time, there were Jews within this spectrum of religious affinities who cared even less about the call of the traditional Sabbath rest and transformed Saturday from a day of repose to an occasion for shopping. But even these unabashed consumers who frequented neighborhood Jewish-owned stores were also not completely uncommitted to the calls of tradition. Though the weekly Sabbath cycle passed unnoticed, certain critical days in the Jewish calendar, most notably Passover and the High Holidays, moved them toward observance—even if they bought their special suit or dress at a Saturday sale advertised in honor of the upcoming festival.[26]

Moreover, when these immigrant Jews got all dressed up for shul, they may have ended up sitting in the sanctuary—men downstairs, women in the balcony—next to Jews who, at first blush, would seem to be unlikely attendees at services. Much to the chagrin of their ideologically true leaders, rank and file members of the *Arbeter Ring* (Workmen's Circle), whom the rest of the year identified with varying forms of atheistic socialism, felt the tugs both of their people's longest-standing religious traditions and of more immediate personal demands. Some, it was said, who never really abandoned their belief in God, even if they habitually did not follow many of the commandments, "went trembling and shaking to shul to pray, due to fear of judgment." Though free to live as they chose, at these contemplative and reflective moments, they identified ideologically with Orthodoxy. They were far from liberated from the ancient belief that on those momentous days a supreme being evaluated the actions of all people over the past year and determined who would live and who would die. While perhaps, as Liebman suggested, these "socialists" may have spent much of their time in shul conversing with their fellow Jews rather than communing with their Creator, still, their very presence in God's house bespoke a dimension of commitment to the faith.[27]

A comparable continuum of commitments characterized the religious values of the descendents of east European immigrants, those whom Liebman and I had called the "nonobservant" Orthodox, as these second- and third-generation Jews both affirmed and disdained a range of *halakhic* teachings. Certainly, over the succeeding decades, many of those who frequently or occasionally attended Orthodox synagogues lost contact with what that tradition demanded of them even as they persisted in identifying with such congregations. For example, in the 1930s, men and women, seated in their respective pews at the Young Israel of Newark, New Jersey, a branch of an Orthodox congregational movement, were either unaware of or unconcerned with Sabbath *halakhic* proscription. Otherwise the synagogue's leadership—drawn from among the more committed members who followed the rigors of the commandments—would not have published a printed guide to "Synagogue Etiquette and Procedures," which called upon the deviants within their midst not to display "pocketbooks on Sabbath and Holidays" or to "jingle" or "open[ly] display money" or to "drive to the synagogue." These actions are all unqualified violations of rabbinic strictures.[28]

At the same time, the problem of Sabbath work frustrated many who very much wanted to be in shul on the Sabbath and may well have been concerned with strictly following *halakhic* regulations. This seemingly unbridgeable dilemma was magnified during the Great Depression, when economic exigencies loomed largest. Sometimes, "'the more strict' chose to 'absent themselves' from their shops . . . leaving them in the hands of their children or hired hands." But those who were at rest perhaps suffered the guilt pangs of contributing to their scion's and possibly to other Jewish employees' transgressions. Regrets about the weakness, but surely not the absence, of personal religious commitment was also the lot of Orthodox Sabbath laborers during the more prosperous early post-World War II period. The frustrations of these Jews was brought home for a Yeshiva University official when, in the late 1940s and early 1950s, he visited an Orthodox outpost in a New England mill town and saw "a line of men's jackets hung neatly on a long row of hooks . . . in shul when there was no one then in the building." The local rabbi explained that "these are Shabbos jackets. They belong to the storekeepers who comprise most of our Shabbos minyan. On Shabbos, we *daven* [pray] at seven o'clock. We are finished by nine," permitting worshippers to then put in a full work day.[29]

Although these conflicted Jews were a significant segment of those who still predominated in Orthodox synagogues when Liebman characterized all such non-Sabbath observers as the "nonobservant," a winnowing of the ranks of Orthodoxy was by then well underway. Some of the previous rank and file ensconced themselves comfortably within Reform, Conservative, and Reconstruction congregations, most noticeably within the burgeoning frontiers of suburbia. For those with a palpable desire to uphold more than a modicum of Sabbath traditions, a decision by the Conservative Rabbinical Assembly in 1950 was particularly meaningful. It "construed" driving a motor vehicle "for the purpose of Sabbath attendance . . . when a family resides beyond reasonable walking distance from a synagogue" as no "violation of the Sabbath." Rather, such attendance was commended as "an expression of loyalty to the faith." Arguably, those who were heartened religiously through that enactment would constitute a core of observant, committed, and guilt-free Conservative Jews in that and future decades. At the same time, others who previously had affiliated with Orthodox synagogues capitalized on the openness of postwar American society and not only drifted away from their ancestral allegiances but chose not to link up with any form of Judaism. In any event, during the twenty-five years after World War II, Orthodoxy lost its numerical supremacy among religious identifying American Jews. However, most of those who then remained in its fold—and those who continued to uphold that form of the faith—tended to be more committed to the *halakhah* than most of their ancestors.[30]

Needless to say, the massive growth of contemporary Orthodoxy's "sectarian" component, composed primarily of the children and grandchildren of immigrant Jews that fled or survived the Holocaust and who have preserved the strictest religious values, profoundly contributed to the transformation of Orthodoxy's makeup.[31] Concomitantly, however, Liebman's prediction about the "modern Orthodox" also has proved prescient, as extensive day school education has drawn many children from less committed families into the ranks of the punctilious. However, in gauging religious values and performances among this group, there are, again, degrees, nuances, and levels of dedication. As late as the 1990s, a study of Orthodox day school families reported that some thirty thousand to forty thousand boys and girls—constitut-

ing between 15 percent and 20 percent of all Jewish youngsters in
Orthodox day schools—were from so-called "nonobservant" homes.
Whether the reasons were cultural, social, or economic, they did not
keep the Sabbath. Seemingly, many parents were attracted to these
schools out of reverence for their "excellent general studies programs"
that were superior to many of the best private schools in their locales,
and out of concern over the quality of education at all but the most
select public schools. But these aspirants did not harbor a full range of
profound religious commitments.[32]

Then there were those in the day school mix, whom another Jewish sociologist identified in the 1980s as a "common type who popu-
lates many modern Orthodox synagogues." This less than fully committed Jew "likes to come late to synagogue and talks more than he
prays once he arrives." In his mode of behavior, this attendee presents
as a spiritual descendent of those immigrant *shtibl*–goers earlier in the
century who were, as noted previously, more interested in conversing
with their fellow Jews than in communing with God. Additionally,
he—and I would say, just as well, she—enjoys "play[ing] Frisbee on
Sabbath afternoon (within the eruv [an enclosure than permits carrying in otherwise public domains on the Sabbath], of course)," and
she "is not likely to use a mikveh." The researcher determined that
such a Jew, comfortable with his choices, does "not fall into . . . [the]
category of nonobservant Orthodox because he sends his children to a
yeshivah, has a strictly kosher home, will not eat meat on the outside,
and will generally adhere to the Sabbath laws like not watching televi-
sion or driving a car, though he may cheat a little on the side."[33]

Finally, notwithstanding the predicted decline of Liebman's
"nonobservant" in this contemporary era, pockets of this old-style Orthodox Judaism have persisted. They continue particularly in locales
remote from Orthodoxy's New York-based epicenter. In 1986, a rabbi
who served in Youngstown, Ohio (estimated Jewish population of
five thousand), lamented that "religious observance and knowledge"
among members of Orthodox synagogues in that and other small communities are "in a sorry predicament." He reported that it was his unhappy lot to minister to "non-practicing Jews" who "almost always
view . . . faith in sociological and ethnic terms." Using Sabbath observance—as Liebman had done—as his prime barometer, the rabbi

noted that it was "rare to find a shomer Shabbat family, aside from the Orthodox synagogue clergy and the faculty of the day school, assuming that such an institution existed." On the *kashrut* front, the "minority who claim to follow the rules . . . usually do not mean that they do so when 'eating out.'" For them, "a kosher kitchen at home" was the extent of their commitment. Seeing, as he did, observance and commitment in absolute terms, this critic did not pause to nuance the level of piety among those in his flock who maintained kosher homes against those who did not.[34]

Almost two decades later, in 2004, as part of my study of the one Orthodox synagogue in Charleston, South Carolina (estimated Jewish population of that metro area was 3,500), I found comparable patterns of religious behavior. The most salient proclivity was that some 90 percent of habitual attendees drove their automobiles to Saturday services and parked them out of sight of the front door of the shul. The force of religious traditionalism was still keeping them in their ancestral religious home, even though their personal religious values were not so different from those who prayed in that city's Conservative synagogue and had religious permission to park where they pleased. These loyalists' nuanced Orthodox allegiances were, of course, somewhat different from the one out of fifteen affiliates of the Orthodox synagogue who belonged simultaneously to the Conservative congregation and the more than one family that also pays dues to Charleston's Reform temple. In communities like this, American Orthodoxy's longest-enduring tradition lives on: the presence of Jews who respect its teachings but who are only partially committed to the strictures of the *halakhah*.[35]

The United States in Abba Hillel Silver's World View

Allon Gal

Abba Hillel Silver's Zionist path and his contribution to political efforts toward the establishment of the State of Israel have been much discussed in the historical literature. By shaping American Jewry into an independent political body, Silver procured a special place for himself in Zionist history. Together with Emanuel Neumann, he rescued Jewish political power from its traditional ties to the Democratic Party, and brought it out into the open political arena where it could pursue Jewish interests autonomously and fashion its actions in response to changing needs.[1]

This independent Jewish course emerged and took shape against the background of United States estrangement from the plight of European Jewry throughout the Holocaust years and America's compliance with Britain's anti-Zionist foreign policy (since 1938). Silver acted courageously and persistently toward the establishment of a Jewish state; he became identified as the foremost American Zionist leader due to his heroic efforts to attain Jewish sovereignty in the Land of Israel.[2]

Silver's political struggle was aimed at public opinion; he tried, with success, to fashion a pro-Zionist force "from the bottom up." For the most part he rejected more diplomatic lobbying techniques, constantly repeating his well-known mantra: "Put not your trust in princes!" Silver apparently followed an "antiestablishment" path.[3]

Thus, a series of questions arise: Did this stance, at the basis of his militant Zionism, actually reject the United States and its polity? Did Silver believe that the United States was not "good enough" for the Jews? And what, in essence, was Silver's "version of America"? Clarification of these questions will help us better understand the overall ideology of one of the most prominent personalities of the American Zionist Movement, and will shed light both on his personal Zionist path and on the uniqueness of American Zionism. A study of Silver's various positions during his early years of activity will teach us much about his initial identification with the United States and the American ethos.

I

Three hundred years after the Puritans settled in North America, Silver, in November 1920, gave a celebratory and comprehensive sermon on that historic event at his reform synagogue, "The Temple," in Cleveland. Based on historical chronicles and on his own thoughts, he presented, one by one, all the principles the pilgrims brought to the United States—focusing primarily on freedom of religion and political liberty. Silver, a Zionist Reform rabbi, stressed that the Hebrew Bible was a central source of inspiration for those Puritan founders. He presented various events throughout the history of the People of Israel, focusing on the non-centralized natures of the periods of the Judges and the Kingdom of Israel, and concluded that "the pilgrims—the Puritans—were the Hebrew Christians. Because the Puritans lived in the spirit of the Old Testament, their form of government was democratic and their sense of righteousness and social justice was absolute and complete." Thus, the social message of the American founders was comprehensive and ennobling, with an emphasis on the principle of "absolute religious freedom and toleration." Following World War I and the Bolshevik Revolution signs of intolerance towards minorities in the United States began to appear, and Silver warned of this danger in the name of the legacy of American Puritanism.[4]

Another value promulgated by the founding fathers (this time likened to Abraham, the Patriarch), was that of idealism and, in this instance, also the pioneer spirit—the design of a new social order based on daring, hard work, enterprise, persistence, self-reliance and moral responsibility, and created by free people in an unsettled land. The most faithful spokesman for this spirit was, according to Silver, Theodore Roosevelt. Silver considered Roosevelt—a progressive Republican in matters of domestic policy, yet a self-proclaimed imperialist in regard to foreign policy— a distinctive American patriot, and called on those of his listeners who would seek a meaningful life to pay attention to the path set by Roosevelt, and to refine and enrich it in their own pursuits.[5]

However, Theodore Roosevelt did not fully reflect Silver's Americanism. In 1924, after the death of Woodrow Wilson—the Democratic president who tried to be progressive in international issues as well as to show sensitivity to the fates of small people and minorities in the United States—Silver gave a memorial talk in which he identified with Wilson's social and international goals. Wilson was worthy of praise because he understood the United States and provided the highest expression of its power—deep-rooted spiritual tradition and idealism. Silver quoted Wilson extensively in defense of civil rights and promoted his resistance to discriminatory immigration quotas, as well as his honest support of equal opportunity and his humanistic approach to new citizens. Wilson had a sympathetic attitude toward the Jews, and tried to help them establish their rights in Europe and to promote their rights in the United States, supporting, for example, Louis D. Brandeis for a position on the Supreme Court. According to Silver, Woodrow Wilson—for his spiritual, social and moral greatness—sets an eternal example for the United States.[6]

Silver, the Zionist, believed that the United States would eventually achieve a 'Wilsonian' regime which would be comfortable for minorities in general and for the Jews in particular. Thus, during the 1920s, while fighting against draconian immigration laws with their antisemitic sting, Silver expressed confidence in the victory of American tolerance. He claimed that the American-Jewish response to these discriminatory immigration laws should be constructive, and that they should reflect the deepening pluralism in the United States. The "melting-pot theory" was passé, and, instead, Silver asserted, we must understand that "Today, we are a people of many peoples." The Jews, and especially those Zionists who correctly understand the United States, should take action for a "more American America"—an

America more loyal to its founding principles and more inclusive of its Jews.[7]

Silver developed his approach to pluralism in a sermon entitled "Making America Safe for Differences," which was given at "The Temple" in 1936. Just as there is only one Bible, which has "70 different interpretations," Silver opined, similarly, there is only one United States, incorporating many different religions and religious groups. These differences must be accepted and the free and equal religious development of these groups must be assured. Nonetheless, we must beware of chaos; all ethnic groups must make it their task to stay in harmony with the United States regime, and care must always be taken to avoid, directly or indirectly, those matters that might lead to unrest.[8]

In the summer of 1940, Silver gave a talk, as part of a series of lectures on pluralism at Harvard University, entitled "In the Midst of Many Peoples." A discussion of the democratic-pluralistic tradition of the ultimate American poet, Walt Whitman, and quotes from his works, served as Silver's introduction to an analysis of the situation of the Jews in the United States, and to relevant aspects of American society which pertained to them. American society is unique, he declared, founded by immigrants from various countries and possessing a complex form of nationalism ("We, in the United States, are a composite people").[9]

To paraphrase Silver, the United States gains strength from being a society composed of different social groups, each with its own racial and cultural characteristics. Cultural uniformity, he warned, is not a prerequisite for a harmonious, democratic society—in fact, cooperation and good-will on behalf of different groups serves the country by promoting national goals. If the United States wants to be loyal to its ideals and to avoid fascism and antisemitism, it must continue to nurture pluralistic patterns: Cultural uniformity is just as disastrous a slogan to raise in modern society as racial uniformity. In fact, the one inevitably leads to the other. In Nazi Germany they were merged into one. Too many human ideals are being broken in our day upon the wheel of totalitarian obsessions, for we who value individualism and exalt personality, to permit ourselves to champion unification in American life. We must learn to accept differences and to find bases of co-operation and spiritual unity in spite of these differences and because of them.[10]

On the eve of the outbreak of World War II and through the war's early years, Silver gave many sermons on the theme of the United States' opposition to Nazi ideology. These sermons, given at "The Temple," created reverberations across the State of Ohio. One of the sermons, given to the Ohio Educators Association, was entitled "The Strength Which Is America." This sermon (later published as an article in a leading Ohio professional journal in the field of education), which speaks for itself, clearly presented three basic elements of American culture:

First—*the importance of the individual.* Each individual has inalienable rights, which the state cannot rescind and the majority cannot diminish. All human beings, regardless of race or creed, are equal under the law. Any and all attempts to subordinate an individual or to discriminate against him/her before the law, due to that individual's race or belief, is a frontal, mortal assault on American ideology.

Second—*government is by consent*, not by coercion, and is from within, not from without. American genius, Silver explained, strives to attain a better life for the greatest number of citizens by means of their voluntary enterprises, via free experimentation, and by processes of gradual development and trial and error. American genius rejects all miraculous, millennial formulas touted (or brandished) by revolutionaries or dictators, preferring the slower and less flashy path of democracy. It also avoids all the atrocities committed by revolutionary regimes: cleansings and assassinations, terrorism and boycotts, espionage and slavery.

Third—*the mercifulness of tolerance which comes from the United States as an aggregate nation.* Many races participated in the discovery of this great land, in its settlement and development. From the moment of its establishment the American nation has been a nation of immigrants. American life can be thought of as a fine mosaic, in which many separate racial and religious identities are grouped into one noble pattern. Barring a few perversions, the overwhelming attitude in the United States, according to Silver, is one of good will, tolerance and cooperation. The American genius is expressed by the softening and reduction of separate groups, which breaks them down into their individual human components. Europe is busy with minority rights, but the United States is busy with human rights.[11]

Silver did not always automatically extend his positive attitude toward the United States and its polity to American society and economics as they actually developed. Until 1932 Silver did not support either of the major political parties, because he was not satisfied with what he saw as their superficial reactions both to his opinions and to serious social problems. Then, against the background of the Depression and in light of the social policies backed by Franklin Roosevelt, Silver became one of Roosevelt's avid supporters. Roosevelt, in turn, after a few months as President, appointed Silver to the National Citizens' Committee—part of the 1933 "Mobilization for Human Needs." In the spring of 1934 Silver summarized and praised Roosevelt's first year in office, and, in 1936, in a sermon at "The Temple" entitled "Achievements and Failures," he claimed that many significant goals had been attained. Later, during the elections at the end of 1936, Silver praised Roosevelt's social programs and again voted for him for president.[12]

However, in 1940 Silver objected to Roosevelt's presidency, partly because he objected, in principle, to a third term of office. His decision to back Wendell Willkie, though (see below), was not just based on his opposition to a third term, but was the considered result of Zionist strategy. When Silver presented the Jewish public with the Democrat, Roosevelt, and his Republican opponent, Willkie, both candidates were deemed worthy of the Jewish voter's trust. In this way, Silver clarified his social-political criteria and his relation to the United States.[13]

Silver claimed to have thoroughly checked both Roosevelt's and Willkie's social platforms (Willkie was suspected by many Jews to be overly conservative and even reactionary), and found no significant differences between them. Both faithfully represented the values of wise and active citizenship. Roosevelt was known as a liberal, but Willkie also fought for the rights of American Blacks, and had fought against the racist Ku Klux Klan years before he considered running for president. During his presidential campaign, Willkie rejected help from anyone even vaguely tainted by suspicion of racism or religious prejudice. He adhered to the tradition of equality upheld by another great Republican leader—Abraham Lincoln.[14]

Roosevelt was popular as a standard-bearer for the struggle against totalitarianism, and was especially supportive of various minorities in the United States, particularly those ethnic minorities suffering from Nazism and fascism in Europe (such as the Jews, the Poles and Czechs). But in such matters as well Willkie did not lag behind and also showed concern for the common people and lower classes in general.[15] Possibly Silver went too far in his comparisons. But in any case and to a great extent he remained loyal to the social criteria and political ideologies that guided the typical Jewish voter, who in those years tended to be a social-liberal.

II

The period in which Silver's Zionism was most radical was, more or less, in the decade from 1940–1950. During the summer and fall of 1940 Silver was personally disturbed by the alienating behavior of the State Department for Jewish Refugees in Europe, and, at this same time, the British, anti-Zionist, White Paper policy was also at its peak. In October 1940 he met with David Ben-Gurion, and together they reached a political understanding which resulted in a combative Zionist policy applicable during World War II and afterwards. On the other hand, Silver's ties to Weizmann dwindled. The political understanding between Ben-Gurion and Silver was strengthened by a growing radicalization of American Jewry and American Zionism, whose political goal was explicitly defined: the establishment of the State of Israel. Even the date for Israel's establishment—the end of World War II—was determined and publicly declared. The main means to this end was a massive call-up both of American Jewry and of the American public in general. Silver undermined the dependence of American Jewry on Roosevelt, and, together with Emmanuel Neumann, acted within the various layers of the community, and within the different organizations and their bulletins, to sway public opinion and exert pressure on the policy decision-makers.[16]

Milestones during this decade included: 1) decisions made by the United Palestine Appeal (UPA) in January 1941, headed by Silver, on the right to establish the Land of Israel as a sovereign Jewish Commonwealth; 2) support for this decision by the Zionist Biltmore Conference in May 1942, attended by both Ben-Gurion and Weizmann; 3) Silver's combative leadership at American Zionist Emergency Council (AZEC), where he overpowered Stephen Wise from 1943–1948; 4) the overwhelming majority support of the American Jewish Conference in August 1943 for Silver and the Biltmore decisions; 5) the activist alliance with Ben-Gurion at the 22nd Zionist Congress in December 1946, which caused Weizmann's ouster from the presidency of the World Zionist Agency, and, 7) Silver's persistent and sophisticated battle in the United States and the United Nations toward the establishment and foundation of the State of Israel between 1947–1949. This period ended after the establishment of the State, and in the Spring of 1950 Silver gave a talk at Hebrew Union College in Cincinnati where he announced the end, in his opinion, of the "Herzlian period" of Zionism. The period of salvation and the establishment of a national refuge were over, and the "Ahad ha-Am period" was beginning—a period which emphasized cultural and spiritual values, cooperation with the Diaspora, and the universal mission of the Jewish state.[17]

One might wonder how Silver's relationship with the United States fared during this radical "Herzlian decade." A survey of his Zionist political appearances during the 1940s teaches us that, despite all his criticism of the United States and its policy, he always maintained a basic faith in the United States, and did not feel compelled to dissociate himself from its general values. Usually, his criticism was specific, focused on the United States' estrangement from and neglect of the disaster befalling European Jewry, and on the United States' lack of sufficient support of the Zionist solution. But Silver never gave up, throughout the entire period, on the possibility of changing the United States' positions and of gaining full support for the establishment of the Jewish state.[18]

Nonetheless, there is no doubt that, especially during the 1940s, one can find some bitterness in Silver's connection to the United States. For example, at the start of 1942 he gave a general talk before the Central Conference of American Rabbis (CCAR) in which he presented Judaism as being the epitome of humanistic and universal values—in total opposition to Nazi ideology. He claimed that the United States was becoming too similar to Europe; it was becoming more obtuse, losing its soul, becoming more technocratic and vulgar; and most dangerous of all, it was losing regard for human dignity and individual rights. The Zionist Reform rabbi declared that Jewish self-assertion and the revival of the historic national homeland was the Jewish people's ultimate answer to murderous and degrading Nazi ideology, and their response to a lowering of values in the United States.[19]

Silver gave many similar Zionist talks during the 1940s. He delivered these talks in a "European format," which—in this case—meant that he approached his subject as a "message of despair" on behalf of society at large. However, more precise scrutiny reveals that there continued to remain a thread of hope connecting Silver and American society. First of all, there was always hope of a democratic Zionist struggle in the United States, and second, though Silver waved the flag of proud Judaism and assertive Zionism, his conceptual framework was, whether discrete or blatant, often in line with American ideals. For instance, during that same landmark Zionist speech of 1942 (mentioned above, which opened with rabbinical quotations and closed with Hebrew verses), he began with references to Lincoln's legacy and asked whether it still had a chance. Later, in the middle of his talk, Silver praised the spiritual values of American communal enterprises and of various eminent personalities, especially Ralph Waldo Emerson. He claimed that this American heritage was not being given its proper place, and called on liberal Jewry in the United States to redeem this threatened heritage. His appeal, and all the Zionist passion in his speech, in no way either demeaned the United States or expressed despair over it. Silver spoke with respect about the American leaders of the past, and claimed that their legacy was a great and ever-valid one. The question only remained as to whether this cultural legacy and its values could still be preserved.[20]

In conclusion, taking a stance similar to that he held before 1940, Silver *did not* call upon American Jewry to replace the general legacy that had failed; instead, he challenged Jewish liberals to *save* that fundamentally American legacy. This was to be *a shared challenge* (although it was of particular weight to the Jews), and part of a great American undertaking, which, if undermined, would be disastrous for everyone.

Silver's Zionist approach, calling for cooperation in "repairing" America during those dark years, should not be surprising. We already saw that the subject of democracy—always at the core of Silver's value-system—led him to seek connections between Judaism and the American Puritan tradition. Throughout this period we find Silver persistently continuing to extol Judaism—versus Nazism—as the cradle of the idea of democracy. In virtually every discussion he held during the 1940s Silver raised this cardinal issue, noting that the historical root of political democracy is based on freedom of religion; in this regard, the Protestants, especially those who came to North America and founded the United States, played a crucial role. This was his main thesis when he lectured before the Union of American Hebrew Congregations in 1939, and was also included in his article published in 1941:

These doctrines [of religious liberty and equality] of the Anabaptists were carried over to Holland and England, and to the American Colonies. The Founding Fathers of our country adopted many of the doctrines of these religious "fanatics." When they wrote into the Declaration of Independence: "We hold these truths to be self-evident—that all men are created equal, that they are endowed by their Creator with certain unalienable rights, that among these are Life, Liberty and the pursuit of Happiness," they were giving political expression to seminal religious Anabaptist doctrines…. When they engraved upon the Liberty Bell the Biblical proclamation: "And Thou shalt proclaim freedom through the land unto all the inhabitants thereof," or when they placed on the first seal of the newborn republic of the United States the figure of Moses leading the children of Israel out of Egypt, they were marshalling religious truth, religious authority and religious tradition to underwrite and sanction their political revolution.[21]

Every year on the 4th of July, Silver had an opportunity to enlighten his audience about this deep historical bond linking Judaism and Puritanism in the development of democracy. On American soil, this partnership created a distinct, thriving democracy, intrinsically humanistic in nature. Silver's "conceptual America"—even during the terrible times of the World War—offered the legacy of religious freedom and human dignity.[22]

Throughout the years after the Holocaust and the war Silver repeatedly praised the American regime—and not only for its democracy. In a New Year's talk he gave in 1949, Silver asked his audience: "What is America? What does America mean?" He answered that America is a historical-geographical phenomenon, but, at the same time, it is also a phenomenon filled with ideas and values—with "the American dream." America is more than just a land, or a population or material wealth. America is a revolution, carrying a banner engraved with the basic concepts of freedom, equality, human rights, freedom of religion, freedom of the press, freedom of speech and the right to assembly. Silver expanded this line of thought beyond the workings of mere democracy, and eloquently depicted America as the pilgrim's carriage, the pilgrim spirit, the very assurance of human progress. America is the "Fair Deal" and the "Square Deal" (two programs for economic reform from the Truman and Roosevelt periods), and is ideally a partnership between the "haves" and the "have-nots." America represents tolerance, goodwill and cooperation between human beings.[23]

This talk went beyond "Americanism" in its historical-geographic aspect to instill the conceptual meaning of and claims about the American ethos in a style saturated with emotion—distinctly and overwhelmingly expressing Silver's deep affinity for the United States and its culture and values.

As the middle of the century neared, Silver gave a series of lectures titled "One Hundred Years of History," one of which was a comprehensive talk on "One Hundred Years of American History." Now, he declared, the United States is leading the world as a result of its pioneering impulse, its spirit of enterprise, its tempo, its inventiveness, its technological skill, organizational capacity, and courageous vision. Here in the United States a free people was pouring all its drive into the profitable use of the resources of a continent and was building up its own way of life—an effort which will remain an epic of extraordinary challenge and grandeur in the annals of mankind.[24]

Silver continued to sketch American history, displaying both his knowledge and his deep affinity for it. However, he also received a fair share of criticism, particularly from those who regarded his efforts to decrease the distance between the social classes with suspicion. Nonetheless, Silver fondly described the efforts of the public to reduce the power of the American plutocracy and to struggle for workers' rights and economic security, although this path was rife with setbacks and failures. But, he stressed, under American circumstances, this was a fight with a good chance of success. Thus, from 1933 on (the start of Roosevelt's term of office), social reform began to take root and have an effect. With the New Deal the United States met many social goals, such as the implementing of various types of social security and a rise in the general standard of living.[25] Silver stressed that these social achievements were attained in a non-socialist manner. He believed that a non-socialist course of reform is more suited to America, and also expressed his certainty that this course would also prove itself in the future.[26]

Although the United States made major advancements in the areas of equality for women and civil rights in general, there were also failures, especially in the case of American Blacks. The social status of various ethnic and religious minority groups (Catholics, Germans, Irish) also continued to present a large and very problematic issue, and these groups were still quite sensitive to the lower regard in which they were held by the generally more powerful Anglo-Americans. But, those suffering most from various forms of discrimination and violence were American Blacks. American democracy, Silver asserted, must hasten to correct these problems with serious and non-superficial solutions.[27]

By the mid-twentieth century, Silver claimed, American democracy was faced with the threat of Communism. The answer to this threat, he felt, should not be the spreading of fear internally nor the instigation of witch-hunts—"solutions" which would be harmful to democracy. Silver believed in the deep-rooted strength of American democracy and maintained his completely optimistic-liberal approach. He believed that American democracy must remain true to itself, and that this constancy would be the best and most basic response to Communism. Under the circumstances of this perceived threat the United States must be even more creative, flexible and constructive—under no circumstances might it use undemocratic or other methods, even

in self-defense. Silver preached against all extremist political movements. The end does not justify the means, and only completely democratic methods can serve and solidify American democracy.[28]

Silver concluded his talk passionately, asserting that America
promised a bright future for its youth, and that the United States would
become the leading moral force in the world. He also believed that the
previous hundred years of America's history showed that these high
hopes were likely to be realized.[29]

A week later, Silver gave a sermon which complemented his prior
lecture (above) dedicated to "One Hundred Years of Jewish History."
In this sermon he again distinctly set out his positive image of America, and spoke about a great moment in Jewish history—when the
balance of Jewish life "shifted from the horrible hate-soaked, blood-
soaked land of Europe to the New World where traditions of human
freedom and tolerance and brotherhood had been dominant for more
than one hundred years."

Silver saw America as a country where tensions are usually resolved without violence— as an essentially enlightened society, that,
by virtue of its positive nature, enables Jews to live in it with dignity
and equality.[30]

III

World War II, the Holocaust, estrangement by the State Department and Roosevelt's evasive policy—plus tension and suspicion in
his relations with Truman—all led Silver, during the 1950s, to a more
particularistic Zionism and to the platforms of the Republican Party.[31]
Despite these changes, though, it is doubtful whether his basic views
on America—both as a Zionist leader and as a Reform rabbi—had
altered significantly.

We have already discussed Silver's programmatic talk in which he
noted the end of the "Herzlian period" in Zionist history; the precise
date of that Founder's Day address, which celebrated the seventy-fifth
anniversary of the founding of Hebrew Union College by Isaac Mayer
Wise, was 12 March 1950. During this address Silver stated that a
criticism of Wise's anti-Zionist stance was not a concern for modern
Jews, and that the time was ripe for reviving the eternal foundations
of the Wise legacy in order to clarify and extol those universal values

of American culture and Judaism which were so important to Wise. Alongside his wish to return to Wise's Reform ideals, we also find Silver identifying with Wise's own deep admiration of the United States as a land of freedom which aimed to uphold those same values which are expressed in Judaism's moral commandments.[32]

A number of years later (in 1954), on the 300th anniversary of the arrival of Jews to the United States, Silver expounded further on America as a home for Judaism, and he lavished praise on the country, its mode of government, and its values. In a comprehensive talk he gave in Detroit in October that same year, Silver opened with one of his usual descriptions of America as having a "colorful, unique, and noble mosaic pattern" and noted the ongoing prosperity of its Jewish inhabitants. This pluralistic commentary on America may have stood somewhat in opposition to the "Eisenhower version of America" of the 1950s, but nonetheless, Silver stuck to it.[33] He repeated the motif that the Jewish pilgrims (i.e., immigrants with a religious mission) had come to America three hundred years earlier to a land of religious freedom. However, the Jews, as active partners, not only enjoyed the situation, but actually helped *shape* the United States and its institutions. Jews, Silver stated, can be proud of the future in store for the United States:

> The coming age will be a great age for America. The next hundred years at least seem likely to be known, I believe, as 'The American Century,' in the same sense as the nineteenth century was 'The Century of Great Britain.' Destiny has singled out our beloved country, the foremost democracy on earth, to give leadership to the world and to lead mankind out of the grave social, political and economic predicament in which it finds itself.[34]

Despite his identification of American Jewry with the United States and his affinity for Republicanism during the 1950s, Silver explicitly refused to use forceful, military tactics in American policy. He stressed his belief in coexistence, in the central role of the United Nations, and in the possibility of American influence in the world, both by setting an example and by offering constructive help to other nations.[35]

During the early 1950s Silver came out against McCarthyism. Obviously, he rejected Communism, but he also objected to its comparison with fascism and Nazism. Fascism, according to Silver, is a persistent enemy of the entire American value-system, and fighting against it is unavoidable. Communism, however, in part raises good causes, and one can and must cooperate with it in various matters. Silver objected to the exacerbation of the Cold War and to the continuing international polarity between the two sides. He sided with constructive American action in Third World countries, and rejected the old, depressing and condescending European-style imperialism. He claimed that America's international economic activity would improve world economy, contribute to the realization of peaceful coexistence, and, in the end, become effective in weakening Communism.[36]

On the home front, Silver warned, McCarthyism was likely to damage all layers of American life. He called for intensive democratic action against McCarthyism and its threat to American values, in order both to preserve the many hues of American society and the nature of the American citizen, and for the sake of the educational system and its ability to instill democratic values in coming generations. He claimed that the answer to McCarthyism, in the long run, is not a political struggle per se, but rather an extension of the rights of the individual and a deepening of democratic education.[37]

During the later years of Silver's active life, i.e. 1950–1963, he returned to his habit of writing, from time to time, about inspiring American personages who influenced his thoughts and whose legacies he thought worthy of adoption and promotion. In January 1956, for example, he gave a long, warm talk about Benjamin Franklin (commemorating his 250th birthday) in which he emphasized Franklin's objection to slavery and his aversion to war, and his jealous support of democracy and his adamant support of popular education. Benjamin Franklin was a man of faith, a deist. He had a sensitive and developed moral code, and, as such, was close in spirit to Judaism and fostered ties with the Jewish community.[38]

Silver was also careful to mention Benjamin Franklin's important place in American history—a place of honor he attained despite, or perhaps because of, his strong and colorful personality and his avid individualism. Silver concluded: "… how fortunate it was for the future of the Republic of the United States in those decisive years to have as one of those at its helm a personality so rich in wisdom, and understanding and love of humanity, and tolerance, and good will, as Benjamin Franklin."[39]

After the assassination of John Kennedy, Silver prepared a sermon on the late Democratic president, analyzing his path and the legacy he left for America and the world. This sermon was meant to be given at "The Temple" on Sunday morning, 1 December 1963. But, on Thanksgiving Day, 28 November, Abba Hillel Silver died suddenly of a heart attack. Kennedy's eulogy, thus, eventually became sort of a farewell speech by Silver himself, a last lecture in which he expressed his values and hopes for America and Americanism. In the wake of his deep shock at the assassination and in light of his close relationship with Kennedy and what he symbolized, Silver filled his eulogy with appreciation for Kennedy's spiritual and innermost inclinations [40] (There is also much symbolism in the fact that Silver's last sermon concerned both the Jewish community and overall American society as well.) In the end, the final sermon was published as part of a eulogy of Kennedy in the local *Cleveland Press*.[41]

Silver's eulogy of Kennedy revolved around Kennedy's loyalty to the vision of the Founding Fathers—from the writers of the Declaration of Independence to the authors of the Bill of Rights, and through to the legacy of another assassinated president, Abraham Lincoln. The vision Kennedy shared with these statesmen was that of a "New Jerusalem"—of a society which gave greater freedoms to all people, in order that all might realize in their own lives the basic human rights regarded by American democracy as irrevocable, self-evident truths.[42]

Furthermore, Silver spoke favorably about Kennedy's realism and praised his sharp perception of the boundaries of power. By virtue of these traits Kennedy was well aware of the inanity and danger of nuclear warfare, and did all he could to prevent it. In general, Kennedy was in a race for peace, rather than a race toward war. He supported the development of weak countries, the fight against poverty and backwardness in various parts of the world, and projects such as the Alliance for Progress and the Peace Corps.[43]

Kennedy had a domestic agenda as well. He fought against the monopoly in the steel industry, had high hopes for and endless dedication to the improvement of the lot of Black Americans and promoted a new, comprehensive law regarding civil rights. He also had great concern for far-reaching improvement of the American educational system.[44]

Towards the end of Silver's eulogy, he claimed that Kennedy had acted on behalf of the sublime mission of "justice, fairness, freedom and peace." These were not just honorific words spouted "following the deaths of saints," but were expressions of Silver's genuine appreciation of this statesman, one who charted his mandated path in both internal and foreign affairs.[45]

It is possible, perhaps, to find additional symbolism in the manner in which Silver concluded his last sermon—in the way he brought in both Jewish-American and American culture. After a poetic passage on Kennedy's civil and political paths, Silver ended with a quotation from David's lament for Jonathan in Samuel II 1:17–27. Silver considered "John," the assassinated American president, to be like a twin brother to the Biblical Jonathan; the president, murdered by a wrong-doer, was a fountain of inspiration and one who continued the path of Jonathan, felled by the profane Philistines. Silver said that the Jewish community mourned Kennedy's death in the name of its tradition of liberty and progress, and on behalf of the Biblical values of spiritual strength and freedom: "Jonathan upon thy high places is slain! I am distressed for thee, my brother Jonathan...How are the mighty fallen...!"[46]

IV

It seems that Silver's radical Zionism did not exclude him from the "classic American Zionist tradition" fashioned by personalities such as Israel Friedlander, Kallen, Brandeis, Henrietta Szold, Stephen Wise and Mordecai Kaplan—a tradition which had a deep affinity with the American ethos.[47] Although Silver's perception of Zionism consequent to the Holocaust and World War II became more particularistic and he became less interested in social questions, it seems right to conclude that his "New Zionism," 1) did not relinquish its identification with the United States, and 2) never doubted its basic affinity with American liberal ideologies.

Silver, who identified with America, wanted to see it as an especially liberal land, a comfortable place where Jews might prosper and where full Zionist activity might be possible. Both these aspects are expressed succinctly, regarding Silver, by Israel Goldstein.

Goldstein, who held many key positions in American Zionism, knew Silver well throughout all his years of activity. In Goldstein's autobiography, he sketches Silver and his activities, and suggests that "Zionism and Hebrew culture were the main causes to which Abba Hillel Silver devoted his energies, yet he also took a leading part in the civic affairs of his [general] community."[48] This testimony, taken from a contemporary, vouches for the conclusion that Silver's Zionism served, at least as a matter of principle, as a complement to—not a replacement for—his integrally American life and thought.

As for the version of America in Silver's political vision, Goldstein emphasizes Silver's tendency toward the Republican Party (during the 1950s), but adds and stresses that "In his firm support of organized labor, civil liberties, and other social causes, Dr. Silver was more liberal than most people gave him credit for being."[49] Goldstein's testimony strengthens the assumption that "Silver's America" was, and remained, basically, a socially liberal land.

In Silver's thought, a deep internal bond remained between his commitment to the existence of a Jewish community in the United States and his involvement in deepening democracy in American society in general. It must be emphasized that Silver continued to see the United States—even during his radical Zionist period and to his last day—as a home for American Jews, and, indeed, he longed for a democratic and enlightened home. Obviously, Silver's liberalism did not have the progressive impulse of the liberalism of, for example, Louis Brandeis or Henrietta Szold. However, Silver, throughout his entire life, believed in an enlightened America which was true to itself—an America dedicated to the Puritan-Biblical heritage of freedom, justice and humanism. He was an avowed optimist in regard to "this kind of America"—an America that affirmatively allowed, amongst other things, for the development of a free and proud Jewish community.[50]

In our discussion we have uncovered the apparent paradox of radical Zionism and enthusiastic American patriotism existing together. The solution to this paradox is found both in the nature of the American democratic regime itself and in the broad and creative interpretations of American Zionists, including Silver. Most American Zionists (at least during the period discussed in this article), perceived America as being basically a pluralist democracy which would allow for the successful promotion of Zionist goals and the establishment and support of a Jewish state—goals always carried out in a manner compatible with the democratic tenets of the American ethos.

In the end, one must always remember that Rabbi Abba Hillel Silver was, first and foremost, a religious personality, and that it was, indeed, the religious element within him that worked to subtly synthesize his radical Zionism and avowed Americanism.[51] We began this article by analyzing Silver's early sermon establishing the spiritual legacy of the Hebrews as akin to that of the Pilgrim Fathers, and we concluded our discussion with his eulogy of Kennedy, which he interwove with the Biblical lament of the fallen Jonathan. Indeed, Silver avidly believed that the American ethos, at its best, was deeply rooted in the Jewish ethical-religious legacy. It was this belief, I suggest, that fundamentally allowed him to boldly and nobly integrate his passionate Zionism and his everlasting Americanism.

Heschel and the Roots of Kavanah

David Ellenson and Michael Marmur

Responsibility and *Kavanah* in Postwar America

The second half of the life of Abraham Joshua Heschel was spent in the United States of America. During the thirty-two years which elapsed from his arrival as part of the Refugee Scholars Project of the Hebrew Union College until his premature death at sixty-five in 1972, Heschel rose to great prominence among North American Jewry. His legacy has been enduring and his impact profound.[1]

Heschel's view of Jewish life in the America of the 1950s and 1960s combined enthusiasm and dismay. His enthusiasm was sparked by the renaissance of interest in Judaism he identified in the younger generation. In 1962, in fact, he proclaimed that "[w]e are living through one of the great hours of history. The false gods are crumbling, and the hearts are hungry for the voice of God."[2] In 1965 he expressed amazement that "together with a decline of affection for being a Jew on the part of our older people we witness a rise of appreciation on the part of many of our younger people ... [who are] disturbed at parents who are spiritually insolvent. They seek direction, affirmation; they reject complacency and empty generosity."[3] Comments to this effect can be found in Heschel's writings from the mid-1950s on.[4]

Although he was buoyed by evidence of a search for spiritual meaning among the younger generation, Heschel was greatly dismayed both by the state of the established Jewish community as well as by the state of contemporary religion and of American society in

345

general. Already in 1948 he had bemoaned what he called "the ba-
nalization of Judaism ... the tumult of arrogant not-knowing and not
wanting to know."[5] In unpublished remarks made in 1955, Heschel is
recorded as having excoriated much of what he saw in Jewish life in
postwar America, and as having added that had he grown up in the
modern American synagogue, he probably not would have remained.[6]
One such child of the 1950s, Arnold Eisen, wrote of the exhilaration,
inspiration and surprise he experienced upon reading these first words
of *God In Search of Man*:

> It is customary to blame secular science and anti-religious
> philosophy for the eclipse of religion in modern society. It
> would be more honest to blame religion for its own defeats.
> Religion declined not because it was refuted, but because it
> became irrelevant, dull, oppressive, insipid.[7]

Heschel's enthusiasm and his dismay shared a common source: his
sense that the enormous potential offered by North America was being
squandered. In his view, laxity was being promoted rather than liberty,
entertainment rather than celebration,[8] vulgarity instead of seriousness
of purpose, and platitudes in place of genuine gratitude. Heschel was
not afraid to frame his critique in prophetic terms:

> To paraphrase the words of the prophet Isaiah: What to me
> is the multitude of your organizations? says the Lord. I have
> had enough of your vicarious loyalty. Bring no more vain of-
> ferings: generosity without wisdom is an evasion, an alibi for
> conscience.[9]

In this article we will emphasize two of the concepts which played a
central role in the mature Heschel's spiritual and social agenda: responsibility and *kavanah*. Although these are by no means the only
themes to be found in Heschel's work, they are of particular interest.
An analysis of the early material presented here will raise the question
of the origins of these particular Heschelian concerns.

The very last days of Abraham Joshua Heschel say much about
how the concept of personal responsibility had become a central te-

net of his life. The last known photograph of Heschel shows him and Daniel Berrigan on their way to Philip Berrigan's release from the Danbury Correctional Institute on 20 December 1972. Heschel had decided that his teaching, research, and even his health, were less urgently significant than his involvement in the great social struggles of the day—in this case, his commitment to Clergy Concerned About Vietnam.[10]

Throughout his final years Heschel was to be found calling for an end to apathy and intransigence. He was at the forefront of the civil rights movement, and, in addition to many other involvements, was also a voice of conscience for Soviet Jewry and a vociferous opponent of the war in Vietnam.

The classic Heschelian statement on Responsibility is to be found in the English version of his work on the prophets:

Above all, the prophets remind us of the moral state of a people: Few are guilty, but all are responsible. If we admit that the individual is in some measure conditioned or affected by the spirit of society, an individual's crime discloses society's corruption.[11]

This statement was later to reappear with relation to race[12] and Vietnam.[13] Time and again, Heschel prevailed upon his fellow Jews and his fellow Americans to hear the call to action and not to shirk responsibility. In a rare autobiographical passage, he recalled his fear as a seven year old upon studying the tale of the Binding of Isaac that the angel might intervene too late. With a mixture of sadness and outrage, Heschel added: "An angel cannot be late, but man, made of flesh and blood, may be."[14] For Heschel, responsibility is not some abstract commitment. It is an urgent and relentless call, and if it remains unheeded the implications are ominous indeed.

In order to find a useful translation of the second of the concepts under discussion, one may consult the dictionary of philosophical terms compiled by Heschel himself in 1941, not long after his arrival at the Hebrew Union College in Cincinnati. In that work כּוונה (*kavanah*) is translated as "intention; methodicalness; attention; aim, purpose, meaning, significance; turning toward a certain place."[15] We find this term used often in Heschel's work, and for a variety of purposes. It is not surprising to find considerable attention paid to the concept in Heschel's leading work on prayer, *Man's Quest for God*. In fact, two different mini-chapters in different sections of that work bear the identical name: 'The Nature of *Kavanah*.'[16] The entire book is suffused with discussions of this term, which Heschel renders in English as "inner devotion."[17]

At one juncture in *Quest* Heschel makes a thinly-veiled pejorative reference to Mordecai Kaplan and Reconstructionism, indicating that "[t]here are some people who believe that the only way to revitalize the synagogue is to minimize the importance of prayer and to convert the synagogue into a social center." His refutation of this position demonstrates the significance Heschel attached to *kavanah*: "A synagogue in which men no longer aspire to prayer is not a compromise but a defeat; a perversion, not a concession. To pray with *kavanah* (inner devotion) may be difficult; to pray without it is ludicrous."[18] Heschel was keen to suggest that *kavanah* was in essence the same whether it was being applied to prayer or in a wider sense: "Our great problem … is how not to let the principle of regularity impair the power of spontaneity (*kavanah*). It is a problem that concerns not only prayer but the whole sphere of Jewish observance."[19] Later in the work we find *kavanah* described as "more than a touch of emotion," but rather as "insight, appreciation." It is the "unique task" of the rabbi "to be a source of inspiration, to endow others with a sense of *kavanah*."[20] The term comes to refer to all that is opposed to a dry instrumentalist reading of the function and purpose of Judaism. A stultified and stagnant Judaism must give way to a Judaism of *kavanah*, which is taken to include a number of desiderata: inner devotion, insight, appreciation, spontaneity and more.

Kavanah was pressed into service in the cause of Heschelian polemics. The motivation for his fervent opposition to symbolic thinking remains a matter of debate.[21] In any case, it is clear that this constituted one of Heschel's most persistent bugbears. He was keen to emphasize the "difference between symbolic understanding and what tradition means by *kavanah*":

Kavanah is awareness of the will of God rather than awareness of the reason of a *mitzvah*. Awareness of symbolic meaning is awareness of a specific idea; *kavanah* is awareness of an ineffable situation ... It is *kavanah* rather than symbolic understanding that evokes in us ultimate joy at the moment of doing a *mitzvah*.[22]

Heschel is sensitive to the possibility that a notion of inwardness might be used to brand traditional Judaism as a religion of mechanical performance and conformity as opposed to one of intentional and meaningful deed, or alternatively that a misreading of *kavanah* could be used to encourage antinomian trends. In the course of one year—1953—we find Heschel exhorting the Conservative rabbinate to serve as exemplars of *kavanah*, while warning the Reform rabbinate of its dangers. In this latter address, he launched a blistering attack against the notion that Judaism can be understood exclusively in terms of intention, with action relegated to obsolescence, or to the category of custom and ceremony. He asks whether the statement that God wants the heart can be taken to mean that He asks for the heart only. Unlike certain Oriental traditions, and also unlike Paul and Kant, Judaism rejects the notion that the right intention by itself can suffice. Indeed, "the crisis of ethics has its root in formalism, in the view that the essence of the good is in the good intention. Seeing how difficult it is to attain it, modern man despaired. In the name of good intentions, evil was fostered."[23]

This assault on a notion of unrealized intention was not sufficient. Heschel also rejected the trend to replace disembodied ethical probity with "customs and ceremonies." By relating to Jewish observance as a subject of anthropological interest, a heavy price was to be paid: "A religious act is something in which the soul must be able to participate; out of which inner devotion, *kavanah*, must evolve. But what *kavanah* could I entertain if entering the *sukkah* is a mere ceremony?"[24] In Heschel's very last work we find mention of the relation between performance of the deed and the intention behind the deed. While legalists have pondered what a person should do, and philosophers and kabbalists alike have debated what a person should think, "Hasidim have chiefly been absorbed by the problem of how a man should think while acting."[25] In the parallel Yiddish volume, the allusion to *kava-*

nah is quite explicit, and the question of whether *mitzvot* require *kavanah* is explicitly mentioned.[26] Until the last period of his life, this question remained in his thoughts.

If one book from Heschel's mature oeuvre were to be chosen as his major theological work, it would be that same work which had evoked such a strong response in the young Arnold Eisen: *God In Search of Man*.[27] We find *kavanah* playing a prominent role in that work: the tension between kavanah and deed is listed as one of the key exemplars of "a *polarity* which lies at the very heart of Judaism."[28]

Two chapters of *God In Search of Man* are devoted to *kavanah*, and each of them presents a central problem associated with the concept. Chapter 38, "The Problem of Integrity," grapples with a major religious challenge, highlighted most particularly in the Hasidic tradition: "If *kavanah* is as intrinsic to the service of God as impartiality of judgment is to scientific investigation; if, in other words, it is not only essential what one does but also what one is motivated by, the possibility of true service, of genuine piety may be questioned."[29] Heschel marshals a range of sources, predominantly from Hasidic literature but also from Rabbinic and medieval texts, in order to grapple with the eternal quest for religious integrity.

Chapter 31 is entitled "Kavanah." After briefly reviewing the term's etymology and commonly accepted meanings, Heschel goes on to emphasize *kavanah*'s dimensions of attentiveness, appreciation and integration, before he ends the chapter with a section entitled "Beyond Kavanah." Here he is keen to assert that the mitzvah is not coterminous with its intention: "A mitzvah is neither a substitute for thought nor an expression of kavanah. A mitzvah is an act in which we go beyond the scope of our thought and intention."[30] It appears that the same concerns he had expressed in his 1953 speeches to the Reform and Conservative rabbis were still exercising Heschel. On the one hand, he is aware that an emphasis on intention might be interpreted as an excuse for non-performance of *mitzvot*. On the other, he is critical of an approach to religious life which douses the fire of intensity and purpose.

Poised between the Scylla and Charybdis of a spiritualized abstract Judaism on one side and religious behaviorism on the other, Heschel ends the chapter by championing a third way: "When superimposed as a yoke, as a dogma, as a fear, religion tends to violate rather than to nurture the spirit of man. Religion must be an altar upon which the fire of the soul may be kindled in holiness."[31] Appended to this closing sentence we find the longest footnote in the entire book, running from page 317 through page 319. Just as remarkably, the genre discussed in the footnote is neither ethical literature nor Hasidic teachings. Instead, the footnote relates to *halakhic* discourse, citing "an ancient controversy among scholars of Jewish law whether the presence of kavanah—of the right intention in carrying out one's duty—is absolutely required for the performance of all religious acts." The classic example of this question which Heschel chooses to mention is that of the person who inadvertently hears the Shofar blown on Rosh Hashanah—does physical performance of the act without intention constitute its fulfillment?

Reviewing examples taken from the Temple cult and from the Laws of Divorce, Heschel presents a relatively detailed survey of the different views relating to the necessity of intention for the validity of the performance of commandments. He provides the following summary: "...the presence of proper intention is required for the act; the presence of improper intention (in some cases) invalidates the act; the lack or absence of intention, proper or improper, while not desirable, does not invalidate the act." The last section of the footnote leans heavily on Joseph Engel's *Athvan Deoraitha*. Engel, who has been described as "one of the most brilliant and underestimated figures of the pre-World War II generation,"[32] was without doubt beyond the reach of the great majority of Heschel's readership. Neither he nor the close *halakhic* argumentation in which he specialized would have been familiar or accessible to most modern Jews (let alone non-Jews) in America in the 1950s. Nevertheless, he closes the mammoth footnote with a conclusion taken directly from that work:

...the deed without the kavanah is considered as if it had been done with kavanah, for where no intention is consciously entertained, it may be assumed the deed was done for its proper purpose. Consequently, in the case of improper intention, wherein that assumption cannot be maintained, the deed is not valid because of the absence of kavanah.[33]

The message at the heart of this footnote is of keen relevance to American Jewish life in Heschel's day (and in ours). He is suggesting that performance without explicit intention is to be preferred over performance when accompanied by a perverse or contrary motivation. Whether this last possibility represents a sideswipe at such approaches as Reconstructionism, which offered a model of religious performance devoid of a basis in Faith, remains an open question.[34]

Yet, however the content of the note is understood, its form and length are remarkable. This is a long *halakhic* excursus at the heart of a work which, while replete with sources, contains very few which exemplify the argumentation of Jewish Law.

From Heschel's perspective, both *kavanah* and responsibility served as rallying calls for an alternative to the mediocrity and apathy of much of American Jewry in the postwar period. What can be learned about the provenance of these terms in Heschel's lexicon? What are the earliest traces of this concern? Perhaps they belong to the American phase in his career, or perhaps the seeds were planted during his decade in Weimar Germany during the Nazi rise to power. However, it is our assertion that the roots of Heschel's concern with these notions go back still further— back to Warsaw, the city of his birth. The remainder of this article will demonstrate this claim by presenting and analyzing two remarkable Hebrew notes his older contemporary Shalom Joseph Halevi Feigenbaum wrote in response to two questions Heschel posed on the issues of *kavanah* and responsibility when he was yet a teenager in Poland.

Heschel the Teenage *Halakhist, Kavanah* and Responsibility

Fifty years before his death, at the age of fifteen, Abraham Joshua Heschel (1907–1972) was first published. The piece, two short paragraphs in length, was followed in subsequent months by two others, all of them in the *Bet Midrash* section of the journal known as *Shaarei Torah*.[35] Although the existence of these pieces has been noted by Heschel's biographers, little interest has been shown in them.[36] It is our view that a renewed interest in this earliest layer of Heschel's life and work may yield useful insights into his self-understanding and motivation.

We turn now to a remarkable piece of literary evidence from this early stage of Heschel's intellectual and religious development that bears on our topic in this essay. The article in question is a piece comprising two responsa by Rabbi Shalom Joseph Halevi Feigenbaum, which was published in the same journal, *Shaarei Torah*, in the Tevet-Adar edition for the year 5684 (1924).[37] These two responsa are dedicated to "the learned and acute descendant of illustrious lineage, Mr. Abraham Heschel, may his light shine, from Warsaw," and they relate to questions posed by Heschel, who was then seventeen.

The full Hebrew text of these responsa is appended to this article. Of particular interest here are Heschel's questions. To be sure, they are not framed in the young Heschel's own style: we have to rely on the accuracy of Feigenbaum's account. Nonetheless, an echo of Heschel's teenage voice—a voice in transition to maturity—may be heard here.

In the first of these two responsa, Feigenbaum states that Heschel asked him the following question. Inasmuch as the question appears to reflect the words of Heschel himself, it is worthwhile to translate this part of the query in full. Heschel is reported as asking:

> … There is an individual whom [the congregation] honored during Sukkot by having him serve as *shaliach tzibur* (prayer leader) for the recitation of *Hallel* (Psalms of Praise) and the waving of the lulav and etrog [as mandated by Jewish law during that part of the prayer service]. However, he has not yet recited the blessing, *'al n'tilat lulav* – on the taking of the lulav,' and he wants to wait and not recite the blessing that accompanies the act [of taking (*l'kikhah*) the lulav] until a beautiful etrog (*etrog m'hudar*) arrives after the prayers are recited. Is it permissible for the [*shaliach tzibur*] who leads in the recitation of *Hallel* and the ritual of waving the lulav [*na'anu'im* that takes place during the recitation of this prayer] to state explicitly that he will intentionally not fulfill the halakhic obligation to [recite the blessing associated with *l'kikhah* – the taking of the lulav – even as he fulfills the ritual of waving the lulav] until the 'beautiful etrog' arrives?[38]

There are a number of Jewish legal concerns that are involved in this question, and they reflect the world of *halakhic* discourse in which Heschel was raised. Heschel knew that Leviticus 23:40, which states, "On the first day (of Sukkot), you shall take (*l'kakhtem*) [1] the product of *hadar* (goodly) trees, [2] branches of palm trees, [3] boughs of leafy trees, and [4] willows of the brook, and you shall rejoice before the Lord your God seven days," demanded that each Jew recite a blessing over the Four Species (Kinds) mentioned in this verse. However, as the response Feigenbaum issued to the question posed by his young student indicates, Heschel was keenly aware that rabbinic literature described the fulfillment of this commandment in a multilayered and nuanced way.

Within Jewish legal tradition, one major ritual issue surrounding the fulfillment of the Levitical commandment is whether the *na'anu'im* are an integral part of the commandment; another revolves around the "quality of beauty" (*hadar*) that the Four Species—unquestionably the etrog—must or ought to possess. While a description of all the laws surrounding this ritual are surely beyond this paper, some understanding of these particular strands of Jewish law is most helpful for illuminating the concerns that occupied the teenage Heschel.

As the Bible makes clear, "taking" of the lulav is surely a required part of the commandment. Therefore, in *Peshahim* 7b, the Talmud holds that the act of taking (*l'kikhah*) the lulav in hand requires that the blessing of "'*al n'tilat lulav*—on the taking of the lulav," be recited immediately prior to lifting the lulav. This follows from the explicit words found in Leviticus 23:40, "You shall take." It is a biblical commandment. In contrast, most authorities regard the "waving – *na'anu'im*" as a rabbinic commandment. The *halakhic* issue that remains is whether the waving (*na'anu'im*) is nevertheless regarded as part of the mitzvah of "taking," or whether it is an act separate and apart. No less an authority than the Rosh (Rabbi Asher ben Yehiel, 14th Century) considers the *na'anu'im* to be a separate requirement and he therefore—in keeping with the logic of Pesachim 7b—states that the blessing must be recited immediately prior to grasping the lulav. He allows for recitation of the blessing prior to the "waving" only if an individual has for some reason failed to recite the blessing prior to the 'taking.'" On the other hand, authoritative legal figures such as Maimonides (Hilchot Lulav 7:9) and the Ran (Rabbi Nissim Gerondi, 14th Century) regard the act of "waving"—albeit a rabbinic enactment—as an essential part of the "taking," and allow for the blessing to take place subsequent to the "taking." Nevertheless, both camps would assert—whatever the differences that divide them concerning the constituent parts of the commandment—that the recitation of the blessing over the lulav and etrog take place prior to the "*na'anu'im*" of the Hallel. Thus, it would seem that there is no way to delay offering the blessing prior to the "waving" of the Four Species during the Hallel service if one serves publicly as *shaliach tzibur*. As Rabbi Feigenbaum observed in the first part of his responsum, inasmuch as the Four Species are in the hands of the *shaliach tzibur* during the recitation of the Hallel, "in my humble option, it is impossible" for the *shaliach tzibur* to avoid the commandment of "taking the Four Species—*n'tilat arba minim*,"—and presumably reciting the blessing over them beforehand.

However, this discussion does not settle the matter. Rosh (Sukkah 3:33) states that an individual fulfills a mitzvah in an optimal way, "*min hamuvhar*," in Hebrew, by observing the highest standard of the commandment. From this perspective, there is some possibility for delaying the recitation of the blessing even after lifting the lulav if the highest standard has yet to be observed. In the case of the Four Species, the Talmud does assert that such a "highest standard" exists. Based on Leviticus 23:40, which describes the etrog as "*p'ri eitz hadar* – the product of goodly (*hadar*) trees," the rabbis, in Sukkah 31a, all concur that the etrog must be *m'hudar* (beautiful) if it is to be ritually qualified for use during Sukkot. Furthermore, in Sukkah 29b, the rabbis state that a lulav that is "dry - *yavesh*" is rendered invalid for ritual use, as they assert that lulav as well as the etrog must possess the trait of "*hadar* – beauty," and, in Sukkah 31a, they extend this standard of *hadar* to all of the Four Species. Otherwise, the species are ritually disqualified for usage in the performance of the commandment. Consequently, as Rabbi Feigenbaum notes at the conclusion of his responsum, it is "possible to say that one can delay [recitation of the blessing] so that one can fulfill the essence of the commandment of "taking" by employing 'beautiful species – *m'hudarim*.'" There are warrants in Jewish law that would allow for postponement of offering the blessing in light of the conditions that Heschel outlined in his question to his rabbi—especially since every single Jewish legal source agrees that the etrog must be *m'hudar*.

Before commenting on the significance of these *halakhic* considerations for our essay, it should also be noted that Heschel's question itself may well reflect a literary trope that he adapted from his Hasidic background, and that it does not reflect an actual situation in which either Heschel himself or someone else was involved. In his *Circle of the Baal Shem Tov: Studies in Hasidism*, Heschel, years later, related a story regarding Rabbi David Ostrer, a Hasid who would visit the Baal Shem Tov each year during Sukkot.[39] When the Baal Shem fell ill, Ostrer asked whom he should now turn to as "his master." The Baal Shem told him he should seek out the Maggid of Mezritch and R. Pinchas of Koretz. As Ostrer was accustomed to send a beautiful *etrog* each year to the Baal Shem Tov, he now had one sent to both the Maggid and R. Pinchas. However, Ostrer went to the court of the Maggid, for R. Pinchas did not yet "preside" over a court of disciples "in the first years after the death of the Baal Shem." Heschel then continues his narrative with the following tale:

> It once happened that the Gentile messenger bearing the etrog was delayed, so that he still had not arrived in Koretz the day before Sukkot. Heavy rains and flooded roads, which had contributed to a general shortage of etrogs, now left the community of Koretz without a single one!
>
> The congregation was already in the midst of their prayers on the morning of the first day of Sukkot, when R. David's messenger at last arrived. R. Pinchas made the blessing over the etrog [after he had put it together with the palm branch, myrtles, and willows, comprising the four kinds of plants used on Sukkot]. Subsequently, the rest of the congregation also fulfilled the commandment of the "four kinds." R. Pinchas then went to the prayer-reader's stand, recited the *Hallel* psalms, and made the required *na'anu'im* [while reciting the Hallel psalms, the "four kinds" are "shaken" in sequence toward all directions of the compass, as well as upward and downward, reflecting the omnipresence of the Divine].

R. Pinchas remarked that until then he had not wished to take upon himself the onus of being a leader, but during the holidays he had recognized that a pact had been made in Heaven for him to accept the yoke. From that point on, he began to "preside."[40]

To be sure, there are significant differences between the question posed in the responsum and the story told in the Hasidic tale. In the Koretz story, there was not a single etrog available prior to the holiday. In the responsum, etrogim were available. The issue was whether the prayer-leader could both lead the service and intentionally delay his recitation of the blessing over the "Four Species," aware that a more "beautiful" etrog that would allow him as an individual to fulfill the commandments of the holiday more fully would soon arrive. In the Hasidic story, the matter of delaying recitation of the blessing was also not at issue. Finally, in the tale, the appearance of the messenger just at the moment that was required for the recitation of the blessing was taken as a divine sign that Heaven desired that R. Pinchas "accept the yoke" of public leadership over a circle of disciples in his native city of Koretz. While it may be that the literary trope suggested by this story did not prompt Heschel to ask his rabbi the *halakhic* query he posed, the parallel between the story—which surely was known to Heschel from his youth—and the question he asked are clearly striking and do not allow us to rule out the possibility that the question was inspired by the story.

Whatever the case, it is evident that the notion of intentionality and responsibility in matters of prayer and leadership and the dilemmas associated with them had begun to occupy Heschel even during his youth, and that he drew upon and expressed these tropes in a *halakhic* genre. However one would adjudicate the *halakhic* arguments and counter-arguments that mark the question of whether lack of appropriate intentionality (*kavanah*) can allow a *shaliach tzibur* to delay the recitation of a blessing over the "Four Species," the fact that he posed this question as a seventeen-year-old indicates that his concern with the issue of *kavanah* and religious devotion had its roots in his youth. What would ultimately lead Heschel to label this requirement as "attentiveness to God" beyond the demands of "paying attention to the text of the liturgy or to the performance of the mitzvah"[41] had already begun to occupy him during his formative years.

The second question the teenage Heschel posed to Rabbi Feigenbaum indicates that his adult concern for the issue of responsibility also found expression in his adolescence. In this responsum, Feigenbaum reports that Heschel asked him for an explication of the Talmudic principle, "Sin, in order that your friend may gain merit—*hato k'dei she'yizkeh haverkha*" (Shabbat 4a). As Feigenbaum wrote, "And he (Heschel) asked in addition, whether (*ha*) the principle, 'We do not say to man, Sin, in order that your friend may gain merit,' [is actionable] even [in an instance] where the many will derive merit [from the sinful act performed by the individual]."[42]

In the Talmudic passage (Shabbat 4a) where this principle is found, the issue revolves around the case of an individual who, in ignorance of Jewish law, placed a loaf of bread in an oven and thereby violated the prohibition that forbids baking on the Sabbath. During the course of the discussion, Rabbi Shila raises the possibility that an individual other than the one who placed the loaf in the oven ought to commit the "minor sin" of removing the loaf from the oven in order to "rescue" his unaware friend from the "more severe sin" of baking on the Sabbath. Rabbi Shesheth, however, immediately objects, stating, "Is a person then told, 'Sin, in order that your friend gain merit.'"

The concern voiced in this responsum may or may not have been directly related to the issue raised in the first question Heschel posed to Feigenbaum. To be sure, it is admittedly unlikely that the concerns voiced in this responsum were linked to the first question Heschel posed about *kavanah*. After all, neither Heschel nor Feigenbaum made any such direct linkage and it is surely possible to treat both matters separately. However, it is possible that Heschel posed this additional question to his rabbi because he wanted to clarify the responsibility that the *shaliach tzibur* had to the entire congregation. After all, if the *shaliach tzibur* led the congregation in prayer and recited the *brachah* over the *arba minim* prior to the Hallel for the sake of leading the community in prayer while at the same time wishing he could have delayed recitation of the blessing until the "choice etrog (*m'hudar*)" arrived, he would surely have committed the "sin" of reciting a blessing that lacked appropriate "*kavanah*." The "responsibility" to lead the congregation in prayer and thereby "grant merit" to the community may have well have been employed as a sufficient justification to permit the commission of what could then have been labeled "a minor transgression."

The issue involved here is one of responsibility—of whether individual piety and observance can be sacrificed in specific and discrete instances for the sake of a greater good. The principle invoked by Rabbi Shesheth seems to affirm that this is categorically forbidden. However, there are a number of passages in the Talmud and in later Jewish legal literature (e.g., Berachot 47b and the *Tosafot* on Shabbat 4a among others) cited by Feigenbaum in his response to Heschel that indicate that a "sinful act" by an individual can be countenanced in instances where the larger community will derive benefit from a relatively "minor transgression." Moreover, one sees this principle invoked quite often in the responsa literature to countenance a "sinful act" on the part of an individual or a rabbinic court of three for the sake of the merit that such an act will bestow upon other individuals or the larger Jewish community. For instance, Rabbi David Tzvi Hoffmann (1843–1921) of Berlin, in his *Melammed L'ho'il, Yoreh De'ah* #83, deals with the question of whether a rabbinic court ought to commit "the minor sin" of accepting an individual who is likely to be nonobservant subsequent to his conversion for the sake of his Jewish wife and the children who will issue from the union. R. Hoffmann cites the dictum of R. Sheshet in Shabbat 4a as offering a possible warrant for not accepting the man. However, he cites the *Tosafot* (medieval commentators on the Talmud) on this dictum in Shabbat 4a as providing grounds for the rabbinic court to commit what R. Hoffman labels the "minor sin" (*issura zuta*) of accepting this man into Judaism for the sake of the greater benefits that will flow to the woman, the children, and the larger Jewish community from his acceptance as a convert. Clearly, this principle places responsibility upon the individual Jew to engage in a "moral calculus" that can require the Jew to commit a "minor infraction" of the Law for the sake of the advantages that such an act will confer upon either the larger community or specific individuals. This principle evokes an unavoidable burden of responsibility, and the query Heschel posed to his rabbis indicates that he was sensitive to this concern from his earliest years in Poland.

Any claim that the issue of *halakhic* responsibility is identical to the later Heschel's emphasis on social responsibility is unsupportable, and unnecessary, as there is little doubt that the historical experience of pre-war Berlin and postwar America had a profound impact on Heschel. Indeed, it is possible to demonstrate that much of Heschel's distinctive emphasis on the need for daring action in pursuit of justice was a relatively late development.

One important source mandating an approach which may be termed "moral interventionism" is Psalm 119:126: עת לעשות לה' הפרו תורתך. As Heschel pointed out in a small chapter devoted to this verse in his work on Rabbinic theology, the meaning of this verse is susceptible to a variety of interpretations. We may render it here as: It is time to act for the Lord/for the Lord to work; make void Your Torah/ they have made void Your Torah.

This verse was introduced explicitly into Heschel's repertoire only in the 1960s, and it may be seen as a Biblical foil to his growing political activism. He devoted a mini-chapter of his work on Rabbinic theology to the verse,[43] in which he noted that it "served as a firm foundation for a modest measure of flexibility in the legal construction of mitzvoth."[44] Yet, as the chapter proceeds, the interpretations seem less and less modest. In the fifth of five interpretations of the verse, Heschel enumerates a number of bold legal decisions predicated on the notion, to quote Rashi on Berakhot 54a, that "There are times when one cancels the words of Torah in order to act for the Lord." Having mentioned some of the classical applications of the legal principle, such as greeting on the Sabbath and committing the Oral Law to writing, Heschel then brings a tradition from Mishnah Keritot, according to which Rabban Simeon ben Gamliel changed the price and scope of a bird sacrifice in the Temple in a year when prices were prohibitively high, explaining his social intervention with reference to our verse.[45]

Heschel's next comment is of great significance: "This fifth interpretation is audacious, and it should not be entrusted to any but the wisest of Sages, who truly understand contemporary times."[46] The risk inherent in the provision of a mandate for overruling the strictures of *halakhah* is self-evident: who is to decide when a particular situation justifies the abrogation of norms? A special capacity to fathom the times in which we live, specifically bestowed upon the elite of each generation, is necessary to ensure that this *halakhic* flexibility does not lead to licentiousness. At the end of this chapter, Heschel brings in *halakhic* applications of the verse from Maimonides, and readings of a quite different nature in the name of the Ba'al Shem Tov and the Kotzker Rebbe.

Heschel's growing involvement in his later years with life outside his study room, forced him to confront many issues relating to his commitments as a traditional Jew. One example may prove instructive. Heschel was pictured next to Rabbi Maurice Eisendrath of the Union of American Hebrew Congregations (Reform) carrying a Torah scroll in an anti-war mobilization at Arlington Cemetery. Many Orthodox Jews protested that this represented a clear infraction of Jewish law. Heschel was at pains to offer a defense for his actions using both *halakhic* and other criteria.[47] In his last works, too, we find Heschel struggling with the question of how to deal with a conflict between the word of God and the demands of Torah.

Rather than suggesting a direct continuity between Warsaw and New York, it is our intention to point out that the roots of Heschel's call for social involvement and responsibility run deep. We do not suggest that Heschel's concern with responsibility in Warsaw in the 1920s is identical with the mature Heschel's call for action in post-war America. However, the questions of the teenage Heschel may be read as foreshadowing his later passions.

In fact, these early writings do unquestionably indicate that Heschel had already begun to consider the themes of intention and responsibility during his Warsaw youth. The concerns voiced in these legal writings anticipate what would be a lifetime of reflection on these notions, and the adult Heschel would articulate these matters in a voice that possessed unparalleled depth, and in a life that would provide unsurpassed inspiration for countless American decades later.

Writing in postwar America, Abraham Joshua Heschel stated that "[t]eaching a child is in a sense preparing him for adolescence. We have to teach him ideas which he can carry over to maturity."[48] It appears that some of the ideas and insights to which the young Heschel was exposed did indeed carry over into his later life, and provided the basis for what was to follow. Arthur Green has shown how a reading of his early poetry can yield many insights into Heschel's life project,[49] and we hope that in this article an even earlier stratum can be considered worthy of interest. Heschel's methodology and terminology were to change during his long journey from Muranowska Street via Vilna, Berlin and London, all the way to Selma, Alabama and the Vatican. We are grateful for the opportunity to present some of the legal and ethical questions which occupied the mind of the youth described simply as "Abraham Heschel of Warsaw." We have tried to demonstrate that despite the differences of context and genre separating Warsaw and New York City, core insights such as the centrality of *kavanah* and the importance of responsibility were established during Heschel's earliest years.

Appendix: The *Sha'arei Torah* material in full
[We have interpreted the acronyms and abbreviations of Heschel's
pieces in parentheses]

1. Vol. 13, no.1, Tishrei-Kislev 5683 (1922–1923) [discussed and
translated above]

סימן עח

איתא בב"ק (דס"ב) דכפל נוהג בדבר המטלטל וגופ[ו] ממון ולפי המסקנא שם (דס"ג)
לא ילפינן מכלל ופרט אלא מריבוי ומיעוט וממילא נתמעט דבר שאינו מסויים ולפ"ז
[ולפי זה] הקשו על הרמב"ם דלא הזכיר לפטור שאינו מסויים ובפי' [ובפירוש]
המשניות כתב הרמב"ם דילפינן כלל ופרט להפך מהמסקנא וכן קשה שלא הזכיר
הא דר' חייא ב"א [בר אבא] אמר ר"י [ר' יוחנן] שנתרבה לכפל לפי המסקנא
עיי"ה [עיין התם] כל הסוגיא.

ונלע"ד לתרץ כי הרמב"ם לשיטתו לא ס"ל הא דתנא בי חזקי' (דס"ג ע"ב) שהרי לבי'
חזקי' מסיק שם (ס"ד ע"ב) דמודה בקנס ואח"כ באו עדים חייב והרמב"ם ס"ל דפטור
וא"כ [ואם כן] לא ס"ל [סבירא ליה] כוותיה ולפ"ז [ולפי זה] ניחא ע' גמרא דס"ג
[גף ס"ג] שהכריחה דלא דרשינן כלל ופרט משום דכל פרט כלל ופרט באפי נפשיה
הוא ופרש"י כתנא דבי חזקי' להלן דס"ד [דף ס"ד] אבל בלא"ה [בלאו הכי] דרשינן
כלל ופרט וא"כ [ואם כן] כיון שהרמב"ם לא ס"ל כתב"ח א"ש [סבירא ליה כתנא דבי
חזקיה אתי שפיר] לשיטתו דייף כלל ופרט ונכון מאד בס"ד [בסיעתא דשמיא] והשאר
מובן מאליו

אברהם יהושע העשיל במ' משה מרדכי ז"ל

2. Vol.13, no.2, Tevet-Adar 5683 (Early Spring 1923):

סימן צח

בשע"ת ח"י [בשערי תורה חלק י] הקשה כ"ג [כבוד גאונו] על הרא"ה [ר' אהרון
הלוי] ז"ל דס"ל [דסבירא ליה] דבקנין דאורייתא קונה אפילו אם אין רוצה לקנות
והקשה מב"ק דס"ז דאיתא התם דיאוש אינו קונה באינו רוצה לקנות וע"כ צ"ל של"ה
[ועל כורחו צריך לומר שלא הוי] קנין דאורייי' וא"כ [ואם כן] מאי מספקא ליה לרבא
אי יאוש קונה מה"ת [מן התורה] או לאו ואמאי לא איפשיט ליה מהכא והניח בצ"ע
[בצריך עיון] ונראה לי דידוע מה שכתב הנתיבות דיאוש ל"מ [לא מהני] להוציא
מרשות הבעלים וכל זמן שלא זכה בו אחד הבעלים יכולים לחזור בו ולפ"ז [ולפי זה]

ניחא דלא אמר הרא"ה דיני אלא בהפקר ושאר קנין דמהני לגמרי להוציאו מרשות
הבעלים ומשו"ה [ומשום הכי] כתב דקונה שלא ברצונו ויאוש גרע כיון שלא יצא
עוד מרשות הבעלים ומשו"ה [ומשום הכי] צריך דעת הזוכה אע"פ שהוא מה"ת [מן
התורה] וז"פ [וזה פירושו].

אברהם יהושע העשיל במהור"ר משה מרדכי ז"ל.

3. Vol.13, no.3, Nisan-Iyar 5683 (Late Spring 1923)

סימן קח

א] ב"ב דכ"ו רש"י ד"ה [בבבא קמא דף כ"ו רש"י דיבור המתחיל] קוצץ בעומק ג'
טפחים וקai על בור שיח ומערה והוא פלא גדול שהרי כל החילוק בין סיפא לרישא
דכאן קיצץ אפילו עמוק מאד וכן איתא בהדיא בגמרא אצל עובדא דרב פפא ור"ה וכ"כ
הרמז"ל [ורב הונא וכתב כך הרמב"ם ז"ל] וכל הפוסקים וא"כ [ואם כן] קשה מדוע
כתב רש"י ג' טפחים.

ב] בב"ק דכ"ח [בבבא קמא דף כ"ח]: איתא בגמרא שור ולא אדם ה"מ בקטלא אבל אם
ניזק חייב וכתב רש"י אבל בכלים אמרינן שבירתן זו מיתתן ופטור וק"ל [וקיימא לן]
והלא כשננקטעה יד הכלי עדיין ראוי למלאכה ול"ש [ולא שנא] לומר זו מיתתו וא"כ
[ואם כן] אמאי פטור משתשלומין וצ"ע [וצריך עיון].

אברהם יהושע העשיל ב"מ משה מרדכי ז"ל

4. Vol. 14, no.2, Tevet – Adar 5684 (Early Spring 1924)

סימן ב

לכבוד החו"ב מגדולי היחוס מר אברהם העשיל נ"י מווארשא.

א] אשר עלה ונסתפק באחד שכיבדוהו בימי החג לירד לפני התיבה בתור ש"ץ באמירת
הלל ועשיית הנענועים בארבעת המינים, אכן הוא עוד לא בירך על נטילת לולב ורוצה
להמתין על אתרג מהודר שיבא לו אחר התפלה, אי שפיר דמי שיאמר ההלל ויעשה
הנענועים ויכוין בפירוש שלא לצאת בזה עד[?] יד"ח נטילה, עד שישיג את המהודר,
והביא שבסי' תקפ"ט תקפ"ט מבואר בב"י או"ח שד"ז פלוגתא דרבוותא היא אם תועיל הכוונה
שלא לצאת עכתו"ד ,והנה אמת שהרב"י שם סיים דלא חיישינן לדעת הרא"ה ז"ל
דהוא יחידאה נגד רבנו שמואל והרשב"א ורבותינו הצרפתים ובעל אהל מועד, ויש לי

בזה אריכות דברים בכתובים עמדי וגם ביחס לדעת היש"ש שאעפ"י דקיי"ל להלכה
דשחיטת חולין א"צ כונה, מ"מ אם מכוין בפירוש לשם נחירה, שחיטתו פסולה, (ע'
ביו"ד בסי' ג' באחרונים בזב, ובמלא הרועים), ואמ"ל, אכן בנידן זה, ברור לע"ד
דא"א לכוין שלא לצאת יד"ח נטילת ד"מ אעפ"י שיכוין לצאת יד"ח מצות הנענועים,
ולא מיבעא בכל ימי החג לבד מראשון, דנטילת ד"מ דרבנן במצות הנענועים, אלא
אפילו ביום הראשון דנטילת ד"ח דאורייתא, ומצות עשיית הנענועים דרבנן, מ"מ אידי
ואידי כולא חדא מצוה ושם מצות נטילת ד"מ נקרא עליה, כי גם מצות הנענועים
היינו בלקיחה, וא"א לנענועים בלי לקיחה, וכשמכוין למצות הנענועים בהכרח מכוין
גם ללקיחה, ואפילו ירצה לבכר את מצות הנענועים דרבנן על פני מצות לקיחת ד"מ
דאורייתא, שזה באמת בל"ה לא נכון לעשיות כן, לא מהני כונתו, דבעל כרחו הרי מכוין
ללקיחה, ע"כ אין זו תקנה, וגם להיפוך האתרג בשעת הנענועים א"א כי א"כ גם יד"ח
הנענועים לא יצא דגם בנענועים צריך כדרך גדילתן, ובעיקר דין זה אם נכון להשהות
המצוה ולהמתין קצת על ד"מ מהודרים, או דשיהוי מצוה לא משהינן, ע' תרומת הדשן
סי' ל"ו לענין שיהוי קידוש לבנה, והביא מיבמות ל"ד, שיהוי מצוה לא משהינן, וע'
במג"א סי' כ"ה סק"ב, ובבאה"ט סי' צ' ס"ק י"א הביא מהאחרונים בזה, וע' בחת"ס
האו"ח סי' ר"ת ד"ה ומ"ש דפורים, ובהגהות מהר"ץ חיות ביומא ל"ג ד"ה אין מעבירין
עהמ"צ, ובגליון מהרש"א ביומא ו' ע"א, והנה בסוכה כ"ה: ברש"י ד"ה שחל שביעי
שלהן בע"פ, אלמא מצוה קלה הבאה לידך אינך צריך לדחותה מפני חמורה עתידה
לך עכ"ל, ויש לחלק ודו"ק, וע' באה"ע רס"י תרמ"ח ובשע"ת סי' תרנ"א סקי"ז, וע'
פמ"ג בפתיחה הכוללת סוף חלק ה', ויש לי בזה אריכות דברים בספרי נתיב הדעת
(כת"י) ביו"ד סי' ש"ה לענין פדיון בכור ואכמ"ל, ונראה להלכה ולמעשה דלהמתין
על מהודרים שיבואו לאחר שעה ושתים, אין מחוסר זמן לבו ביום ומשהינן שפיר כדי
לעשות מן המובחר, וע' גם בבאה"ט ושע"ת ריש סי' תרע"ג, אכן קצ"ע אם יזדמן
כה"ג שבד"מ אלו שאינם מהודרים כ"כ יוכל לצאת שם ידי מצות הנענועים בשעת
ההלל, ומשא"כ במהודרים שיביאו לו אחר זמן התפלה וההלל, ואפילו אם יוכל לעשות
בהן גם הנענועים מ"מ יפסיד ע"י זה אמירת ההלל ועשיית הנענועים בצבור, אם ג"כ
ימתין, ואפשר לומר דימתין כדי לקיים עיקר מצות לקיחה במהודרים אפי' ביום ב'
בלקיחה נמי דרבנן, ויש לפלפל בזה.

ב) ואשר שאל עוד אם הא דאין אומרים לאדם חטא כדי שיזכה חברך, הוא אפילו אם
יזכו רבים, דבר זה מבואר בכמה דוכת' בתוס', ע' שבת ד'. ד"ה וכי שכתבו ג' תירוצים
וחילוקים. א', דדוקא היכי דע"י שזה לא יחטא יבא חברו לידי חטא וכעין הא דעירובין
ל"ב: מוטב דליעבד חבר איסורא זוטא כי היכי דלא ליעבד ע"ה רבה, הוא דאומרים
לאדם חטא בשביל שיזכה ולא יחטא חברך, וכ"ה דעת הרשב"א ז"ל הובא בב"י או"ח
סי' ש"ו עיי"ש והב"י שם בשו"ע, וע' ט"ז שם, ובמ"א ס"ק כ"ט, ס"ל כתי' ב' דהיכי
דלא פשע חברו אומרים לזה חטא בשביל שיזכה חברך שלא פשע ע"ש, וכן במג"א
סי' תרנ"ה, ובחי' ג' רחבו, וכן בעירובין שם ופסחים פ"ח: וגיטין מ"א: ד"ה כופין,

דבמצוה דברים אמרינן ליחיד חטא בשביל שיזכו הרבים מוש"ה שיחרר ר"א עבדו ועבר בעשה כדי שיזכו הרבים להתפלל בעשרה, אך בב"ב י"ג. כתבו דשאני התם דרבי אליעזר עצמו גם כן זכה שהתפלל בעשרה וכה"ג לאו חטא בשביל שיזכה חברך הוא אלא כדי שתזכה בעצמך יע"ש, וכונתם דכה"ג הוי רק משום דעשה חמור דוחה עשה קל, ע' פסחים נ"ט. נמצא שדין זה אם אומרים לאדם חטא בשביל שיזכו הרבים תלוי בתירוצי התוס' הנ"ל ודו"ק. והרשב"א ז"ל דס"ל דס"ל היכא דלא פשע חברו אין אומרים לאדם חטא בשביל שיזכה חברו, איך יפרנס הא דמעשה בשפחה שנהגו בה מנהג הפקר וכפו את רבה ועשאוה בת חורין, דלא יועיל לדידיה תירוץ התוס' שתירצו דחשיבי כאנוסים ולא כפושעים, אע"כ יתרץ דכדי להציל ולזכות הרבים שאני וכן ראיתי עתה ברדב"ז ח"ג סי' אלף ה' (תקט"ו) וז"ל, שאלה, יהודי שכתפס בבית הסהר בשבת ואין לו מה לאכול אם מותר לאחר לומר לנכרי להוליך לו לאכול או מותב שיתענה בשבת כו' תשובה, אומר אני שדבר זה מותר, ולא משום שהוא הולך אצל אכילה וצרכי חולה שאב"ס נעשים ע"י נכרי בשבת חדא דאין זה זה חולה דכמה בנ"א מתענים יום אחד ואינם חולים, ותו דאין מתירין אמירה לנכרי כדי שלא יבא החולי ועדיין לא בא, ואי משום עונג שבת אין אומרים לזה חטא באמירה לנכרי שבות כדי שיזכה זה בעונג שבת, אלא הטעם דמצרים כולה דלתותיה נעולות בלילה והיא רשות היחיד כו' עכ"ל. ודוחק לומר דמיירי שהיהודי שנתפש פשע בזה ובפשיעתו נתפס דהו"ל לפרש הכי, אלא ודאי אפי' אינו פושע ואשם בדבר תפיסתו ס"ל לרדב"ז דאין אומרים לאדם חטא בשביל שיזכה חברו וכרשב"א ז"ל. וע' בנוב"ת חאהע"ז סי' קכ"ז סי' קנ"ז ובתשו' הרשב"א שהביא שם ודו"ק, ואחשוב שנמצא אריכות בחקירה זו בספר שדי חמד בחלק הכללים שאין ת"י.

הק' שלום יוסף הלוי פייגענבוים חופ"ק לאקאטש.

The Postwar Pursuit of American Jewish History and the Memory of the Holocaust

Hasia Diner

In 1947, when the Hebrew Union College in Cincinnati launched the American Jewish Archives (AJA), a repository of original documents and a library of published works, it projected the Holocaust into its institutional rationale. The director of the AJA, historian Jacob Rader Marcus, enumerated in the first issue of the archives' journal the various reasons why American Jewry needed to collect and study the documents of its past, and among them he declared, "American Jewry is at this moment the largest surviving body of Jews in any one country." The fact of its "surviving," for Marcus, cast the founding of the research institution into the Holocaust context. Marcus extended this theme further, at the very beginning of the article, stating bluntly, "These United States today shelter 5,000,000 Jews, almost one-half of the 11,000,000 who have survived the Hitler era."[1]

That Marcus placed this archival undertaking, devoted to the study of the American Jewish past, into the reality of the horrific events of the "Hitler era" reflected much about American Jewish culture during the early postwar period. With a twinned sense of foreboding and obligation, the Jews of the United States—teachers, writers, community leaders, scholars, and rabbis, among others—recognized some hard facts that went beyond a sense of collective anguish over the mammoth losses endured by the Jewish people, although that anguish pervaded the Jewish public arena.

Europe, which had provided American Jews with rabbis, teachers, intellectuals, ideas, and texts, for all intents and purposes no longer existed. For centuries, American Jewry, long considered a cultural and intellectual backwater in the Jewish world, took, and Europe gave. That dynamic, which had in fact been more complicated than that, had come to grinding halt, however. Now the Jews of the United States could only rely upon themselves for all that they had once imported from the "mother lode" of Europe. As they repeatedly stated, American Jews, through their schools, seminaries, publications, and other agencies for the production of cultural works, had to fill the void left by the Germans' violence. They had to move in and occupy the space once peopled by the Jews of Europe.

In the postwar era, Jewish community leaders in the United States, across a broad spectrum of ideologies and opinions as to what constituted the essence of Jewishness, asked themselves and the Jewish public repeatedly whether they had the cultural wherewithal to shoulder the burden that the gruesome recent history had so dramatically thrust upon them. Across that same spectrum, most admitted, with regret, that as American Jewry then functioned, the answer would have to be no. The Jews who made their home in the open, materialistic, and individualistic environment of the United States did not, as they saw it, possess the Jewish authenticity, collective consciousness, and passion needed for the task. There were, however, partisans for projects of various kinds, including the study of American Jewish history, who offered solutions to the problem they faced, namely, how to invigorate Jewish life in America as an antidote to the losses sustained in Europe.

American Jewry, as represented in the output of its organizations and its organs of public opinion, in the written and spoken words that resounded in the public sphere of what might be labeled, for lack of a better term, "the American Jewish community," fretted over the Jewish future. Those whose words appeared in sermons, speeches, articles, and books, regardless of their ideological orientation—be it Orthodox, Reform, Conservative, Reconstructionist, secular Yiddishist, or Zionist—converged on a recognition that the prospects for creative and dynamic Jewish life in America hung in the balance. They worried over the future of Jewish life in America in part because they understood that only an energized and group-conscious Jewish polity would undertake the many philanthropic and political challenges that the Jewish people, at home and abroad, faced.

Communal activists, again representing a spectrum of opinions, considered among other possible solutions that studying and celebrating the American Jewish past could stimulate Jewish consciousness and might be a way to get "ordinary" American Jews to contribute to Jewish causes and be politically conscious of their place in the American and world contexts. As they marshaled the facts, anecdotes, and details of American Jewish history, they also turned to the Holocaust, bringing these two together in ways that might on the surface have seemed to stretch the imagination.

In this context, the field of American Jewish history, as both a scholarly enterprise and a matter of popular interest in the Jewish world, owed its origins in part to the devastating impact of the deaths of Europe's six million Jews. That it "took off" in terms of ever-more publications, projects, and public awareness in the years immediately after the end of World War II than in previous decades ought not to be seen as just an accident of history. Marcus announced AJA's opening just two years after the war had come to an end, a moment in time when America and American Jewry recognized the brutal fact that one-third of the Jewish people, 90 percent of those who lived in Europe, had been murdered. He made amply clear in his statement that the need for an archive that housed the raw material on American Jewish history and that stimulated the scholarly use of it could not be disassociated from the recent tragedy.

While the AJA might have come into being even without the horror of the Holocaust, the European "catastrophe," a word commonly used in to denote the Holocaust in the early postwar years, played a role in stimulating interest in the history of American Jews. It also played a role in communal leaders across the spectrum of American Jewish life calling for even more such knowledge. Whether they envisioned an efflorescence of "pure" scholarship or whether they tied references to American Jewish history with references to the catastrophe, Jewish leaders, in their lectures, speeches, articles, and pedagogic works for Jewish children, made clear that the details of American Jewish history needed to be understood in light of the Holocaust.

Clearly, the roots of American Jewish history, in both its amateur and semi-academic forms, lay in an era more distant than the postwar period. The founding of the American Jewish Historical Society (AJHS) in 1892 showed that the Holocaust had no part in its creation and early development. The Society and its members produced books and articles on various aspects of American Jewish history long before the 1930s and 1940s.[2]

But like many other American Jewish projects of the postwar years, the stark turn of events on the world stage made an impact upon undertakings launched earlier and under different circumstances. The Holocaust lent new urgency to preexisting Jewish cultural ventures, gave them a boost, and provided them with a new rationale.[3]

The catastrophe of European Jewry that left an immediate and tangible mark on American Jewry did, however, stimulate historians and other Jewish communal activists to think about American Jewish history, refer to it, and use it as a way to keep alive the memory of the tragic events in Europe. From the late 1940s into the early 1960s, these historians and activists employed American Jewish history in ways that they had not before and integrated it into their communal activities with direct citation to the European tragedy.

Marcus was actually not the first historian to exhort American Jews to study their history in the name of the extirpated Jews of Europe. Columbia University historian Salo Baron had preceded him in this, and Baron had not waited until the end of World War II, with the full revelation of the exact scope of the slaughter, to connect the catastrophe with the desideratum of furthering the study of American Jewish history. At a 1942 event celebrating the 450th anniversary of Columbus's "discovery of America," as the ominous news from Europe made its way to America, Baron called upon American Jews to study their own history. While he noted that the moment, with the gloom of the war and the unfolding tragedy of European Jews in front of them, seemed inauspicious for American Jews to think about themselves and their past, he warned that since "the fate of the Jewish people is being decided now for generations to come," American Jews needed to contemplate and systematically study their own history. Baron predicted that American Jewry would, as a result of the Nazi juggernaut, emerge as the largest Jewish community in the world and would therefore dominate world Jewish events. A community with such a responsibility, he believed, needed to have a sense of its own history, the study of which ought not to be relegated to amateurs and pushed to the margins of communal concern.[4]

This kind of thinking resounded among the makers of American Jewish culture. The Jewish Publication Society (JPS) of America issued a press release in 1948, advertising the publication of Lee M. Friedman's *Pilgrims in a New Land*, a history of American Jewry. That document stated directly, "History has now forced us, for the first time, into a dominant role in the life of world-Jewry. Whether we are mature enough or not . . . leadership is ours. . . . The heart-rending duties of fund-raising for our brethren in the DP camps and for resettlement in Palestine will demand . . . less of our time and energy." The time had come, JPS said, to "develop our genuinely creative American Jewry."

Publication projects of all kinds in the postwar years made the point that the Holocaust's bitter reality demanded that American Jews know something about themselves and where they came from. In 1947, Rabbi Abraham Scheinberg, editor of *American Jews: Their Lives and Achievements*, justified his book in terms of the "six million European Jews [who] have perished in an orgy of mass murder unparalleled in history" and the fact that "the five-and-a-quarter millions of American Jews," who constituted "a half of the total world Jewish population" are "the most numerous, the most prosperous, the freest among all the Jewries of the Diaspora." Scheinberg asked the era's ubiquitous American Jewish question: "Now that European Jewish life lies in ruins, what do we here in the United States have in the way of human material that makes for Jewish vitality and Jewish survival here and elsewhere? What are we contributing to Jewish life in our own country?" To find the answer, he suggested, not surprisingly, that American Jews learn more about themselves by turning to his book.[5]

Two years later, the AJHS announced the first observance of "Jewish

History Week," taking as its cue the interrelated phenomena that most of the "great communities of Europe" had ceased to exist and that the American Jewish community had reached its "coming of age."[6]

On the surface, the writing of American Jewish history, particularly in the decades immediately following the Holocaust, had no place for those tragic events. They had not only played out far from the United States, but they also comprised only a small portion of a history that spanned several hundred years. Historical works that covered the middle of the seventeenth century onward had few pages to devote to the events in Europe in the 1930s through the middle of the 1940s.

But, writers found ways to weave the Holocaust into their master narrative, a tricky project that required intellectual ingenuity. Anita Lebson, in her 1950 *Pilgrim People*, proved to be particularly creative. When writing about the sympathy expressed by the broad American public to the Jewish victims of the Russian pogroms at the end of the nineteenth century and the early twentieth, she interjected, "Perhaps some day the historian of the future will be wise enough to explain why Americans took the Jewish massacres of 1881–1906 to heart and not those of 1933–1945." She dubbed the 1930s as the eve of "destruction and annihilation," and in her chapter on that grim period, she celebrated American Jewry's rescue efforts, including the work of Henrietta Szold, the founder of Youth Aliyah, which saved children from Hitler's Europe. Szold, Lebson wrote, "knew the anguish of deepest mourning for the millions who died in the crematoria and concentration camps of Germany."[7]

Elma Ehrlich Levinger's 1954 *Jewish Adventures in America* brought the Holocaust into communal celebration of three hundred years of American Jewish history. Writing about philanthropist Nathan Straus, who had been dead several years before Hitler gained power, Levinger described Straus's relief for European Jewry during World War I. "His death," she consoled her readers, "spared him the knowledge of the horrors of the Hitler persecution." To Levinger, the history of American Jewry could not be disassociated from recent history, when "six million Jews, not only those of German birth but . . . from German-conquered territory, perished in cattle cars, in concentration camps and crematoria."[8]

1954 and the Tercentenary: A Chance to Tell the Story

The American Jewish tercentenary proved particularly opportune for Jews to write the Holocaust into their American lives. Levinger's book, a text very much part of the three hundredth anniversary output, provided one such example. Another came from Harvard University historian Oscar Handlin, who put the Holocaust on the first page of his 1954 *Adventures in Freedom: Three Hundred Years of Jewish Life in America*. Published by McGraw-Hill, one the country's most prestigious presses, Handlin's volume opened by quite whiggishly asserting that American Jews deserved to feel quite self-congratulatory as a result of "our record of achievements; the great deeds performed, the contributions to the welfare of our fellow man, the prosperity, recognition and status we have attained." He then shifted gears, however, and went on in a decidedly different tone as he introduced his history, in fact the first scholarly history of the Jews of the United States and, for sure, the first published by a professor at a major American university:

Yet we should be remiss in our duties to ourselves were we to limit our commemoration to these thoughts. The year we celebrate is 1654; but we cannot forget that the year in which we celebrate is 1954. Nor can we, in the midst of our joy and well-being, blot out from memory the tragic decade that has just closed. Honesty demands that as we celebrate we have in mind the stark facts of our present situation. Jews have recovered from the shock of the six million victims of the European catastrophe.[9]

So too the public programming surrounding the 1954 celebrations of 1654, the speeches and gatherings, drew a direct connection between those three centuries of Jewish life in America and the shadow that the Holocaust cast on the Jewish present. Rabbi Israel Goldstein over the course of 1954 delivered a set of lectures around the country and abroad about the meaning of the anniversary. Published as *American Jewry Comes of Age*, this relatively small book abounded with Holocaust references. Their profusion indicated the degree to which those who thought about the experience of Jews in the United States in the 1950s refracted it through the lens of the catastrophe. Because of its fortunate history, Goldstein declared, "American Jewry . . . should bear its good fortune . . . with humility toward all other Jewries, and especially toward European Jewry at whose breast it had nursed. Alas, so many Jewish centers in Europe are only a shadow of their former selves—Vilna, Warsaw, Vienna, Prague, Frankfurt, Amsterdam, Antwerp. . . . Can American Jewry make up . . . for these casualties?" In valorizing American Jewish charity and communal activism, he bemoaned that "no effort of ours could have availed to save the six million who were destroyed by Hitler," and as he described the first Jews who arrived in New Amsterdam in 1654, Goldstein noted, "They were refugees. After them there came successive waves . . . down to the recent chapter of our time with its black Hitler era."[10]

In the mid-1950s, as part of the tercentenary, individuals who called for the systematic study of American Jewish history referred to the catastrophe as one reason to do so. At the April 1953 conference to plan the nationwide history project, sponsored by mainstream organizations such as the American Jewish Committee, Goldstein reminded those assembled that in the years since the 250th celebration at the beginning of the century, "the greatest shock which these fifty years brought has been Nazi Germany's demonstration of the lowest depths to which human nature can sink. . . . The Jewish people . . . has felt the progress of these years and has suffered as the chief 'man of sorrows' from the tragedy of these years. . . . Of Europe's nine to ten million Jews, two-thirds fell victim to Nazi extermination." And "because of these casualties Jewish life can never be the same in the years and generations ahead." Therefore, he said, American Jews needed to contemplate their own past.[11]

Community programming that year paid homage to the Holocaust, integrating it into the history of American Jewry. A speaker at the February 1954 National Federation of Temple Sisterhoods Biennial Assembly gave her version of recent American Jewish history, a history that she asserted fundamentally changed the consciousness of American Jews:

> With the advent of Hitler, even the most apologistic [*sic*] Jew realized that whatever his status in the community in which

he lived, no matter how he had or tried to assimilate, he was a Jew and Hitler and the world intended that he be constantly reminded of this fact. So, many ethnic and assimilationist Jews became intelligent, practicing Jews. They learned or re-learned the story of their people and became strong."[12]

Works of all sorts conjoined the tercentenary and the Holocaust. YIVO Institute for Jewish Research historian Abraham Menes, writing for *Judaism*'s special three hundredth anniversary issue, put the American Jewish experience and the Holocaust together in demographic and nearly religious terms: "Tragic and painful beyond compare as the catastrophe in Europe has been for us," he mourned, "it would have been still more crushing to us as a people had it not been preceded by the miracle of mass immigration from Europe which commenced in the 1880's." Menes made the "pioneers of the East Side," the Jewish women and men who had settled in New York at the turn of the century, into a kind of "saving remnant," since they "played a leading role in bringing about this miracle."[13]

The Zionist magazine *Midstream* entered the world of American Jewish journalism during the tercentenary year, and historian and Zionist philosopher Ben Halpern's article, "America is Different," fittingly appeared in its premier issue. Halpern speculated on the irony that the "celebrations of the American Jewish community . . . chanced to come at a time when we American Jews, after the destruction of the six million who were the main body of Jewry and the immediate source of our traditions, remain as the major part of all the Jews in the diaspora." Halpern considered that destruction to be the defining event of the American Jewish present, as it had transformed Jewish life:

Without European Jewry, the face of the Jewish problem as it appears to American Jews is radically altered and in a way simplified. Hitherto, thoughts about the Jewish problem . . . were based upon our European traditions, and no less, upon our involvement with the European Jewish situation. But now we live in a Jewish world where essentially, we see only two main constituents: ourselves, American Jews, and the State of Israel.[14]

Beyond the Tercentenary

As American Jews wrote and spoke about their communal past, as they presented their histories and as they contemplated their present circumstances, they continually referred to the Nazi's destruction of European Jewry. Rather than seeking to suppress this painful story, they instead searched for and found seemingly limitless opportunities to show what had happened. After 1954, postwar history projects on the experience of Jews in the United States, intended for multiple audiences, placed the Holocaust in that narrative. Morris U. Schappes, in his 1958 *The Jews of the United States: A Pictorial History, 1654– Present*, conformed to the dominant trope. He chronicled in detail what had happened, "The six million dead, victims of Nazism, were two-thirds of the Jews of Europe, and more than one-third of all the Jews in the world." He invoked the "human ashes of the crematoria" and valorized the State of Israel as the by-product of the catastrophe.[15]

Much of the postwar rhetoric that yoked the Holocaust to the study of American Jewish history focused on the rising generation of American Jews. These girls and boys would become the women and men who would lead and contribute to American Jewish life. Rabbis, pedagogues, communal activists, and others hoped that American Jewish stories drawn from the Holocaust era would inspire the next generation to shape and sustain Jewish culture and to take up the reins of Jewish life. Reform leader Albert Vorspan in 1960 published *Giants of Justice*, biographical sketches of American Jews who paid heed to the "prophetic tradition" that exhorted Jews to live by the words, "justice, justice shalt thou pursue." He made much of the tragedy of European Jewry in his heroic portraits of a group of "giants"—American Jews who combined love of their people with public service. Louis Brandeis, Vorspan described, had retired from the U.S. Supreme Court in 1939 but continued to be a public voice:

> [He] was unwilling to rust away his last years in a rocking chair. There was still too much to do. Even before his retirement, the Nazi extermination of Jews had compelled him to break his customary judicial reserve and appeal to the President to do all in his power to prevent the impending termination of immigration to Palestine.

Brandeis failed, but he did not give up and "even in the grim moments of Nazi butchery, he never despaired of the ultimate triumph of the democracies and of the imperishability of Jewish ideals and aspirations." Lillian Wald also spent her final years of life consumed with the "deathly tragedy of Nazism," while Henry Monsky of the B'nai B'rith lobbied, organized, pleaded, and spoke out as he tried to do something about the "savage massacre of European Jewry by Hitler." Vorspan chronicled other American Jewish "giants of justice," too—Henrietta Szold, David Dubinsky, Stephen Wise, Abraham Cronbach, Herbert Lehman—all of whom had led public lives that touched upon the Holocaust. Vorspan wrote this book not purely as history. He hoped to inspire his audience "native-born . . . and middle class," Jews who "have imbibed the values of middle-class America; conformist, complacent, acquisitive, with success and money the gods to be worshipped." He wanted them to advocate for justice in America, not to lapse "into guilty silence and moral neutrality." Vorspan noted that, "[T]his generation has been moved and shaped . . . by the profound experience of Hitlerism and the destruction of 6,000,000 Jews." As to the future, he hoped young American Jews would also consider that tragedy so that when they became adults, they would think about "the survival of Jewish identity and ethical values in Judaism."[16]

From a very different place on the American Jewish scene, advocates for Yiddish education discerned a connection between incorporating American Jewish history in their youth work and the legacy of the *hurban*, "the destruction," the word used most often in Yiddish lectures, publications, and general parlance when referring to the Holocaust. In the early postwar period, Yiddish advocates disseminated the message that they, more often and more effectively than others, linked American Jewry with the martyred millions and here, as in much of their rhetoric, they made American Jewish history part of an organic story. In the 1950s, the Workmen's Circle issued Yiddish and English flyers and pamphlets, "shule" (or "school") propaganda, to convince parents to send their children to Jewish schools, particularly its institutions. One brochure intoned:

Don't neglect your child's Jewish education. The Workmen's Circle School acquaints the child with Jews in America, who in so short a time trod the path from the sweatshop to great accomplishments; with Jews in Palestine who turned swamps and wilderness into a fruitful land and a home for persecuted brethren; with the Jews of Eastern Europe from which we or our parents came and where despite the terrible Hitler atrocities Jewish life will again flourish.

Messages like this fused together three powerful forces—Jewish success in America, the flowering of Jewish life in Israel, and the "Hitler atrocities," and provided the rationale for educating American Jewish children.[17]

Much of the conjoining of the Holocaust and American Jewish history stemmed from a sense of communal urgency, a desire on the part of the leadership to prod American Jews to become "better" Jews and make up for the toll exacted upon the Jewish people, regardless of how much they differed as to what constituted being a "good" Jew. Yet at the same time, more practical needs stimulated that rhetorical twinning.

The Jews of the United States faced a very realistic challenge in the postwar years. They alone, among the worldwide Jewish people, had the numbers and the financial ability to raise money to help the Jews who managed to survive "the terrible Hitler atrocities." Millions had to be raised annually to succor those in the Displaced Persons camps in Europe, those who emigrated to Israel, and those who came to the United States. Moreover, American Jewish agencies drew a connection between the massive fundraising effort on behalf of the survivors and the history of the Jews in America, most of whose parents and grandparents had immigrated as relatively impoverished immigrants. The Jewish Labor Committee (JLC) laid this argument out in the pamphlet *Scope and Theme: American Jewish Tercentenary 1654–1954*, a document for use by unions and other groups affiliated with the JLC "on how to celebrate" the anniversary. The anonymous author began by admitting that, "History has made of the American Jewish community the largest Jewish community in the world. This community, in the American and the Jewish tradition, has had a record of concern for the rights and the well-being of Jews in other parts of the world," particularly as it helped the "refugees and displaced persons during and since the Hitler holocaust." The goal could not be clearer. The JLC hoped that attendees of three hundredth anniversary programs would learn from their history as American Jews about the needs of the Holocaust survivors and would use that knowledge to dig even deeper into their pockets to raise the much-needed money.

This fusion of American Jewish history and the needs of the survivors provided a leitmotif of the postwar period, the early years in particular, when the needs proved to be most acute. This conjoining of the episodes from American Jewish history and American Jews' responsibility to aid the Holocaust survivors took place on the national and local levels and could be heard in communities across the country, as fundraising efforts proceeded.

The Jews of Charleston, South Carolina, for example, employed this rhetorical strategy as they turned to drama to advocate for the Hebrew Immigrant Aid Society (HIAS) to settle survivors in their city. In the winter of 1950, they staged an elaborate, well-financed extravaganza marking the bicentennial of Jewish settlement in the colony, then state. The planning committee hired New York playwright Sam Byrd to write a script on the community's history and staged his work, "For Those Who Live in the Sun," at Charleston's Dock Street Theater. It involved a huge cast of costumed characters, including nineteenth century poet Penina Moïse; Francis Salvador, a hero of the American Revolution, and Judah P. Benjamin, the "Brains of the Confederacy." Roles included Native Americans, British soldiers, Confederate soldiers, late nineteenth century Jewish immigrants, and good-hearted, welcoming non-Jewish Charlestonians. Dancers and singers recreated an 1880s Purim Ball. Local Jewish history provided the motif and rationale for the play.

But, in fact, "For Those Who Live in the Sun" and the entire two hundredth anniversary festivity had been intended to raise both awareness about the survivors of the Holocaust, particularly those who had been brought to Charleston, and to collect money to assist them as they went about the process of building new lives. The play opened in "Barracks 17, Displaced Persons Center, Foehrenwald, Bavaria, and the Center Administrative Office" and took place on "A November night, 1950." As the play moved back to the mid-eighteenth century, narrating two centuries of "the Jews of Charleston," it simultaneously told, over and over again, "the story of the Schumans, the small displaced family from Poland whose hope in life was to reach Charleston." David, Anna, and Lisa Schumann surfaced in every era as time-traveler witnesses to the evolution of this little piece of American Jewish history. The Schuman family portrayed in this historical drama appeared on stage at the end of every scene, each of which corresponded to an era in the history of this Jewish community, and they commented, positively, about what they had just seen. They spoke of finding a place "in the sun," in Charleston or some other American community, for themselves and other survivors. Their words served simultaneously as a tribute to Charleston, a place that had historically manifested low levels of antisemitism and relatively high rates of economic mobility, and as a call to the women and men in the audience to remember the tragedy and to contribute their funds and goodwill to the "new Americans," like the Schumans, who had come to South Carolina.

As if the drama had not been obvious enough, the program book for the play, handed out to all who attended, included a piece written by the executive director of the local Jewish social service agency which made the same point but without drama and much more directly. Holocaust survivors, he told the audience members, had come to Charleston. They need services and the good will of the city's residents who ought to welcome these newest newcomers. Thus, woven into the historic narrative of the Jewish experience in the Palmetto State was the fact that some survivors had begun to find a new life "in the sun," and Charlestonians should help them make that a reality. American Jewish history, in this case a local variant of the national narrative, served then a very practical, indeed urgent, need.

The dramatic device of making Holocaust survivors key characters in a pageant marking two centuries of a southern Jewish community spoke volumes about postwar American Jewry. The play allowed the local Jewish community to show how long it had been present in South Carolina and how crucial a role Jews had played in making American and local history possible. The three-hour extravaganza also allowed them to demonstrate to the estimated two thousand attendees, and the larger number who read reviews in the local newspapers, how deeply they felt their responsibility toward the survivors of the Holocaust, some of whom, in 1950, still found themselves in Foehrenwald, the last of the Displaced Persons Camps, and those who now had resettled in Charleston.[18]

This play, a small detail of relatively little import in and of itself, reflected the communal culture as a whole. Leaders turned to American Jewish history to stimulate Jewish consciousness and to foster financial giving to survivors. They also used it to try to come to terms with what had happened and how the world, including the United States, to which they professed profound loyalty, had allowed the unimaginable—the systematic slaughter millions of Jews—to happen. In the texts they produced from the mid-1940s through the early 1960s, a politically charged era characterized by intense anti-Communism and hyperpatriotism, writers, commentators, and others who referred to the history of the era demonstrated a willingness to point out America's complicity. They did this because they considered that the United States had not asserted any leadership or courage in the face of the Hitler menace, and they did so as a way to analyze the history of American antisemitism. This theme provided historians and those who referred to historical events with a means to integrate the decidedly negative history of anti-Jewish sentiment in America into the otherwise upbeat narrative of the American Jewish past.

Historian Oscar Handlin, who had eloquently introduced his chronicle of three centuries of American Jewish history with his reference to the deaths of the six million, took up this issue of American antisemitism in 1948. He and coauthor Mary Flug Handlin addressed it in an Anti-Defamation League "Freedom Pamphlet," *Danger in Discord: Origins of Anti-Semitism in the United States.* "Hitler," the Handlins wrote, "did not have to rely exclusively upon Germans to do his work for him in the United States." Instead the two historians noted that many Americans had in the 1930s approved of the ways, "the German government plunged ever deeper into the paths of anti-Semitism." This forty-page pamphlet covered the years up to 1941, but two sections, "The Shadow of Hitlerism" and "Elements of American Fascism," briefly but clearly showed how antisemitism in America had operated in tandem with antisemitism in Germany. While the booklet, like much of Handlin's public history work, glorified the American system, it made clear that some Americans, including elected officials, accepted that "the Nazi persecution of the Jews was necessary to save western civilization from the menace of world Jewry."[19] Handlin documented this same history in a 1955 article in the *American Jewish Year Book*, noting that, "clear echoes of the doctrines preached and practiced in Germany" had been uttered on the floor of the U.S. Congress. He carried this theme into his 1954 *Adventures in Freedom,* in which he pointed out how the lethal brew of isolationism, antisemitism, and pro-Nazi sympathies made America a partner in the destruction of European Jewry. "Hitler," wrote Handlin about the years leading up to World War II, had in America, "[N]ative tools, working for their own interests," who "served his purposes," namely, the demonization of the Jews, including those in the United States.[20]

In 1959, Handlin ghostwrote *A Nation of Immigrants,* funded by the Anti-Defamation League and issued under the name of the junior senator from Massachusetts, John F. Kennedy, then seeking the Democratic nomination for the presidency. In this book, Handlin emphasized how some Americans had, during the interwar years, participated in global antisemitism, and how that had led the United States government to abet in the devastation of the Jewish people. The book was Kennedy's campaign call for immigration reform, and several captioned photographs told this story. On a page divided by text, the top featured a snapshot of a Nazi book burning, a "symbol of the Nazi cancer that was to consume so much of Europe," while the bottom showed physicist Albert Einstein and his daughter, taking the oath to become United States citizens. The text between the two images read:

> With the rise of Hitler and virulent anti-Semitism in the 1930's, millions of Jews tried desperately to escape from Germany and Nazi-occupied countries. Many nations of Europe, as well as the United States, were reluctant to admit the despairing multitudes. Before the end, six million Jews had died in concentration camps and gas chambers.[21]

Although Kennedy's face appeared on the book's cover, the voice was Handlin's, as he criticized United States policy in the years surrounding the Holocaust and drew a line that connected immigration policy and the fate of the six million.

Other individuals writing for Jewish publications concurred with this, chiding the United States for its indifference during the Holocaust. In 1954, Irving Lehrman and Joseph Rappaport produced a brochure-length history of the Jews of Miami and told in it of the tragedy of the "S.S. *St. Louis* . . . carrying over nine-hundred Jewish escapees from Hitlerism." U.S. immigration officials denied the ship and its passengers the right to dock, and despite the efforts of the National Council of Jewish Women and the Greater Miami Jewish Federation, the *St. Louis* was "forced to return across the ocean" and became "an ill-fated harbinger of the cataclysm that was soon to strike."[22] The story of the *St. Louis* had entered into American Jewish public culture four years earlier. In October 1950, an episode of "The Eternal Light," a weekly radio program sponsored by the Jewish Theological Seminary, told the story of "Landau," a man living in Israel, who revealed to a friend that as a young man he had wanted to go to the United States rather than Israel. In fact, "I was a passenger on the S.S. *St. Louis*. Before the war we got so close to Florida we could see the men and women bathing at Miami. But we were turned away." When asked if he had gone to Israel immediately, he said no, he had not. Instead, "I went to a Nazi concentration camp."[23]

With the exception of Handlin's writings, none of these statements came from professional historians. Rather, amateurs and community activists began to write and speak about America's less-than-impressive role, indeed, its culpability by inaction, in the tragedy of the Hitler era. Isaiah Minkoff, in a speech he gave many times to Jewish groups in the 1950s, recalled America's isolationist policies of the 1930s. "Nazism could have been destroyed," he told the New Jersey Jewish Community Relations Council in 1956, "but people," meaning Americans, "were apathetic. 'What is it to us?' they asked. Some looked on Hitler as a mere internal German matter, his antisemitism a problem for Jews to worry about. Some said, 'Let the Germans and the Poles beat each other to death: who cares?'" Minkoff then continued. "We," the Jewish people, "paid dearly for this blissful isolationism."[24] Harry Simonhoff, a Miami attorney and travel writer with an amateur's interest in Jewish history, offered a piece in 1959 on "F.D.R. and the Jews." In it, he contrasted "F.D.R.'s reputation as the great friend of the Jews" with the fact that "The Nazi persecutions began cautiously in 1933;

they ended in 1945 with the annihilation of 6,000,000 Jews. Through it all Roosevelt stood out as the most influential public figure in the world." Simonhoff asked his readers to consider, "What did he do to help the victims of sadistic cruelty and terror, of blood-letting and unmitigated torture? . . . Was he *really* a friend?" The brief article, based on no archival documents, answered in the negative, taking America to task for its role in that annihilation.[25] Rabbi Jack Reimer was even more passionate and accusatory. In a 1961 piece on the Eichmann trial in *Conservative Judaism*, Reimer described how, metaphorically, most nations of the world sat in the glass booth with the man who had declared, "I will go to my grave laughing because I have succeeded in killing five million Jews." Reimer did not let the United States off the hook. "When the record of what was done is published, we," meaning here not the Jews but the United States, "will have to answer to ourselves as to how it is that we did so little to stop it. We will have to explain how this country that has been able to find room for so many homeless Cubans and so many exiled Hungarians could find no room in those decisive years for those who had no place on earth to go to."[26]

When contemplating various postwar political matters, Jewish commentators turned back to what they saw as the history of America's culpability through inaction in making the Holocaust possible. For New York's Reform congregation Emanu El's Brotherhood Week in 1949, Rabbi Julius Mark lectured on "Christianity and Judaism—Wherein They Are Similar." That address, which he then reprinted in a 1959 compendium of his best sermons, criticized America's immigration policies when it came to the Jewish survivors. He looked backward in time. "Where," he declared, "were the protests, save among Jewish organizations, when not only one, not 15, but 6,000,000 human beings—men, women and little children—were not jailed, but were shamefully and cruelly done?" Isaac Rosengarten, editor of *The Jewish Forum*, also invoked Holocaust-era policy when writing about the McCarran-Walter Act, a 1952 piece of legislation that both maintained the racially based quotas inherited from the 1920s and facilitated the deportation of "subversives." In his 1959 piece, Rosengarten labeled the act a form of "Hitlerism," and in calling for changes in the law, he recalled that when "the Jews of Hitler's Germany" had found that no country, "including the U.S.A.," opened "its gates to rescue their very lives." Later, in March 1960, Rosengarten, officiating at the Judge Brandeis Awards Ceremony in New York's City Hall, reminded his audience that the United States "dilly-dallied in reacting to [Hitler's] genocidal treatment of the Jews," and now, fifteen years after the Nuremburg trials had "convicted many Nazi leaders of the most heinous crimes, our Government, in administering her supervision over Western Germany, permitted these criminals to regain respectability and return to their former positions of prominence."[27]

At times, talk about the United States as a minor player in the Holocaust spilled over into the realm of partisan politics. Jacob Glenn, a physician with an interest in American Jewish history, offered his opinions to readers of *The Jewish Forum* in the midst of the 1960 presidential campaign. Glenn blamed the Republicans for having "originated, developed and brought into existence something new in American life—the quota system of immigration that hit hard at the influx of Jewish immigration . . . and that subsequently caused the fatal bottling up of the 6,000,000 Jews."[28] Two years later, Ivan Schatten, in *The Detroit Jewish News,* turned the tables on Glenn, asking, "How can any Jew ever believe that the Democratic Party is our 'friend' any more than the Republican party?" He reminded readers that "Franklin D. Roosevelt . . . refused to allow our war-planes to bomb the railroad tracks leading up to the infamous Nazi concentration camps. This of course means that untold numbers of Jews may have been saved from slaughter if the bombings had taken place. Roosevelt and his Democrats had been in office many years, so one can not say that there was Republican influence that made F.D.R. take his action," or lack thereof.[29]

The willingness of American Jews to posit a connection between American history and the tragedy of European Jewry reflected a number of truths: that the Holocaust was central in their thinking; that they were involved in the liberal politics of the day; and that they had a comfort level in conjoining these two. These truths were set against their profound forebodings that today's security could be easily undone. The slaughter of one-third of their people had changed American Jews acutely, and they took it as a given that their place in the Jewish world had changed, as well. To make up for the losses and confront those changes with cultural strength and with wisdom, their leaders said, they needed to know where they had come from, how America had left its mark on them, and what had been the nature of their responses to other crises and tragedies in the past., As a subject to be studied, American Jewish history provided some of them, such as Jacob Rader Marcus, a potential weapon in a looming cultural campaign. They hoped it would equip the Jews of the United States to face the present and future. Although Marcus built one of the most impressive and richest repositories of material to make the study of American Jewish history possible, he hardly stood alone. He was but one American Jew who saw a direct linkage between the history of the Jews in America and the tragedy endured by the Jewish people in Europe at the hands of Germany and its allies in the 1930s and 1940s.

The Historical Consciousness of Mid-Century American Reform Judaism and the Historiography of Ellis Rivkin

Robert M. Seltzer

Wissenschaft des Judentums, the critical study of Judaism and the Jews according to modern historiographical methods, was a decisive influence in the formative decades of Reform Judaism. Abraham Geiger and his colleagues were convinced that the scientific study of Jewish history provided a ground for adjusting Judaism to the "spirit of the times."[1] The importance of modern historical consciousness is evident in the formal Pittsburgh (1875) and Columbus (1937) Platforms of the Reform movement in America. To be sure, its centrality appears to have diminished in the wake of experience-oriented theologies and what has been called "midrashic existentialism," which emphasize direct encounter rather than academic *Wissenschaft*.[2] However, Jewish historical consciousness in the broad, scientific sense was still a prime concern to numerous postwar Reform rabbinical students from the 1940s to at least the 1970s. This essay will deal with aspects of the historiography of Ellis Rivkin, the most comprehensive theorist of the entire Jewish past associated with twentieth-century American Reform Judaism and the history teacher of so many Reform rabbis in the second half of the century.[3]

Rivkin's books, essays, reviews, and published lectures cover a remarkable range of subjects: religious leadership in ancient Israel; the origins of the synagogue; the Pharisees; the crucifixion of Jesus; the religiosity of Paul and the parting of the ways between Christianity and Judaism; Saadia Gaon's rivalry with the exilarch in Baghdad; the Aristotelianism of Maimonides; the putative Jewishness of Conversos (the so-called Marranos) during the heyday of the Spanish Inquisition and the scope of their international trading entrepreneurship; the life and thought of Leon da Modena; and the causal matrix of the Holocaust.[4] Few Jewish historians have done original research in so many diverse topics. As a teacher and lecturer Rivkin excelled. He sought, in his classes and through his popular talks and writings, to bring out the meaning of Jewish history as a whole, an increasingly problematic undertaking. Because of the fragmentation of Judaica into specialized sub-fields and the proliferation of detailed studies, it requires immense effort, time, and concentration to integrate this new scholarship into an exact and comprehensive portrait of Judaism through the ages.[5]

In the last few decades terms have surfaced for a wide variety of general historical sub-fields, such as psychohistory, gender history, demographic history, ecohistory, and even "subaltern" and "sensory history." Among these are also microhistory and macrohistory. Usually, history-writing recounts the interactions of individuals over a significant duration of time in the form of a narrative in which the historian interweaves his or her understanding of relevant decisions, motives, pressures, emotions, immediate "factors" and principal "causes." Microhistory focuses on close-up, small-scale happenings hitherto overlooked by historians, while macrohistory offers sweeping views of a "long durée" in the terminology of the *Annales* School or, at the extreme, a universal account of human past based on or used to substantiate a philosophy of history.[6] The dichotomy of microhistory/macrohistory brings to mind the aphorism of the ancient Greek poet Archilochus via Isaiah Berlin: "The hedgehog knows one big thing, while the fox knows many little things."[7] The fox is the microhistorian, expert in archival and other forms of meticulous research, investigating a delimited historical moment in its uniqueness. The microhistorian seeks to retrieve aspects of the past that offer insight into ordinary life in a town or village at a certain time, or about a minor but representative individual for whom records survived by accident. The hedgehog is the macrohistorian who depicts sweeping processes against the most comprehensive horizon possible, looking for comparative patterns, hidden cycles, and slow drifts that can be perceived at an altitude from which individuals shrink or disappear.

Although Rivkin has written important microhistorical works, as a macrohistorian he is in a class by himself in twentieth-century Jewish historiography.[8] (He himself uses neither term.) As a macrohistorian, Rivkin offered his students a sweeping vision of the entire Jewish past. This paper will attempt to explain Rivkin's influence on a cadre of Reform rabbinical students (and therefore on a generation of Reform rabbis) from the time he became a member of the faculty of Hebrew Union College in 1949 until— and beyond— his retirement in 1988.

* * * *

Ellis Rivkin was born in Baltimore on 7 September 1918 (Rosh Hashanah 5679), to a fervently Orthodox family of *mitnaggedic* (anti-Hasidic) persuasion. His mother was born in the United States and his father came from Lithuania. In Jewish parlance, Ellis is a *Litvak* by descent and by proclivity. He was sent to Hebrew school before he began public school, and, after becoming bar mitzvah, attended services every morning at a synagogue several miles from his home— a synagogue composed of educated people, many of German-Jewish origin. His family was highly respected for its piety, and Ellis's observance became even more intense in his teenage years. There was even talk of sending him to one of the still-flourishing yeshivas of interwar Poland.[9]

After graduating high school, Rivkin studied Talmud with a private tutor and enrolled at the Baltimore Hebrew College. The dean was Dr. Louis Kaplan, a Conservative Jew who, in Rivkin's words, "tried to wean me away from extreme Orthodoxy with philosophy, but I always had an answer for him." Rivkin remembered that "it was not the study of philosophy that changed my mind; it was the study of history. I had acquired a wonderful young teacher, Harry M. Orlinsky, who was doing post-graduate work at Johns Hopkins University."[10] (Orlinsky joined the faculty of the Jewish Institute of Religion (JIR) and later of the Hebrew Union College (HUC) when the latter merged with JIR in 1950. He would become a distinguished biblical scholar.) Orlinsky taught post-biblical Jewish history in a way that opened Rivkin's eyes to the ubiquity of historical change. "The notion of constant development over time forced me to ask how I can sustain the claim that change does not occur in a supernatural Torah. Do not the same historical laws apply to Jewish history as to non-Jewish history? I concluded that they did. . . . Ideas change; beliefs change; the image of God changes. This principle applies to the biblical era as well."[11] As a result, Rivkin accepted that the Torah was a composite work which came into being as a result of a long drawn-out process—a conclusion which shook his religious faith to its foundations.

Rivkin recalled that for a while he led a double life as a secular student of history at Johns Hopkins University on weekdays and a scrupulously observant Jew on Shabbat. In 1941 he received his Bachelor of Arts from Johns Hopkins; in 1943, his Bachelor of Hebrew Letters from Baltimore Hebrew College. In 1946 he received his Ph.D. under the supervision of Frederick C. Lane, an eminent scholar of Italian history at Johns Hopkins, for a dissertation on Leon da Modena, a noted Italian rabbi of the Renaissance who, like Rivkin, straddled the Jewish and non-Jewish worlds intellectually. Rivkin taught Jewish history for three years at Gratz College in Philadelphia (like the Baltimore Hebrew College, a Jewish teachers' training institution) until he was spotted by Jacob Rader Marcus. Impressed, Marcus arranged for his appointment to the faculty of the Hebrew Union College; in 1949 the Rivkins moved to Cincinnati, where they have lived ever since. Rivkin recalled:

> I would have preferred a position teaching Jewish history at a secular institution of higher learning, but there were almost none at the time. . . . I stipulated that I must be free to expound any conclusions about Jewish history that my research and reasoning led to. I would teach Jewish history (even the history of Reform Judaism) . . . as objectively as possible.

President Nelson Glueck graciously responded, 'We would not want you otherwise.'[12]

It is a tribute to the broadmindedness of Marcus and Glueck that they felt no compunction in appointing to the faculty a brash young scholar with an original mind and sharply critical approach. Indeed, under their aegis, HUC had become a home for stimulating and diverse Jewish viewpoints: Zionism and Hebrew literature with Ezra Spicehandler, liturgy and Jewish thought with Jakob Petuchowski, midrash with Eugene Milhaly, Talmud with Alexander Guttman, Hellenistic Judaism and New Testament with Samuel Sandmel, Assyriology and sophisticated biblical scholarship with Julius and Hildegard Lewy, classic and recent trends in philosophy with Samuel Atlas and Alvin Reines. These and others brought a fresh approach to the education of Reform rabbis. This flourishing can be viewed as a result of American Jews' intensification of their Jewish identity after the Holocaust and the establishment of the State of Israel—a redefinition that made the old ideological parameters passé—and can be seen as well as concurrent with the greater prestige of religion in the era of the Cold War.[13]

At HUC Rivkin attracted the loyal devotion of a cadre of rabbinical students attracted by his ability to generate intellectual excitement. Samuel E. Karff wrote: "He was my teacher—not only at HUC, but even earlier at the Gratz College of Jewish Studies in Philadelphia. . . . Those of us who were fortunate enough to have Ellis Rivkin as our teacher know well his brilliant, original, system-building mind."[14] A passionate advocate of his own ideas, he was charming, witty, unfailingly sympathetic to his students' problems, helpful in times of need, and tolerant of their viewpoints when they differed from his own. Michael A. Meyer has written: "What I have always appreciated about Ellis Rivkin is his genuine desire that students both try to understand his ideas and also bring to them their own critical perspectives. He has never insisted that appreciative students become slavish disciples."[15] Rivkin showed that history was a creative activity—not, as students sometimes complain, "memorizing names and dates." For example, he included in his syllabus works such as R. G. Collingwood's *Idea of History,* which presents the historian as a detective who reconstructs the past from evidence, direct or circumstantial, that happens to survive in the present. His classes were investigations of the yet uncertain, rather than regurgitation of what previous scholars had written.

It was Rivkin's comprehensive approach to Jewish history that resonated with that group of students who went on to become Reform rabbis and scholars when the movement was in state of regeneration. American Reform Judaism had broken loose from the stagnation of the twenties and early thirties when it was identified with old-line German Jewish families, and had found support among Jews whose parents had been immigrants from Eastern Europe. In 1950 the Hebrew Union College merged with Stephen Wise's Jewish Institute of Religion, and, except for a rump of Classical Reform Jews, was ready to meet the mid-twentieth century head-on. This transformation had been in the works since the late 1930s and early 1940s, beginning with the emergence of a new generation of rabbis who sought to cope with more contemporary currents of Jewish and American thought—men who combined training in philosophy or the social sciences with considerable knowledge of Judaica and involvement in Jewish politics. Distinguished as spokesmen for Judaism in their communities, these rabbis moved Reform Judaism toward an appreciation of Jewish peoplehood, Zionism, and the symbolic value of aspects of Judaism that had been downplayed previously. Rivkin was able to mark out a place for himself at HUC because his historiography was so dissimilar from that previously ensconced in Reform. His approach found fertile soil in a postwar era characterized by both optimism and anxiety, by respect for intellectuality, and by the discarding, among liberals, of ideological shibboleths. Although his worldview was largely consistent over time, it did change in nuance as he responded to developments in the second half of the twentieth century.

* * * *

In this article we will look at essays Rivkin wrote on American Jewish history during the course of three successive decades of the twentieth century: the fifties, sixties, and seventies. To be sure, American Jewry was never, for him, a subject of primary research. This field was dominated by Jacob Rader Marcus, who had turned from the study of German Jewish history in the late thirties to American Jewish history, and who established the American Jewish Archives in 1947.

Herbert Zafren, director of the Libraries of HUC-JIR for many years and Rivkin's brother-in-law, remarked at a celebration of Rivkin's 80th birthday that his "excursions in American Jewish history seem to be mostly out of duty than personal interest."[16] A reading of these papers indicates that was not precisely the case. Indeed, his views of American Jewry express his conception of modern Jewish history and reflect his overall approach to the development of Judaism as a whole.

The first of his trilogy on American Jewry, "A Decisive Pattern in American Jewish History," appeared in 1958 in a volume entitled *Essays in American Jewish History,* issued in honor of the tenth anniversary of the American Jewish Archives.[17]

From the beginning the fundamental terms in Rivkin's historical analysis were *structure* and *pattern.* In the 1958 piece he explained that "emphasis has been place upon the dynamic elements of structural change, rather than on the particulars which constitute the whole at any given moment."[18] The essay opens with three of his central principles. The first is the connection between Jewry and world history:

> The history of the Jews is a history of involvement. It is not simply the history of a people living in a specific geographical area whose development can be treated as something largely distinct and separate. . . . It is always, at one and the same time, both a history of that which is distinct, that which has its special delineation in time, and of that which is interwoven with the fate of empires and civilizations. The history of the Jews is intermeshed with the history of the ancient Near East, the Hellenistic world, the Roman Empire, the Sassanian dynasty, and the Moslem, Christian, and Western civilizations. It cannot be torn from its larger context.[19]

Rivkin's second principle, for him something of a historical law, is a cyclical pattern that eventually has affected every branch of the diaspora: "The Jews in each case experience a phase of acceptance and well-being linked to the expansion of that society, and a phase of rejection and persecution linked to the disintegration and collapse of that society."[20]

The third and most fundamental factor shaping American Jewry was capitalism. "The history of the United States may be said to be unique in that it manifests a historical evolution which is dominated by the dynamics of expanding capitalism. . . . The uniqueness of Jewish experience is thus to be sought in the relationship of the Jews to capitalism in its purest manifestation."[21]

Rivkin held that capitalism was the only socio-economic system that contains within itself a self-transcending process that results in the systematic creation of wealth, not just its reassignment. The entrepreneurial spirit embodied in rational planning for the continuous accumulation of wealth is dynamic inasmuch as capitalists look for new opportunities to augment their capital, which, in the long run, leads to progress. He acknowledged that capitalism can cause dislocation, suffering, and worse, but insisted that no other system in history facilitated the *growth* of prosperity rather than simply allowing wealth to change hands among social parasites.[22]

Before describing how Rivkin applies this principle to American Jewish history, some comments on the concept of *capitalism* are in order.[23] The term "capital" for accumulated wealth invested by merchants and others appears as early as the seventeenth century, but *capitalism* as a description of an economic system was the coinage of nineteenth-century socialists. From the Marxist perspective, *capitalism* designates the arrangements that permitted possessors of capital to "own" the "means of production," which in turn enabled them to expropriate much of the "economic surplus" that their hired labor produced (this was the source of the moral outrage and ideological ferment that revolutionary socialism sought to capture and channel). According to the Marxists (and Rivkin agreed), capitalism had superseded feudalism and previous systems of subsistence, as well as the dominance of acquiring wealth through military expertise, monopolies of sacred rituals, agricultural toil, or artisanal skills.[24]

Early modern capitalism required a stable legal system of reliable rules which encouraged risk-taking and legitimated simple and clear-cut ownership (*ownership* being a legal notion varying from society to society). Capitalism needed and expressed internalized attitudes motivating reinvestment at the expense of consumption ("deferred gratification"). Economic historians note (and Rivkin emphasizes) that Western capitalism has undergone repeated transformations, from seventeenth-century mercantile capitalism, to nineteenth-century industrial and corporate capitalism, to late twentieth-century post-industrial capitalism. Because these variations entail many specific arrangements, *capitalism* as such is no longer the main explanatory term in economic theory. However, the concept remains useful in a macrohistorical perspective. By emphasizing its centrality in the progress of history, Rivkin stands out as something of an inverted Marxist. Instead of emphasizing the negative features of capitalism, he emphasized its positive effects while calling attention to what he considered the totalitarian implications of some forms of socialism.

In the 1958 article Rivkin traced capitalism to merchant entrepreneurs in seventeenth- and eighteenth-century Europe, including Sephardic Jews (former Conversos) in Amsterdam, London, and Hamburg, as well as Court Jews (*Hofjuden*) in German-speaking Central Europe who had connections to Poland-Lithuania. In the New World Sephardic Jews from Atlantic port-cities and Ashkenazic Jews from Central Europe found a niche as independent merchants, tradesmen, or their agents. "The sprinkling of Jews in the colonies and in the early republic is thus explained by the fact that commercial capitalism determined the character and the extent of emigration and immigration."[25] The number of colonial Jews was small, because they came from lands where Jews had little contact with the peasants who made up the bulk of the settlers.

Rivkin held that Jews encountered no discrimination in colonial times because America was characterized by "an economic structure which encouraged fluidity and mobility, and which rewarded the enterprising and the thrifty. [Capitalism] flourished in a political and ideological framework that was receptive to its needs and responsive to its drive."[26] America did not have a formal established religion, nor were there exclusionary guilds, a hereditary aristocracy, or a permanent un-free white agricultural class like the medieval serfs.[27] According to Rivkin, what made America ideal for capitalist development (and therefore for the Jews who came here), was what it did *not* have. It did not have those medieval features that European societies were not able to completely shake off. What it *did* have was ample land, natural resources, convenient and accessible communication routes, and a native population easy to push aside. For capitalism, British North America was a Brave New World in far more than a geographical sense.

Rivkin emphasized how important it was that the foundational documents of the United States of America appealed to natural law and inalienable rights, not to scriptural authority. The founding fathers, many of whom were deists, prohibited the establishment of a national Church. By contrast, in late eighteenth and nineteenth-century Europe, the Church, the monarchy, and the aristocracy retained enough of their former power to reassert themselves from time to time. "Whenever the development of capitalism called for the dissolution of anomalous classes, its spokesmen were either incapable of marshalling the social strength needed for the venture, or they recoiled at the prospect that they might unleash the very forces which would endanger them."[28] Rivkin insisted that, because medievalism was non-existent in early America, there was no opposition to the presence of Jews. Indeed, they were highly respected in their role as merchants. "When Europe entered upon its capitalist phase encumbered by a Jewish problem that had been spawned by the medieval world and its collapse, the United States, never having known any system of production other than capitalistic or geared to capitalism, was not faced with a Jewish problem."[29] American Jews did not have to be formally emancipated (except with respect to holding public office in some states); in continental Europe Jewish emancipation, for many years, was partially or completely blocked by sectors of the population that never fully made peace with it.

The situation of lower-class German Jews before the massive inroads made by capitalism indicated to Rivkin that "as long as stagnation and decay remained impervious to dynamic [capitalist] change, the Jew was secure in his [traditional, circumscribed economic] role, certain of his future, and geared to expectancies that were as dependable as they were humiliating."[30] Advancing capitalism disrupted these stable, if demeaning relationships, leading large numbers of German Jews to come to America in the middle of the nineteenth century. Before and especially after the Civil War, the economy was expanding. Servile immigrant peasants became free American farmers. Jews with economic skills that had been despised in the Old World were energized by opportunities for "enterprise, imagination, and innovation."[31]

To be sure, there was the potential for backlash. Rivkin has in mind Ulysses S. Grant's Order Number 11 expelling "the Jews as a class" from Mississippi, Tennessee, and Kentucky—an order which, although immediately rescinded by Lincoln, proved to be an ominous ascription of the negative features of capitalism (in this case, smuggling) to Jews. (This attribution was to resurface a few decades later.)

In the latter half of the nineteenth century a third period of American Jewish history commenced, which "again reveal[ed] the interplay of European forces stimulating emigration with forces in the United States encouraging immigration."[32] Capitalism entered a new phase with the spectacular growth of industrialization in Western and Central Europe, the beginning of its penetration into Eastern Europe and, coinciding with the closing of the agricultural frontier in America, in the mushrooming cities of the United States. Some Jews who had come to America earlier now set up factories, department stores, and investment banks. Immigration of large numbers of "proletarianized," "precapitalist" Jews from Eastern Europe during this period led to tensions with Jews largely of German origin: Rivkin opined that "this antagonism between capitalist and precapitalist Jews has made its appearance at every phase in history when two contradictory forms came into opposition with one another."[33] In the 1880s and 1890s came the rooting of antisemitic tendencies among the gentile upper classes of New England who had made their fortunes earlier, as well as among nativist farmers confronted by insolvency and farm foreclosures.

The negative stereotype of impoverished alien Jews of east European origin coincided with the image of parasitic Jewish capitalists who controlled international finance. This combination fostered the image of the Jew as "money power," evoking negative stereotypes of Shylocks and Christ-killers. Rivkin points out that, nevertheless, the upsurge of antisemitism did not affect the inexorable transformation of "precapitalist Jewish immigrants into small capitalists," nor did it halt their Americanization and the concomitant decline of radical socialist ideas among them.

The next section of Rivkin's 1958 article deals with the changing character of American Jews after the closure of large-scale immigration in the mid-twenties. The Jewish proletarian was usually a one-generation phenomenon. Immigrants' children found opportunities in American cities as shopkeepers, white-collar workers, teachers, and professionals. More American Jews made their way into the middle class, despite the introduction of quotas in the professions and the major universities "by presumably the least intolerant segment of society, the community of learning."[34] Nevertheless, Jews remained linked in many minds with international banking and with Bolshevism, further fuelled by the *Protocols of the Elders of Zion* circulated in Henry Ford's *Dearborn Independent.*

According to Rivkin, FDR's New Deal prevented the middle class from collapsing—sparing Jews "some of the cruelest blows" of a difficult period—but "middle-class status did not dissolve [the Jews'] relations with millennia of history that made for vulnerability in distressed societies, *irrespective* of class position [his emphasis]. . . . [Jews] found themselves accused of being the architects of disintegration."[35] The tirades of Father Charles E. Coughlin pulled together the negative characteristics attributed to the "qualitative role" of the Jews so that, for the antisemite, "the depression was not viewed as the outcome of the breaking down of the total complex economy, but as the consequence of external interference with an economy which otherwise would have been immune to breakdown." Rivkin recalled his principle that Jews have "a scapegoat potential that could not be equaled by any other minority."[36] However, during the New Deal "despair was contained by the preservation of some firmness of structure" through innovative measures such as expanding the federal bureaucracy.[37] The concluding sections of the 1958 essay touch on the social and economic shifts immediately following World War II: the even more crucial role the federal government had come to play in "every corner of national life" as a result of military and other preparations during the Cold War, "the rapid growth of large-scale corporate enterprise, and the steady reduction in the significance of small economic units." Rivkin remarks that restrictions on Jewish employment were "relaxed" and eventually disappeared. "The general prosperity of these years offered little fertile soil to anti-Semitic agitators, . . . although should any major crisis emerge in the future, it is to be expected that anti-Semitism will once more be aroused from its momentary dormancy."[38]

In sum, the "decisive pattern" referred to the title of this essay is that the socio-economic structure of the Jewish population confirmed for Rivkin that the destiny of the Jews was dependent upon the fate of capitalism."[39]

* * * *

In 1967 Rivkin gave a talk entitled "The Jew in American Society" in Los Angeles at the annual conference of the Central Conference of American Rabbis. In it he reiterated his theory of the central importance for Jews of "developmental capitalism":

Capitalism can survive only if it grows and develops. It must continuously create capital or wither away. The lure of profit stirs competition, and competition is sustained by the potential of widened markets. Those entrepreneurs whose restless spirits are stirred by the excitement of profit not only undertake risks and hazards, but unleash innovation and undermine the citadels of tradition. In a word, developing capitalism generates permanent revolution.[40]

For Rivkin, the spiral of capitalist development liberates the mind and society from the burden of the past, including capitalism's "own traditional and obsolescent forms."[41] To be sure, inexorable change has agonizing side-effects, such as those resulting from the "ominous business cycle" and rivalries between capitalists of different nations. Shrinking of the overall European market after World War I spawned totalitarian solutions which rendered Jews vulnerable. Rivkin insists that the crucial factor that interfered with continuous capitalist development was "the limiting and obstructive role of the nation-state."[42] At first nationalism had a revolutionary face that encouraged economic development.

In nineteenth-century Europe, Jews had had no difficulty identifying with their respective nation-states, although it was only of limited benefit for them to do so when antisemitic nationalists began to preach that "the role of the Jew in history was to sow the seeds of decay."[43] Nationalism did give birth to Zionism which, Rivkin acknowledged, offered Jews pride in their past, protected self-esteem, and held out hope in dark times for a better future. Rivkin's judgment was that the role of the nation-state in history was as a whole negative, resulting, inter alia, in wars in which the mass armies of nation-states wreaked vast destruction and death.

It was the continental dimension of the United States that enabled capitalist development to escape the limits encountered in divided Europe. The United States showed that the "nation-state form was not a necessity for developing capitalism," confirming "the possibility of a *global* unity that could sustain an almost limitless range of diverse interests."[44] Capitalism fostered cultural creativity: for example, "it was here and here alone, that religion spawned domesticated and wild varieties to prove their fitness by survival."[45] America did not prevent one from disassociating from his or her inherited religion—or from not espousing any religion whatsoever.

By the late 1920s, a saturated domestic market brought economic stagnation to the United States as well. Only after World War II came a "grand reversal."[46] Writing in 1967 Rivkin stated: "It is my contention that the United States did commit itself to . . . a global goal following World War II, and it has been unflagging in pursuing it ever since." What he discerned as the post-war American plan for a global economy was a campaign "against the remnants of nation-state capitalism and imperialism" because the latest form of capitalism must "wage a ceaseless struggle against all traditional societies that strangle economic growth."[47] Rivkin prophesied that this phase promised to be truly "*social* revolutionary."

According to Rivkin, because World War II delivered a crushing blow to the antisemitism amplified by the Depression, American Jews were able to respond to the subsequent economic upswing by taking advantage of "the technological breakthroughs that placed a premium on the very talents and skills that Jews had in large measure by virtue of their flight from proletarianization." Paradoxically, economic development "went hand in hand with spiritual gloom." In an "Age of Anxiety," religion was looked to for emotional answers and, in the McCarthy years, was used for protection against charges of disloyalty. "Capitalism was identified with conservatism; Communism, though brutal and totalitarian, was fantasized as the heir of the radical principle." In this atmosphere, where radicalism lost its cachet and there was a certain religious revival, Jewish ethnic loyalties strengthened. As Rivkin put it rather poetically, yet sarcastically, "A glow within was kindled by the luminous light lustering forth from Bible and Midrash, Talmud and Zohar, the Kuzari and the tales of the Hasidic masters."[48]

When Rivkin prepared this talk, he felt that the so-called post-war religious revival was incongruent with the outward-looking attitude of the American cultural revolution of the later sixties. Perhaps with existentialism or Protestant Neo-orthodox theology in mind, Rivkin countered with the statement that "man's reason could build a world as easily as it could destroy it. God's universe might be problem-laden, but it was not absurd." (The *CCAR Yearbook* includes a question-and-answer period after talks by Rivkin and Will Herberg in which Rivkin drove home that point.) The new critical attitude of the later sixties toward the religious conservatism of the fifties was typified by the "God is dead" theology. A more widespread symptom was the social activism of Reform and Conservative rabbis in the civil rights movement. Especially notable in Rivkin's eyes was the Catholic *Aggiornamento*, reflecting the desire of the Church to respond to the onset of an era of "global, permanent revolution which will not interfere with religion but will not keep it artificially alive." Later in the talk Rivkin posits that "traditional Judaism, be it Orthodox, Conservative, or Reform, will either have to embrace [the spirit of] *aggiornamento* or slowly wither away."[49]

Writing in 1967 Rivkin predicted that Jewish folk identity was doomed to a precarious existence. "The global outlook will be the only one appropriate for the *functional* role that most Jewish youth will be destined to play in their mature years."[50] Jewish ethnicity may not turn out to be durable when ethical codes are problem-oriented rather than tradition-oriented, "with good and evil losing their absolute character and shifting in response to the situational dilemma."[51] Toward the end of the CCAR presentation came Rivkin's most optimistic account of a messianic age in the offing: "The new will be too exciting to barter for the old. Moses, the burning bush, revelation at Sinai, will be appreciated for its historical and anthropological interest, but not for any light it may shed on containing the population explosion, increasing the yield per acre in underdeveloped lands, shaping viable nations out of the chaos of underdevelopment, calculating the optimal rate of economic growth." In a future-oriented world, "the past will be primarily a vast treasure house of man's strivings to attain the good life, and of his persistent failures. It will less and less beckon as an alternative to the treasures that await him."[52] Rivkin did envision a positive role for Reform Judaism if it looked ahead rather than behind. The following extract conveys Rivkin's enthusiasm for what was about to dawn:

> Reform Judaism, however, cannot but greet the emerging global society as the confirmation of its faith that history was development and that Judaism was spiritualization of this process. The founding fathers of our movement were radicals who welcomed the sweeping away of a medievalism that had wracked and despoiled the Jews, hounded them as pariahs, ground down their self-esteem by humiliating and degrading legislation, and turned their Judaism into the caricature of what it might have been. They were excited by the dawn of a new age of human equality and the vistas that science, philosophy, and literature opened for them. They bore the scars of a *halakhic* yoke that had crushed intellectual curiosity with the ban, and that had strained to hold them back from the beckoning call of western civilization. They cast off the yoke, even as they sought to capture Judaism's essence.
>
> And they discovered that this essence was change and development. *Judaism was its history* [emphasis mine], and its history was an adventure with God. Not the anthropomorphic God of Israel's childhood, but that force and power fulfilling itself in the history of mankind in general and the history of Israel in particular. To carry through its mission, Judaism had dared to change. Western civilization was an opportunity for religious creativity, not the death knell of Judaism. . . . Free to draw on the riches of our past, we need no longer be slaves to it. Judaism, for us, is not only a past, but a future. This was and is the message of Reform Judaism.[53]

In the discussion that followed at the CCAR meeting, Rivkin articulated a leitmotif of his later thinking:

I would like to stress that from this vantage point the basic source of strength for Judaism will lie in the recognition that *the idea of unity* [emphasis mine], the concept of one God involves the ultimate achievement of the unification of mankind. In other words, what we are entering upon is the next stage in a process that began when, way back in the patriarchal phase of Jewish history, semi-nomads felt they could organize their experience more effectively through a One than by fragmentizing it through the many. The subsequent history of Judaism has been the elaboration of *the unity principle* [emphasis mine], as new and more complex problems were solved through unity rather than fragmentation.[54]

Rivkin concluded that forces which "began to emerge only around 1958 and picked up considerable momentum with the Kennedy Administration and the signing of the Test Ban Treaty" will "eventually challenge Jewish ethnicity and the recent intensification of religious identity.... I cannot promise you that the Jewish community, as now conceived, will be the Jewish community of thirty or forty or fifty years from now. However, I can point out that the character of the Jewish community has in the past frequently undergone changes of equivalent radical [character]."[55] Rivkin recalled that for the Pharisees the community was not only ethnic: it was also interested in winning Jew and non-Jew alike to a belief in the resurrection of the dead and last judgment—hence their reputation for proselytism. Similarly, modern Jewish nationalism was a radical departure from previous forms of Judaism, as was Reform Judaism.[56]

Ignoring the conflicting emotions generated by the U.S. military involvement in Vietnam and Israel's Six Day War, Rivkin's futuristic historicism reached its height in the late sixties.

* * * *

In 1976 Rivkin took up the analysis of American Judaism once again in a festschrift for Jacob Rader Marcus.[57] By then "the Holocaust" had become reified in the popular consciousness—especially of American Jewry—so Rivkin elaborates on the circumstances that led to it. He reviews the trajectory from growth to stagnation to break-down leading to the escalation of fascist and antisemitic ideologies in Europe after 1929. "The Nazi regime moved in to shore up the col-lapse of German capitalism by smashing the trade unions, dissolving the political parties of the Weimar republic, rearming to make a bid for continental hegemony, impoverishing, degrading, and ultimately physically annihilating the Jews."[58] The sovereign nation-state, "a carry-over from the medieval pre-capitalist world," was the primary reason why capitalism was unable to break out of this cyclical pattern there.[59] Those limits were not apparent throughout most of the nine-teenth century, until post-Bismarckian Germany found itself blocked by France and Great Britain from expansion in Europe and overseas. The resulting competition between European powers set the stage for World War I. Because the European home-markets were not big enough effectively to facilitate the technologies of mass production, European capitalism was a "hybrid" of the nation-state, the boundar-ies of which were restricted by political and cultural factors inherited from earlier times, and an economic system "whose driving principle, the principle of profit, is transnational and global."[60] American pre-dominance after World War II prevented the restoration of these ulti-mately incompatible factors in the West.

One of the "transmutations" (a Rivkinian term) of Jewish identity that had flourished in modern times was Jewish socialism. In 1976 Rivkin wrote that the Jewish experience with functioning Marxist systems has been very negative because these societies came to be governed by elites (in the Stalinist case, an exceptionally ruthless one) whose motivation was power, not development.[61] He gave a quali-fiedly positive evaluation to the State of Israel as a possible integra-tive force in the Middle East, but by and large he did not view it as an optimal solution to Jewish survival.[62]

The setting most conducive the progress of modern Jewry, accord-ing to Rivkin, was the United States. Here developmental capitalism did not confront nation-state obstructions. The creators of the Consti-tution had opted for a federal infrastructure that encouraged the free movement of goods, services, and talent, and thus prevented westward expansion from leading to the creation of independent American na-tion-states. The attempt to create a separate American nation-state by the Confederacy was crushed. Moreover, rights were located in the individual, not the polity or social collectivity. "It was only because the *natural* rights of the colonists had been violated that they had gained the right to establish a state of their own."[63] That the territory of the United States did not develop as a jumble of nation-states made possible a continent-wide market where the key to profits turned out to be heightened worker productivity, which was a breakthrough to a new stage in economic progress.

Post-World War I European states, intent on defending their lands and colonies from American economic penetration, stalled "the directional trust of developmental capitalism."[64] Then, in the 1930s, the further growth of the American economy was stymied—a frustrating situation that threatened to make the Jews expendable. "The seed-bed for totalitarianism would thus be ready for rapid cultivation, and the Jews of the United States would be highly vulnerable to the traditional solution of the Jewish question when an economy stagnates and breaks down: impoverishment, degradation, discrimination, and, as likely as not, expulsion."[65] However, the scarcity of labor during World War II created opportunities for the unemployed. "The fact that the enemy of America was also the arch-enemy of the Jews made for a growing positive image of the Jewish people."[66] By the mid-1970s America had become "the world's first post-industrial society" and its Jews the first "people" able "to develop a post-industrial profile virtually free of agricultural-industrial residuals." (By putting "people" in quotation marks, Rivkin was pointing out that the concept was for him a historical construct that varied from era to era and culture to culture.)[67]

In his 1976 article Rivkin had given a macrohistorical account of why, in his opinion, the Jews turned out to be suited for the new phase of capitalism. In late antiquity Jewry had become largely an urban diaspora, barred from agriculture but granted autonomy on religious grounds. The Jewish belief-system was not tied to priestly intermediation; only the individual's observance and knowledge of divine law determined his reward or punishment in the afterlife. This freedom from the pressures of religious and, to some degree political coercion by the state gave the Jews a greater ability to keep pace with the forces enabling the rise of early modern capitalism. No other "people" were in quite this situation.[68]

Writing in the mid-1970s Rivkin held that Great Britain tried, after the end of World War II, to "sustain the patterns of economic underdevelopment" in the Commonwealth, but it was American capitalism that seeded new growth in the world economy. Using its influence to dissolve nation-state barriers, the United States made possible the intensified global expansion of capitalism. The post-industrial stage of economic development was a shift from "wealth as quantitative (commodities) to that of wealth as qualitative (intellectual and spiritual).[69] The expansion of the profitable service-sector had become evident by the late sixties. "This breakthrough to post-industrialism is the outcome of a political system grounded in natural-rights philosophy that transcended the nation-state, and of an economic system geared more to innovation than to replication."[70] Technologies which had matured in advanced countries could be shifted to less developed lands. Rivkin reminded his readers that Jews were now concentrated in the service and knowledge industries, sectors to which they were "pre-fitted" long before they reached these shores. Jews had not been farmers and were not for very long proletarians; they were "knowledge workers." He concluded:

> If the post-industrial society does indeed spin-off a spiral of development and proves that the barriers to continuous economic growth are surmountable, then the United States will have broken the stranglehold of eternal cycles. Under such circumstances the Jews can anticipate an end to their status as a vulnerable minority. The problem of Jewish survival will no longer be physical but spiritual. . . . When fear [of antisemitism and other anxieties] gives way to free choice, will there be Jewish values worth sustaining and a Jewish identity worth preserving?[71]

* * * *

Rivkin developed these subjects further in the thirty years since the last paper was published. One of these recent pieces is a "Postlude" included in the 2003 reprinting of his 1971 book, *The Shaping of Jewish History.* The new title of the book, *The Unity Principle,* indicates the drift in Rivkin's thinking.[72]

Concerning the "Jewish profile" in the West—mainly the United States—there were changes in nuance only. As readers of his *Globalist Newsletter* know, for many years Rivkin had devoted himself to marshaling evidence debunking the superpower status of the USSR. The disintegration of the USSR, the dismantling of the Soviet empire, and the introduction of capitalism there between 1985 and 1991 were hardly surprising to him (although they were to many prominent Sovietologists). The persistence of what he labeled "hegemonic rivalries" in the global age has been the focus of his structural analysis of the current world scene.

As in his earlier pieces on American Jewry, the 2003 Postlude veers back and forth from world to Jewish history in order to explain what "global developmental capitalism" meant for the Jewish people. (Rivkin was a prescient user of the term "globalization" as he was for "structuralism.") He was now willing to admit that obstacles may prevent the Isaianic teleology he had lauded in the 1960s and 1970s from being actualized, at least in the near future, and diagnosed Fundamentalism as a "counter-revolution" appealing to those who are negatively impacted by the painful changes that accompany globalization. The brief prominence of Louis Farrakhan, for example, showed that virulent antisemitism could resurface. Rivkin tried to explain the reasons for the surge of "ultra-*halakhic* [Jewish] Orthodoxy" and a newly militant Hasidism, neither of which was conspicuous when the first edition of the book was published. "The lines between right-wing Reform and left-wing Conservatism became more and more blurred as Reform ideology lost its cutting edge. Living an 'authentic' Jewish life became as important, if not more so, than being a light to the nations and a beacon to the peoples."[73]

Jews in the diaspora were now almost everywhere on the forefront of a form of capitalism rooted in "knowledge formation." In this economic sector, where human beings "measure themselves and each other primarily for their individual qualities and not their ethnic or religious personae, ... the Jewish people will remain vulnerable to intermarriage and the weakened Jewish identity that intermarriage spins off."[74] Despite all that, Rivkin's optimism reasserted itself. In response to the traditionalistic spirit of "revivalism" taking root in Reform Judaism, Rivkin argued that the future depends, not on "replication" of old patterns or "variations" of them, but on "mutations." "*Judaism in the present as in the past is the outcome of the vicissitudes of historical process and not the outcome of some dogmatic or doctrinal claim* [his italics]."[75] "Adaptability and absorption have always been the genius of Jewish peoplehood. . . . The experience of the Jewish people, like the experience of no other people, has been an experience with history, with what God is or might be—an experience that goes beyond doctrine, dogma, and belief."[76]

In his 2003 Postlude, Rivkin postulated that "although the destiny of Jewish history cannot as yet be conclusively predicted, the metaphysical import of Judaism can be discerned." God may have been powerless to prevent a Holocaust but nonetheless (in his phrase) "God teaches." In this context he meant that we can learn from the study of Jewish history how to assure sustained worldwide economic growth so the preconditions for holocausts do not recur. This destiny was a dynamic process in which "it is up to human beings to discover the preconditions for achieving ideal ends such as peace, tranquility, righteousness, justice, love, and compassion."[77]

The Postlude ended with the most explicit statement yet of Rivkin's Unity Principle, a tenet that had "the generative power at one and the same time to continuously image new concepts of God and elicit new shapes and forms for the Jewish people." The Unity Principle is "a search and not a finding, . . . not [permanently] bound to any transient assumption of what God is." "It is this principle, as it unfolded in the history of a Jewish people, that can claim to be none other than *the God as revealed by history*" [Rivkin's emphasis].[78] For Rivkin the Unity Principle is that which enables mind to discover a rational explanation for diverse phenomena in the past and, at the same time, it is the locus for explaining diversity in the future. As one of his students suggests, Rivkin's Unity Principle is "an evolving, dynamic, universal constant operating within the universe but prior to it, such that the novelty spun off from it leads it to become what it had not been before."[79]

At the end of the Postlude, Rivkin connected the *telos* of history to hallowed Jewish texts, particularly to the creation story of Genesis 1 and the Isaianic vision of the End of Days. It is perhaps indicative of the limits of historiography alone that, for universal values, Rivkin reached back to the Bible for a conception of ethical purpose. Critics have asserted that the study of history cannot generate an ethical system on its own, as the good is always relative to specific circumstances. For a conception of ultimate value Rivkin alluded to ancient Jewish prophecies about social justice, the end of war, and harmony within nature.

* * * *

Among the published critiques of Rivkin's historiography by his admiring students, two are especially pertinent.[80]

In response to Rivkin's position at a 1973 CCAR conference in Atlanta, Samuel Karff gave an appreciative but critical response to a talk by Rivkin entitled "Modalities of Jewish History."[81] For Karff, Rivkin's position is consistent with the Reform idea of "progressive revelation," but does not adequately treat the dimension of continuity in Judaism. For example, Rivkin concludes there was a revolutionary break from Pentateuchal to Pharisaic Judaism, but downplays the deeper interconnections. Karff criticized Rivkin as being so "overcommitted to the principle of repeated transmutation in his modalities of Jewish history so that he has not adequately delineated the organic bond between one stage and another."[82] "Rivkin is led to overstatement" and his version of the central theme of Judaism "can neither differentiate it significantly from other systems nor inspire the commitment of future generations." And, his messianic vision "does not take seriously enough the experience of our recent past."[83]

Michael A. Meyer's critique, "Rivkin on Jewish Modernity and Continuity," opens by citing reviews by Rivkin of noted historians such as Cecil Roth, Oscar Handlin, and John Higham, and an analysis of Rivkin's lengthy and controversial essay on Salo Baron published in 1959.[84] In Meyer's words, Rivkin argued that Baron "failed to impose any unity, any conceptual scheme that could make the course of Jewish history intelligible." While acknowledging the value of Rivkin's contention, for example, that a structural understanding of the Spanish Inquisition undermined the credibility of Converso confessions of secret Judaism because they were extracted by torture, Meyer remarked that historians are leery of "black versus white"—i.e., of overly simple explanations that do not take fully into account the "mixed (economic

and ideal) motives" of historical actors. Not all *Conversos* may have
been completely devoid of Jewish feelings as Rivkin conveys. Meyer
also noted that Rivkin's generalization that "nationalism means fragmentation" accounts for his ambivalence about Zionism. While acknowledging that the State of Israel had been a force for eliminating
imperialism from the Middle East, in the last analysis Zionism "runs
counter to the underlying principle [according to Rivkin] of all Jewish
history: the principle of unity." Meyer sums up: "Having disposed of
what he believes to be false [synchronic and diachronic] constructions
of Jewish unity, Rivkin moved to a striking conception of his own: the
unity of the Jewish people lay in the very idea of unity itself."[85]

* * * *

Being stimulated intellectually by Rivkin hardly meant agreeing
with all his conclusions or confining oneself to his structuralist methodology. One can ask if "structural history" dehumanizes its subjects,
for, in the last analysis, history is about imperfect, sometimes conflicted, human beings, not just impersonal patterns. Does macrohistory reflect the attitudes of the historian more than or as much as "the
bare facts?" Of course, the historian selects those facts that he or she
feels are most relevant, but the more distant the historian is from the
ground-level of events the easier it is to ignore crucial details that do
not fit the grand pattern.

The concern of this paper, however, is not the correctness of
Rivkin's views, but their appeal to a loyal coterie of rabbinical students, an appeal that, until recently, resonated with the centrality of
modern historical consciousness in Reform Jewish theology.

Rivkin's focus on a unity principle operating in history perhaps
mirrored his concurrent attempts to unify his own life. Rivkin's historiography enabled him to forge a bond between his upbringing in
the Orthodox world of Baltimore and his mature years as a professor in a liberal rabbinic seminary in Cincinnati. In this regard, there
are parallels on several levels between Rivkin and the Russian-Jewish
historian and ideologist Simon Dubnow.[86] Rivkin's reconfiguration of
his youthful Orthodoxy into an ideology of Jewish history exemplifies
what Dubnow called "integration of soul," the understanding which
comes from integrating the self's present state of mind with its up-

bringing and development.[87] In his autobiography, Dubnow described how in his twenties he sat compiling his first account of Jewish history ("a new Talmud") a few miles from where his honored grandfather taught the old Talmud in the Mstislavl yeshiva. For Dubnow, history and not religious faith would serve as a sufficiently inspiring basis of a modern Jewish identity. He was a member of a secularized (and secularist) east European Jewish intelligentsia for whom peoplehood was the principal ideological building block. In contrast, "free-thinking" Jews like Rivkin found a congenial home in American Reform Judaism during an era of exuberant expansion when the blatantly secularist Jewish option was dying out.

Rivkin's macrohistory is in line with the writings of Isaac Marcus Jost, Heinrich Graetz, Dubnow, and, on a smaller scale, Cecil Roth (*A Bird's Eye View of Jewish History*) and Solomon Grayzel (*A History of the Jews*)— historians who constructed comprehensive accounts of the Jewish past for a wide public. They each had their expertise but, in areas where they had not done primary research, they relied on secondary sources to construct macrohistorical narratives that made being Jewish personally and collectively meaningful to their readers. Like Dubnow, Rivkin is interested in the socio-economic dimension of Jewish modernization. Whereas for Dubnow, the evolution of Jewish communal structures was the key to Jewish survival, Rivkin called attention to the struggles for power and wealth often lurking behind religious matters. Dubnow had paid special attention to the local *kehillot* and to the overarching Jewish Council of the Four Lands of Poland and Lithuania. Rivkin treated Pharisaism as a "hidden revolution" in religious authority and the (re)conversion of the Marranos to Judaism as an "entrepreneurial" rather than spiritual decision. That there is such cursory discussion in Rivkin's writings of the religious reasons for the emergence of Reform Judaism may be another indication that his historiography is more indebted to the East European stream of Jewish history than the German.[88]

Rivkin follows Dubnow's lead by insisting that a world history of the Jews be organized around those diaspora communities that successfully adapted to their surroundings and whose formidable subcultures influenced Jews in adjacent geographical areas (e.g., the influence of Sephardic Jewry on the Jews of medieval Provence and of medieval Ashkenaz on the Jews of Poland). Rivkin dismissed the way Salo Baron assumed that the Jews were a group analogous to other nationalities. Although neither Dubnow nor Rivkin were Zionists, Dubnow was a diaspora nationalist and Rivkin was not. Dubnow in eastern Europe became the spokesman for "folkist" Jewish identity. The American setting of Rivkin's work led him to reject what now would be labeled an "essentialist" concept of Jewish nationhood; he posited the "affirmation of the diaspora" only along with a version of the doctrine of the "mission of Israel" espoused by nineteenth-century Reform Judaism. Dubnow came to call his history "sociological;" Rivkin is something of a philosophical idealist about history.

Rivkin's appeal to Reform rabbinical students from the 1950s to the 1970s might be explained as follows: First, he valorized reason, not subjectivity. The complete intelligibility of the Jewish experience meant that the inner levels of Jewish history could be uncovered through a delineation of impersonal forces. There is a connection between Rivkin's youthful absorption in talmudic study and his mode of analysis in the HUC classroom. For him, the apparent irrationalities of history, as of international politics, have a simple (some would say simplistic) explanation ascertained through the correct interpretation of the right texts—of certain parts of them. As time went on, Rivkin became more committed to this approach, paying less and less attention to what other historians said. In order to "solve a historical problem" Rivkin parsed the relevant primary sources according their credibility and consistency with an eye to the underlying power structures that determined the surface events. This is evident in his contributions to the crowded field of biblical history, on the place of Jesus in the Judaism of the first century C.E., the Pharisees, on the Conversos—and on post-World War II international rivalries. He made little or no use, for example, of archeological data, Greco-Roman papyri, the writings of the Church Fathers, medieval manuscripts, or the archives of early modern Europe. He preferred to "think through" problems for his students with published materials that he felt were poorly understood.

Second, Rivkin's conception of the uniqueness of the Jewish past in comparative history can be seen as a secular equivalent of the idea of the "chosen people," problematic as it is. To be sure, *asher ba-*

har banu has been drastically reinterpreted and sometimes rejected by various modern Jewish thinkers. Moreover, the Jews are usually treated in general history textbooks as just another small people, albeit one meriting attention in connection with the emergence of monotheism and, subsequently of Christianity and Islam, or in connection with their persecution by Crusaders or Nazis. Rivkin lays bare the factual uniqueness of the Jewish experience, straddling as it does the Ancient Near East, Hellenistic, Roman, Persian, Islamic, feudal Christian, early modern, and modern eras. The evolving Jewish collectivity already in late antiquity and the early Middle Ages underwent social changes which made its profile truly distinctive. Urbanization, a religious scholar class, a predominant merchant sector, and Jewish life as entirely a diaspora minority enabled Rivkin to assert that the remarkable distinctiveness of Jewry was empirically demonstrated.

Third, Rivkin's totalistic vision of Jewish history put primary emphasis on mutability, structural and ideological. His prime example is the sweeping Pharisaic reformulation of the earlier Judaism espoused by the Aaronide priests. Almost every aspect of biblical Judaism was transformed by the Pharisees: the centrality of ritual atonement gave way to an internalized mitzvah system incumbent on each individual, a caste of priestly intermediaries was superseded by a stratum of learned sages from all walks of life; the canonized Written Torah was reframed as a dynamic Oral Torah, and relative silence on existence after death was replaced by the promise (or warning) of personal afterlife in *Gan Eden* or *Gehenna*. According to Rivkin, the Pharisaic revolution that had created the lineaments of rabbinic Judaism was responsible for most of the basic beliefs of Christianity and Islam, and was therefore of world-historical significance. (Incidentally, Rivkin's broadminded treatment of Christian origins was facilitated by the more tolerant postwar American religious scene: nowhere else and at no other time would a liberal Jewish scholar's views on the subject be treated with such respect outside the Jewish fold.[89])

If Judaism "mutated" and "people" is a construct, what is the unifying feature in the history of Judaism of which the historical phases of Jewishness are subsets? The increasing pluralism of American Jewry has concrete implications which are grounded in more abstract ones.

For the Orthodox the core is *halakhah;* as we have noted, Rivkin, addressing Reform rabbinic students, was trying to show this was possible through the lesson of history.

Initially Rivkin's Unity Principle was the methodological assumption that everything that that happens must have a coherent rational explanation, but it also had a philosophical thrust. At the end of the Postlude Rivkin refers to "the *metaphysical* import of Judaism."[90] For him, the Unity Principle became more than a heuristic trope for how Judaism synthesizes diverse dimensions of reality into a coherent and evolving whole at each successive stage of its progress through time. He comes to see this principle as an active force in itself. In conversation he referred to it as the embodiment of his "theology," evoking something of the ultimate meaning which Jews ascribe to God. We recall that in the 1967 paper given at the CCAR, Rivkin had written about the founders of Reform Judaism: "They cast off the yoke [of *halakhah*], even as they sought to capture Judaism's essence. And they discovered that this essence was change and development. Judaism was its history, and its history was an adventure with God. Not the anthropomorphic God of Israel's childhood, but that force and power fulfilling itself in the history of mankind in general and the history of Israel in particular.[91]

Like Gershom Scholem in this regard but more so, Rivkin is not merely the disinterested scholar absorbed in his academic specialty but akin to a philosopher of Judaism. Unlike Scholem who was a professor at the Hebrew University of Jerusalem, Rivkin taught in an American rabbinic college dedicated to conveying the meaning of Judaism to prospective liberal rabbis and their future congregants. In the classroom, at HUC-JIR graduations, and on the lecture circuit, he not only analyzed specific historical developments but preached what he considered the basic impetus of Jewish history, indeed of world history.

At times the Unity Principle is akin to Spinoza's conception of the determinative laws of nature or Hegel's vision of the utter rationality of history as *Geist* moving to achieve full actuality. For Rivkin the "Unity Principle" is that which encouraged Jewish thinkers to incorporate more and more data under a single coherent, overarching explanation. According to Rivkin, this principle had been at work in the clan deity of the biblical patriarchs, in the judgmental God of charismatic prophecy, in the singular deity of the canonized Penta- teuch, in the highly personal *Avinu she-ba-shamayim*, "Our Father who is in heaven," of rabbinic Judaism, in the scientific Prime Mover of the Jewish Aristotelians, as well as in the kabbalists' mystical *Ayn Sof* which emanated the *sefirot*, in Spinoza's *Deus sive natura*, and so forth, down to Rivkin's own philosophy. The Unity Principle brought increasing domains of nature and history under an integrating system, legitimating Reform as a continuation of what is essentially Jewish despite its abandonment of so many traditional religious beliefs and practices.

It is well-known among historians of thought that there is a close tie between Hegel and Spinoza. Is Rivkin a Hegelian? Hegel was a philosopher overwhelmingly aware of historical change, whereas Rivkin is a historian who developed latent philosophical interests. There were other Jewish scholars influenced by Hegelianism, one of the most original being the early nineteenth-century *maskil* Nahman Krochmal.[92] For Krochmal, the deities of a people symbolized its core values; the core idea of Judaism and therefore the God of the Jews was the Absolute Spirit (*ha-ruhani ha-mukhlat*), which explains why Judaism was repeatedly reborn after passing through the fateful cycle of national existence which ended in the extinction of other peoples. In each successive stage the Absolute Spirit/Jewish God achieved fur- ther clarity and comprehensiveness. Marx, early on a Young Hegelian, famously claimed later that he turned Hegel right-side-up so the socio- economic feet of history were on the ground and the idealist head was in the air. There were elements of Marxism in Rivkin's approach with the major difference that, for Marx, capitalism, for all its trans- formative effects, generated class warfare that would ultimately end in communism. For Rivkin, capitalism is far more constructive and long-lasting, being still the driving force for economic advance and the cultural progress of humankind. Without abandoning the material- ity of history, Rivkin sought to revivify the Hegelian *Geist,* the "Idea" that achieves full actualization only in the long course of time.

Rivkin adhered, in his own way, to the famous (or infamous) Hegelian principle that whatever is real is rational and that therefore the rational is real. For Rivkin to bring something under the wings of the Unity Principle is to formulate an explanation that fits into a grand system, so that the Unity Principle will describe how Judaism— or at least certain Jewish thinkers—incorporates increasingly diverse phenomena into a single matrix. If not a Hegelian or a Marxist, he is as close to being a Krochmalian as twentieth-century Jewish thought produced.

Finally, for Rivkin, the Unity Principle underpins the unification of the human race that was a crucial element of the prophetic End of Days. The great problem of the approach of Spinoza, Hegel, Marx, and their ilk was how to find "the *ought*" within "the *is*." Is the assumption of a moral goal to history not deduced from the process but superadded it from other sources? Hegelian thought is said by some commentators to be ethically vacuous because the good is relative to whatever phase of the dialectic into which the *Geist* has moved. Rivkin turns to Jewish texts in the Torah and the Prophets for an ethical teleology which incorporates moral judgments about the global unification of humanity, the fulfillment of the individual, and the triumph of Reason. This is yet another reason why Rivkinism fit so well into American Reform Judaism with its moralism and optimism.

* * * *

"Rivkin's rabbis" were assured by their teacher that Reform had rejuvenated Judaism around Enlightenment reason and progress, individual autonomy, social justice, universalism, and a principle akin to ethical monotheism. His passionate search for rational understanding resonated with the new confidence and intellectual energy of American Reform in a time of resurgent prosperity and national self-confidence. Even though ideologies of secular teleology are now in eclipse and the tone of recent historical theory is ironic, for Rivkin there is a "master narrative" that makes total sense of Jewish history. To be sure, he insists that the students and investigators of history need a realistic conception of the motives and techniques of power and authority. He acknowledges there is no sure guarantee that humanity will actualize the utopian ideals of the classic prophets. Rivkin's students, and readers of his work as well, are indebted to the diversity and extent of his efforts to show that Jewish history makes sense and offers hope. As Ludwig Wittgenstein said of Freud,[93] after studying with him it was impossible to look at the world in the same old way.

Telling the American Story: Yiddish and the Narratives of Children of Immigrants

Rakhmiel Peltz

Are Yiddish Language and Culture Limited To The Immigrant Generation?

In order to better understand the history of Jews in the United States and the history of Yiddish in America as well, it is vital to clarify the relationship that children of east European immigrants have had to Yiddish. Based on new data, I will revise the common picture that paints the second generation only as rejecting their parents' language and culture. Researchers of American Jewish life must both acknowledge and scrutinize the ambivalence expressed by this generation toward the Yiddish culture of their parents.

The varying connection over time between Yiddish language and the ethnic identity of Jews in the United States is an issue of great significance when one attempts to untangle the factors that affect how Jews identify themselves as being Jewish. Generations of speakers have designed their languages as codes and conduits of communication within cultural contexts, and the study of the correspondence between linguistic signs and their associated meanings over time and space has occupied scholars for centuries. However, it is only during the past forty or so years that language use as it relates to changing social factors has developed as a field of inquiry. The awareness of be-

417

ing an American and at the same time a member of the Jewish ethnic group is attributed to a creative act of consciousness of the second generation—the American-born children of immigrants.[1] Deborah Dash Moore, in her history of this generation, underscored the pivotal role it played as a bridge between immigrant parents and future generations who were unfamiliar with immigrant culture. The second generation defined American Jewish identity, according to Moore,[2] by creating a moral community in an urban setting—by interweaving immigrant Jewish culture, with "American culture, middle-class values [and] urban lifestyles." In the immigrant household, Jewish culture was largely imparted to the children by way of the Yiddish language. I have been studying the second generation's use of Yiddish and its attitude toward the language for the past twenty-five years. Based on qualitative data I have collected in various communities, this article will investigate to what degree members of this generation regard Yiddish language as a source both of their Jewish identity and of the moral guidelines that direct their lives.

Because little research has been done on spoken Yiddish in the United States, I chose to begin by investigating the nature of language use in one neighborhood, South Philadelphia. An area of primary settlement, like its analogous neighborhood, New York City's Lower East Side, this neighborhood retained more of its ethnic character than did areas of secondary settlement. The positive identification with place on the part of the residents facilitated my ethnographic research, which included work in residential and shopping areas as well as in synagogues and the local Jewish senior center. I also performed archival research on settlement and institutional history. In my ethnographic research I came in contact with about four hundred neighborhood residents, 123 of whom were identified by name in my files, and thirty of whom I interviewed in depth. I estimated the Jewish population of the neighborhood in 1985 to number three to four thousand. At that time I was interested in the entire Jewish community, but found that by that date about three quarters of the Jewish residents were native born. In this aging Jewish community a majority of the residents were older than sixty.

When I returned to do active fieldwork in South Philadelphia in 1997 I met only a few people at the senior center who were born in

Europe, and these individuals were mostly Holocaust survivors. In the early 1980s, the European-born Jews in the neighborhood had largely come to the United States as part of the mass immigration. When I perused the senior center membership list in 1997, I recognized only about five percent as having been members twelve years earlier. During 1984–1985, I convened the *Gleyzele tey* (Glass of Tea) Yiddish discussion group at the senior center on a weekly basis. All sessions were in Yiddish, with almost all the participants speaking in Yiddish. (I spoke very little during the sessions.) From the beginning of 1997, I facilitated the group once again on a weekly basis, changing to once a month in the fall of 1997 through the summer of 2010. In 1997, most of the group members could speak Yiddish, but, by 2010, fewer than half of the attendees speak Yiddish, although almost all of them understand the language. I now participate heavily in the Yiddish discussions and cultural presentations.

Subsequent to my initial fieldwork years in South Philadelphia, I facilitated another Yiddish conversation group, *Glezele tey* (Glass of Tea, pronunciation according to the *litvish*—northeastern European Yiddish—dialect that is characteristic of New England), from 1986–1996 in the Conservative synagogue, Congregation B'nai Israel, in Northampton, Massachusetts. The group consisted of elderly children of immigrants. Some of the participants could not speak Yiddish, but even they insisted that all monthly meetings be held in Yiddish and about Yiddish. They wanted to hear the language. These Yiddish meetings constituted all the senior citizen activities in the synagogue. From 1993–1996, I also facilitated a monthly Yiddish-speaking group of elderly children of immigrants in Orthodox Congregation Rodphey Sholem, *Di gantse mishpokhe* (The Whole Family), in Holyoke, Massachusetts. More participants spoke Yiddish in the Holyoke group than in Northampton. During 1986–1987, I facilitated occasional Yiddish groups in a variety of institutions in Worcester, Massachusetts, and, in addition, I led seminars and Yiddish discussion groups in different locations in the United States over the years. Furthermore, I have interviewed scores of individuals and recorded group conversations in Yiddish among elderly children of immigrants. If these interviews could not be carried out in Yiddish, English was used. Case studies from a selection of these interviews will be presented below.

How Do The Children Of Immigrants View Their Parents' Culture?

In my research, the elderly children of Jewish immigrants expressed a positive attitude to Yiddish, independent of whether they grew up in a large urban Jewish neighborhood or in a town with a small Jewish population. They related to Yiddish as a core component of their Jewish identity, along with belief in God and keeping kosher. They would identify these beliefs and behaviors as integral to being Jewish, even when they did not speak Yiddish, believe in God, or keep kosher. These children of immigrants at this age and in this time, independent of their own practice, associate the core elements of being Jewish with the household of their immigrant parents.[3]

These findings initially took me by surprise. I had been familiar with the way that historical accounts depicted children of immigrants as distancing themselves from the world of their parents geographically, intellectually, and emotionally. I assumed that this would be reflected in this generation's attitude toward Yiddish at the end of the twentieth century. Irving Howe, the author of the most detailed presentation of the culture of east European Jews in the United States, terms this commonly accepted interpretation as a rupture—"a *Kulturkampf* between the generations"—but at the same time he realizes the ambivalence that characterizes the children's view of their parents:

> The sense of embarrassment derived from a half-acknowledged shame before the perceived failings of one's parents, and both embarrassment and shame mounted insofar as one began to acquire the tastes of the world. And then, still more painful, there followed a still greater shame at having felt ashamed about people whom one knew to be good.[4]

This ambivalence, or love-hate-relationship, characterized, at the same time, the children's attitude to Yiddish.[5]

The historians of American Jewry, however, consistently document that the children of immigrants turned their back on Yiddish. For example, Henry Feingold cites a survey of twenty New York City families taken in 1940, which found that knowledge of Yiddish, except for a few phrases, had almost disappeared among the American-born children. More interesting, in light of our finding later in history, was the survey's report that second and third generation Jews viewed Jewishness as shaped by "matters of the heart," rather than by a specific religion or culture[6]—that the realm of emotions is the location for ethnic identity. Another history that focuses on the years after World War II describes the younger generations as non-participants in the organized Yiddish cultural institutions that published or performed the Yiddish word—except in the world of the *yeshiva* where traditional Talmud study proceeded in Yiddish as it had for centuries.[7]

One of the historical sources for studies of the life of east European immigrants has been the Yiddish press, and particularly the *Bintl briv* (Bunch of Letters) column of the *Forverts* (*Jewish Daily Forward*), wherein immigrants turned to the editor for advice. In the section dealing with Yiddish language in the first anthology of the column published in English, a child of immigrants complains, in 1933, that his parents embarrass him and his brothers by insisting on using Yiddish when they are out together—even if they are in a store on Fifth Avenue. The son claims that the brothers are not ashamed of their parents, but that the parents should limit their Yiddish to the home, and not use the language "among strangers and Christians." The editor takes a middle road, viewing the parents as reasonable and "not fanatics" in their insistence on Yiddish, but encouraging them also to use English, since "people should and must learn the language of the country." Implied here is that the struggle between the languages and generations within the family is a complex issue.[8]

Turning to the realm of literary creativity, we find that the children of immigrants are painted in more nuanced colors. For example, in Sholem Ash's novel *Onkl Mozes*, which probably more than any other Yiddish novel stressed that immigrant life was modeled on a way of life transplanted from the European hometown, the roles of the different generations in the family are corrupted. The hometown becomes a sweatshop under the control of one *landsman* (townsperson), Uncle Moses. The children are depicted as smarter than the parents—who themselves are degraded to powerless children[9]—and the family is split apart and leaves tradition behind. The children replace the fervor of traditional belief with devotion to secular gods, such as socialism, fathers are symbolized as either elderly or as children, and the European hometown serves only as a burial ground to which those who are ready to die return. As America seduces the children away from their families and discards the elderly, the collective from the hometown becomes a "machine" in New York City and can only appreciate life by thinking about the good old days in the old country. Writing in 1918, Sholem Ash saw the children of immigrants as sacrificing themselves for their parents, and depicted this situation especially through *Onkl Mozes*'s heroine, Masha. In this book, the children of immigrants serve as parents for their own immigrant parents, but they do not embrace their language or culture.[10]

The best example of a literary portrayal of the complex language situation of the Jewish immigrant family remains Henry Roth's English-language novel, *Call It Sleep*. Writing in 1934, Roth sets the events, as narrated by the son of the family, David, in New York City between 1907 and 1913. The major language of the immigrant home is Yiddish—written in the book as standard English–the accented English of the Jewish and non-Jewish adult immigrants, the Hebrew and Aramaic of the religious school, and the Polish that David's mother uses to keep secrets from her son.[11] David controls all the elements of this orderly language system. Although there are linguistic indicators of familial strife and fears vis-à-vis the outside world, for David, the immigrant child, language remains a supportive and caressing feature of home and hearth.[12] In a brilliant analysis of the language of the novel, Werner Sollors points out that the English text as mediated by the narrator's translation reveals a Yiddish language that is rich and full of lyrical expression, but represents "a world made accessible … but not fully recuperable."[13] While Roth is implying throughout the novel that the child is developing the power to decode systems of different and often opposing languages and cultures, David's love for his mother, her language, and her world are constant. Sollors analyzes a scene in which David demonstrates his language loyalty to Yiddish, when Aunt Bertha offers him "suddeh vuddeh" (Soda Water) through accented English words. David rejects the offer with pure Yiddish words, in the native language of his aunt and mother.[14] In later writings and interviews, Roth shared his great discovery that the everyday memories of the Lower East Side could be transformed into art "by the alchemy of language."[15]

Roth also revealed that his view of the early immigrant years should be grasped from the vantage point of the time of its writing, 1934.[16] At that time it was becoming clear that, as Europe was vociferously rejecting the Jew, a loving son might want to preserve, through literature, an immigrant world that was no more. So, too, in this essay which treats the memories of children of immigrants, we should remember that memories grow from the historical context and life cycle stage at the time of remembering.

Moving away from historical studies and literary works, census data on claiming Yiddish as a mother tongue yield another picture during the twentieth century. Yiddish was among the "big six" languages claimed in the United States census of 1940 and 1960. Yet, by the end of those twenty years it experienced a forty-five percent loss of claimants, while Spanish, for example, experienced an increase of seventy-three percent.[17] Second- and third-generation claimants decreased for most languages, but Fishman understood that complex psychological factors influenced both claiming and under claiming.[18] The analysis of mother tongue claiming between 1960 and 1970 revealed dramatic increases—for Yiddish the reported increase was sixty-five percent.[19] Obviously such an increase could not be explained by the birth of new speakers or by the influence of new immigrants. In the United States in general, the climate for involvement in ethnic affairs had become markedly favorable in the 1960s. This, along with positive associations with Israel's victory in the Six Day War, swelled the ranks of those Jews with positive ethnic identification. In such an affirmative atmosphere for Jewish affiliation, second, third, and fourth generation Jewish Americans, when given the opportunity, expressed their Jewishness with a response that declared that their mother tongue was Yiddish. The change from 1970 to 1979, on the other hand, was a decrease of twenty-four percent claiming Yiddish, illustrating "the rise and fall of the ethnic revival."[20] The spike of Yiddish claimants in 1970 is not insignificant, but rather can serve as an indicator of the general attitude of American-born Jews to Yiddish at various times in history.

Researchers on ethnicity in the United States, and specifically scholars of language and ethnicity, have underscored the malleability and mutability of ethnic identity, as well as its emblematic aspects.[21]

These concepts point to the meaning of ethnic identity for both scholars and ethnic group members at the end of the twentieth century. Furthermore, in order to identify strongly with ethnic language, one does not have to understand or speak it, but needs only feel associated with it, since "language is an aspect of our self-ascription."[22] The respondents in the census who declared Yiddish as their mother tongue included fluent speakers along with people who had never been exposed to Yiddish.

One might conclude that what is happening with Yiddish is also being experienced by all other immigrant languages. Every case in history, however, reflects the traditional position of the specific language within its society, the immigration history of the group, the time when immigration commenced, or concluded, its ongoing status, and the life cycle stage of its speakers at the time of focus. For Yiddish, the traditional multilingualism of its speakers has involved different languages. Therefore, even in America, when a child of immigrants is asked to identify her mother tongue, she may for various reasons choose Hebrew, English, Polish (or some other east European tongue like Hungarian or Russian), or Yiddish. A language chosen at any time may reflect both its use within the life of the Jewish family and its value and emotional significance in relation to the claimant's Jewish identity. After the cessation of east European immigration to the United States in 1924, Yiddish speakers were only replenished in small numbers by way of immigration from Holocaust survivors and older Jews from the Soviet Union. With the Yiddish homeland wiped off the face of the earth starting in 1939, the reflexes related to Yiddish speech and identification relate to the fate of the language and culture of pre-1924 immigrants. With regard to the life cycle, children of immigrants generally report a period of intensive exposure to the immigrant culture in their parents' household, relatively little exposure in middle age, and in some cases increased involvement in later life.

By the late 1960s and early 1970s, at a time in history when most of the Jewish immigrants from the mass immigration were no longer alive but the United States was ripe for expression of ethnic identity, the second generation did not only declare themselves in favor of Yiddish in the census, but also organized around Yiddish in their communal institutions, community centers, synagogues, and senior citizen centers. Hundreds of Yiddish culture clubs sprouted from grass roots initiatives across the country, which were not financed by the budgets of the communal institutions.[23] Looking at community-based innovations which started within the Jewishly involved population, it can be argued that this was probably the major Jewish cultural change at the time. However, largely supported by an elderly group of organizers and focusing on Yiddish—a language that had been deemed peripheral or dead for quite some time—this change did not receive notice or publicity. By 1976 a world congress in support of Yiddish culture was organized in Jerusalem, and was attended by hundreds of second generation delegates from the Yiddish culture clubs in the United States and other world communities.[24] Perusing the October 1996 issue of a monthly newsletter *Der Bay*, subtitled *The Golden Gate to the Yiddish Community*, one finds, in addition to local meetings in the San Francisco bay area— not exactly the largest Jewish population center in the United States— fifty-six meetings listed, taking place at locations as widespread as Des Moines, Iowa; Kansas City, Kansas; Fort Worth, Texas; and Mercer Island, Washington. No other ethnic group in the United States rallied around its ethnic language and culture in this manner.

If indeed this positive attitude toward Yiddish reflected a general return of ethnic elderly citizens to involvement with the language and culture of their youth, one can search for analogous signals in the general research on ethnic aging. The results are, however, mixed. We have reports of second generation Polish Americans seeking out a retirement environment in Arizona where they can express their ethnic identity and appreciate and use more Polish.[25] Confirmation also comes from Mary Doi's work on increased ritual observance of the sixtieth birthday celebration among children of Japanese immigrants in California.[26] There are many reports of increased identification of older Native Americans with their ethnic religion, language and culture, but the most striking examples relate to the migration of urban Native Americans back to the reservation after retirement.[27] A role that these individuals play which Jewish Americans rarely assume nowadays is that of cultural conservator and instructor of the grandchildren. The parallels with Japanese Americans and Polish Americans have to be further studied, since immigration restrictions in the 1920s affected them together with the European Jews, and the confluence of age and immigration history may influence the observed behavior.

However, before jumping to conclusions, we must remember that the studies we have obviously do not all indicate a positive attitude to the language and culture of these ethnic Americans' youth. For example, in Micaela di Leonardo's work with second generation Italian Americans in northern California, attenuation and not enhancement of cultural involvement was predominant.[28] Furthermore, Mark Luborsky and Robert Rubinstein warn that revitalization may also activate anxieties associated with loss of family members and cultural heritage.[29] We may also question whether the phenomenon of return will be characteristic of aging children of immigrants in the future. In each case, the historic development of contemporary behavior must be scrutinized carefully.

Autobiographical Narratives in the American Jewish Archives

I was most fortunate to benefit from two periods of research at the American Jewish Archives in Cincinnati.[30] Largely due to the collecting genius of Jacob Marcus, the AJA is a magnificent repository of autobiographies, especially those of children of immigrants. My research was greatly aided by reference to those collections, which included both written accounts of "everyday" Jews who were raised in smaller communities away from the hustle and bustle of larger East Coast Jewish communities, and the autobiographies of Reform and Conservative rabbis, which often reflect the traditional American households in which they were raised in the first half of the twentieth century.

Marcus himself shared, in an interview in 1990, that while he was growing up in a small town near Pittsburgh he heard only Yiddish from his Lithuanian-born parents—but he could not recall speaking it. Nor did he remember his friends speaking Yiddish, although their parents spoke the language as well. At Hebrew Union College, many of his fellow students knew Yiddish, but Marcus never heard them speak it. From the time he began teaching at Hebrew Union College (HUC), however, he would use Yiddish words and phrases in his lectures, and his students always understood. However, at the time of this interview he found that none of his students could understand Yiddish.[31]

Reform Rabbi Herman Elliot Snyder, of Springfield, Massachusetts, was born in New Bedford, Massachusetts, and was the son of a rabbi. He associated Yiddish with *shabbes*—the Sabbath. On *shabbes* his father would test him on translating the Bible portion into Yiddish, his mother would read the children stories from the whole week's worth of daily Yiddish newspapers, as well as the Yiddish classics that in later years she read to them in English translation, and would also recite to them, before *havdole*— the prayer that ushers in the new week at the end of the Sabbath—*"Got fun Avrom"* (God of Abraham)—the woman's prayer in Yiddish that begs God for a good week to come.[32] Conservative Rabbi Simcha Kling, of Louisville, Kentucky, grew up in Newport, Kentucky in a household in which English was spoken but where Yiddish was heard at family gatherings and young Simcha understood the conversation. As a young teen he learned to read his father's daily Yiddish paper and later on improved his understanding in order to use the language in his research. Kling associated Yiddish with home and family, along with keeping kosher and observing the Sabbath—lighting candles and abstaining from writing, cooking, or sewing—although his father worked and the children went to the movies on Saturday afternoon. After a move to Cincinnati and his bar mitzvah, both Kling and his mother became strictly *shomer shabbat*— observant of the Sabbath. Kling's experience clearly shows Yiddish as an important and determinative ingredient of Jewish family life.[33]

It was common for children of immigrants who grew up with Yiddish in their households to recall that their parents would read to them from the daily newspaper, which would arrive in the hinterlands from New York City. Furthermore, Yiddish-language activities in the family included, for example, the mother reading the *Tsena urena* (Yiddish commentary on the bible for women) and reciting Psalm 91 in Yiddish, the children learning their lullaby in Yiddish and performing Yiddish theater, the eldest daughter writing home to Europe to the grandparents in Yiddish, and the son delivering his bar mitzvah speech in Yiddish. But despite its presence in the home, there also was tremendous ambivalence attached to the use of Yiddish. The youngsters resented the flaunting of the Yiddish paper in full public view in Altoona, Pennsylvania, for example, and for young Lionel Koppman, not only disliked being called *"Labeleh"* by his parents, "but all others—Jews and non-Jews alike—called me, until I went to public school, simply "Laby." Imagine being called "Laby" in a town like Waco, Texas. I recall being unmercifully teased with taunts like "Laby, the cry baby," and much worse."

But what this generation most often retains from their childhood is the "ethical will" that is encapsulated by the Yiddish words that ring in the ears of the children for a lifetime. Koppman remembers that *his* mother taught him assertiveness. "'*Zay shtolts!*' (Be proud), I hear her saying."[34]

Yiddish and the Narrative of Personal Experience

In searching for signs of the enduring presence of the European Yiddish culture of Jewish immigrants in succeeding generations, one locus of investigation is the narrative of personal experience told by children of immigrants. Children of immigrants to the United States, with the exception of the fairly recently arrived Spanish speakers, are known in general for not speaking their immigrant tongue and rarely transmitting it to future generations. However, especially since this generation generally understands the mother tongue, one cannot assume that its members have not been profoundly touched by the lives and culture of their parents. The fact that my fieldwork in different types of Jewish communities since the early 1980s has consistently found a strong, positive, emotional identification with the Yiddish language among elderly children of immigrants can help in reassessing the attitude of this generation to the immigrants in American Jewish history.

In recent years, I have explored the stories that elderly children of immigrants tell about their relationship to the world of their parents, and have especially emphasized their attitude to their parents' culture. At this time in history—after the center of vibrant Yiddish culture in eastern Europe was wiped off the face of the earth by the Nazis—the stories of the children of parents who had lived in Europe, as well as those of the few survivors of eastern European society still alive, become a source for learning about that culture. I will present information I have gleaned from group discussion sessions in Yiddish as well as individual audiotape-recorded ethnographic interviews.[35]

The analysis of the narrative of personal experience has served as a uniting concern of both the humanities and the social sciences during recent decades. From the early work of William Labov and Joshua Waletzky, this analysis moved from defining minimal narratives consisting of sequential clauses to underscoring the importance of evaluation by the speaker.[36] Later work probed what the point of the narrative was and how it reflected cultural values and norms. Livia Polanyi, in her volume, *Telling the American Story*, recognized a core of common concerns among Americans. Americans, according to her study, consist of all those who consider themselves to be American. Such self–ascription can prove to be deceptive, but Polanyi describes her stance clearly. Namely, neither Polanyi's mother, an Italian Roman Catholic American, nor her immigrant father, a Hungarian Jewish American, considered themselves American. "They knew they did not share the values of a lot of people whom they categorized as Americans, but those people who consider themselves Americans do share a set of values."[37] Polanyi, however, the American-born daughter, considers herself American. Her study

is based on the idea that stories are rooted in what you know to be true and that telling a story to someone who does not share your presuppositions about the world as expressed in that story means that (s)he will not really know what you are talking about or care. When you talk to people who can't understand you, your story gets lost and what happens is that the people you are talking to know that you are not one of them.[38]

I differ with Polanyi in that I do not accept that children of immigrants are Americans like everyone else. Their interpretation of their parents' cultures links them as a discrete group that has its own presuppositions about the world that are molded by their parents' cultures. The evaluations that I will extract from my recent collection of narratives of American-born children of eastern European Jewish immigrants follow my earlier ethnographic studies of this generation in an old urban neighborhood of primary settlement, and in small towns in New England. In the earlier studies, I found that the focus of this generation regarding their Jewish American identification was neither the synagogue, the Jewish communal federation of organizations, nor the State of Israel— it was, rather, the experiences and values of the Yiddish culture of the immigrant household of their youth.[39] This is a far cry from our assumptions that these children distanced themselves from their parents physically and emotionally—as we learned from historical studies.[40] It also carries a very different message from the image of the launching of a sophisticated generation of intellectuals and writers, based on the early experience of Malamud, Bellow, Howe, and the like—all children of immigrants.

I hold the view, based on my recent studies, that this generation is in constant and continuous dialogue with their immigrant parents, even when they are seemingly estranged, or when the parents are long deceased. I also argue that to assume that we can understand a culture from its written and published literature, either in Yiddish or English, is naïve at best and destructive and distorting at worst. At this time in history it is incumbent upon us to hear the stories that are shared orally and to learn from them. To provide some continuity for the vibrant Yiddish culture of eastern Europe and immigrant America—be it only second hand through educational opportunities—I maintain that the lessons of that culture cannot be learned without studying these narratives. In some ways these stories teach us more about Yiddish culture than the best of its sophisticated published literature.

The Group

It is 10 February 1997, and twenty-nine elderly adult children of Jewish immigrants are attending a Yiddish conversation group meeting at a senior center in Philadelphia. They are discussing: "Parents and Children—To Be a Child in an Immigrant Household." Several of the participants have known each other for years; a few, however, new to the senior center, have been attracted by this opportunity to speak Yiddish. Everyone can understand the language, but not everyone can speak it. I facilitate the group meeting, but allow them to speak as much as possible, without my comments or questions. I start the group by asking what they remember most about their parents when they were growing up. What enduring lessons did their parents teach them?

The responses came quickly, and were largely about their parents' lives—about who their parents were. We also heard about the moral values parents conveyed, chiefly by example.

One of the speakers, Dvoyre, was the eldest of eight children born to parents who came from Ukraine. For her, the parental motto was, first and foremost, *"tse zayn a mentsh"* ("to be a good person"), and second, to be a religious Jew. Dvoyre does not see herself as having been the teacher of her parents—as their guide to Americanization. Her mother did not want to change and was content to remain in her old ways, while her father, on the other hand, made his own way into the new society. As an example of her father's Americanization, Dvoyre recalled his becoming president of an American fraternal lodge, the Golden Chain Lodge. Strongly influenced by her parents, Dvoyre accepted the *shidekh* (match) with her first husband, a partnership that her parents had previously arranged.

Elke is herself an immigrant, who came to the United States from Cuba in the 1950s after marrying an American serviceman who had been stationed there. Her mother was born in Cuba, but her father came from a small city in Belorussia. She credits them with giving her a Jewish education at a Cuban Yiddish school. Although her parents were not strictly observant, they attended a Reform synagogue where she became a bat-mitsvah, *"azey vi in amerike"* ("like in America"), she says. Yet, she is most proud of the fact that her father studied Spanish in order to do the bookkeeping for his business, and could speak it without an accent. Yiddish became the language of secrets in Elke's family, and she recalled that her parents switched to Yiddish in their store when they did not want the non-Jewish customers to understand.

Khane came to the United States from Moscow in 1930, a time when mass immigration from Eastern Europe was legally restricted (beginning in 1924). Her father, a rabbi, had secured a pulpit in Philadelphia. One of five siblings, she recalled with enthusiasm that whenever the children asked their parents anything, an answer was always forthcoming. They could even ask about sex, and they received replies based on the Bible. Khane and her siblings did not have to go to other people for information. She and her brothers and sisters sat around the table with their parents—fortunate children who were not embarrassed to ask, with parents who were not ashamed to answer. From her view, all the children in her family had respect for their parents and all learned by example. The greatest value was education, and the parents made clear that the entire family was to study and learn, and to include a mastery of English as one of their achievements.

Even without a yearning for learning and acculturation, immigrant parents remained towering figures nevertheless. Beyle remains impressed with her parents, citing their ability to manage so well in business without knowing English. Her father had come to America all alone, without family, at age fourteen, and never received an education. Nonetheless, as a self-educated person he achieved much. He sang with the most famous cantors, was president of his *farayn* (hometown society), helped raise money to build the Jewish Orphan's Home, and, in his last years, was president of a senior citizens' club. Beyle is proud of the fact that, a tinsmith by trade, her father had made the Jewish stars on the elegant large synagogue in the neighborhood. For Beyle, her father was a model of achievement, even though the areas in which he excelled were far from her own interests.

Esther, one of the few attendees who cannot speak Yiddish because her own parents did not use Yiddish at home, recalled her grandfather. Like other children of newcomers who also had immigrant grandparents, Esther has used the behavior of the earlier generation as a guide for her own choices. Two incidents remain with her. When her grandfather did not receive an invitation to a wedding in the family, his response was indicative of his character: "If I am invited, let them live 120 years, and if I'm not invited, let them live 120 years." Esther inferred from this family myth that it is important not to get angry and not to get insulted; most issues are just not worth it. The second pivotal scene that stayed with her is set in her grandparents' kitchen. Her grandmother realized, while grandfather was eating his soup, that she had cooked the *fleyshik* (meat) soup in the *milkhik* (dairy) pot. The grandmother said: "give it to me, I'll throw it out." But the grandfather responded: "let me finish the soup, then you can throw the pot out." Esther calls these "warm memories"—memories that have to do with flexibility, with being slow in bringing anger to relationships, and being lenient in Jewish religious practices. These approximate her own behavior, and she reconstructs her roots accordingly.

In this group setting, and speaking in Yiddish, the children of immigrants called up memories of their immigrant parents and grandparents that are replete with role models to follow and ethical messages that guide them today. To understand the process of remembering and forgetting, of selecting from the past in developing guidelines for behavior and of establishing and reestablishing a usable past, the "memory practices" of the individual and the group must be analyzed.

I have chosen three case studies, based on ethnographic interviews with elderly adult children of immigrants that illustrate different ways that these children continue the culture of the immigrant household. These cases were selected to demonstrate both a continuum of association with Yiddish over a lifespan, and a wide range of shared stories within the family. In the first case, in an adult life that exhibited little Jewish affiliation, the elderly child had very little active connection or use of Yiddish. In the second case, Yiddish was one component at all life stages of the child's Jewish involvement. In the third case, the parents, having rejected other aspects of Jewishness, clung to Yiddish and Yiddish culture. This informant's (and her husband's) Jewish participation is likewise entirely in the sphere of Yiddish culture. In the first case, in contrast with the other two cases, little close sharing within the immigrant family was reported. In each example, however, we find that the link to the family is an intense engagement with parents from the vantage of the child's old age, even if the parents are long deceased.

Dovid, the Unaffiliated Ethnic

Fieldwork in Jewish neighborhoods and organizational settings skews the populations I encounter; it is the ethnically affiliated Jew who typically hears me out. In posing my questions about attachments to the immigrant household, I must be sure to locate a diverse set of individuals who share in common this kind of upbringing, independent of their present place of residence or organizational membership. In this regard, the city of Holyoke, Massachusetts has attracted me for many years. Jews have continued to reside in Holyoke, a small paper and silk mill city in western Massachusetts, as a small minority up until today, amongst a heavily Roman Catholic population composed of Irish, Polish and French Canadian Americans, and, additionally,

Puerto Ricans, who settled in Holyoke after World War II. Although contiguous to the city of Springfield and its larger Jewish community, Holyoke remains independent, and supports an Orthodox and a Conservative synagogue and its own United Jewish Appeal campaign. In years gone by Holyoke also supported a Jewish Community Center and an array of Zionist, fraternal and youth groups.

Dovid lived in Holyoke through the end of high school. Sitting in his university office in Boston, Dovid—an accomplished researcher and professor of biological sciences, dean of the graduate school of arts and sciences, fellow of a college at Oxford, and summer researcher at the prestigious Marine Biological Laboratory in Woods Hole— shares clear memories about Holyoke and strong judgments about who his immigrant parents were. Born in 1924, the only child of a young immigrant couple who had met in New York City, Dovid watched his parents closely, free from the distractions that siblings or close relatives can generate. The fact that he never lived in Holyoke after high school left Dovid with an unmuddled and unconfused picture of his childhood which was unaffected by subsequent changes in the city. In addition, his mother died when he was twenty and she was thirty-nine. This informant's telescopic view isolates the stories he tells of his early years in a manner that sets them off from any other narratives I have heard.

"My life really began when I went to college. I was not supposed to go to college." None of Dovid's friends, not even the Jewish ones, thought about going to college. Their dream of the future was to be an assistant manager at the A&P, and to own a car and a house. Dovid's father was a tailor, with a shop opposite the main hotel in town. An important economic advisor in Washington who was a consultant to the Holyoke mills would stay at the hotel and have Dovid's father make his suits. He took an interest in Dovid and recommended him to Clark University. According to Dovid, as soon as he entered college he felt perfectly at home in the world of ideas, and never left it. He has no clue, however, of what factors in his earlier life would account for this successful acculturation to the academic world. All we have is his expressed desire to leave an unhappy home and a city for which he does not seem to have too much affection. In fact, if anything, Dovid finds it "eerie" to evoke memories of the city and its people. Recalling images of his parents, on the other hand, yields distinct and lucid portraits of the two. They seem to exist in their son's mind's eye as discrete individuals who had tremendous formative influences on the boy, yet they do not appear in these images to occupy the same household or to be creating a family ambience. Dovid, the young boy and the mature adult, is forthright about his dislike for his father and his love for his mother.

"I never particularly liked my father...I kept my distance.... He was a complainer... he really wasn't a very nice person.... He was the absolute—*ungeshpart* (obstinate)—is that the word?... He liked being isolated, independent....What's the word I want—a misanthropic person?...He wasn't a family man." Although his father had four sisters and two brothers in Holyoke they did not get along, and congregated together at most once a year for Passover. Dovid is outspoken: his father did not like people, identified with no ideology, and remained frustrated and unhappy his whole life. But it is more pity for his father than hatred that Dovid conveys. "I feel so bad that any human being can go through life and never enjoy anything."

His father belonged to the Harmony Club, a men's social club consisting only of Jews, although with no particular religious character. In the evenings, the men would get away from their wives to drink, gamble, and play card games, be it pinochle or poker. He was allowed to go there with his father, to "*shmaye* around" ("wander aimlessly"). Dovid describes a world in which children were little adults, in which there was no notion of protecting children. The only taboos that were kept hidden from children had to do with sex. Otherwise, "if you were old enough you could go to work." Dovid sometimes did go to work in his father's shop, and hated it. But on the way home, he would enter the local bar with his father to drink beer and eat from the smorgasbord. Dovid was also exposed to "the biggest bookie joint" in town, run by the head of the Board of Aldermen. Although he never identified spiritually or emotionally with his father, Dovid does picture his father as "a natty guy – squeaky clean—that I got from him."

His mother, as Dovid tells it, was a "stunning woman ... a romantic," who had come alone from Denmark as a young girl and was adopted by her uncle. Unlike the other immigrants, Dovid's mother spoke English without an accent and attended high school. His father, on the other hand, could hardly write Yiddish or Hebrew, and could only read English sign names and numbers. "My cultural background was nil … there were no books in my house." Culture existed in the sports page or at the movies. His mother worked in a department store, which was very unusual for a Jewish woman at the time. She had an uncle in New York who would rent a hotel in the Catskill Mountains and manage it during the summer. For her vacation she would take Dovid with her to the hotel. She was a fan of music and theater, and it was in the summer resorts that Dovid developed his passion for performance, singing and dancing. It was in these hotels, too, that Dovid was initiated into sex and manhood. Therefore, he credits his mother for this liberation from the provincialism of Holyoke. In college and after graduation, he acted in theater and has maintained this love for performance.

Although I was clear in my questions about cultural life, Dovid chose mainly to recount his emotional response to his parents. The details of their Jewish involvement in Holyoke only revealed that his father was an atheist, and that they lived in a neighborhood that was sparsely populated by Jewish families. In their apartment complex of 150 units, for example, they were the only Jewish family. He did not attend the large Hebrew school at Zion Hall, but his parents hired a private tutor for him. Obviously, even though they did not attend synagogue, they were concerned about their son's Jewish education. Dovid claims that he learned very little, only picking up his knowledge of *yiddishkeit* (Jewishness) from the Passover seder and through the family. His father's mother, who died the same year as his own mother, lived in Holyoke and only knew Yiddish. But the contrast with the ethnic vibrancy of a big urban center was obvious to Dovid. When he went to visit his mother's family in the Bronx, "it was like going to Israel."

Although surrounded mostly by non-Jews, Dovid also had Jewish friends. In the summers he attended day camp at Zion Hall—a camp run by a "pro-Palestine" (Zionist) activist—and he "got a lot of *yiddishkeit* there." This was also the headquarters for many organizations during the school year, and Dovid belonged to the Amigo Club, a teen Jewish club, played on the ping-pong team and went to dances. He felt good about being with Jewish young people. On the High Holidays he would go to the Orthodox synagogue with friends to meet the girls. Although not religiously affiliated, young Dovid identified positively with Jewish culture and his Jewish community. "It was hard growing up as a Jew in Holyoke ... it was such a Catholic city." Ethnic gang wars prevailed, antisemitic slurs were acceptable in everyday parlance, and public schools were more like Catholic parochial schools. Thus, antisemitism also reinforced his Jewish consciousness.

In response to my question asking who, in Holyoke, the role models for his own life were Dovid has no answer. He entered the science professions because the two nicest people he knew were science instructors. His mother's romantic nature and her devotion to theater and the arts shaped his love of writing—even grant proposals. Yet the concept of parents as role models is not one that he really embraces. "I'm a role model ... my son is a carpenter and musician ... and my daughter is a huckster."

Dovid has a wealth of memories ready to be shared with someone eager to learn about Holyoke. But, unprovoked, he rarely retrieves these memories, privately or in social meetings. The strong emotional attachments to his parents, both the positive and the negative ones, appear to overwhelm what one might expect to be the cultural memories about growing up in a Jewish household and in a Jewish community in a small New England city. Although parents and family are generally the source for initial enculturation within the ethnic group, Dovid's initiation took place in relative isolation from other ethnic group and family members. This path lays the groundwork for a different scenario, where the distinct and separate lives of his parents allow his private interaction with them to become so much more vital to him than their potential roles as communicators of an immigrant Jewish culture. This is also largely a result of their own decision not to affiliate with organized Jewish life or to live in a Jewish neighborhood. Dovid does not seem to retain very many lucid memories of Jewish moments in his parents' household. But then again, because he is so taken with his parents as strong individuals who only on occasion interacted with him, I learned little about the culture of the household from the interview. However, there is no doubt that life decisions made by the second generation reflect in great measure their interaction with immigrant parents.

Tsine: An Extension of the Immigrant Household

We are sitting in Philadelphia in Tsine's home of fifty years. She lives down the street from the house her family lived in for almost seventy years—where she grew up, where her parents continued to live until their deaths, and which her younger sister still occupies. Tsine was born in 1924, the same year as Dovid, but just as Dovid feels distant from the neighborhood of his childhood, Tsine, in contrast, never left. As in the case of Dovid, Tsine, too, is emotionally bound to her parents, especially to her mother. These living ties of memory, however, are closely linked to the experience of the ethno–religious household, which remained alive for Tsine because of her decision to live close to her parents. Her strength of emotion and the extent of her shared memories definitely focus on her mother, even though her father lived an independent, active life for fourteen years after her mother's death. At several junctions, her husband Berl had wanted to leave the neighborhood, but Tsine could not agree to that decision. "I don't think that I could stay away—my mother and I were girlfriends. I loved her as a mother... but I... she was my confidante." Although her four sisters were all close to their mother, it was Tsine who was most influenced by her from the beginning. "If my mother said it was dark out there and it wasn't dark, I said to myself, well, what's the difference, she says it's dark, let it be dark."

Tsine's parents hailed from a shtetl near Vinitse, Ukraine. Her father came before World War I and her mother and the family's first child were separated from him for ten years. They arrived in Philadelphia in 1923, and Tsine was the first of four American-born daughters. Neither parent had parents or siblings in the United States, and Tsine understands this to be the reason for the closeness of the immediate family. "I think that maybe because we had nobody else, we cleave— we were closer to one another, at that time … and there were a lot of good, good times." The closeness of those first years is recalled by Tsine only in positive terms, although the family was poor. But she remembers a house full of delicious foods. This was her mother's domain:

> My mother was really a mother, and that was her station in
> life. She sewed for us, she cooked for us, she baked for us, and

cleaned for us, and that was her whole life. I don't remember my mother ever having free time; I don't remember her ever having any pleasure. It was a very—ah—she had nobody to confide in … My mother was very introverted—quiet, unassuming, none of us take after her— we are all extroverted.

Although she identifies with her mother, she has a different personality. Tsine's father is the extrovert, "a people person." At age eighty-eight he helped the kosher butcher on the shopping street cut up meat and would socialize with all the customers. "He was out flittering, seeing people." He had worked for most of his life as a paperhanger, using a cart that he locked in front of his house, and never driving a car. After World War II he declared that he was going back to tradition and no longer worked on the Sabbath nor ate at non–kosher establishments. "He was very, very religious, to a point where it was a fault." Her mother, who was Orthodox and never cooked or shopped on the Sabbath was, however, more pliable. For example, she would eat some things in a non–kosher restaurant. As a schoolgirl, Tsine and her sisters stayed home from school for all Jewish holidays, as did Tsine's children.

Her father attended synagogue Friday nights and Saturdays and her husband, Berl, would go with him, even though he had grown up in a less traditional, non-kosher home. Tsine's mother kept a strictly kosher kitchen, as did Tsine after marriage. She also always lit Sabbath candles. But before each holiday she spent a lot of time in her mother's kitchen, helping her prepare the traditional dishes. For Passover, they would bring home one hundred pounds of potatoes, fifty pounds of onions, and thirty dozen eggs. She and Berl did all the work for the extended family meals. Because it had always been a part of her, Tsine was much more oriented to synagogue life than was Berl. As a schoolchild she recalls coming home from Friday evening services and crying to her mother, complaining about not being allowed, as a girl, to go up to the *bimah* (the platform in front of the ark that contains the Torah scrolls). She had studied in the local, modern *Talmud Torah* (supplementary religious school for children), where Sunday classes were devoted to writing and reading Yiddish. Interestingly, although Tsine had received a Jewish education, she did not enroll her eldest daughter in any Jewish school, although her younger daughter did attend Hebrew school. In the first years of their marriage, Tsine and Berl were not active in synagogue life, but after the children were grown both she and Berl became leaders in a local Conservative synagogue. The death of her mother coincided with the time that they became very active in the shul. Different ethnic and religious experiences may prevail during specific age and life cycle stages.

Although Tsine credits her parents for her love of *yiddishkeit*, the lessons she ascribes most to her mother's influence are the moral ones, dealing with how to treat people and make life decisions. Tsine is proud that she never hurts anyone intentionally. Describing the destructive behavior of a senior center worker, she recalls her mother's words: "But you know what my mother used to say, '*tsen mul a kish, in eyn mul a patsh, iz nokh nit glaykh*'" ("ten kisses do not make up for one slap"). "*In di mame ot ekhet gezukt, befor de vort farlozt dayn moyl bisti de balebus, en nu(kh) dem iz yener der balebus* ("And my mother also said, before the word leaves your mouth you are in charge, and after that, it's no longer yours to account for, the other person is responsible"). And this is how I lived all my life." Although it was her father who told stories about Europe and about how strong he was as a young man, the life stories that Tsine recounts are the ethical lessons of her mother.

The security of a proud ethical position affords Tsine the ability to overlook the economic insecurity and poor financial position that characterized her entire married life. Most of the time Berl worked as a roofer. Tsine, who claims that she never worked outside the home, actually helped Berl in all his business ventures. When she married Berl, his parents were against the marriage. Her in-laws were not loving people, according to Tsine, especially the father-in-law, whom she calls "a Jewish brute," "an abuser." She could have separated Berl from his parents, but her mother insisted that "because you love your husband, you respect his family." Tsine made it clear to her children that they had to visit their father's parents. Tsine says this was a direct influence of her mother. For her mother family was very important, and Tsine feels that this was probably largely because her mother left her family at a young age and never saw them again. She knows that her mother served as her model when she and Berl were establishing their family life. Tsine recalled another example of her mother's moral influence: when Tsine's father-in-law was not well enough to drive, his children decided to write to the motor vehicle bureau to revoke his license. Tsine wrote the letter for them, but her father-in-law found out and blamed her. She did not want to talk to him, but her mother prevailed, telling her that he was an old man and should be forgiven. Her mother kept all communication lines open within the family.

This closeness to her mother and, indeed, reverence for her were carried over to Tsine's children. Her older daughter used to come home from school and go into her grandmother's house first. "She and my mother—they loved each other desperately." The story that stands out among those that link the generations in Tsine's family is one that binds Tsine's daughter—when she gives birth to her first child—with her grandmother who is about to die. As the granddaughter, having just given birth, is lying in her hospital bed in New York City, she receives a phone call from her grandmother. The grandmother says that the reason she has not come to New York to see the baby is that she is preparing for Passover, and that she will see the baby soon. The grandmother had actually been calling from the hospital, but did not want to worry her grandchild and ruin her joy. Three days later the grandmother dies. The granddaughter is devastated and the next time she comes to Philadelphia she is unwilling to go into her grandparents' house. Obviously, Tsine had allowed her mother to serve as a role model for her daughter.

There are other important stories that circulated within the family which were closely connected to historical and biographical events. Tsine heard stories about pogroms from her mother. One can well imagine the fright and suffering of a mother alone with a child through war, revolution and its aftermath. Tsine knew, for example, that her mother would hide in the woods with her daughter. She tells of how a Bolshevik soldier came to her mother, who was a seamstress, and forced her to move the material that was on the entire inside of the coat to the outside of the coat. She also remembers hearing of the money that her grandfather sent to bring his family over, and of how the Bolsheviks confiscated the mail so the money never reached her mother. These were frightening tales for a young girl to hear. But the terrifying experiences of her mother, who had survived for ten years with her first daughter and without a husband through World War I, the Russian Revolution, and the subsequent pogroms, were translated into life lessons, and surfaced, sometimes, in the situations of daily life. Her mother was always fearful, for example, that her daughters would get hurt and forbade them to ride on roller skates or bicycles.

Most of all, Tsine's love for her parents' household is conveyed through her memories of the tastes and sounds of the home. Although Tsine would open a can of tuna fish for a meal, because Berl "was not an eater," for her mother, every meal had to be cooked. A dairy meal consists at least of hot soup, cooked fish, potatoes and two freshly cooked vegetables. The seasonal specialties included *schav* (sorrel) borscht with rhubarb and cherry *varenikes* (dumplings) in the summer, and *povidle* (preserves) and sour tomatoes in the winter. The culture of her mother's home that she took with her was encapsulated in the Yiddish language that Tsine loves, as much as it was in the special recipes. There was always Yiddish in the house, but as the girls grew older there was also English. They usually answered their parents in Yiddish, but it did not matter which language was used, because, according to Tsine, both were permissible and understood. Their father read the Yiddish newspaper and never learned English well, but their mother, although she arrived in the United States ten years after her husband, learned English much better. Tsine enjoys singing Yiddish songs and treasures her mother's wise Yiddish proverbs.

In recent years, since her husband's death, Tsine has been spending a lot of time reviewing life together with her neighborhood friends, whom she meets regularly at the synagogue and the senior center. The constant cues provided by the street on which she grew up and still resides form a lavish bank for her memory repertoire. The memories she conjures up are most vivid when they are physically reinforced, as on the occasions when she prepares her mother's recipes for her son-in-law, who is "an eater." Telling stories and quoting proverbs are cultural sources for Tsine's memory practices, ones that bring to life her past and her life partners, long gone. When I listened to her memories of her mother and husband, it seemed that she was not addressing me, but them.

Although Tsine was born in the same year as Dovid, they experienced their youth, at least from the vantage of old age, in different ways. Tsine identifies with her immigrant household and has remained bound to it for almost her whole life, whereas Dovid abandoned his immigrant roots rather early. The towering figures of immigrant parents, however, do not dissipate, even after their death. Dovid is vicariously engaged with the negative personality of his father as much as Tsine is turning to the wisdom of her mother for guidance.

Malke: Another Generation?

We sit in Malke's sixteenth floor apartment overlooking Philadelphia's elegant Rittenhouse Square. Yiddish stories and songs from the immigrant years are alive each and every day in the lives of Malke and her husband Reuvn, a real estate attorney. Both have mothers who are still alive at ages ninety-five and one hundred. Malke was born in 1935 to immigrant parents from the shtetl Shargorod, not far from Vinitse—the same Ukrainian area of origin as Tsine's parents. I search in Malke's account of her immigrant household for a different pattern of values and experiences, for she is relatively young in relation to the other adult children of immigrants I have encountered so far. Is she, therefore, as if from another generation? Or is there an enduring cultural inheritance for all children of immigrants?

The story Malke tells of her parents' lives does follow a pattern. Both came to the United States alone as young singles, without parents or siblings. Her mother was soon joined by a father and two younger siblings, but Malke's father remained without any close relatives on this side of the ocean. The two had known of each other in Shargorod, but first met after arriving in the United States in 1921, and were married in 1927. Malke, more than Dovid and Tsine, remembers hearing stories of European Jewish life from her mother. The most vivid are the harrowing stories about the war, which extended into Ukrainian territory well into the 1920s, and included the brutal pogroms that her mother endured. She recalls hearing about the confusion over which army was coming and which army was leaving at any given time. To identify the armies, children were sent out to identify the color of the hats, "reds, whites, Cossacks, or Denikintses (followers of the Ukrainian white general)." When the Cossacks came, they approached the women and insisted that they hand over their rings, or they threatened to cut off the finger, barking, "the ring or the finger!" Jews hid in fear in the shul, which the attackers burned down. Frightening episodes for young Malke to hear.

Perhaps the most influential of her mother's narratives for Malke is the one in which her strong-willed mother sets herself against her family's wishes. The family made an arrangement to marry her off, and gave her a dowry. But Malke's mother was not in love and had no desire to be stuck with this person. She went to her father and said, "instead of the dowry, give me the money to go to America." Several others from the *shtetl* were leaving for America and she was so insistent that the family relented and let her go. The story obviously was a source of honor for her mother, one that she told about herself with pride, and one that confirmed her role as a model for Malke.

Malke grew up during the years of the Depression and World War II. "I never realized how poor we really were until years later. I was happy." She shared bicycles with friends and received hand-me-down clothing. "I was very proud of hand-me-down clothes. I thought that's the way it was." Her mother, a seamstress, changed workplaces from a garment factory to a lampshade factory because of what we now call sexual harassment. After Malke's brother was born two years after her marriage, she stopped working, although during the war years, when her husband became an inspector in a factory that made military clothing, she ran the family candy store. Because of the store, they lived in a neighborhood that was largely non-Jewish.

But even when they lived in a Jewish neighborhood, Malke's parents did not attend synagogue. In fact, they called all those who went to shul hypocrites. Nevertheless, Malke was part of a girls' club at the local shul, the T. I. (Tikvah Israel) Stars. The household had no room for religious ritual—no Sabbath or holiday observance, no kosher kitchen—and mixed meat and milk and had one set of dishes, "we did not eat ham, but we ate bacon." Her parents were the first generation to leave traditional Jewish life. "I think they were escaping constraints." In fact, Malke remembers her mother's father, who was a *shames* (sexton) in a Philadelphia shul.

In the new neighborhood, recognizing Jewish letters on a storefront, Malke stumbled upon a local Yiddish school and begged her mother to send her there, according to her mother's version of the story. Supposedly, she said to her mother: "I understand Yiddish and can speak it; I want to learn to read and write." Later, she also went to supplementary Yiddish high school outside of her neighborhood, and only there did she find friends who could share in the Yiddish culture of her household. Yiddish is the primary link to the Jewish nature of her home. Her parents spoke only Yiddish at home, and Malke remembers worrying about going to public school for the first time because she only knew the common words for spoon, fork, and knife in Yiddish. This is a classic story that children of immigrants retell, and Malke too was part of that tradition.[41] At home her parents read the Yiddish newspaper and listened to Yiddish records and Yiddish radio. Her mother is a masterful singer of Yiddish and Russian folksongs. The apartment was full of Yiddish books when she was growing up, but not one English book. This was Malke's Jewish heritage. She interprets her parents' clinging to Yiddish culture as a result of it being all that was left to them once they had discarded religion and rejected political involvement.

As a child, Malke recalled reciting the classic poem by I. L. Peretz on the radio, while the announcer held the paper for her in order that it should not rattle: "*Vayse, broyne, shvartse, gele. Ale mentshn zaynen brider*" ("White, brown, black, yellow. All people are brothers"). Differences within the political factions of the Yiddish cultural arena and its institutions—the schools and summer camps—were not clear to the young Malke. Her parents were left wing, but not as radical as her mother's younger sister and brother. The sister, who was an officer of the Communist Party, they called "*farbrent*" (extreme), and the brother was continually taking trips to the Soviet Union. He was quite wealthy, and one summer paid for Malke to attend a Communist-oriented Yiddish camp. She attended the Socialist Yiddish elementary school, the Communist-affiliated Yiddish high school, and spent one summer at the Socialist Yiddish summer camp. Only later in life did Malke become aware of the problems attached to extreme leftist positions. Her aunt was anti-Israel, for example, but her mother was not. The positive aspects of the progressive orientation of her family, however, remained with Malke.

I didn't become aware of this until much later and I think that's why I went into geriatric social work, why I worked at

Jewish agencies like HIAS, with the new Russian immigrants
… why I still feel so connected to these people ….Somehow
the ideology came through—social justice, make a better
world—it's all there in the music and songs and poems—it
stays with you. It does have an impact, even when you do not
realize it is happening.

The saying of her mother that underlines their cultural devotion
to Yiddish is: *"Rekhts tsi links, abi yidish"* ("Be it right or left, as long
as it's Yiddish"). Malke believes that her parents sent her to the Yiddish high school as a way of keeping her connected to them. "They
were doing what was comfortable for them … I don't think they had
an awareness of what it would be like for their children growing up
in America." These are parents struggling in their day-to-day existence, with little time for envisioning their children's future. "I always
thought my parents were different … Reuvn and I decided that we
wanted our family to grow up in the mainstream because we felt out
of it, so we joined the synagogue." In point of fact, when Malke introduced religious ritual into her home, it was not difficult for her mother
to accept and it was familiar to her from her youth.

The first time that I lit candles was when I had children. I
wanted them to know what shabbos candles were. My mother
was over for dinner. I wanted to put the food there and that the
children should not burn themselves. I moved the candles and
she criticized me— "you're not supposed to move candles."
My mother bought me a white porcelain dish that said, "shabbos."

Malke had been left with the Yiddish culture of the immigrant
generation at a time when almost all of her school and neighborhood
friends were *grandchildren* of immigrants, with no knowledge of Yiddish. "I felt very alone with it." Once at a friend's house, the parents
were telling secrets in Yiddish, not realizing that Malke understood. In
this way, she belonged to a different generation from her friends. Her
parents were indeed older than her friends' parents, but they seemed
much older because of their immigrant background. "My mother never

wore make-up, never dressed up, never wore high heels. I remember going to Woolworth's when I was twelve and telling my mother that she should wear some lipstick." Malke was able to remain devoted to the culture of her parents' home because she married Reuvn, who not only shared a similar cultural background, but who also valued Yiddish culture as she did.

Malke's family was also different because they remained tied to Europe. During World War II her parents would read her newspaper stories and discuss them— they would tell her about what was happening in the war; about families being separated and finding each other. Whenever her parents met *landsleit* (fellow townspeople) the same frenetic sharing of local stories would proceed, and Malke would hear time and time again the same phrases, "*shnayderishe shul*" ("tailors' synagogue"), "*aribern brik*" ("across the bridge"), and "*ver voynt vi?*" ("who lives where?"). And there were her uncle's continual trips, reports, and contacts with family as well. In 1978 Malke and her mother, who still have relatives in Russia and Ukraine, visited Shargorod together. For this family, unlike most American Jewish families, the ties to the old country have never been cut.

When asked by me to identify the lasting myths and values that she learned from her parents, Malke, like Tsine, comes up with the moral lessons that guide behavior, not the political ideology or the Jewish historical linkage. Her mother was the sole family member to maintain relations with various factions in the extended network: "A lot of people in the family were nasty to each other and didn't speak to one another, but my mother spoke to everyone." Malke learned the family value, that "blood is thicker than water."

The example of Malke brings to the fore a case in which Yiddish remains the sole ethno-religious focus for the second generation. In Malke's family, the memory practices carried on by telling Yiddish stories, singing Yiddish songs, and keeping the bond to Europe alive were those more characteristic of an earlier period in history. The larger ethnic group at the time had moved away from Yiddish and Europe. For most families, the myths of the immigrant neighborhood, like New York's Lower East Side and the experiences of the American servicemen in World War II, had taken over. In this case, we see a contrast between the individual memory repertoire and the collective way of remembering. For Malke and Reuvn, on the other hand, their own unique pattern of hooking up to their cultural heritage, especially to Yiddish music, as their family matured, directed many of their decisions about new friendships, leisure time activities, and even place of residence. For Malke, as for older second-generation Jews, the richness of historic Yiddish culture provides a reservoir of potential memory practices. However, as in all other cases, the immigrant parent remained a towering figure and ethical beacon.

Fitting the Memory Practices of Adult Children of Immigrants into the History of Yiddish in America

The realm of family-specific memory practices and their role in individual and group identification has not received much scholarly attention. Marea Teski found that a person's identity is intimately linked to the memories of childhood that are remembered as being important. As these memories are retained or activated, they reinforce current evaluations of self. Moreover, Teski documented that individuals who were exposed to large repertoires of remembering develop their own diverse repertoires. Children learn to talk about memories. The significant practices which are often specific for certain families include storytelling, retelling of family events, and picture taking. In families that talk about memories and frequently share them in an open fashion, family members report a feeling of closeness within the family. Sharing and retelling memories is a learned phenomenon. If one has experienced this in the family as a child, one is likely to be able to mimic this behavior with one's own children in the next generation.[42] Furthermore, Teski found that different cultures talk about early memories in unique ways and value the development of a memory repertoire distinctively.[43]

In the selected sample I have studied in this chapter I document family differences. Although Dovid was a keen observer of parental character, he offered relatively few family memories or stories. According to the above analysis, we might expect to find little feeling of intimacy within the family. Indeed, the picture he paints is one of three separate individuals, not of a collective family culture. Moreover, his retrospective evaluations depict him as not being able to wait to leave the household. Tsine, in contrast, comes from a family with closeness and sharing of memories, especially as illustrated by their living close to one another and the frequent family events. Malke's family is smaller and more isolated in the history of the Jewish family cycle in the United States, but nonetheless, more than the other families, their practices include sharing memories of the past through folksong and through narrative. This exercise in family and immigration history aims to show how memories of the first years are applied to the way that individuals think about themselves in adulthood. In addition, the narratives collected from the second generation describe the cultural factors and behaviors in which Yiddish is enmeshed within immigrant family life.

The case studies also serve to highlight that, although the nature of family involvement with the Jewish community may vary both for the immigrant family and for the family life that the children later construct for themselves, and that although after leaving their parents' home and its strong dose of Yiddish the children may chart different courses in relation to Yiddish over their lifespan, the emotional attachment to immigrant parents remains strong. This conclusion has not been stressed in the historical accounts of the second generation.

In my research with members of this generation, the use of Yiddish today has signified, and sometimes awakened, deep feelings about being Jewish. Time and again I have been told that Yiddish is a factor that relates to the heart of their being, and specifically to the core of their Jewish identity.[44]

In attempting to probe the meaning of the results of my fieldwork with elderly children of immigrants, the intense emotional bonding to parents may in part indicate the effects of the recent death of parents. The elderly often experience parental loss. This may account for the extent of the emotional response and is indicative of the type of consideration that should be weighed in this complex effort to write a history of this generation's ties to the world of their parents.

The lessons learned from elderly children of Jewish immigrants at the end of the twentieth century should guide us in more carefully scrutinizing the role of the second generation throughout history. The importance of Yiddish relates to its position as the ethnic mother tongue, but it also must be seen in specific association with its structure and function as it evolved in a multilingual Jewish society vis–à–

vis Jewish and non–Jewish languages. The ambivalent attitude toward Yiddish and behavior connected to its language use on the part of the children of immigrants reflect in part long-standing and complex historical relationships that Jews have developed and have internalized in relation to Hebrew and to the non-Jewish languages of their neighbors. This is not a story that simply mimics that of other immigrant languages. From my recent research with Holocaust survivors as well as from the findings that characterize the second generation, it is clear that we must further investigate the history of the ethical will that is transmitted to the next generation within the family via Yiddish. Moral lessons tended to overwhelm the details of the immigrant household in all the interviews I have conducted. Such lessons relate to how to treat people, deal with family, and make life decisions. Informants have demonstrated pride in these ethical positions, which were often identified with the Yiddish language.

The research literature on Yiddish in America has largely concentrated on the literary output of the immigrant generation—the creation of diverse *belles lettres* limited to this single generation. We also possess studies of Yiddish theater and the press. However, language and culture permeate the entire population and are not restricted to sophisticated writers, the corpus they create, and its audience. I have attempted to describe the context for Yiddish language and culture in the everyday life of the masses through its reflection in a focused group of informants of adult children of east European immigrants. Their lives are American stories in that they illustrate a pattern of integrating the immigrant culture into American ethnic culture. This generation is a bridge between the immigrants and future generations, between those who knew the old country and those who choose not to remember or teach about the old country. The members of this generation understand each other's assumptions and cultural values. However, the narrative they tell is not the same as that of subsequent generations of Americans.[45]

I have planned this review and research project as an expansion of the types of sources that are turned to in order to chronicle the history of Yiddish in the United States. For a broader understanding, we cannot limit our research to the analysis of immigrant institutions, such as the press, *belles lettres*, and theater. Besides evaluating accounts in the general histories of American Jewry and the portrayal of the second generation in literature, I have also updated the picture to include the activities of the second generation at the end of the twentieth and start of the twenty-first centuries. In addition, I point to the qualitative data gleaned from diaries and ethnographic interviews, the quantitative information analyzed in census results, and the perspectives garnered from an understanding of the relation of life cycle changes to cultural expression and cultural memory. The latter angle is enriched with the insights gained both from contemporary conceptions of ethnic identification and comparisons from the experience of the second generation of other ethnic groups.

Yiddish has been the main vernacular of the Jewish immigrants to the United States throughout American Jewish history. Although in the early colonial period Sephardic Jews were a sizable portion of the immigrants, by the 1700s most Jews were Yiddish speakers. Moreover, most of the early immigrants from Germany were either from former Polish lands or were Yiddish speakers from Germany. Only toward the middle of the nineteenth century did German-speaking Jews, who had recently experienced language shift from Yiddish to German, arrive in the United States.[46] Since the first boats with masses of Yiddish-speaking Jews from Russia arrived by 1882, we see that Yiddish was indeed the main spoken language of the Jewish immigrants except for relatively short periods. However, by the end of the twentieth century very few Yiddish-speaking immigrants were still alive, and those who remained were mostly the last of the Holocaust survivors and older immigrants from the Soviet Union. Most Yiddish speakers at the present time are descendants of Hasidic immigrants—secular Yiddish speakers are hardly present in the contemporary Jewish population in the United States.[47] Moreover, the pervasiveness of Yiddish throughout the population, crossing all lines in the Jewish community, as I have implied to be the case within the immigrant generation, is a generalization of the past. The overall increase in those declaring Yiddish as their mother tongue in 1970 seems to reflect an ethnic revival that was followed by a fall. Currently, Yiddish speakers are largely concentrated in ultra-Orthodox communities. A recent estimate of Yiddish speakers in New York City reported three thousand secular speakers and three hundred thousand ultra-Orthodox speakers.[48]

Much of the nature of contemporary American Jewry has been determined by the second generation, the children of immigrants. To limit our understanding of this generation as a group which voluntarily distanced themselves from the world of their parents is an oversimplification. I have shown that the evidence speaks for an ambivalent attitude from the beginning. All along, the locus of involvement with Yiddish is in the domain of the intimate family and the emotional sphere to which such attachments belong. Historical perspective also begs for the inclusion of inferences based on ethnographic work with this last cohort in the history of that generation. The concept of generation is only significant within an historical context. Children of immigrants born in the 1880s may share characteristics with those born in the 1930s; however, appeal to memory practice and reconstruction depends on contemporary conventions and accepted principles. This was an insight of Maurice Halbwachs, as was his brilliant observation of the collective framework for memory: "Collective frameworks are … precisely the instruments used by the collective memory to reconstruct an image of the past which is in accord, in each epoch, with the predominant thoughts of the society."[49] Both the psychological awareness of the formative influence of parents and the generative family on the personality of the individual, and the positive associations with ethnic group in the United States during the past four decades, may recast the ways in which the second generation views both its connection to its first generation parents and to their culture. Starting in the 1970s Jewish communal life witnessed an explosion in local Yiddish language and culture groups across the nation.[50] These clubs were formed mostly by adult children of immigrants. Such a framework was not thinkable forty years earlier.

The heart of every culture, which is carried over from generation to generation, is found in the primary institution of the family. To study the essence of Yiddish culture, *dos pintele yidish,* researchers must search in the realm of the family of Yiddish-speaking Jews. Children watch their parents very closely. They internalize a culture and often unknowingly transmit it to the next generation. Yiddish permeated the report of the discussion group and the recollections of Malke and Tsine. Dovid obviously understands Yiddish, but does not seem to have spoken the language. I have found that the Yiddish language today is different from that of the immigrant parents. Sometimes the use of Yiddish does not involve speaking or comprehension. The language exists in some cases without language usage, as a symbol of cultural identity and allegiance. The long history of Yiddish in America must be documented in the future to include more complete information from the biographies and autobiographies of earlier children of immigrants and the ethnographies of the ambience for Yiddish in contemporary ultra–Orthodox families.

This report, by culling from different lines of evidence, reviews the complex connection of children of Jewish immigrants to their mother tongue, Yiddish. In many different types of communities across the United States at the end of the twentieth century, this generation indicated that Yiddish language was at the heart of their individual and group identities. The history of this crucial generation, the bridge between European and immigrant cultures on the one hand and an American ethnic culture on the other hand, must be written with more attention to the realm of the intimate, primary institution, the immigrant family. Communication within the family, as well as the absence thereof, was mediated by Yiddish. This research project underscores the active dialogue that contemporary adult children of immigrants maintain with their parents. In families that share narratives and ethical wills, the intergenerational dialogue format is perpetuated from generation to generation.

Henrietta Szold:
The Making of an Icon

Shuly Rubin Schwartz

"Henrietta Szold, 1860–1945, was an educator, social pioneer, editor and visionary figure in modern American and Jewish history." Thus reads the citation in the National Women's Hall of Fame describing Szold's accomplishments. In October 2007, she and nine other inductees joined 217 outstanding American women whose accomplishments have been recognized at the hall in Seneca Falls, New York. On the one hand, it is gratifying that Szold's achievements have gained this public, national recognition. On the other hand, it is surprising that it took until 2007— thirty-eight years after the hall's founding—for Szold to garner this distinction.[1] In fact, this was the second attempt by Hadassah, the Women's Zionist Organization, to secure Szold's induction. In 1999, an effort spearheaded by Hadassah's then executive director, Laura Schor, had failed to secure Szold's recognition. In preparation for a second nomination, Roberta Elliott, Hadassah's public affairs director, attended the 2005 induction ceremony to see what she could learn about the process. As a result, to enhance Szold's chances of acceptance, Elliott focused the 2007 nomination application on her American activities.[2] When inducted that year, Szold followed other Jewish women who had already joined the Hall of Fame, including Hannah Greenebaum Solomon, Ernestine Rose, Lillian Wald, and Rosalyn Yalow.[3]

This decision to emphasize Szold's contributions to American life did not begin with Hadassah's campaign for induction into the Hall of Fame. As this article will demonstrate, Hadassah had long recognized and championed Szold as an American Jewish leader whose accomplishments spanned both the Jewish and the American scenes.

One of the best-known American Jewish women, Szold achieved distinction in many areas.[4] Early in her life, Szold focused her efforts on facilitating the Americanization of newly arrived Jewish immigrants from Eastern Europe. She founded a night school in Baltimore to teach English language and American citizenship; this school became a model for night schools and immigrant education programs throughout the United States.

Probably the most Jewishly learned woman in the United States in her time, Szold deeply enriched Jewish cultural life as well. She had gained her intensive Jewish knowledge from her father, Rabbi Benjamin Szold. With him, she studied biblical and rabbinic texts and learned Hebrew, Aramaic, German, and French. She applied her learning by teaching children in her father's congregation and serving as editor and translator of his articles and studies. Drawing on her fine secular education from Baltimore's Western Female High School, Szold began to devote herself to editorial work with the Jewish Publication Society, the first successful publication society dedicated to producing Jewish cultural works in English for American Jews. The only female member of the publications committee, Szold became the society's first full-time editor in 1893. Though she held the title "secretary," Szold actually oversaw, edited, and/or translated most of the works that the society published during this period, including Heinrich Graetz's *History of the Jews* and Simon Dubnow's *Jewish History*. Szold played an instrumental role in the success of the *American Jewish Year Book*. This annual publication, which first appeared in the fall of 1899, quickly became the premier reference work surveying facts and trends in the American Jewish community and beyond. She served officially as coeditor with Cyrus Adler for two years, then sole editor for an additional two years. Whether up front or behind the scenes, Szold devoted hundreds of hours of work over an entire decade to ensure the accuracy, quality, and depth of analysis of this increasingly influential work.[5]

Of course, Szold is best known for her role as the founder of Hadassah. Thanks to her strong, effective leadership, Hadassah became the largest Zionist group in the United States and the most successful American Jewish women's volunteer organization. Under her direction, Hadassah established a visiting nurse system, medical unit, and social services in Palestine. Szold also directed Youth Aliyah, the ambitious program that rescued thousands of children from Nazism and helped them acclimate to new lives in Palestine.[6]

In building her organization, Szold consciously chose not to model it on existing Zionist organizations that focused on political and diplomatic advocacy as well as general philanthropy. Rather, Szold drew from her knowledge of the effectiveness of women's benevolent societies and the female-led settlement houses founded by Jane Addams, Lillian Wald, and others. Determined to find a way to realize the progressive ideals that she believed in, Szold focused on developing an urban public health model for Palestine that would provide social welfare services to both Jews and Arabs. This kind of "practical philanthropy" resonated with American Jewish women, and they were attracted to an organization that recognized the special contribution that women could make to the Zionist cause.[7]

Szold also understood Hadassah as a powerful instrument for deepening the Jewish identity of American Jewish women. Through study groups, lectures, and gatherings, this organization educated women about Judaism and Zionism, which served to deepen their dedication to the Jewish people. By influencing American Jewish women to devote their energies to advancing the Zionist cause through a separate women's organization that championed its own independent agenda, Szold also demonstrated a commitment to women's empowerment through learning, organizing, and volunteerism.[8]

Moreover, Szold inspired women through her own example. Though she moved to Palestine in 1920, returning to the United States in subsequent years only to visit, Szold continued to have a profound influence on American Jewish women. She embodied the best of what many wanted to be by modeling just how much one educated, motivated, determined woman could accomplish. Many Hadassah leaders idolized Szold and emulated her in their roles as teachers, public speakers, advocates for Jewish life, and promoters of Zionism. As Sophia Ruskay, one of Szold's colleagues and a member of the first board of Hadassah, recalled, Szold "electrified everybody . . .

it was the humanity and the knowledge. . . . Nothing was ever said about women's rights but we had the feeling she was living women's rights."[9]

Given Szold's manifold accomplishments and popularity among American Jews, it is not surprising that when a group of Jewish studies scholars met in the 1990s to discuss which women to feature for the inaugural poster series of Ma'yan/ Jewish Women's Archive, Szold immediately came to mind. The Szold poster features her quote, "Dare to Dream, and When you Dream—Dream Big." This was a clever way to link Szold to Theodor Herzl, the extraordinary male leader and founder of political Zionism, whose well-known motto was, "If you will it, it is no dream."[10] The poster reinforces the notion that, like Herzl, Szold was a visionary leader who advanced the Zionist cause not only through her own efforts but also by inspiring others to work for the realization of the Zionist dream.

But how did Szold become the iconic figure who has served as inspiration and role model for generations of American Jewish women? One might think that this happened automatically, that her fame spread as a natural outgrowth of her accomplishments—that her deeds spoke for themselves. And on one level this is true. Closely identified with the accomplishments of Hadassah, Szold enjoyed celebrity status among its members. Hadassah women flocked to see her whenever she returned to the United States, and those who visited Palestine stopped off to visit her in her Jerusalem home.[11] Even in her lifetime, Szold's fame extended beyond Hadassah. She received honorary degrees from the Jewish Institute of Religion and Boston University and was mentioned by *The Nation* magazine as one of the most significant Americans in 1936.[12]

Yet this recognition only partly accounts for Szold's continued standing within Hadassah and beyond. That she remains among the best-known, most respected American Jewish women can be attributed largely to the desire of Hadassah's leaders to foster an iconic image of Szold. These efforts began even during Szold's lifetime. Despite her discomfort with it, the organization engaged in what Szold saw as "myth-worship." Hadassah mounted celebrations of Szold's sixtieth, seventieth, seventy-fifth, and eightieth birthdays, and leaders from around the world offered tributes and congratulations.[13] Yet this was only the beginning of Hadassah's efforts to secure Szold's reputation. Szold continued to gain in stature after her death not only because of her merits but also because Hadassah's leadership deliberately cultivated her as an icon over time. They consciously worked to publicize her accomplishments, to educate the younger generation of Hadassah women about her, and to help the larger public appreciate her pioneering role in Hadassah and beyond. The leadership did this not only to preserve Szold's legacy but also to enlarge the reputation of their organization. They understood that elevating Szold's rank within the Jewish community would boost Hadassah's gravitas, helping to distinguish it from other Jewish women's groups. They also knew that Szold's accomplishments in American life and the recognition that she garnered in the secular world helped raise the standing of Hadassah in the eyes of its members, the Zionist community, and the world at large.

The way that Hadassah cultivated Szold's reputation can best be seen by focusing on its efforts in the fifteen years after her death, for this set the pattern that would result in the Seneca Falls induction in 2007. In 1949, Hadassah established the annual Henrietta Szold Award, a humanitarian prize awarded to individuals who best represent Szold's ideals and beliefs. By choosing world-renowned elected officials, Jewish leaders, and other humanitarians as recipients of the award, Hadassah leaders helped ensure that Szold would be identified both parochially with prominent leaders of the Jewish people and broadly with internationally known humanitarians. The award entwined her prestige with theirs, thereby securing her continual elevation in stature. The first recipient was the popular former first lady Eleanor Roosevelt, a woman known for her humanitarian efforts throughout the world and particularly for her role as the head of the National Youth Aliyah Advisory Committee of Hadassah. Two years later, Hadassah bestowed the prize on President Harry S. Truman. Over the years, recipients included Mordecai M. Kaplan, David Ben-Gurion, Golda Meir, Elie Wiesel, and Hillary Clinton; and dual recipients Yitzhak Rabin and Shimon Peres, and Rabbi Irving and Blu Greenberg.[14]

In the 1950s, efforts to enhance Szold's prestige galvanized around the upcoming centennial of Szold's birth. This 1960 milestone provided a perfect opportunity to solidify Szold's image as a quintessential American Jewish leader. From the start, Hadassah recognized that the centennial ought not be a women's event alone. Rather, it should be international in scope and extend beyond the Jewish community. Toward that end, Hadassah began its planning in 1957 with the creation of an international presidium to oversee the centennial. This group consisted of Nahum Goldmann, the newly elected president of the World Zionist Organization; Golda Meir, then the State of Israel's minister for foreign affairs; and Tamar de Sola Pool, a past national president of Hadassah.[15] The three leaders represented the three key constituencies—Zionist organizations, the State of Israel, and Hadassah—essential to launching a successful centennial celebration within the Jewish community. The involvement of Goldmann and Meir—however symbolic—added luster and legitimacy to the centennial. As for Pool, she was the obvious choice to envision and manage the centennial for Hadassah. Editor of the *Hadassah Newsletter* for many years in addition to serving as the organization's president, Pool had worked closely with Szold during her lifetime, especially with Youth Aliyah. She also chaired Hadassah's birthday celebrations for Szold and the 1945 memorials after her death.[16] As Pool explained, she was compelled to take on the planning for this celebration to preserve Szold's reputation as the linchpin of the organization:

> I think of Hadassah's work for Israel as of an estuary, every branch of which of which [*sic*] brings down its rushing waters to the source of the beloved land. If we ascend these branches we find that they come together flowing from a mighty stream which finds its source in the great spirit that was Henrietta Szold. Everything that we have discussed and all the work that we do partakes of her mind's clear vision, the warm humanity of her heart and her soul's unshakeable faith.[17]

In Pool's view, the centennial celebration was a historic opportunity to educate the larger world about Szold because:

> Outside the circles of Hadassah, Youth Aliyah and those who worked with her in the Land of Israel, she was virtually

unknown. . . . Keenly, therefore, do I feel that we should think of the Centennial in a big way and not merely as just one more, perhaps enlarged, birthday party.[18]

To make this happen, Pool contacted Eleanor Roosevelt to enlist her support. Pool convinced Roosevelt to chair a group of "Honorary World Sponsors," and in that capacity, Roosevelt wrote to all the past Nobel Peace Prize winners asking them to join her as honorary sponsors of Szold's centennial.[19] Pool clearly believed that associating as many world-renowned leaders as possible with the event would enlarge Szold's stature exponentially. Pool also felt this would bolster the emphasis on Szold's impact on American life and society at large. Through her planning of the centennial celebration, Pool helped shape Szold's legacy in a way that emphasized the qualities of intellect, faith, and humanitarianism, while also touching on her Jewishness, her gender, and her organizational work.

Hadassah leaders understood that to convey a wide-ranging message about Szold's extensive influence, they would need to employ various media and venues. They also recognized that doing so would help them expose a maximum number of people to Szold's life and achievements. To accomplish this, Hadassah launched several initiatives. It arranged for the Szold tribute that Hadassah president Miriam Freund had delivered on the occasion of the centennial to be entered into the U.S. Congressional Record.[20] The organization commissioned Irving Fineman to write a definitive biography of Szold.[21] In Israel, Hadassah leaders successfully lobbied to have the highway leading to Kiryat Hadassah named "Henrietta Szold Road"[22] and also effectively influenced the Israeli government to issue a commemorative postage stamp that depicts Szold with background images of Hadassah Hospital and dancing children.[23] Additionally, Hadassah leaders enlisted the support of rabbis around the world, encouraging them to give special sermons to highlight Szold's "deep religiosity, her loyalty to Judaism as a faith and a way of life, and the ethical and prophetic principles of human oneness which she pursued."[24]

Finally, Hadassah leaders realized that they would reach the greatest number of people through film. This, their most ambitious idea, began percolating in 1957. Pool contacted Murray Silverstone, president of Twentieth Century-Fox, who agreed to produce a motion picture on Szold. As Pool explained, she knew "of no better way of bringing to the millions of human beings throughout the world the inspiration of her life of idealism and human service than through the medium of a vivid and eloquent film which will depict the dramatic changes she wrought."[25]

In its earliest conception, then, the film was meant to emphasize the universal over the particular, the humanitarian nature of Szold's service rather than its significance for Jewish life and its future.

It was not surprising that Silverstone expressed interest in the project, as both he and his wife Dorothy—who served as the film's associate producer—were supporters of the State of Israel, and Dorothy already had experience producing a documentary about Palestine. Together with her three daughters, she had produced *The Magnetic Tide*, a film about Jews and Arabs living together. Distributed nationally by Twentieth Century-Fox, the film generated proceeds for Children to Palestine, an interfaith group founded to save Jewish children in Europe during World War II. Murray Silverstone met with Freund, and Hadassah leaders began to develop a list of Szold's qualities, experiences, and accomplishments that they hoped to emphasize in such a film. By the end of 1959, Silverstone had agreed to assume complete artistic and financial responsibility for the film.[26]

In keeping with Pool's overarching view of the centennial, the list developed for the film highlights not Szold's Jewishness or her Zionism but rather her Americanism, feminism, and humanism. The first item on the list links Szold to a core American event by recounting her first memory: sitting on her father's shoulder watching Abraham Lincoln's funeral cortège pass by. The subsequent script emphasized that this recollection remained a continuing focus for Szold throughout her life.[27]

The list also featured the seventy-fifth birthday tribute to Szold by New York City mayor Fiorello LaGuardia, in which he emphasized her pivotal contribution to America. It includes LaGuardia's words that acknowledge. "I would not be receiving you today as Mayor of the City of New York but for the work that you did fifty years ago. Had it not been for those evening classes through which my parents were Americanized we would be facing today a new kind of slavery, an industrial slavery."[28]

Szold's Jewish learning and editorial work are presented in the list as feminist breakthroughs: "the first woman student in the Jewish Theological Seminary . . . editor of the Jewish Publication Society in the early 1890's. She organized a wartime overseas unit. All these are firsts for women." On the health front, Szold is credited with no less than countering "witch medicine with twentieth century creative standards of medical practice, healing, and teaching."[29]

Szold's work with Youth Aliyah is praised as an act of defiance against evil, without explicitly mentioning that its raison d'être was the saving of *Jewish* children from Hitler's grasp: "Against the backdrop of world history she defied the destruction of Hitler with construction; and the gas chambers with the exquisite rehabilitation movement known as Youth Aliyah."[30]

In terms of her character, the list praised Szold's work ethic, explaining that she toiled until her death, going so far as to work in an office that adjoined her hospital room. The list also stressed her world-wide reach, noting that she lived, worked, and touched the lives of Jews and gentiles in Israel, Germany, Poland, Russia, Tehran, Shanghai, and Cyprus, "as well as in the free lands of the West."[31]

Given this broad focus, it is not surprising that the subsequent script likens Szold to "Florence Nightingale in courage and mercy... like Jane Addams as a humanitarian... like Clara Barton to inspire a following." In a similar vein, the script suggests that the narration of Szold's visit to Palestine be illustrated with a ship passing by the Statue of Liberty. The following words accompany this image: "On this voyage, like the inspiring statue, Miss Henrietta herself was to light the way for hundreds of thousands of benefactors for all mankind." By driving home the connection between Szold and Lady Liberty, the script broadened Szold's appeal and elevated her reputation.[32]

Not everyone was happy with the universalistic emphasis of the script. In particular, Chanoch Reinhold, educational director of Youth Aliyah, opposed this approach. "Whilst fully appreciating the attempt to stress the humanitarian element . . . I cannot accept the little that is said about her contribution as a Jewess to Jewish national enterprises. . . . It . . . was actually the '*Jewish* Publication Society'" . . . *Jewish* immigrants that she worked with " *Jewish* youth of Germany. . . . the holocaust struck particularly at <u>Jews</u>. . . . " Similarly, Reinhold criticized the section on Youth Aliyah for its emphasis on "uniting the families" after the war, when in reality—and regretfully—in only a few cases could this be accomplished. He urged that the film emphasize more accurately the true mission of Youth Aliyah, which was "to make our wards independent so that they could create their own happiness after their families had been lost or fallen on evil days."[33]

While some of Reinhold's concerns were incorporated into the film—they did identify Szold's place of employment as the Jewish Publication Society—the film's basic universality remained intact. This is to be expected, both because of Hadassah's larger goals for the film and because this approach mirrored the prevailing 1950s Hollywood modus operandi of downplaying the Jewishness of Jews that it portrayed.[34] Thus, in the Szold film, the Holocaust is described in some detail, yet not once are the victims identified as Jews. In depicting Youth Aliyah, the film did not incorporate Reinhold's suggestions. On the contrary, it expressed an optimistic tone and depicted a couple searching for their child in the various youth centers.[35]

Finally, Reinhold and others suggested changes that would more accurately portray Szold, the person. Szold was never referred to as "Miss Henrietta" during her lifetime, and Reinhold suggested changing the script to call her "Miss Szold." The film does use other appellations for Szold, but it still occasionally refers to her by the affected title "Miss Henrietta." Similarly, the film does not incorporate suggestions that it emphasize Szold's modesty and impartiality. It does delete the phrase that Szold was "married to the cause of helping others," heeding Reinhold's warning that this was in bad taste. However, the film adds several references to her unmarried, spinster, and childless state, reflecting prevailing gender stereotypes of the time that viewed unmarried women with suspicion, pity, or both. Thus, though the film highlights Szold's universalism and humanitarianism, it is less effective in portraying her as a feminist leader who promoted gender equality. By incorporating the gendered attitudes that it does, the film undermines its feminist goals.[36]

Upon the film's completion, Silverstone expressed pleasure that it would enable people to "know about the very wonderful humanitarian,

Henrietta Szold, who did so much for our people and brought distinction to the United States, the land of her birth, and to Israel."[37] *Call of the Holy Land*[38] was shown in theaters first in New York City and then throughout the Unites States, often accompanying the movie *Can-Can,* starring Frank Sinatra and Shirley MacLaine. It also played in Canada; London, England; and Sydney, Australia; often at benefit performances for Youth Aliyah. At the time, Silverstone estimated that eventually 150 million people would see it.[39]

Once the plans for the centennial had been set in motion, the presidium issued a call for its observance. That call, like the film itself, highlights Szold's "pioneering achievements along the expanding frontiers of education, social welfare, public health and the rehabilitation of youth." It underscores that Szold's "spiritual roots reach deeply into the ideas of American democracy and the ethical, social and religious teachings of the Hebrew prophets." Finally, the call—more clearly and unambiguously than the film—stresses that Szold "elevated the status of women and gave enlarged dimensions to voluntary work." The members of the presidium explained that the aim of the centennial was "to imprint upon the memory and the minds of all, and especially of youth, the knowledge of her life and to focus the light of history upon her place amongst the great humanitarians."[40]

In many different ways, then, the centennial celebration constructed an identity for Szold that stressed American, humanitarian, and, to a lesser degree, feminist themes. Szold had done much to advance the Jewish learning, leadership qualities, and self-respect of American Jewish women; she had been instrumental in establishing modern medical care in what would become the Jewish state; and she had played a critical role in the successful efforts of Youth Aliyah to save thousands of Jewish children from certain death by the Nazis. Yet she was celebrated in 1960 primarily for accomplishments framed in a more universalistic manner. This did not necessarily negate her more parochial achievements. Rather, it enabled them to gain recognition before a broader audience. As we have seen, Hadassah leaders deliberately chose this path, hoping to enhance Szold's reputation and, ultimately, their own.

The decision to induct Szold into the Hall of Fame in 2007 thus flows directly from the deliberate efforts on the part of Hadassah leaders many decades earlier to enshrine Szold as the quintessential American as well Jewish leader.[41] Thanks to their efforts, Szold has become a beloved icon appropriated by feminists, Americans, Zionists, and Jews as they seek inspiration from past leaders and strive to create new realities for the future.

Yentl: From Yeshiva Boy to Syndrome

Pamela S. Nadell

"Yentl-you have the soul of a man."
"So why was I born a woman?"
"Even Heaven makes mistakes."
Isaac Bashevis Singer (1964) [1]

Now it's Yentl's turn to run the damn yeshiva.
Danya Ruttenberg (2001) [2]

In 1991, in the *New England Journal of Medicine*, Bernadine Healy, then director of the National Institutes of Health, coined the term the "Yentl Syndrome." Two articles in that issue of the journal, one of medicine's flagship publications, had discovered "sex bias in the management of coronary heart disease." Healy explained: The "Yentl Syndrome" referred to the medical phenomenon that "once a woman showed that she was just like a man," in this case, "by having severe coronary artery disease or a myocardial infarction, then she was treated as a man would be." [3] The "Yentl Syndrome," as a term, caught on in medical literature. Not only did cardiologists use it, but pediatricians, studying Swiss children, analyzed the "Yentl Syndrome in Childhood Asthma." [4]

Meanwhile, Yentl began to make unexpected appearances elsewhere as well. The *New York Times* headlined its report on the first women to complete Drisha Institute's Talmudic program "You've Come a Long Way, Yentl." [5] The *Forward* crowed that a female cantor

467

is "no longer the curious Yentl in a man's domain,"[6] and third-wave Jewish feminists titled a collection of essays *Yentl's Revenge*.[7]

How did the name Yentl become so iconic of the feminist struggle against gender bias that physicians, journalists, and feminists evoke it to signal gender discrimination— and not only in Jewish contexts? Yentl, a fictional character created by the Nobel laureate Isaac Bashevis Singer (1904–1991), made her first appearance in English as "Yentl, the Yeshiva Boy" in 1964.[8] However, Yentl owes her fame as the exemplary victim of patriarchal bias to the 1983 film *Yentl*, the directorial debut of superstar Barbra Streisand. How did this film— on the one hand enormously financially successful and on the other harshly criticized, particularly by Singer himself—emerge as an iconic image of the feminist struggle of modern times?

In order to understand the film, we must begin with the short story on which it is based. Singer first published "Yentl, the Yeshiva Boy" in Yiddish in 1962. He was, of course, one of the towering giants of Yiddish literature, and the only Nobel laureate ever to write in that language. Born in 1904, in Leoncin, Poland, the son of a Hasidic rabbi and a rationally inclined mother, Singer grew up in Warsaw in a family which also produced two other distinguished writers: his elder brother Israel Joshua Singer (1893–1944) and his elder sister (Hinde) Esther Singer Kreitman (1891–1954). In 1935, I.B. Singer immigrated to New York and eventually began to write for the Yiddish daily *Forward*. Most of his stories initially appeared in the Yiddish press, and his novels were serialized there as well. His first collection of stories in English, *Gimpel the Fool*, came out in 1957, and, from then on, Singer published widely in English, re-working, with his translators, his Yiddish originals. In 1978 the Nobel Prize for Literature recognized "his impassioned narrative art which, with roots in a Polish-Jewish cultural tradition, brings universal human conditions to life." Singer considered the "high honor bestowed…a recognition of the Yiddish language—a language of exile, without a land." He opened his Nobel address in Stockholm in Yiddish, "because no one has ever spoken Yiddish here in this hall and only Gott knows if someone is going to speak Yiddish here again."[9]

In "Yentl, the Yeshiva Boy," Singer, the creator of often fantastical Yiddish stories and novels, imagines Yentl, a young woman of marriageable age born with "the soul of a man and the body of a woman...thirst[ing] for Torah."[10] "Yentl knew she wasn't cut out for a woman's life. She couldn't sew; she couldn't knit. She let the food burn...." Instead of seeing that she learned to cook and sew, her bedridden father, evidently a widower, had, over the years, secretly taught her the sacred texts of Jewish law. After his death, Yentl, who also in appearance was "unlike any of the girls in Yanev—tall, thin, bony, with small breasts and narrow hips"—succeeds in escaping a life of drudgery at the noodle board. She cuts her braids, fashions sidelocks, puts on her father's clothes, and saunters off into the world as a man, bent on studying in a yeshiva.

At an inn, Yentl, for the first time in her life, "found herself alone in the company of young men." There, taking the name Anshel, she meets Avigdor, follows him to his yeshiva in Bechev, becomes his study partner, and falls in love with him. For his part "Avigdor grew more and more attached to this boy, five years younger than himself, whose beard hadn't even begun to sprout." In time, he confesses that they are "like the story of Jacob and Benjamin: my life is bound up in your life."

Before Avigdor met Anshel, arrangements had been made for him to wed. But, when the father of Hadass, his "destined one," discovered that Avigdor's brother had hanged himself tainting the groom's family with the scandal of suicide, he called off the engagement. Out of despair Avigdor agrees to marry the shopkeeper Peshe, "a cow with a pair of eyes" and a "husband-killer"—her first husband died the year they married—and begs Anshel to wed Hadass. When Anshel asks, "What good would that do *you*?" Avigdor replies: "Better you than a total stranger."

Although convinced "that what she was about to do was sinful, mad, an act of utter depravity," Anshel agrees to marry Hadass, entangling them both in a "chain of deception." After the wedding, Anshel "found a way to deflower" Hadass, who, "in her innocence, was unaware that things weren't quite as they should have been." Meanwhile, Avigdor, loathing Peshe, began taking his meals with Anshel and Hadass.

For Anshel, "lying with Hadass and deceiving her had become more and more painful. Hadass's love and tenderness" shames Anshel/

Yentl. Moreover, the town began to gossip. Why didn't Anshel go the baths before the Sabbath? Why hadn't his beard yet sprouted?

Passover approached. It was local custom for young men boarding at their in-laws to travel to nearby cities during the holiday's intermediary days. Anshel, promising "to reveal an astonishing secret," persuades Avigdor to journey with him to Lublin. There, confessing "I'm not a man but a woman," Yentl disrobes to convince the disbelieving Avigdor. Hearing her story, he asks "What will you do now?" Yentl answers: "I'll go away to a different yeshiva."

Before she leaves, Yentl encourages Avigdor to divorce Peshe and marry Hadass. As they replay, for the last time, their old patterns of arguing the law, Avigdor "saw clearly that this was what he had always wanted: a wife whose mind was not taken up with material things. His desire for Hadass was gone." Although Avigdor broaches marriage with Yentl, "it was too late for that. Anshel could not go back to being a girl, could never again do without books and a study house."

Avigdor returns to Bechev; Anshel sends Hadass a writ of divorce; and the town puzzles over the great mystery. In time, Avigdor divorces Peshe and marries Hadass, but without joy. Within a year she gives birth to a son. Avigdor names him Anshel.

In writing of the "human condition" of the masquerade, Singer employs a time-honored literary device. Shakespeare, for example, repeatedly played with the disguise of cross-dressing: Portia as a lawyer in *The Merchant of Venice*, Viola as Cesario in *Twelfth Night*, and Rosalind as Ganymede in *As You Like It*. Cultural critic Marjorie Garber finds echoes of these characters rippling throughout Singer's tale.[11]

Yet, others locate Singer's inspiration for "Yentl, the Yeshiva Boy" closer to his own cultural milieu, asserting that the life and legend of the story of Hannah Rochel Werbermacher (1806–1888?), the Maid of Ludomir inspired him. Renowned in Hasidic circles as the only woman ever esteemed as a rebbe, the Maid of Ludomir won acclaim for her deep piety, her learning, and her healing and mystical gifts. Until she was pressured into a short-lived marriage she acted like a man—wearing *talit and tefilin,* building her own *shtibl,* holding gatherings, teaching Torah, and leading prayer. Eventually, she settled in Israel, where she continued to attract a following, and where her grave remains a site of pilgrimage.[12]

But, beyond literary and historical sources, Singer had his own real-life inspirations for "Yentl, the Yeshiva Boy." His biographer, Janet Hadda, argues that "everyone in the [Singer] family ... experienced considerable confusion over gender roles" and that this problem "subsequently absorbed Singer in many of his works." His great-grandmother Hindele reputedly "wore ritual fringes just like a man," and was so remarkable that the Belzer rebbe "'offered [her] a chair when she came to visit him' — an unheard of honor for a woman." Singer's mother, Basheve Zylberman Singer, "knew much more about scholarly matters than other women of similar background and standing." Her father "often decried the fact that she hadn't been born a man." Her daughter, Hinde Esther, described her mother androgynously: "Pale, thin, and with those large grey eyes of hers, she looked like a Talmudist who spends his days and nights and years in study, rather than a woman." Married to a Hasidic rabbi, Basheve was utterly unsuited to the role of *rebbetsin*. On Krochmalna Street in Warsaw, where she lived, she was "like an alien plant," "unable to socialize" with the women, "to gossip, to find satisfaction in the housewifely tasks that filled their lives." And they couldn't enter the realm of her powerful intellect.[13]

Finally, the eldest child in the family, Singer's sister Hinde Esther, also aspired to the knowledge reserved for men and was deeply dissatisfied with the lot of a daughter denied the privileges her brothers had. Her novel *Deborah* loosely fictionalizes the Singer household—a household illuminated not only by Isaac Bashevis's memoir *In My Father's Court*, but also by his eldest brother, Israel Joshua Singer, in his masterful memoir *Of a World That Is No More*.[14] Israel Joshua Singer recalled: "When my sister asked Mother what *she* would be when *she* grew up, Mother answered her question with another: 'What *can* a girl be?'"[15]

Whatever sources may have inspired the story, critical reception was mixed. When *Yentl* appeared in 1964 in Singer's *Short Friday and Other Stories*, the *New York Times* reviewer Orville Prescott decided that "even as artful a writer as Mr. Singer can't maintain a uniformly high standard." Of the several stories in the book which he found "flat and tiresome...'Yentl, the Yeshiva Boy'...comes perilously close to being silly."[16] Yet, the story ultimately captivated another far more influential reader, the "actress who sings," Barbra Streisand.[17]

By the time *Yentl* opened in theatres in the United States in November 1983, Streisand had been involved with the project for fourteen years. She first read Singer's story in 1968, and shortly afterward acquired the film rights. In the late 1970s, having already rejected Singer's screenplay adaptation as well as others' attempts, she wrote her own film treatment. Production finally went forward after the movie was reconceived to allow Streisand, the best-selling female recording artist of all time, to sing a series of songs which become Yentl's interior monologues.[18] Streisand co-authored the film, co-produced it, staged its musical numbers, starred in the title role, and made her directorial debut with *Yentl*.[19]

The film opened to mixed reviews. *Newsweek's* David Anson thought it gave Streisand "her best vehicle since *Funny Girl*."[20] *Chicago Sun-Times*'s Roger Ebert went into the movie "expecting some kind of schmaltzy formula romance," and found himself "quietly astonished" by its "special magic." He was also convinced that the Hollywood scuttlebutt that *Yentl* would prove "too Jewish" for middle-America was dead wrong. "Like all great fables," he wrote, "it grows out of a particular time and place, but it takes its strength from universal sorts of feelings. At one time or another, almost everyone has wanted to do something and been told they couldn't and almost everyone has loved the wrong person for the right reason."[21] As the *New York Post*'s Rex Reed put it, "The movie is like rye bread; you don't have to be Jewish to love it."[22]

Ebert and Reed were right. The film had wide appeal. It earned five Academy Award nominations—for Amy Irving as best supporting actress as Hadass, for art direction, and for two of its songs—and won the Oscar for Best Original Score. Streisand was snubbed in the Academy's major categories of director, leading actress, and best film, but she won Golden Globes for her directorial debut and for producing the best film in the musical or comedy category.[23] Moreover, *Yentl*, which cost twenty million dollars to make, grossed forty million dollars in the U.S. and earned more money abroad.[24]

But other critics were not impressed. John Simon found *Yentl* "totally despicable...a monstrous rubber pterodactyl, inflated with an egomania more monumental than Miss Streisand's beak."[25] Janet Maslin wrote in the *New York Times* that Streisand's "musical talents—in fact, all of her talents—have been far better used elsewhere."[26] The exceedingly thoughtful Jewish cultural critic Ilan Stavans, editor of the three-volume *Isaac Bashevis Singer: Collected Stories* (2004), called it "atrocious."[27] Surely, the best remembered criticism came from I.B. Singer. Interviewing himself in the *New York Times* Singer decried the film's lack of "artistic merit," its directing, Streisand's monopolization of the camera, the singing —"there was too much singing in this movie, much too much" —and especially the ending.[28]

The film script indeed tampered with the original story.[29] In the film, Peshe virtually disappears. We actually have to read the screen credits to learn that she is the bakeshop keeper lewdly leering at Avigdor, but in the movie they never marry. Moreover, Streisand imagines a new ending. In Singer's story Yentl goes away; we never learn what happens to her. But in the film, she sets off for America, dressed once again as a woman, striding across the steerage deck singing at the top of her lungs (à la Streisand's *Funny Girl* Fanny Brice belting out "Don't Rain on My Parade" on the prow of a tugboat).[30]

Singer felt that the alterations in Streisand's adaptation of his story lacked "any kinship to Yentl's character, her ideals, her sacrifice, her great passion for spiritual achievement."[31] As for the ending, he said: "Well, for a woman like her to go to America—especially in those years—is as far from my writing as can be."[32] The last scenes in Singer's screenplay couldn't differ more in mood from the film's ultimately optimistic affirmation of self-discovery and adventure. In Singer's original screenplay Yentl, after revealing herself to Avigdor, leaves town, and, still dressed as Anshel, spends her last ruble to rent a private room at an inn. Astonished, the innkeeper mocks Anshel, exclaiming that he's never "heard of a Yeshiva boy asking for a room for himself," and telling him: "You're simply mad." In the middle of the night a local squire arrives, and the night clerk, assuming the room occupied by Yentl to be vacant, unlocks the door. Stunned to find Yentl in her nightshirt, a man's clothes, and no man in the room, the squire challenges her: "Are you a man, a woman or a devil?" Yentl, dressing quickly in Anshel's clothes, bolts. The scene ends with the camera following a "solitary figure down the street until it disappears in the blinding snow."[33]

Of Streisand's decision to end the film by sending Yentl to America, Singer wrote:

> Let's imagine a scriptwriter who decides that Mme. Bovary should end up taking a cruise along the Riviera or that Anna Karenina should marry an American millionaire instead of committing suicide, and Dostoyevski's Raskolnikov should become a Wall Street broker instead of going to Siberia. That is what Miss Streisand did by making Yentl, whose greatest passion was the Torah, go on a ship to America, singing at the top of her lungs. Why would she decide to go to America? Weren't there enough yeshivas in Poland or in Lithuania where she could continue to study? Was going to America Miss Streisand's idea of a happy ending for Yentl? What would Yentl have done in America? Worked in a sweatshop 12 hours a day where there is no time for learning? Would she try to marry a salesman in New York, move to the Bronx or Brooklyn and rent an apartment with an ice box and a dumbwaiter?[34]

In a terrific essay on the film, Stephen Whitfield shows us that these arguments over the transformation of this work from fiction to film give us entrée into the creation of American Jewish culture. Streisand's Yentl sings: "Where is it written what it is I'm meant to be?,"[35] and the film answers that *Yentl* could be other than what I.B. Singer imagined. For Whitfield, the clash between Singer and Streisand replays the "clash between the Old World and the New... between the sensibilities of a Warsaw-born man and a Brooklyn-born woman a generation younger." *Yentl*'s "refusal to be confined— either by the religious norms.... or by the genre in which her fate was first imagined—is one way of summarizing the individualism and experimentalism... personal freedom and assertion..." that have become hallmarks of the Jewish experience in America.[36]

Although Singer and many critics disdained the ending — Janet Maslin thought it "dreadful;" Roger Ebert said that "Yentl sailing off for America seemed like a cheat;" Pauline Kael, who found most of *Yentl* "glorious," called the ending "a flat-out mistake"[37]—Whitfield found it "cogent." He perceived "a logic" in the geographic arc of the film as it traced "Yentl's trajectory"—propelling her from one shtetl to the next, then on to the city of Lublin, "and finally across the Atlantic to another continent, where at its other end Hollywood" and its filmic imagination lay. Filming *Yentl* allowed for "new artistic choices"— for a re-visioning of the story. A film, Whitfield argues, "should not be judged only by its fidelity to a text": successful film adaptations enlarge and enrich cultural life, and *Yentl*, according to Whitfield, stands among them.[38]

Other scholars, too, have used *Yentl* as a prism for reading late twentieth-century American culture, and their arguments also hinge on the movie's choice to send Yentl to America. In *Roots Too: White Ethnic Revival in Post-Civil Rights America*, American studies scholar Matthew Frye Jacobson explores how, in the 1960s, the once-dominant gospel of American life, the melting pot, gave way to ethnic particularism, making room for white ethnics' proud identification with their immigrant pasts. Their new "roots obsession," he observed, "was not some quirky, momentary identity quest...Rather, in their loving recovery of an immigrant past, white Americans reinvented the 'America' to which their ancestors had journeyed." Mass culture played a key role in promoting this ethnic pride, which focused on America as "'a nation of immigrants' — a national 'we' whose point of origin is the steerage deck of the European steamer." Jacobsen reads films like *Yentl*—and like *Fiddler on the Roof* (1971), *The Godfather I* and *II* (1972, 1974), and *Titanic* (1997)—as "ratifying th[is] conception." Thus Yentl's parade among the steerage passengers on the S.S. *Moskva* "melds Yentl's historical moment with Streisand's 'assimilated' present a century later...to project an affiliation with steerage as the very soul of 'Americanism.'"[39]

For theater professor Henry Bial, *Yentl* speaks to the Jewish share in this white ethnic revival. In *Acting Jewish: Negotiating Ethnicity on the American Stage and Screen*, he locates *Yentl* among a series of films which include Woody Allen's *Play It Again Sam* (1969) and *The Way We Were* (1973), another Streisand vehicle. He argues that as the "strength of the melting pot waned," performances created by those clearly identified in the public eye as Jews, like Streisand (and also Allen), consciously "shifted toward the Jewish-specific end of the spectrum."[40]

In the latter decades of the twentieth century, as antisemitism became a negligible factor in American life and ethnic pride surged, Jews felt increasingly comfortable "acting Jewish." Baseball-logo *yarmulkes*, Hebrew names, and imposing outdoor menorahs, including the one lit on the Ellipse on the National Mall, all affirmed that Jews were no longer inhibited by public displays of Jewishness. Bial explains that *Yentl*, with its warm depiction of Jewish learning, openly "embrace[s] Jewishness…communicating a specific message of Jewish continuity to a Jewish audience." The ending, then, for an American audience, is crucial to the message of the film: "When Yentl is forced to abandon her masquerade," Bial writes, "she does not stand and fight for a reconsideration of gender roles in Russian Jewish culture but instead emigrates to America."[41] *Yentl* thus affirmed and celebrated for American Jews that in this land they could both Jewish and American, and in diverse ways.

But, rather than focusing on the adaptation of story to film, on the tensions between art forms, or on how the film mirrors late twentieth century American culture and the place of American Jews within it, I am much more intrigued by the issue of the film's popular reception. Somehow *Yentl* emerged in the American imagination as shorthand for gender discrimination—and not only in Jewish contexts. The film, even though he hated it, surely gave Singer his greatest public exposure. The same year it opened, Singer's publisher, Farrar, Straus and Giroux, brought out a beautifully illustrated book containing just *Yentl, the Yeshiva Boy*. Nevertheless, far more people met Yentl through the film or its album, which sold three million copies, or through its songs, which have remained a staple of Streisand's oeuvre and which were prominently featured in her first-ever concert tour in 1993.[42] In the popular imagination Yentl became synonymous with the film, not with Singer's story.[43] When the *New York Times* columnist Maureen Dowd wrote about Charlton Heston—forever identified with his role in *The Ten Commandments* (1956)—and Streisand wrangling over gun control, she titled her column "Yentl vs. Moses." Her readers understood exactly who she was talking about, and it was not I.B. Singer.[44]

* * * *

To mark the 350th anniversary of Jewish life in America, the National Foundation for Jewish Culture (today the Foundation for Jewish Culture), with funding from the National Endowment for the Humanities, created a nationwide lecture series on American Jewish icons, inviting its audiences to consider "What Makes an American Jewish Icon?" The lecturers nominated an eclectic group of texts for consideration—A.M. Rosenthal's 1958 the *New York Times Magazine* essay "There is No News from Auschwitz;" *Fiddler on the Roof*; the Jewish Palestine Pavilion at the 1939 New York World's Fair; the 1966 and 1996 *Commentary* magazine symposia "The Condition of Jewish Belief;" the U.S. Holocaust Memorial Museum; Mordecai M. Kaplan's *Judaism as a Civilization*, and *Yentl*.[45] What gave *Yentl* a place on this roster is that it stands, much as journalist Ari Goldman argued for A.M. Rosenthal's 1958 essay, as an underappreciated text. Goldman regarded "There Is No News from Auschwitz" as "a groundbreaking article...a departure from the journalism of the day," and he located it as a pivotal event in the growing "public awareness of the Holocaust."[46] Likewise, *Yentl*, is also an undervalued text. It broke new ground for the film industry of its day and helped deepen public awareness of second-wave feminism.

This is not the place to write the history of the second wave of American feminism. Suffice it to say that the movement burst forth out of a series of events in the 1960s, which began when President John F. Kennedy's 1961 Commission on the Status of Women "implicitly recognized the existence of gender-based discrimination in American society."[47] Betty Friedan's 1963 best-seller *The Feminine Mystique* galvanized hundreds of thousands to do something about "the problem that has no name."[48] And, perhaps even to the surprise of the congressman who amended the original draft of Title VII of the 1964 Civil Rights Act to add the word sex, the act passed, banning discrimination in employment on the basis of both race and sex.[49] Then, in 1966, with the founding of the feminist civil rights organization, the National Organization of Women, the "world split open." Soon thereafter, the first meetings between second-wave feminism and American Judaism occurred. In 1972, the Conservative Jewish women of Ezrat Nashim issued "Jewish Women Call for Change," demanding equal access to Jewish ritual, Jewish leadership, and Jewish communal life, and Reform's Hebrew Union College ordained a woman rabbi.[50]

A decade later *Yentl* hit the screen, and its story of the subterfuges required of a girl who wished to learn resonated deeply in a world increasingly sensitized to gender discrimination. *Yentl* was, as noted by scholars Allison Fernley and Paula Maloof, "the first major American film directed, co-produced, and co-written by a woman—who is also its star."[51] Those championing second-wave feminism have repeatedly chronicled triumphant "firsts": the first woman to sit on the Supreme Court (Sandra Day O'Connor, 1981); to become Secretary of State (Madeline Albright, 1997); to win a Golden Globe for directing (Barbra Streisand, 1984); to receive an Oscar for directing (nominees, 1927–2009, 3; winners, 0).[52] American Jews keep their own lists as well: the first women to become rabbis (Reform, 1972; Reconstructionist, 1974; Conservative, 1985); the first to have a solo pulpit; to lead a large congregation; to find a position in a seminary; and to head a rabbinical association.

Streisand was well aware of the challenges she faced cracking the directorial ceiling with *Yentl*. She spoke on camera for the American Film Institute's series *The Directors*, of how, in Hollywood, when she tried to make the movie in 1980 there was

> a feeling of women, actresses, singers, they should stay in their place...Don't try to be too ambitious; don't reach out beyond your limitations...There is also an inclination to believe actresses could be flighty, not fiscally responsible, responsible for money, finances...[53]

Streisand saw her challenge linked to Yentl's exclusion from the world of the yeshiva. The "only way to study was to be part of a man's world, because women weren't permitted to study, and I was feeling the same feelings...I wasn't permitted to direct."[54]

Moreover, not only was the making of *Yentl* a feminist first from behind the camera, but, as Fernley and Maloof argue, what ended up on screen made "accessible to a large audience ideas" of second-wave feminism about gender and identity previously "broached only in the works of 'serious' female fiction writers and academic feminist theorists." Singer saw Yentl's confused sexual identity as "evil" and perverse; Streisand treated Yentl's gender "confusion with an extraordinary empathy."[55]

For Streisand, one of the central questions of the film was "What it feels like to be male, female?"[56] She wanted her audience to question its "easy assumptions and presuppositions about life."[57] Anshel thrives intellectually and also emotionally with Avigdor as her study partner, while at the same time Yentl/Anshel learns from Hadass and admires her beauty, womanliness, grace and domestic gifts. In the film, she comes to love them both—Anshel and Hadass eventually kiss. None of this homoerotic behavior is portrayed as perverse. Instead, Yentl's masquerade allows her to discover herself. Streisand described how she deliberately had Yentl cross bodies of water—a small puddle in the opening of the film, later a canal, a river, eventually an ocean— to signify each stage of Yentl's growth.[58] By the end of the film, Yentl refuses to live any longer in the shadows. She must listen to the voice deep inside: "to see myself, to free myself, to be myself at last.... No matter what happens, it can't be the same anymore."[59] She has emerged as "a confident and independent self," one who has transcended the rigid sex role limitations of the world she must now abandon because it offers her no alternative but to marry Avigdor and darn his socks. Given this interpretation, the ending flows naturally. Yentl, dressed once more in a woman's clothes, is ineluctably drawn to a "new place...the traditional symbol of discovery, change, and promise, America."[60]

Even to those unfamiliar with feminist theory and how its turn to gender complicates our understanding of the sexes and the construction of sex roles, the film's entire premise speaks openly of the feminist struggle for equal access. At its core, Singer's story had subverted the traditional notion that women lacked the intellectual capacity for serious study.[61] Streisand was drawn to make a film about this theme, which would expose assumptions, and ask the question why gender should "impact the nature of learning anything." Streisand, again identifying with Yentl, described her father, who had died when she was fifteen months old and whose spirit she felt hovered over her as she made this film, as a religious and learned man. She believed that, had he lived, he would have taught her.[62] Nearly a quarter century after *Yentl* first appeared, two scenes in particular stand out for how they spoke to second-wave feminism and its demand for equal access.

The film opens with a still frame on which appear the words: "In a time when the world of study belonged only to men there lived a girl called Yentl." Then, riding into the world of the *shtetl* atop a bookseller's wagon, we, the audience, encounter the rigidly gendered world of Jewish tradition. We enter the synagogue, and the first words heard on screen are men's prayers. As the viewer exits the synagogue and heads out into the bustling square, the film cuts back and forth between shots of men and women. Men huddle together excitedly discussing what they have learned from their books—both the permitted and the forbidden. Women, on the other hand, stand in the marketplace hawking fish, chickens, and flowers. They wash clothes in the river as their children splash about. They gossip about fish and engagements while the men speculate about the mysteries of creation.[63]

Meanwhile, Yentl and the bookseller have a heated exchange. Yentl approaches him:

Yentl: I'd like to buy this one please.
Bookseller: Sacred books are for men.
Yentl: Why?
Bookseller: It's a law, that's why.
Yentl: Where is it written?
Bookseller: Never mind where, it's a law.
Yentl: Well, if it's a law, it must be written somewhere, maybe in here, I'll take it.
Bookseller: Miss, do me a favor, do yourself a favor…uh, here…buy a nice picture book; girls like picture books.
Yentl: What if I tell you it's for my father?
Bookseller: Why didn't you say? Fifteen kopeks and if you want to know where that's written, it's inside the cover.[64]

By 1983, the critique implicit in this depiction of a society so determinedly gendered and so explicitly inimical to women's learning was utterly familiar to *Yentl*'s American audience, which sympathized with Yentl as she lied to the bookseller. By the time the film appeared, the changes wrought by feminism's demand for women's full access to higher education and all that that would come to signify were well underway. Only a little more than a decade before, the all-male preserves of the elite Ivy League had opened their admission gates to women.[65] Already unprecedented numbers of women were entering professional schools which, in the past, had never had more than token female representation.[66] These women battled discrimination not only in college and university admissions policies, but also in their demands for equality once they were on campus. In 1970, the Women's Equity Action League insisted that the U.S. government require institutions of higher education holding federal contracts to comply with antidiscrimination regulations. By the end of that year more than 160 such institutions had been taken to court over compliance.[67] These changing patterns in American education made headlines.

Such blatant denial of women's access to equal education also hit close to home in the Jewish world. Only weeks before *Yentl* opened, the Conservative movement's Jewish Theological Seminary had voted, after a decade-long acrimonious public debate, to ordain women as rabbis. That debate had begun with Seminary Chancellor Gerson Cohen conceding "Qualifying her to teach...is one thing. Ordaining her as a rabbi is quite another." It concluded with Cohen applauding his movement's determination to "overcome inhibitions of centuries...to take a major step in the equalization of women in Jewish religious life."[68] *Yentl*'s desire to learn spoke to audiences, Jewish and Gentile, many of whom had experienced first-hand or through their daughters, wives, and mothers, the repercussions of women's new educational opportunities.

The second scene from the film which invites a feminist reading takes place after Anshel, having followed Avigdor to his yeshiva, passes the rabbi's entrance exam. For the first time in her life, Anshel proclaims: "I'm a student." Streisand then launches into one of her private musical commentaries, which reviewer Stanley Kaufman likened to a diary.[69] As she sings, "This is one of those moments that you remember all your life...,"[70] a montage of student life in the yeshiva appears on screen. Meanwhile, over the dialogue, the song, which the actors cannot hear, continues.

The images and dialogue of the world of the yeshiva contrast pointedly with the world of women depicted in the film's opening scene. Here, we see men and boys heatedly arguing with one another while Streisand's song celebrates Anshel joining herself to that chain of tradition: "I can travel the past and take what I need to see me through the years. What my father learned and his father before him will be there for my eyes and ears." As the scene continues, Avigdor, from atop a ladder, pulls books off the shelves and throws them down to Anshel, while the song exults: "There are certain things that once you have no man can take away....and now they are about to be mine." In this world of men and boys exuberance reigns; students grab and toss Anshel's hat; and Anshel, confident, thumbs his nose at them. As he and Avigdor head out into the rain, even the drizzle cannot dampen their spirited discussion.

As the scene climaxes, Anshel enters the yeshiva courtyard where the rabbi teaches. Descending a long staircase, he moves from the periphery of the crowd of students to its very center. The rabbi asks: "Where in the Talmud does it say possession is nine-tenths of the law?" The students give wrong answers; Avigdor comes closest; he has the right tractate—but only Anshel knows the exact page (*daf*).

This passage from periphery to center crystallizes the film's feminist message. The first wave of American feminism, in the 1910s and 1920s, failed to move women into the center of American life. Women won the right to vote, but made only token gains in the political, economic, educational, and social spheres. Feminism's second wave, though, came far closer to transforming American society. Its gains — the disappearance of separate "help wanted" ads for men and for women, the infusion of funding into girls' sports,[71] and the insistence that affirmative action include women — thrust women into the center of American life.

The second wave of American feminism also paved the way for an emerging Jewish feminism, which, in a few short decades, has transformed American Judaism. Jewish feminism propelled women onto the *bimah* as rabbis, cantors, and laity; embraced new rituals such as the women's seder and adult bat mitzvah; and has both invented a number of new settings and opened older ones where women are fully welcome to encounter the texts of Jewish tradition.[72] Today, a woman whose "soul thirst[s] for Torah" has an array of choices before her, and she, unlike "Yentl, the Yeshiva Boy," need not mask herself in order to pursue them.

As Yentl moved from the periphery to the center, she represented, in the popular imagination, women's battle against gender discrimination. Film critic Pauline Kael derided Streisand for "want[ing] Yentl to be—gulp—a role model....a contemporary heroine..."[73] Yet, despite the disdain of critics, that is just what Yentl became. As a result of Streisand's film, Yentl has entered our lexicon. Physicians have discovered the "Yentl syndrome"; journalists have coded stories about Jewish women's growing access to learning and leadership with her name; and the editor of *Yentl's Revenge* exclaimed: "Now it's Yentl's turn to run the damn yeshiva. She knows enough. She's got the necessary tools.... Yentl's back—and this time it's personal."[74]

Yentl, a landmark of second-wave feminism, and a film infused with its sensibilities and messages, gave us Yentl, feminist icon. As she sang—"The time had come....to try my wings...What's wrong with wanting more? If you can fly, then soar."— Yentl gave voice to feminism's aspirations, ambitions, and complexities.[75] Although NIH Chief Bernadine Healy had hoped that the Yentl syndrome would "slip back into history as a curiosity of times gone by,"[76] newspapers as far away as Glasgow and London are still using "Yentl syndrome" to refer to the unfortunate phenomenon.[77] Meanwhile, in Dublin, a feature writer, despairing over the violence women continue to face in the world, remarked on the "great distance" women have traveled "since Yentl" and ruefully mused how far they have yet to go "on a shockingly dangerous road."[78] In Florida, too, a journalist probing the "khaki ceiling" and roadblocks to women in the military, remarked, "Today, women don't have to go all Yentl to join the military."[79] These references to Yentl affirm her iconic status as the archetypical victim of patriarchal bias, and suggest that she's likely to remain so for the foreseeable future.

Notes

Chapter 1 - After Sixty Years: An Appreciation

1. See his "Zionism and the American Jew," in *The Dynamics of American Jewish History: Jacob Rader Marcus's Essays on American Jewry*, ed. Gary Phillip Zola (Hanover and London: University Press of New England, 2004), 61–75.

Chapter 2 - Jacob Rader Marcus and the Archive He Built

1. "The Program of the American Jewish Archives," *American Jewish Archives* 1, no. 1 (June 1948): 2.

2. For additional background and biographical information on Marcus, see Jonathan D. Sarna, "Jacob Rader Marcus," *American Jewish Year Book* 97 (1997): 633–640. For an extensive analysis of Marcus's scholarship, see Gary P. Zola's introduction in *The Dynamics of American Jewish History: Jacob Rader Marcus's Essays on American Jewish History*, ed. Gary Phillip Zola (Hanover, NH: Brandeis University Press, 2004), xii–xxxi. Many studies have been written on the development of the American archival profession. One of the best is Richard J. Cox, *American Archival Analysis: The Recent Development of the Archival Profession in the United States* (Metuchen, NJ: Scarecrow Press, 1990).

3. Salo Wittmayer Baron (1895–1989) taught at Columbia University from 1930–1963. Emphasizing communal social history, Baron's most famous work was his multi-volume *A Social and Religious History of the Jews*. For a full study of Baron see Robert Liberles, *Salo Wittmayer Baron: Architect of Jewish History* (New York: New York University Press, 1995). Oscar Handlin (b. 1915) joined the faculty at Harvard in 1939. His most famous book is *The Uprooted* (1951), for which he won a Pulitzer Prize.

4. As quoted in Sarna, "Jacob Rader Marcus," 638–640; see also, "Program of the American Jewish Archives," 2–5. Jeffrey Gurock has noted the importance of Marcus's historical "spadework" as a key ingredient in the development of a methodical and systematic approach to the writing of American Jewish history. See Jeffrey S. Gurock, *American Jewish History: A Bibliographical Guide* (New York: Anti-Defamation League of B'nai B'rith, 1983), xvi–xx. See also, Zola, *The Dynamics of American Jewish History*, xiii–xiv.

5. Rebecca Hirsch, "The Permanence of Provenance: The 'Two Traditions' and the American Archival Profession," accessed on 22 April 2009 at http://www.archivists.org/publications/proceedings/researchforum/2008/RebeccaHirsch-SAA-ResearchForum-2008.pdf; Richard Pearce-Moses, *A Glossary of Archival and Records Terminology* (Chicago: Society of American Archivists), accessed on 22 April 2009 at http://www.archivists.org/glossary/term_details.asp?DefinitionKey=789.

6. Richard C. Berner, *Archival Theory and Practice in the United States: A Historical*

Analysis (Seattle: University of Washington Press, 1983), 1–2. Beyond Berner's work, much has been written in archival literature on the historical manuscripts tradition. See, for example, Luke J. Gilliland-Swetland, "The Provenance of a Profession: The Permanence of the Public Archives and Historical Manuscripts Traditions in American Archival History," *American Archivist* 54, no. 2 (Spring 1991): 160–175; James M. O'Toole, *Understanding Archives and Manuscripts* (Chicago: Society of American Archivists, 1990); and Frank G. Burke, *Research and the Manuscript Tradition* (Lanham, MD: Scarecrow Press, 1997).

7. Gilliland-Swetland, "The Provenance of a Profession," 161–163, 172–175.

8. "The Program of the American Jewish Archives," 2. In preferring the informational value of a document over its intrinsic value, Marcus was, again, instinctively reflecting an ongoing archival debate then taking place among contemporary archival theorists such as Theodore R. Schellenberg. See Schellenberg's *Modern Archives: Principles and Techniques* (Chicago: University of Chicago Press, 1956), 133–160 for an extended discussion of the differing values of documents. For an analysis of documentation strategy theory, past and present, see Doris J. Malkmus, "Documentation Strategy: Mastodon or Retro-Success?" *American Archivist* 71, no. 2 (Fall/Winter 2008): 384–409. Writing both in his introduction to the AJA in 1947 and again in 1960, Marcus foretold key components of documentation strategy theory (i.e., institutional cooperation in collecting and the importance of documenting events as they happen) when he foresaw a natural division of collecting spheres among Jewish archives based on geography and stated that the AJA "sets itself to collect contemporary materials, so that scholars years hence can turn with confidence to its files in writing what will then be the history of our own day. The Archives does not propose to wait for the materials of the present to be assembled by the scholars of the future," "The Program of the American Jewish Archives," 2–3, and Jacob R. Marcus, "The American Jewish Archives," *The American Archivist* 23, no. 1 (January 1960): 61.

9. David M. Zielonka, *Manual of the American Jewish Archives* (Cincinnati: American Jewish Archives, 1961). In matters of arrangement and description, the AJA was utilizing (out of necessity) methods of economy and practicality during the 1950s that were espoused decades later in archival literature and are now the rage in archival theory and practice; see, Mark A. Greene and Dennis Meissner, "More Product, Less Process: Revamping Traditional Archival Processing," *American Archivist* 68, no. 2 (Fall/Winter 2005): 208–263.

10. Thanks to Jonathan D. Sarna for his advice and input in this area.

11. In the *Moment Magazine* interview, Marcus was asked about his principles in accepting or rejecting materials for inclusion in the American Jewish Archives. He responded that the material "should throw light on the Jewish social experience....I'm interested in criminals just as I am in rabbis." *Moment* interview, A82.

12. Elisabeth Kaplan, "We Are What We Collect, We Collect What We Are: Archives and the Construction of Identity," *American Archivist* 63, no. 1 (Spring/Summer, 2000): 134–138.

13. Jacob R. Marcus, "From Peddler to Regimental Commander in Two Years: The Civil War Career of Major Louis A. Gratz," *Publications of the American Jewish Historical Society* 38, no. 1 (September 1948): 22–44.

14. "Program of the American Jewish Archives," 2.

15. Kaplan, "We Are What We Collect," 150. See also Jeffrey S. Gurock's extensive history of the American Jewish Historical Society's publications, "From Publications to American Jewish History: The Journal of the American Jewish Historical Society and the Writing of American Jewish History," *American Jewish History* 81, no. 2 (Winter 1993–1994): entire volume. In reading Gurock's study, it is easy to draw comparisons between the AJHS and Marcus's efforts at the AJA and to better understand Marcus's efforts in the context of the AJHS's work.

16. Marcus, "The American Jewish Archives," 58; "Program of the American Jewish Archives," 2, 5.

17. Marcus's famous quote on this topic is: "the fact scrubbed clean is more eternal than perfumed or rouged words. The historian's desk is an altar on which he must sacrifice his most cherished prejudices...", cited in *The Writings of Jacob Rader Marcus: A Bibliographic Record*, comp. Herbert C. Zafren and Abraham J. Peck (Cincinnati: American Jewish Archives, 1978), forward material. See also the introduction in Zola, *The Dynamics of American Jewish History*, along with 11–12, 24, 33, and 127, for a discussion of Marcus's views of "scientific" scholarship together with his own words on the subject.

18. "Program of the American Jewish Archives," 5.

19. Kaplan, "We Are What We Collect," 150.

20. During Marcus's tenure as director, the AJA published a series of brochures, monographs, posters, and other volumes on American Jewish history, totaling nearly one hundred titles in all. Included among these were scholarly studies of American Jewish life, reprints of special issues of the AJA's journal, handbooks on beginning a synagogue archive and researching Jewish genealogy, as well as multi-volume catalogs of the AJA's manuscript, photograph and sound recordings collections.

21. Marcus, "The American Jewish Archives," 60. The Tercentenary issues were, *American Jewish Archives* 6, no. 2 (June 1954) and 7, no. 1 (January 1955); the "Western Issue" was *American Jewish Archives* 8, no. 2 (October 1956). The "imposing monograph" was written by Leonard J. Mervis (1912–1988), a 1939 graduate of Hebrew Union College and one of Marcus's students there; later, rabbi of Oak Park Temple B'nai Abraham Zion in suburban Chicago, as his doctoral thesis at the University of Pittsburgh: "The Social Justice Movement and the American Reform Rabbi," *American Jewish Archives* 7, no. 1 (June 1955): 171–230.

22. Morris U. Schappes, *A Documentary History of the Jews in the United States, 1654–1875* (New York: Citadel Press, 1950).

23. Ellis Rivkin, "A Documentary History of the Jews in the United States, 1654–1875: A Review Article," *American Jewish Archives* 4, no. 2 (June 1952): 89; "Rejoinder of Morris U. Schappes to Ellis Rivkin," *American Jewish Archives* 5, no. 1 (January 1953): 32.

24. "Letter to the Editor," *American Jewish Archives* 5, no. 1 (June 1953): 120.

25. Jacob R. Marcus to Ellis Rivkin, 1 and 8 August 1952, American Jewish Archives records, MS 687, Box 39, folder 5, AJA, Cincinnati, OH.

26. Stanley F. Chyet (1931–2002) was ordained at HUC-JIR in 1957 and received his Ph.D. there in 1960, the same year he was appointed to the College-Institute's faculty. From 1960–1976 he was the Associate Director of the American Jewish Archives. He then transferred to the College-Institute's Los Angeles campus where he remained for the rest of his life.

27. "Civil War Centennial (Southern Issue)," 8, no. 1 (April 1961); "Civil War Centennial (Northern Issue)," 8, no. 2 (November 1961); "Union of American Hebrew Congregations Centennial—A Documentary," 25, no. 1 (April 1973); "The Hebrew Union College-Jewish Institute of Religion—A Centennial Documentary," 26, no. 2 (November 1974). In a notice observing the twenty-fifth anniversary of the AJA, Chyet revealed his poetic spirit in an assessment of where the AJA had been, and might go: "How much of what has been accomplished—not only at the Archives but in Jewish academia generally—deserves to be seen as more than quantitative? How much of it has been exploited with passion and imagination to foster the growth of a Jewish spirituality?...As Ludwig Lewisohn once wrote, 'Not what you do matters, but what your soul makes of the thing you do.' The soul? Is there within Jewish academia something historians—or anyone else—might recognize as a soul? Maybe the next twenty-five years of the American Jewish Archives will see a positive answer to that question." "After Twenty-Five Years," *American Jewish Archives* 24, no. 1 (April 1972): 5.

28. Abraham J. Peck (b. 1946) earned a Ph.D. in European history from University of East Anglia (U.K.) and an M.A. in international relations from American University in Washington, DC. He served as Associate Director of the American Jewish Archives from 1977–1997. Peck is now on the faculty in the Department of History at the University of Southern Maine.

29. Other thematic issues that appeared during Peck's editorship include: "The East European Immigrant Jew in America (1881–1981)," with guest editor Uri D. Herscher, 33, no. 1 (April 1981); "Young Scholars on the American Jewish Experience," 34, no. 1 (April 1982); "New Perspectives on Latin American Jewry," with guest editor Judith Laiken Elkin, 34, no. 2 (November 1982); "Forgotten Fiction: American Jewish Life, 1890–1920," 37, no. 1 (April 1985); and "Historical Perspectives on Israel, the United States, and American Jewry," 40, no. 1 (April 1988).

30. My thanks to Jonathan D. Sarna for bringing many of these points to my attention and for his perspective on Marcus's work.

31. When asked in the *Moment* interview who was his role model, Marcus said, "my model is Jacob Rader Marcus....I think that my approach [is] unique, that the Jews are unique." Concerning the possibility of writing a memoir, Marcus said, "...if you have strength to write a memoir, then you have strength to finish your scientific work. That has to be done first." *Moment* interview, A82–A84.

32. "After Twenty-Five Volumes," *American Jewish Archives* 26, no. 1 (April 1974): 3.

33. Marcus, "American Jewish Archives," 61; Kaplan, "We Are What We Collect," 151; Jonathan D. Sarna, *American Judaism: A History* (New Haven: Yale University Press, 2004), xx.

Chapter 3 - "A Land That Needs People for Its Increase:" How the Jews Won the Right to Remain in New Netherland

1. I am greatly indebted to Robert Emery, Mary Wood, Colleen Osteguy, and Robert Begg of the Albany Law School library for their extraordinary efforts in helping me with the development of this article. I also thank Gillian Berchowitz, Charles Gehring, Jonathan Sarna, and Lance Sussman for their helpful comments. The writing of this article was partially supported by a summer research grant from Albany Law School and a grant from The Jacob Rader Marcus Center of the American Jewish Archives.

I thank Kevin Proffitt and Dana Herman at the AJA for their help. While this essay is part of a symposium in honor of the birthday of the American Jewish Archives and a decade of leadership by Gary Zola, I would like to also add a minor dedication to Samuel Oppenheim, who gathered material on Jews in early New York and wrote about them more than a century ago. Oppenheim (1859–1928), a native of New York, was an attorney and public servant, the recording secretary of the American Jewish Historical Society, and a prolific author of books and articles on the history of Jews in the New World. His work remains the place to start on this subject.

2. Hyman Grinstein's seminal work *The Rise of the Jewish Community of New York* (Philadelphia: Jewish Publication Society, 1945), 21, 39, devotes but a few lines to the Jews of the Dutch period. Henry L. Feingold, *Zion in America: The Jewish Experience from Colonial Times to the Present* (New York: Twayne Publishers, 1974), 20–24 presents an excellent, but short, discussion of the New Amsterdam experience. See also Jacob Rader Marcus, *Early American Jewry: The Jews of New York, New England, and Canada, 1649–1794* (Philadelphia: The Jewish Publication Society of America, 1951), 24–33. The most comprehensive volume is the dated but still useful Samuel Oppenheim, *The Early History of the Jews in New York, 1654–1664: Some New Matter on the Subject* [hereinafter *Early History*] Publications of the American Jewish Historical Society, No. 18 (1909). This pamphlet was also published in *American Jewish Historical Society Journal* (*AJHSJ*) 18 (1909): 1–91. The pagination in both versions is identical. Contrary to my argument, James Homer Williams argues that the history of the Jews in New Amsterdam "has received a great deal of attention—far beyond the actual number of people involved warrants." James Homer Williams, "An Atlantic Perspective on the Jewish Struggle for Rights and Opportunities in Brazil, New Netherland, and New York," in *The Jews and Expansion of Europe to the West, 1450–1800*, ed. Paolo Bernardini and Norman Fiering (New York and Oxford: Berghahn Books, 2001), 370. The most serious, and best, attention to the first Jews in a larger study is Jonathan Sarna, *American Judaism: A History* (New Haven: Yale University Press, 2004).

3. Saul S. Friedman, *Jews and the American Slave Trade* (New Brunswick, NJ: Transaction Publishers, 1998), 104.

4. In addition to Friedman, *Jews and the American Slave Trade*, the traditional account appears in the most recent general history of New Netherland, Russell Shorto, *The Island at the Center of the World: The Epic Story of Dutch Manhattan and the Forgotten Colony That Shaped America* (New York: Doubleday, 2004), 275. Letter from the Directors at Amsterdam to the Director General [Stuyvesant] and Council, 26 April 1655, in Charles T. Gehring, ed., *New Netherland Documents Series, Vol XII, Correspondence, 1654–1658*, [hereinafter *NND*] (Syracuse: Syracuse University Press, 2003), 48–49. This letter is also printed with slight variations in punctuation, spelling and italics, as The Directors of the W.I. Co., Dept. of *Amsterdam*, J. Bontemantel and Edward Man to Director [Petrus] *Stuyvesant* and Council in *New Netherland*, 26 April 1655, Berthold Fernow, ed., *Documents Relating to the Colonial History of the State of New York* (Albany, NY: Weed, Parsons, and Company, 1883), (Old Series) XIV: 315.

5. Rev. Johannes Megapolensis to the Classis of Amsterdam, 18 March 1655, in Hugh Hastings, ed., *Ecclesiastical Records of the State of New York* [hereinafter *Ecclesiastical Records*] (Albany: James B. Lyon, State Printer, 1901), 1:335–336. Berthold Fernow,

ed., *The Records of New Amsterdam: From 1653 to 1674* (1897, reprint Baltimore, MD: Genealogical Publishing Co., Inc., 1976), 244. Leo Hershkowitz argues that there were not even twenty-three Jews that came from Recife, but I am unconvinced by his argument. See Leo Hershkowitz, "New Amsterdam's Twenty-Three Jews – Myth or Reality," in *Hebrew and Bible in America: The First Two Centuries*, ed. Shalom Goldman [hereinafter "Myth or Reality"] (Hanover and London: Brandeis University Press, and Dartmouth College, 1993), 171–181.

6. Daniel M. Swetschinski, *Reluctant Cosmopolitans: The Portuguese Jews of Seventeenth-century Amsterdam* [hereinafter *Reluctant Cosmopolitans*] (London: The Littman Library of Jewish Civilization, 2000), 117. Jews were never huge participants in the company, constituting just over five percent of the stock holders in the 1670s. Friedman, *Jews and the American Slave Trade*, 64–65. See also Eli Faber, *Jews, Slaves, and the Slave Trade: Setting the Record Straight* (New York: New York University Press, 1998), 21.

7. Petition to the Honorable Lords, Directors of the WIC, January 1655, published in Oppenheim, *Early History*, 9.

8. Van Cleaf Bachman, *Peltries or Plantations: The Economic Policies of the Dutch West India Company in New Netherland, 1623–1639* (Baltimore, MD: Johns Hopkins University Press, 1969), 50–51; Rex H. Hudson, ed., *Brazil: A Country Study* (Washington, DC: Federal Research Division, Library of Congress, 1997), 22; Swetschinski, *Reluctant Cosmopolitans*, 114; Lewis Samuel Feuer, *Spinoza and the Rise of Liberalism* (Boston: Beacon Press, 1958), 28; Sarna, *American Judaism*, 6; I.S. Emmanuel, "New Light on Early American Jewry," *American Jewish Archives* 7 (1955): 5.

9. Swetschinski, *Reluctant Cosmopolitans*, 115.

10. "Favorable Reply from the States-General," in I.S. Emmanuel, "New Light on Early American Jewry," Appendix F, 43–44. Letter from the Directors to Stuyvesant, 21 March 1651, in Fernow, ed., *Documents Relating to the Colonial History* (Old Series) XIV: 135.

11. The best discussion of the details of *how* the Recife Jews made it to New Amsterdam is Leo Hershkowitz, "By Chance or Choice: Jews in New Amsterdam 1654," *AJA* 57 (2005): 1–15; Feuer, *Spinoza and the Rise of Liberalism*, 28–29. Leo Hershkowitz argues there were probably not twenty-three Jews, asserting that "With a good deal of imaginative arithmetic that figure can be reached." Hershkowitz, "Myth or Reality," 172. His argument is based on the fact that we do not have the names of all twenty-three, but there is no reason to believe that the names of any of the children, or probably all of the women in this group, would have been noted in any records. Indeed, had the Jews not been sued by the ship captain, we might not have as many of the names of the adult Jewish men on the ship.

12. Hershkowitz, "By Chance or Choice," 4.

13. Sarna, *American Judaism*, 6.

14. Rev. Johannes Megapolensis to the Classis of Amsterdam, 18 March 1655, in *Ecclesiastical Records*, 1:335–336. See also Oppenheim, *Early History*, 2.

15. Samuel Oppenheim, "More About Jacob Barsimson, The First Jewish Settler in New York," *Publications of the American Jewish Historical Society* 29 (1925): 39. Leo Hershkowitz, "Some Aspects of the New York Jewish Merchant and Community, 1654–1820," *American Jewish Historical Quarterly* 66 (1976–1977): 10 and "By

Chance or Choice: Jews in New Amsterdam 1654," *AJA* 57 (2005): 1, spells the name "Barsimon." However, the most recent investigations by the New York State Library find that in the written records of the colony the name is always Barsimson.

16. Leo Hershkowitz makes this argument in "By Chance or Choice," 1. Hershkowitz, "Myth or Reality," 171–181.

17. Oppenheim, *Early History*, 3; Oppenheim, "More About Jacob Barsimson," 41–42; Marcus, *Early American Jewry*, 24.

18. Oppenheim, "More About Jacob Barsimson," 39.

19. Karina Sonnenberg-Stern, *Emancipation and Poverty: The Ashkenazi Jews of Amsterdam, 1796–1850* (London: Macmillan, 2000), 27–28.

20. Friedman, *Jews and the American Slave Trade*, 5. Sonnenberg-Stern, *Emancipation and Poverty*, 28–29; C.R. Boxer, *The Dutch Seaborne Empire, 1600–1800* (New York: Alfred A. Knopf, 1965), 130; Lewis Samuel Feuer, *Spinoza and the Rise of Liberalism*, 7.

21. Information on this is found at the Jewish Museum of Amsterdam. See also http://www.jewishencyclopedia.com/view.jsp?artid=197&letter=N&search=Dutch%20Citizenship#578 and http://www.jewishencyclopedia.com/view.jsp?artid=248&letter=N&search=Dutch%20West%20Indies%20Company#737 accessed on 18 September 2008.

22. Jonathan Israel, "Introduction," in *Dutch Jewry: Its History and Secular Culture (1500–2000)*, ed. Jonathan Israel and Reinier Salverda (Leiden, Netherlands: Brill, 2002), 10.

23. Marcus, *Early American Jewry*, 14.

24. Leo Hershkowitz, in "By Chance or Choice," 4, argues they were delayed in Spanish Jamaica or possibly Spanish Cuba.

25. Berthold Fernow, ed., *The Records of New Amsterdam: From 1653 to 1674* (1897, reprint Baltimore: Genealogical Publishing Co., Inc., 1976), 1: 240, 241, 244, 249. This record provides some of the names of the Jews, including Abram Israel, Judicq de Mereda, David Israel, and Moses Ambrosius.

26. Rev. Johannes Megapolensis to the Classis of Amsterdam, 18 March 1655, *Ecclesiastical Records*, 1:335–336.

27. Ibid.

28. As it turned out, most of these first Jews did not stay very long in New Amsterdam. Leo Hershkowitz, "Myth or Reality," 171–181.

29. Stuyvesant to the Amsterdam Chamber, 22 September 1654, reprinted in Samuel Oppenheim, *Early History, 4–5*. Oppenheim provides only an extract of Stuyvesant's letter. Unfortunately, Oppenheim does not provide a source for this letter, indicating the extract was "recently found by the writer [Oppenheim] in a clearly written Dutch MS. of the period." Ibid., 4. This extract also appears in Jacob R. Marcus, *The Jew in the American World: A Source Book* (Detroit: Wayne State University Press, 1996), 29. This volume also fails to give a source for this letter.

30. Ibid.

31. Ibid.

32. Swetschinski, *Reluctant Cosmopolitans*, 51, notes that by the end of the seventeenth century Jews began to get similar economic, social, and even political rights in Bordeaux and London.

33. Ibid.

34. George L. Smith, *Religion and Trade in New Netherland: Dutch Origins and American Development* (Ithaca: Cornell University Press, 1973), 98, 103.

35. This directive is quoted in Henri and Barbara Van Der Zee, *A Sweet and Alien Land: The Story of Dutch New York* (New York: Viking Press, 1978), 91–282.

36. Literally the "Nineteen Lords Directors."

37. Smith, *Religion and Trade in New Netherland*, 64.

38. Also on this cutting edge was Roger Williams, the founder of Rhode Island, where the second Jewish Community in the North American Colonies would emerge. See Paul Finkelman, "School Vouchers, Thomas Jefferson, Roger Williams, and Protecting the Faithful: Warnings from the Eighteenth Century and the Seventeenth Century on the Dangers of Establishments to Religious Communities," *Brigham Young University Law Review* Vol. 2008 (2008): 525.

39. Smith, *Religion and Trade in New Netherland*, 64.

40. John Webb Pratt, *Religion, Politics, and Diversity: The Church-State Theme in New York History* (Ithaca, NY: Cornell University Press, 1967), 6.

41. Henri and Barbara Van Der Zee, *A Sweet and Alien Land*, 91–92.

42. Oliver A. Rink, *Holland On the Hudson: An Economic and Social History of Dutch New York* (Ithaca, NY: Cornell University Press, 1986), 223.

43. Ibid., 225.

44. Patricia U. Bonomi, *Under the Cope of Heaven: Religion, Society, and Politics in Colonial America* (New York: Oxford University Press, 2003), 25.

45. Stuyvesant to the Amsterdam Chamber, 22 September 1654, reprinted in Oppenheim, *Early History*, 4–5.

46. Colonial Albany Social History Project at http://www.nysm.nysed.gov/albany/lutheran.html, accessed on 18 September 2008.

47. Revs. Megapolensis and Drisius to the Classis of Amsterdam, 6 October 1653, *Ecclesiastical Records*, 1:317–318.

48. Classis of Amsterdam to Revs. Megapolensis and Drisius, 23 February 1654, Ibid. 1:322–323.

49. Expulsion of Swedish Ministers from Delaware, 25 September 1655, Ibid., 1:340.

50. The Directors to Stuyvesant, 14 June 1656, Fernow, ed., *Documents Relating to the Colonial History*, 14 (Old Series): 351. A placaat, or placat, is "a form of subordinate or inferior legislation." J.W. Wessels, *History of the Roman-Dutch Law* (Grahamstown, SA: African Book Co., 1908), 208. According to Grotius "the general written law consists of enactments of the States, i.e. of the knights, nobles and representatives of the large towns; or placaats of the heads of provinces (lands hoofden) to whom such power has been lawfully granted by the States under the title of counts, lords, governors or chief magistrates." Ibid.

51. The Directors to Stuyvesant, 14 June 1656, Fernow, ed., *Documents Relating to the Colonial History*, 14 (Old Series): 351.

52. Petitions of the Lutherans to the Governor and Council, 24 October 1656; and letter from the Directors to Stuyvesant, 7 April 1657, *Ecclesiastical Records*, 1:358–360; 372–373 and 377–378.

53. The Classis of Amsterdam to the Consistory of New Netherland, 25 May 1657, *Ecclesiastical Records*, 1:378–381.

54. Petition of Revs. Megapolensis and Drisius to the Burgomasters, etc. Against Tolerating the Lutherans, 6 July 1657; Report of the Mayor and Aldermen of New

Amsterdam Upon the Petition of the Ministers Against Allowing Lutheran Service, 14 July 1657, Ibid., 1: 386–388; 388–390.

55. Ibid.

56. Letter from the Directors to Stuyvesant, 20 May 1658; Fernow, ed., *Documents Relating to the Colonial History,* 14 (Old Series), 417–418.

57. Revs. Megapolensis and Drisius to the Director-General and Council of New Netherland, 23 August 1658 and Revs. Megapolensis and Drisius to the Classis of Amsterdam, 24 September 1658, *Ecclesiastical Records*, 1:428–430 and 432–436.

58. Revs. Megapolensis and Drisius to the Classis of Amsterdam, 10 September 1659 and Acts of the Calssis of Amsterdam, 3 November 1659, *Ecclesiastical Records*, 1:449–450 and 454.

59. Rev. Gideon Schaats to the Classis of Amsterdam, 22 September 1660, *Ecclesiastical Records*, 1: 482–483 and response by the Classis, Ibid., 504–505 and 515–516. "Letter from the Governor in Regard to the Lutherans," 13 October 1666, Ibid., 583.

60. Revs. Megapolensis and Drisius to the Classis of Amsterdam, 5 August 1657, *Ecclesiastical Records*, 1: 393–400.

61. Pratt, *Religion, Politics, and Diversity*, 19.

62. Sydney E. Ahlstrom, *A Religious History of the American People*, 2 vols. (Garden City, NJ: Doubleday, 1975), 1:229, 230.

63. Revs. Johannes Megapolensis and Samuel Drisius to the Classis of Amsterdam, 14 August 1657, *Ecclesiastical Records*, 1: 399–400. Frederick J. Zwierlein, *Religion in New Netherland* (Rochester, N.Y.: John P. Smith, 1910), 213–242.

64. Ibid.

65. In 1657, Dutch authorities in New Netherlands tortured the Quaker Robert Hodgson in a variety of ways, including dragging him behind a horse cart, placing him in a vermin filled dungeon, and severely whipping him and "chaining him to a wheelbarrow in the hot sun until he collapsed." He was later hung by his hands in a prison cell and "whipped until he was near death." After two days in solitary confinement, he was again whipped until near death. Hodgson's ordeal ended when Stuyvesant's own sister convinced him to release Hodgson from prison and expel him from the country. Smith, *Religion and Trade in the New Netherlands*, 223. See also Zwierlein, *Religion in New Netherland*, 213–246.

66. "Remonstrance of the Inhabitants of Flushing, L.I., Against the Law Against Quakers," 1 January 1658, in *Ecclesiastical Records*, 1:412–413.

67. Directors of the Dutch West Indies Company to Stuyvesant, 16 April 1663, *Ecclesiastical Records*, 1:530.

68. Other evidence suggests that the actions of Stuyvesant were often in tension with the goal of the Directors to increase the population of the colony and to preserve basic liberties. For example, the Directors reprimanded Stuyvesant for inserting a clause "in the printed passports, given to freemen sailing from here [Holland] to *New-Netherland*" which required "that they must remain there [New Netherland] for a certain number of years." The directors noted this was "offensive to many," "antagonistic to the liberty of free people" and "an obstacle to the increasing of the population." The letter to Stuyvesant ended: "You will govern yourself accordingly." Directors to Stuyvesant, 30 July 1654, Fernow, ed., *Documents Relating to the Colonial History*, 14 (Old Series), 280. See also The Directors of the W.I. Co., Dept.

of *Amsterdam*, David van Baerle, Edward Man. and Abr. Wilmerdonx to Director [Petrus] Stuyvesant and Council in *New Netherland*, 13 March 1656, in Ibid., 341, ordering Stuyvesant to allow the ship *Scots* to sail "to and fro ... because for the sake of increasing the population, trade and its freedom must not be hampered with, but ought to be relieved from all restrictions."

69. Directors of the Dutch West Indies Company to Stuyvesant, 16 April 1663, in *Ecclesiastical Records*, 1:530.

70. Rev. John Megapolensis to the Classis of Amsterdam, 6 October 1653, in *Ecclesiastical Records*, 1:334–336. Although unhappy with their presence in his domain, Megapolensis gave some charity to the Jews, who arrived destitute. Van Der Zee, *A Sweet and Alien Land*, 290–291.

71. Ambassador Nieupoort to the States General, 31 December 1655, and Nieupoor to States General, January 1656, in E.B. O'Callaghan, ed., *Documents Relative to the Colonial History of the State of New York* (Albany, NY: Weed, Parsons, and Company, 1856), 1:578–559; 582–583.

72. Stuyvesant to the Amsterdam Chamber, 22 September 1654, reprinted in Oppenheim, *Early History*, 4–5.

73. Petition to the Honorable Lords, Directors of the WIC, January 1655, published in Oppenheim, *Early History*, 9.

74. Ibid.

75. Stuyvesant sent two additional letters to the Directors on 2 September and 27 October. Letter from the Directors at Amsterdam to the Director General [Stuyvesant] and Council, 26 April 1655, in Gehring, ed., *NND*, Vol. XII: 48–49. The Directors of the W.I. Co., Dept. of *Amsterdam*, J. Bontemantel and Edward Man to Director [Petrus] Stuyvesant and Council in *New Netherland*, 26 April 1655, Fernow, ed., *Documents Relating to the Colonial History* 14 (Old Series), 315.

76. Letter from the Directors at Amsterdam to the Director General [Stuyvesant] and Council, 26 April 1655, in Gehring, ed., *NND*, Vol. XII: 48–49.

77. Letter from the Directors at Amsterdam to the Director General [Stuyvesant] and Council, 26 April 1655, in Gehring, ed., *NND*, Vol. XII: 48–49. Part of this translation is now in dispute. The traditional translation by Berthold Fernow, which the new Gehring edition confirms, and which has been repeated by almost all scholars, included this line: "and also because of the large amount of capital, which they have invested in shares of this Company." But more recently, the scholar Jaap Jacobs has argued that this line should actually be translated as: "the large sums of money for which they are still indebted to the Company." See Jaap Jacobs, *New Netherland: A Dutch Colony in Seventeenth-Century America* (Leiden: Brill, 2005), 375–376. If Jacobs is correct, then my interpretation here is strengthened. However, there appears to be no consensus at the moment on this new translation, and even Jacobs admits that "the case for this completely different translation is not without weaknesses." He notes that there is "no other occurrence known" of interpreting the words as he does. Ibid., 376.

78. Petition to the Honorable Lords, Directors of the WIC, January 1655, published in Samuel Oppenheim, *Early History*, 9.

79. The Directors to Stuyvesant, 13 March 1656, Fernow, ed., *Documents Relating: to the Colonial History* 14 (Old Series), 341.

80. Sarna, *American Judaism*, 9–10.

81. Paul Finkelman, "School Vouchers, Thomas Jefferson, Roger Williams, and Protecting the Faithful," 525.

82. Pratt, *Religion, Politics, and Diversity*, 24.

83. Pratt argues that the failure to resolve the tension and contradiction between Stuyvesant and the West India Company officials undermined the Dutch colony. *Religion, Politics, and Diversity*, 25. This may be true, although it seems unlikely that a consistent policy of either tolerance or repression would have prevented English seizure of the colony. Petition to the Honorable Lords, Directors of the WIC, January 1655, published in Samuel Oppenheim, *Early History*, 10.

84. E.B. O'Callaghan, ed., *Documents Relative to the Colonial History of the State of New York*, 2:251.

85. Pratt, *Religion Politics and Diversity*, 26–35, . O'Callaghan, ed., *Documents Relative to the Colonial History of the State of New York*, 3:218.

86. *Colonial Laws of New York*, 1:115.

87. Pratt, *Religion Politics and Diversity*, 34–35.

88. Jacob R. Marcus, *The Colonial American Jew, 1492–1776* (Detroit: Wayne State, 1970).

89. "Answer of Governor to Enquiries About New York," 16 April 1678, *Ecclesiastical Records*, 1: 709.

90. "Governor Dongan's Report on the State of the Province," 1684, *Ecclesiastical Records*, 2:879–880; Douglas Greenberg, *Crime in the Colony of New York* (Ithaca, NY: Cornell University Press, 1978), 26; Edwin Scott Gaustad, *Historical Atlas of Religion in America* (New York: Harper and Row, 1962), 2.

91. Oppenheim, *Early History*, 9. See also Oppenheim, "More About Jacob Barsimson," 39; Leo Hershkowitz, "Some Aspects of the New York Jewish Merchant and Community, 1654–1820," *American Jewish Historical Quarterly* 66 (1976–1977): 10; Leon Hühner, "Asser Levy: A Noted Jewish Burgher of New Amsterdam," *AJHS Journal* 8 (1900): 99.

Chapter 4 - Architecture of Autonomy: The Blessing and Peace Synagogue of Suriname

1. Frederik Oudschans Dentz, "Wat er overbleef van het kerkhof en de synagoge van de Joden-Savanne in Suriname," *De West-Indische Gids* 7–8 (July-August 1948): 210–225, 214; David Baruh Louzada et al., *Beschryving van de Plechtigheden nevens de Lofdichten en gebeden, uitgesproken op het eerste Jubelfeest van de synagoge der Portugeesche Joodsche Gemeente, op de Savane in de Colonie Suriname, genaamd Zegen en Vrede op den 12 den van Wynmaand des Jaars MDCCLXXXV* (Amsterdam: Hendrik Willem en Cornelis Dronsberg, 1785), passim and, for the poem, 3–5 in the Hebrew section. The date coincided with Wednesday, 8 Heshvan 5546. See Alan Corré's excellent "Perpetual Jewish/Civil Calendar" at http://www.uwm.edu/~corre/.

2. A discussion of the messianic import of Jodensavanne's layout and the architecture of its synagogue first appeared in Rachel Frankel, "Antecedents and Remnants of Jodensavanne: The Synagogues and Cemeteries of the First Permanent Plantation Settlement of New World Jews," in *The Jews and the Expansion of Europe to the West, 1450–1800*, ed. Bernardini and Fiering (New York and Oxford: Oxford University Press, 2001), 394–436, and is more amply considered here from an architectural-historical perspective.

3. Iberian-origin Jews in Suriname are more seldom identified as members of the "Portuguese and Spanish Jewish nation." "Portuguese Jews" is employed in this article for the sake of brevity. The idiosyncratic spelling and pronunciation of Hebrew in this article are drawn from communal archives.

4. Wim Klooster, *The Dutch in the Americas, 1600–1800* (Providence, RI: The John Carter Brown Library, 1997), 68.

5. This is the argument of Jacob Rader Marcus in his edited volume, *Historical Essay on the Colony of Surinam, 1788* (Cincinnati: American Jewish Archives, 1974), ix–x. Marcus also states that this was the first time since Rome bestowed citizenship on all of its subjects in the third century that Jews received "such substantial rights and liberties." See also his *The Colonial American Jew, 1492–1776*, 2 vols. (Detroit: Wayne State University Press, 1970), I: 152. Marcus's statement appears to be true in the sense that nowhere else in the western world had Jews been granted a semi-autonomous settlement. It is difficult to definitively compare the civil and political privileges bestowed upon the Jews of Curaçao and Suriname since the 1659 document of privileges granted to Isaac da Costa by the Directors of the West India Company at Amsterdam is missing. See Isaac Emmanuel and Suzanne Emmanuel, *A History of the Jews in the Netherlands Antilles*, 2 vols. (Cincinnati: American Jewish Archives, 1970), I: 48–49 and 335.

6. The Temple was dramatically expanded under the rule of King Herod in the first century B.C.E. See Lee I. Levine, *The Ancient Synagogue: The First Thousand Years*, 2nd ed. (New Haven, CT: Yale University Press, 2005), 43.

7. David P. Cohen Paraira, "A Jewel in the City: The Architectural History of the Portuguese-Jewish Synagogue," in *The Esnoga: A Monument to Portuguese-Jewish Culture*, ed. Judith C. E. Belinfante, et al. (Amsterdam: D'Arts, 1991), 41–68, 56.

8. Cohen Paraira, "A Jewel in the City," 56–58. In various places and time periods, Jews were concerned with the permissibility of modeling diasporic synagogues after the ancient Temple. See the responsum of Ezekiel Landau (1713–1793) and relevant discussions in Vivian B. Mann, ed., *Jewish Texts on the Visual Arts* (Cambridge: Cambridge University Press, 2000), 8 and 95–96. Inspiration from Iberia's synagogues is more difficult to ascertain, but similarities include the connection of the synagogue to a complex of public buildings, such as a study room, student quarters, and ritual bath. See Yom-Tov Assis, "Synagogues in Mediaeval Spain," *Jewish Art* 18 (1992): 7–29, 14. Ornamental detail in Iberia's synagogues, however, was distinct from that of the western Sephardic diaspora, as suggested by the private house of worship Samuel Halevi Abulafia commissioned in the fourteenth century. Today known as El Tránsito synagogue, it displays predominantly Islamic (*mudejar*) influence, similar to the Alhambra. Esther W. Goldman, "Samuel Halevi Abulafia's Synagogue (El Tránsito) in Toledo," *Jewish Art* 18 (1992): 59–69, 60, and Mann, *Jewish Texts*, 76.

9. Cohen Paraira, "A Jewel in the City," 58–61, and Cornelis Christiaan Goslinga, *The Dutch in the Caribbean and in the Guianas, 1680–1791* (Assen/Maastricht, the Netherlands and Dover, NH: Van Gorcum, 1985), 508. The 1730 building was designed by architects Pieter Roggenburg and Hendrik Schielagh, who likely modeled it after Amsterdam's *esnoga*, while imbuing it with local accents. Curaçao's first synagogue was built in 1674 in Willemstad, and then rebuilt in 1690 and 1696. Of the successor to these structures, erected in 1703, little is known, as neither images nor descriptions have been preserved, but it may have been modeled after the *esnoga* in Amsterdam.

Bernard R. Buddingh, *Van Punt en Snoa: Ontstaan en groei van Willemstad, Curaçao vanaf 1634, De Willemstad tussen 1700 en 1732 en de bouwgeschiedenis van de synagoge Mikvé Israël-Emanuel 1730–1732* (n.p.: Aldus Uitgevers, 1994), 167, 176, and 182, and Emmanuel and Emmanuel, *History of the Jews of the Netherlands Antilles*, 123.

10. Cohen Paraira, "A Jewel in the City," 46. The architects of Portuguese synagogues in Italy, the Netherlands, England, and North Germany were all Christian. In Eastern Europe, however, many synagogues were designed by Jews. Franz Landsberger, *A History of Jewish Art* (Cincinnati: The Union of American Hebrew Congregations, 1946), 226 and 246.

11. Victor Enthoven, "Suriname and Zeeland: Fifteen Years of Dutch Misery on the Wild Coast, 1667–1682," in *International Conference on Shipping, Factories and Colonization*, ed. J. Everaert and J. M. Parmentier (Brussels: Koninklijke Academie voor Overzeese Wetenschappen, 1996), 249–260, 253–255. It was hard to secure personnel, and all kinds of private initiatives were necessary to hire a workforce. Agents of planters in the United Provinces, from 1669–1679, contracted craftsmen such as carpenters, mill builders, coopers, and bricklayers, and, in the 1670s, founding members of the Jodensavanne community hired Dutch mill makers and carpenters from the Netherlands. Testimony of Abraham Drago of Amsterdam, procurator of Samuel Nassy, living in Suriname, Amsterdam, 30 June 1671, Not. Arch. No. 2903, Gemeentearchief Amsterdam (henceforth GAA); Dienstcontract Suriname van de broers Jacob Corneliss van Boelen, timmerman/molenmaker en Hendrick Corneliss, scheppstimmerman bij Samuel Nassy op Suriname [Suriname service contract of the brothers Jacob Corneliss van Boelen, carpenter/mill maker, and Hendrick Corneliss, ship carpenter, by Samuel Nassy in Suriname], 10 July 1671, Not. Arch. 2904, GAA; testimony of Jacob Pereyra, 31 January 1680, Not. Arch. 3245, fol. 139, GAA. When contracted workers from abroad did not suffice, Surinamese Jews presumably drew upon slave labor. In 1684, the year prior to the construction of Beraha VeSalom, there were 163 Jews in Suriname and 972 Africans enslaved to them. On the other hand, David Cohen Nassy implied in 1788 that Jews in Jodensavanne manufactured the bricks themselves, out of boiling vats used for sugar refining. Marcus, ed., *Historical Essay*, I: 29.

12. Thirty-eight buildings in Recife were built by Jews (*"fabricadas pelo Judeo o por Judeos"*). Hannedea van Nederveen Meerkerk, *Recife: The Rise of a 17th-Century Trade City from a Cultural-Historical Perspective* (Assen and Maastricht: Van Gorcum, 1989), 157.

13. Cohen Paraira, "A Jewel in the City," 46–47 and 53, and J.H.J. Hamelberg, *De Nederlanders op de West-Indische eilanden* (Amsterdam: Emmering, 1979), I: 64. Similar restrictions were common in Jewish communities elsewhere and in other times. Opposition was to the building of synagogues as the highest structure of a town or the embellishment of houses of worship was common. See Salo Wittmayer Baron, *The Jewish Community: Its History and Structure to the American Revolution*, 3 vols. (Philadelphia: The Jewish Publication Society of America, 1942), 2: 138–139, and Israel Abrahams, *Jewish Life in the Middle Ages* (Philadelphia: The Jewish Publication Society of America, 1896), 27. Jodensavanne's Jews had even more architectural freedom than their Jewish contemporaries elsewhere in the Caribbean. When the Jews of St. Eustatius petitioned the Dutch colonial authorities in 1737 for

permission to build a synagogue, this was conceded with the caveat that their house of worship be situated so that "the divine service of the Jews would not hinder the one of the Christians." See Johannes Hartog, *The Jews and St. Eustatius: The Eighteenth Century Jewish Congregation Honen Dalim and Description of the old Cemetery* (St. Maarten, Netherlands Antilles: n.p., 1976), 5.

14. There were 543 male and 429 female enslaved Africans. Enthoven, "Suriname and Zeeland," 255.

15. Enthoven, "Suriname and Zeeland," 255.

16. Edward van Voolen, "A 'miniature sanctuary': The history and function of the synagogue," in *The Esnoga: A Monument to Portuguese-Jewish Culture*, ed. Judith C. E. Belinfante, et al. (Amsterdam: D'Arts, 1991), 34–39, 37.

17. David Cohen Nassy, *Essai Historique sur la Colonie de Surinam* (Amsterdam: S. Emmering, 1968 [Paramaribo, 1788]), part I, 44 and 63.

18. Johannes Menne Postma, *The Dutch in the Atlantic Slave Trade, 1600–1815* (Cambridge; New York: Cambridge University Press, 1990), 185.

19. Peter Mark and José da Silva Horta, "Two Early Seventeenth-Century Sephardic Communities on Senegal's Petite Côte," *History in Africa* 31 (2004): 231–256, 248–249.

20. Diogo Fernandes and his wife, Branca Dias, for example, immigrants from Portugal and alleged judaizers, launched sugar plantations in Brazil by the mid-sixteenth century and were accused of establishing a crypto-Jewish center, complete with a synagogue and Torah. Arnold Wiznitzer, "The Jews in the Sugar Industry of Colonial Brazil," *Jewish Social Studies* 18, no. 3 (July 1956): 189–198, 192. Given the scrutiny of the Inquisition, the synagogue was likely located in a private house. For a multitude of other examples of worship in private homes see Bruno Feitler, *Inquisition, juife et nouveaux-chrétiens au Brésil: Le Nordeste XVIIe et XVIIIe siècles* (Leuven/Louvain, Belgium: Leuven University Press, 2003), 147–148.

21. Ibid., 230; Günther Böhm, "The First Sephardic Synagogues in South America and in the Caribbean Area," *Studia Rosenthaliana* 22, no. 1 (Spring 1988): 1–14, 5; Arnold Wiznitzer, *The Records of the Earliest Jewish Community in the New World* (New York: American Jewish Historical Society, 1954), 55–56. Tânia Neumann Kaufman [*Passos Perdidos História Recuperada: A Presença Judaica em Pernambuco* (Recife: Ensol e Bagaço, 2000), 24] improbably speculates that this building was modeled after Amsterdam's *esnoga*. Recent archaeological excavations suggest that Brazil's first synagogue was discreet, at least from the exterior. Recife's synagogue was likely situated in two houses, numbers 197 and 203 of present-day Rua do Bom Jesus (formerly, Jodenstraat). An inventory describes it as: "Humas cazas grandes de sobrado da mesma banda do rio, com fronteira para a rua dos Judeos [*sic*], que lhes servia de synagoga, a qual he de pedra e cal com duas lojas por baixo, que de novo fabricarão ditos Judeos [*sic*]." [Some large, multi-level houses on the same side of the river, facing Jews' Street, that served as their synagogue, and which is of stone and lime, with two stores on the main floor, which these Jews also built.] The transcription is from Egon Wolff and Frieda Wolff, *Quantos Judeus Estiveram no Brasil Holandês* (Rio de Janeiro: Instituto Histórico e Geográfico Brasileiro, 1991), 96. Compare the transcription of Gonsalves de Mello, *Gente da Nacao*, 230. A similar translation appears in Arnold Wiznitzer, "The Exodus from Brazil and Arrival in New Amsterdam of the Jewish Pilgrim Fathers, 1654," *Publications of the American Jewish Historical*

Society 54, no. 2 (December 1954): 80–97, 83. Zacharias Wagner (1614–1668), who produced an illustration in ca. 1638 of what would become known as Jodenstraat (Jews' Street), provides a hint of what Brazil's first synagogue looked like. Archival documents show that nearly every house on this street featured a store on its first floor. In Recife, the combined residential/shop building was most prevalent in buildings constructed and inhabited by Jews. Van Nederveen Meerkerk, *Recife*, 137, 157, 168, 169, 174–175. A museum with a "probable replica of the synagogue" was inaugurated on the original site in 2002. Y. David Weitman, *Bandeirantes Espitiuais do Brasil: século XVII* (n.p.: Editora Maayanot, 2003), XIX and XXI. We thank Odette Vlessing for this source.

22. Feitler, *Inquisition, juife et nouveaux-chrétiens au Brésil*, 145.

23. Ibid., 150–156. Compare José Antônio Gonsalves de Mello, *Gente da Nacao: Cristãos-novos e judeus em Pernambuco 1542–1654* (Recife: Fundação Joaquim Nabuco, Editora Massangana, 1989), 231.

24. Rochelle Weinstein, "Sepulchral Monuments of the Jews of Amsterdam in the Seventeenth and Eighteenth Centuries," doctoral dissertation (New York University, 1979), 97, and Emmanuel and Emmanuel, *History of the Jews of the Netherlands Antilles*, I: 51, 59. These two latter authors also indicate parenthetically (I: 59, n. 41) that the island's Jews built "a proper synagogue" in the city in 1674 and that a synagogue near the Jewish plantations was erected between 1679 and 1682 to replace the earliest makeshift house of prayer. We are unaware of architectural descriptions of these edifices.

25. Jonathan I. Israel, "The Jews of Dutch America," in *The Jews and the Expansion of Europe to the West, 1450–1800*, ed. Paolo Bernardini and Norman Fiering (New York and Oxford: Berghahn Books, 2001), 335–349, 346; Jacob Rader Marcus, *The Colonial American Jew, 1492–1776* (Detroit: Wayne State University Press, 1970), I: 146–147; Frederik Oudschans Dentz, *De Kolonisatie van de Portugeesch Joodsche Natie in Suriname en de Geschiedenis van de Joden Savanne* (Amsterdam: M. Hertzberger, 1927), 5–6; Herbert Ivan Bloom, *The Economic Activities of the Jews of Amsterdam in the Seventeenth and Eighteenth Centuries* (Williamsport, PA: The Bayard Press, 1937), 150.

26. On this day, David Nassy obtained permission from the West India Company to establish a colony "on Cayenne and in the adjacent lands." Letter by J. Rijckaert and David van Baerle, West India Company, Chamber of Amsterdam, to the States General, Amsterdam, 21 February 1664, p.1., Staten-Generaal, inv. nr. 5767, Nationaal Archief, the Hague, the Netherlands (henceforth NAN). We thank Wim Klooster for this information, which confirms the document discussed and reproduced in Nassy, *Essai Historique*, part I, 13; part II, 113–122. See also Emmanuel and Emmanuel, *History*, 44.

27. James Rodway, *Chronological History of the Discovery and Settlement of Guiana* (Georgetown, Demerara: "Royal Gazette" Office, 1888), 146; Zvi Loker, "On the Jewish Colony at Remire, French Guiana," *Judaica Latinoamericana: Estudios Histórico-Sociales*, vol.2 (Jerusalem: AMILAT, 1993), 9–15, 10.

28. Nassy, *Essai Historique*, part II, 114.

29. Stewart L. Mims, *Colbert's West India Policy* (New York: Octagon Books, 1977), 65–66.

30. Günter Böhm, "The Synagogues of Surinam," *Journal of Jewish Art* 6 (1978): 98–104, 99.

31. David de Sola Pool, *Portraits Etched in Stone: Early Jewish Settlers, 1682–1831* (New York: Columbia University Press, 1952), 119.

32. Québec Spanish and Portuguese Synagogue (corporate author), *History of the Corporation of Spanish and Portuguese Jews "Shearith Israel" of Montréal, Canada: One Hundred and Fiftieth Anniversary of the Spanish and Portuguese Jews of Montréal* (Montreal: s.n., 1918).

33. Nassy, *Essai Historique*, part I, 50.

34. Baron, *The Jewish Community*, 2, no. 139, and Robert Goldenberg, "The Synagogue as Sacred Space," *Conservative Judaism* 38, no. 2 (Winter 1985–1986): 19–22, 20.

35. Levine, *The Ancient Synagogue*, 114, 302, 305.

36. Rachel Frankel in conjunction with Caribbean Volunteer Expeditions (C.V.E.) volunteers, 1997 field survey.

37. Cohen Paraira, "A Jewel in the City," 48. For information on seating capacity in Amsterdam's *esnoga* see Geoffrey Wigoder, *The Story of the Synagogue: A Diaspora Museum Book* (San Francisco: Harper and Row, 1986), 117.

38. Nassy, *Essai Historique*, part II, 49–50.

39. Ibid., 51.

40. Ibid. Coenraad Liebrecht Temminck Groll, *De Architektuur van Suriname, 1667–1930* (Zutphen: De Walburg Pers, 1973), 303. The modern Dutch word for brick is *baksteen*.

41. Cohen Paraira, "A Jewel in the City," 54.

42. Pierre Jacques Benoit, *Voyage à Surinam* (Brussels: Société des Beaux-Arts-Gérants: De Wasme et Laurent, 1839).

43. In England's seventeenth-century Irish settlements, for example, chimneys served to distinguish English dwellings from "the cabins of the 'mere Irish.'" James Robertson, "Jamaican Architectures before Georgian," *Winterthur Portfolio* 36, nos. 2/3 (2001): 73–95, 90.

44. Cohen Paraira, "A Jewel in the City," 46.

45. An inventory list of 1821 suggests that, during the period of Jodensavanne's decline, these four gateways contained four separate doors made of "bruynhard" wood. Inventarissen van gewijde voorwerpen en andere goederen in het gebedhuis S.V.S. te Paramaribo en in en buiten de synagoge B.V.S. op de Savanne [Inventories of the sacred artifacts and other goods in the prayer house S.V.S. in Paramaribo and in and outside the Synagogue B.V.S. at the Savannah], 1821, Nederlands-Portugees-Israëlitische Gemeente in Suriname, inv. nr.141, NAN.

46. On this observation for Amsterdam's *esnoga*, see Cohen Paraira, "A Jewel in the City," 53.

47. Humberto Rodríguez-Camilloni, "Utopia Realized in the New World: Form and Symbol of the City of Kings," in *Settlements in the Americas: Cross-Cultural Perspectives*, ed. Ralph Bennett (Newark: University of Delaware Press/London and Toronto: Associated University Presses, 1993), 28–52, 28.

48. On Indian and maroon attacks before and around 1680 see Cornelis Ch. Goslinga, *The Dutch in the Caribbean and in the Guianas, 1680–1791* (Assen/Maastricht, The Netherlands: Van Gorcum, 1985), 270; S. W. de Groot, *From Isolation towards*

Integration: the Surinam Maroons and their Colonial Rulers: Official Documents Relating to the Djukas, 1845–1863 (The Hague: Martinus Nijhoff, 1977), 6–7; Rosemary Brana-Shute, "The Manumission of Slaves in Suriname, 1760–1828," doctoral dissertation (University of Florida, 1985), 46, 63; and Richard Price, *The Guiana Maroons*, 23–24, 28.

49. Gerald L. Burke, *The Making of Dutch Towns; a Study in Urban Development from the Tenth to the Seventeenth Centuries* (London: Cleaver-Hume Press, 1956), 33–52; Anthony Edwin James Morris, *History of Urban Form: Before the Industrial Revolutions* (New York: John Wiley and Sons, 1979), 123, 185–188. Burke (31) dates the rise of Dutch medieval town planning to the fifteenth century, and acknowledges Dutch towns as "comparative late-comers in Europe."

50. John Archer, "Puritan Town Planning in New Haven," *Journal of the Society of Architectural Historians* 34 (1975): 140–49, 140, 144–145. We thank James Robertson for pointing us to this source.

51. Archer, "Puritan Town Planning in New Haven," 140, 144–145. Archer's analysis of New Haven's grid is an interpretation the authors find convincing. For other interpretations, see idem, 140.

52. David de Sola Pool, ed. and trans., *Book of Prayers According to the Custom of the Spanish and Portuguese Jews*, 2nd ed. (New York: Union of Sephardic Congregations, 1997). We have slightly modernized the translation.

53. The translation is from *JPS Hebrew-English Tanakh*, 2nd ed. (Philadelphia: The Jewish Publication Society, 1999), 944.

54. On the infrequency of manumission see Brana-Shute, "The Manumission of slaves in Suriname."

55. For this and other examples of the use of the *spaansche bok* in Jodensvanne see Wieke Vink, "Creole Jews: Negotiating Community in Colonial Suriname," doctoral dissertation (Erasmus Universiteit Rotterman, 2008), 157, and Richard Price, *Alabi's World* (Baltimore and London: The Johns Hopkins University Press, 1990), 175, 177. Note the protest of Mahamad leaders and the shock of foreign visitors who witnessed these scenes. This form of torture, widespread throughout the colony, is often described by John Greenwood in his "2 Diaries or Notebooks," Unpublished manuscript, Manuscript Department, New York Historical Society, New York.

56. Baron, *The Jewish Community*, 2:140; Abrahams, *Jewish Life*, 26; and Emily Taitz, "Kol Ishah-The Voice of Woman: Where Was It Heard in Medieval Europe?" *Conservative Judaism* 38, no. 3 (Spring 1986): 46–61, 54–55. Synagogue complexes in Spain, inventoried after the Expulsion of 1492, describe not only women's galleries, but also specific areas designated for women's ritual ceremonies—sometimes referred to as "Jewish women's synagogue," "house of Jewesses," or "women's synagogue." Isidro G. Bango, *Remembering Sepharad: Jewish Culture in Medieval Spain* (State Corporation for Spanish Cultural Action Abroad, 2003), 93–94.

57. Carol Herselle Krinsky, *Synagogues of Europe: Architecture, History, Meaning* (New York: Architectural History Foundation and Cambridge, MA: MIT Press, 1985), 29. A few medieval synagogues of Spain featured a women's gallery, usually on one side of the main hall only, but most reserved a room or hall adjacent to the main sanctuary, often for use as an *ezrat nashim* (women's room). Assis, "Synagogues," 17–18.

58. Uri Kaploun, ed., *The Synagogue* (Philadelphia: Jewish Publication Society of America, 1973), 84. Abrahams (*Jewish Life*, 27) dates this transformation to the end of the thirteenth century. Prayer rooms for women, he writes, appeared "at the side of and a little above the men's synagogue, with which the rooms communicated by a small window or balcony."

59. Nonetheless, there are exceptions among Iberian-origin Jews of Amsterdam. Krinsky (*Synagogues of Europe*, 390) writes: "in the synagogue [of Amsterdam] of 1639, some of the gallery space was reserved for men; at least one of the galleries which ran around three sides of the interior held men."

60. Krinsky, *Synagogues of Europe*, 6.

61. Kaploun, *The Synagogue*, 67–68. On the numinous properties of spaces see Louis Jacobs, "Holy Places," *Conservative Judaism* 37, no. 3 (Spring 1984): 4–16.

62. This word denotes a pavilion or palace and refers to the repository and abode of the law. Bango, *Remembering Sepharad*, 94.

63. Kaploun, *The Synagogue*, 93; Wigoder, *The Story of the Synagogue*, 75. Cohen Paraira ("A Jewel in the City," 59) states just the opposite: that the prestige of Amsterdam's *esnoga* influenced the bipolar arrangement of Sephardic synagogues in Leghorn (c.1700), London (1701), Willemstad (1732), Paramaribo (1737), Naarden (1759), Newport, Rhode Island (1763), and New York (1897).

64. Krinsky, *Synagogues of Europe*, 48–50; Kaploun, *The Synagogue*, 83 and 93–95. Landsberger (*History of Jewish Art*, 31) postulates that this layout offered the "beauty of a wide space which would have been spoiled by a center platform" and appealed to a sense of balance by giving the Torah ark and the reader's platform "equal importance in position and size."

65. An area for further research is seating arrangement in the women's section of the synagogue. This information may indicate how common it was for Surinamese women to attend services, and whether social discord played itself out spatially. In Amsterdam, London, and Recife, where few females attended synagogue, there was scant need for pre-arranged seating. In New York, Jewish women tended to imitate their Protestant sisters who frequented church services, and reserved seating became a necessity for the congregation. Limited space in Shearith Israel's women's section stimulated class conflicts about preferred seating, and eventually a special area was specifically designated for the "elite women of the Gomez clan." Jonathan D. Sarna, *American Judaism: A History* (New Haven, CT: Yale University Press, 2004), 18.

66. Inventarissen van gewijde voorwerpen en andere goederen in het gebedhuis S.V.S. te Paramaribo en in en buiten de Synagoge B.V.S. op de Savanne [Inventories of the sacred artifacts and other goods in the prayer house S.V.S. in Paramaribo and in and outside the Synagogue B.V.S. at the Savannah], 12 December 1848, inv. nr. 141, Nederlands-Portugees-Israëlitische Gemeente in Suriname, NAN.

67. Epitaph of Rachel Mendez Meza (?–1715), Cassipora Creek Cemetery, grave number 61, field research of Aviva Ben-Ur and Rachel Frankel, 1998.

68. Baron, *The Jewish Community*, 2:140. There is no evidence in Jewish history to indicate when the woman's gallery or separate seating for women in the synagogue came into existence. Shmuel Safrai, "Was There a Woman's Gallery in the Synagogue of Antiquity?" (Hebrew), *Tarbiz* 32 (1963): 329–338.

69. Inventarissen van gewijde voorwerpen en andere goederen in het gebedhuis S.V.S. te Paramaribo en in en buiten de Synagoge B.V.S. op de Savanne [Inventories of

the sacred artifacts and other goods in the prayer house S.V.S. in Paramaribo and in and outside the Synagogue B.V.S. at the Savannah], 4 March 1822, Nederlands-Portugees-Israëlitische Gemeente in Suriname, inv. nr. 141, NAN. A thirteenth-century responsum from Spain refers to a women's praying quarter as "*beit ha-kneset shel ha-nashim*" (women's synagogue). In Barcelona, the women's section was called "*scola de les dones*" (synagogue of the women) and "*sinagoga menor*" (smaller synagogue), strikingly parallel to Suriname's communal records, which refer to the women's gallery as "*esnoga de mulhers*" and "*vrouwen appartement.*" Evidence from medieval Spain (Assis, "Synagogues," 18) demonstrates that these were not separate synagogues. Here, too, the locution describing these rooms supports the existence of prayer services parallel to those of men in the main sanctuary. Assis ("Synagogues," 22) also notes that in some Iberian Jewish communities, adults called to read from the Torah wore silver crowns, as did children in medieval Barcelona when the scrolls were led to and from the synagogue. This may provide another explanation for the copper crowns noted in the women's balcony of Beraha VeSalom.

70. Inventarissen van gewijde voorwerpen en andere goederen in het gebedhuis S.V.S. te Paramaribo en in en buiten de Synagoge B.V.S. op de Savanne [Inventories of the sacred artifacts and other goods in the prayer house S.V.S. in Paramaribo and in and outside the Synagogue B.V.S. at the Savannah], 25 June 1821, Nederlands-Portugees-Israëlitische Gemeente in Suriname, inv. nr. 141, NAN. The locution is "*da Esnoga de Homme.*"

71. Cassipora Creek Cemetery, grave number 158, field research of Aviva Ben-Ur and Rachel Frankel, 1998.

72. Jodensavanne Cemetery, grave number 341, field research of Aviva Ben-Ur and Rachel Frankel, 1999.

73. Isaac S. Emmanuel, *Precious Stones of the Jews of Curaçao* (New York: Bloch Publishing Co., 1957), 381.

74. Figures based on Enthoven, "Suriname and Zeeland," 255. This would make the synagogue space comparable to Curaçao's Mikvé Israel, which in 1690 offered room for at least 200 males and 80 for females in the women's gallery. Emmanuel and Emmanuel, *History of the Jews of the Netherlands Antilles*, 93.

75. Recall that the ruins of Beraha VeSalom measure 94 feet along its east-west axis and 43 feet across its north-south width (4,042 square feet or 375 square meters). A plot of land purchased by Port Royal's Jews in 1676/1677 measured 63 by 26 feet (1,638 square feet), while another plot purchased in 1704 measured 64 by 32 feet (2,048 square feet). Jacob A. P. M. Andrade, *A Record of The Jews in Jamaica From the English Conquest to the Present Time* (Kingston, Jamaica: The Jamaica Times, 1941), 40. Likewise, the synagogue of St. Eustatius, consecrated in 1739, measured 40 by 27 ½ feet or 1,100 square feet (12.75 x 8.5 meters). Hartog, *The Jews and St. Eustatius*, 5–6. At its peak in 1781, the island's Jewish community numbered about 100 adult males. *Publications of the American Jewish Historical Society* XI (1903): 152. New York's Mill Street synagogue, built in 1728, measured a mere 35 square feet and stood 21 feet high. De Sola Pool, *Portraits Etched in Stone*, 119. Curaçao's synagogue was dimensionally more similar to Beraha VeSalom. See n. 65.

76. The full verse reads: "Therefore say, 'Thus says the Lord God; Although I have cast them far off among the nations, and although I have scattered them among the countries, I have been to them a little [or: lesser] sanctuary in the countries where they

have come...."' This translation is based on Harold Fisch, ed., *The Holy Scriptures* (Jerusalem: Koren Publishers, 1989). On Talmudic and other rabbinic interpretations of "little sanctuary" see Krinsky, *Synagogues of Europe*, 7–11, and Joseph Gutmann, "Return in Mercy to Zion: A Messianic Dream in Jewish Art," in *The Land of Israel: Jewish Perspectives*, ed. Lawrence A. Hoffman (Notre Dame, IN: University of Notre Dame Press, 1986), 234–260; 254, n. 14. An Iberian precedence for a diminished synagogue modeled on the Temple occurs in Córdoba, whose fourteenth-century synagogue is adorned with a stucco dedication plaque referring to the building as a "lesser sanctuary." See Assis, "Synagogues," 15.

77. Of course, the limited architectural use of a huge expanse of land may have also been dictated by financial constraints.

78. Gershom G. Scholem explores this theory in his *Major Trends in Jewish Mysticism* (New York: Schocken Books, 1974 [1941]), 156–204.

79. Midrash Hane'elam, Bereshit, Parshat Hayei Sarah, in Shimon bar Yochai (traditionally ascribed author), *Sefer HaZohar* (Vilna: Wdowa I Bracia Romm [the widow and brothers Romm], 1923), 125a. We thank Jonathan Sarna for pointing out this source, which supports our idea of actualized, as opposed to, anticipatory messianism. On the Midrash Hane'elam see Scholem, *Major Trends*, especially 188.

80. Enthoven, "Suriname and Zeeland," 255. However, according to a late eighteenth-century chronicler, in 1690, Suriname was home to ninety-two Jewish families, ten to twelve German Jews related to the Portuguese there by bonds of marriage, and fifty bachelors who did not belong to these families (a total of about 575 people). Of the black slaves, there were said to be at least 9,000. Nassy, *Essai Historique*, part I, 48. By contrast, according to Postma (*The Dutch in the Atlantic Slave Trade*, 185), the population of Suriname in 1684 was no more than 4,000 in total, and by 1695, the total population was still less than 5,000.

81. This is a tricky historiographical issue due to the reticence of sources. A master manumitting a slave child often cited his desire to acknowledge the enslaved mother's loyal service, but left unarticulated the precise nature of his relationship with these individuals. However, it is usually safe to assume that these children, particularly when designated as Jews, were sons and daughters of their masters. See Aviva Ben-Ur, "A Matriarchal Matter: Slavery, Conversion, and Upward Mobility in Colonial Suriname," in *Atlantic Diasporas: Jews, Conversos, and Crypto-Jews in the Age of Mercantilism, 1500–1800*, ed. Richard Kagan and Phillip Morgan (Baltimore, MD: Johns Hopkins University Press, 2009), 152–169 and 270–279. Rape of African-origin slave women was rarely discussed and even then only euphemistically. See, for example, F. A. Kuhn, *Beschouwing van den Toestand der Surinaamsche Plantagieslaven: Eene Oeconomisch-Geneeskundige Bijdrage tot Verbetering Deszelven* (Amsterman: C. G. Sulpke, 1828), 3. Kuhn, a physician in Suriname, subtly indicates that sailors would sexually assault African women and girls aboard slave ships, thus transmitting to them sexual diseases. From the extensive diary of the eighteenth-century Jamaican planter Thomas Thistlewood, we know that enslaved women sometimes initiated or manipulated sexual relations with their white masters to the enslaved's advantage. See Trevor Burnard, *Mastery, Tyranny, and Desire: Thomas Thistlewood and his Slaves in the Anglo-Jamaican World* (Chapel Hill: University of North Carolina Press, 2004), 28–29, 162, 217, 226–227, 266.

82. Ascamot, 1755, Nederlands-Portugees-Israëlitische Gemeente in Suriname, inv. nr. 102, Tractate 19, article 4, NAN.

83. Ascamot, 1748, Nederlands-Portugees-Israëlitische Gemeente in Suriname, inv. nr. 99, Tractate 26, article 1, "On not admitting Mulattoes as *jehidim* to the synagogue nor whites married to mulattoes," NAN.

84. Yosef Kaplan, "Political Concepts in the World of the Portuguese Jews of Amsterdam During the Seventeenth Century: The Problem of Exclusion and the Boundaries of Self-Identity," in *Menasseh Ben Israel and His World*, ed. Yosef Kaplan, Henry Mechoulan, and Richard H. Popkin (Leiden; New York: E. J. Brill, 1989), 45–62, 58.

85. Ibid., 57–58.

86. Ascamot, Nederlands-Portugees-Israëlitische Gemeente in Suriname, inv. nr. 101, tractate 2, article 6, NAN.

87. Memorandum of Eurafrican Jews (literally, "the coloreds") to Governor Frederici, 2 September 1793, Oud Archief Suriname, Gouvernements Secretaries, inv. nr. 528, NAN; Robert Cohen, *Jews in Another Environment: Surinam in the Second Half of the Eighteenth Century* (Leiden: E. J. Brill: 1991), 156–174; Aviva Ben-Ur, "Peripheral Inclusion: Communal Belonging in Suriname's Sephardic Community," in *Religion, Gender, and Culture in the Pre-Modern World*, ed. Alexandra Cuffel and Brian Britt (New York: Palgrave Macmillan, 2007), 185–210.

88. Memorandum of Eurafrican Jews (literally, "the coloreds") to Governor Frederici, 2 September 1793, Oud Archief Suriname, Gouvernements Secretaries, inv. nr. 528, NAN. Eurafrican Jewish women were also classified as *congregantes*; it is unclear how this may have affected their ritual participation or privileges.

89. Vink, *Creole Jews*, 295. Vink suggests that the "rather sudden turn to halakha" in the community at this time may have been a mask to cover color discrimination.

90. Cohen, *Jews in Another Environment*, 173.

91. The earlier building was referred to as the "Casa de Oração." Böhm, "The First Sephardic Synagogues," 10–11, and n.a., "...en de oudste synagoge," *Suralco Magazine* 17, no. 1 (1985): 4–7, 6–7. The High German Jewish community dated the founding of its synagogue building to 1837. N.a., *Feestdienst ter gelegenheid van het 75 jarig bestaan der synagoge Newé Sjalom van de Ned. Israël. Gemeente in Suriname op maandagavond 20 Mai 1912/5 Siwan 567*, p.2, Archief van Philip Abraham Samson Bibliotheca Rosenthaliana, Universiteit van Amsterdam. It is unclear where the women sat prior to the gallery addition. Neveh Salom was likely named after one of the Portuguese congregations in Amsterdam that in 1639 united with Bet Jacob and Bet Israel, forming Congregation Talmud Torah. The new congregation moved into the recently renovated building formerly occupied by Bet Israel and became "the first in the country to be recognized as an official synagogue building." Weinstein, "Sepulchral Monuments," I: 141–142. Curaçao's second synagogue was also named Neveh Salom and considered part of its predecessor, Congregation Mikvé Israel. "Ascamot ou ordennança," c. 1750, Stukken betreffende gemeenten te Amsterdam, Curaçao, Suriname en Constantinopel [Pieces concerning the communities in Amsterdam, Curaçao, Suriname and Constantinople]," 334, fo. 1029, GAA. According to communal archives, Sedek VeSalom had a women's gallery by at least 1821. Minuut-notulen van vergaderingen van de Senhores de Mahamad

(Parnassijns) en van de Junta (Parnassijns en ouderlingen) [Minutes of meetings of the Gentlemen of the Mahamad (*parnasim*) and of the Junta (*parnasim* and elderly), 9 February 1821, 52, Nederlands-Portugees-Israëlitische Gemeente in Suriname, inv. nr.11, NAN.

92. Fragment van een Askamothboek [Fragment of an *askamot* book], 1678, Nederlands-Portugees-Israëlitische Gemeente in Suriname, inv. nr. 98, NAN. As late as 1821, Sedek VeSalom was referred to as the *gebedhuis* and Beraha VeSalom as the *gemeente* or *kahal*. Inventarissen van gewijde voorwerpen en andere goederen in het gebedhuis S.V.S. te Paramaribo en in en buiten de synagoge B.V.S. op de Savanne [Inventories of the sacred artifacts and other goods in the prayer house S.V.S. in Paramaribo and in and outside the Synagogue B.V.S. at the Savannah], 1821, Nederlands-Portugees-Israëlitische Gemeente in Suriname, inv. nr. 141, NAN. Inspiration for this regulation no doubt derived from Dutch-occupied Brazil, where Congregation Tsur Israel mandated in 1648 that the newly drafted communal ordinances would apply to all Jews residing in Brazil at the time or who would in the future migrate to that colony. Yet, the Brazilian congregation was not as hegemonic as that of Amsterdam, permitting, with Tsur Israel's permission, the establishment of future independent congregations. Arnold Wiznitzer, "The Minute Book of Congregations Zur Israel of Recife and Magen Abraham of Mauricia, Brazil," *Publications of the American Jewish Historical Society* 42, no. 2 (December 1952): 217–302, 221 and 229.

93. The Surinamese regulation against the establishment of additional synagogues parallels the Rabbinic discomfort with replacing the Temple with the synagogue, exemplified through the eschewal, until modern times, of the word "*beit mikdash*" (Temple) to describe a house of prayer. See Goldenberg, "The Synagogue as Sacred Space," 21. Also in some ways parallel was the Jerusalem Temple, constructed under King Solomon's reign in the tenth century B.C.E. According to the Hebrew Bible (Deuteronomy 12: 13–14), God legally designated one site—rabbinically interpreted as the locale of Jerusalem's *beit-hamikdash*—as the only place where ancient Israelites were permitted to offer burnt offerings, rites later replaced in the diaspora by daily prayer. Goldenberg, "The Synagogue as Sacred Space," 19. Later, the Talmud forbade reproducing the Temple in whole or in part, or any of its implements (Babylonian Talmud, Rosh ha-Shanah 24a). The ancient precept was periodically violated, with the rise of Jewish sacrificial temples on the island of Elephantine on the Nile River and at Leontopolis. Raymond Scheindlin, *A Short History of the Jewish People* (New York: Oxford University Press, 1998), 28; 36–37. At the synagogue of Sideh, Pamphylia, two seven-branched candelabra were crafted. Samuel Krauss, *Synagogale Altertümer* (Hildesheim: Gg. Olms, 1966), 236.

94. Böhm, "The Synagogues of Surinam," 104; Oudschanz Dentz, *De Kolonisatie van de Portugeesch Joodsche Natie*, 28.

95. N.a., "Joodse Kleurlingen in Suriname," *De West-Indische Gids* 13–14 (1955). The prayer house was located at the end of Dominéstraat at the intersection of Zwartenhovenbrugstraat. By 1955, the square still bore the name *sivaplein*.

96. In 1794, B.M. Meza and Samuel de Robles thrice advertised for the sale of the Jewish Eurafrican *Gebeed-huys* (prayer house). *Weeklyksche Surinaamsche Courant*, inv. nr. 48 (29 May 1794), 8; inv. nr. 49 (5 June 1794), 7; inv. nr. 50 (12 June 1794), 8.

97. Paramaribo's Sephardic synagogue has recently been rented out as a cyber-cafe

and computer store. N.a., "Centuries-Old Synagogue Becomes Computer Center," *Hampshire Weekend Gazette* (10–11 February 2001): D7. The interior of Sedek VeSalom was removed and sent to the Israel Museum in Jerusalem in 2000.

98. "Creolization" denotes the cross-fertilization that takes place when different cultures interact and individuals select particular elements from the other culture, endowing these with new meanings and merging them with their own traditions.

99. On building materials as suggestive of social status and degree of adaptation to colonial life, see Robertson, "Jamaican Architectures," 75.

100. N.a., "Beschrijving van de Joden-Savanah," *Surinaamsche Almanak, voor het Jaar 1833* (Amsterdam: C. G. Sulpke, 1833), 287–291, 288–289.

101. Nassy, *Essai Historique*, part II, 51.

102. Ibid.

103. Inventarissen van gewijde voorwerpen en andere goederen in het gebedhuis S.V.S. te Paramaribo en in en buiten de synagoge B.V.S. op de Savanne [Inventories of the sacred artifacts and other goods in the prayer house S.V.S. in Paramaribo and in and outside the Synagogue B.V.S. at the Savannah], 7 August 1827, Nederlands-Portugees-Israëlitische Gemeente in Suriname, inv. nr. 141, NAN.

104. N.a., "Beschrijving van de Joden-Savanah," 287.

105. Again, this spelling reflects Portuguese Jewish pronunciation of Hebrew.

106. Intekenlijst van gelden tot herstel van gebouwen op de Savanne, 1838 [Financial subscription list for the recovery of buildings on the Savannah, 1838], Paramaribo, 28 August 1838, Nederlands-Portugees-Israëlitische Gemeente in Suriname, inv. nr. 481, NAN.

107. Ibid.

108. Inventarissen van gewijde voorwerpen en andere goederen in het gebedhuis S.V.S. te Paramaribo en in en buiten de synagoge B.V.S. op de Savanne [Inventories of the sacred artifacts and other goods in the prayer house S.V.S. in Paramaribo and in and outside the Synagogue B.V.S. at the Savannah], inventory dated Jodensavanne, 12 December 1848, Nederlandse Portugees-Israëlitische Gemeente in Suriname, inv. nr. 141, NAN.

109. Monty Jacobs, "A Jewish Shrine in Surinam," *Jewish Heritage* (Summer 1962): 33–35, 33.

110. Wim Klooster, "The Caribbean and the Atlantic World," in *The Cambridge History of Judaism, Vol. 7: The Early Modern Period, c.1500–c.1815*, ed. Jonathan Karp and Adam Sutcliffe (Cambridge: Cambridge University Press, 2010).

111. Todd M. Endelman, *The Jews of Britain, 1656 to 2000* (Berkeley: University of California Press, 2002), 21.

112. Egon Wolff and Frieda Wolff, *Dicionário Biográfico I: Judaizantes e Judeus no Brasil, 1500–1808* (Rio de Janeiro, 1986), 77; Emmanuel and Emmanuel, *A History of the Jews in the Netherlands Antilles*, I: 42.

113. Dave Verdooner and Harmen Snel, *Trouwen in Mokum: Jewish Marriage in Amsterdam, 1598–1811*, 2 vols. (Gravenhage: Warray, n.d.), I: 42.

114. Swetschinski, *Reluctant Cosmopolitans*, 138–140, 215, n. 170, 279; Herbert Friedenwald, "Material for the History of the Jews in the British West Indies," *Publications of the American Jewish Historical Society 5* (1897): 45–101, 58.

115. Wim Klooster, "Networks of Colonial Entrepreneurs: The Founders of the Jewish Settlements in Dutch America, 1650s and 1660s," in *Atlantic Diasporas:*

Jews, Conversos, and Crypto-Jews in the Age of Mercantilism, 1500–1800, ed. Richard Kagan and Philip D. Morgan (Baltimore, MD: The Johns Hopkins University Press, 2009): 31–49, 43.

116. Consider, for example, the English settlement of Providence Island, off the coast of Central America. By 1638, most of the island's population was enslaved. Alison Games, *Migration and the Origins of the English Atlantic World* (Cambridge: Harvard University Press, 1999), 210; Karen Ordahl Kupperman, "Errand to the Indies: Puritan Colonization from Providence Island through the Western Design," *The William and Mary Quarterly*, Third Series, 45, no. 1 (January 1988): 70–99.

Chapter 5 - David Nassy's "Furlough" and the Slave Mattheus

1. Nationaal Archief, The Hague, the Netherlands (henceforth NAN), Archief der Nederlands-Portugees-Israelitische Gemeente in Suriname (henceforth ANPIG) 87, 947–954 (American Jewish Archives microfilm [henceforth AJAmf] 67n).

2. NAN, ANPIG 799, 8 January 1790 (AJAmf 67c). Biographical material on David Nassy can be found in R. Bijlsma, "David de Is. C. Nassy, Author of the *Essai Historique sur Surinam*," in *The Jewish Nation in Suriname*, ed. Ruobert Cohen (Amsterdam: S. Emmering, 1982), 65–73 and Robert Cohen, *Jews in Another Environment. Surinam in the Second Half of the Eighteenth Century* (Leiden and New York: E. J. Brill, 1991). I will be treating David Nassy further in my forthcoming study *Braided Histories: Slavery and Sociability in Colonial Suriname*.

3. NAN, ANPIG 87, 754 (AJAmf 67n). [David Nassy], *Essai Historique sur la Colonie de Surinam*, 2 vols. (Paramaribo, 1788 [*sic* for Amsterdam: Hendrik Gartman, 1789]), 1: xv.

4. NAN, Suriname Oud Notarieel Archief (henceforth SONA), 788, 1r–4v; SONA 789, 29–30, 41–42, 81–84 ; SONA 791, no. 8, 22 March 1786 (AJAmf 67b).

5. NAN, ANPIG 155 (AJAmf 179). *Beschryving van de Plechtigheden nevens de hofdichten en gebeden, uitgesproken op het eerste Jubelfeest van de Synagoge der Portugeesche Joodshe Gemeente, op de Savane in de colonie Suriname, genaamd Zegen en Vrede* (Amsterdam: H. Willem and C. Dronsberg, 1785).

6. [Nassy], 1: 176; Cohen, *Jews*, 146–153.

7. Cohen, *Jews*, 181–239. [Nassy], 2: 79.

8. [Nassy], 1: 165–166, 2:77–80. Michiel van Kempen, *Een Geschiedenis van de Surinaamse Literatuur*, 2 vols. (Breda: Uitgeverij De Geus, 2003), 1: 251–283.

9. [Nassy], 1: v-xxiv. Bijlsma, 70. NAN, ANPIG 156 (AJAmf 179).

10. NAN, ANPIG 420 (Registrar dos Sepultados), 45r. Robert Cohen, "Patterns of Marriage and Remarriage among the Sephardi Jews of Surinam, 1788–1818," *Jewish Nation*, 92, 99. Sarah Cohen Nassy died unmarried in 1803 at age thirty-six (ANPIG 20, 5564 Kislev 25; 10 December 1803).

11. NAN, ANPIG 257, session of 27 June 1786; ANPIG 179, receipt of 30 November 1787 (AJAmf 183); ANPIG 87, p. 949 (AJAmf 67n).

12. NAN, ANPIG 87, pp.753, 948 (AJAmf 67n). Cohen, *Jews*, 156–172. See further on the relation between colonial Jewish communities and converts of color in the important book by Jonathan Schorsch, *Jews and Blacks in the Early Modern World* (Cambridge: Cambridge University, 2004), chap. 9.

13. NAN, ANPIG 87, 948 (AJAmf 67n).

14. [Nassy], 1: 167, 179–82, 103–13; 2: 22, 78–9. Bijlsma, 70. David Nassy, *Lettre-*

Politico-Theologico-Morale sur les Juifs (Paramaribo: A. Soulage Jr., 1799), lxxvi.
15. NAN, ANPIG 87, pp. 949–952 (AJamf 67n). Nassy's salary as secretary for the community was listed as 1600 guilders in the budget for 1792 (NAN, ANPIG 194; [AJAmf 184]). Schiltkamp, "Jewish Jurators in Surinam," in *Jewish Nation*, 62.
16. NAN, ANPIG 87, 952–953 (AJamf 67n). J. A. Schiltkamp and J.Th. de Smidt, *Plakaten, Ordonnantiën en andere Wetten, uitgevaardigd in Suriname*, 2 vols. (Amsterdam: S. Emmering, 1973), 2: 971–972, no. 811 (ordinance of 10 February 1780).
17. NAN, ANPIG 167, Boedel David B. Louzada (AJAmf 149). No plantation is listed under the Louzada name in any of the eighteenth-century Suriname maps, which cover all the rivers and creeks. David Hisquiau Baruch Louzada, who was born at Jodensavanne in 1750 and who became *hazzan* of the synagogue there in 1777, was surely a relative of David Baruch Louzada. The younger man, David Hisquiau, also had associations with David Nassy; we find him, for instance, as one of the appraisers of Nassy's estate in 1782. (Z. Loker and Robert Cohen, "An Eighteenth-Century Prayer of the Jews of Surinam," *Jewish Nation*, 75–77; NAN, SONA 789, 41, 71 [AJAmf 67b]). But the older David Baruch Louzada willed either his entire estate or else just the slaves from his estate to the Portuguese Jewish community, which collected the payments for the rental of the slaves.
18. [Nassy], *Essai*, 2:25. NAN, Raad van Politie, Requeten 417, 64–65. Norval Smith, "The history of the Surinamese creoles II: Origin and differentiation," in *Atlas of the Languages of Suriname*, ed. Eithene B. Carlin and Jacques Arends (Leiden: KITLV Press, 2002), 139–142. I have also treated the language spoken on the Jewish plantations in Natalie Zemon Davis, "Creole Languages and their Uses: The Example of Colonial Suriname," *Historical Research* 82 (2009): 268–284. Jewish converts in Suriname are discussed in Aviva Ben-Ur, "A Matriarchal Matter: Slavery, Conversion, and Upward Mobility in Suriname's Jewish Community," in *Atlantic Diasporas: Jews, Conversos and Crypto-Jews in the Age of Mercantilism, 1500–1800*, ed. Richard Kagan and Philip D. Morgan (Baltimore, MD: Johns Hopkins University Press, 2009).
19. Public Record Office, London, WO 1/146, f. 1v; [Nassy], *Essai*, 2: 38–39. Cohen, *Jews*, 164–166. P. J. Benoit, *Reis door Suriname* (Zutphen: De Walburg Pers, 1980), figs. 12–14, 16, 18–19, 24–25.
20. *De Weekelyksche Woendaagsche Surinaamse Courant* (1 April 1783): announcement by the Regents of the Portuguese Jewish Nation of the sale of a group of slaves from the estate of the late David Baruk Lousada [*sic*]. NAN, ANPIG 190 (AJAmf 184) Conta e Descargo do Boedel de David Baruch Louzada, 1788: David de Isaac Cohen Nassy pays for the rental of Mattheus, Sebelle and Dagon. Dagon first appears on a 1784 account as rented out to Joseph Cohen Nassy, who had leased the other family in the Louzada estate (NAN, ANPIG 167, Boedel David B. Louzada, [AJAmf 67n]). Four years later he was leased to David Nassy.
21. Philippe Fermin, *Traité des maladies les plus fréquentes à Suriname et des remèdes les plus propres à les guérir* (Maestricht: Jacques Lekens, 1764), chaps. 17–18; Fermin practiced as a physician in Suriname from 1754–1762. Bertrand Bajon, *Mémoires pour server à l'histoire de Cayenne et de la Guiane Françoise*, 2 vols. (Paris: Grangé, 1777–1778), vol. 1, memoirs 8–9. Anthony Blom, *Verhandeling van den landbouw in de Colonie Suriname* (Amsterdam: J. W. Smit, 1787), 339–342.

22. [Nassy], *Essai*, 2: 64–69.

23. NAN, SONA 799, 2 April 1792, 12 April 1792 (AJAmf 67c); NAN, ANPIG 196, Boedel David B. Louzada (1794); ANPIG 197 (1795): Abraham Benito da Mesquita, secretary at 500£ per year (AJAmf 185).

24. NAN, SONA 737, 530–31 (May 1784). AJA, ms. 13500 (23 December 1794).

25. [Nassy], *Essai*, 1: 97.

26. NAN, Societeit van Suriname 210, Journal, 1076.

27. Mikveh Israel Archives, Financial Records (1792), 28 September 1792 [12 Tishrei 5553], received from David Nassy payment in full for 5552. On the Jews of Philadelphia, see Edwin Wolf and Maxwell Whiteman, *The History of the Jews of Philadelphia from Colonial Times to the Age of Jackson* (Philadelphia: The Jewish Publication Society, 1975).

28. On Solomon Marache, see Mikveh Israel Archives, Minute Book no. 1, p. 26; Wolf and Whitemen, 61–62, 99, 110, 121–122, 146, 166, 175, 222–224, 431 n. 63. Nassy, *Lettre*, 43.

29. Wolf and Whiteman, 190–192; Full text of "Centennial anniversary of the Pennsylvania Society, for Promoting the Abolition of Slavery," accessed on 22 February 2009 at http://www.archive.org/stream/centennialannive00penn/. Frances J. Dallett, "Family of Mrs. Robert Smith: A Commentary on Genealogy of Esther Jones," *Pennsylvania Genealogical Magazine* 33, no. 4 (1984): 307–324; Mary Smith Holton Marache was the daughter of the Quaker Esther Jones Smith, and all her relatives on the Jones side were Friends. Her cousin, the abolitionist George Aston, was close to her and to the children she had in her second marriage with Marache.

30. Historical Society of Pennsylvania, *Manumission Book of the Pennsylvania Society for the Abolition of Slavery*, Book A, ff. 134–135.

31. Gary B. Nash, *Forging Freedom: The Formation of Philadelphia's Black Community, 1720–1840* (Cambridge, MA: Harvard University Press, 1988), 60–62.

32. Wolf and Whiteman, 200. David Nassy, *Mémoire sur les Moyens d'Ameliorer la Colonie de Suriname* (1795), 23–25, NAN, Eerste Afdeling Aanwinsten 1935, Inv. VIII.

33. Nash, 98–137. Absalom Jones and Richard Allen, "To the People of Colour," in *A Narrative of the proceedings of the Black People during the Late Awful Calamity in the Year 1793* (Philadelphia: William Woodward, 1794), 26–27.

34. Mathew Carey, *A Short Account of the Malignant Fever, Lately Prevalent in Philadelphia*, 2nd ed. (Philadelphia: Mathew Carey, 1793), 76–77; Jones and Allen's publication is a response to Carey. Nash, 121–125. David Nassy, *Observations sur la Cause, la Nature et le Traitement de la Maladie Epidémique, Qui Règne à Philadelphie* (Philadelphia: Mathew Carey, 1793), 34–40. Wolf and Whiteman, 193–194.

35. *Early Proceedings of the American Philosophical Society for the Promotion of Useful Knowledge* (Philadelphia: McCalla and Stavely, 1884), 207, 212. Background note to and description of Peter Legaux's *Journal of the Vine Company of Pennsylvania*, manuscript in the American Philosophical Society Library, Accessed on 22 February 2009 at http://www.amphilsoc.org/library/mole/l/legauxvine.htm. On Jean Pierre Blanchard's aerial voyage from Philadelphia: http://www.historynet.com/jean-pierre-blanchard-made-first-us-aerial-voyage-in-1793.htm accessed on 22 February 2009.

36. Wolf and Whiteman, 191. They give Moline's arrival date as 1793, but he is already listed along with Benjamin Nones among those Philadelphians subscribing to

a turnpike road between Philadelphia and Lancaster in June of 1792 (Charles I. Landis, *The First Long Turnpike in the United States* [Lancaster, Pa., 1917], 136). Moline's decision not to indenture his manumitted slaves may have been made from conviction or simply from his having passed the six-month deadline for such an arrangement.

37. Jean Devèze, *Recherches et Observations, Sur les Causes et les Effets de la Maladie Epidémique qui a régné à Philadelphie* [printed in French and English translation] (Philadelphia: Parent, 1794), 2–3. Nassy mentions their friendship during the epidemic in his *Observations*, 44.

38. On the influx of about 500 slaves from Saint Domingue and their manumission in the years 1793–1796, see Nash, 141–142.

39. For the model developed in the French colonies in the wake of the revolution, see Laurent Dubois, *A Colony of Citizens: Revolution and Slave Emancipation in the French Caribbean, 1787–1804* (Chapel Hill: University of North Carolina Press, 2004). For the model of freedom in the Maroon communities of Suriname, see Richard Price, *Alibi's World* (Baltimore, MD: The Johns Hopkins University Press, 1990).

40. John Carter Brown Library, Providence, Rhode Island, Brown Papers (1795), 26 April 1795.

41. *Early Proceedings*, 232. Bijlsma, 71. Judah M. Cohen, *Through the Sands of Time: A History of the Jewish Community of St. Thomas, U.S. Virgin Islands* (Hanover, NH: Brandeis University Press, 2004), 14–16. NAN, ANPIG 198, 4, 9 August 1796 (AJAmf 185).

42. David Nassy, *Programma de Huma Caza d'Educaçao, ou Seminario de Criaturas na Savana de Judeus* [trilingual text in Portuguese, Dutch, and French] (Paramaribo: A. Soulage, Jr., 1796).

43. Among examples of Jewish *congregaten* who had once belonged to a Nassy: Joseph de David Cohen Nassy, Simcha de Jacob Nassy. An example from the Reformed Church in 1787: Vrije Janiba van Adjuba van Nassy (Januba was the daughter of Adjuba, who had been manumitted earlier by David Nassy). For an image of such shops, see Benoit, fig. 32.

44. Jones and Allen, 26–27.

Chapter 6 - The Democratization of American Judaism

This essay honors Dr. Gary P. Zola on the tenth anniversary of his becoming executive director of the Jacob Rader Marcus Center of the American Jewish Archives. Our deep and productive friendship extends over almost thirty years. An earlier version of this paper was delivered as the 2008 Lapidus Lecture in American Jewish Studies at Princeton University.

1. Nathan O. Hatch, *The Democratization of American Christianity* (New Haven, CT: Yale University Press, 1989), 6, 64.

2. Jacob R. Marcus, *To Count A People: American Jewish Population Data, 1585–1984* (Lanham, MA: University Press of America, 1990), 237.

3. Jonathan D. Sarna, *American Judaism: A History* (New Haven, CT: Yale University Press, 2004), 30.

4. Ibid., 31–61; Jonathan D. Sarna, "What Is American About the Constitutional Documents of American Jewry?," in *A Double Bond: The Constitutional Documents of American Jewry*, ed. Daniel P. Elazar, Jonathan D. Sarna, and Rela G. Monson (Lanham, MD: University Press of America, 1992), 35–55; Jonathan D. Sarna, "The

Impact of the American Revolution on American Jews," *Modern Judaism* 1 (1981): 149–160.

5. Myron Berman, *Richmond's Jewry, 1769–1976* (Charlottesville, VA: University Press of Virginia, 1979), 6. Berman claims that Cohen arrived "a year after the war," but this cannot be right since he was already in Richmond in 1781 when he did business with Daniel Boone and because by the time he came to Philadelphia he was described as being from Virginia; see Jonathan D. Sarna, "Jacob I. Cohen," *Dictionary of Virginia Biography* 3 (Richmond, VA: Library of Virginia, 2006): 345–347 (a footnoted copy is in the American Jewish Archives); Herbert T. Ezekiel and Gaston Lichtenstein, *The History of the Jews of Richmond From 1769 to 1917* (Richmond, VA: Ezekiel, 1917), 15; and Aaron Baroway, "The Cohens of Maryland," *Maryland Historical Magazine* 18 (1923): 359.

6. Jacob I. Cohen Papers, American Jewish Historical Society (AJHS), New York; Leon Hühner, "Some Additional Notes on the History of the Jews of South Carolina," *Publications of the American Jewish Historical Society (PAJHS)* 19 (1910): 151–156. The oft-repeated tale that Cohen was taken prisoner during the Revolution seems to be baseless; see my discussion in "Jacob I. Cohen and the 350th Anniversary of American Jewish Life," *Generations* 11 (May 2005): 1,3,8,14.

7. See Ezekiel and Lichtenstein, *History of the Jews of Richmond*, 14.

8. Berman, *Richmond's Jewry*, 1–12; Ezekiel and Lichtenstein, *History of the Jews of Richmond*, 15–16.

9. The Mikveh Israel minutes from this period are reprinted in Jacob R. Marcus, *American Jewry: Documents, Eighteenth Century* (Cincinnati: Hebrew Union College Press, 1959), 120–121.

10. Gratz Mordecai, a descendant, reported that Moses Mordecai "married in England, Elizabeth Whitlock, who previously became a convert to the Jewish faith, which she ever afterwards adhered to in the strictest manner." "Notice of Jacob Mordecai...," *PAJHS* 6 (1897): 40. However, the English rabbinate had a firm policy of not approving conversions, for fear of breaching the agreement under which Jews had been readmitted into England; see Todd M. Endelman, *The Jews of Georgian England 1714–1830* (Philadelphia: Jewish Publication Society, 1979), 145–146; and Joseph R. Rosenbloom, *Conversion to Judaism From the Biblical Period to the Present* (Cincinnati: Hebrew Union College Press, 1978), 75–76. Under the British Penal Laws, moreover, conversion from Protestantism to Catholicism, at least, was strictly punished. See F.P. Moran, *The Catholics of Ireland Under the Penal Laws in the Eighteenth Century* (London: Catholic Truth Society, 1899), 16–18. Perhaps Whitlock traveled to Holland, where conversions were easier to obtain. Emily Bingham, *Mordecai: An Early American Family* (New York: Hill and Wang, 2003), 13, implies that the marriage took place in America and suggests that Mordecai came to America as a convict.

11. Shulhan Aruch, *Even Ha-Ezer*, 6:8; see also the discussion in Maimonides, Book of Holiness, Laws of Forbidden Marriages, 18:3.

12. For a parallel case in England in 1825, which is strikingly similar to our case, see Endelman, *The Jews of Georgian England*, 145.

13. Marcus, *American Jewry: Documents*, 121–124. On this issue, as on so many others, Haym Salomon and Jonas Phillips clashed. Whether this was the "unrecorded

quarrel" that prompted Phillips's decision to be buried in New York is unclear. See Samuel Rezneck, *The Saga of an American Jewish Family Since the Revolution: A History of the Family of Jonas Phillips* (Washington, DC: University Press of America, 1980), 15–16.

14. On Haym Salomon, see Jacob R. Marcus, *United States Jewry 1776–1985* (Detroit: Wayne State University Press, 1989), 66–77; and Edgar J. McManus, "Haym Salomon," *American National Biography Online* (accessed 23 June 2008) ; on Mordecai Sheftall, see Malcolm Stern, "Sheftall," in *Encyclopaedia Judaica* 18, 2nd ed., ed. Michael Berenbaum and Fred Skolnik (Detroit: Macmillan Reference USA, 2007), 433; and on Israel Jacobs, see Edwin Wolf II and Maxwell Whiteman, *The History of the Jews of Philadelphia from Colonial Times to the Age of Jackson* (Philadelphia: Jewish Publication Society, 1956), 30 *passim*; and *Poulson's American Daily Advertiser* (6 March 1810): 3.

15. A copy of the original *ketubbah*, located in the Jewish National Library in Jerusalem, is found in small collections file, SC-6277, American Jewish Archives, Cincinnati, OH. I am most grateful to Mr. Kevin Proffitt for sending me a copy.

16. Sidney M. Fish, "The Problem of Intermarriage in Early America, *Gratz College Annual of Jewish Studies* 4 (1975): 85–95. The article reproduces the original text and provides an English translation. An abbreviated translation along with other valuable material may be found in Malcolm H. Stern, "Two Jewish Functionaries in Colonial Pennsylvania," *American Jewish Historical Quarterly* 57 (September 1967): 41–46.

17. E. Slijper, "Saul Loewenstamm," *Jewish Encyclopedia* 8 (New York: Funk and Wagnalls Co., 1901–1906), 194; Louis I. Rabinowitz, "Loewenstamm," in *Encyclopaedia Judaica* 2nd ed., 13, 167–168. Presumably, the congregation turned to Loewenstamm in Amsterdam because it would have been unthinkable, so soon after the American Revolution, to seek rabbinic guidance from England.

18. Stern, "Two Jewish Functionaries," 35–48, contains the most complete biography of Mordecai.

19. Hatch, 179–183.

20. Fish, "Problem of Intermarriage," and Wolf and Whiteman, *History of the Jews of Philadelphia*, 128–131. No reply from Loewenstamm has been located.

21. Fish, "Problem of Intermarriage," 93–94.

22. Sarna, "What Is American about the Constitutional Documents?," 37.

23. For the text of Beth Shalome's constitution, see *American Jewry: Documents*, 145–146; and Elazar et al., *A Double Bond*, 112.

24. Elazar, et al., *A Double Bond*, 105 (article 12).

25. Shearith Israel broadened its franchise under its 1805 constitution; see ibid., 105–111 (where the term *yachid* is replaced by "elector.")

26. See the Shearith Israel minutes reprinted in *PAJHS* 21 (1913) and Jacob R. Marcus, *The Colonial American Jew*, II (Detroit: Wayne State University Press, 1970), 897–911. For Europe, see Salo Baron's discussion of "growing plutocracy" in his *The Jewish Community: Its History and Structure to the American Revolution*, II (Philadelphia: Jewish Publication Society, 1945), 50–51; and for Amsterdam, see Miriam Bodian, *Hebrews of the Portuguese Nation* (Bloomington: Indiana University Press, 1997), 51–52. In London, kinsmen "unto the third generation" were not permitted to hold office together at the Spanish and Portuguese Synagogue, but there

was no apparent objection to business partners serving together; see Neville Laski, *The Laws and Charities of the Spanish and Portuguese Jews Congregation of London* (London: Cresset Press, 1952), 5.

27. Jacob ben Meir (Rabbenu Tam) in the twelfth century had advocated an even more extreme model of communal consensus, but his view remained a minority one; see Menachem Elon, *Jewish Law: History, Sources, Principles* (Philadelphia: Jewish Publication Society, 1994), 715–723. Colonial American Jews, by contrast, promoted the principle of deference to authority; see Sarna, *American Judaism*, 14.

28. For a list of the congregation's *parnasim*, see David and Tamar de Sola Pool, *An Old Faith in the New World: Portrait of Shearith Israel* (New York: Columbia, 1955), 503. Their birth dates can be found in Jacob R. Marcus, *The Concise Dictionary of American Jewish Biography*, 2 vols. (New York: Carlson Publishing, 1994), and the resulting calculation is my own.

29. Quoted in Robert J. Dinkin, "Seating the Meeting House in Early Massachusetts," *New England Quarterly* 43 (1970): 450.

30. Jonathan D. Sarna, "Seating and the American Synagogue," in *Belief and Behavior: Essays in the New Religious History*, ed. Philip R. Vandermeer and Robert P. Swierenga (New Brunswick, NJ: Rutgers University Press, 1991), 189–206, esp. 191–192.

31. Pool, *Old Faith in the New World*, 44.

32. Sarna, "Seating and the American Synagogue," 192.

33. Sarna, *American Judaism*, 45–61.

34. Ibid., 47–49; Karla Goldman, *Beyond the Synagogue Gallery: Finding a Place for Women in American Judaism* (Cambridge: Harvard University Press, 2000), 38–54.

35. The letter was first printed in Isaac Goldberg, "Mr. Noah, American," *Menorah Journal* 24 (Autumn 1936): 287–288, and reprinted in Isaac Goldberg, *Major Noah: American-Jewish Pioneer* (Philadelphia: Jewish Publication Society, 1938), 51–52. I have supplied material in brackets to aid readability. James W. Hagy, *This Happy Land: The Jews of Colonial and Antebellum Charleston* (Tuscaloosa: University of Alabama Press, 1993), 79–80 supplies valuable background on Carvalho and links this description to some 1811 court cases concerning synagogue assaults in Charleston. But since Noah's 1812 letter refers to developments "within this last week," the association seems doubtful. Those cases, instead, underscore the many different social tensions within the congregation.

36. Jeremiah J. Berman, *Shehitah: A Study in the Cultural and Social Life of the Jewish People* (New York: Bloch, 1941), 285–287; Samuel Oppenheim, "The Question of the Kosher Meat Supply in New York in 1813: With a Sketch of Earlier Conditions," *PAJHS* 25 (1917): 54–57; Sarna, *American Judaism*, 50.

37. In theory, the ultimate authority available to the synagogue was the dreaded "excommunication," but in practice this punishment was almost never meted out in North America; see Sarna, *American Judaism*, 16.

38. Sarna, *American Judaism*, 53–54; Elazar, et al., *Double Bond*, 116; Hagy, *This Happy Land*, 63–64, 70–71.

39. "Democratization," *Oxford English Dictionary* (second edition, 1989), http://dictionary.oed.com accessed on 20 July 2008.

40. Sarna, *American Judaism*, 52–61 sets forth the "synagogue community" to "community of synagogues" model. For a critique, see Holly Snyder, "Rethinking

the Definition of 'Community' for a Migratory Age 1654–1830," in *Imagining the American Jewish Community*, ed. Jack Wertheimer (Waltham, MA: Brandeis University Press, 2007), 3–27.

41. Among the best sources are L.C. Moise, *Biography of Isaac Harby* (Columbia, SC: R.L. Bryan, 1931); Lou H. Silberman, *American Impact: Judaism in the United States in the Early Nineteenth Century*, B.G. Rudolph Lectures in Judaic Studies (Syracuse, NY: Syracuse University Press, 1964); Robert Liberles, "Conflict Over Reforms: The Case of Congregation Beth Elohim, Charleston, South Carolina," in *The American Synagogue: A Sanctuary Transformed*, ed. Jack Wertheimer (Cambridge: Cambridge University Press, 1987), 274–296; Hagy, *The Happy Land*, 128–160; Michael A. Meyer, *Response to Modernity: A History of the Reform Movement in Judaism* (New York: Oxford University Press, 1988), 228–233; and Gary P. Zola, *Isaac Harby of Charleston, 1788–1828* (Tuscaloosa, AL: University of Alabama Press, 1994), 112–149.

42. Quotes are from the documents published in Moise, *Isaac Harby*, 52, 61.

43. Quotes are from ibid., 71, 118.

44. What follows is based on Sarna, *American Judaism*, 55–57; for key documents, see Joseph L. Blau and Salo W. Baron, *The Jews of the United States 1790–1840: A Documentary History* (New York: Columbia University Press, 1963), 540–545; for other accounts, see Hyman B. Grinstein, *The Rise of the Jewish Community of New York* (Philadelphia: Jewish Publication Society, 1945), 40–49 and Pool, *Old Faith*, 436–437.

45. Israel Goldstein, *A Century of Judaism in New York: B'nai Jeshurun 1825–1925* (New York: B'nai Jeshurun, 1930), 55–56 reprints the preamble.

46. See James G. Heller, *As Yesterday When It is Past: A History of the Isaac M. Wise Temple, K.K. B'nai Yeshurun of Cincinnati, in Commemoration of the Centenary of Its Founding* (Cincinnati: Isaac M. Wise Temple, 1942), 26–27; and Joshua Trachtenberg, *Consider the Years: The Story of the Jewish Community of Easton, 1752–1942* (Easton, PA: Centennial Committee of Temple Brith Shalom, 1944), 237.

47. Hatch, 64.

Chapter 7 - Jonas Phillips Levy: A Jewish Naval Captain in the Early Republic

1. Edwin Wolf II and Maxwell Whiteman, *The History of the Jews of Philadelphia from Colonial Times to the Age of Jackson* (Philadelphia: Jewish Publication Society of America, 1959), 84, 96, 116–127, 146, 149, 151.

2. Ibid., 220, 225, 227. The authors identify Levy as supporting the Whigs in the election of 1810, but that would have been impossible as the Whig party was not founded until the 1830s. In Philadelphia, the Federalists were forerunners of the Whigs and took the positions the Whigs would later hold.

3. Melvin Urofsky, *The Levy Family and Monticello, 1834–1926* (Charlottesville, VA: Thomas Jefferson Memorial Foundation, 2002). For Jefferson Monroe Levy, see http://www.jewishvirtuallibrary.org/jsource/biography/JLevy.html accessed on 28 February 2009 and for Jonas's relation to Monticello, "Correspondence re: Monticello, 1869–1974," Jonas P. Levy Papers, P-412, Box 1, folder 3, American Jewish Historical Society (AJHS), New York.

4. For Phillips's nurturing spouse, see Aviva Ben-Ur, "The Exceptional and the Mundane: A Biographical Portrait of Rebecca Machado Phillips," in *Women and*

American Judaism: Historical Perspectives, ed. Pamela Nadell and Jonathan Sarna (Waltham, MA: Brandeis University Press, 2001), 46–80.

5. Jonas Phillips Levy, "Autobiography," 1, typescript copy in SC-7049 at The Jacob Rader Marcus Center of the American Jewish Archives (hereafter AJA), Cincinnati, OH. For convenience, future references to this work appear in parentheses in the text. In 1977 Samuel Rezneck published a summary of the autobiography with connecting comments as "The Maritime Adventures of a Jewish Sea Captain, Jonas P. Levy, in Nineteenth-Century America," *American Neptune* 37 (1977): 239–252.

6. An excellent biography of Uriah Levy was written by the late Ira Dye, *Uriah Levy, Reformer of the Antebellum Navy* (Gainesville, FL: University of Florida Press, 2006).

7. "Capt. Jonas P. Levy," *The New York Times* (15 September 1883): 5. General Talavera may in fact be Felipe Santiago de Salaverry.

8. List of Documents, Jonas P. Levy vs. Mexico, 5 February 1874, Claims vs. Mexico folder, P-412, Box 1, folder 4, AJHS, New York.

9. Nelson Reed, *The Caste War of the Yucatan* (Stanford, CA: Stanford University Press, 1964), chs. 1–2.

10. For Evans, see http://www.cavaliergalleries.com/artist_bio.php?artist_id=847 accessed on 27 February 2009.

11. Minutes, Congregation B'nai Jeshurun, New York, microfilm copy at AJA, Cincinnati. The salaries for the two rabbis are found in the 1847 minutes. Abraham Mitchell was a liquor merchant: see his Daybook, Historical Society of Pennsylvania, Philadelphia. Jonas's wife, Frances Allen Mitchell Levy, was born in 1823 and died in 1893 as noted on the tombstone she shares with her husband at Shearith Israel Cemetery, Cypress Hills, Brooklyn, NY.

12. Samuel Owen, *The New-York Legal Observer: Containing Reports of Cases Decided in the Courts of Equity and Common Law...* (New York: for the author, 1845), 163–166.

13. Memorial of Jonas P. Levy to the Honorable Senate and House of Representatives, 29 January 1850, SC-7049, AJA. For Uriah's wealth, see Marc Leepson, *Saving Monticello: The Levy Family's Epic Quest to Rescue the House that Jefferson Built* (New York: Free Press, 2001), 76. Leepson identifies August Belmont, who was an Episcopalian by this time, as the wealthiest Jew.

14. Jonas P. Levy "To the Honorable Senate and House of Representatives," 17 January 1852; Jonas P. Levy to W. H. Wadsworth, 3 August 1873; Jonas P. Levy vs. Mexico, 5 February 1874; P-412, Box 1, folder 4, Claims Re: Mexico, AJHS, New York.

15. Jonas P. Levy to Secretary of the Treasury H. McCulloh, 28 July 1867; Whittesley quoted in Jonas P. Levy to W. H. Wadsworth, 3 August 1873. Both in P-412, Box 1, folder 4S, Claims Re: Mexico, AJHS, New York.

16. Petition of Jonas P. Levy to Congress of the United States, February, 1856, P-412, Box 1, folder 4, AJHS, New York.

17. "Correspondence in Claim Re: Mexico, folder, 1851–1859, 1868–1882," and "Petitions to Congress, n.d., 1856, 1882," P-412 Box 1 folder 4, AJHS, New York.

18. Marc Lee Raphael, *Towards a "National Shrine": A Centennial History of the Washington Hebrew Congregation* (Williamsburg, VA: Department of Religious Studies, College of William and Mary, 2005), 1–2.

19. Jerry Klinger, "The Swiss Treaty and the Washington Hebrew Congregation," accessed on 29 February 2009 at http://www.jewishmag.com/110mag/swissbill/swissbill.htm.

20. The full story is told in Sol M. Strook, "Switzerland and the American Jews," *Publications of the American Jewish Historical Society* 11 (1903): 7–52, reprinted in Abraham J. Karp, ed., *The Jewish Experience in America, III: The Emerging Community* (Waltham, MA: American Jewish Historical Society, 1969), 77–122. Strook reprints all the important documents. For the petition, Levy's letter to Lewis Cass, and Cass's reply, see *Occident* 12 (1854): 97–100.

21. Lewis Cass (10 July) to Jonas P. Levy and Levy to Cass, 12 July 1858, *Occident* 16 (1858): 259–260.

22. Jonas P. Levy to Lewis Cass (6 April) and Cass to Levy, 12 April 1859, *Occident* 17 (1859): 30.

23. The list of witnesses Uriah P. Levy assembled to support his claim that he was fit to command a ship and ought to be reinstated in the navy included at least three of the nation's most powerful Democrats: Augustus Schell, a presidential appointee as head of the New York Customs' House (the most lucrative source of graft in the nation) and future Chairman of the National Democratic Party, James Gallatin, President of the Bank of New York, and the famous historian George Bancroft, successively Secretary of the Navy and War under Democrat James Polk. In 1846 Bancroft ordered Commodore Stockton and General Taylor to be prepared to move on California and disputed territory in Northern Mexico, respectively, thereby provoking the Mexican War. Benjamin F. Butler, *Defence of Uriah P. Levy: Before the Court of Inquiry, held at Washington City, November and December, 1857* (New York: Wm. C. Bryant, 1858), table of contents.

24. Minutes of the Board of Delegates of American Israelites, 28 March 1860, SC-1194, AJA, Cincinnati.

25. Abraham Simon, "Notes of Jewish Interest in the District of Columbia," *Publications of the American Jewish Historical Society* 26 (1918): 218–219; *Occident* 17 (1859): 214.

26. Jonas P. Levy to Isaac Leeser (1 April) and Leeser to Levy (7 April), 1859, reprinted in *Occident* 17 (1859): 11–12.

27. Raphael, 4, quoting *National Intelligencer* (23 May 1859): 3.

28. Jonas P. Levy to Henry Hart, President of the Board of Delegates of American Israelites, 23 January 1860, *Occident* 18 (1860): 92, copy in Bertram W. Korn papers, MS 99, Box 28, folder 14, "Prayers Offered by Jews in 19th Century Legislatures," AJA, Cincinnati.

29. Raphael, 5.

30. *Occident* 17 (1860): 275, 287; *American Jewish Messenger* 7, no. 5 (1860): 37, copy in MS 99, Box 28, folder 14, AJA, Cincinnati.

31. *Occident* 17 (1860): 310.

32. Embossed advertisement, 1857, Arnold and Deanne Kaplan Collection of American Judaica, Allentown, PA.

33. Several of Levy's memorials are found in the Mexican Claims folder in P-412, Box 1, folder 4 at the AJHS, and/or his Biography folder at the AJA. The final one, dated 1882, is in the Arnold and Deanne Kaplan Collection of American Judaica, Allentown, PA.

34. Ibid.

35. Board of Delegates of American Israelites, Minutes, 30 and 31 May 1860, SC-1194, AJA, Cincinnati.

36. Cited by Bertram Korn, *Eventful Years and Experiences: Studies in Nineteenth Century American Jewish History* (Cincinnati: American Jewish Archives, 1954), 104. For the Jewish political group, see *Occident* 18 (1860): 197, 226; Jerome Mushkat, *Fernando Wood: A Political Biography* (Kent, OH: Kent State University Press, 1990), 112–113.

37. Jonas P. Levy to Jeremiah S. Black (12 December 1860) and Black to Levy (21 December 1860), *Occident* 18 (1861): 253–254.

38. Bertram W. Korn, *The Early Jews of New Orleans* (Waltham, MA: American Jewish Historical Society, 1969), 326.

39. Jonas P. Levy accounts, 9 and 11 March 1865 and letter to Lt. Colonel Boyd (Raleigh, NC), 8 August 1865, P-412, Box 1, folder 1, Civil War Claims; Jonas P. Levy to Senate Committee on Foreign Relations, 15 June 1874, P-412. B-412, Box 1, folder 4, Claims Re: Mexico, AJHS, New York.

40. Certified Copy of the Will of Uriah Phillips Levy (filed under Levy, Uriah Phillips), SC-7146, AJA. It is well summarized in Dye, 241–246. For the statue controversy, see Leon Hühner, *The Life of Judah Touro (1775–1854)* (Philadelphia: Jewish Publication Society of America, 1946), 120–122, 180–182; Leepson, 98–100.

41. Memorial by Mr. Tillotson, 22 September 1868, P-412, Box 1, folder 3, Miscellaneous Correspondence re: Monticello, AJHS, New York.

42. Leepson, 74, 76, 94.

43. William Robertson to Jonas P. Levy, 4 February 1868, 13 February 1868, 18 March 1868, 21 December 1868, P-412, Box 1, folder 6, Robertson Correspondence file, AJHS, New York; Edward P. Cannon to Jonas P. Levy, 16 July 1869; James Alfred Jones to Jonas P. Levy, 7 November 1870, 13 November 13, 1872, P-412, Box 1, folder 3, Miscellaneous Correspondence re: Monticello, AJHS, New York. Whether Uriah Levy's marriage was valid in Virginia may be of more than academic interest as the state Virginia would not recognize the intermarriage of blacks and whites until 1959, and of course does not recognize gay marriage today.

44. Leepson, 98–100; George Carr to Jonas P. Levy, 23 December 1868, P-412, Box 1, folder 2, Carr Correspondence file, AJHS; Jonas P. Levy to William Robertson, 28 September 1868, P-412, Box 1, folder 2, Robertson Correspondence file, AJHS, New York; Edward P. Cannon to Jonas P. Levy, 16 July 1869, P-412, Box 1, folder 3, Miscellaneous Correspondence re: Monticello file, for case of Levy v. Levy, AJHS, New York.

45. George Carr to Jonas P. Levy, 23 December 1868, 28 April 1873, 7 November 1875, P-412, Box 1, folder 2, Carr Correspondence file, AJHS, New York; William Robertson to Jonas P. Levy, 20 March 1873, 11 June 1873, 21 November 1875, P-412, Box 1, folder 6, Robertson Correspondence file, AJHS, New York.

46. Jonas Philips Levy to William Robertson, 13 May 1873, 7 June 1873, 15 June 1873, 21 November 1875, Robertson Correspondence file; Petition to Congress, including "History of Monticello 1765 On," P-412, Box 1, folder 3, Miscellaneous Correspondence re: Monticello, February 1874, AJHS, New York.

47. Petition to Congress, including "History of Monticello 1765 On," and response by House of Representatives Committee on Buildings and Grounds, February 1874,

P-412, Box 1, folder 3, Miscellaneous Correspondence re: Monticello, AJHS, New York.

48. Ibid; Leepson, 109–111.

49. Stationery heading on Jonas P. Levy to George Carr, 5 April 1873, P-412, Box 1, folder 2, George Carr Correspondence folder, AJHS, New York.

50. A portrait of Levy is owned by the Washington Hebrew Congregation, and one of his wife by the American Jewish Historical Society in Newton Centre, MA, but as hers is considerably larger, they are not the matching set. For Fanny Mitchell Levy's portrait, see online entry under her name in Art Inventories Catalogue, Smithsonian Institution Retrieval Information System.

51. Leepson, 109–111.

52. Marriages and Deaths, 15 January 1879, p. 16, Congregation Shearith Israel, New York, Congregation Shearith Israel Manuscripts. Microfilm 1-D, AJA, Cincinnati. Rothschild was a name found, although not frequently, among American Jews at this time, and did not necessarily imply a link to the famous European family.

53. *Occident* 12 (1853): 275; Broadside, Invitation of B'nai Jeshurun Educational Institute to Inaugural Ceremony, Arnold and Deanne Kaplan Collection of American Judaica, Allentown, PA.

54. Treasurer's Book and Seat Holders, 3, 7, 13, and 24 (1861–1862), Congregation Shearith Israel, New York, microfilm 1-D, AJA. Uriah contributed $105 per year in increments of $35 until his death; then his widow paid $20.25 in increments of $6.75; she also donated $15 when her husband died.

55. *Occident* 18 (1860): 204.

Chapter 8 - Beyond the Parochial Image of Southern Jewry

1. This essay could not have been completed without the extraordinary assistance of several archivists and archives. I wish to thank Kevin Proffitt, Vicki Lipski, Lisa Frankel, Dana Herman, and the American Jewish Archives, Cincinnati, OH; Deborah Weiner and the Jewish Historical Society of Maryland, Baltimore, MD; Adina Anflick and the American Jewish Historical Society, Center for Jewish History, New York, NY; Charlotte Bonelli and the American Jewish Committee Archives, New York, NY; Cheryl Kempner and the B'nai B'rith Klutznick National Jewish Museum, Washington, DC; Casey Green and the Rosenberg Library, Galveston, TX; and Catherine Kahn and the Touro Infirmary Archives, New Orleans, LA. Rabbi James Kessler of Temple B'nai Israel of Galveston, TX, Bryan Edward Stone, and Hollace Ava Weiner generously provided an amazing number of citations and leads from their extensive knowledge of Texas Jewish history.

My first contact with Gary P. Zola took place indirectly when I read and greatly admired his study of Isaac Harby, the leader of the Reformed Society of Israelites and, as Gary shows, a cosmopolitan figure in educational and literary circles. Gary's is a landmark biography placing Harby within time and place and greatly increasing our knowledge and understanding of the origins of Reform Judaism in the United States. Through the years Gary has penned articles on Rabbi Perry Nussbaum and civil rights; the Southern Conference of Rabbis, forerunner of the Central Conference of American Rabbis; and "Why Study Southern Jewish History" under my editorship and he has reciprocated by editing and publishing three of mine as well as graciously providing two fellowships for me to use collections at the Archives. See Gary

P. Zola, *Isaac Harby of Charleston, 1788–1828* (Tuscaloosa: University of Alabama Press, 1994); "What Price Amos: Perry Nussbaum's Career in Jackson, Mississippi," in *Quiet Voices: Southern Rabbis and Black Civil Rights*, ed. Mark K. Bauman and Berkley Kalin (Tuscaloosa: University of Alabama Press, 1997; paperback: 2007), 230–257; "Southern Rabbis and the Founding of the First National Association of Rabbis," *American Jewish History* 85 (December 1997): 353–372; reprinted in *Dixie Diaspora: An Anthology on Southern Jewish History*, ed. Mark K. Bauman (Tuscaloosa: University of Alabama Press, 2007), 33–54, and "Why Study Southern Jewish History?" *Southern Jewish History* 1 (1989): 1–21. Mark K. Bauman, "The Transformation of Jewish Social Services in Atlanta, 1928–1948," *American Jewish Archives Journal* 53 (2001): 83–111; "Variations on the Mortara Case in Midnineteenth-Century New Orleans," *American Jewish Archives Journal* 55 (2003): 43–58; "A Century of Southern Jewish Historiography," *American Jewish Archives Journal* 59, nos. 1 and 2 (2007): 3–78.

2. See, for example, Melvin I. Urofsky, "Preface: The Tip of the Iceberg," in *Turn to the South: Essays on Southern Jewry*, ed. Melvin I. Urofsky and Nathan Kaganoff (Charlottesville: University Press of Virginia, 1979), xi–xiii; *Commonwealth and Community: The Jewish Experience in Virginia* (Richmond: Virginia Historical Society and Jewish Community Federation of Richmond, 1997); Harry Golden, *Our Southern Landsman* (New York: G.P. Putnam's Sons, 1974); Eli N. Evans, *The Provincials: A Personal History of Jews in the South* (Chapel Hill: University of North Carolina Press, 2005; orig. pub. 1973); Mark I. Greenberg, "Becoming Southern: The Jews of Savannah, Georgia," *American Jewish History* 86 (March 1998): 55–75; Eric Goldstein, *The Price of Whiteness* (Princeton, NJ: Princeton University Press, 2007). Marcie Cohen Ferris and Mark I. Greenberg, eds., *Jewish Roots in Southern Soil: A New History* (Hanover, NH: Brandeis University Press, 2007), passim.

3. Lee Shai Weissbach, "Stability and Mobility in the Small Jewish Community: Examples from Kentucky History," *American Jewish History* 79 (Spring 1990): 355–375; "Kentucky's Jewish History in National Perspective: The Era of Mass Migration," *Filson Club Historical Quarterly* 69 (1995): 255–274; *Jewish Life in Small-Town America* (New Haven, CT: Yale University Press, 2005); Mark K. Bauman, "The Southerner as American: Jewish Style" (Cincinnati: American Jewish Archives, 1996).

4. See Juliet Lapidus, "South vs. North," *Forward* (15 June 2007): B2, for an exchange between Mark I. Greenberg and me where it is extremely difficult to discern differences of opinion between us.

5. For the growing literature on western Jewry see Moses Rischin and John Livingston, *Jews of the American West* (Detroit: Wayne State University Press, 1991); Marc Dollinger and Ava F. Kahn, *California Jews* (Waltham, MA: Brandeis University Press, 2003); Ava F. Kahn, ed., *Jewish Life in the American West* (Seattle: University of Washington Press, 2000); Jeanne Abrams, *Jewish Women Pioneering the Frontier Trail* (New York: New York University Press, 2006); Ellen Eisenberg, Ava F. Kahn, and William Toll, *Jews of the Pacific Coast: Reinventing Community on America's Edge* (Seattle: University of Washington Press, 2010).

6. I explored some of the themes raised here more on the grass-roots level in Mark K. Bauman, "A Multithematic Approach to Southern Jewish History," in *The Columbia*

History of Jews and Judaism in America, ed. Marc Lee Raphael (New York: Columbia University Press, 2008), 263–290.

7. My original research on Rosanna Dyer Osterman was undertaken as a Starkoff Fellow at the American Jewish Archives as part of a broader study, "Southern Jewish Women and Their Social Service Organizations," *Journal of American Ethnic History* 22 (Spring 2003), 34–78, especially 41.

8. The original family name was Nachman. John Dyer was also born in Mainz/Mayence, Eytinge-Nachman Family file, Jewish Museum of Maryland, Baltimore, MD (hereafter cited as JMM); Leon Dyer Papers, 1836–1850, Document file, The Jacob Rader Marcus Center of the American Jewish Archives, Cincinnati, OH (hereafter cited as AJA); Isadore Blum, *The Jews of Baltimore* (Baltimore, MD: Historical Review Publishing Company, 1910), 9–11; Adolf Guttmacher, *A History of the Baltimore Hebrew Congregation Nidche Israel, 1830–1905* (Baltimore, MD: Lord Baltimore Press, 1905), 28–31. For the Dyer children see Henry Cohen, "Settlement of the Jews in Texas," *Publications of the American Jewish Historical Society* (hereafter cited as *PAJHS*) 2 (1894): 147–149 and appendix (which lists excerpts from Isadore Dyer's and Rosanna Dyer Osterman's wills); Natalie Ornish, *Pioneer Jewish Texans* (Dallas: Texas Heritage Press, 1989), 21, 85, 105–106, 171–173, 246–249 (on this and following); James Lee Kessler, "BOI, A History of Congregation B'nai Israel, Galveston, Texas," doctoral dissertation (Hebrew Union College, 1988); A. Stanley Dreyfus, "A Hebrew Benevolent Society: A Saga of Service," 10 page typescript of speech given at ceremony commemorating the centennial of the founding of Galveston Hebrew Benevolent Society, Temple B'nai Israel, 30 October 1966, Rosanna Osterman Collection, SC 9350, AJA, Cincinnati, OH. Dreyfus indicates that Isadore married an Episcopalian woman in 1842 and regularly contributed to her church. Consequently Dreyfus grants credit to Rosanna for providing "the impetus for Jewish worship and Jewish benevolence" rather than to Isadore.

9. Discussion of these opposing historical frameworks begins with Oscar Handlin, *The Uprooted: The Epic Story of the Great Migrations That Made the American People* (New York: Atlantic-Little, Brown Books, 1951) and John Bodner, *The Transplanted: A History of Immigrants in Urban America* (Bloomington: Indiana University Press, 1985).

10. See Joseph Osterman Dyer, "Mrs. Rosanna Osterman," typescript, 1923, SC-9351, AJA, Cincinnati, OH (original in Rosenberg Library, Galveston, TX); Dyer, "Some Foreign Pioneers," *Galveston Daily News* (18 December 1921); Dyer, "An Old Galveston Home, Now Y.W.C.A. Residence," *Galveston Daily News* (6 March 1921): 26, columns 1–8; "Former Fever Times," *Galveston Daily News* (9 June 1907): (for the frequent yellow fever epidemics in the city during the 1840s and 1850s); Bobbye Robinson, "Jewish 'Saga of Service' Recounted," *Galveston Daily News* (31 October 1966): A, 1, 5 (recounts speech by A. Stanley Dreyfus, former rabbi of the congregation, at centennial of Temple B'nai Israel); Ornish, *Pioneer Jewish Texans*, 171–173; Hollace Ava Weiner, *Jewish Stars in Texas; Rabbis and Their Work* (College Station: Texas A&M University Press, 1999), 60. Dyer, whose date I have used, disagrees with Henry Cohen on the year of death of Joseph Osterman, the latter putting it at 1861, as well as the year of marriage which Cohen gives as 1825. Cohen indicates that Osterman died from an accidental gunshot wound fired by a worker in a gunsmith shop. Cohen, "The Jews in Texas," *PAJHS* 4 (1896): 16.

11. 1966 clipping; June Angerstein, "Immigrants Came When Texas Was Republic," *Galveston Daily News* (22 February 1970): C10; Dreyfus, "Hebrew Benevolent Society."

12. On this and following see excerpts from Rosanna Dyer Osterman's will in Henry Cohen, "Early Jewish Settlements in Texas," in *One Hundred Years of Jewry in Texas*, ed. Henry Cohen, David Lefkowitz, and Ephraim Frisch (Dallas: Jewish Advisory Committee for the Texas Centennial, 1936), 10–11; Cohen, "Settlement of the Jews in Texas," 153–156; Ornish, *Pioneer Jewish Texans*, 246–247; Elizabeth Hayes Turner, "Osterman, Rosanna Dyer," http://www.tshaonline.org/handbook/online/articles/00/fos8.html accessed on 5 August 2008. See also J. Angerstein, "Immigrants Came When Texas Was Republic." Rosanna Osterman's obituary (Galveston *Tri-Weekly News* [14 February 1866]: 2) reflected the imagery of the women's sphere. The following is from a letter from the "committee on the part of the sick of Col. Hobby's Reg't": "Mrs. Osterman was refined, cultivated and unostentatious—a blessing to a community and state; an honor and ornament to her sex.... Her life and deeds afford on the highest type of woman's excellence and usefulness." Colonel Alfred M. Hobby included a poem dedicated to Osterman in *The Serfs of Chateny and Miscellaneous Poems* that was originally published with this obituary. This, other tributes and obituaries are in the Osterman biography files.

13. "Testament of Judah Touro," New Orleans, 6 January 1854, copy, SC-12411, AJA, Cincinnati, OH. For a published copy of excerpts see Max J. Kohler, "Judah Touro, Merchant and Philanthropist," *PAJHS* 13 (1905): 104–111.

14. Touro bequeathed $410,000 to the indigent Jews of Jerusalem. The donation brought together Gershom Kursheedt and Moses Montefiore who were in charge of executing the bequest. Kursheedt traveled from New Orleans to London where he and Montefiore continued on to Palestine in 1855. During their first trip together they decided to build a hospital but when the Rothschilds constructed one, their plans became obsolete. With a second trip in 1857 they laid plans for an alms house. Kursheedt made a solo stay in 1860, the year the North American Relief Society for Indigent Jews of Jerusalem opened the first alms house bringing Jews outside of the Old City of Jerusalem. The facility (*Batei Mishkenot Sha-Ananim*) is credited with "laying a foundation for a *modern* Jerusalem." Kursheedt has been called "the first American Jew to play a substantial role in the Jewish protests against the Damascus blood libel incident." Kursheedt's trips would have been widely discussed within the New Orleans Jewish community and would likely have come to the attention of Rosanna Dyer Osterman. Kursheedt followed his father's example. In 1834 as a leader of New York Jewry, Israel Bar Kursheedt had initiated the creation of the *hevrat trumat hakadosh*, a central clearing house to collect and distribute funds to Jews in need overseas. He also led "Americans to the Development of the State of Israel," Shelomo Alfassa, "Sephardic Contributions strengthening of the Yishuv in Palestine," http://www.alfassa.com/contributions.pdf accessed on 28 August 2008 (first quotation);"Mishkenot Sha-Ananim: From Alms House to Cultural Centre – Jerusalem's First Building Outside the Old City's Walls," *The Israeli Review of Arts and Letters* (1996) reprinted in Israeli MFA Library, http://www.mfa.gov.il/MFA/MFAAArchive/2000_2009/2003/9/M accessed on 6 September 2003; no author, "Mishkenot Sha-ananim," http://www.jewishvirtual library.org/jsource/societyauthor_&_culture/geo/mishkenot.html accessed on 13 March 2009. During the late 1850s Kursheedt and Montefiore also collaborated in

protesting the Edgardo Mortara incident. Kursheedt represented most of the Jewish communities in the United States in this dialog. See Bertram W. Korn, *American Reaction to the Mortara Case, 1858–1859* (Cincinnati: Hebrew Union College, 1957); Bauman, "Variations on the Mortara Case;" Kenneth Libo and Abigail Kursheedt Hoffman, *The Seixas–Kursheedts and the Rise of Early American Jewry* (n.c.: Bloch Publishing Company, 2001). Kursheedt is another exemplar of the themes depicted in this article.

15. Jonathan D. Sarna informs me that Osterman must have copied from Touro's will since the Hebrew Foreign Mission Society was no longer extent by 1868. See Michael Pollak, *Mandarins, Jews, and Missionaries: The Jewish Experience in the Chinese Empire* (Philadelphia: Jewish Publication Society, 1980); Jacob Kellner "The Formative Years of American Support for the Jewish Community in Palestine, 1833–1881," *Shalem* 1 (1974): 377–426 (Hebrew). I am indebted to Professor Sarna for these citations and numerous insights.

16. See, for example, Abraham J. Peck, "'That Other Peculiar Institution': Jews and Judaism in the Nineteenth Century South," *Modern Judaism* 7 (February 1987): 99–114; "Between Myth and Reality—Jews and Judaism in the Nineteenth Century American South," *Proceedings of the Ninth World Congress of Jewish Studies*, division b, 3 (Jerusalem, 1986), 119–126.

17. Isaac Harby led Charleston's Reformed Society of Israelites but, like members of the Labbatt, Harby, and Hyams families, in New Orleans his relatives joined the traditional, Portuguese rite, Dispersed of Judah congregation when it opened. The move from the Reformed Society of Israelites to New Orleans to a Reform and then to a Sephardic congregation similar in function to KK Beth Elohim prior to the Reform schism points to the problem of labeling people as Reform versus traditional during this period. For activities of Harby relatives in New Orleans see Bertam W. Korn, *The Early Jews of New Orleans* (Waltham, MA: American Jewish Historical Society, 1969), 182–187, 189–190, 202, 212, 226, 241, 245, 248, 321–332. Isaac Harby's son Julian migrated to Texas in time to participate in its war for independence from Mexico in which he was joined by his uncle Levy Charles Harby. See Ornish, *Pioneering Jewish Texans*, 29, 44.

18. Abraham Cohen Labbatt married Caroline Hyams the day after he signed the Reformed Society of Israelites' constitution. He pioneered as a Jewish business trader in Texas and in 1849 went to California with the gold rush. The following year he helped establish and served as the first full term president of San Francisco's Congregation Emanuel. The family returned to New Orleans and then to Texas during the 1860s. A.C. Labbatt's son Henry, born in New Orleans, married Emily Dyer Labbatt (Rosanna Dyer Osterman's niece). Like his father he went to California and returned to Texas where he served in the state House of Representatives and actively participated in Galveston's Temple B'nai Israel. See Ornish, *Pioneering Jewish Texans*, 139–140, 246, 249, 264–265. For A.C. Labbatt's activities in New Orleans see Korn, *Early Jews of New Orleans*, 337 n. 10. While in San Francisco, Henry served as secretary of that city's first Hebrew Benevolent Society and was active in Congregation Emanuel. Another of A.C. Labbatt's sons, Samuel K., held office in New Orleans' Hebrew Benevolent Society before founding (with his brother Joseph and fellow Charlestonian Solomon N. Carvalho) and presiding over the same institution in Los Angeles, the city's first Jewish organization. Samuel K. petitioned for the city's first

Jewish cemetery. Samuel and Joseph acted as their father's business agents and then returned with the family to Texas. William M. Kramer and Norton B. Stern, "Samuel K. Labbatt: Sephardic Founder of the Los Angeles Jewish Community, 1830–1870," *Western States Jewish History* 28 (July 1996): 337–345; William M. Kramer, "Samuel K. Labbatt: Los Angeles' First Jewish 'President,' 1854," *Western States Jewish Historical Quarterly* 7 (January 1975): 151–153. For a rabbi who filled pulpits in the South including K.K. Beth Elohim in Charleston, served in San Francisco and Portland, Oregon, and illustrates the rabbinical aspect of the internal migration theme see Joshua Stampfer, *Pioneer Rabbi of the West: The Life and Times of Julius Eckman* (Portland, OR: Institute of Jewish Studies, 1988).

19. Samuel Hyams and his son Henry M. were members of the Reformed Society of Israelites. Samuel Hyams served as a trustee of New Orleans's congregation Shangarai Chasset before he joined Dispersed of Judah. Henry M. Hyams moved to Donaldsonville and served in the state Senate, and in 1859 won election as Lieutenant-Governor of Louisiana, the first Jew to hold such a position in any state government. He also served as vice president the Hebrew Widows and Orphans Home. Numerous other Reformed Society family members migrated to New Orleans. Dr. Edwin Warren Moïse served as attorney-general and speaker of the Louisiana legislature. Hyams's cousin, Phillip Benjamin, joined the Reformed Society. Judah P. Benjamin, Phillip's son, attended Isaac Harby's Academy. Judah P. Benjamin, unlike the others, played virtually no part in the New Orleans Jewish community. On these and other relocated Charlestonian Jews see Korn, *Early Jews of New Orleans*, 187–190, 189, 227, 232, 237, 248. Zola, *Isaac Harby*, 232–233, n. 32. Judah P. Benjamin started a successful legal practice in New Orleans, became a plantation owner, served as U.S. Senator, and then held three positions in the Confederate cabinet. After the war he relocated to London where he became a barrister and wrote legal texts. Eli N. Evans, *Judah P. Benjamin: The Jewish Confederate* (New York: Free Press, 1988).

20. Unless otherwise noted, for Levi's family and life see Robert W. Shook, "Abraham Levi, Father of Victorian Jewry," *Western States Jewish Historical Quarterly* 9 (January 1977): 144–154 ; Henry Cohen, "Introduction and Biography," in I.O.B.B., *Leo N. Levi Memorial Volume* (Chicago: Hamburger Printing Co, 1905), 12–15, served as the basis for Cohen's treatment of Levi in "Early Jewish Settlements in Texas," 24–25; Ornish, *Pioneer Jewish Texans*, passim.

21. *The American Israelite* (31 January 1879): 6, reported on Levi's receipt of gold medals in 1875 and 1876 and degree from the University of Virginia as well as his position at the Flournoy, Scott, and Levi law firm. The article indicates that "Mr. Levi is well known to our readers as a welcome contributor to these columns." Correspondents like Levi helped Isaac M. Wise, the newspaper's editor and institution builder of Reform Judaism, unify American Jewry through the flow of information. This reference provides an early indication of Levi's actions in the same regard.

Letters from Levi under the pseudonym "Themis" and describing Jewish activities in Galveston appeared 30 November 1877: 6; 4 January 1878: 5–6. In the first of these Levi explained Jewish involvement in business in relation to the Jews' history of persecution and then explained that they had now attained a more advanced state of participation in a variety of economic, professional, and political affairs. He used the wealth and position of Galveston Jews, whom he described as critical to the success of their island, as illustrative, finally pointing to a $4,000 donation to "the Theological University in Cincinnati" as proof. For a twenty-one year old, both this letter and the second, which disparaged the spiritual state of Galveston's Jews and is discussed below, displayed insight and maturity. He returned to these themes repeatedly in the future. Copies of *The American Israelite* articles were graciously provided by AJA as were other periodicals. I am indebted to Bryan Edward Stone for the identification of Levi as Themis. For advertisement, see *Galveston Daily News* (26 September 1884): 9.

22. Levi wrote a letter, "Contemporary History of American Israelites, Duty of Collecting Data and Material, Suggestions to the Executive Committee and Lodges," to *Menorah* 5 (July–December 1888): 122–127, advocating the collection of information on American Jewish history and specifically the conducting of an American Jewish census every decade by the I.I.O.B. that influenced Cyrus Adler's call for the creation of the American Jewish Historical Society. Levi and Cohen were charter members of the latter. Levi's advocacy of an extensive Jewish census was ahead of his time but in keeping with his interpretation of the contemporary concept of scientific charity. To him philanthropy could neither be rendered effectively nor evaluated appropriately without statistical verification. The American Jewish Committee subsequently published annual statistics on Jewish population in its *Yearbook,* but collection of more complete data awaited the era of the Second World War efforts of the Jewish Federation and Welfare Fund national network. See Jeffrey S. Gurock, "From Publications to American Jewish History," *American Jewish* History 81 (Winter 1993–1994): 155, no. 1 (for the influence of Levi's article on Adler); Bauman, "A Century of Southern Jewish Historiography," (for Cohen's participation in the AJHS).

23. Levi used his access to Roosevelt occasionally to disagree with policies he and other Jewish leaders perceived negatively. When, for example, the State Department considered classifying Jews as a race for immigration purposes, a classification at odds with the position of most Reform Jewish leaders although they often used the term themselves, Levi argued that this would open "a Pandora's box" dividing Jews besides classifying them differently from other immigrants. Then as later, Jewish leaders framed their arguments in general human rights terms and sought equal treatment of Jews with other groups.

24. Restrictionists charged that many eastern European immigrants including Jews labored in the cities as industrial workers rather than what were viewed as more productive farmers. Levi thus supported Jewish agricultural colonies in New Jersey. When it became obvious that few would or could settle in these, "colonization" or "removal" to the hinterland, as exemplified by the programs of the organizations with which Levi was involved, served as the next logical step. Levi exchanged correspondence with attorney George D.M. Peixotto concerning the possibilities of Jewish agricultural colonies and the program of the Jewish Agricultural and Industrial Aid Society presided over by Cyrus L. Sulzberger. Levi indicated that he had obtained a financial backer and land in Texas for such a venture several years previously. The well-equipped farms manned by Jewish settlers "obtained favorable harvests." "It was impossible, however, to keep them on the farms. One by one they deserted and drifted back to the towns, so that, at the end of two years, there was not a Jewish farmer left in the settlement." After careful study and following "the consensus of opinion," Levi had concluded "that any general plan to make Jewish agriculturalists must prove a failure." Levi praised the work of Chicago Rabbi A.R. Levy who made loans to individual farmers who then had a stake in their enterprise but criticized Sulzberger's efforts.

Levi attributed the failure of Jewish agricultural settlements to the background experiences of the eastern European Jewish immigrants. Levi to Peixotto, 1 April 1903, Levi N. Levi Papers, B'nai B'rith Klutznick National Jewish Museum, Washington, DC (hereafter cited as BBKNJM).

25. For this and following see the general sources on Levi cited above, as well as the Louis Lipsky Collection, Levi-Simon Wolf correspondence, Simon Wolf Collection, and the Baron de Hirsch Fund Collection, all at the Center for Jewish History, American Jewish Historical Society, NY (hereafter cited as AJHS). Simon Wolf chaired the Board of Delegates of American Israelites for many years, among his many Jewish defense activities. Esther L. Panitz, *Simon Wolf: Private Conscience and Public Image* (London and Toronto: Associated University Presses for Fairleigh Dickinson University Press, 1987), 86–91, 148–150, gives inordinate credit to Wolf. The Levi-Simon Wolf correspondence illustrates close collaboration with Wolf advising but also carrying out Levi's wishes and following his opinions. Peter Romanofsky, "'…To Rid Ourselves of the Burden…'": New York Jewish Charities and the Industrial Removal Office, 1890–1901," *American Jewish Historical Quarterly* 64 (June 1975): 331–343, especially 337–341, gives substantial credit to Levi for the removal program. The next level of the colonization scheme, the Galveston Movement in which Henry Cohen played a prominent role, started after Levi's death. See Bernard Marinbach, *Galveston: Ellis Island of the West* (Albany: State University of New York Press, 1983); Samuel Joseph, *History of the Baron de Hirsch Fund: The Americanization of the Immigrant* (Philadelphia: Jewish Publication Society, 1935), 186–191. Sheldon Morris Neuringer, *American Jewry and United States Immigration Policy* (New York: Arno Press, 1980), 62–63; Naomi W. Cohen, *Jacob H. Schiff: A Study in American Jewish Leadership* (Hanover, NH: Brandeis University Press, 1999), 84–85; *Not Free to Desist: A History of the American Jewish Committee, 1906–1966* (Philadelphia: Jewish Publication Society, 1972). Jack Glazier, *Dispersing the Ghetto: The Relocation of Jewish Immigrants Across America* (Ithaca and London: Cornell University Press, 1998), especially 48–54, 57–58, 147–148, provides a thorough background for the issues addressed here and below and gives Levi substantial credit.

26. Leo N. Levi, "A Layman's Open Letter to the Rabbis," *Menorah* July 1887 reprinted in *Leo N. Levi Memorial Volume*, 150–158. This and the addresses and articles discussed below appear in this volume.

27. *Twenty-first Annual Report of the Union of American Hebrew Congregations, December 1894* (Cincinnati, OH: The Bloch Company, 1895), 3374; David Philipson, "Julius Freiberg," *PAJHS* 19 (1910): 202–205. AJA special projects archivist Vicki Lipski graciously brought this and several other citations to my attention.

28. Leo N. Levi, "Judaism in America from the Standpoint of a Layman," speech delivered at the UAHC council meeting in New Orleans in December 1894, *Levi Memorial Volume*, 63–89 (quotation on 64).

29. Ibid., 74–79.

30. Ibid., 73, 82, 65.

31. Ibid., 83, 88–89.

32. Henry Cohen, "Portrait of a Rabbi," in *Henry Cohen: Messenger of the Lord*, compiled by A. Stanley Dreyfus (New York: Bloch Publishing Co, 1963), 12–14, 31 (the author of the chapter was the rabbi's son and namesake). After Levi's death, IOBB established a charity hospital in Hot Springs, Arkansas, so that patients could

benefit from the local springs. Henry Cohen worked diligently on the project, named the Leo N. Levi Memorial Hospital. See *Galveston Daily News* (27 October 1913) for cornerstone laying ceremony and tribute to Levi. The issue of 14 January 1904 of the same newspaper carries a Levi obituary. Still the rabbi and layperson did not always agree. Cohen supported the Pittsburgh Platform.

33. "Proceedings of the Fourteenth Council," *Twenty-first Annual Report of the UAHC* (Cincinnati, OH: The Bloch Company, December 1894), 3374–3375, 3416.

34. Isaac M. Wise, David Philipson, Charles S. Levi, "Protest Against the Address," ibid., 3416.

35. Levi defined Jews as a race, but not one based on hereditary physical and mental characteristics. Therefore when he attacked the attempt to define Jews as a race for immigration purposes, he was not being inconsistent. He argued that Jews were a people with divergent national allegiances like any other religious group.

36. Osterman's spying activities for the South and the prominent roles played by members of the Hyams and Benjamin families in the Confederacy obviously illustrated espousal of regional causes.

Chapter 9 - An Ambivalent Relationship: Isaac M. Wise and the Independent Order of B'nai B'rith

1. Cornelia Wilhelm, "Community in Modernity —Finding Jewish Solidarity within the Independent Order of B'nai B'rith," *Simon Dubnow Institute Yearbook* 1 (2002): 297–319.

2. Michael A. Meyer, "German Jewish Identity in Nineteenth-Century America," in *Toward Modernity*, ed. Jacob Katz (New Brunswick, NJ: Transaction Books, 1987), 253.

3. See Cornelia Wilhelm, *Deutsche Juden in Amerika: Bürgerliches Selbstbewusstsein und jüdische Identität in den Orden B'nai B'rith und Treue Schwestern, 1843–1914* (Stuttgart: Steiner Verlag, 2007), 11ff.

4. Jacob Katz, *Jews and Freemasons 1723–1939* (Cambridge: Harvard University Press), 11ff. For individual leadership see Jacob Katz, "Samuel Hirsch, Rabbi, Philosopher and Freemason," in *Emancipation and Assimilation*, ed. Jacob Katz (Farnborough: Gregg International Publishers Limited, 1972), 159–172; and Samuel Hirsch, *Die Humanität als Religion, in Vorträgen, gehalten in der Loge zu Luxemburg* (Trier: C. Troschel, 1854), passim. For the influence of masonic organization on modern Jewish societies see also Jacob Toury, *Soziale und Politische Geschichte der Juden in Deutschland 1847–1971: zwischen Revolution, Reaktion und Emanzipation* (Düsseldorf: Droste, 1977), 211ff.

5. Isaac M. Wise, *Reminiscences*, translated from the German and edited with an introduction by David Philipson (Cincinnati: Leo Wise and Co., 1901), 198.

6. Wise, *Reminiscences*, 265.

7. Ibid., 187–188.

8. *Sinai* I (August 1856): 203–205; Max Lilienthal, "Erster Vortrag im Vereine der Freunde," *Israel's Herold* (20 April 1849): 26–27; and Max Lilienthal, "Erster Vortrag im Vereine der Freunde," *Israel's Herold* (27 April 1849): 34–35. See also "'The Convention,' *Israel's Herold*, Dr. Lilienthal, The Society of Friends," *The Occident* VII (June 1849): 139–143; and Wise, *Reminiscences,* 90–91, where Wise clearly down-

plays his defeat; see also James G. Heller, *Isaac M. Wise: His Life Work and Thought* (New York: UAHC, 1965), 166–167.

9. Wilhelm, *Deutsche Juden*, 77ff.

10. See also Carl Wittke, *Refugees of Revolution, German Forty-Eighters in America* (Philadelphia: University of Philadelphia Press, 1952), 122ff.; Jörn Brederlow, *"Lichtfreunde" und "freie Gemeinden," Religiöser Protest und Freiheitsbewegung im Vormärz und in der Revolution von 1848/49* (München, Wien: Oldenbourg Verlag, 1976). See also Bruce Levine, *The Spirit of 1848, German Immigrants, Labor Conflict, and the Coming of the Civil War* (Urbana and Chicago: University of Illinois Press, 1992), 48–49.

11. Michael A. Meyer mentions a connection between the Jewish "Reformfreunde" in Frankfurt and the larger "Lichtfreunde" Movement in pre-revolutionary Germany. Michael A. Meyer, "Alienated Intellectuals in the Camp of Religious Reform: The Frankfurt Reformfreunde, 1842–1845," *Association for Jewish Studies Review* (*AJS Review*) 6 (1981): 61–86. Sylvia Paletschek, *Frauen und Dissens* (Göttingen: Vandenhoeck und Ruprecht, 1990), 43ff. and 53ff.

12. Jacob Rader Marcus, *United States Jewry, 1776–1985*, Vol. III (Detroit: Wayne State University Press, 1993), 67, 760 (n. 19).

13. Hyman Grinstein, *The Rise of the Jewish Community of New York, 1654–1860* (Philadelphia: Jewish Publication Society of America, 1945), 202.

14. Wilhelm, *Deutsche Juden*, 77ff.

15. Meyer, *Response*, 243ff.

16. Alan Silverstein, *Alternatives to Assimilation: The Response of Reform Judaism to American Culture 1840–1930* (Hanover, NH: Brandeis University Press, 1994), 42–45; Meyer, *Response*, 243ff. See also Jonathan Sarna, *American Judaism* (New Haven: Yale University Press, 2004), 110.

17. Maurice Mayer to Bernhard Felsenthal, 9 May 1867, P-21 (Bernhard Felsenthal Papers), Box 2, American Jewish Historical Society (AJHS), New York. See also "Dr. Einhorn in Baltimore und seine Feinde," *Sinai* V (1860): 65–69, and Bernhard Postal, "A Century of Service," *American Jewish Year Book* (*AJYB*) 45 (1943–1944): 97–116.

18. Isidor Busch, "The Jewish Orphan Asylum, Cleveland O.," *The Menorah* (July 1888): 24–26.

19. *Constitution des Unabhängigen Orden B'nai B'rith, revidiert und angenommen in der General-Versammlung der Constitution Gross-Loge im Jahre 1851* (New York: Mühlhäuser, 1851), MS 508 (Records of B'nai B'rith District Grand Lodge No.6, 1895–1914), Box SR 1, The Jacob Rader Marcus Center of the American Jewish Archives (AJA), Cincinnati, OH. See also Wilhelm, *Deutsche Juden*, 129ff.

20. See Meyer, "A Centennial History," passim.

21. Wise, *Reminiscences*, 331.

22. Julius Bien, "History XXVI," *The Menorah* (July 1888): 48. "The College," *The Israelite* (18 January 1867): 4.

23. Baruch Rothschild and Maurice Mayer, 2 June 1865, IOBB-Archives, Box 96. Washington, DC.

24. Bien, "History XXXIII," *The Menorah* (March 1889): 173ff. Before, the Constitution Grand Lodge used to be "mobile" and met in the capital city of the district of the national president.

25. Bernhard Postal, "B'nai B'rith, A Century of Service," *AJYB* 45 (1943–1944): 97–116.

26. "*Dr. Einhorn in Baltimore und seine Feinde,*" *Sinai* (April 1860): 65–69. Maurice Mayer to Bernhard Felsenthal, 9 May 1867, P-21, Box 2, AJHS.

27. Wilhelm, *Deutsche Juden,* 164–165. See also telegraph Clara Brückner to IOBB, Convention Richmond VA, 1900, 3 June 1890, in Proceedings of the General Convention, IOBB, 1890, 100 (MS 508, Box SR 2), AJA.

28. Report of Annual Proceedings of DGL # 2, IOBB, 1863, 26, MS 36 (Records of B'nai B'rith District Grand Lodge No. 2, 1851–1907), Series B, Box B 30, AJA.

29. Baruch Rothschild to Maurice Mayer, 2 June 1865, IOBB-Archives, Box 96.

30. Ibid.

31. Bien, "History 539 XXIV," *The Menorah* (May 1889): 267.

32. Report of the Annual Proceedings of District Grand Lodge (DGL) # 2, IOBB, 1863, 26, MS 36, Series B, Box B 30, AJA.

33. Report of the General Convention of the Independent Order B'nai B'rith (IOBB), 1862, 13, MS 508, Box SR 1, AJA; Report of the Annual Meeting of DGL # 2, IOBB, 1862, 6ff., MS 36, Series B, Box B 30, AJA. Report of the Annual Proceedings of DGL # 2, IOBB, 1863, 25, MS 36, Series B, Box B 30, AJA; Baruch Rothschild to Maurice Mayer, 2 June 1865, IOBB-Archives, Box 96. Report of the Annual Proceedings of DGL # 2, IOBB, 1863, 26, MS 36, Series B, Box B 30, AJA.

34. "Convention of the Constitution Grand Lodge, IOBB," *The Israelite* (7 August 1863): 44.

35. On the situation in Chicago see Tobias Brinkmann,"*Von der Gemeinde zu' Community': Jüdische Einwanderer in Chicago, 1840–1900,*" *SHM* 10 (2002): 225ff.

36. Report of the Proceedings of DGL # 2, IOBB, 1862, 12, MS 36, Series B, Box B 30, AJA. ("...to make it an open society for the promotion of the interests of Judaism and the effective practice of charitable and benevolent purposes").

37. "Meeting of the Constitution Grand Lodge IOBB at Philadelphia, July 31, and August 1 and 2," *The Israelite* (12 August 1864): 52.

38. Report of the Proceedings of DGL # 2, IOBB, 1862, 14, MS 36, Series B, Box B 30, AJA.

39. Ibid.

40. "Meeting of the Constitution Grand Lodge IOBB at Philadelphia, July 31, and August 1 and 2," *The Israelite* (12 August 1864): 52.

41. *To the Several Lodges of the IOBB in the State of Illinois: Joint Report of their Representatives at the Annual Session of District Grand Lodge No. 2, at Milwaukee, July 14–17, 1867,* 10ff., IOBB-Archives.

42. "The Convention," *The Occident* (September 1868): 280.

43. *To the Several Lodges of the IOBB in the State of Illinois: Joint Report of their Representatives at the Annual Session of District Grand Lodge No. 2, at Milwaukee, July 14–17, 1867,* 22f, IOBB-Archives.

44. Proceedings of the Constitution Grand Lodge IOBB, 1867, 39, MS 508, Box SR 1, AJA. See Maurice Mayer to Bernhard Felsenthal, 9 May 1867, P-21, Box 2, AJHS. District No. 5 broke off from District No.3, and comprised Maryland, District of Columbia, Virginia, the Carolinas and Georgia; District No. 6 broke off from District No. 2 and comprised Illinois, Wisconsin, Minnesota, Iowa, Nebraska and Michigan.

45. "Work done for the Union of American Hebrew Congregations," *Israelite* (13 February 1874): 4; and "Die Convention des Bene Berith Ordens in Chicago," *Die Deborah* (13 February 1874): 2; "The General Convention of IOBB" *Israelite* (13 February 1874):6.

46. Proceedings of the General Convention, IOBB, 1874, 73, MS 508, SR 1, AJA.

47. Work done for the Union of the American Hebrew Congregations," *The Israelite* (13 February 1874): 4; and "Die Convention des Bene Berith Ordens in Chicago," *Die Deborah* (13 February 1874): 2. See also "The General Convention of IOBB," *The Israelite* (13 February 1874): 6.

48. I. M. Wise to Simon Wolf, 1 November 1898, Microfilm 2827, AJA.

49. See Wilhelm, *Deutsche Juden*, 269ff.

Chapter 10 - The Odyssey of a Liturgist: Isaac S. Moses as Architect of the *Union Prayer Book*

1. Marcus Jastrow (1829–1903) and Adolph Huebsch (1830–1886) are good examples of those who caught the revolutionary fervor and joined forces with the Spring of Nations.

2. *'Olat Tamid/Gebetbuch fuer israelitische Reform-Gemeinden* (Baltimore: E.W. Schneidereith, 1858), by David Einhorn (1809–1879) formed a key exception to this rule.

3. Enunciated first at the 1855 Cleveland Conference, Isaac Mayer Wise's dream of a fixed homogeneous liturgy to serve all the synagogues of America was not to be—at least not for a while. His close colleagues in the liturgy-making enterprise, Leo Merzbacher (1810–1856) and Adolph Huebsch, went off to create successful *siddurim* of their own.

4. The handsomely reworded prayer for Jerusalem by Merzbacher for Benediction 14 of his elegantly emended *Shemoneh 'Esreh* in his *The Order of Prayer* (p. 104) was ruled out altogether by Samuel Adler in his 1860 revision (p. 70), no doubt to obviate any suspicion of being unpatriotic in the new land. (See below for bibliographical details of both editions.)

5. While on the whole faithful to the text of his father-in-law David Einhorn's *'Olat Tamid*, Emil G. Hirsch's (1851–1923) 1896 English translation (*Dr. David Einhorn's 'Olat Tamid: Book of Prayers for Jewish Congregations*, after the German Original [Chicago: S. Ettlinger, 1896]) parted company with Einhorn's text insofar as he added a Sunday morning service (euphemistically labeled "Service for the Days of the Week") with a fine complement of new prayers. Others, like Gustav Gottheil (1829–1903) of Congregation Emanu-El in New York City, and Joseph Krauskopf (1858–1923) of Congregation Keneseth Israel in Philadelphia, produced wholly innovative services for the one day of the week when the overwhelming majority of their congregants could take off from work and attend worship services. Gottheil's manual was *Morning Prayers* (New York: Philip Cowen, 1889), and Krauskopf's, *The Service Ritual* (Philadelphia: J.B. Lippincott, 1888).

6. For lack of a full-scale biography of Isaac S. Moses, we resort to a meager outline in the hope that the details of his liturgical/literary activity that follow will help towards a more adequate portrayal of the man. Scanty available data may be found in the *American Jewish Year Book* 5 (1903–1904): 83, and the *Universal Jewish Encyclopedia* Vol. 8 (1941), 13–14, as cited by Gary P. Zola in his valuable

The Americanization of the Jewish Prayer Book and the Liturgical Development of Congregation Ahawath Chesed, New York City (New York: Central Synagogue, 2008), 82, n. 101. A kind of verbal daguerreotype is Joseph Stolz's warmhearted obituary tribute mentioned in the next note.

7. In his memorial tribute to Moses, younger colleague Stolz admirably put in a nutshell Moses' career in liturgy-making:

> Like so many other rabbis of the latter half of the nineteenth century endeavoring to adapt the old ritual to a new country and the new age, Isaac Moses published his own modified prayer-book [.........] He was among the first to advocate and support the idea of a Union Prayer Book. When the matter came officially before our Conference [Central Conference of American Rabbis], Dr. Wise appointed him a member of the first commission to prepare the manuscript. After the lapse of many months, it looked as if nothing would ever be accomplished because of the diversity of opinion and standard, whereupon of his own accord, upon his own initiative, at his own expense, without the thought of gain or glory, Isaac Moses published the manuscript which, after much discussion was, in 1892, accepted by the Conference as the unrevised basis of the future Union Prayer Book (*CCAR Yearbook* 37 [1927]: 254).

The ins and outs of this process, including the politics and the personalities, are gone into, with detail and precision, by Lou H. Silberman in his "The Union Prayer Book: A Study in Liturgical Development," in *Retrospect and Prospect: Essays in Commemoration of the Seventy-Fifth Anniversary of the Founding of the Central Conference of American Rabbis*, ed. Bertram W. Korn (New York: CCAR, 1965), 46–80. The most recent succinct treatment of the *Union Prayer Book*'s formative years may be found in Zola's *The Americanization of the Jewish Prayer Book*, 58–65.

8. Not included in this list are Moses's pedagogical works on which his brother Adolph Moses, also a rabbi, collaborated. Working with children and youth—as reflected in his Sabbath School hymnals, another educational tool—yielded him continual satisfaction. In 1880 he also authored a catechism for confirmation.

9. For the 1860 and 1864 editions of *The Order of Prayer*, Adler introduced further generally slight textual changes, while as a rule preserved the style and intent of his precursor. On the other hand, some major revamping did occur such as the uprooting of Deut. 11:13–21 and Nu. 15:37–41 from the *Shema*.

10. On this prayerbook and its many editions, see Jakob J. Petuchowski, *Prayerbook Reform in Europe: The Liturgy of European Liberal and Reform Judaism* (New York: World Union for Progressive Judaism, 1968), 4–18, 58–66.

11. Eric Friedland, "Leopold Stein: A Liberal Master of Prayer," in *Aspects of Liberal Judaism: Essays in Honor of John D. Rayner*, ed. David J. Goldberg and Edward Kessler (London and Portland, OR: Vallentine Mitchell, 2004), 49–72.

12. The temple, after a merger with Shaar Hashamayim, was eventually renamed Central Synagogue. Moses pastored the joint congregation during the last years of his service in the active rabbinate.

13. Merzbacher (1855) did retain a number of psalms and scriptural readings from the *Pesuqey de-Zimrah*, but without either of their attendant benedictions, *Barukh she-Amar* or *Yishtabbach*. He did, however, retain *Elohay Neshamah* and *Vi-Yhi Ratson...*

she-targilenu (of the Preliminary Benedictions)—and the *Shema*—for the private Morning Service at home.

14. One of the major concerns of Reform—and Reconstructionist—liturgies, notably in America and England, has been to go beyond the customary choices and to find fresh, ampler ways of using the Psalms.

15. The Sephardim have adhered to a similar practice, albeit with a very different assortment of psalms for each of the holy days. (Of these Merzbacher picked the Sephardic Ps. 81 for his New Year Evening Service only.) They normally recite the pilgrimage Ps. 122 after the evening *'Amidah* on all the Festivals apart from Passover. For his introductory psalms, Adler chose Ps. 134 for all evening services without exception (as did his predecessor), Ps. 124 for Hanukkah as well as Purim, Ps. 29 ("Ascribe to the LORD, O heavenly beings") for the Three Festivals, Ps. 121 for Rosh Hashanah, Ps. 92 (but not Ps. 93) for the Sabbath (Adler, 4–9), and Ps.130 for Yom Kippur (Adler, vol. 2 [1863], 4–5).

16. This is no less true of the Progressive prayerbooks produced in England, especially under the auspices of Liberal Judaism all the way from *Liberal Jewish Prayer Book* (ed. Israel Mattuck; London: Liberal Jewish Synagogue, 1926) and *Service of the Heart* (eds. Chaim Stern and John D. Rayner, London: Union of Liberal and Progressive Synagogues, 1967), to the unexcelled *Machzor Ruach Chadashah*, ed. Andrew Goldstein and Charles H. Middleburgh (London: Liberal Judaism, 2003).

17. After being systematically kept out of all the various versions of the *Union Prayer Book* and each of the *Gates* series, the restorationist phrase (*va-havi'enu le-shalom... ve-tolikhenu qomemiyyut le-artsenu*) in *Ahavah Rabbah* has been brought back in *Mishkan T'filah: A Reform Siddur* (New York: Central Conference of American Rabbis, 2007), 62, 230, 316, 456.

18. The same obtains in *Mishkan T'filah*, though not elsewhere throughout the prayerbook, as in the unchanged *attah vechartanu* ("You have chosen us from all peoples... and exalted us above all tongues") starting off the Intermediate Benediction of the Festival *'Amidah*.

19. *Ordnung der oeffentlichen Andacht fuer die Sabbath- und Festtage des ganzen Jahres nach dem Gebrauche des Neuen-Tempels-Vereins in Hamburg*, ed. S.I. Fraenkel and M.I. Bresselau (Hamburg: self-published, 1819), 54–60.

20. Ps. 24:9–10, instead of the standard Ashkenazic *Eyn Kamokha*.

21. Eric L. Friedland, "Why Do We Still Pray Anti-Goyism," *CCAR Journal: A Reform Jewish Quarterly* (Fall 2002): 49–57; Jakob J. Petuchowski, *Prayerbook Reform in Europe*, 198–306.

22. Just the same, for the English, Moses (*Ms. 1891, Ms. 1892, UPB 1892*) went for David Einhorn's prefatory: "It is our duty to render praise and thanksgiving unto the Creator of heaven and earth, who delivered us from the darkness of false belief and revealed to us the light of His truth. He is our God and there is none besides" (cf. Einhorn 1858, 26; the entire prayer is deleted from Hirsch's 1896 translation).

23. Anyone who has grown up on the *Union Prayer Book* will instantly recognize in the start of its Adoration ("Let us adore the ever-living God....") locutions from the English of Merzbacher's *'Aleynu*.

24. *Tefillot Beney Yeshurun Minhag Amerika*: The Daily Prayers. Part I, revised and compiled by the Committee of the Cleveland Conference, translated by Isaac M. Wise (Cincinnati: Bloch, 1857), 37 [Hebrew], 31–32 [English], 43–44 [German]. It is to

be recalled that during the Cleveland Conference Merzbacher served on the same committee with Wise for the creation of the then-envisioned uniform American rite, *Minhag Amerika*. W. Gunther Plaut, *The Growth of Reform Judaism: American and European Sources until 1948* (New York: World Union of Progressive Judaism, Ltd., 1965), 19.

25. On the Hebrew side in Merzbacher we have *Hishtachavayah*, which is a mite odd as the term, literally translated, means prostration, which obviously was not the regular praxis at Temple Emanu-El. After all is said and done, it is particularly noteworthy that a prayer title that Moses latched onto become utterly entrenched in the Reform liturgy until the 1970s, with the advent of the *Gates* series, wherein its former appellation, *'Aleynu*, is reclaimed.

26. Worthy of discussion, another time perhaps, is Merzbacher's literarily adroit retreatment of the Intermediate Benedictions of the weekday *Shemoneh 'Esreh*. Another example of Merzbacher's skill in the use of the Hebrew language is discussed in my "An Unusual Reform *Eyn K-Eloheynu*," *CCAR Journal: A Reform Jewish Quarterly* (Fall 1994): 43–53.

27. The German has the more chaste, psalm-like "*So sei gepriesen, Ewiger, unser Gott, in all Deinen Walten; geheiligt Dein Name in Ewigkeit,*" which is of course *yitgaddal ve-yitqaddash shemeih rabba* in paraphrase. (For the text of this entire section, see *Order of Prayer in the House of Mourners* [New York: M. Thalmessinger, 1871], 12–15).

28. *MS 1892* and *UPB 1892* (both, 186–187).

29. For a detailed account of Einhorn's path blazing endeavors in the area of liturgy, see the first chapter, "David Einhorn and *Olath Tamid*," in my *Were Our Mouths Filled with Song; Studies in Liberal Jewish Liturgy* (Cincinnati: Hebrew Union College Press, 1997), 17–49.

30. Or trumpet or any other brass instrument, as the case may be.

31. Which, typically, Einhorn brings to a close (in Emil G. Hirsch's 1896 translation, p. 43) with: "May soon every nation become Thy people, the whole earth Thy Jerusalem; that fulfilled be Thy covenant with the fathers and through their descendents be blessed all the families of the earth."

32. For his part, Adler (124–127) amalgamated all the three sections (which Merzbacher for the most part maintained) and distilled them unto a single paragraph iterating, however, the anticipatory, hopeful theme of the Shofarot segment and favoring its climactic benedictory seal (*shome'a qol teru'at 'ammo yisra'el be-rachamim*). In adopting Adler's newly-worded passage for his fusion of the three sections, whether in Hebrew or in English, Moses stuck exclusively to its futuristic motif enkindled by the *Shofarot* section.

33. Huebsch (*Seder Tefillah: Gebete fuer den oeffentlichen Gottesdienst der Tempelgemeinde Ahawath Chesed* Vol. 2 [New York: A. Sommers, 1872]) originally put his *Teqi'at Shofar* (with its associated two blessings and a single string of notes), followed by *Zikhronot* and *Shofarot* (minus their expected blasts) after the Return of the Scroll to the Ark (immediately following the sermon and a German hymn), in a kind of residual *Musaf* (120–130). The *Malkhuyot* stays exclusively within the *'Amidah* of *Shacharit* as its Intermediate Benediction (90–94).

34. *Avodat Israel: Israelitish Prayer Book* (1873), 529, 84–85, 206.

35. For an illuminating exposition of European Progressive Judaism's handling

of this quandary, see Jakob J. Petuchowski's "Reform Benedictions for Rabbinic Ordinances," *Hebrew Union College Annual* XXXVII (1966): 175–189.

36. For his benediction for kindling the light of Hanukkah, Wise put in his *Minhag Amerika* the startling amalgam *Barukh attah..ha'olam shehecheyanu ve-qiyyemanu vehiggi'anu la-zeman ha-zeh le-hadliq ner shelachanukkah* [*sic*!] (with no mention of the commandment to kindle), followed by *she-'asah nissim* and a complete (!) *Ha-Nerot Hallalu*. (pp. 112–113 [Hebrew], 98 [English], 133 [German]). Moses took this up in *Ms. 1892* and in *UPB 1892*, but with *Ha-Nerot Hallalu* abridged. Wise's amalgamated benediction has never been replicated anywhere else since then.

37. There is, however, in the Merzbacher volume (292–293) a *Birkat ha-Mazon*, made up of the traditional first two paragraphs. The first paragraph (*ha-zan et ha-kol*) takes the place of the grace before the meal (*Ha-Motsi*). The second paragraph (*'al ha-arets ve-'al ha-mazon*) serves as the sole after-dinner benediction. Very symmetrical and cut-and-dried, indeed. For his *Ms. 1892* (213–214) and *UPB 1892* (225–226) Moses reintroduces *Ha-Motsi* before the meal as well as the invitatory *Zimmun*, bringing the two postprandial *berakhot* back together in their customary spot. Also one may find another two benedictions (*Ha-Mappil* and *Vi-Yhi Ratson...she-Tashkiveni*) in a very concise *Qeriat Shema' 'al ha-Mittah* (Prayers before Retiring at Night), essentially the same in all three volumes (Merzbacher, 294–295; *Ms. 1892*, 211; *UPB 1892*, 223).

38. In his translation and modulation of Leopold Stein's Passover *Haggadah* (1841; included as well in the second edition of the latter's *Seder ha-'Avodah*, Vol. 1, 161–198), which Moses took it upon himself to include in *UPB 1892* (227–257)—apparently to the consternation of his fellow ritual committee members of the CCAR—he revives the *asher qiddeshanu* benedictory form for the *Kiddush* (227) and for eating the *matsah* and the *maror* (247). Moses's haggadah also was published as a free-standing booklet, *Seder Haggadah: Domestic Service for the Eve of Passover* (Chicago, 1893).

39. *Seder Tefillah: Prayers for the Divine Services of Congregation Ahawath Chesed* Vol. 2, ed. Adolph Huebsch; trans. Alexander Kohut (New York: A.L. Goetzl, 1889). In a similar vein, those very benedictions (*lishemo'a qol shofar and shehecheyanu*) were not to be reinstated until the 1945 edition of *Union Prayer Book II* (79).

40. This winning prayer made its way into the domestic part of the newly revised 1940 edition, towards the end of the volume (375). Meanwhile each formal service on *Leyl Shabbat* is prefaced by a lighting of the Shabbat candles—near the beginning of the book (7)—accompanied by the time-honored blessing, in Hebrew and in English. None of this should come as a surprise when one realizes that there was already a respectable tradition of women's prayers in the vernacular, as in the many editions of Fanny Neuda's *Stunden der Andacht* (1855) and in their Yiddish antecedents.

41. Two first-rate essays that deal with Geiger's liturgical work are David Ellenson's "The *Israelitische Gebetbuecher* of Abraham Geiger and Manuel Joel" in his *After Emancipation: Jewish Religious Responses to Modernity* (Cincinnati: Hebrew Union College Press, 2004), 193–222, and Jakob J. Petuchowski's "Abraham Geiger and Samuel Holdheim: Their Differences in Germany and Repercussions in America" in his *Studies in Modern Jewish Theology and Prayer*, ed. Elizabeth R. Petuchowski and Aaron M. Petuchowski (Philadelphia/Jerusalem: The Jewish Publication Society, 1998), 257–282.

42. *Gebetbuch der Genossenschaft fuer Reform im Judenthum. Erster Theil: Allwoechenlichen Gebete und hausliche Andacht; Zweiter Theil: Die Festgebete* (Berlin: Im Selbst-Verlage der Genossenschaft, 1848).

43. This prayer first appeared in the very first liturgical work of this group, *Gebete und Gesaenge zu dem von der Genossenschaft fuer Reform im Judenthum eingerichten Gottesdienst in Berlin, fuer das Neujahrsfest des Weltjahres 5606* (Berlin: Selbstverlag der Genossenschaft, 1845, als Manuscript gedruckt), 8, 27, 45.

44. The first edition of the *Union Prayer Book*, both vols. I (1895, 54, 164, 230) and II (1894, 36, 84), offer this as a possibility for a closing benediction—unfortunately, for the last time.

45. *CCAR Yearbook* 19 (1909): 82. And see below, n. 52. Stein's German original first appeared in *Chizzuk ha-Bayit: Gebete und Gesaenge zum Gebrauche bei der oeffentlichen Andacht der Israeliten. Oder: Bausteine zur Auferbauung eines veredelten Synagogengottesdienstes.* Vol. 1 (Erlangen, 1840), 81–84. (Pasted at this point into the copy from the Edward Birnbaum Collection in the Klau Library, HUC-JIR, Cincinnati, is a musical setting, following the *Kol Nidre* melody, for four male voices, "arrangé par J.M. Ochs.") Frederick L. Hosmer's genial rendition of Stein's celebrated German adaptation of *Kol Nidre* in all three parts debuted in *Ms. 1893* (81–82).

46. The full text, part of which is cited here, is in *Ms. 1893* (81–82). *UPB II* 1894 (89) and the revision of 1922 (95) include only a portion of the original. The second revision of 1945 drops this text entirely in favor of a paraphrase of the actual *Kol Nidre* the Aramaic text of which additionally appeared in the first printing but was eliminated in subsequent printings.

In addition, Moses was responsible for translating a fair number of Huebsch's hymns from the German for the last congregation he devotedly ministered to, such as hymns #126, #129–#131 in his *Hymns and Anthems 1904*.

47. He also gave us the comparably lyrical and perennial favorite "Rock of Ages" for the Hanukkah hymn, *Ma'oz Tsur*.

48. *Hymns and Anthems*, 56–57; *Union Hymnal* (1932), 137; The [Conservative] Rabbinical Assembly of America and the United Synagogue of America, *Sabbath and Festival Prayer Book/Seder Tefillot Yisrael* (1946), 373.

49. Here's the charming first stanza in the uncluttered original:

> *Lobt den Herrn*
> *Nah und fern*
> *Alle Schoepfungsheere!*
> *Lieder singt!*
> *Preist und bringt*
> *Ihm allein die Ehre*
> *Alle Welt,*
> *Treu gesellt,*
> *Seinen Ruhm vermehre!*

50. Moses also turned into English verse Stein's German adaptation of *Ki Lo Na'eh, Ki Lo Ya'eh and Va-Yehi ba-Chatsi ha-Laylah* (*UPB 1892*, 251–256). Henry Berkowitz, supporter of Moses's "sketch-prayerbook" (*Ms. 1891*), wrote a different translation of Stein's broad paraphrase of the last-named, "And It Came to Pass at Midnight," and converted the Frankfurter rabbi's endearing musical toast *So Hebt die Becher*

Feierlich into "The Festive Cup," both of which renditions appear in the 1908 and 1923 editions of *The Union Haggadah* (1908, 72–74, 14–15; 1923. 115–117, 14–15).

51. His eulogist uses the term "auto-didact" with extraordinary "native gifts." *CCAR Yearbook* 37 (1927): 251. All the same, during a keynote address to his peers in the CCAR, right at a time when a volume of theological essays was on the verge of being completed by the Committee on Systematic Jewish Theology, Moses proclaimed: "We need more spirituality and less theology; we need the stimulating and vitalizing influences of art, architecture, music the inspiring power of symbolism, feeding the imagination with sublime sentiments and strengthening the will by noble resolutions." ("Sources of Spirituality—Conference Sermon," *CCAR Yearbook* 27 (1916): 231.

52. "The only new feature of this book is the appended collection of Psalms for responsive reading. No modern prayer can compare in depth of feeling and simplicity of expression with the Psalms of the Hebrew bards. In them breathes the living spirit of prayer. Their variety, too, recommends them to universal use. There is hardly a state of feeling that finds not expression in one or another of these ancient songs. Some of the Psalms in this collection may be rendered by the Choir alone, for which abundant compositions are extant."

53. In anticipation of Buber's I-thou philosophy, one might say.

54. Literally, "magnificence and faithfulness." It is a *qerovah* in the form of a litany inserted in the repetition of the *'Amidah* during *Shacharit* on Yom Kippur. In mystical and Hasidic circles it may be said on Sabbath and Festival mornings before *Barukh She-Amar*. The prayer/poem is derived from the sixth-century *Heykhalot Rabbbati*. Is Isaac S. Moses at this juncture pointing back to a Hasidic background, let alone an Orthodox upbringing?

55. Now intended for use in the synagogue and the home, not just Sunday School.

56. Later in the same discourse he remarks, "I am not inveighing against my own calling when I say that in the interest of Jewish religiousness we might well spare a dozen preaching rabbis yearly in the place of an equal number of capable, religiously and musically trained cantors who would lead the service."

57. A desideratum remains a close study of all the newly-composed prayers and meditations in each of the Moses *siddurim* that derive from neither the Hebrew nor the German.

58. It is interesting that as late as 1907 Moses preached a sermon at a Concluding Service on Yom Kippur in German! *"Hoffnung und Trost"—Skizze der Neila-Predigt*, MS 122, Isaac S. Moses file, American Jewish Archives, Cincinnati, OH.

59. In 1916, remarkably enough, Moses served on the CCAR's committee for the revision of the *Union Prayer Book*.

60. As a consequence of a consolidation with another synagogue in 1922, it was renamed Congregation Emanu-El B'nei Jeshurun.

61. Founded in 1847, it became known as KAM Isaiah Israel as the result of a merger in 1971.

62. It doubtless helped that Bernhard Felsenthal (1822–1908), high-minded and forthright Jewish polymath and the first co-translator (with David Einhorn) of *'Olat Tamid* (Baltimore and New York, 1872), was one of the two to ordain Moses; and that Emil G. Hirsch, who collaborated with Moses and his brother Adolph on a short-lived biweekly family newspaper in Milwaukee, *Der Zeitgeist* (1880–1882), was to be responsible for a second, improved translation in 1896. Hirsch, Einhorn's son-in-law

and a scholar in his own right, is gratefully credited in the preface to the latter's *Huebsch 1916* with giving Moses useful advice regarding textual and procedural detail in that prayerbook.

63. Moses explains his rationale thus, in part, on the first page of the preface to *Tefillat Yisrael 1887*: "After a trial of over two years, the English Ritual published by the undersigned [Isaac S. Moses] in 1884 has been found inadequate to the wants of our congregation. The majority of those who regularly attend divine service are accustomed to the Hebrew as the language of prayer, while those for whom the English Ritual was intended do not take that interest in our public worship....To satisfy the demands of both, the old and the young generation, the undersigned has recast his former publication adding all the principal prayers in the Hebrew language contained in the older Prayer-book [i.e. the Merzbacher/Adler rite], yet making the English rendition on the opposite page an independent Ritual, thus enabling the worshipper to follow the service intelligently whether using the Hebrew or the English part."

64. I am grateful to Professor Richard Sarason for his constant support and, especially, for drawing my attention to the handwritten dedication to Isaac M. Wise—with whom Moses, the Einhorn partisan he long was, had previously engaged in controversy—in a copy of *UPB 1892* among the holdings of the Klau Library, HUC-JIR, Cincinnati. The jubilant tribute reads (italics supplied):

> To the Master of American Judaism,
> the father of the *Union* of Hebrew Congregations
> and the founder of the *Union* Hebrew College
> from the maker of this *Union* Prayer Book as a
> sign of highest esteem and grateful love.
>   Isaac S. Moses

Chapter 11 - Modern Maccabees: Remaking Hanukkah in Nineteenth Century America

1. I am grateful to Jonathan Sarna, Hasia Diner, Melissa Klapper, Richard Drucker and the anonymous reader for their comments on earlier versions of this article. I am also grateful to the National Endowment for the Humanities, the Gilder Lehrman Institute, the Hadassah-Brandeis Institute, and Rowan University for supporting research used in this essay. Material on Penina Moise in this work also appeared in my essay, "Quick to the Party: The Americanization of Hanukkah and Southern Jewry," *Southern Jewish History* 12 (2009): 1–38.
R. Lawrence Moore, *Religious Outsiders and the Making of America* (New York: Oxford University Press, 1986).

2. Jakob J. Petuchowski, "The Magnification of Chanukah" *Commentary* 29 (January 1960): 38–46; Jonathan D. Sarna, "Is Judaism Compatible with American Civil Religion? The Problem of Christmas and the National Faith," in *Religion and the Life of the Nation*, ed. Roland D. Sherrill (Urbana: University of Illinois Press, 1990), 152–173; Jenna Weissman Joselit, *Wonders of America* (New York: Hill and Wang, 1994), 227–244; Andrew Heinze, *Adapting to Abundance: Jewish Immigrants, Mass Consumption, and the Search for American Identity* (New York: Columbia University Press, 1990), 74–79.

3. Leigh Eric Schmidt, *Consumer Rites: The Buying and Selling of American Holidays* (Princeton, NJ: Princeton University Press, 1995), 105–191; Karal Ann Marling,

Merry Christmas: Celebrating America's Greatest Holiday (Cambridge: Harvard University Press, 2000); Penne Restad, *Christmas in America: A History* (New York: Oxford University Press, 1995).

4. Gerald Sorin, *Tradition Transformed: The Jewish Experience in America* (Baltimore, MD: Johns Hopkins University Press, 1997), 3. Several scholars have made this point. See, for example, Marshall Sklare, *Conservative Judaism: An American Religious Movement*, 2ⁿᵈ ed. (New York: Schocken, 1972); Leon Jick, *The Americanization of the Synagogue: 1820–1870* (Hanover, NH: Brandeis University Press, 1976; 1992); Jonathan D. Sarna, *American Judaism* (New Haven: Yale University Press, 2004).

5. Sarna, *American Judaism*.

6. Ellen M. Litwicki, *America's Public Holidays 1865–1920* (Washington, DC: Smithsonian Institution Press, 2000).

7. "Thoughts from Denver Colorado," *American Israelite* 31 (2 January 1885): 2.

8. Marc Lee Raphael, *Profiles in American Judaism: The Reform, Conservative, and Reconstructionist Traditions in Historical Perspective* (San Francisco: Harper and Row, 1984), 197; Board of Delegates of American Israelites, survey. Others count the ratio differently. Hasia Diner estimates that by 1880 "only twelve synagogues— out of two hundred—had not affiliated" with Reform's Union of American Hebrew Congregations. Diner, *The Jews of the United States 1654–2000* (Berkeley: University of California Press, 2004), 122. Gerald Sorin also claims most of the country's "well over 200 congregations" were Reform. Sorin, *Tradition Transformed* (Baltimore, MD: Johns Hopkins University Press, 1997), 29. Sarna and Sorin both agree that no one paid much attention to the "small number of newly formed congregations established by arriving Eastern Europeans." Sorin, *Tradition Transformed*, 29; Sarna, *American Judaism*, 101–102.

9. Arthur Kiron, "Golden Ages, Promised Lands: The Victorian Rabbinic Humanism of Sabato Morais," doctoral dissertation (Columbia University, 1999), 108.

10. Ibid., 282.

11. Benjamin Rabinowitz, "The Young Men's Hebrew Association, 1854–1913," *Publications in American Jewish History* 37 (1947): 221–232.

12. Jonathan D. Sarna, "A Great Awakening: The Transformation That Shaped Twentieth Century American Judaism and Its Implications for Today," (Council for Initiatives in Jewish Education, 1995); Kiron, "Golden Ages, Promised Lands."

13. *Jewish Messenger* 14 (4 December 1863): 21.

14. Sarna, *American Judaism*, 75.

15. Jonathan D. Sarna, "The Cult of Synthesis in American Jewish Life," *Jewish Social Studies* 5 (Fall/Winter 1999): 52–79.

16. William R. Hutchison, *The Modernist Impulse in American Protestantism* (Durham, NC: Duke University Press, 1992), 102; Lance J. Sussman, "The Myth of the Trefa Banquet: American Culinary Culture and the Radicalization of Food Policy in American Reform Judaism," *American Jewish Archives Journal* LVII, nos. 1 and 2 (2005): 42.

17. Henry Ward Beecher, "The Advance of a Century," *New York Tribune*, extra no. 33, Independence Day Orations (4 July 1876): 37–44, reprinted in *Democratic Vistas, 1860–1880*, ed. Alan Trachtenberg (New York: G. Braziller, 1970), 70; T. J. Jackson

Lears, *No Place of Grace: Antimodernism and the Transformation of American Culture, 1880–1920* (Chicago: University of Chicago Press, 1981), 7.

18. Lears, 17.

19. Hasia R. Diner, *A Time for Gathering*, 44–48; Lee Shai Weissbach, *Jewish Life in Small Town America* (New Haven: Yale University Press, 2005).

20. Edith Gelles, ed., *The Letters of Abigaill Levy Franks, 1733–1748*, xviii; Sarna, *American Judaism*, 45.

21. Shaye Cohen, *From the Maccabees to the Mishnah* (Westminster: John Knox Press, 1987, 1989), 37–38.

22. Cyrus Adler and Louis H. Levin, "Szold, Benjamin," http://www.jewishencyclopedia.com/view_friendly.jsp?artid=1232&letters=S.

23. I. Leeser, "The Demands of the Times, *Occident and American Jewish Advocate* 1, no. 12 (March, 1844).

24. Sarna, *American Judaism*, 78; Sussman, *Isaac Leeser*, 162.

25. Sussman, 175.

26. Sarna, *American Judaism*, 95.

27. Philip Kieval, "The Talmudic View of the Hasmonean and Early Herodian Periods in Jewish History," doctoral dissertation (Brandeis University, 1970), 122.

28. Daniel Boyarin, "Tricksters, Martyrs, and Collaborators: Diaspora and the Gendered Politics of Resistance" in *Powers of Diaspora*, ed. Jonathan Boyarin and Daniel Boyarin (Minneapolis: University of Minnesota Press, 2002), 53–55.

29. 2 Maccabees 6:19; 4 Maccabees 6:3–7; Boyarin, 63; *Avodah Zarah* 17b.

30. *Avodah Zarah* 17b.

31. Boyarin, 62.

32 Yosef Hayim Yerushalmi, "'Servants of Kings and Not Servants of Servants': Some Aspects of the Political History of the Jews," Tenenbaum Family Lecture Series in Judaic Studies, Emory University, 8 February 2005.

33. Salo Wittmayer Baron, *A Social and Religious History of the Jews*, 2nd rev. ed. (New York: Columbia University Press, 1952–1983), 4:36–43; Yerushalmi, "Servants of Kings," 4.

34. Joseph Heinemann, *Prayer in the Talmud: Forms and Patterns* (Berlin: Walter De Gruyter, 1977), 35.

35. Catherine Bell, *Ritual: Perspectives and Dimensions* (New York: Oxford University Press, 1997), 138–139.

36. Joseph Caro, *Shulchan Arukh, Orach Chaim*, 670:2.

37. Moses ben Israel/Isserles. *Encyclopedia Britannica*. 2008. Encyclopedia Britannica, http://britannica.com/eb/article-9042992 accessed on 9 March 2008; Solomon B. Freehof, "Ceremonial Creativity Among the Ashkenazim," *Jewish Quarterly Review* (1967): 210.

38. Robert Bruce Mullin, *Miracles and the Modern Religious Imagination* (New Haven: Yale University Press, 1996), 31–50.

39. Jakob J. Petuchowski suggested that the Enlightenment and ensuing political revolutions made all miracles seem implausible. Petuchowski, "The Magnification of Chanukah," *Commentary* 29 (January 1960): 38.

40. Naomi Cohen, "Pioneers of American Jewish Defense," *American Jewish Archives* 29, no. 2 (November 1977): 134.

41. Max Lilienthal, "The Festival of Chanuckah," *Occident* IV, no. 12 (March 1847); "The Jews in China," *Occident* I, no. 4 (July, 1843); "The Cincinnati Hebrew Benevolent Society," *Occident* IV, no. 11 (February 1847); "The New York Hebrew Benevolent Society," *Occident* III, no.9 (December 1845); "Manifesto of German Rabbis" translated from the Hebrew by Mr. Neumegen, *Occident* VIII, no. 4 (July 1845).

42. Michael A. Meyer, *Response to Modernity: A History of the Reform Movement in Judaism* (New York: Oxford University Press, 1988), 248; Alan Silverstein, *Alternatives to Assimilation: The Response of Reform Judaism to American Culture 1840–1930* (Hanover, NH: Brandeis University Press, 1994), 10; Sarna, *American Judaism*, 43–44.

43. Jacob Rader Marcus, ed., *American Jewish Biography*, vol. 2 (Brooklyn: Carlson Publishing Co., 1994), 569.

44. "The Pittsburgh Liberal Religious Platform, November 16–19, 1885," in *The Jew in the American World: A Source Book*, ed. Jacob Rader Marcus (Detroit: Wayne State University Press, 1996), 241–243.

45. Benny Kraut, "Judaism Triumphant: Isaac Mayer Wise on Unitarianism and Liberal Christianity," *Association for Jewish Studies Review* 7 (1982): 179–183.

46. I.M. Wise, *Israelite* (28 July 1865): 29; and *Israelite* (23 December 1887): 4; James Gutheim Heller, *Isaac M. Wise: His Life, Work, and Thought* (New York: UAHC, 1865), 534–564.

47. Isaac M. Wise, "Hanucah: the Dedication Feast" *Israelite* (18 December 1857): 18.

48. Isaac M. Wise, "Thoughts from Denver, Colorado," *American Israelite* (2 January 1885): 2.

49. The new, more reform worship in turn offended traditionalist members who left to form their own congregation, Shearith Israel. Gary Philip Zola, *Isaac Harby of Charleston* (Tuscaloosa: University of Alabama Press, 1994), 112–150; Gary P. Zola, "The first Reform Prayer Book in America: The Liturgy of the Reformed Society of Israelites," in *Platforms and Prayer Books: Theological and Liturgical Perspectives on Reform Judaism*, ed. Dana Kaplan (Lanham, MD: Rowman and Littlefield, 2002), 20; *Pocket Guide to Kahal Kadosh Beth Elohim and Charleston Jewish History* (June 2005), 4. Penina Moïse, *Fancy's Sketch Book* (Charleston, SC, 1833). This was the first book of verse published by an American Jewish woman.

50. Psalm 30, *The Jewish Study Bible* (Oxford: Oxford University Press, 1985, 1999), 1430, Jewish Publication Society translation.

51. Christine Leigh Heyrman, *Southern Cross: The Beginnings of the Bible Belt* (New York: Knopf, 1997).

52. Rebecca Samuel (Petersburg, VA, 1790) in *The Jews in America: A Treasury of Art and Literature*, ed. Abraham Karp (Southport, CT: Hugh Lauter Levin Associates, 1994), 48–50; Hasia R. Diner and Beryl Leiff Benderly, *Her Works Praise Her* (New York: Basic Books, 2002), 15–16.

53. Meyer, 3.

54. Abraham Geiger, *Judaism and Its History*, trans. Charles Newburgh (New York: Bloch Publishing Co., 1911). Originally published in 1865, the manuscript was reprinted in New York that same year.

55. Joseph Caro, *Shulchan Arukh, Orach Chaim*, 670:2.

56. New RSV *Oxford Annotated Bible*, AP 341; Peter Kirby, "4 Maccabees" *Early Christian Writings* (8 June 2007).

57. Advertisement, *The Israelite* (23 November 1860): 166.

58. R. Glanz, "Where the Jewish Press Was Distributed in Pre-Civil War America," *Western States Jewish Historical Quarterly* 5 (1971–1972): 1–14.

59. Isaac M. Wise, *The World of My Books*, trans. Albert H. Friedlander (Cincinnati: American Jewish Archives, 1954), 21.

60. Isaac M. Wise, *The History of the Israelitish Nation from Abraham to the Present Time* (Albany, 1854).

61. Eric Friedland, *"Were Our Mouths Filled With Song": Studies in Liberal Jewish Liturgy* (Hebrew Union College Press, Cincinnati, 1997); *Minhag America* from Sefton D. Temkin, *Isaac Mayer Wise: Shaping American Judaism* (Oxford: Oxford University Press, 1992), 276: "The 17th benediction, in which traditional form petitions for restoration of the Temple service...reads *veheshev shechinatcha lidvir betecha* - let the glory of thy majesty return to the hall of thy house; ...the penultimate benediction has the narrative part of the insertions for Hanukkah and Purim, but not the introductory prayer *Al Hanissim* – Wise did not believe in miracles"; Isaac M. Wise, *History of the Israelitish Nation* (Albany, 1854).

62. Virginia Larkin Redway, "Handel in Colonial and Post-Colonial America (to 1810)," *The Musical Quarterly* (1935): 192.

63. Alexander L. Ringer, "Handel and the Jews," *Music and Letters* 42, no. 1 (Jan., 1961): 22.

64. Ringer, "Handel and the Jews," 27.

65. Brad Leissa and David Vickers, accessed on 3 February 2007 at http://gfhandel.org/faqs.htm.

66. Georg Fredrich Handel, *Judas Maccabeus: A Sacred Drama* (1747), words by Thomas Morell, Act One, accessed on 30 June 2007 at http://opera.stanford.edu/iu/libretti/judas.htm; Alexander L. Ringer, "Handel and the Jews," 17–29.

67. Handelian FAQs, accessed on 30 June 2007 at http://gfhandel.org/faqs.htm.

68. E. Hayter, "Music in America," *The Musical Times and Singing Class Circular* (May 1888): 303–304.

69. Loring B. Barnes, "Musical Progress in the United States," *The Musical Times* (1 February 1887): 110.

70. I am grateful to Jonathan M. Hess for pointing this out to me. Jonathan M. Hess, "Leopold Kompert and the Work of Nostalgia: The Cultural Capital of German Jewish Ghetto Fiction," *Jewish Quarterly Review* 97, no.4 (Fall 2007): 577; Emil Lehmann, "Zum Weihefeste," *Der Orient* 9 (1848): 412.

71. Ludwig Philippson, "Literarischer Wochenbericht," *Allegemeine Zeitung des Judemthums* 46 (1882): 750–751. For a comparison of that genre with ghetto tales see Jonathan M. Hess, "Leopold Kompert." On Jewish Historical fiction see Jonathan Skolnik, "Writing Jewish History Between Gutzkow and Goethe," and Skolnik, "Writing Jewish History at the Margins of the Weimer Classics: Minority Culture and National Identity in Germany, 1837–1873," in *Searching for Common Ground: Diskurse zur deutschen Identitat 1750–1871*, ed. N. Vaszonyi (Cologne: United Nations, 2000), 227–238, and Skolnik, "'Who Learns History from Heine?': The German-Jewish Historical Novel as Cultural Memory and Minority Culture, 1824–1933" doctoral dissertation (Columbia University, 1999).

72. "Hanucah The Feast of Dedication," *The Israelite* X, no. 24 (11 December 1863): 188.

73. Isaac M. Wise, "The First of the Maccabees" *The Israelite* (1860). An advertisement for the novel in book form ran in *The Israelite* (23 November 1860): 166.

74. Michael Satlow, *Creating Judaism* (New York: Columbia University Press, 2006), 115–187.

75. Dianne Ashton, *Rebecca Gratz: Women and Judaism in Antebellum America* (Detroit: Wayne State University Press, 1997), 121–169.

76. Isaac Leeser, "Festival Observance," *Occident* 48 (1861): 285.

77. Sussman, *Isaac Leeser and the Making of American Judaism*, 200–201.

78. See for example H. A. Henry "Festival Observance: Sermon delivered at Shearith Israel synagogue, San Francisco, on feast of Hanukkah 5627" *Occident* 25 (1867): 290.

79. Samuel Isaacs, *Jewish Messenger* (18 December 1857): 100.

80. Sussman, *Isaac Leeser*, 80–104, Kiron, "Golden Ages, Promised Lands," 275–318; Sarna, *American Judaism*, 80–81.

81. Kiron, "Golden Ages, Promised Lands," 284.

82. Sarna, *A Great Awakening*, 4.

83. Ibid., 16.

84. "Chanucka," *American Hebrew* 9, no. 3 (16 December 1881): 50.

85. David Glassberg, *American Historical Pageantry*, 9–15.

86. David Kaufman, *Shul With A Pool: The Synagogue Center in American Jewish History* (Hanover, NH: Brandeis University Press, 1999), 69.

87. Mark C. Carnes, *Secret Ritual and Manhood in Victorian America* (New Haven, CT: Yale University Press, 1989), 10–23.

88. See Front Page and "Our Philadelphia Letter," "Our Baltimore Letter," *American Hebrew* 5, no. 4 (10 December 1880): 39.

89. David Glassberg, *American Historical Pageantry: The Uses of Tradition in the Early Twentieth Century* (Chapel Hill: University of North Carolina Press, 1990), 39.

90. "The Festival of Chanucka," *Frank Leslie's Illustrated Newspaper* (3 January 1880): 317.

91. John B. Jentz review of Joshua Brown, *Beyond the Lines: Pictorial Reporting, Everyday Life, and the Crisis of the Gilded Age* (Berkeley: University of California Press, 2003) in *Journal of American History* 90, no. 3 (December 2003): 68, 80.

92. Alan Silverstein, *Alternatives to Assimilation: The Response of Reform Judaism to American Culture 1840–1930* (Hanover, NH: Brandeis University Press, 1994), 82.

93. Paula Hyman, *Gender and Assimilation in Modern Jewish History* (Seattle: University of Washington Press, 1995), 139–140.

94. E. Anthony Rotundo, *American Manhood: Transformations in American Manhood from the Revolution to the Modern Era* (New York: Basic Books, 1993), 246.

95. Some evidence suggests that Longfellow composed his poem after seeing a full performance of Handel's *Judas Maccabeus* in Europe. Wilbert Snow, "Review of *The Diary of Clara Crowninshield: A European Tour with Longfellow 1835–1836* by Andrew Hilen," *Modern Language Notes* 73, no. 5 (May 1958): 367–368.

96. "Christmas" *Philadelphia Inquirer* (26 December 1879): front page.

97. *Frank Leslie's Illustrated Weekly* (27 December 1879): 293 and Supplement (3 January 1880): 338.

98. Ellen Litwicki, *America's Public Holidays 1865–1920* (Washington, DC: Smithsonian Institution Press, 2000), 9–10.

99. Harley Erdman, *Staging the Jew: The Performance of An American Ethnicity 1860–1920* (New Brunswick, NJ: Rutgers University Press, 1997), 42–79; Stephen J. Whitfield, "The Politics of Pageantry, 1936–1946," *American Jewish History* 84, no. 3 (September 1996): 221–252.

100. *American Hebrew* 5, no. 4 (10 December 1880): 39.

101. Erdman, *Staging the Jew*, 40–62.

102. Max Cohen to Solomon Solis-Cohen, 14 October 1879, Solomon Solis-Cohen Collection, National Museum of American Jewish History, Philadelphia, PA.

103. *Libretto of the Chanucka Entertainment Given at Lexington Ave. Opera House, Dec 28, 1878.* Text by Julius Frank., NY 1878. Includes sections from Handel's oratorio *Judas Maccabeus.* Owned by Cornell University.

104. Solomon Solis-Cohen, "Chanuka," *American Hebrew* 37, no. 4 (30 November 1888): 34; Jonathan Boyarin and Daniel Boyarin, *Powers of Diaspora*, 4.

105. Sarna, *American Judaism*, 136; Sarna, "The Making of an American Jewish Culture," in *When Philadelphia Was the Capital of Jewish America*, ed. Murray Friedman (Philadelphia: Balch Institute for Ethnic Studies, 1993), 149; Max Cohen to Solomon Solis-Cohen (22 December 1879) Solis-Cohen Papers, National Museum of American Jewish History.

106. Philip Cowen, *American Hebrew* 37, no. 3 (23 November 1888): front page.

107. Rachel Oliveri, "Guide to the Collection of the Purim Association of New York City" (1862–1902) I-20, American Jewish Historical Society Papers, 1865–1906, AJHS, New York.

108. Jonathan M. Hess, *Germans, Jews, and the Claims of Modernity* (New Haven: Yale University Press, 2002), 2–27.

109. For more on this trend see Beth S. Wenger, "'Rites of Citizenship:'" Jewish Celebrations of the Nation," in *The Columbia History of Jews and Judaism in America*, ed. Marc Lee Raphael (New York: Columbia University Press, 2008), 366–383.

110. Jonathan D. Sarna, "The Cult of Synthesis in American Jewish Culture," *Jewish Social Studies* 5, nos. 1/2 (1998–1999): 52–79.

111. Anon. "Jews in the Union Army: Sketches from the Seat of War, by a Jewish Soldier," *The Jewish Messenger* 11, no. 5 (7 February 1867): 41.

112. Litwicki, *America's Public Holidays*, 241.

113. Benny Kraut, "Jewish Survival in Protestant America" in *Minority Faiths and the American Protestant Mainstream*, ed. Jonathan Sarna (Urbana: University of Illinois Press, 1998), 16.

Chapter 12 - "The Spirit of Jewish History:" From Nachman Krochmal to Ahad Ha'am

1. Max Nussbaum, "Nachman Krochmal: The Philosopher of Israel's Eternity," *American Jewish Year Book* 44 (1942–1943): 83; on the Galician *Haskalah* and Krochmal, see P. Lachower, *Toledot ha-Sifrut ha-Ivrit ha-Hadashah*, vol. 2 (Tel Aviv: Dvir Pub. Co., 1951), 24ff.; see also Julius Guttmann, *Philosophies of Judaism* (New York: Holt, Rinehart and Winston, 1964); Eliezer Schweid, *A History of Jewish Thought in Modern Times* (Jerusalem: Kibbutz Hameuhad and Keter Publishing House, 1977), 172–201 (Hebrew); Yehoyada Amir, "The Perplexity of Our Time: Rabbi Nachman

Krochmal and Modern Jewish Existence," *Modern Judaism* 23, no. 3 (2003): 264–301; Jay Michael Harris, *Nachman Krochmal: Guiding the Perplexed of the Modern Age* (New York: New York University Press, 1991).

2. The work appeared in 1851, eleven years after Krochmal's death. Krochmal, in his will, expressly requested Zunz to edit his work. See Shalom Spiegel, *Hebrew Reborn* (New York: Macmillan Co., 1930), 98.

3. Bernard J. Bamberger, "The Beginnings of Modern Jewish Scholarship," *CCAR Yearbook* 42 (1932): 219.

4. Solomon Schechter, *Studies in Judaism* (Philadelphia: The Jewish Publication Society of America, 1938), 52. We shall use here Simon Rawidowicz, ed., *Kitvei Rabbi Nachman Krochmal* (Berlin: Aj'anoth, 1924) with its excellent introduction and critical notes.

5. Schechter, 65.

6. Rawidowicz, ed., 272–283.

7. Simon Rawidowicz, "War Nachman Krochmal Hegelianer?" *HUCA* 5 (1938): 535–582. Rawidowicz pointed out that there were fundamental differences between the philosophic viewpoints of Krochmal and Hegel, despite their use of similar or identical terminologies. Ibid., 562. This issue is treated in greater detail in *Kitvei Rabbi Nachman Krochmal*, 160–200. Rawidowicz's opinion is shared by a number of scholars; e.g., Natan Rotenstreich, "Muhlat ve-hitrahashut be-mishnato shel RANAK," *Kenesset* 6 (1941): 339; "Tfisato ha-historit shel RANAK," *Zion* 7 (Sept., 1941): 35ff.; Meyer Waxman, *A History of Jewish Literature*, vol. 3 (New York: Bloch Publishing Co., 1945), 461f.; Spiegel, 11f.

The difficulty in identifying Krochmal's thought with that of Hegel, particularly with regard to Krochmal's concept "*ha-ruhani ha-muhlat*" compared to the Absolute Spirit as delineated by Hegel, is summarized by Abraham I. Katsch, in "Nachman Krochmal and the German Idealists," *Jewish Social Studies* 8 (April 1946): 87ff. In Katsch's view, the comparison between both concepts is

> …specious, Krochmal's Absolute Spirit having nothing in common with Hegel except the bare name. In the first place, it is not a dialectical proposition, issuing out of any schematic triad of thesis, antithesis and synthesis…. For Hegel, the Absolute Spirit (Reality) is the key to the world—nay the essence of it, the sum total of things, realized in three successive stages of the 'of itself,' 'outside itself' and 'of and for itself.' It is the essential result of its own activity in transcending immediacy, (one might want to check out the original here—the trans. was ungrammatical) negating it and returning within itself. All these dialectical and metaphysical elements are absent from Krochmal's conception. Ibid., 91.

This difficulty is also understood by Rotenstreich, who sees a further problem in the philosophic basis for a relationship between the two concepts. Rotenstreich's views, however, are refuted by Guttmann, 323. Guttmann stresses that Rotenstreich's difficulty exists only if Krochmal did indeed identify *ha-ruhani ha-muhlat* with the Absolute Spirit of Hegel. If, however, it can be held that for Krochmal the spirit of the Jewish people, as well as the other national spirits, are but "manifestations" of the Absolute Spirit, this difficulty falls away. Guttmann, nevertheless, would reinforce that while for Krochmal the spirit of the other nations were but manifestations of "specific metaphysical powers," that of the Jewish people was directly related to the Absolute Spirit. Guttmann, 447, n. 68.

8. See Guttmann, 324; Julius Guttmann, "Yesodot ha-Mahshavah shel rabbi Nachman Krochmal," *Knesset* 6 (1941): 262–263; Mordecai M. Kaplan, *The Greater Judaism in the Making: A Study of the Modern Evolution of Judaism* (New York: Reconstructionist Press, 1960), 201ff., follows Guttmann's view of pervasive Hegelian influence on Krochmal; see also Joseph Klausner, *Historiah shel ha-Sifrut ha-Ivrit ha-Hadashah*, vol. 2 (Jerusalem, 1937), 201–208; Ismar Schorsch, "The Philosophy of History of Nahman Krochmal," *Judaism* 10 (Summer 1961): 239–245; Jacob Taubes, "Nachman Krochmal and Modern Historicism," *Judaism* 12 (Spring 1962): 150–164.

9. Katsch, 87–102; Jacob B. Agus, "Nationalistic Philosophies of Judaism," *Judaism* 5 (Summer 1956): 256–259.

10. Wilhelm Windelband, *A History of Philosophy*, Vol. 2 (New York: Harper and Brothers, 1901), 527.

11. Patrick Gardiner, *Theories of History* (Glencoe: The Free Press, 1959), 37.

12. Ibid., 39.

13. Ibid., 40.

14. Ibid., 41–42.

15. Ibid., 42.

16. Ibid., 42–43.

17. Ibid., 42.

18. A summary of the scholarship reflecting Herder's influence on Krochmal, as well as that of Giambattisto Vico (1668–1744), whose work, *The New Science* (1725), anticipated the basic ideas of Herder, is found in Rawidowicz's introduction to *Kitvei Rabbi Nachman Krochmal*, 170ff. Cf., Martin Buber's essay "Goyim ve-elohav," *Knesset* 6 (1941): 287. According to Abraham I. Katsch, of all the influences working upon Krochmal that of Herder was foremost. See Katsch, 87ff.

19. Guttmann, *Philosophies of Judaism*, 321.

20. Rawidowicz, ed., 7–8.

21. Ibid., 7–10.

22. Ibid., 12.

23. Ibid., 13–15.

24. Ibid., 29.

25. For the problems involved in the use of the concept 'Absolute Spirit' by Hegel and by Krochmal, see n. 7.

26. Ibid., reference to Isa. 46:4.

27. Guttmann, *Philosophies of Judaism*, 325.

28. Rawidowicz, ed., 30.

29. Guttmann, *Philosophies of Judaism*, 325.

30. Ibid., 326–327.

31. Rawidowicz, ed., 31.

32. Spiegel, 11.

33. Taubes, 159.

34. Kaplan, 201.

35. Rawidowicz, ed., 34f.

36. Ibid., 35.

37. Ibid., 37.

38. Jer. 10:16.

39. Rawidowicz, ed., 37–38. *Ein Sof* is a favorite kabbalistic term for God.

40. Ibid., 38.

41. Ibid., 44.

42. Ibid., 40.

43. Ibid., 40–41. (Cf., Psalms, 20:9)

44. Ibid., 41–44.

45. Ibid., 44–47.

46. Ibid., 47–49.

47. Ibid., 50–59.

48. Ibid., 60–82.

49. Ibid., 82.

50. This last period is covered by Krochmal in only three quarters of a page (Ibid., 112). This instance of abbreviation cannot be torn out of its total context, when it is recalled that what we have of *Moreh nevukhei ha-Zeman* is a compendium of notes and essays on diverse subjects in various stages of completion. While empirical history is important in Krochmal's research, it is, after the depiction of the first two cycles of history in which ample empirical material is presented, only additional clay for the mold that has already been set as a philosophical system.

51. Ibid., 112.

52. Schorsch, 242.

53. Katsch, 97.

54. Taubes, 160.

55. Ibid.

56. Ibid., 161.

57. "*U-ba ahar ha-zman ha-gadol ha-nizkar mo'ed shelishi liyeridah...*" ("Then came after the long above mentioned period the third phase of decline...") Rawidowicz, ed., 112.

58. Nahum Sokolow, *Hibbat Zion* (Jerusalem: Ludwig Mayer, 1934), 49.

59. See "The Spiritual Revival," in *Ahad Ha'am, Selected Essays*, ed. Leon Simon (Philadelphia: The Jewish Publication Society of America, 1962), 253–305. On Ahad Ha-Am, see Aryeh Simon and Joseph Heller, *Ahad Ha'am, ha-Ish, po'olo ve-torato* (Jerusalem: The Hebrew University Press, 1955); Steven Zipperstein, *Elusive Prophet: Ahad Ha'am and the Origins of Zionism* (Berkeley: University of California Press, 1993); Joseph Goldstein, *Ahad Ha'am* (Jerusalem: Keter, 1992).

60. See Joseph Heller, *The Zionist Idea* (New York: Schocken Books, 1949), 53.

61. *Kol Kitvei Ahad Ha'am* (Tel Aviv: Dvir, 1947), 135–138, 313–320, 337–341.

62. Spiegel, 108.

63. Simon, 289–290.

64. "What is now already visible in Eretz Israel entitles one to say with confidence, Surely, Eretz Israel is destined to become a national spiritual center of Judaism, dearly beloved by all the people, unifying it and knitting it together; a center of Torah and wisdom; of language and literature, of physical labor and purification of soul, a true representation in miniature of the Jewish people as it ought to be." "Sakh ha-kol," in *Kol Kitvei Ahad Ha'am*, 427.

65. "Ha-kongress ha-tsioni ha-shlishi," in *Kol Kitvei Ahad Ha'am*, 300. Herzl's address and the transactions of the Congress are recorded in *Stenographisches Protokoll*

der Verhandlungen des III Zionisten-Kongresses (Wien: Verlag des Vereines Erez Israel, 1899), 234.

66. "Ha-kongress ha-tsioni ha-shlishi," in *Kol Kitvei Ahad Ha'am*, 300.

67. "Pirkei Zikhronot," in *Kol Kitvei Ahad Ha'am*, 495; see also Simon and Heller, 244.

68. "Leshe'elat ha-lashon," in *Kol Kitvei Ahad Ha'am*, 96.

69. See Guttmann, *Philosophies of Judaism*, 324; Simon and Heller, 162.

70. "T'hiya ubriya," in *Kol Kitvei Ahad Ha'am*, 292–293.

71. "T'hiyat ha-ruah," in *Kol Kitvei Ahad Ha'am*, 181; "Ha-mussar ha-leumi," in *Kol Kitvei Ahad Ha'am*, 162; "Dr. Pinsker u-mahbarto," in *Kol Kitvei Ahad Ha'am*, 46–47.

72. Ibid.

73. Simon and Heller, 201.

74. Yehezkel Kaufmann, "Hefez ha-kiyyum ha-leumi," *Miklat* 4 (1920): 175.

75. Agus, 258.

76. Simon and Heller, 162.

77. Me'ir Turtel, *Bissus ha-leumiut be-Kitvei Ahad Ha'am* (Jerusalem: Hebrew University Press, 1942), 33ff.

78. Yehezkel Kaufmann, "Ikarei De'otav shel Ahad Ha'am," *Hatekufah* 24 (1928): 421–439. Yehezkel Kaufmann, "Hefez Ha-kiyum Ha-leumi," *Miklat* 4 (1930): 175–199.

79. Ezra Spicehandler, "Reflections on Ahad Ha'am," *Midstream* (Winter 1959): 52.

80. Ibid.

81. W.R. Sorley, *A History of English Philosophy* (Cambridge: Cambridge University Press, 1920), 270.

82. See George H. Mead, *Movements of Thought in the Nineteenth Century*, ed. Merrit H. Moore (Chicago: University of Chicago Press, 1936), 373.

83. See Katsch, "Nachman Krochmal and the German Idealists," 100.

84. "Higia ha-sha'a, first letter," in *Kol Kitvei Ahad Ha'am*, 383.

85. "Pirkei Zikhronot," in *Kol Kitvei Ahad Ha'am*, 495.

86. "Bassar Varuah," in *Kol Kitvei Ahad Ha'am*, 350.

87. "Al shtei ha-se'ipim," in *Kol Kitvei Ahad Ha'am*, 363; "Shinui ha-arakhim," in *Kol Kitvei Ahad Ha'am*, 159; "Mukdam u-me'uhar bahayim," in *Kol Kitvei Ahad Ha'am*, 78ff.

88. "Torah she-balev," in *Kol Kitvei Ahad Ha'am*, 51–54; "Mukdam u-me'uhar bahaim," in *Kol Kitvei Ahad Ha'am*, 78–83.

89. "Al shtei ha-se'ipim," in *Kol Kitvei Ahad Ha'am*, 373.

90. "Torah she-balev," *Kol Kitvei Ahad Ha'am*, 53.

Chapter 13 - Creating Cultural Space: Jews and Judaism at a Public University in the 1920s

1. A widely-read book, Charles Silberman, *A Certain People, American Jews and Their Lives Today* (New York: Summit Books, 1985), 51–55, discusses Jewish entry into higher education in the 1910 to 1930 period almost entirely within the context of elite private schools and discrimination. Scholars examining quotas at elite schools have said little about how Jews who did not face quotas, primarily at large public schools, created a Jewish life. See for example, Hasia R. Diner, *The Jews of the United*

States 1654 to 2000 (Berkeley: University of California Press, 2006), 209–210. John Higham, *Send These to Me, Jews and Other Immigrants in Urban America* (New York: Atheneum, 1975), 159–161, does note the open admissions at public universities, but his focus on discrimination did not lend itself to discussing the dilemmas of cultural adjustment for students who attended these institutions.

2. Heywood Broun and George Britt, *Christians Only, A Study in Prejudice* (New York: Vanguard Press, 1931), 74; Harold S. Wechsler, *The Qualified Students, A History of Selective College Admission in America* (New York: John Wiley & Sons, 1977), 134,148,155–156,168; Marcia G. Synnott, *The Half-Opened Door, Discrimination and Admissions at Harvard, Yale and Princeton, 1900–1970* (Westport, CT: Greenwood Press, 1979), 14, 20. By the late 1920s Rutgers, whose procedures were complicated because it received public financing, did much the same. See Michael Greenberg and Seymour Zenchelsky, "Private Bias and Public Responsibility: Anti-Semitism at Rutgers in the 1920s and 1930s," *History of Education Quarterly* 33, no. 3 (1993): 295–320.

3. Naomi W. Cohen, *Jacob H. Schiff, A Study in American Jewish Leadership* (Hanover, NH and London: Brandeis University Press, 1999), 76–77. The [Portland] *Scribe* (26 October 1928), reported that Mrs. Nathan Miller of New York had just given $250,000 to Columbia University to establish a chair in Jewish History and that Lucius N. Littauer had previously provided funds for a chair in Jewish Studies at Harvard.

4. Paul Ritterband and Harold Wechsler, in *Jewish Learning in American Universities, the First Century* (Bloomington and Indianapolis: Indiana University Press, 1994), 10, note that in the late nineteenth and early twentieth centuries, "American Jews also saw university recognition as a route to social and cultural inclusion." Arnold J. Band, "Jewish Studies in American Liberal-Arts Colleges and Universities," *American Jewish Yearbook 67* (1966): 6, noted that all five scholars appointed to American universities between 1886 and 1902 to teach "Judaica or closely related subjects," were Jewish, and their appointments gave some prestige to local Jewish communities. Since their courses were offered largely in graduate programs, relatively few Jewish students could have benefited from them.

5. On the philosophy of the Menorah Society, as expressed through the *Menorah Journal*, which initiated publication in 1915, see Seth Korelitz, "The Menorah Idea: From Religion to Culture, From Race to Ethnicity," *American Jewish History* 85, no. 1 (March, 1997): 73–100.

6. Horace M. Kallen to Henry Hurwitz, 31 August 1915, 1 January, 22 March, 21 April, 10 October 1916, Henry Hurwitz Papers, MS 2, Box 23, File 2, The Jacob Rader Marcus Center of the American Jewish Archives (hereafter AJA), Cincinnati, OH.

7. Henry Hurwitz, Tentative Memorandum on Scope and Plans of the Quinquennial Convention (Dec. 26th–31st, 1917)," MS-2, Box 68, File 1, AJA.

8. Higham, *Send These to Me*, 160; Ritterband and Wechsler, *Jewish Learning*, 26.

9. David O. Levine, *The American College and the Culture of Aspiration, 1915–1940* (Ithaca: Cornell University Press, 1986), 39, 191.

10. Stephen Steinberg, *The Academic Melting Pot: Catholics and Jews in American Higher Education* (New Brunswick, NJ: Transaction Books, 1974), 21; Higham, *Send These to Me*, 160.

11. Sherry Gorelick, *City College and the Jewish Poor, Education in New York, 1880–1924* (New Brunswick, NJ: Rutgers University Press, 1981), 169.

12. On Berkeley Hillel's early years see articles in the *Scribe* (23 September 1927), (28 October 1927), (23 December 1927), (19 October 1929). UCLA, which was upgraded from a teacher's college to a branch of the University of California in the mid-1920s, had a Menorah Society by 1926. Local rabbis lectured on campus and offered courses on the Hebrew language. See *B'nai B'rith Messenger* (14 May 1926).

13. *Scribe* (12 November and 3 December 1920) note activities of Menorah Societies at Reed College and the University of Washington respectively.

14. Ritterband and Wechsler, *Jewish Learning*, 16.

15. Fred Rosenbaum, *Architects of Reform, Congregational and Community Leadership, Emanu-El of San Francisco, 1849–1980* (Berkeley, CA: Western Jewish History Center, 1980), 45–54, 84; Ritterband and Wechsler, *Jewish Learning*, 62–63.

16. Ritterband and Wechsler, *Jewish Learning*, 20.

17. Dan A. Oren, *Joining the Club: A History of Jews and Yale* (New Haven, CT: Yale University Press, 1985), 40. The prominent presidents of the University of Chicago, Johns Hopkins and Harvard felt that including Jewish learning in their curriculum would reinforce scientific Biblical scholarship and attract Jewish philanthropic support. See, Ritterband and Wechsler, *Jewish Learning*, x. As late as 1945, only about a dozen positions in Jewish studies of any kind existed at American colleges and universities. See Jonathan Sarna, *American Judaism: A History* (New Haven, CT and London: Yale University Press, 2004), 329.

18. Hand written card providing summary enumeration of student denominational affiliation, in President's Office Correspondence, 1919, folder labeled "Religion," University of Oregon Archives, Eugene, OR. All future references to the President's Office Correspondence will be indicated as PLC Papers, referring to the president from 1903 to 1926, Prince Lucien Campbell.

19. Rosenberg spoke on "A Debt of Honor Unpaid," see folder on "Failing-Beekman Orations," 1920–1921. At the commencement in June, 1918, Amy E. Carson spoke on "The Jew and His Heritage," folder on "Failing-Beekman Orations," 1917–1918, PLC Papers.

20. University of Oregon Faculty Meeting, 2 March 1916, accessed on 27 March 2008 at www.uoregon.edu/~assembly/AssemblyRecordsVol3/Vol-3-337.pdf.

21. Prince Lucien Campbell to Renwick B Knox, 24 July 1923. PLC Papers.

22. Rev. Edwin V. O'Hara to Dear Friend, 10 May 1921, PLC Papers.

23. Karl Onthank to Reverend G L Clark, Corvallis, 26 November 1919; Prince Lucien Campbell to Bishop Walter T. Sumner [Episcopal Diocese of Oregon], 2 March 1923, Sumner to Campbell 9 March 1923; Bruce J. Giffen to Dear Friend, 18 February 1924, PLC Papers.

24. L P Putnam, General Secretary of the University of Oregon YMCA, to Frank Sheldon 24 August 1922, Dean Colin Dyment to Prince Lucien Campbell, 12 November 1923, PLC Papers.

25. Karl Onthank to H.W. Stone, YMCA Portland, 24 April 1923, PLC Papers.

26. Prince Lucien Campbell to Board of Regents, 29 October 1915, PLC Papers.

27. Allen M. Eaton, *The Oregon System, the Story of Direct Legislation in Oregon* (Chicago: A.C. McClurg & Company, 1920), 141–147.

28. Sadie Orr-Dunbar to Prince Lucien Campbell, 8 November 1918, Jonah Wise to Campbell, 20 May 1919, PLC Papers.

29. On Selling's continual suspicion of the university's faculty and students see, Karl Onthank to Mrs. Susan Campbell, no date, but filed in 1924 folder, PLC Papers.

30. *Scribe* (21 October 1927) notes that the ZBT chapter of the University of Washington was composed largely of Jewish students from Portland whose "family members used the B'nai B'rith Center." This center for social and athletic activities was located near the homes of Portland's wealthier Jewish families, and ZBT around the country catered to the sons of wealthy families. See Marianne R. Sanua, *Going Greek, Jewish College Fraternities in the United States, 1895–1945* (Detroit: Wayne State University Press, 2003), 69; William Toll, *The Making of an Ethnic Middle Class, Portland Jewry Over Four Generations* (Albany: State University of New York Press: 1982), 127–128.

31. *Scribe* (6 January 1922) notes that twenty Jewish college students (though not necessarily all from Portland) were currently enrolled at Reed College. To suggest the close relationship between some elite Portland families and Reed College, in 1930 Herbert Swett was elected president of the alumni society. See *Scribe* (20 June 1930). As early as 1916, both schools had active Menorah Societies to provide cultural stimulation.

32. Prince Lucien Campbell to Jonah Wise, 9 December 1915, PLC Papers.

33. Karl Onthank to Jonah Wise, 10 December 1919, Wise to Onthank, 26 December 1919, Onthank to Miss Florence Reed, 5 May 1920, Onthank to L.E. Bassett, 9 October 1920, PLC Papers.

34. Horace M. Kallen, "The Roots of Anti-Semitism," *The Nation* (28 February 1923): 242.

35. Boas quickly developed a national reputation by publishing two essays on anti-semitism in the *Atlantic Monthly*. See Ralph Philip Boas, "Jew-Baiting in America," *Atlantic Monthly* (May, 1921): 658–665, and Boas, "Who Shall Go to College," *Atlantic Monthly* (October, 1922): 441–448.

36. S.C. Kohs to Dr. E.S. Conklin, 20 May 1920, PLC Papers.

37. Karl Onthank to President's Office, Michigan Agricultural College, 23 July 1920, is identical to many other letters in the file. See President's Office File, 1920, PLC Papers.

38. Karl Onthank to Jonah Wise, 23 November 1920, PLC Papers.

39. Jonah Wise to Karl Onthank, 26 November 1920, Prince Lucien Campbell to Jonah Wise, 7 December 1920, PLC Papers.

40. Faculty Meeting minutes can be found online at www.uoregon.edu/~assembly/AssemblyRecordsVol3/Vol-3-337.pdf accessed on 27 March 2008.

41. On Bert Treiger's innovative teaching of Modern Hebrew at the Portland Hebrew School, see *Scribe* (1 October 1920).

42. *Scribe* (6 January 1922).

43. Prince Lucien Campbell to George Rebec, 10 January 1922, PLC Papers.

44. Jonah Wise to Karl Onthank, April 21, 1920, Prince Lucien Campbell to Jonah Wise, 31 October 1921, PLC Papers.

45. Karl Onthank to Mrs. Susan Campbell, March 19, 1926 PLC Papers.

46. *Scribe* (14 February 1930).

47. *Scribe* (2 May 1930).

48. Ritterband and Wechsler, *Jewish Learning*, 60–63 describes the faculty, course offerings, and funding for the UC program from 1894 through the 1930s.

49. Band, "Jewish Studies," 6–14.

50. *University of Oregon Catalogue 1936–1937* (Eugene: University of Oregon Press, June 1936), 131,135, 142, 147.

51. Ibid., 142.

52. *University of Oregon Catalogue, 1935–1936* (Eugene: University of Oregon Press, June 1935), 31, 137.

53. *Scribe* (24 November 1927). Broun and Britt, *Christians Only, A Study in Prejudice*, 95, notes a survey in 1930 by a *Jewish Daily Bulletin* that found nineteen Jews out of thirty-five hundred students at Oregon Agricultural College. *The Scribe* never mentioned Jewish student life at OAC.

54. A few Jewish students did stay in the dorms and accumulated debts. See "Student Problems" folder, 1919–1920, PLC Papers.

55. *The University of Oregon Announcement, 1922–1923* (Eugene: University of Oregon Press, April, 1922), 44–46.

56. Sanua, 146–147.

57. *Scribe* (16 December 1927).

58. For an extended presentation of Rabbi Benjamin Goldstein's views see *Scribe* (23 December 1927). A brief sketch of the array of colleges at which Jewish students enrolled, their activities on campus, and contacts between campuses is provided in William Toll, "A Regional Context for Pacific Jewry, 1880–1930," in *The Columbia History of Jews and Judaism in America*, ed. Marc Lee Raphael (New York: Columbia University Press, 2008), 231, 233.

59. *Scribe* (24 February 1928).

60. Scheinbaum's graduation is noted in Minute Book, Hebrew School [Portland, Oregon] 30 March 1924, Minute Book at Oregon Jewish Historical Society. When Scheinbaum graduated from the University and went to study at Cornell in the fall of 1929, Manuel Schnitzer, also from Portland, became director of the Sunday School See *Scribe* (4 October 1929).

61. *Scribe* (16 March), (20 April 1928), (8 March 1929).

62. *Scribe* (21 September 1928).

63. *Scribe* (14 December 1928), (7 February 1929).

64. *Scribe* (11 January 1929).

65. The Portland Hebrew School was supported by Portland's Federated Jewish Societies, with student tuition voluntary. See Minute Book, Hebrew School (8 November 1927), (12 February 1931).

66. *Scribe* (31 August 1928).

67. *Scribe* (12 October 1928). Enrollment in the school varied, but reached one hundred sixty-seven in the spring of 1927. It declined to about 125 in February, 1930, but by then a branch in East Portland enrolled at least thirty. See Minute Book, Hebrew School [Portland, Oregon] 28 April 1927, 13 January 1929, 28 February 1930, Jewish Historical Society of Oregon (merged with Oregon Jewish Museum).

68. The Portland Hebrew School was housed at the Jewish community's Neighborhood House in South Portland and was supported not by synagogues but by the Port-

land Jewish Federation. See *Scribe* (9 March 1928), (12 October 1928), (28 December 1928), (1 February 1929).
69. *Scribe* (1 February 1929).
70. In September 1928, over a dozen graduates of the school (including Scheinbaum) formed an alumni group which intended to meet every Monday night to study Hebrew. *Scribe* (21 September 1928). In February 1930, Rabbi Parzen was elected president, and Rabbi Rubin second vice-president of the Portland branch of the Zionist Organization of America. See *Scribe* (28 February 1930).
71. Minutes, Jewish Education Association of Portland, 24 October 1927, 12 January 1928, 15 August 1928. Jewish Education Association Papers, Jewish Historical Society of Oregon (merged with Oregon Jewish Museum).
72. *Scribe* (1 February 1929).
73. A list of fraternity members by class, with accompanying photographs of most members, appeared in the annual issues of the University of Oregon's yearbook, *The Oregana*, starting in 1928. Membership data has been gathered from those sources. *The Oregana* is held in Special Collections at the University of Oregon Library.
74. Sanua, *Going Greek*, 69, Appendix A. Rabbi Meyer Rubin's affiliation with Neveh Tzedek, a synagogue whose members held a Conservative view of Judaism, is seen in *Scribe* (25 October 1929), *Scribe* (7 February 1930), notes that the SAM chapter at the University Oregon was the last of a "chain" along the Pacific Coast, including California, Washington, University of Southern California, and Utah.
75. See photographs in *Oregana*, 1939.
76. William Toll, "Voluntarism and Modernization in Portland Jewry: The B'nai B'rith in the 1920s," *The Western Historical Quarterly* 10, no. 1 (January 1979): 21–38.
77. William Toll, "Ethnicity and Stability: South Portland's Italians and Jews, 1900–1940," *Pacific Historical Review* 54 (May, 1985): 161–189. See also the observation by Bert Treiger, principal of the Portland Hebrew School in 1929, that so many families had moved away from South Portland that the school felt lucky to retain enrollment. *Scribe* (8 March 1929).

Chapter 14 - Robert King Merton, His Science, and the Promise of the Enlightenment
1. It was in the American Jewish Archives, while working in the papers of Horace Meyer Kallen regarding his disputes over the scientific value of the work of Immanuel Velikofsky, that I ran across a provocative reference to Robert King Merton. However, it was only on the urging of my colleague David Hollinger that I decided to look more closely at Merton's career and ideas. Professor Hollinger had written a paper on Merton ("The Defense of Democracy: Robert King Merton's Formulation of the Scientific Ethos," in *Knowledge and Society: Studies in the Sociology of Culture Past and Present* Vol. 4, ed. Robert Alan Jones and Henrika Kuklick [Greenwich, CT, and London: JAI Press, 1983], 1–15), and decided that Merton was a complex figure who deserved another and perhaps different approach. That is what I have done in this essay. In addition to Hollinger's, there is another perceptive discussion of Merton by Everett Mendelsohn, "Robert K. Merton: The Celebration and Defense of Science," *Science in Context* 3, no. 1 (1989): 269–289.
2. My understanding of the Enlightenment is particularly influenced by the brilliant essay with which Isaiah Berlin introduces his anthology *The Age of Enlightenment*

(New York: George Braziller, 1957), 11–29, as well as the perceptive and learned work of Henry F. May, *The Enlightenment in America* (New York: Oxford University Press, 1976). Because Professor May intends to be comprehensive, he presents a much more complex discussion than is needed here. I have also gained much from Norman Hampson's *The Enlightenment* (London: Penguin, 1990) and Dorinda Outram's *The Enlightenment*, 2nd ed. (Cambridge: Cambridge University Press, 2005), as well as more specialized works. Among them Louis Dupre's *The Enlightenment and the Intellectual Foundations of Modern Culture* (New Haven and London: Yale University Press, 2004) was quite helpful.

3. Betty Jo Teeter Dobbs and Margaret C. Jacob, *Newton and the Culture of Newtonianism* (Atlantic Highlands, NJ: Humanities Press, 1995); Thomas L. Hankins, *Science and the Enlightenment* (Cambridge: Cambridge University Press, 1985). The quote from Alexander Pope is in Basil Willey, *The Eighteenth Century Background* (London: Chatto and Windus, 1949), 5.

4. For a good general discussion, see Larry Stewart, *The Rise of Public Science* (Cambridge: Cambridge University Press, 1992). See also Simon Schaffer, "Natural Philosophy and Public Spectacle in the Eighteenth Century," *History of Science* 21 (1983): 1–43. The most comprehensive contemporary discussion of the orrery can be found in Abraham K. Rees, ed., *The Cyclopaedia, or, Universal Dictionary of Arts, Sciences, and Literature* [microform] 1st American ed. (Philadelphia: Samuel F. Bradford, 1805–1825), Early American imprints, Second series, no. 9234. See articles on "Orrery" and "Planetary Machines." An informative study is Harold E. Gillingham, "The First Orreries in America," *Journal of the Franklin Institute* 229 (January 1940): 81–99. On Rittenhouse, see Brooke Hindle, *David Rittenhouse* (Princeton: Princeton University Press, 1964). The Latin inscription is from Howard C. Rice, Jr. *The Rittenhouse Orrery* (Princeton: Princeton University Library, 1954), 88.

5. For a clear sense of how geographically varied the Enlightenment was and of its lack of influence among the lower classes, see Derek Beales, *Enlightenment and Reform in Eighteenth-Century Europe* (London: IB Tauris, 2005), 7–27. On the Declaration and the Constitution as Enlightenment documents, see May, 96–101; 163–167; Bernard Bailyn, "Political Experience and Enlightenment Ideas in Eighteenth Century America," *American Historical Review* 67 (1962): 339–351.

6. The recent literature on the impact of the Enlightenment upon European Jews balances its benefits with its cultural costs and resulting emotional turmoil. See Shmuel Feiner, *The Jewish Enlightenment* (Philadelphia: University of Pennsylvania Press, 2004), 21–84, 87–182, and Pierre Birnbaum and Ira Katznelson, eds., *Paths of Emancipation* (Princeton, NJ: Princeton University Press, 1995), as well as some good special studies: David Sorkin, *The Transformation of German Jewry, 1780–1840* (Oxford: Oxford University Press, 1987); Steven M. Lowenstein, *The Berlin Jewish Community, Enlightenment and Family Crisis, 1770–1830* (Oxford: Oxford University Press, 1993); and Jay Berkovitz, "The French Revolution and the Jews: Assessing the Cultural Impact," *AJS Review* 20 (1995): 25–86. See also David B. Ruderman, *Jewish Enlightenment in an English Key* (Princeton, NJ: Princeton University Press, 2000). Washington's letter can be found in George Washington, *Writings*, ed. John H. Rhodehamel (New York: Library of America, 1997), 706–707. For a European contrast, see Ole Peter Grell and Roy Porter, eds., *Toleration in Enlightenment Europe* (Cambridge: Cambridge University Press, 2000). Abigail Franks to Naphtali Franks,

17 October 1739, *Letters of the Franks Family (1733–1738)*, ed. Leo Hershkowitz and Isidore Meyer (Waltham, MA: American Jewish Historical Society, 1968), 66.

7. Some of the papers of Robert King Merton (1910–2003) are deposited at Columbia University Library in the division of Manuscripts and Archives, New York, NY. The archivist expects that the papers may be available to scholars by the summer of 2009. The most valuable manuscript materials available for this essay were in the Talcott Parsons Papers in the Pusey Library, Harvard University Archives, Cambridge, MA. There is an extensive personal correspondence between Merton and Parsons. In addition, there are some letters from Merton in the P.A. Sorokin Papers in the Pusey Library at Harvard. In 1945 Parsons tried to bring Merton on to the faculty in Harvard. There is a very useful file on this endeavor (UAV 870.2700), which the chairman of the Sociology Department allowed me to examine. There is a folder (UAV 161 .201 xx) of Merton's Graduate School record in the Harvard Archives of the Pusey Library, which I was not granted permission to examine. Ms.Vanessa Merton kindly granted me an extended interview. She is not responsible for the view expressed in this essay. Merton's own reminiscences are an essential source: *A Life of Learning* (New York: American Council of Learned Societies, 1994). This should be compared with Morton M. Hunt, "Profile," *New Yorker* 36 (28 January 1961): 39–63.

8. Skimming through the *Saturday Evening Post* of the 1920s brings us such articles as: A.W. Parker, "Immigration Control," 192 (28 February 1920): 8; I.F. Marcosson, "Checking the Alien Tide," 135 (5 May 1923): 18; K.L. Roberts, "Slow Poison," 196 (24 February 1924): 8–9; L. Stoddard, "The New Realism about Science," 197 (6 September 1924): 38; H.H. Curran, "Fewer and Better," 197 (15 November 1924): 6; "More Deportations Needed," 198 (3 April 1926): 34; H.W. Child "Whose County Is This?" 198 (22 May 1926): 6–7; R. Crawford, "Halt who's there?" 200 (7 January 1928): 33; "Why Not Register Them?" 202 (22 March 1930): 24; "Arithmetic and Unemployment," 203 (2 August 1930): 18; "Crime and Immigration," 203 (9 August 1930): 26.

9. Robert C. Bannister, "Principle, Politics, Profession: American sociologists and Fascism, 1930–1950" in *Sociology Responds To Fascism*, ed. Stephen P. Turner (London and New York: Routledge, 1992), 196–198; Edwin B. White to Talcott Parsons, 12 May 1939, Talcott Parsons Papers, Edwin B. White folder, Pusey Library, Harvard University, Cambridge, MA. For a recent discussion of the immigration acts and their effects, see Roger Daniels, *Coming to America* (New York: Harper Collins, 1990), 265–284, 287–306. Leonard Dinnerstein describes the rising antisemitic sentiment and restrictions against Jews in this era, in *Anti-Semitism in America* (Oxford: Oxford University Press, 1994), 78–149. On social dances at the University of Chicago, see Jerry Gershenhorn, *Melville J. Herskovits and the Racial Politics of Knowledge* (Lincoln: University of Nebraska Press, 2004), 14. Students were sometimes more unequivocal in their desire to exclude Jews than the administrators. See W.T. Ham, "Harvard Student Opinion on the Jewish Question," *Nation* 115 (6 September 1922): 225–227 and (18 October 1922): 412. On the Jewish Fraternities' internalization of antisemitism, see Marianne R. Sanua, *Going Greek* (Detroit: Wayne State University Press, 2003), 28, 152–157.

10. See Ernest Maass, "Integration and name changing among Jewish refugees from Central Europe in the United States," *Names* 6 (September 1958): 129–171; Arthur Scherr, "Change-of-Name Petitions of the New York Courts," *Names* 34 (Septem-

ber 1988): 285–302. Benzion Kaganoff, *A Dictionary of Jewish Names* (New York: Schocken, 1977), 66–76. For German Jews, see Rudolf Glanz, *Studies in Judaica Americana* (New York: Ktav, 1970), 278–313. Of course, the ease of changing one's name in the United States compared to changing one's name in Europe was a factor. For the dismal effect of restrictions on name changing in Germany, see Diez Bering, *The Stigma of Names* (Ann Arbor, MI: University of Michigan Press, 1992).

11. The most detailed available description of Merton's early life is in *Life of Learning*, 2–7.

12. Young Merton was an amateur magician and an admirer of the Jewish escape artist Houdini (Harry Weisz, son of a rabbi). As Merton chose to remember it, he adopted the stage name Merlin, which evolved into Merton. Friends began calling him by his stage name, which he liked, so he decided to change it legally. See *Life of Learning*, 8–9.

13. Pitirim A. Sorokin, *A Long Journey* (New York: Rowman and Littlefield, 1963), 241–268. "The Sorokin-Merton Correspondence on Puritanism, Pietism, and Science, 1933–1934," *Science in Context* 3 (1988): 293–300. Robert King Merton, "Remembering the Young Talcott Parsons," *The American Sociologist* 15 (May 1980): 68–71. Howard Brick, "Talcott Parsons's Shift Away from Economics, 1937–1946," *Journal of American History* 87 (Sept. 2000): 490–514. Uta Gerhardt, *Talcott Parsons* (Cambridge: Cambridge University Press, 2002), 1–128.

14. Sarton may have been of Jewish origin, although his daughter, May Sarton, who had antisemitic inclinations herself, ardently tried to prove that this was not true. Margot Peters, *May Sarton* (New York: Knopf, 1997), 214. George Sarton, "August Comte, Historian of Science," *Osiris* 10 (1952): 328–357. Robert K. Merton, "George Sarton, Episodic Recollections of an Unruly Apprentice," *Isis* 76 (1985): 477–486. Robert K. Merton and Arnold Thackray, "On Discipline Building, The Paradoxes of George Sarton," *Isis* 63 (December 1972): 473–490. Robert K. Merton and Arnold Thackray, "George Sarton," *Dictionary of Scientific Biography*, Vol. 12, ed. Charles C. Gillespie (New York: Charles Scribner's Sons, 1975), 107–114. For a clear description of Comte's thought (no minor achievement!), see Raymond Aaron, *Main Currents in Sociological Thought*, Vol. 1 (New York: Penguin, 1998), 73–143.

15. Sarton had Merton's dissertation, "Science, Technology, and Society in Seventeenth Century England," published in *Osiris* 4, no. 2 (1938): 360–362. It was republished as a book in 1970, as well as in a new edition in 2001, with new prefaces, a new author's introduction, and an expanded and updated list of readings. For a discussion of its "Weberian" aspects, see I. Bernard Cohen, ed., *Puritanism and the Rise of Modern Science: The Merton Thesis* (New Brunswick, NJ: Rutgers University Press, 1990). For a discussion of the "Marxist" aspects of the thesis, see Harriet Zuckerman, "The Other Merton Thesis," *Science in Context* 3 (1989): 239–267. In part because of his lack of familiarity with Marxist lingo, Steven Shapin is led to diminish the influence of Marx and Marxists upon Merton's dissertation. When Merton disparages "vulgar materialism," and "vulgar Marxism," he is not attacking the Marxists, but rather adopting their terms and categories. It is strange and revealing that this self-appointed "vanguard of the working class" used the term "vulgar" as a term of deprecation. "Vulgar materialists" and "vulgar Marxists" were usually labels applied to economic determinists who believed that people acted primarily from personal economic motives. This was too simple for the Marxists who argued that people

acted from diverse motives but that those were shaped by class perspectives. "Vulgar materialism" was rejected for something they called "dialectical Materialism." See Steven Shapin's argument in "Understanding the Merton Thesis," *Isis* 79 (December 1988): 594–608. Merton published an excerpt from his dissertation, "Science and the Economy of Seventeenth Century England," in *Science and Society: A Marxist Quarterly* 3 (Winter 1939): 3–27.

16. In the five years between receiving his Ph.D. at Harvard and arriving at Columbia, Merton published his dissertation and wrote sixteen scholarly articles as well as forty book reviews. It has been estimated that one of these articles, "Social Structure and Anomie," *American Sociological Review* 3 (1938): 672–682 has been one of the most frequently cited in American sociology. Stephen Cole, "The Growth of Scientific Knowledge," in *The Idea of Social Structure*, ed. Lewis A. Coser (New York: Harcourt Brace Jovanovich, 1975), 175.

17. Robert K. Merton, "Fact and Factitiousness in Ethnic Opinionnaires," *American Sociological Review* 5 (1940): 13–28. For the methodological debate in this same volume, see George Lundberg, "Note," 38–39; Jessie Bernard, "A Communication," 415–417; Robert K. Merton, "A Communication," 647–648. With regard to the four Merton papers discussed here, it is always necessary to read them in their original printings. These papers have often been reprinted, but usually with omissions and modifications.

18. Robert K. Merton, "Intermarriage and Social Structure," *Psychiatry* 4 (August 1941): 361–374. For a comparison of the statistics on Jewish/Gentile intermarriage and Black/White intermarriage, see Julius Drachsler, *Intermarriage in New York City* (New York: Columbia University, 1921), 46, 50; Merton, "Intermarriage," 374; Merton, "Intermarriage," 368–371.

19. Robert K. Merton and M. F. Ashley Montagu, "Crime and the Anthropologist," *American Anthropologist* 42 (July–September, 1940): 384–408. For an appreciative obituary of Montagu, see Susan Sperling, "Ashley Montagu (1905–1999)," *American Anthropologist* 102 (September 2000): 583–588.

20. Robert K. Merton, "Social Structure and Anomie," *American Sociological Review* 3 (October 1938): 672–682.

21. Robert K. Merton, "Science and the Social Order," *Philosophy of Science* 5 (July 1938): 321–337. The reference to the "White Jew," Heisenberg, is on p. 323; see also n.7. Merton's cautious observation is on p. 337. Merton published a much-discussed article, "The Self-Fulfilling Prophecy," in *The Antioch Review* 7 (Summer 1948): 193–216. Towards the end of the essay there is a paragraph discussing Jews and antisemitism and another discussing Negroes and Negrophobia. The essay was incorporated into all three editions of Merton's *Social Science and Social Structure.* Oddly enough, Negro and Negrophobia were entries in the subject index for all three editions. Jew and antisemitism appeared in none of the subject indexes, although the paragraph on Jews remained in all editions.

22. Robert K. Merton, "A Note on Science and Democracy," *Journal of Legal and Political Sociology* 1 (October 1942): 115–126, especially 115–117. There is an important change in the 1973 reprint of this essay in Robert K. Merton, *The Sociology of Science*, ed. Norman Storer (Chicago: University of Chicago Press, 1973), 269, where the 1942 "not" becomes the 1973 "not only." But since this emendation fits

more closely to the overall argument of the essay, it is most likely a correction of a typo than a change of mind.

23. For Jefferson's view of the role that "the light of science" (as against "monkish ignorance and superstition") would play in the spread of human rights, see his letter to Roger C. Weightman, 24 June 1826, in *The Life and Selected Letters of Thomas Jefferson*, ed. Adrian Koch and William Peden (New York: the Modern Library, 1944), 729–730. For Rittenhouse, science has a direct tendency to "dilate the heart with universal benevolence and to enlarge its views … [for it lays] the foundation of our eternal improvements and happiness" (*Oration delivered February 24th, 1775*, 21, 27). See also Merton's review of Julian Huxley's "Science and Social Needs" in *Isis* 24 (December 1935): 188–189.

24. Merton, "A Note on Science and Democracy," 117–121.

25. Ibid., 124–126.

26. Ibid., 121–124. For a later statement of his notion of "communism" in science, see Robert K. Merton, "The Matthew Effect in Science II," *Isis* 79 (December 1988): 620. On Babeuf, see R.B. Rose, *Gracchus Babeuf* (Stanford, CA: Stanford University Press, 1978), 35, 166, 182. Babeuf drew his inspiration from Rousseau and other members of what Henry F. May calls the Revolutionary Enlightenment (see May's *The Enlightenment in America*, 165ff). In contrast, James Madison, whom May classifies as part of "Moderate Enlightenment," proposed to advance science in America through the enlightened self-interest of a patent law provision in the Federal Constitution. See *Federalist* 43, ed. Jacob E. Cooke (Middletown, CT: Wesleyan University Press, 1961), 288.

27. Merton's endeavors drew oblique support from the rising influence of logical positivism (often called logical empiricism) in the departments of philosophy of the major American universities of the day. Logical positivism was a stripped down version of the Enlightenment, ostensibly sans moralism and metaphysics yet maintaining scientific knowledge as the exemplar of all meaningful knowledge. Rudolph Carnap, perhaps this philosophical movement's most influential thinker, was an ardent advocate of some of the Enlightenment's most cherished ideals—that of social progress and the scientific education that would help bring it about. See Gurol Irzik, "Changing Conceptions of Rationality," in *Logical Empiricism*, ed. Paolo Parrini (Pittsburgh, PA: University of Pittsburgh Press, 2003), 343–344; Friedrich Stadler, "The Vienna Circle: Context, Profile, and Development," in *the Cambridge Companion to Logical Empiricism*, ed. Alan Richardson (New York: Cambridge University Press; 2007), 27–30; Hans Joachim Dahms, "Vienna Circle and French Enlightenment," in *Encyclopedia and Utopia*, ed. Elisabeth Nemeth (Dordrecht, The Netherlands: Kluwer Academic Publishers, 1996), 53–61; Gerald Holton, "From The Vienna Circle to Harvard Square," in *Scientific Philosophy: Origins and Development* ed. Friedrich Stadler (Dordrecht, The Netherlands: Kluwer Academic Publishers, 1993), 47–72.

28. For Merton's scientific aspirations for the discipline of sociology that "startled" his close friend and colleague, see Paul F. Lazarsfeld to Dr. Talcott Parsons, 26 September 1944, in the Merton folder of the Harvard University Department of Sociology (UAV 870.2700) Pusey Library, Harvard University Archives, Cambridge, MA.

29. For Merton's demonstration of the points of agreement between functional analysis and dialectical materialism in all three editions of his textbook, see Robert K.

Merton, *Social Theory and Social Structure* (Glencoe, IL: Free Press, 1949), 41–43; 2nd ed., revised and enlarged (1957) 39–42; 3rd ed., revised and enlarged (1968) 93–96. Merton often gave his classes in the late afternoon or evening, making them accessible to working students. See Nathan Glazer, "From Socialism to Sociology," in *Authors of Their Own Lives*, ed. Bennett M. Berger (Berkeley: University of California Press, 1990), 198–199. For a particularly informative discussion of the sociology department at Columbia when Merton figured prominently on the faculty, see James N. Coleman, "Columbia in the 1950s," in *Authors of Their Own Lives*, 75–103. From the accounts of the leading sociologists who graduated in this era, it would be easy to romanticize the vibrancy of graduate student life in sociology at Columbia without considering its costs. The bulk of these students lived as lumpen-intellectuals and *luftmenschen*. Of the graduate students entering between 1940 and 1956 on the average, five percent received the Ph.D. The average time for completion was 10.1 years. Compared with students in the sciences, graduate students in sociology received little financial support. See the tables in Hans Rosenhaupt and Thomas J. Chinlund, *Graduate Students: Experience at Columbia University, 1940–1956* (New York: Columbia University Press, 1958), 59, 60, 75. For a suggestive discussion of the relationship of Merton and Lazarsfeld to their graduate students, see Terry N. Clark, "Clientelism and Universalism," *The Tocqueville Review* 17 no.2 (1996): 183–204.

30. This "central orientation" remains unchanged in all three editions of *Social Theory and Social Structure*. In the 1st ed. (1949), 47; 2nd ed. (1957), 46–47; 3rd ed. (1968), 100–101.

31. Robert K. Merton, "Discussion," *American Sociological Review* 13 (April 1948): 168.

32. The cited "Discussion" is part of a forceful critique of a paper presented by Talcott Parsons. "The Position of Sociological Theory" was read before the annual meeting of the American Sociological Society in December 1947 and printed in *The American Sociological Review* 13 (April 1948): 156–164. It was Merton's attempt to save functionalism from the functionalist by extracting its bias toward the status quo. In later years many sociologists came to the conclusion that the endeavor was unsuccessful.

33. Merton, *Social Theory and Social Structure* (1949), 53; (1957), 52–53; (1968), 107.

34. Merton, *Social Theory and Social Structure* [epigraph] (1949), 3; (1957), 3; (1968), 1. "On Sociological Theories of the Middle Range" in *Social Theory and Social Structure* (1949), 5–16; (1957), 5–16; (1968), 39–72.

35. These two Mertonians, Cynthia Fuchs Epstein and Jonathan R. Cole, investigated the "low representation of women in science." See their essays in *The Outer Circle: Women in the Scientific Community*, ed. Harriet Zuckerman, Jonathan R. Cole and John T. Bruer (New York: Norton, 1991). See also Jonathan R. Cole, *Fair Science* (New York: Free Press, 1979) and Cynthia Fuchs Epstein, *Deceptive Distinctions* (New York: Russel Sage Foundation, 1988). Perhaps toward the end of his career, Merton lost some of his optimism about integrating sociological theory and practice. The subtitle of the first edition of his textbook, "toward the codification of theory and research," disappears in the later editions. Moreover, the last book that Merton wrote, published posthumously, *The Travels and Adventures of Serendipity* (Princeton, NJ: Princeton University Press, 2004), suggests that Merton's sense of reality was coming closer to that of William James.

36. For the work of Vannevar Bush, see Bruce L. R. Smith, *American Science Policy since World War Two* (Washington, DC: Brookings Institution Press, 1990), 36–107. G. Paschal Zachary, *Endless Frontier: Vannevar Bush, Engineer of the American Century* (Boston: MIT Press, 1997) is a good biography, emphasizing the broader implications of Bush's career.

37. The sad story of Boris Hessen is well-told by Loren R. Graham in "The Socio-Political Roots of Boris Hessen: Soviet Marxism and the History of Science," *Social Studies of Science* 15 (November 1985): 705–722. Merton relied on Hessen at many points in his dissertation, but he was persuaded (in part by G.N. Clark's work) that Hessen's sense of the social setting was too narrowly focused. Merton, *Science, Technology, and Society in Seventeenth Century England,* 2nd ed. (New York: H. Fertig, 1970), 206. For Hessen's paper see *Science at the Crossroads; Papers Presented to the International Congress of the History of Science and Technology,* 2nd ed. (London: F. Cass, 1971), 150–212.

38. Karl Marx, "A Contribution To The Critique Of Political Economy," in *A Handbook of Marxism,* ed. Emile Burns (London: V. Gollancz Ltd., 1935), 372.

39. Merton, *Social Theory and Social Structure,* (1949), 217–264; (1957), 456–508; (1968), 510–562.

40. Robert K. Merton, "Priorities in Scientific Discovery," *American Sociological Review* 22 (December 1958): 633–659; Robert K. Merton, "Making It Scientifically" [Review Essay on *The Double Helix*], *The New York Times Book Review* (25 February 1968): 1, 41–43. Robert K. Merton (with Harriet Zuckerman), "The Matthew Effect in Science," *Science* 198 (5 January 1968): 55–62. Robert K. Merton, "The Matthew Effect in Science, II," *Isis* 79 (December 1988): 606–623. Robert K. Merton (with Harriet Zuckerman), "Patterns of Evaluation in Science" *Minerva* 9 (January 1971): 66–100. Merton later assigned the topic of peer review to his students Stephen Cole and Jonathan R. Cole, who then wrote *Peer Review in the National Science Foundation: phase two of a study* (Washington, DC: National Academy Press, 1981). This work was judged as being too uncritical by some. See Ian A. Mitroff, "Peer Review at the NSF" *Social Studies of Science* 9 (May 1979): 199–232. Daryl Chubin and Edward J. Hackett, *Peerless Science: Peer Review and U.S. Science Policy* (Albany, NY: SUNY Press, 1990). Merton's claim that scientists embody some of the prime values of civilization can be found in his essay "The Behavior Patterns of Scientists," *The American Scholar* 38 (Spring 1969): 213–220.

41. For a detailed study of the student revolt at Columbia, see Jerry L. Avorn, *Up Against the Ivy Wall* (New York: Atheneum Press, 1968). The revolt at Columbia came somewhat late. The Berkeley student upheaval had started in 1964 and was followed by similar events on other campuses. The students at Columbia borrowed tactics, issues, and even some of the flavor of the other student revolts. For a comprehensive survey, see Seymour Martin Lipset, *Rebellion in the University* (Boston: Little, Brown, 1972). For some of the prevalent issues raised by the students and faculty sympathizers, see Sheldon S. Wolin and John H. Schaar, *The Berkeley Rebellion and Beyond: Essays on Politics and Education in the Technological Society* (New York: New York Review and Vintage Books, 1970). Early in his career, Merton looked upon science and technology as great progressive forces. He seemed to agree with the British and American Marxist scientists that it was capitalism, at this stage, that blocked their growth. See his reviews of Frederick Soddy, ed., *The Frustration of*

Science, in *Isis* 25 (1936): 274; of B.J. Stern, *The Frustration of Technology* in *Isis* 29 (1938): 567; of J.D. Bernal, *The Social Function of Science* in *American Journal of Sociology* 16 (1941): 622–623. After WWII, when American industrial productivity grew rapidly, Merton set aside this notion. For a while, he became concerned that new technologies might be turned against workers, but proposed that the problem could be handled by worker-management negotiation! Merton, *Social Theory and Social Structure* (1949), 317–328; (1957), 562–573; (1968), 616–627. In his dissertation, Merton had written about military uses of science and technology in the seventeenth century, yet the new ominous linkage between government, the military, science, and technology in the twentieth century seems to have been invisible to him.

42. Recognition of the moral ambiguousness of science grew rapidly in the years following World War II. This awareness was fed by diverse events and disclosures that seemed to discredit the cheerful notion that science, democracy, and goodness marched forward hand in hand. Among all the other disclosures, the finding that science had prospered mightily under Nazism, and that some of Germany's leading scientists had willingly lent their expertise to the campaign to murder millions of innocent Jews and others, was deeply disturbing. See Benno Muller-Hill, *Murderous Science*, translated from the German edition (New York: Oxford University Press, 1988) and the work of his student Ute Deichmann, *Biologists Under Hitler*, translated from the German edition (Cambridge, MA: Harvard University Press, 1996). Muller-Hill is an eminent German geneticist who took on this historical study as a personal obligation. For some of the responses see Robert N. Proctor, "Review of *Murderous Science*," *Science* 241, no.4866 (5 August 1988): 730–731; Michael H. Kater, "Review of *Murderous Science*," *Isis* 80, no. 4 (December, 1989): 722–723; William Seidelman, "Mengele Medicus: Medicine's Nazi Heritage," *The Milbank Quarterly* 66, no.2 (1988): 221–239.

43. Preeminent among these neo-Marxist critics was Alvin W. Gouldner, a former student and friend. Both Merton and Gouldner tried to maintain their friendship despite their sharp disagreements. For Merton's version of his friendship with his "spikey" critic, see Robert K. Merton, "Alvin W. Gouldner: Genesis and Growth of a Friendship," *Theory and Society* 11 (November 1982): 915–938. Two of Gouldner's most pertinent works are *The Coming Crisis of Western Sociology* (New York: Basic Books, 1970) and *For Sociology* (London: Allen Lane, 1973).

44. Warren O. Hagstrom's empirical study of *The Scientific Community* (New York: Basic Books, 1965) found little trace of Merton's scientific ethos. See also Randall Collins and Sal Restivo, "Development, Diversity, and Conflict in the Sociology of Science," *Sociological Quarterly* 24 (Spring 1983): 188–189. They argued that Merton's Functionalism "provided an ideology for scientists to defend their turf." More generally, they announce "the end of the Mertonian Hegemony" (193). See also Robert A. Rothman, "A Dissenting View of the Scientific Ethos," *British Journal of Sociology* 25 (March 1972): 102–108. Michael Mulkay, an earlier follower, deserted Merton on the grounds that his notion of science was outmoded (*Science and the Sociology of Knowledge* [London: G. Allen and Unwin, 1979] and *Sociology of Science: A Sociological Pilgrimage* [Philadelphia: Open University Press, 1991]). Stephen Cole presented the odd memorial speech, "Merton's Contribution to the Sociology of Science," *Social Studies in Science* 34 (December 2004): 829–843. Randall Collins,

Robert K. Merton On Social Structure and Science, ed. Piotr Sztompka in *American Journal of Sociology* 103 (July 1997): 275–277.

45. Morton M. Hunt, "How Does It Come To Be So?" *New Yorker* 36 (28 January 1961): 39–63. Werner J. Cahnman, "Robert King Merton," in *Encyclopaedia Judaica*, Vol. 11 (Jerusalem: Keter, 1972), 1394–1395. Merton, Robert K., "Curriculum Vitae," in *R.K. Merton Papers* [a webpage with links to a small selection of printed materials by and about Merton], accessed on 19 March 2009 at http://www.garfield. library.upenn.edu/merton/list.html. The two Israeli scholars were Joseph Ben David and Yehuda Elkana. See Gad Freudenthal and J.L. Heilbrun, *Eloge: Joseph Ben David, 1920–1986* in *Isis* 80 (December 1989): 659–683. When the author of this paper taught in the American Studies Department of the Hebrew University, in the fall of 1989, the story of Merton's *hora* was retold with relish. Merton's autobiographical account can be found in *A Life of Learning* (1994), Charles Homer Haskins Lecture. American Council of Learned Societies Occasional Papers, no. 25, *passim*. See also the detailed and changing entries that Merton supplied to *Who's Who in America*, 1950–2003.

46. At the height of the radicalism of the 1960s (1964–1974), a group of young Black sociologists argued that their growing up Black gave them a special entry for understanding the sociology of the Black community. Merton opposed this argument. Growing up Black might possibly blinker them with a special parochialism. They needed the "outsider's" perspective and disinterestedness. Merton ended his address with a peroration alluding to a famous outsider and universalist—"Insiders and Outsiders unite. You have nothing to lose but your claims. You have a world of understanding to win." Robert K. Merton, "The Perspectives of Insiders and Outsiders" in *The Sociology of Science*, ed. Norman W. Storer (Chicago: University of Chicago Press, 1973), 136.

47. For some of the uses and abuses to which various kinds of cognitive skepticism regarding science have been put, see John H. Zammito in *A Nice Derangement of Epistemes* (Chicago: University of Chicago Press, 2004). Professor Zammito writes from the position of "moderate historicism." The ramifications of Godel's "incompleteness" have been interpreted in divergent ways. See Rebecca Goldstein, *Incompleteness* (New York: W.W. Norton, 2005); Roger Penrose, *Shadows of the Mind* (New York: Oxford University Press, 1994), 64–126; Solomon Feferman, "Godel, Nagel, Minds and Machines," Ernest Nagel Lecture delivered at Columbia University, 27 September 2007, accessed on 19 March 2009 at http://math.stanford.edu/~feferman/ papers/godelnagel.pdf. Godel himself became a philosophical Platonist.

Chapter 15 - When Harry Met Max

1. Harry M. Orlinsky, "On the Present State of Proto-Septuagint Studies," *Journal of the American Oriental Society* (*JAOS*) 61 (1941): 81 (introductory note).

2. For Margolis's life and scholarship, see Leonard Greenspoon, *Max Leopold Margolis: A Scholar's Scholar* (Atlanta: Scholars Press, 1987).

3. Unless otherwise noted, all letters cited in this article to or from Orlinsky are found in MS Collection No. 661, Harry Meyer Orlinsky Papers, of the American Jewish Archives (AJA), Cincinnati, OH. I offer my sincerest thanks to the AJA staff, who, over the years, have welcomed me warmly and helped me more than words can

adequately describe. My thanks also to the Graduate School at Creighton University for its support for my travel and research in Cincinnati.

4. Jonathan D. Sarna, *JPS: The Americanization of Jewish Culture 1888–1988* (Philadelphia: JPS, 1989), esp. 113–116; and Jonathan D. Sarna and Nahum M. Sarna, "Jewish Bible Scholarship and Translations in the United States," in *The Bible and Bibles in America*, ed. Ernest S. Frerichs (Atlanta: Scholars Press, 1988), 100–103.

5. For this expression, see Greenspoon, *Margolis*, 110, where another expression of Margolis's, this one of unalloyed affection, is cited; namely, his description of his daughter as "the contemporary of my work on Joshua." Margolis authored numerous scholarly articles on the Septuagint. Four parts of his magnum opus, *The Book of Joshua in Greek*, were published between 1931 and 1938. The fifth part, long considered irretrievably lost, appeared in print in 1992. The full introduction to this work has never been found.

6. Orlinsky to Richardson, 30 November 1980, 661/13/2, Richardson, G. P. 1980–1983.

7. Ibid.

8. Adler to Orlinsky, 25 March 1931, 661/1/8, Adler, Cyrus, 1931–1940.

9. Orlinsky to Gentlemen, Dropsie College, 30 March 1931, 661/1/8, Adler, Cyrus, 1931–1940.

10. Adler to Orlinsky, 16 June 1938, 661/1/8, Adler, Cyrus, 1931–1940.

11. Oral interview with Orlinsky, cited in Greenspoon, *Margolis*, 37f.

12. Adler to Orlinsky, 16 June 1938, 661/1/8, Adler, Cyrus, 1931–1940.

13. Orlinsky to Kramer, 1 April 1989, Ms. 661/9/15, Kramer, Samuel N., 1951–1985. For a full exposition of Orlinsky's views on this issue, see his "The Masoretic Text: A Critical Evaluation," which served as the Prolegomenon to the reprinting of Christian D. Ginsberg, *Introduction to the Massoretico-Critical Edition of the Hebrew Bible* (New York: KTAV, 1996), I–XLV. Ginsberg's study had originally appeared in 1897.

14. Orlinsky to Montgomery, 8 June 1940, 661/11/3, Montgomery, James A., 1939–1945.

15. Published as *Max Leopold Margolis: Scholar and Teacher* (Philadelphia: Alumni Association, Dropsie College for Hebrew and Cognate Learning, 1952).

16. Orlinsky to Albright, 21 May 1951, 661/1/11, Albright, William F., 1941–1971.

17. This was Mrs. Margolis's shorthand method of referring to her husband's magnum opus, *The Book of Joshua in Greek* (see above).

18. Margolis to Orlinsky, 11 July 1941, 661/10/10, Margolis, Max Leopold, 1941–1942, 1951–1953. In general, Orlinsky felt that Margolis's understanding of the Septuagint was a vast improvement over most of those who preceded him and many of his contemporaries. There were, not unexpectedly, points at which Orlinsky differed with his teacher. With respect to the Septuagint version of Joshua, Margolis pictured the Greek translator as working with a consonantal text that was, for all intents and purposes, equivalent to the Masoretic Text (MT). In Margolis's analysis, differences between the MT and the LXX in the book of Joshua were almost always attributable to the translator himself, who typically curtailed the MT-type Hebrew with which he was working (see his remarks in "Specimen of a New Edition of the Greek Joshua," in *Jewish Studies in Memory of Israel Abrahams* [New York: Jewish Institute of Religion, 1927] 307–323). Orlinsky disagreed. In his opinion, the translator responsible for LXX Joshua adopted a mostly word-for-word approach to the task of rendering the

Hebrew into Greek. Thus, MT–LXX differences should be sought in the Hebrew that lay before the translator (that is, his *Vorlage)*, rather than linked to any initiative on the part of the translator (see especially Harry M. Orlinsky, "The Hebrew *Vorlage* of the Septuagint of the Book of Joshua," in *Congress Volume [Rome, 1968]* [Leiden: Brill, 1969], 187–195). This sort of disagreement among LXX scholars continues, in one form or another, to this very day.

19. Orlinsky to Margolis, 17 February 1942, 661/10/10, Margolis, Max Leopold, 1941–1942, 1951–1953.

20. Letter dated 19 January 1953, 661/10/10. Margolis's wife, Evelyn Aronson, was from a prominent Jewish family in San Francisco. She was a (much older) first cousin of Barry Goldwater.

21. Isaac Leeser, *The Twenty-Four Books of the Holy Bible: Hebrew and English* (Philadelphia: L. Johnson and Co., 1853–1854).

22. When the RSV Old Testament appeared in 1952, its editors, Orlinsky included, were subjected to searing criticism; in addition, copies of the book were burned. Critics of Orlinsky did not hesitate to mention his religion. Thus, Carl McIntire, "The New Bible [RSV]: Why Christians Should Not Accept It" (Collingswood, NJ: Christian Beacon, 1952), 15: "The committee actually included in its membership a Jew, Harry M. Orlinsky....A Jew does not accept the deity of Christ, but is Unitarian in belief, and this helps to explain the Unitarian emphasis dealing with the passages referring to the Messiah." And Joseph Hoffman Cohn, "The Revised Standard Version—A Sad Travesty: A Review" (New York: American Board of Missions to the Jews, Inc., 1952), 5: "One of these translators is a noted Jewish scholar, who, by very tradition, is bitterly opposed to the Christ as having been sent of God to bring to the world redemption....Was there assigned to this particular Jewish scholar the dominant control over how the principal Jewish passages that deal with the Lord Jesus Christ... should be interpreted? It is difficult to explain otherwise to our own satisfaction how there could have come about this strange perversion of divine truth." (I located copies of these and other pamphlets in the Archives of the Yale Divinity School, New Haven, Connecticut: MS 70, Papers of the Standard Bible Committee, 12/225 [for McIntire] and 12/226 [for Cohn].)

23. Orlinsky to Montgomery, 20 July 1945, 661/11/3.

24. Albright to Orlinsky, 6 August 1945, 661/1/11, Albright, William F., 1941–1971.

25. Orlinsky to Albright, 9 August 1945, 661/1/11, Albright, William F., 1941–1971.

26. Orlinsky to Weigle, 4 April 1951, 661/17/3, American Standard Bible Committee. Correspondence, 1945–1965.

27. See especially the relevant chapters in Harry M. Orlinsky, *Essays in Biblical Culture and Bible Translation* (New York: Ktav, 1974).

28. Grayzel to Weigle, 21 March 1955, 661/17/3, American Standard Bible Committee. Correspondence, 1945–1965.

29. It was in the 1960s that the Torah portion of the new translation began to appear in print. The entire translation was first published in 1985 as *TANAKH. A New Translation of THE HOLY SCRIPTURES According to the Traditional Hebrew Text* (it contained revisions from earlier publications of the Torah, the Prophets, and the Writings). In 1999 the JPS produced the first edition of its *TANAKH* with Hebrew and English texts on facing pages.

30. Draft letter to the Editor, *The Jewish Chronicle*, 23 October 1962, 661/16/26, Zussman, Lesser, 1962–1963.

31. This volume appeared in 1969 as Harry M. Orlinsky, *Notes on the New Translation of the Torah* (Philadelphia: Jewish Publication Society, 1969).

32. Orlinsky to Grayzel, 6 September 1963, Ms. 661/1/31, Baron, Salo, 1963, 1980–1987.

33. Orlinsky to Ulrich, 27 June 1980, 661/15/26, Ulrich, Eugene, 1979–1982.

34. Orlinsky to Metzger, 8 December 1980, 661/10/24, Metzger, Bruce, 1969, 1976–1990.

35. Orlinsky to Metzger, 9 November 1983, 661/10/24, Metzger, Bruce, 1969, 1976–1990.

36. Orlinsky to Potok, 5 July 1990, 661/12/22, Potok, Chaim, 1984–1990. This volume appeared as Harry M. Orlinsky and Robert G. Bratcher, *A History of Bible Translation and the North American Contribution* (Atlanta: Scholars Press, 1991). An entire chapter (chapter VII, "Male Oriented Language Originated by Bible Translators," 267–277) is devoted to the issue of inclusive-language Bibles.

37. Leonard Greenspoon, "On the Jewishness of Modern Jewish Biblical Scholarship: The Case of Max L. Margolis," *Judaism* 39 (1990): 82–92. Margolis had written and spoken quite forthrightly on these issues. Among the evidence I adduced in support of this view are Margolis's private statements—e.g., in a letter to Kaufmann Kohler (April 1905), "If Christian scholars, like Kittel and Budde, bluntly assert that their exegesis of the OT is and must be Christian, well then...my understanding of the OT is and must be Jewish"—and observations in scholarly publications—e.g., in an article titled, "The Scope and Methodology of Biblical Philology" (*JQR* n.s. 1 [1910/11]: 32f), "Only a Jew who knows himself at one with the Bible religion can adequately interpret the Scriptures....Only a Jew can say on approaching Holy Writ: This is the flesh of my flesh, and bone of my bones."

38. Orlinsky to Albright, 661/1/11, Albright, William F., 1941–1971.

39. Orlinsky to Elliger, 15 November 1951, 661/4/23, Elliger, D. Karl, 1951, n.d.

40. Orlinsky to Weigle, 18 January 1955, 661/17/3, American Standard Bible Committee. Correspondence, 1945–1965. It is difficult to suppress the thought that, had Margolis lived to see Orlinsky's career flourish, he would have applied to his student the title "Jewish expounder of the Bible," one who is (in Margolis's words, taken from the *JQR* article cited in the previous note) "at home in patristic literature as well as in Mishnah and Talmud and Midrash....There is not a verse, there is not a word in the Bible that has not a long history of interpretation behind which one must know, and know at once for immediate use." There is a real kinship here (often in the Jewish tradition, as early as the Hebrew Bible, the relationship between teacher and student is described in terms of parent-child): Each of these men had, in his own way and in his own circumstances, faced and overcome opposition from both Jews and non-Jews about the validity and significance of their choice—as Jews and as academic scholars—to focus so much of their attention and efforts on the Bible.

41. Jacobs to Orlinsky, 3 December 1982, 661/8/9, Jacobs, Maurice, 1959, 1979–1982.

Chapter 16 - Rethinking the History of Nonobservance as an American Orthodox Jewish Lifestyle

1. Charles S. Liebman, "Orthodoxy in American Jewish Life," *American Jewish Year Book* 66 (1965): 27–28, 30–31, 34–36, 48, 67, 90.
2. Jeffrey S. Gurock, *From Fluidity to Rigidity: The Religious Worlds of Conservative and Orthodox Jews in Twentieth Century America* (Ann Arbor, MI: Jean and Samuel Frankel Center for Judaic Studies, University of Michigan, 1998), 5–6; idem; "Twentieth-Century American Orthodoxy's Era of Non-Observance, 1900–1960," *The Torah u-Madda Journal* 9 (2000): 87–88. On other definitions of "non-observance," see for example, Jacob J. Schacter, "Preface," in *Jewish Tradition and the Non-traditional Jew,* ed. Jacob J. Schacter (Northvale, NJ: Jason Aronson, 1992), xiv–xvii. On response to competing movements defined as nonobservant, see also in that volume Judith Bleich, "Rabbinic Responses to Nonobservance in the Modern Era," 37–115. See also Adam S. Ferziger, *Exclusion and Hierarchy: Orthodoxy, Nonobservance and the Emergence of Jewish Identity* (Philadelphia: University of Pennsylvania Press, 2005), which, like my work, speaks of personal deviants even as it focuses on delineating Orthodox responses to them in Europe.
3. Gurock, *Orthodox Jews in America* (Bloomington, IN: Indiana University Press, 2009).
4. On the problem of corruption in kosher meat industries, see, for example, Harold P. Gastwirt, *Fraud, Corruption and Holiness: The Controversy over the Supervision of Jewish Dietary Practice in New York City, 1881–1940* (Port Washington, NY: Kennikat Press, 1974). On rabbinical violations of Prohibition, see Hannah Sprecher, "'Let *Them* Drink and Forget *Our* Poverty': Orthodox Rabbis React to Prohibition," *American Jewish Archives* (Fall/Winter 1991): 135–179. On the issue of recalcitrant husbands, see, for example, www.agunahinternational.org for the activities of those who oppose this abuse of the *halakhah.*
5. For this case study and discussion, see Gurock, *Orthodox Jews*, prologue.
6. For a learned discussion of the chronology for the term "Orthodoxy" as applied initially to eighteenth and nineteenth century Europe, see Jacob Katz, "Orthodoxy in Historical Perspective," *Studies in Contemporary Jewry* 2 (1986): 3–17.
7. Jacob Rader Marcus, *The Jew in the American World: A Source Book* (Detroit: Wayne State University Press, 1996), 142–143. On the use of this source as evidence of the lack of observance in eighteenth century America, see for example, Jonathan D. Sarna, *American Judaism: A History* (London and New Haven: Yale University Press, 2004), 45–46; Abraham J. Karp, *Haven and Home: A History of the Jews in America* (New York: Schocken Books, 1985), 22–23; Howard Sachar, *A History of the Jews in America* (New York: Knopf, 1992), 27.
8. I.J. Benjamin, *Three Years in America, 1859–1862* Vol. 1, trans. Charles Reznikoff (Philadelphia: Jewish Publication Society, 1956), 79–80, 235–36; Vol. 2, 95.
9. Hyman L. Meites, *History of the Jews of Chicago* (Chicago: The Jewish Historical Society of Illinois, 1924), 40.
10. Abram Vossen Goodman, "A Jewish Peddler's Diary," *American Jewish Archives* (June, 1951): 98, 99, 107. Kohn's statement about his religious problem can be characterized as the "classic" statement on the subject, since virtually every historian who has attempted to highlight this issue of identity has relied on this diary as representative of the thousands of immigrant merchants who were so perturbed. See, for ex-

ample, Lee Max Friedman, "The Problems of Nineteenth Century American Jewish Peddlers," *Publications of the American Jewish Historical Society* 44 (1954):1–7; Sarna, 70; Hasia Diner, *A Time for Gathering: The Second Migration, 1820–1880* (Baltimore and London: Johns Hopkins University Press, 1992), 67; Marcus, *Memoirs of American Jews, 1775–1865*, Vol. 3 (Philadelphia: Jewish Publication Society, 1956), 6–8; Leon Jick, *The Americanization of the Synagogue, 1820–1870* (Hanover, NH: The University Press of New England, 1992), 34–36.

11. Goodman, 97.

12. Diner, 67–69.

13. Jeremiah J. Berman, "The Trend in Jewish Religious Observance in Mid-Nineteenth Century America," *Publications of the American Jewish Historical Society* (1944):39–41.

14. On the ethnic and socioeconomic backgrounds of most Jews who migrated to midcentury America, see Diner, 21–24. On the implications of their being unaware of liberalization of Judaism in Germany see Jick, 30, 41–42.

15. Kimmy Caplan, *Orthodoxy in the New World: Immigrant Rabbis and Preaching in America (1881–1924)* [Hebrew] (Jerusalem: Zalman Shazar Center for Jewish History, 2002), 215–217.

16. Ibid.

17. On the ideology and activities of the eastern Jewish Enlightenment (Haskalah) see, for example, Michael Stanislawski, *For Whom Do I Toil?: Judah Leib Gordon and the Crisis of Russian Jewry* (New York and Oxford: Oxford University Press, 1988), 5–7, 25–27. On the decline of ritual observance among enlightened Jews of this time period in eastern Europe, see ChaeRan Y. Freeze, *Jewish Marriage and Divorce in Imperial Russia* (Waltham, MA: Brandeis University Press, 2002), 196–98; See also Salo W. Baron, *The Russian Jew under Tsars and Soviets* (New York: Macmillan, 1964), 126–131, 137–140, 144–146.

18. Elias Tcherikower, ed., *The Early Jewish Labor Movement in the United States*, trans. and ed. Aaron Antonovsky (New York: YIVO, 1961), 254, 266.

19. For Rabbi Jacob David Willowski's negative evaluation of American Jews, see *American Hebrew* (4 January 1901): 236.

20. For an early twentieth century sociologists' understanding of the social pressures that led men to cut their beards, see Julius Greenstone, "Religious Activity," in *The Russian Jews in the United States*, ed. Charles Bernheimer (Philadelphia: John C. Winston, 1905), 158.

21. Joshua Hoffman, "The Institution of the *Mikvah* in America," in *Total Immersion: A Mikvah Anthology*, ed. Rivkah Slonim and Liz Rosenberg (Northvale, NJ: Jason Aronson, 1997), 78, 83. See also Asher C. Oser, "The Promotion of *Mikvah* Ritual, 1900–1920," seminar paper (University of Connecticut, 2007).

22. Ephraim Lisitsky, *In the Grip of Cross Currents*, quoted in excerpt form in Irving Howe and Kenneth Libo, eds., *How We Lived: A Documentary History of Immigrant Jews in America, 1880–1930* (New York: Richard Marek, 1979), 96.

23. On this family phenomenon in an immigrant community in a small town outside of New York, see Ewa Morawska, *Insecure Prosperity: Small-Town Jews in Industrial America, 1890–1940* (Princeton, NJ: Princeton University Press, 1996), 156–157.

24. On the phenomenon of early Saturday morning services for workers about to go to their labors, see Herbert S. Goldstein, ed., *Forty Years of Struggle for a Principle: The*

Biography of Harry Fischel (New York: Bloch Publishing Company, 1928), 17–19, cited in Sarna, *American Judaism*, 163.

25. Hutchins Hapgood, *The Spirit of the Ghetto: Studies of the Immigrant Quarter of New York* (New York: Funk and Wagnalls, 1902), 125–126.

26. Andrew R. Heinze, *Adapting to Abundance: Jewish Immigrants, Mass Consumption and the Search for American Identity* (New York: Columbia University Press, 1990), 65–66.

27. Tony Michels, *A Fire in their Hearts: Yiddish Socialists in New York* (Cambridge, MA and London: Harvard University Press, 2005), 184, 186. See also Annie Polland, "The Sacredness of the Family: New York's Immigrant Jews and their Religion, 1890–1930," doctoral dissertation (Columbia University, 2004), 72, 75, 77.

28. William B. Helmreich, *The Enduring Community: The Jews of Newark and Metrowest* (New Brunswick, NJ: Transaction Publishers, 1999), 247.

29. Samuel Koenig, "The Socioeconomic Structure of an American Jewish Community" in *Jews in a Gentile World: The Problem of Anti-Semitism*, ed. Isacque Graeber and Stuart Henderson (New York: Macmillan, 1942), 227, 229; Victor B. Geller, *Orthodoxy Awakens: The Belkin Era and Yeshiva University* (Jerusalem and New York: Urim Publications, 2003), 34.

30. On the numerical decline of Orthodoxy in the early postwar period, see Bernard Lazerwitz and Michael Harrison, "American Jewish Denominations: A Social and Religious Profile," *American Sociological Review* (August, 1979): 659–661. On the hegemony of Conservativism during this same period, see Jack Wertheimer, "The Conservative Synagogue" in *American Synagogue: A Sanctuary Transformed*, ed. Jack Wertheimer (New York: Cambridge University Press, 1987), 123–126. See also Marshall Sklare, *Conservative Judaism: An American Religious Movement* (Glencoe, IL: University of Illinois Press, 1955), 199–212. On that significant rabbinical decision on driving, see "Responsum on the Sabbath," *Rabbinical Assembly Proceedings* 14 (1950):112–118.

31. On the transplantation and impact of these sectarian Jews see, for example, William Helmreich, *The World of the Yeshiva: An Intimate Portrait of Orthodox Jewry* (New York: Free Press, 1982); Jerome R. Mintz, *Hasidic People: A Place in the New World* (Cambridge: Harvard University Press, 1992).

32. Alvin I. Schiff, "Worlds in Collision or Collaboration: Synagogues, Schools and Yeshivot," presentation to the Rabbinical Council of America (June, 1993), 4, noted and discussed in Wertheimer, "Jewish Education in the United States," *American Jewish Year Book* (1999): 60.

33. Helmreich, "Trends within Contemporary Orthodoxy," *Judaism* (Fall 1981): 381–382.

34. Shmuel Singer, "Orthodox Judaism and the Smaller American Community," *Tradition* (Spring 1986): 59–63.

35. Gurock, *Orthodoxy in Charleston: Brith Sholom Beth Israel and American Jewish History* (Charleston, SC: College of Charleston Library, 2004), 74.

Chapter 17 - The United States in Abba Hillel Silver's World View

1. This article is a revised edition of my Hebrew publication in *Michael: On the History of the Jews in the Diaspora* 15, ed. Robert Rockaway and Shlomo Simonsohn (Tel Aviv: Diaspora Research Institute, 2000), ix–xxv.

Allon Gal and Ofer Shiff, "Abba Hillel Silver: Judaism and Zionism," (Hebrew) *Iyunim Bitkumat Israel: Studies in Zionism, the Yishuv and the State of Israel* 8 (1998): 687–698; see also *The Journal of Israeli History* 17, no. 1 (Spring 1996) devoted to Abba Hillel Silver, esp. Hasia Diner's, "Zion and America: The Formative Visions of Abba Hillel Silver," 45–69; David H. Shpiro, *From Philanthropy to Activism: The Political Transformation of American Zionism in the Holocaust Years, 1933–1945* (Oxford: Pergamon Press, 1994), *passim*; H. L. Feingold, *The Jewish People in America: A Time for Searching, Entering the Mainstream 1920–1945* (Baltimore and London: Johns Hopkins University Press, 1992), 189–265; Marc Lee Raphael, *Abba Hillel Silver: A Profile in American Judaism* (New York: Holmes and Meier, 1989), 77–217; Allon Gal, *David Ben Gurion and the American Alignment for a Jewish State* (Bloomington and Jerusalem: Indiana University Press and Magnes Press, 1991), 99–208; Zvi Ganin, *Truman, American Jewry, and Israel, 1945–1948* (New York: Holmes and Meier, 1979), *passim*; Melvin I. Urofsky, *We Are One!: American Jewry and Israel* (Garden City, NY: Anchor Press, 1978), 17–254.

2. See n. 1.

3. Ibid.

4. Abba Hillel Silver, "The Spiritual Legacy of the Pilgrim Fathers" (sermon). The Temple, 14 November 1920. Papers of Rabbi Abba Hillel Silver (microfilm edition), Series IV, Folder 84/44, Sede Boqer Campus: Ben-Gurion Research Institute, Ben-Gurion University, Israel (hereafter referred to as the Silver Archive).

5. Ibid.

6. Abba Hillel Silver, "Woodrow Wilson" (sermon), The Temple, 10 February 1924, in *A Word in Its Season: Selected Sermons, Addresses and Writings of Abba Hillel Silver,* Vol. 2, ed. H Weiner (New York: World Publishing Co., 1972), 351–358.

7. Abba Hillel Silver, "What Has Become of the Melting Pot?" (sermon), The Temple, 22 October 1922, Series IV, Folder 145/138, Silver Archive.

8. A.H. Silver, "Making America Safe for Difference" (sermon), The Temple, 23 February 1936, Series IV, Folder 497/447, Silver Archive.

9. Abba Hillel Silver, "In the Midst of Many Peoples," in his *The World Crisis and Jewish Survival: A Group of Essays* (New York: R.R. Smith, 1941), 143–193, esp. 171–177.

10. Ibid., 189–190.

11. Abba Hillel Silver, "The Strength...Which Is America," *Ohio Schools* (Sept. 1940): 314–315, 336–337.

12. Raphael, 35–41, 109.

13. Ibid. See also n. 14, 15.

14. Abba Hillel Silver, "Thoughts on the Coming Elections" (sermon), The Temple, 27 October 1940, Series IV, Folder 159/614, Silver Archive.

15. Ibid.

16. Gal, *David Ben Gurion*, 65–83 on Silver's political career.

17. Silver's lecture dividing the history of Zionism into periods: "Problems and Prospects of American Judaism," lecture delivered at The Hebrew Union College, 12 March 1950, reprinted in *Therefore Choose Life: Selected Sermons, Addresses, and Writings of Abba Hillel Silver* Vol. 1, ed. Herbert Weiner (Cleveland: World Publishing Co., 1967), 404–417.

18. For the most conspicuous political speeches by Silver during the 1940s see Abba Hillel Silver, *Vision and Victory: A Collection of Addresses, 1942–1948* (New York: Zionist Organization of America, 1949), esp. 1–193.

19. Abba Hillel Silver, "Spiritual Return and National Redemption" in *Central Conference of American Rabbis 53rd Annual Convention, 24 February–1 March 1942*, Vol. 7 (Cincinnati: CCAR, 1942), 239–253, 247.

20. Ibid., esp. 240–243.

21. Regarding the centrality of democracy in the thought and personality of Silver, and also in his role as a Reform rabbi, see his book, *The Democratic Impulse in Jewish History* (New York: Bloch, 1928); Abba Hillel Silver, "The Rediscovery of Judaism" in *World Crisis and Jewish Survival*, quotation from 68 and esp. 63–70.

22. See, for example, his sermon on Independence Day, "The Religious Roots of Democracy," Cain Park Sunday evening service, 4 July 1943, Series V, Folder 638/43, Silver Archive.

23. Ibid. "The New Year, 1949" (sermon), The Temple, 1 January 1949, Series IV, Folder 167/117, Silver Archive.

24. Abba Hillel Silver, "One Hundred Years of American History" (sermon), The Temple, 30 October 1949, reprinted in *A Word In Its Season*, 280.

25. Ibid., 284–285.

26. Ibid., 285–286.

27. Ibid., 286–287.

28. Ibid., 286–288.

29. Ibid., 288.

30. Abba Hillel Silver, "One Hundred years of American History" (sermon), The Temple, 6 November 1949, reprinted in *A Word In Its Season*, 289–297.

31. The changes in Silver's Zionism are only beginning to be studied; meanwhile, it is possible to suggest that what are typical of the post-Holocaust period are his impressions of his visit to Israel and of the American Zionist Agency Conference in 1951. Both of these influences caused Silver to take note of the vitality, the dynamic quality, and the signs of national pride which arose against the background of the Holocaust and the harsh economic situation See his "Writings: ZOA, 1951," 76–85, Series V, Folder 183/813, Silver Archive. In regard to his Republican affinity during the 1950s, see Raphael, 197–201.

32. Abba Hillel Silver, "Problems and prospects" reprinted in *Therefore Choose Life*, esp. 407–408.

33. Abba Hillel Silver, "The Questions that Await Us," Tercentenary Address, Detroit, 17 October 1954, reprinted in *Therefore Choose Life*, 299ff.

34. Ibid., 300–302.

35. Ibid., 302.

36. Abba Hillel Silver, "A Great Age and a Frightened America" (sermon), The Temple, 6 April 1952, reprinted in *A Word In Its Season*, 241–248.

37. Ibid.

38. Abba Hillel Silver, "Benjamin Franklin" (sermon), The Temple, 22 January 1956, reprinted in *A Word in its Season*, 398–404.

39. Ibid., 403–404.

40. Ibid. See the editor's note on 614.

41. Ibid.

42. Abba Hillel Silver, "John F. Kennedy," in *A Word In Its Season*, 417.

43. Ibid., 420–421.

44. Ibid.

45. Ibid., 422.

46. Ibid.

47. Allon Gal, "The Mission Motif in American Zionism (1898–1948)," *American Jewish History* LXXV, no. 4 (June 1986): 363–385; Allon Gal, "ha-Tsiyonut ha-Amerika'it Bein Shetei Milhamot ha-Olam: Me'afyenim Ra'ayoniyim," (Hebrew) *Yahadut Zemanenu* 5 (1989): 79–90.

48. Israel Goldstein, *My World as a Jew: the Memoirs of Israel Goldstein* Vol. 2 (New York: Herzl Press, 1984), 342.

49. Ibid., 342–343.

50. For background see Allon Gal, "ha-Tsiyonut ha-Amerika'it," esp. 81–83.

51. Michael A. Meyer, "Abba Hillel Silver as Zionist within the Camp of Reform Judaism," *Journal of Israeli History* 17, no. 1 (Spring 1996): 9–31.

Chapter 18 - Heschel and the Roots of *Kavanah*

1. See Michael A. Meyer, "The Refugee Scholars Project of the Hebrew Union College" in *A Bicentennial Festschrift for Jacob Rader Marcus*, ed. Bertram W. Korn (New York: Ktav, 1976), 359–375. On the impact of Heschel in America, see S. Daniel Breslauer, *The Impact of Abraham Joshua Heschel as Jewish Leader in the American Jewish Community from the 1960s to His Death: A Social, Psychological and Intellectual Study*, doctoral dissertation (Brandeis University, 1974); Hillel Goldberg, "Abraham Joshua Heschel And His Times," *Midstream* 28, no. 4 (1982): 36–42; Hillel Goldberg, *Between Berlin and Slobodka: Jewish Transition Figures From Eastern Europe* (Hoboken, NJ: Ktav, 1989), especially 115–136; Robert G. Goldy, *The Emergence of Jewish Theology in America* (Bloomington and Indianapolis: Indiana University Press, 1990); Edward K. Kaplan, *Holiness In Words: Abraham Joshua Heschel's Poetics of Piety* (Albany, NY: State University of New York Press, 1996), 7–18; and most comprehensively, Edward K. Kaplan, *Spiritual Radical: Abraham Joshua Heschel in America* (New Haven and London: Yale University Press, 2007). For compelling evidence of the impact of Heschel on rabbinical students in the 1960s, see Charles S. Liebman, "The Training of American Rabbis," *American Jewish Year Book* 69 (1968): 84–85.

2. "Idols in the Temples" in *The Insecurity of Freedom* (Philadelphia: Jewish Publication Society, 1966), 66.

3. "Existence and Celebration," in *Moral Grandeur and Spiritual Audacity*, ed. Susannah Heschel (New York: Farrar, Straus and Giroux, 1996), 27.

4. See "Teaching Religion to American Jews" [1956] as reprinted in *Moral Grandeur*, 148.

5. Quoted in Morris M. Faierstein, "Abraham Joshua Heschel and the Holocaust," *Modern Judaism* 19 (1999): 269.

6. Samuel H. Dresner, *Heschel, Hasidism and Halakha* (New York: Fordham University Press, 2002), 92.

7. *God In Search of Man* (New York: Farrar, Straus and Cudahy, 1956), 3. Arnold M. Eisen, *Taking Hold of Torah: Jewish Commitment and Community in America* (Bloomington and Indianapolis: Indiana University Press, 1997), 17–18. The com-

ment is worth recording here: "'My God!' I exclaimed ... 'He's been to my shul!' Heschel knew! I noted excitedly that he had not excluded Judaism from the category of religion gone stale. My anger was legitimate. I was not supposed to be tolerant of what I saw all around me!"

8. See "Carl Stern's Interview with Dr. Heschel" (1972) as reprinted in *Moral Grandeur*, 412.

9. "Existence and Celebration," 27.

10. Heschel chose to close *The Insecurity of Freedom* with a translation of the last chapter of his 1934 biography of Maimonides, which he wrote in Germany. The account of the late Maimonides spending more and more time engaged in the ills of his patients and away from his books mirrored his own journey from the book-lined study to the barricades. See *The Insecurity of Freedom*, 285–298.

11. *The Prophets* (Philadelphia: Jewish Publication Society, 1962), 16.

12. "Religion and Race," (1963) as reprinted in *The Insecurity of Freedom*, 93.

13. "The Reasons for My Involvement in the Peace Movement," (1973) as reprinted in *Moral Grandeur*, 225.

14. "A Prayer for Peace," (1971) as reprinted in *Moral Grandeur*, 232.

15. *A Concise Dictionary of Hebrew Philosophical Terms* (mimeographed, Cincinnati, 1941), 34.

16. *Man's Quest for God: Studies in Prayer and Symbolism* (New York: Charles Scribners Sons, 1954), 11–14; 84–85.

17. Ibid., 34, 53, 64.

18. Ibid., 53. See Mordecai M. Kaplan, *Judaism as a Civilization* [1934] (Philadelphia: Jewish Publication Society, 1984), 425–430; Mel Scult, *Judaism Faces the Twentieth Century: A Biography of Mordecai M. Kaplan* (Detroit: Wayne State University Press, 1993), 154–178; David Kaufman, *Shul With A Pool* (Hanover, NH: Brandeis University Press/University Press of New England, 1999), especially 242–274.

19. *Man's Quest for God*, 65. See also Heschel's *Heavenly Torah: As Refracted through the Generations* (New York and London: Continuum, 2005), 200–207. The Hebrew original of this section was published in 1962. See Gordon Tucker's comment, 204, n. 37.

20. *Man's Quest for God*, 85. Significantly, this comment was originally made in a 1953 address to the Rabbinical Assembly of America. See "The Spirit of Jewish Prayer," (1953) as reprinted in *Moral Grandeur*, 121. See also Kaplan, *Spiritual Radical*, 146–156.

21. See Aaron L. Mackler: "Symbols, Reality and God: Heschel's Rejection of a Tillichian Understanding of Religious Symbols," *Judaism* 40, no. 3 (1991): 290–300; Edward K. Kaplan, *Holiness in Words*, 75–89; Michael Marmur, "In Search of Heschel," *Shofar* 26, no.1 (2007): 38–40.

22. *Man's Quest for God*, 136–137. The complex question of what Heschel has in mind in his disparaging remarks about "symbolic thinking" lie outside the range of this article.

23. "Toward An Understanding of Halacha," (1953) as reprinted in *Moral Grandeur*, 140.

24. Ibid., 143.

25. *A Passion for Truth* (New York: Farrar, Straus and Giroux, 1973), 42.

26. *Kotzk: The Struggle for Integrity* (Tel Aviv: Ha-Menorah, 1973), 35–37.

27. Interestingly, Eisen himself has warned against "undue concentration" on this work, and calls for a shift "away from an exclusive reliance on *Search*." See Arnold Eisen, "Re-reading Heschel on the Commandments," *Modern Judaism* 9, no.1 (1989): 1–3. For an early example of the view regarding *Search* as Heschel's *Summa*, see Franklin Sherman, "Abraham Joshua Heschel: Spokesman for Jewish Faith," *Lutheran World* 10 (1963): 400–408.

28. *Search*, 341.

29. Ibid., 387.

30. Ibid., 316.

31. Ibid., 317.

32. Norman Lamm, *Seventy Faces: Articles of Faith*, Vol.1 (Hoboken, NJ: Ktav, 2001), 61. The passage in question is from *Athvan Deoraitha* (Lemberg, 1891), Chapter 23, from 35b. Heschel provides a highly selective reading of Engel's argument.

33. *God in Search of Man*, 319.

34. Particularly interesting in this light is a phrase employed by Heschel in a private letter to Kaplan in February 1943 [located in the Heschel Papers, Box 2, at the Jewish Theological Seminary Archives (JTSA), New York]. He asserts that despite their differences, "the community of *kavanah* is more decisive than the difference of *nusach*."

35. The conditions in which these pieces were written have been evoked by Heschel's biographers, and are the subject of a forthcoming article by Michael Marmur, "Heschel the Teenage Halakhist in Warsaw." Having been tutored first by Bezalel Levy and then by the noted rabbi Menahem Zemba, Heschel was also linked with the Metivta Yeshiva in Warsaw. The journal *Shaarei Torah* had its offices on 4 Muranowska Street near—and actually on the same street as—the Heschel family home. Originally, Rabbi Shlomo Altman had established *Bet Midrash* as a separate publication in 1922, designed to challenge young men studying at the Metivta and elsewhere to sharpen their pilpulistic skills and demonstrate their capacity for *halakhic* creativity. Soon the decision was taken to publish *Bet Midrash* as a supplement to *Shaarei Torah*, a publication established in 1913 by Yitzhak Hacohen Feigenbaum and continued by his son, Yisrael Isser Feigenbaum. During the year 5683 (1922–1923) five editions of *Sha'arei Torah* with the *Bet Midrash* supplement were published. Abraham Joshua Heschel, who turned sixteen in the course of that year, published in three successive editions of the journal. It may be the case that this consistency says something about the regard in which he was held, at least by the editor of *Bet Midrash*, Rabbi Shlomo Altman. It is clear from comments made in the journal that competition among young scholars to have their novellae published was fierce. In the Av 5682 (1922) edition, Altman issued a stern warning that any attempts to apply undue pressure so that a particular piece be included would come to nought. To give a sense of how remarkable the appearance of three consecutive pieces by one young man was, it is worth noting that in those three editions some thirty-eight young scholars published in *Bet Midrash*: only Heschel and one other young man, Issac Katz of Rippin, had three pieces published. Another young man, Mendel Sirkes of Warsaw, however, had five pieces published in the space of two years. Most of the students just had one piece included by the editor. In 1922 we find the journal offering a prize of two thousand marks to the provider of the most convincing and harmonious explanation of a *halakhic* conundrum. For a brief mention of this journal and the circle of R. Isaac Feigenbaum (p.366) and for much useful information, see Abraham Zemba, "Metivta of Warsaw" [Hebrew] in

Jewish Institutions of Higher Learning in Europe; Their Development and Destruction [Hebrew], ed. Samuel K. Mirsky (New York: Ogen, 1956), 363–380.

36. Edward K. Kaplan and Samuel H. Dresner, *Abraham Joshua Heschel: Prophetic Witness* (New Haven and London: Yale University Press, 1998), 38–50.

37. Feigenbaum, an inhabitant of Lokacz, was associated with *Shaarei Torah* from 1910, the year in which the publication first appeared. He was one of its most prolific contributors. In 1931 he published a selection of responsa, all of which are dedicated to rabbis and emerging scholars. See *Meshiv Shalom* (Bilgoray: Kronenberg, 1931). It is interesting to note that Feigenbaum did not include the present responsa in his collection.

38. This is our translation of the text found in the appendix, which is taken from the journal, *Shaarei Torah*, aleph.

39. See Abraham Joshua Heschel, *The Circle of the Baal Shem Tov: Studies in Hasidism*, ed. Samuel H. Dresner (Chicago and London: The University of Chicago Press, 1985), 9–10. The article on R. Pinchas of Koritz was originally published in Hebrew, "Le-Toldot R. Pinchas MiKoritz," in *Alei Ayin, Essays in Honor of Zalman Shicken* (Jerusalem: Schocken Press, 1948–1952), 213–244.

40. Ibid.

41. *God in Search of Man*, 315.

42. This is our translation/explication of the text found in the appendix, which is taken from the journal, *Shaarei Torah*, B.

43. *Torah min Hashamayim be-Aspeklaria Shel Ha-Dorot*, vol.3 (New York and Jerusalem: Jewish Theological Seminary, 1995), 120–122. Quotations from this work are taken from Gordon Tucker, ed., *Heavenly Torah*, 736–739. See also ibid., 594. The full extent of Heschel's deployment of this verse falls beyond the scope of our current article.

44. Tucker, ed., *Heavenly Torah*, 736.

45. Ibid., 738. In a footnote Heschel points out that according to one commentary this was not a one-time ruling.

46. Ibid., 738.

47. See *Spiritual Radical*, 323–324.

48. A.J. Heschel, "Jewish Education," [1953] as reprinted in *The Insecurity of Freedom*, 235. In a 1956 article ("Confusion of Good and Evil," as reprinted in *Insecurity of Freedom*, 139), Heschel paraphrases a tradition from *Midrash Tehillim* and adds his own interpretation: *There is not a single mitzvah which we fulfill perfectly...*except circumcision and the Torah that we study in our childhood, for these two acts are not infringed upon by "alien thoughts" or impure motivations. This statement implied a special status to the material considered in this article. It refers to a period before puberty and complexity changed the nature of his study.

49. Arthur Green, "Three Warsaw Mystics," *Jerusalem Studies in Jewish Thought* 13 (1996): 1–58. For the translated poems, see *The Ineffable Name of God: Man*, trans. Morton M. Leifman (London and New York: Continuum, 2004).

Chapter 19 - The Postwar Pursuit of American Jewish History and the Memory of the Holocaust

1. Jacob Rader Marcus, "The Program of the American Jewish Archives," *American Jewish Archives* 1 (1948): 2; Marcus continued into the 1950s to refer to the destruc-

tion of the larger portion of European Jewry as a reason—although certainly not *the* reason— to study American Jewish history. In one of his writings during the tercentenary year, he noted, "[S]ometimes . . . in the quiet and the solitude of our thoughts, we lift up our eyes and we recall what has happened abroad since 1939, particularly in central Europe. We are disturbed by the fact that a Jewry that we thought was secure has been destroyed, that five million Jews have been destroyed. We sometimes ask ourselves, How can we attain security? How can we survive as Jews and as an integral part of this great American Republic?" Marcus, "Three Hundred Years in America," in *The Dynamics of American Jewish History: Jacob Rader Marcus's Essays on American Jewish History*, ed. Gary P. Zola (Waltham, MA: Brandeis University Press, 2004), 124.

2. Jeffrey Gurock, "From Publications to American Jewish History: The Journal of the American Jewish Historical Society and the Writing of American Jewish History," *American Jewish History* 81 (Winter 1993/1994): 155–271.

3. A more detailed statement appears in my new book, *We Remember with Reverence and Love: American Jews and the Myth of Silence after the Holocaust, 1945–1962* (New York: New York University Press, 2009).

4. Salo Baron, *Steeled by Adversity: Essays and Addresses in American Jewish Life* (Philadelphia: Jewish Publication Society, 1971), 15.

5. Abraham Scheinberg, *American Jews: Their Lives and Achievements: A Contemporary Biographical Record* (New York: Golden Book Foundation of America, 1947), viii.

6. Philip Goodman to Bernard Bamberger, 17 November 1949, Synagogue Council of America (SCA) Papers, I-68, Box 27, "Jewish History Week" folder, AJHS, New York.

7. Lee M. Friedman, *Pilgrims in a New Land* (Philadelphia: Jewish Publication Society of America, 1948), 9, 113, 365, 367, 374–375; Anita Libman Lebson, *Pilgrim People* (New York: Harper and Brothers, 1950), 4, 409–410, 444–445, 455, 476, 460–461,480–487; see also Rufus Learsi, *The Jews in America: A History* (Cleveland: World Publishing, 1954), 291, 293, 295, 297–298, 301–305, 312; Oscar Handlin, *Adventures in Freedom: Three Hundred Years of Jewish Life in America* (New York: McGraw-Hill, 1954), vii–viii, 260; Morris U. Schappes, *The Jews in the United States: A Pictorial History 1654 to the Present* (New York: Citadel, 1958), 219–281.

8. Elma Ehrlich Levinger, *Jewish Adventures in America: The Story of 300 Years of Jewish Life in the United States* (New York: Bloch, 1954), 233–235, 238–240, 277.

9. Handlin, vii–viii.

10. Israel Goldstein, *American Jewry Comes of Age: Tercentenary Addresses* (New York: Bloch, 1955), 74, 90, 97, 127, 192–193, 146.

11. A dissident group, representing Jews further to the left than the "official" planning committee, also made use of the Holocaust in their "Declaration." "When we draw upon the bloody reckoning of World War II, of the numberless victims exacted from the Jewish People, we remember not only the martyrs murdered in the ghettoes and Hitler's slaughter camps, but also those Jews who wrote a chapter in the book of Jewish heroism. . . . We remain true," they wrote, "to the watchword: 'Never to forgive, Never to forget.' On this solemn occasion," they continued, "we recall with deepest pain the memory of the six million Jews who perished at the hands of the Nazis."

"Declaration: 300 Years of Jewish Life in America," Committee for the 300th Anniversary of Jewish Settlement in the USA, Adopted 19 June 1954 by the Preliminary Conference of the Committee for the 300th Anniversary of Jewish Settlement in the USA, American Jewish Tercentenary Collections, I–11/6/8, AJHS, New York.

12. "The Sisterhood Caravan Rolls On," *Biennial Assembly, National Federation of Temple Sisterhoods, February 13–17, 1954*, 53. [not listed]

13. Abraham Menes, "The East Side Matrix of the Jewish Labor Movement," *Judaism* 3 (Fall 1954): 366–380.

14. "Statement of Purpose," 1; Julius Horwitz, "Dachau—1955," 2–4; Ben Halpern, "America is Different," *Midstream* 1, no.1 (Autumn 1955): 39–52.

15. Morris U. Schappes, *The Jews of the United States: A Pictorial History 1654 to the Present* (New York: Citadel Press, 1958), 219, 225, 271; Schappes, given his Communist sympathies, could not resist using this history book and, in particular, the matter of the "six million" to venture out in a distinctive and combative mode. He used his book to condemn the American Jewish "plutocracy," the American Jewish Committee, and the B'nai B'rith during the Hitler years for their inaction. "Organizations like the B'nai B'rith were virtually paralyzed by this approach, and bestirred themselves mainly, as did the American Jewish Committee, with vain programs of research and publications." (225)

16. Albert Vorspan, *Giants of Justice* (New York: Union of American Hebrew Congregations, 1960), 39, 74, 111–116, 121–126, 186–187, 209, 241, 253; see also Philip Klutznick, *No Easy Answers* (New York: Farrar, Straus and Cudahy, 1961), 7, 9, 39, 67, 111.

17. "Send Your Child to One of the 145 AR Schools," "Jewish Education for Your Child," 2, Shul Propaganda" Jewish Labor Committee Collection, Box 2, "Shul Propaganda" folder, YIVO Archives, New York.

18. *The Souvenir Book of the Bicentennial: 1750–1950: The Story of the Celebration of the Bicentennial of the Charleston Jewish Community, November 19 through November 26, 1950* (Charleston, SC: Bicentennial Committee, 1951), 29, 83, 87, 91–92, 99, 103, 141. The official program book for the bicentennial included an address by the head of the local Jewish Community Center on the need to donate money to assist the survivors who were coming to Charleston.

19. Oscar Handlin and Mary Flug Handlin, *Danger in Discord: Origins of Anti-Semitism in the United States* (New York: Anti-Defamation League, 1948), 33–37; see also Handlin and Handlin, "A Century of Jewish Immigration to the United States," *American Jewish Year Book* 50 (1948/1949): 1, 13, 78, 80.

20. Handlin and Handlin, "The Acquisition of Political and Social Rights by the Jews in the United States," *American Jewish Year Book* 56 (1955): 84; Handlin, *Adventures in Freedom*, 207–209.

21. John F. Kennedy, *A Nation of Immigrants* (New York: Anti-Defamation League, 1959), 41.

22. Irving Lehrman and Joseph Rappaport, *The Jewish Community of Miami Beach* (New York: American Jewish History Center, 1954).

23. "A Duty of Conscience," *The Eternal Light* [Radio Program] (New York: The Jewish Theological Seminary of America, 8 October 1950), 3–4.

24. Speech, 19 February 1956, Minkoff Papers, Box 12, folder 11, Wagner Labor Archive, New York.

25. Harry Simonhoff, "FDR and the Jews," *Jewish Spectator*, 24, no. 8 (October, 1959): 10–12.
26. Jack Riemer, "Contemporary Issues: Eichmann," *Conservative Judaism* 15, no. 3 (Spring 1961): 35–36.
27. "Un-American Proposal," *Jewish Forum* 42, no. 3 (March, 1959): 32; "Justice Brandeis Award Ceremony," *Jewish Forum* 42, no. 3 (March, 1960): 32.
28. Jacob Glenn, "The Republican Record and the Jewish Vote," *Jewish Forum* 43, no. 10 (October, 1960): 172.
29. Ivan Schatten to *The Detroit Jewish News*, Box 1, "Correspondence as Jewish News Editor" folder, Philip Slomowitz Papers, P-84, AJHS, New York.

Chapter 20 - The Historical Consciousness of Mid-Century American Reform Judaism and the Historiography of Ellis Rivkin
1. See Michael A. Meyer, "Two Persistent Tensions within *Wissenschaft des Judentums*," in *Modern Judaism and Historical Consciousness: Identities, Encounters, Perspectives*, ed. Andreas Gotzmann and Christian Wiese (Leiden and Boston: Brill, 2007), 72–89, especially 73–76, 80–83.
2. I owe the term "midrashic existentialism" to Lance Sussman.
3. I am grateful to have been invited to contribute to this volume in honor of signal anniversaries of the American Jewish Archives, its journal, and of Gary Zola as its executive director. Dr. Zola and his staff have augmented with skillful dedication what our teacher Jacob Rader Marcus created, ensuring that the AJA holds a leading position in American Jewry's self-understanding and raising the field of American Jewish studies to a full-fledged and respected status in general historical scholarship. Congratulations. I would like to thank the following for reading versions of this essay and offering suggestions: Rabbis Jack Bemporad, Sanford Ragins, Lawrence Siegel, Mayer Selekman, and Judith Lewis. Also, I am grateful to Hunter colleagues Jack Salzman, Howard Chernick, and Richard Belsky for discussing various pertinent matters with me in connection with the piece. All the errors it contains are mine.
4. A selected bibliography of Rivkin's major works can be found in *My Life of Jewish Learning and Other Essays*, Occasional Papers in Jewish History and Thought, No. 24 (New York: Hunter College of The City University of New York, 2005), 47–49. A comprehensive account of Rivkin's oeuvre is Francis Barry Silberg's dissertation, *Aspects of the Life and Work of Ellis Rivkin: An Intellectual Biography with Annotated Bibliography* (Milwaukee: University of Wisconsin, 2004). It contains a chronological and topical bibliography of Rivkin's work (236 items, ranging from 1941 to 2004) with summaries and analyses of each piece, including unpublished works, some of which Silberg reconstructed from scattered notes. It also contains a glossary and an appendix on Rivkin's *Globalist Newsletter* as published from November 1975 to June 1994. A copy of Silberg's book is in the Klau Library of HUC-JIR in Cincinnati.
5. Robert M. Seltzer, *Jewish History after the End of Ideology*, Hunter Occasional Papers in Jewish History and Thought No. 9 (New York: Hunter College of The City University of New York, 2000), 7–12. I note that the integration of Jewish studies into academia has resulted in greater exactitude of research but a narrowing of purview.
6. There is a small but growing literature on this subject, for example, Johan Galtung and Sohail Inayatullah, eds., *Macrohistory and Macrohistorians: Perspectives in Individual, Social, and Civilizational Change* (Westport, CT: Praeger, 1991); Paul

Costello, *World Historians and Their Goals: Twentieth-Century Answers to Modernism* (DeKalb, IL: Northern Illinois University Press, 1993); Randall Collins, *Macrohistory: Essays in the Sociology of the Long Run* (Stanford, CA: Stanford University Press, 1999). I tried to apply the concept to Jewish history in "Since Graetz and Dubnow: The Dialectics of Macrohistory," *Jewish Studies Network* 2, no. 1 (Spring 1988): 1–4.

7. Isaiah Berlin, *The Hedgehog and the Fox: An Essay on Tolstoy's View of History* (Chicago: Ivan R. Dee, 1993), 3.

8. Among Rivkin's works of microhistory are articles and books defining the Pharisees, his book on the crucifixion of Jesus, and his examination of inquisitional sources connected with Converso confessions of secret Judaism. His main work of macrohistory is *The Shaping of Jewish History, A Radical New Interpretation* (New York: Charles Scribner's Sons, 1971), reprinted in 2003 by Behrman House under the title *The Unity Principle: The Shaping of Jewish History* with a foreword by Robert M. Seltzer and edited by Seymour Rossel.

9. The biographical information is drawn largely from Rivkin's presentation "My Life of Jewish Learning: An Odyssey from God to God," in *My Life of Jewish Learning and Other Essays*, 6–13. It should be supplemented by the more detailed account in Barry Silberg, *Aspects of the Life and Work of Ellis Rivkin*.

10. Ellis Rivkin, *My Life of Jewish Learning and Other Essays*, 9.

11. Ibid., 10–11.

12. Rivkin, *My Life of Jewish Learning and Other Essays*, 11.

13. Rivkin became full professor of Jewish history in 1953; Adolph S. Ochs Professor of Jewish History in 1965. As mentioned, he retired in 1988. For more biographical details, see the web page of the Rivkin Society at http://www.rivkinsociety.org/biography.html.

14. Samuel E. Karff, "Modalities of Jewish History" in the *Yearbook of the Central Conference of American Rabbis* LXXXIII (1973): 139.

15. Michael A. Meyer, "Rivkin on Jewish Modernity and Continuity," in *Structural Analysis: The Historiographical Method of Ellis Rivkin*, ed. Allen Podet (Potsdam, Germany: The Abraham Geiger College, and Diepenau, Germany: Goettert-Verlag, 2002), 218.

16. Herbert C. Zafren, "Ellis Rivkin's Development as a Scholar," in Podet, *Structural Analysis*, 385.

17. The book in which this article appeared was, appropriately, edited by Jacob Rader Marcus (Cincinnati: American Jewish Archives, 1958): 12–61. The two other pieces Rivkin wrote on the subject are "The Jew in American Society," *Yearbook of the Central Conference of American Rabbis* LXXVII (1967): 200–226; and "The American and American-Jewish Experience: A Study in Uniqueness" in *A Bicentennial Festschrift for Jacob Rader Marcus*, ed. Bertram Wallace Korn (Waltham, MA: American Jewish Historical Society and New York: Ktav Publishing House, 1976): 453–472. Two other related articles by Rivkin are a review of a book by Morris U. Schappes, "A Documentary History of the Jews in the United States, 1654–1875," *American Jewish Archives* (1952): 88–99; and "The Uniqueness of the American Jewish Experience" in *Jews in a Free Society: Challenges and Opportunities*, ed. Edward A. Goldman (Cincinnati: Hebrew Union College Press, 1978): 43–55.

18. See the footnote on p. 26 of "A Decisive Pattern in American Jewish History."

The rest of that footnote deals with the relationship of structural phases to each other.

19. Ibid., 23.

20. Ibid., 24.

21. Ibid., 25.

22. On p. 225 of his 1967 paper Rivkin remarked: "I could have tried to use another term than capitalism, so that it would be more acceptable, but I would be falsifying. What is developing is capitalism. Take a look at the Wall Street Journal and you see that capitalism is not withering away."

23. A convenient brief summary of the history of the concept is found in Raymond Williams, *Keywords: A Vocabulary of Culture and Society*, revised edition (New York: Oxford University Press, 1983): 50–52.

24. To be sure capitalists are found in pre-modern and in some non-European societies, for example in Sung China and Tokugawa Japan. There is a long-standing discussion among historians as to why China did not surge permanently ahead of Western Europe despite its head-start as an urbanized, commercial, and proto-industrial economy. A discussion that substantiates many of Rivkin's points is Randall Collins, "An Asian Route to Capitalism," in *Macrohistory*, 207–237.

25. "Decisive Pattern," 28.

26. Ibid., 29–30.

27. Rivkin does not discuss black slavery, which was a capitalist form of forced labor as property, not a medieval survival of serfdom.

28. Ibid., 31.

29. Ibid., 33.

30. Ibid., 36.

31. Ibid., 37.

32. Ibid., 38.

33. Ibid., 43.

34. Ibid., 51.

35. Ibid., 53

36. Ibid., 56.

37. Ibid., 57.

38. Ibid., 60.

39. Ibid., 61.

40. Rivkin, "The Jew in American Society," 200–201.

41. Ibid., 201.

42. Ibid., 204.

43. Ibid., 205.

44. Ibid., 206.

45. Ibid., 205.

46. Ibid., 207.

47. Ibid., 207–210.

48. Ibid., 213.

49. Ibid., 216. He was referring to the "bringing up to date" of Pope John XXIII's Second Vatican Council.

50. Ibid., 214.

51. Ibid., 215.

52. Ibid., 215–216.

53. Ibid., 216–217.
54. Ibid., 219.
55. Ibid., 222.
56. Ibid., 222–223.
57. *A Bicentennial Festschrift for Jacob Rader Marcus*, 453–482.
58. Ibid., 457–458.
59. Ibid., 458.
60. Ibid.
61. Ibid., 459–461.
62. E.g., Rivkin, "The Jew in American Society," 215; *Unity Principle*, 271–276.
63. "The American and American Jewish Experience," 462.
64. Ibid., 463.
65. Ibid., 464.
66. Ibid., 464.
67. Rivkin seems to mean that, on ibid., 454 at the top.
68. Ibid., 456.
69. Ibid., 466.
70. Ibid., 467.
71. Ibid., 468–469.
72. I will not be dealing in any detail with Rivkin's attitude toward the State of Israel, which he predicted would be in the future a Middle Eastern equivalent of Hong Kong, i.e., a key financial center in a regional common market that he expected to emerge in the process of globalization. He was writing this during the Oslo Accords of 1992.
73. Rivkin, *Unity Principle*, 307.
74. Ibid., 293.
75. His italics, 308.
76. Ibid., 316.
77. Ibid., 323–324.
78. Ibid., 325–326.
79. I thank Mayer Selekman for this definition. To me it sounds very Spinozistic, Spinoza being a philosopher whom Rivkin greatly admires. (Useful in this regard is D. D. Raphael, "Spinoza," in *Jewish Philosophy and Philosophers*, ed. Raymond Goldwater (London: The Hillel Foundation, 1962): 104–123. In Rivkin's formulation a sense of history is brought into Spinoza's conception of nature, which was what Hegel and the later Hegelians had sought to do. Pertinent is the account of the career of Hegelian thought in twentieth-century France: Michael S. Roth, *Knowing and History: Appropriations of Hegel in Twentieth-Century France* (Ithaca, NY: Cornell University Press, 1988) and his *The Ironist's Cage: Memory Trauma, and the Construction of History* (New York: Columbia University Press, 1995). Roth's books about the decline of Hegelianism in the post-war intellectual milieu suggest parallels with the declining appeal of Rivkin's approach to Jewish history among Reform rabbinical students in recent decades. Bringing Hegel in line with Jewish history, rather than Jewish history in line with Hegel, is Emil L. Fackenheim, "Moses and the Hegelians: Jewish Existence in the Modern World," in *Encounters Between Judaism and Modern Philosophy: A Preface to Future Jewish Thought* (New York: Basic Books, 1973): 79–169.
80. Robert M. Seltzer and Jack Bemporad, "Ellis Rivkin on Judaism and the Rise of

Christianity," in Podet, *Structural Analysis*, 304–323, especially 321–323. Also Robert M. Seltzer, "Foreword," to *The Unity Principle: The Shaping of Jewish History*," vii–xiii. Many of the essays in the Podet volume have pertinent critiques of Rivkin.

81. Samuel Karff, "Modalities of Jewish History," *CCAR Yearbook* Volume LXXVII (1973), 139–144.

82. Ibid., 139.

83. Ibid., 143.

84. Michael A. Meyer, "Rivkin on Jewish Modernity and Continuity," in Podet, *Structural Analysis*, 218–239. Ellis Rivkin's review-essay of Salo Baron, "The Writing of Jewish History," was published in New York by Futuro Press, n.d. It is a thirteen page reprint "with additions" of his piece in *The Reconstructionist Magazine* 25, no. 2 (15 June 1959):13–18 and 25, no. 10 (26 June 1959): 24–27. Rivkin's review was ostensibly of volumes two and three of the second, expanded edition of Baron's *Social and Religious History of the Jews* but actually dealt with Baron's historiography as a whole.

85. Meyer, "Rivkin on Jewish Modernity and Continuity," 223, 225, 229, 231. Both Karff's and Meyer's incisive critiques should be read in their entirety. I want to thank Rabbi Karff for going to the trouble of locating the original version in his personal archive, which allows me to claim that this piece for the American Jewish Archives is based on archival research.

86. It is "not accidental," as the Marxists used to say, that I wrote my dissertation on Dubnow after having earlier studied with Rivkin.

87. See Robert M. Seltzer, "Coming Home: The Personal Basis of Simon Dubnow's Ideology," *AJS Review* 1 (1976): 283–301.

88. Rivkin taught us to appreciate the work of Raphael Mahler, for example, who used a Marxist approach to investigate class conflicts within the Jewish community, such as between the Karaites and the Rabbanites or between the Galician *maskilim* and Hasidism. In a similar vein, when working on my master's thesis on the rise of Hasidism, Rivkin directed me to the valuable work of Benzion Dinur, who investigated tensions with the eighteenth-century East European *kehillot*, an important element in the rise of Beshtian Hasidism.

89. In *My Life of Jewish Learning and Other Essays*, Rivkin himself claimed to remember that as a child he was intrigued by Paul's agonies about his salvation in relation to his militant Pharisaism.

90. Rivkin, *Unity Principle*, 332.

91. "The Jew in American Society," 216–217.

92. On Krochmal, see Julius Guttmann, *Philosophies of Judaism: The History of Jewish Philosophy from Biblical Times to Franz Rosenzweig*, trans. David W. Silverman (New York: Holt, Rinehart, and Winston, 1964), 321–344. Also Robert M. Seltzer, *Jewish People, Jewish Thought* (New York: Macmillan, 1980), 570–579. The classic article on Krochmal's reputed Hegelianism is "Was Nachman Krochmal a Hegelian?" in Simon Rawidowicz, *Studies in Jewish Thought*, ed. Nahum N. Glazer (Philadelphia: Jewish Publication Society, 1974), 350–384.

93. I owe this comparison to Jack Bemporad, who heard about Wittgenstein's qualified admiration for Freud from the intellectual historian Stephen Toulmin. On this theme, Jacques Bouveresse, *Wittgenstein Reads Freud: The Myth of the Unconscious*, trans. Carol Cosman (Princeton, NJ: Princeton University Press, 1996), 3–20.

Chapter 21 - Telling the American Story: Yiddish and the Narratives of Children of Immigrants

1. Deborah Dash Moore, *At Home in America: Second Generation New York Jews* (New York: Columbia University Press, 1980), 10–11, 241.

2. Ibid., 11.

3. For a further discussion of these conclusions, see Rakhmiel Peltz, *From Immigrant to Ethnic Culture: American Yiddish in South Philadelphia* (Stanford: Stanford University Press, 1998), 173–217.

4. Irving Howe, with Kenneth Libo, *The World of Our Fathers* (New York and London: Harcourt Brace and Jovanovich, 1976), 262.

5. Peltz, 185–188.

6. Henry Feingold, *A Time for Searching: Entering the Mainstream, 1920–1945* (Baltimore and London: The Johns Hopkins University Press, 1992), 88.

7. Edward S. Shapiro, *A Time for Healing: American Jewry since World War II* (Baltimore and London: The Johns Hopkins University Press, 1992), 66–67.

8. Isaac Metzger, ed., *A Bintel Brief* (Garden City, NY: Doubleday and Co., 1971), 158–159. Although some of the most influential studies of Jewish immigrant life have relied on the Yiddish press, none have based their conclusions on archival studies of the newspapers' unpublished files and records, but rather have relied on published reports. Thus, we have little knowledge of the correspondence of the editors with authors or the public. Relying on published reports, the historians or editors cannot establish if the *Bintl briv* letters, for example, have been fabricated by the editors.

9. Sholem Ash, *Onkl Mozes* (Buenos Aires: Ateneo Literario en el IWO, 1973 [1918]), 22, 27. First published in 1918, this Yiddish novel was made into a popular 1932 Yiddish film in the United States starring Maurice Schwartz.

10. Ibid., 208.

11. Henry Roth, *Call It Sleep* (New York: Noonday Press, 1991 [1934]).

12. Peltz, 188–189.

13. Werner Sollors, "'A World Somewhere, Somewhere Else.' Language, Nostalgic Mournfulness, and Urban Immigrant Family Romance in *Call It Sleep*," in *New Essays on Call It Sleep*, ed. Hanna Wirth-Nesher (Cambridge and New York: Cambridge University Press, 1996), 130.

14. Ibid., 135.

15. Ibid., 160.

16. Ibid., 181–182, n. 84.

17. Joshua A. Fishman, with V.C. Nahirny, J.E. Hoffman, R. G. Hayden et al., *Language Loyalty in the United States* (The Hague: Mouton, 1966), 44.

18. Ibid., 43.

19. Joshua A. Fishman, ed., *The Rise and Fall of the Ethnic Revival: Perspectives on Language and Ethnicity* (Berlin: Walter de Gruyter, 1985), 130.

20. Ibid., 147.

21. Werner Sollors, *Beyond Ethnicity: Consent and Descent in American Culture* (New York: Oxford University Press, 1986), 37, 230; George De Vos and Lola Romanucci–Ross, "Ethnicity: Vessel of Meaning and Emblem of Contrast," in *Ethnic Identity: Cultural Continuities and Change*, ed. George De Vos and Lola Romanucci–Ross (Palo Alto, CA: Mayfield Publishing Company, 1975), 369.

22. Carol M. Eastman and Thomas C. Reese, "Associated Language: How Language and Ethnic Identity Are Related," *General Linguistics* 21 (1981): 110.

23. Rakhmiel Peltz, "The Changing Ethnic Identity of the New Jewish Elderly," *Journal of Aging and Judaism* 5 (1990): 65–69; Peltz, *From Immigrant to Ethnic* Culture, 212.

24. Joshua A. Fishman, "*Yerusholaymer 'velt-konferents far yidisher kultur' fun a sotsyo–lingvistishn kukvinkl*" (Jerusalem 'World Conference for Yiddish Culture' from a Sociolinguistic Viewpoint), *Yidishe shprakh* 35 (1976): 1–3, 16–31.

25. Veronika F. Rempusheski, "Caring for Self and Others: Second Generation Polish American Elders in an Ethnic Club," *Journal of Cross–Cultural Gerontology* 3 (1988): 223–271.

26. Mary L. Doi, "The Transformation of Ritual: The Nisei 60th Birthday," *Journal of Cross–Cultural Gerontology* 6 (1991): 153–163.

27. Joan Weibel–Orlando, "Indians, Ethnicity as a Resource and Aging: You Can Go Home Again," *Journal of Cross–Cultural Gerontology* 3 (1988): 323–348; Weibel–Orlando, "Grandparenting Styles: Native American Perspectives," in *The Cultural Context of Aging: Worldwide Perspectives*, ed. Jay Sokolovsky (New York: Bergin and Garvey, 1990), 109–125; Weibel–Orlando, *Indian Country, L.A.: Maintaining Ethnic Community in Complex Society* (Urbana: University of Illinois Press, 1991).

28. Micaela di Leonardo, *The Varieties of Ethnic Experience: Kinship, Class, and Gender among California Italian–Americans* (Ithaca, NY: Cornell University Press, 1984).

29. Mark R. Luborsky and Robert L. Rubinstein, "Ethnic Identity and Bereavement in Later Life: The Case of Older Widowers," in Sokolovsky, ed., 238.

30. American Jewish Archives, Loewenstein/Wiener Fellowship, summer 1984; AJA, Starkoff Fellow, 1989–1990.

31. Jacob Rader Marcus, interview by the author, Cincinnati, 8 August 1990.

32. Typescript Autobiography, Rabbi Herman Elliot Snyder, "Memories" attached at end, written December 1982, Manuscript Collection 598, Box 22, folder 4, American Jewish Archives (AJA), Cincinnati, Ohio.

33. Autobiography, Rabbi Simcha Kling, written 1982, Biographies Collection, AJA.

34. Transcript of Oral Memoir, Ruth Greenstein Feinberg, who grew up in Hartford, Connecticut, 4 February 1975, Biographies Collection, AJA; Bound Book, Florence Berman Karp, who grew up in Altoona, Pennsylvania, *Roses in December: A Memoir of My Parents* (Pittsburgh, PA: Wolfson Publishing Co., 1983), 30, 34–36, Biographies Collection, AJA; Published Booklet, Min Klein, who grew up in Greensboro, North Carolina, "This I Remember" (Greensboro, North Carolina, August 1981), 17–19, Histories Collection, Klein Family, AJA; Handwritten Autobiography, Lionel Koppman, who grew up in Waco, Texas, 12 May 1985, "What I Remember," written in Jackson Heights, New York City, quotations, pages 1, 6, Biographies Collection, AJA.

35. The initial work in this project that focuses on the narratives of children of immigrants was done while I was a Fellow of the Center for Judaic Studies, University of Pennsylvania (1996–1997). I also acknowledge the support of a fellowship from the Feinstein Center for American Jewish History, Temple University, Philadelphia, PA.

36. William Labov and Joshua Waletzky, "Narrative Analysis," in *Essays on Verbal and Visual Arts*, ed. June Helm (Seattle: University of Washington Press, 1967), 12–

44; William Labov, *Language in the Inner City: Studies in the Black English Vernacular* (Philadelphia: University of Pennsylvania Press, 1972).

37. Livia Polanyi, *Telling the American Story: A Structural and Cultural Analysis of Conversational Storytelling* (Cambridge, MA: MIT Press, 1989), 199.

38. Ibid., 198.

39. Peltz, *From Immigrant to Ethnic* Culture.

40. For example, see Moore, *At Home in America*.

41. Peltz, *From Immigrant to Ethnic Culture*, 122, 188.

42. Marea C. Teski, "Memory Practices: Growing Memories in Childhood Experience and Training," unpublished paper, 94th Annual Meeting (Washington, DC: American Anthropological Association, November 1995).

43. Marea Teski, "The Dynamics of Holographic Memory Repertoire in American, European, and Middle Eastern Individuals," Abstract, 95th Annual Meeting (San Francisco, CA: American Anthropological Association, November 1996).

44. Peltz, *From Immigrant to Ethnic* Culture, 182–184.

45. Polanyi, 199.

46. Kalmen Weiser, *"Di 'prehistorye' fun yidish in amerike"* (The 'Pre–History' of Yiddish in America), unpublished Paper, Yiddish Studies Program, Columbia University, 1996.

47. For a recent review of the work of Joshua Fishman on Yiddish speakers in the United States during the second half of the twentieth century and the beginning of the twenty-first century, including a discussion of the different engagement with Yiddish by secular and ultra-Orthodox Jews, see Rakhmiel Peltz, "The History of Yiddish Studies: Take Notice!," in *Language Loyalty, Continuity and Change: Joshua A. Fishman's Contributions to International Sociolinguistics*, ed. Ofelia Garcia, Rakhmiel Peltz, and Harold Schiffman (Clevedon: Multilingual Matters, 2006), 69–108.

48. Joshua A. Fishman, "A Decade in the Life of a Two–in–One Language: Yiddish in New York City (Secular and Ultra–Orthodox)," in *Can Threatened Languages Be Saved*, ed. Joshua A. Fishman (Clevedon: Multilingual Matters, 2001), 74–100.

49. Maurice Halbwachs, "The Social Frameworks of Memory," in *Maurice Halbwachs: On Collective Memory*, ed. and trans. Lewis A. Coser (Chicago: University of Chicago Press, 1992 [1925]), 40.

50. Peltz, 1998, op. cit., 191–192.

Chapter 22 - Henrietta Szold: The Making of an Icon

1. Accessed on 13 July 2008 at http://www.greatwomen.org/history.php.

2. Roberta Elliott, email to Barbara Spack, Natalie Silverman, et al., 2 February 2007; and Susan Woodland, email to Shuly Rubin Schwartz, 10 September 2008.

3. Accessed on 2 September 2008 at http://www.greatwomen.org/women.php?action=viewAll.

4. Over the years, many biographies have been written about Szold, including Joan Dash, *Summoned to Jerusalem: The Life of Henrietta Szold* (New York: Harper & Row, 1979); Irving Fineman, *Woman of Valor: The Life of Henrietta Szold, 1860–1945* (New York: Simon and Schuster, 1961); Elma Ehrlich Levinger, *Fighting Angel: The Story of Henrietta Szold* (New York: Behrman House, 1946); Marvin Lowenthal, *Henrietta Szold: Life and Letters* (New York: Viking Press, 1942); and Baila Round

Shargel, *Lost Love: The Untold Story of Henrietta Szold* (Philadelphia: Jewish Publication Society, 1997).

5. Jonathan D. Sarna, *JPS: The Americanization of Jewish Culture* (Philadelphia: Jewish Publication Society, 1989), 47–74.

6. Accessed on 13 July 2008 at http://www.hadassah.org/pageframe.asp?section= about&page=archives/archives_chron1.html&header=chronology&size=50; and http: //jwa.org/exhibits/wov/szold/youth.html.

7. Erica Simmons, "Playgrounds and Penny Lunches in Palestine: American Social Welfare in the Yishuv," *American Jewish History* 92 (September 2004): 263–266; idem, *Hadassah and the Zionist Project* (New York: Rowman & Littlefield, 2006), 2–3; and Mary McCune, "Social Workers in the Muskeljudentum: 'Hadassah Ladies,' 'Manly Men' and the Significance of Gender in the American Zionist Movement, 1912–1928," *American Jewish History* 86 (June 1998): 135–138.

8. Joyce Antler, "Zion in Our Hearts: Henrietta Szold and the American Jewish Women's Movement," in *Daughter of Zion: Henrietta Szold and American Jewish Womanhood*, ed. Barry Kessler (Baltimore: Jewish Historical Society of Maryland, 1995), 41–44.

9. Dash, 106.

10. Accessed on 6 July 2008 at http://jwa.org/discover/inthepast/posters/viewposters/ hszposter.html.

11. Rebecca Brickner to Barnett Brickner, 12, 15, and 18 April 1932, personal files of Balfour Brickner; and Erica Simmons, *Hadassah and the Zionist Project* (Lanham, MD: Rowman & Littlefield, 2006), 125.

12. Jewish Women's Archive, "Henrietta Szold: Legacy," http://www.jwa.org/exhibits/ wov/szold/legacy.html, accessed on 23 February 2007; and Shulamit Reinharz, s.v., "Szold, Henrietta," in *Encyclopaedia Judaica* 2nd ed., 19, ed. Michael Berenbaum and Fred Skolnik (Detroit: Macmillan Reference USA, 2007), 409–411.

13. Antler, 35; and Record Group (RG) 7/21/257, Hadassah Archives (HA), New York.

14. List of Henrietta Szold Awardees, RG 13/22/5; http://www.hadassah.org/news/ content/news-view.asp?pr_id=536, accessed on 6 July 2008; Henrietta Szold Citation, 10 February 1949, RG 3/101, HA, New York.

15. Chaim Yahil, s.v., "Goldmann, Nahum," 7: 714–716; and Susan Hattis Rolef, s.v., "Meir (Myerson, Née Mabovitch), Golda," in *Encyclopaedia Judaica* 13: 777–779; and National board minutes, 7 Aut [*sic*] 1957, RG 13/21/7, HA, New York.

16. Accessed on 13 July 2008 at http://www.hadassah.org/about/content/president_ bios/TamardeSolaPool.pdf.

17. Memo 24 October 1957 from [Tamar] cc. Dr. Freund, Mrs. David Levine, Ms. De Sola Pool, RG 13/21/4, HA, New York.

18. Tamar to Miriam Freund, 19 May 1959, RG 13/21/1, HA, New York.

19. Pool to Eleanor Roosevelt, 24 August 1959; Miriam Warburg to Pool, 15 February 1960; and Pool to Zena and Abe Harman, 18 February 1960, 21:1; and Miriam Freund, August 1960, RG 13/21/4, HA, New York.

20. National board minutes, 17 March 1960, RG 13/21/1, HA, New York.

21. Pool to Freund, 12 February 1958, RG 13/21/1, HA, New York.

22. National board minutes, 30 April 1958; and Moshe Pearlman, "All Roads Lead to Hadassah," *Hadassah Newsletter* (April 1959), RG 13/21/10, HA, New York.

23. Pool to Golda Meir, 30 April 1959, RG 13/21/1, HA, New York.

24. "Proposed Opening of the Henrietta Szold Centennial," outline, n.d., RG 13/21/1, HA, New York.

25. Pool to Miriam Freund, 26 June 1957, 21:4; and Pool to Murray Silverstone, 10 February 1958, 22:1, RG 13, HA, New York.

26. "Dorothy Silverstone," *The New York Times* (23 March 1993): accessed on 4 August 2008 at http://query.nytimes.com/gst/fullpage.html?res=9F0CEED81030F9 30A15750C0A965958260&scp=1&sq=Dorothy%20Silverstone%201993&st=cse; and Tamar to Murray Silverstone, 10 February 1958, RG 13/22/1; minutes, Henrietta Szold Centennial Committee, 24 March 1959, RG 13/21/5; and Pool to Miriam Freund, 24 December 1959, RG 13/22/1, HA, New York.

27. Pool to Dr. Freund, Mrs. Schoolman, Myrtle Karp, 30 October 1957, RG 13/21/4, HA, New York. Irving Fineman, in the biography that he produced for the centennial, refuted the veracity of some of the details of this story. Szold's father took part in the funeral procession and, thus, could not have been holding Henrietta on his shoulder to watch the cortège. But the story continued to retain its symbolic importance. Fineman, 435.

28. Pool to Dr. Freund, Mrs. Schoolman, Myrtle Karp, 30 October 1957, RG 13/21/4, HA, New York.

29. Ibid.

30. Ibid.

31. Ibid.

32. Script of the film, 4 Aug 1959, RG 13/22/1, HA, New York.

33. Emphasis is mine. Harry Gilroy, "Farm Units Mark Jubilee in Israel," *The New York Times* (21 February 1954): 19; and Chanoch Reinhold, "Notes on Narration of the Henrietta Szold Film," attached to Zev Weiss to Miriam Freund, 15 May 1960, RG 13/22/1, HA, New York.

34. Patricia Erens, *The Jew in American Cinema* (Bloomington, IN: Indiana University Press, 1984), 198.

35. Reinhold, "Notes on Narration."

36. Reinhold "Notes on Narration"; and Lotte Beyth, remarks to "Miss Henrietta," 10 May 1960, both attached to Weiss to Freund, 15 May 1960, RG 13/22/1, HA, New York.

37. Murray Silverstone to Miriam Freund, 9 March 1961, RG 13/22/1, HA, New York.

38. *Call of the Holyland*, 35 mm, 19 min. (Los Angeles: Twentieth Century-Fox Film International, 1960).

39. Silverstone to Freund, 9 March 1961, RG 13/22/1, HA, New York.

40. "A Call," 15 April 1959, RG 13/21/4, HA, New York.

41. Accessed on 6 July 2008 at http://www.hadassah.org/pageframe.asp?section= news&page=newsus.asp&header=newsus&size=50.

Chapter 23 - *Yentl:* From Yeshiva Boy to Syndrome

1. Earlier versions of this essay were presented as public lectures for the series "American Jewish Icons." I am deeply grateful to Jonathan D. Sarna for his comments on an earlier draft.

Isaac Bashevis Singer, *Yentl, the Yeshiva Boy*, trans. Marion Magid and Elizabeth Pollet (New York: Farrar, Straus and Giroux, 1983), 8.

2. Danya Ruttenberg, *Yentl's Revenge: The Next Wave of Jewish Feminism* (Seattle: Seal Press, 2001), xx.

3. Bernadine Healy, "The Yentl Syndrome," *New England Journal of Medicine* 325, no. 4 (1991): 274–276.

4. Anne K. Eckman, "Beyond 'the Yentl Syndrome:' Making Women Visible in Post–1990 Women's Health Discourse," in *The Visible Woman: Imaging Technologies, Gender, and Science*, ed. Paula Treichler, Lisa Cartwright, and Constance Penley (New York: New York University Press, 1998), 130–170; Michael A. Crilly et al., "Gender Bias in the Clinical Management of Women with Angina: Another Look at the Yentl Syndrome," *Journal of Women's Health* 17, no. 3 (2008): 331–342; Claudia E. Kuhni and Felix H. Sennhauser, "The Yentl Syndrome in Childhood Asthma: Risk Factors for Undertreatment in Swiss Children," *Pediatric Pulmonology* 19, no. 3 (1995): 156–161.

5. Rosalie A. Radomsky, "You've Come a Long Way, Yentl: Women as Talmud Scholars," *The New York Times* (18 August 1996): CY7.

6. Michael Isaacson, "A Strong Voice Quietly Changing the Cantorate," *Forward* (9 July 2008): http://www.forward.com/articles/13728/ accessed 24 February 2009.

7. Ruttenberg, *Yentl's Revenge: The Next Wave of Jewish Feminism*.

8. Isaac Bashevis Singer, *Short Friday, and Other Stories* (New York: Farrar, Straus and Giroux, 1964).

9. Isaac Bashevis Singer, "Nobel Lecture," accessed on 3 August 2008 at http://nobelprize.org/nobel_prizes/literature/laureates/1978/singer-lecture.html.

10. Singer, *Yentl, the Yeshiva Boy*. All quotations come from this edition. The story was copyrighted in 1962 and first appeared in English in Singer, *Short Friday, and Other Stories*.

11. On transvestism in western culture, see Marjorie B. Garber, *Vested Interests: Cross-Dressing and Cultural Anxiety* (New York: Routledge, 1992). She compares Yentl to both Rosalind and Viola, 82.

12. Rebecca T. Alpert, *Like Bread on the Seder Plate: Jewish Lesbians and the Transformation of Tradition*, Between Men—Between Women (New York: Columbia University Press, 1997), 136–138. Michele Aaron, "The Queer Jew and Cinema: From Yidl to Yentl and Back and Beyond," *Jewish Culture and History* 3, no. 1 (2000): 23–44. On the Maid of Ludomir, see Nathaniel Deutsch, *The Maiden of Ludmir: A Jewish Holy Woman and Her World* (Berkeley: University of California Press, 2003).

13. Janet Hadda, *Isaac Bashevis Singer: A Life* (New York: Oxford University Press, 1997), 18–30.

14. Esther Singer Kreitman, *Deborah*, rpt. ed. (New York: Feminist Press at CUNY, 2004); Isaac Bashevis Singer, *In My Father's Court*, rpt. ed. (New York: Farrar, Straus and Giroux, 1991); Israel Joshua Singer, *Of a World That Is No More* (New York: Vanguard Press, 1971).

15. Cited in Hadda, 40.

16. Orville Prescott, "Demons, Devils, and Others," *The New York Times* (14 December 1964): 33.

17. *The Directors—Barbra Streisand*, Robert J. Emery, 2000.

18. This is discussed in Stephen J. Whitfield, "Yentl," *Jewish Social Studies* 5, nos. 1/2 (1998/1999): 154–176. See also: Barbra Streisand Biography, accessed on 16

February 2006 at http://www.sonymusic.com/artists/BarbraStreisand/bio_bio_pg2. html.

19. Film credits are published on the International Movie Data Base at http://www. imdb.com/title/tt0086619/ accessed 4 August 2008. *Yentl* was released on DVD in 2009 (*Yentl: Two Disc Director's Cut*, MGM Entertainment, 2009).

20. Quoted in Whitfield, "Yentl."

21. Roger Ebert, "Yentl," *Chicago Sun-Times* (9 December 1983): accessed on 4 August 2008 at http://rogerebert.suntimes.com/apps/pbcs.dll/article?AID=/19831209/ REVIEWS/312090302/1023.

22. Rex Reed quoted in Henry Bial, *Acting Jewish: Negotiating Ethnicity on the American Stage and Screen* (Ann Arbor: University of Michigan Press, 2005), 106.

23. Barbara Streisand Biography, accessed on 16 February 2006 at http://www. sonymusic.com/artists/BarbraStreisand/bio_bio_pg2.html.

24. Box Office Mojo, accessed on 10 August 2008 at http://www.boxofficemojo. com/movies/?id=yentl.htm; Whitfield claims it earned 50 million domestically and an equivalent amount abroad; Whitfield, "Yentl," 158. Another source says it earned 22.8 million in the foreign box office in 1984; "Yentl-15 years: Chronology," accessed on 22 July 2008 at http://www.bjsmusic.com/Yentl15/chronology.html.

25. John Simon, "Men Aloft, Woman Adrift," *National Review* (27 January 1984): 54–57.

26. Janet Maslin, "Film: 'Yentl,' a Drama with Barbra Streisand," *The New York Times* (18 November 1983): C10.

27. Ilan Stavans, "What Melting Pot? Multiculturalism and American Jews: Essay," *Forward.com* (16 September 2005): accessed on 24 February 2009 at http://www. forward.com/articles/what-melting-pot.

28. Isaac Bashevis Singer, "I.B. Singer Talks to I.B. Singer About the Movie 'Yentl,'" *The New York Times* (29 January 1984): H1. Note that *Yentl* was also adapted by Singer, in collaboration with Leah Napolin, for the stage. It opened at the Eugene O'Neill Theater on Broadway in 1975 and ran for 223 performances. It starred Tovah Feldshuh, who was nominated for a Tony Award for her performance; accessed on 12 August 2008 at http://www.ibdb.com/production.php?id=3762.

29. For a very perceptive essay which shows how many of the changes are based on the 1936 Yiddish cross-dressing movie *Yidl Mitn Fidl*, see Aaron, "The Queer Jew and Cinema: From Yidl to Yentl and Back and Beyond," 34.

30. Maslin, "Film: 'Yentl,' a Drama with Barbra Streisand."

31. Singer, "I.B. Singer Talks to I.B. Singer About the Movie 'Yentl.'"

32. Harlan Jacobson, "Singer, Not the Song," *Film Comment* 20, no. 1 (January/ February, 1984): 53.

33. Isaac Bashevis Singer, "Film Script for Yentl: Excerpts," *Yiddish* 14, nos. 2/3 (2006): 129–142, 131–138.

34. Singer, "I.B. Singer Talks to I.B. Singer About the Movie 'Yentl.'"

35. Michel Legrand, Alan Bergman, and Marilyn Bergman, "No Matter What Happens," (SONY Music Entertainment, 1983).

36. Whitfield, "Yentl," 154–155.

37. Maslin, "Film: 'Yentl,' a Drama with Barbra Streisand;" Ebert, "Yentl;" Pauline Kael, "The Current Cinema," *The New Yorker* (28 November 1983):170–176.

38. Whitfield, "Yentl," 161, 163, 165, 16 8, 174.

39. Michel Legrand, Alan Bergman, and Marilyn Bergman, *A Piece of Sky* (Sony Music Entertainment, 1983), song; Solvej Schou, "Unprecedented 4 Women Nominated for Screenwriting Oscars," Associated Press State and Local Wire, LexisNexis Academic (22 February 2008), accessed 24 February 2009; Matthew Frye Jacobson, *Roots Too: White Ethnic Revival in Post-Civil Rights America* (Cambridge: Harvard University Press, 2006), 7–8, 72, 84–85.

40. Bial, *Acting Jewish: Negotiating Ethnicity on the American Stage and Screen*, 27, 105–106, 155–156.

41. Ibid., 27, 105.

42. Singer, *Yentl the Yeshiva Boy*. The statistic comes from Whitfield, "Yentl," 158. A *Yentl* medley also appears on the CD *Barbra: The Concert* (Sony, 1994).

43. On this point, see Whitfield, "Yentl," 174.

44. Maureen Dowd, "Yentl vs. Moses," *The New York Times* (6 May 1998): A23.

45. This list appeared at http://www.jewishculture.org/programs/350/icons/ accessed on 14 February 2006; this page is no longer available.

46. Ari Goldman's lecture was posted at American Jewish Icons, accessed on 14 February 2006 at http://www.jewishculture.org/programs/350/icons/. This page is no longer available.

47. Quoted in Whitfield, "Yentl," 135.

48. Betty Friedan, *The Feminine Mystique* (New York: Norton, 1963).

49. Ruth Rosen, *The World Split Open: How the Modern Women's Movement Changed America* (New York: Viking, 2000).

50. "Jewish Women Call for Change, 1972," in *The American Jewish Woman: A Documentary History*, ed. Jacob Rader Marcus (New York: Ktav, 1981), 894–896.

51. Allison Fernley and Paula Maloof, "Review of Yentl by Barbra Streisand," *Film Quarterly* 38, no. 3 (Spring 1985): 38–46, 38.

52. Schou, "Women Break Record in Writing Nominations at Oscars."

53. *The Directors—Barbra Streisand.*

54. Ibid.

55. Fernley and Maloof, "Review of Yentl by Barbra Streisand," 38–40.

56. *The Directors—Barbra Streisand.*

57. Fernley and Maloof, "Review of Yentl by Barbra Streisand," 38–40.

58. *The Directors—Barbra Streisand.*

59. Legrand, Bergman, and Bergman, "No Matter What Happens."

60. Fernley and Maloof, "Review of Yentl by Barbra Streisand," 38–40.

61. Miriam Herman Maltz, "Ambiguity in Isaac Bashevis Singer's 'Yentl the Yeshiva Boy,'" *Jewish Affairs* 55, no. 4 (Summer 2000): 7–12, 11.

62. *The Directors—Barbra Streisand.*

63. *Yentl*, Barbra Streisand, 1983.

64. Ibid.

65. Jerome Karabel, *The Chosen: The Hidden History of Admission and Exclusion at Harvard, Yale, and Princeton* (Boston: Houghton Mifflin, 2005).

66. For example, as one of nine women attending Harvard Law School in 1955, Ruth Bader Ginsburg, who would later become Associate Justice of the Supreme Court, had to explain, as did each of the women, "how she justified taking a place in the class that would otherwise have gone to a man;" Malvina Halberstam, "Ruth Bader Ginsburg,"

in *Jewish Women in America: An Historical Encyclopedia*, ed. Paula Hyman and Deborah Dash Moore (New York: Routledge, 1997), 515–520.

67. Rosalind Rosenberg, *Divided Lives: American Women in the Twentieth Century* (New York: Hill and Wang, 1992), 209.

68. Gerson D. Cohen, "Women in the Conservative Movement," *Outlook* (Winter 1973): 6; Gerson Cohen quoted in Charles Austin, "Conservative Group Votes to Admit Women as Rabbis," *The New York Times* (25 October 1983): A20.

69. Stanley Kauffmann, "Streisand on the Roof," *The New Republic* (19 December 1983): 22–23.

70. Michel Legrand, Alan Bergman, and Marilyn Bergman, "This Is One of Those Moments," (SONY Music Entertainment, 1983).

71. That transformation was the result of Title IX of the Education Amendments of 1972 to the Civil Rights Act of 1964. It reads: "No person in the United States shall, on the basis of sex, be excluded from participation in, or denied the benefits of, or be subjected to discrimination under any educational program or activity receiving federal assistance;" "What is Title IX?"; http://www.american.edu/sadker/titleix.htm accessed 7 March 2006.

72. These are discussed in Pamela S. Nadell, "A Bright New Constellation: Feminism and American Judaism" in *The Columbia History of Jews and Judaism in America*, ed. Marc Lee Raphael (New York: Columbia University Press, 2008), 385–405.

73. Pauline Kael, "The Current Cinema," *The New Yorker* (28 November 1983): 170–176.

74. Ruttenberg, *Yentl's Revenge: The Next Wave of Jewish Feminism*, xx.

75. Legrand, Bergman, and Bergman, *A Piece of Sky*.

76. Healy, "The Yentl Syndrome," 275.

77. Ibid. Alison Chiesa, "Women Suffer Lower Level of Angina Care, Claims Survey; 'Cultural Factors' Blamed for Divide," *The Herald (Glasgow)* (4 April 2008): News, 8; "Angina Treatment for Women 'Is Second-Best,'" *Daily Mail (London)* (4 April 2008): 1st, 27. In the interests of full disclosure, I must note that Healy cited Singer's short story and not the film when coining the "Yentl syndrome." However, these articles in *The Herald* and the *Daily Mail*, which, given their similarity, must be based on a press release, both credit the film for inspiration for the syndrome.

78. Fiona Looney, "How Do You Tell Children Why Baiba Was Killed?" *Daily Mail (London)* (21 November 2007): Ireland, 15.

79. Robyn E. Blumner, "Women's Khaki Ceiling," *St. Petersburg Times (Florida)* (22 May 2005): Perspective, 1.

Contributors

Dianne Ashton is professor of religion and director of the American studies program at Rowan University. She is the author of *Rebecca Gratz: Women and Judaism in Antebellum America* and *Jewish Life in Pennsylvania* and co-editor of *Four Centuries of Jewish Women's Spirituality,* which is newly revised. Her essays on American Jewish history have appeared in many collections and encyclopedias. She is currently working on a history of Hanukkah in America, to be published by New York University Press.

Mark K. Bauman took early retirement as professor of history at Atlanta Metropolitan College and later taught as Mason Fellow for a semester at the College of William and Mary. He edited or co-edited three special issues of *American Jewish History* and is the founding and current editor of *Southern Jewish History*. Bauman has also written forty-five articles and is the author or editor of five books.

Aviva Ben-Ur is associate professor in the department of Judaic and Near Eastern studies at the University of Massachusetts Amherst. She is the author of *Sephardic Jews in America: A Diasporic History* (New York University Press, 2009) and co-author, with Rachel Frankel, of *Remnant Stones: The Jewish Cemeteries of Suriname*, Vol. 1 (Hebrew Union College Press, 2009). Her current book project focuses on Eurafrican Jews in colonial Suriname.

Natalie Zemon Davis is Henry Charles Lea Professor of History emeritus at Princeton University and adjunct professor of history at the University of Toronto. Her books include *Society and Culture in Early Modern France*, *The Return of Martin Guerre*, *Women on the Margins: Three Seventeenth-Century Lives* (Glikl Hamel is one of the three women), *The Gift in Sixteenth-Century France*, *Slaves*

591

on Screen, and most recently, *Trickster Travels: A Sixteenth-Century Muslim Between Worlds*. Among other courses at Princeton, she taught in the Jewish studies program.

Hasia Diner is the Paul S. and Sylvia Steinberg Professor of American Jewish History and director of the Goldstein-Goren Center at New York University. She has written numerous books in the fields of American Jewish history, immigration and ethnic history, and the history of American women, and her most recent work, *We Remember With Reverence and Love: American Jews and the Myth of Silence After the Holocaust, 1945–1962*, was released in the spring of 2009 by New York University Press.

David Ellenson is president of Hebrew Union College–Jewish Institute of Religion and also serves there as the Grancell Professor of Jewish Religious Thought. His book, *After Emancipation: Jewish Religious Responses to Modernity*, won the National Jewish Book Award in 2005.

Paul Finkelman is the President William McKinley Distinguished Professor of Law and Public Policy and senior fellow in the Government Law Center at Albany Law School. He is the author, co-author, or editor of more than twenty-five books and more than one hundred and fifty scholarly articles on topics ranging from constitutional law, Thomas Jefferson and slavery, the war on drugs, and American race relations. He has held fellowships and grants from the National Endowment for the Humanities, the American Philosophical Society, the American Bar Foundation, The Japan Society of the Promotion of Science, the Jacob Rader Marcus Center of the American Jewish Archives, Yale University, Harvard Law School, the Gilder Lehrman Institute, and the Library of Congress. In 2008 he was a visiting scholar at the Graduate School of Law and Politics at Osaka University.

Rachel Frankel is an architect in New York City. Her essay, "Antecedents and Remnants of Jodensavanne: The Synagogues and Cemeteries of the First Permanent Plantation Settlement of New World Jews," appeared in *The Jews and the Expansion of Europe to the West,*

1450–1800 (Berghahn Books, 2001). She is co-author, with Aviva Ben-Ur, of *Remnant Stones: The Jewish Cemeteries of Suriname*, Vol. 1 (Hebrew Union College Press, 2009).

Eric L. Friedland was the Harriet Sanders Professor of Judaic Studies at three universities and one seminary in the Dayton, Ohio, area for thirty years. During his tenure, he published a book on progressive Jewish prayer books in the United States and abroad called *"Were Our Mouths Filled With Song": Studies in Liberal Jewish Liturgy* (HUC Press, 1997) as well as monographs and many articles in scholarly journals, festschriften, yearbooks, and the popular press. Now retired, he lectures on the Jewish-Muslim nexus, an old-new interest of his, and continues undauntedly to explore the countless instances of cross-fertilization between European and American non-Orthodox rites throughout the nineteenth century.

Allon Gal is professor emeritus in the history department and a senior research fellow at the Ben-Gurion Research Institute, Ben-Gurion University of the Negev, Israel. He is on the editorial board of *Studies in Contemporary Jewry, Bialik Institute, Journal of Modern Jewish Studies*, and *American Jewish History*. He is a contributor to and editor of the three-volume work *World Regional Zionism: Geo-cultural Dimensions* (Jerusalem: Shazar Center and Ben-Gurion University Press, 2009 [Hebrew]); co-author, with A.S. Leousssi and A.D. Smith, of *The Call of the Homeland: Diaspora Nationalisms, Past and Present,* to be published by Brill, Leiden and Boston; and co-author, with M. Lissak, of *The Historical Foundations of Israeli Democracy,* to be published in Hebrew by Yad Izhak Ben-Zvi, Jerusalem. He is currently working on the role of Western Zionism in the democratic course of the *Yishuv* and the State of Israel.

Leonard Greenspoon, a native of Richmond, Virginia, holds the Klutznick Chair in Jewish Civilization at Creighton University, where he is also professor of classical and Near Eastern studies and of theology. Many of his publications deal with aspects of Bible translation, with topics ranging from the earliest translation, the Septuagint, to recently composed versions of the Bible. He has also been involved as editor or consultant in three Bible translation projects. In his research and writing, Greenspoon is especially interested in the way Bible translators reflect the historical, social, cultural, political, as well as religious environments in which they work. In this connection, he wrote a biography of Max L. Margolis and is now working (with Jason Kalman) on a biography of Harry M. Orlinsky, as well as a history of Jewish Bible translations (to be published by the American Bible Society).

Alfred Gottschalk *z"l* served as president (1971–1995) and then chancellor of Hebrew Union College–Jewish Institute of Religion. He was Distinguished Professor of Bible and Jewish Religious Thought and the John and Marianne Slade Professor of Jewish Intellectual History. Dr. Gottschalk joined the HUC-JIR faculty following his ordination from HUC-JIR and was Dean at HUC-JIR, Los Angeles. He earned his doctorate in philosophy and the history of religion.

Jeffrey S. Gurock is Libby M. Klaperman Professor of Jewish History at Yeshiva University and chairs the Academic Council of the American Jewish Historical Society. His most recent book is *Orthodox Jews in America* (Indiana University Press, 2009).

Samuel Haber teaches in the history department at the University of California, Berkeley. He has published in the fields of American Jewish history and American intellectual history. He welcomes comments on this essay at Zanvil@Socrates.Berkeley.edu.

Michael Marmur is assistant professor of Jewish theology at the Hebrew Union College–Jewish Institute of Religion in Jerusalem. He also serves as the vice-president for academic affairs of HUC-JIR. His doctoral dissertation focused on the work of Abraham Joshua Heschel, and he teaches and writes on Heschel and other modern Jewish thinkers, as well as on Jewish education.

Pamela S. Nadell is the Inaugural Patrick Clendenen Professor of History and director of the Jewish studies program at American University. She is the author of, among others, *Women Who Would Be Rabbis: A History of Women's Ordination, 1889–1985,* and editor of

American Jewish Women's History: A Reader. She is past chair of the Academic Council of the American Jewish Historical Society and a consultant to the permanent exhibition of the National Museum of American Jewish History.

Rakhmiel Peltz is professor of sociolinguistics in the department of culture and communication and founding director of Judaic studies at Drexel University. His research specialty is the social history of Yiddish language and culture. He authored *From Immigrant to Ethnic Culture: American Yiddish in South Philadelphia* (Stanford University Press, 1998) and produced the documentary film, *Toby's Sunshine: The Life and Art of Holocaust Survivor Toby Knobel Fluek* (2008). Currently he is editing the work of Uriel Weinreich on the language and culture of Jews in eastern Europe in order to make it accessible to a new generation of Yiddish researchers in training.

William Pencak is professor of history and Jewish studies at the Pennsylvania State University. He has been the recipient of the Wiener-Lowenstein and Bernard and Audre Rapoport fellowships at The Jacob Rader Marcus Center of the American Jewish Archives. His book, *Jews and Gentiles in Early America: 1654–1800*, published by the University of Michigan Press, was runner-up for the National Book Award in American Jewish History for 2005. He is currently working on a sequel, *Jews and Gentiles in the Early Republic: 1800–1865*.

Kevin Proffitt is senior archivist for research and collections at The Jacob Rader Marcus Center of the American Jewish Archives, director of its fellowship program, and sits on the academic advisory and editorial board of *The American Jewish Archives Journal*.

Jonathan D. Sarna is the Joseph H. and Belle R. Braun Professor of American Jewish History at Brandeis University. He also chairs the academic advisory and editorial board of the Jacob Rader Marcus Center of the American Jewish Archives and is chief historian of the National Museum of American Jewish History in Philadelphia. Author or editor of more than twenty books on American Jewish history and life, his most recent book is *A Time to Every Purpose: Letters to a*

Young Jew. His *American Judaism: A History* won the 2004 "Jewish Book of the Year Award" from the Jewish Book Council. In 2009, Dr. Sarna was elected to the American Academy of Arts and Sciences.

Shuly Rubin Schwartz is the Irving Lehrman Research Associate Professor of American Jewish History, dean of the Albert A. List College of Jewish Studies at The Jewish Theological Seminary, and author of *The Emergence of Jewish Scholarship in America: The Publication of the* Jewish Encyclopedia. Schwartz also lectures and writes widely on American Jewish life, American Judaism, and Jewish women's experiences. Her most recent book, *The Rabbi's Wife*, won the National Jewish Book Award in the area of modern Jewish thought. She serves on the Academic Council of the American Jewish Historical Society and the academic advisory boards of the Jacob Rader Marcus Center of the American Jewish Archives, the Hadassah Research Institute on Jewish Women, and the Jewish Women's Archive.

Robert M. Seltzer is a professor of history at Hunter College and the Graduate School of The City University of New York. He is also director of Hunter's Jewish social studies program and has served as president of the Association for Jewish Studies. He holds degrees from Washington University, Yale University, Columbia University, and HUC-JIR and is author of *Jewish People, Jewish Thought: The Jewish Experience in History*, as well as many articles on Jewish intellectual history. He is currently concerned with the relationship among modern concepts of history, comparative religion, and Jewish faith.

Lance J. Sussman is the senior rabbi of Reform Congregation Keneseth Israel in Elkins Park, Pennsylvania. The author of *Isaac Leeser and the Making of American Judaism* (1995), Sussman has taught at Binghamton University, Rutgers University, Hunter College of the City University of New York, the Hebrew Union College–Jewish Institute of Religion in New York, and Princeton University. He also serves as a trustee of the Katz Center for Advanced Jewish Studies at University of Pennsylvania and the Delaware Valley College in Doylestown, Pennsylvania. Rabbi Sussman is the national chair of the Central Conference of American Rabbis Press and is a founding member of the academic advisory and editorial board of the Jacob R. Marcus Center of the American Jewish Archives. He is also a member of the B'nai Yaakov Council.

William Toll earned his doctorate in U.S. history at UC Berkeley (1972) under Professor Kenneth Stampp. He currently teaches American Jewish history as an adjunct professor at the University of Oregon and resides in Eugene. He has written several books, including *The Resurgence of Race: Black Social Theory from Reconstruction to the Pan-African Conferences* (1979); *The Making of an Ethnic Middle Class: Portland Jewry Over Four Generations* (1982); and *Jews of the Pacific Coast: Reinventing Community on America's Edge* (2009) [with Ellen Eisenberg and Ava Kahn]. He has contributed essays to many edited volumes and scholarly journals, including *The Journal of Southern History*, *The Pacific Historical Review*, *The Journal of American Ethnic History*, *The Western Historical Quarterly*, *The Pacific Northwest Quarterly*, *American Jewish History*, and *The American Jewish Archives Journal*.

Cornelia Wilhelm currently teaches at Ludwig-Maximilians-Universität (LMU) in Munich. She has taught both as Aresty Visiting Scholar and LMUexcellent Visiting Professor and Liaison North America at the Bildner Center and the History Department of Rutgers University. She has also been a visiting professor of American history at the historical seminar of the University of Innsbruck, Austria. She has published widely on migration, religion, gender, and social history in a transnational and transatlantic perspective. Her second book, *Deutsche Juden in Amerika: Bürgerliches Selbstbewusstsein und jüdische Identität in den Orden B'nai B'rith und Treue Schwestern, 1843–1914,* has recently been published by the German Historical Institute (GHI) in Washington, DC, and will soon be published in English by Wayne State University Press. The GHI has also recently published her reference guide to archival holdings on German Jews in the United States.

Index

#

22nd Zionist Congress, 332

A

Aaron, Michele, 586n12, 587n29
Aaron, Raymond, 555n14
Aboab, Isaac, 76
Abrahams, Israel, 497n13, 501n56, 501n58
Abrahams, Jacob, 104
Abrams, Jeanne, 520n5
Abulafia, Samuel Halevi, 496n8
Academy of Music (New York), 219, 222
Acting Jewish: Negotiating Ethnicity on the American Stage and Screen
    (Henry Bial), 475
Addams, Jane, 457, 463
Adler, Cyrus, 218, 291–93, 456, 525n22
Adler, Henry, 171
Adler, Samuel, 170, 178–79, 182–84, 194, 530n4, 531n8–9, 533n32
Adventures in Freedom: Three Hundred Years of Jewish Life in America
    (Oscar Handlin), 373, 382
African Episcopal Church, 90
Agus, Jacob B., 242, 545n8, 547n75
Ahad Ha-Am, 238–45, 332
Ahavai Shalom synagogue, 265–66
Ahlstrom, Sydney E., 493n62
AJAJ. See American Jewish Archives Journal
AJAr. See American Jewish Archives Journal
AJHS. *See* American Jewish Historical Society
Albright, Madeline, 478
Albright, William Foxwell, 294, 296, 302
Alfassa, Shelomo, 522n14
Alger, Horatio, 278
Allen, Louis, 120
Allen, Richard, 90, 93, 510n33, 511n44
Allen, Woody, 476

599